*Critical Perspectives on Housing*

# Critical Perspectives on Housing

*Edited by*

*Rachel G. Bratt*

*Chester Hartman*

*Ann Meyerson*

Temple
University
Press

*Philadelphia*

Temple University Press, Philadelphia 19122
© 1986 by Temple University. All rights reserved
Published 1986
Printed in the United States of America


*Library of Congress Cataloging-in-Publication Data*
Main entry under title:
Critical perspectives on housing.
  Bibliography: p. 634
  Includes index.
  1. Housing—United States—Addresses, essays,
lectures.  2. Public housing—United States—
Addresses, essays, lectures.  3. Labor and
laboring classes—Dwellings—United States—
Addresses, essays, lectures.  I. Bratt, Rachel G.,
1946–    .  II. Hartman, Chester W., 1936–
III. Meyerson, Ann, 1949–
HD7293.C738    1986          363.5′0973          85-17274
ISBN 0-87722-395-5
ISBN 0-87722-396-3 (pbk.)

# Contents

# Acknowledgments

The project of creating a compendium of the best analytical thinking and programmatic ideas of progressive "housers" originated at the founding conference of The Planners Network in May 1981. The Network, of which all three editors are active members, is a national organization of progressive urban and rural planners housed at the Institute for Policy Studies in Washington, D.C.

The editors would like to thank Emily Paradise Achtenberg, Bob Beauregard, Charlotte Brady, Michael Bratt, Judith Feins, Amy Fine, Ann Gerroir, Arville Grady, Michael Krinsky, Amanda McMurray, Joel Rubenzahl, Kim Vaugeois, and Patricia Watson for their assistance in creating this collection. We are especially indebted to Michael Ames of Temple University Press for his early and continuing support of the project and to Mary Capouya of the Press for her skillful shepherding of the manuscript through its various stages. The work of putting the book together was shared equally among the editors, whose names are listed alphabetically.


We dedicate this book to our children, who are listed chronologically: Joanna Bratt, Jeremy Bratt, Joshua Meyerson Krinsky, Samuel Isaac Meyerson Krinsky, and Jeremy Fine Hartman.

# Editors' Introduction

America is in the midst of a deep and long-term housing crisis. Its signs and signals have been protracted, diffuse, and at times camouflaged. Nonetheless, they amount to a qualitatively altered future housing picture for Americans.

The nation's consciousness of housing conditions, however, is still very much shaped by the extraordinary performance of the housing sector in the post–World War II decades when there was a dramatic increase in home-ownership (from 44 percent in 1940 to 66 percent in 1980), particularly of freestanding, single-family suburban houses, and an equally dramatic decrease in substandard physical conditions and overcrowding—feats that tend to obscure the high numbers of urban and rural poor still living in slum conditions and the deterioration of large portions of central-city neighborhoods.

But over the last two decades, as the nation suffered severe economic jolts—what some economists have called a "crisis in U.S. capitalism" (see Bowles et al., 1983)—the housing conditions of those who experienced housing problems during the 1950s, 1960s, and 1970s have worsened, and new problems and victims have appeared. Since the mid-1960s, the amount of income households have available to spend on housing has been squeezed by the effects of declining growth in the nation's economy, producing unemployment and inflation, as well as by shifts in the structure of the labor market away from manufacturing and toward managerial–professional–technical and service jobs. At the same time, the cost of producing and maintaining housing has risen dramatically, with land and financing costs the leading culprits.

Thus, at one level, the gap between the haves and have-nots in America is widening, and housing, as the central expenditure for most lower-income families, reflects this polarization most acutely. For various subpopulations, such as those with very low incomes, female-headed households, and minorities, the housing crisis takes on larger proportions: a higher incidence of poor physical conditions and overcrowding and a lack of available units, in addition to severe cost burdens. At another level, for a large and growing segment of middle-income consumers, owners and renters alike, securing decent, affordable housing is becoming problematic. And at a third level, there are serious and increasing problems for some major institutional actors in the housing picture, most notably credit providers, the real estate industry, and government.

This assessment of the current state of the housing problem is by no means widely shared by housing analysts and policymakers. It explicitly departs from both the prevailing conservative and liberal perspectives. More concretely, the analytic perspective that guided the commissioning and selection of the chapters in this collection[1] embraces these recognitions:

• The housing crisis is most usefully understood with reference to the interests and actions of the principal actors involved—financial institutions; developers, owners, and managers of real estate; and government at all levels. The pressures and constraints exerted by these private- and public-sector actors shape consumer behavior.

• The central role that the state has played in U.S. housing policy has been to aid the private sector in its profit-making endeavors.

• The housing crisis can be understood only in the context of the broader economic forces at work in the country and internationally.

The approach to solutions that informs this collection can be further expressed in these propositions:

• Decent, affordable housing is a *right* that all Americans should have, and, like all rights, its acceptance in society will come about only through political struggle.

• Quantum leaps, both in the amount of government expenditures and kinds of state intervention in the workings of the housing market, are essential, particularly to meet the needs of lower-income households.

• Political mobilization and organization of those not adequately served by the existing housing system is a precondition for change and for the development of a government role in housing that is responsive to the needs of consumers.

• Many examples exist, both in the United States and abroad, that can offer direction and models for restructuring the U.S. housing system.

The conservative and liberal perspectives on housing, in contrast, may be characterized in the consciously oversimplified but, we think, accurate terms that follow. Conservatives either reject the notion that a housing crisis exists or acknowledge its existence for only a small, clearly identifiable segment of society; they maintain that, overall, the market functions well to meet the nation's housing needs. As such, they oppose direct federal subsidies to produce new or rehabilitated housing. Their solution is to use incentives to induce the market to meet a wider spectrum of needs, to free the market from government regulation as far as is practicable, and to inject market-attuned housing allowances to meet at least a portion of the need that cannot be met directly by free-market suppliers. [*See Chapter 21 by*

*Chester Hartman.*] Yet they will not support any widespread use of such allowances because of their budgetary impact, and they reject the notion that decent housing or housing subsidies are an entitlement. Instead, they favor a reduction of housing standards and expectations, particularly on the part of middle- and lower-income people.

The liberal perspective more honestly acknowledges the extent of housing problems in society and is more favorable to solutions that require government intervention and spending, with at least some funds going to programs that depart from or challenge the dominant market-supplied housing system (public housing is the most notable example of this). But liberals fail to recognize the structural causes of the housing crisis, do not embrace the concept of decent housing as a right, and are unwilling to advocate the expenditures required to provide every American with an affordable, decent place to live. Like the conservatives, liberals do not propose or support social welfare programs that require massive budgetary reallocations and radically different fiscal policies. They are therefore willing to put forth only those solutions that by and large accept the market-based housing economy, rather than build on a structural analysis of the housing crisis to devise and propose alternatives to that system.

A more detailed picture of the current dimensions of the housing crisis supports the approach we take in this book.[2]

## Availability

Available, affordable rental units are needed all across the country. Using 1980 census data, the National Low Income Housing Coalition estimates that for very-low-income renter households there is a gap of 1.2 million units between the number of such households and the number of rental units available at rents representing 30 percent of their incomes (Dolbeare, 1983b). The experiences of many would-be housing voucher recipients confirm these nationwide statistics. In major cities like Boston and New York, often as many as half the vouchers are returned to the local housing authorities because adequate, affordable rental units cannot be found. In addition, landlord abandonment, arson, the conversion of rental units to condominiums and cooperatives, and changes of land use cause the existing housing stock to shrink as ongoing investment in older rental properties for in-place tenants becomes increasingly unprofitable. Indeed, a government report of a few years ago described rental housing as an "endangered species" (U.S. Comptroller General, 1979; see also Downs, 1983; LeGates and Murphy, 1984).

The supply of available housing units in general—both for rent and individual homeownership—is not keeping up with the growing population. The 10-year goal established in the 1968 Housing Act of producing 26 million units, 6 million of which were to be subsidized, fell far short of achievement; only 17.6 million units were built, 201,000 of which were publicly owned (U.S. Bureau of the Census, 1984f, table 1328). National housing production goals are no longer even being officially set by the government.

## Affordability

Housing costs have been consuming an increasingly large proportion of disposable family income, making this aspect of the housing problem the most important measure of the current crisis. For renters, median gross rent as a percentage of median income rose from 22 to 29 percent from 1973 to 1983 (U.S. Bureau of the Census, 1983d). More than 10 million renter households paid 35 percent or more of their income for rent in 1983; 6.3 million paid 50 percent or more; and 4.7 million paid 60 percent or more. While less severe, the problem exists among homeowners too: 3.1 million households paid 50 percent or more of their income in housing costs in 1983. The affordability problem of course hits lower-income people hardest: The *median* rent-to-income ratio for renter households earning less than $3,000 was a stratospheric 60+ percent (the *Annual Housing Survey* does not provide more specific figures at this level); for renter households in the $3,000–6,999 income class, the *median* ratio was 55 percent; and for renter households in the $7,000–9,999 class, the *median* ratio was 39 percent (U.S. Bureau of the Census, 1983d).

When so high a proportion of disposable income must be advanced for housing, it is impossible for lower-income households to achieve minimum standards of living with respect to other necessities, and the lower the overall income and the larger the household size, the truer this is. [*See Chapter 3 by Michael E. Stone.*]

Homeownership is becoming an increasingly difficult proposition, particularly for newly formed households. In 1983, for the first time in more than 20 years, the nation's homeownership rate fell; although it was a small drop, from 65.6 percent to 64.6 percent, it is an important signal that the "American dream" is becoming less attainable (U.S. Bureau of the Census, 1984e). Mortgage interest rates in the 11 to 14 percent range seem to be a fixture now, whereas as recently as 1975 they averaged 8.75 percent, and in 1968 were 6.83 percent. When combined with rapidly escalating house prices, monthly mortgage payments rise geometrically, far faster than incomes:

• In 1975, the average-price, new single-family house cost $44,600, and the contract interest rate for a conventional first mortgage averaged 8.75 percent. With an 80 percent mortgage and housing costs at 25 percent of income, a family in 1975 would have needed a down payment of $8,920—65 percent of median family income that year—and, on a 30-year level-payment mortgage, would have had a monthly mortgage payment of

$280.69, which in turn required a minimum annual income of $13,473—2 percent below the nation's median family income that year.

• In 1981, the average-price, new single-family house cost $94,100, and the contract interest rate for a conventional first mortgage averaged 14.1 percent. With an 80 percent mortgage and housing costs at 25 percent of income, a family in 1981 would have needed a down payment of $18,820—84 percent of median family income that year—and, on a 30-year level-payment mortgage, would have had a monthly mortgage payment of $897.93, which in turn required a minimum annual income of $43,101— nearly double the nation's median family income that year (calculated from U.S. Bureau of the Census, 1981c, 772; and U.S. Bureau of the Census, 1981b, table 2).

For taxpayers who itemize, these out-of-pocket payments are partially offset by end-of-the-year tax deductions, albeit in a highly regressive fashion [*see Chapter 15 by Cushing Dolbeare*].

The new adjustable (variable) interest-rate mortgage, which rapidly is replacing the fixed-rate, fixed-payment mortgage, shifts the risk and burden of inflation from lender to borrower, decreases security of tenure, and makes it less possible for the homeowner to save for upward housing mobility or old age. [*See Chapter 4 by Ann Meyerson.*]

Utility costs are placing a great burden even on homeowners with no or low mortgage costs. The Consumer Price Index (CPI) for fuel oil, coal, and bottled gas rose from 110.1 in 1970 to 685.8 in mid-1981; in that same 11-year period, electricity prices rose by 175.7 points, compared with a 152.7 point rise in the CPI for all items (U.S. Bureau of the Census, 1981c, 468). Permanently high oil and electricity prices, deregulation of natural gas, and aggressive rate-increase campaigns by utility companies all indicate that these costs will continue to consume a too-high proportion of the family budget.

Local property taxes also are increasing dramatically as local and state governments experience severe fiscal crises and the federal government continues to cut back traditional aid programs. Since the property tax—in effect, a sales tax on housing services—is inherently highly regressive, low-income households are hit hardest. The median real estate tax bill for the 1.5 million homeowners with incomes under $3,000 in 1983 was $326, or more than 10 percent of their total income (U.S. Bureau of the Census, 1983d). Renters of course are equally burdened by such taxes, although they do not show up as direct payments but are folded into the rent payment to the landlord.

## Quality

One in 13 households still lives in dilapidated units or in units lacking basic plumbing facilities. Although the number of occupied inadequate units has decreased markedly in recent decades, millions of Americans, most of whom are poor, are currently living in housing unacceptable by the standards of U.S. society in the 1980s. In 1979, 24 percent of renters and 19 percent of homeowners had insufficient heat. And 32 percent of all rental units and 10 percent of all owner-occupied units were rated by their residents as being in poor or fair condition (U.S. Bureau of the Census, 1982b, table A-2).

Newly arising or newly recognized housing-related health problems have surfaced, such as neurological damage to children by lead poisoning from ingestion of lead-based paint, the cumulative effect of which is heightened by increasing levels of lead in the air and dirt children play in, from gasoline, and from other sources; fires and asphyxiation caused by improperly installed and vented heating devices used to cope with cold weather and high heating bills; hypothermia resulting from the absence of adequate heating, in turn attributable to an inability to pay heating bills and the subsequent shut-off of utilities; death and injury from fires set to collect insurance awards or empty buildings for redevelopment.

Nearly 3 million households were reported living in overcrowded conditions (1.01 or more persons per room) in the 1983 *Annual Housing Survey*, 700,000 in conditions of extreme overcrowding (1.51 or more persons per room). As is to be expected, overcrowding is most common among lower-income renters: For renter households with incomes under $3,000 a year, 7 percent were overcrowded; and among renter households with incomes of $3,000–6,999 a year, 6 percent were overcrowded (U.S. Bureau of the Census, 1983d). The *Annual Housing Survey* data for 1980 showed that only 5 percent of all renter households with incomes under $3,000 were overcrowded (Dolbeare, 1983b). The New York City Housing Authority reported in 1983 that as many as 17,000 families in the city's public housing projects were illegally doubling up, a problem that, according to the Housing Authority chair, is "growing geometrically" (Rule, 1983). And it is almost a certainty that official overcrowding statistics underreport reality, since respondents understandably are reluctant to report doubling up to census takers and other investigators, for fear of getting into trouble with landlords, housing code officials, welfare workers, and immigration authorities.

The most serious problem of housing quality concerns neighborhood conditions. In 1979, 73 percent of renters and 67 percent of homeowners regarded their neighborhoods as deficient in one or more respects (e.g., too much litter, noise, or crime, or streets needing lighting or repairs). Forty-five percent of renters and 50 percent of homeowners were dissatisfied with schools, police protection, public transportation, or other services (U.S. Bureau of the Census, 1982b, tables A-2, A-3).

# Security

Forced displacement annually affects some 2.5 million Americans (LeGates and Hartman, 1981). The reasons run the gamut: gentrification, undermaintenance, formal eviction, arson, rent increases, mortgage foreclosures, property-tax delinquency, speculation in land and buildings, conversion of low-rent apartments to luxury units or condominiums or nonresidential uses, demolition, "planned shrinkage" (i.e., intentional withdrawal of city services that forces the population to move and readies the area for redevelopment), historic preservation (Hartman, Keating, and LeGates, 1982). The victims are almost always lower-income persons, with a disproportionate number of nonwhites and the elderly (LeGates and Hartman, 1981). The results almost always are higher housing costs and sociopsychological disruption in personal and family life, with a disturbingly high proportion of displacees winding up in inferior and overcrowded dwellings as well (Hartman, 1964, 1971).

The rise of outright homelessness, the most extreme result of forced displacement, is a phenomenon that is evident in most cities and some towns and rural areas. While precise numbers are inherently difficult to derive, informed estimates put the national figure at somewhere around 2 million people, and growing (U.S. Congress, House, Subcommittee on Housing and Community Development, 1982).[3] Numbers aside, local reports indicate clearly that the people showing up at overnight shelters represent a full range of household types, ages, and races; no longer are derelicts and alcoholics the only ones to be counted among the homeless. Homelessness is caused by a variety of interacting factors, including poverty, unemployment, the deinstitutionalization of mentally disturbed persons, reduction of government benefit programs, and the loss and lack of production of low-rent housing. [*See Chapter 2 by Kim Hopper and Jill Hamberg.*]

Moreover, homelessness is not confined to former renters. Homeowners too are increasingly vulnerable to mortgage foreclosure, resulting in eviction. Mortgage delinquencies are higher than at any time since the 1930s,[4] and with such delinquencies comes the likelihood of default and foreclosure. In the third quarter of 1984, slightly over 6 percent of all home mortgage loans were 30 days or more past due, and in the high-unemployment states of the Midwest and Mid-Atlantic the rate was considerably higher—9.57 percent in Illinois, for example (Rosenblatt, 1984). In the first half of 1982, foreclosure—a step that lenders generally resort to most reluctantly—took the homes of 1 out of every 400 mortgagors in the United States (Mariano, 1983).

# Inequality

Minorities face significantly more severe housing problems than the rest of the population. On all standard measures of housing conditions (affordability, physical inadequacy, overcrowding, and rates of homeownership), blacks and other minorities are consistently found to be worse off than whites. For certain minority groups, such as Native Americans and Hispanics, housing conditions are among the worst in the nation. Nearly one-fourth of all Hispanic and Native American households live in substandard housing; more than half of the Native American families living in reservation areas inhabit substandard housing (Treuer, 1982). Despite passage of the 1968 Civil Rights Act, discrimination is still widely practiced and severely limits housing opportunities for minorities (Feins and Bratt, 1983; U.S. HUD, 1979c). [*See also Chapter 18 by the Citizens Commission on Civil Rights.*] Female-headed households also tend to suffer greater housing problems than the majority of the population: 10 percent live in housing officially rated as inadequate, as opposed to 7.5 percent of all households (President's Commission on Housing, 1982, 9).

But these groups suffer more than simply inadequate, insecure, and unaffordable housing conditions. As Achtenberg and Marcuse (1983, 207) state, "Housing, after all, is much more than shelter: it provides social status, access to jobs, education and other services, a framework for the conduct of household work, and a way of structuring economic, social and political relationships." Thus, minorities are held back educationally, in terms of employment opportunities, and in countless other ways by inadequate and segregated housing. Further, women tend to be confined to the traditional division of labor within the family and to limited labor force participation, in part as a result of housing design and locational patterns [*see Chapter 13 by Dolores Hayden*]. And housing patterns tend to keep classes, races, and subcultures separate and antagonistic, and thus less able to join forces in combating their common enemies. "In this way, the housing crisis today expresses and perpetuates the economic and social divisions that exist within the society as a whole" (Achtenberg and Marcuse, 1983, 207).

The housing crisis also reflects fundamental institutional problems:

1. The central element in the provision of mortgage credit in the United States, the thrift industry, ran into deep trouble, beginning with the steep inflation that characterized the second half of the 1960s. Long-term, fixed-rate mortgages would not yield adequate profits in inflationary times, and competition from other savings instruments and institutions left the thrifts with insufficient funds to lend to potential mortgagors. As thrifts chalked up huge losses and failures mounted, Congress took steps to restructure the housing finance system and the banking system generally. These changes likely will lead to increased concentration within the financial industry and increased domination of the financial system by large commercial banks, to a possible shortage of housing credit, and to higher-priced mortgages, thereby exacerbating the problems of low-, moderate-, and middle-income housing consumers. [*See Chapter 4 by Ann Meyerson.*]

2. Largely because of its dependence on adequate, reliable, and reasonably priced sources of credit, the residential construction industry is increasingly unable to meet the nation's housing needs. Since 1970, production levels have experienced severe peaks and troughs, with a particularly deep trough moving into the 1980s (LeGates and Murphy, 1984). The industry's all-time-high production figure came in 1972, with 2.4 million units. In 1980 it was down to 1.3 million units, a precipitous drop from the previous year's figure of 1.8 million units. In 1981 and in 1982, only 1.1

million units were produced each year. The 1.6 million units in 1984 were still way below both the figure of a dozen years earlier (when the total number of households was considerably smaller) and the units needed for new household formation and replacement of the existing stock. Unemployment in the construction industry is always among the highest of any sector of the economy: 14.2 percent in November 1984, an astounding 21.9 percent in November 1982 (U.S. Department of Labor, 1982, 1984).

3. The federal government is rapidly withdrawing from its traditional role of directly subsidizing housing production. In recent years, virtually all programs that directly add, through new construction or rehabilitation, to the stock of housing available to lower-income households have been terminated; federal subsidies to those living in government-aided housing have been reduced, by requiring residents to pay 30 percent instead of 25 percent of their incomes; plans are under way to demolish, convert, or sell off substantial portions of the existing subsidized stock; and the move to housing allowances is giving a small proportion of the needy an inadequate sum to compete on the open market for a dwindling (and in some areas nonexistent) supply of decent, moderate-priced vacancies. [*See Chapter 21 by Chester Hartman for a detailing of these Reagan administration moves.*]

The chapters in Parts 1 and 2, somewhat artificially divided into "private sector" and "public sector" treatments (artificial because the private sector in the United States almost never operates without some significant level of support from the public sector, and because the public sector by and large exists to provide that support), describe and analyze various manifestations of the nation's housing crisis and the role the principal actors have played in it. Part 3 offers possible strategies for change. Chapters cover the potential and limitations of political organization of tenants and homeowners, as well as the various actions and programs around which they can be organized. The book then presents a more holistic set of possible solutions, all of which proceed from the goal of "decommodifying" housing—converting it from a commodity that is developed, bought, sold, and managed exclusively or primarily for profit maximization to a "use good," something developed and managed exclusively for the purpose of meeting a basic human need in the most efficient and satisfactory fashion. In this context, the final chapters analyze a range of current and historical experiences from other countries—some capitalist, some socialist. Americans tend to examine insufficiently the social welfare systems and programs of other countries, and perhaps nowhere is this truer than in housing.

At a time when past solutions have either been inadequate or have failed, and when prevailing ideas and programs seem patently unable to meet the challenge of a real and growing housing crisis in the United States, a critical analysis of what is wrong and a bold presentation of alternatives is particularly appropriate. We predict that things will get a lot worse. But with the analytic tools and programmatic ideas offered here, they *can* get better. At the least, it is time to address the root causes of the nation's housing crisis.

# Notes

1. Of the 33 chapters herein, 15 were written specially for this volume or are being published for the first time: Hopper–Hamberg, both Meyerson articles, Schlesinger–Erlich, Appelbaum–Gilderbloom, Sánchez, Orfield, Kravitz–Collings, Bratt, McAfee, Borgos, Schifferes, Appelbaum, Marcuse (on Vienna), and Hamberg–Schuman; 8 have been revised or updated specially for this book: Stone, Marcuse (on the myth of the benevolent state), Dolbeare, Schur–Robbins, Hartman, Kolodny, Schuman, and Hartman–Stone.

2. The housing crisis schema that follows, along with some data and phrasing, have been adopted from Achtenberg and Marcuse, 1983.

3. In the spring of 1984, HUD issued a study estimating the number of homeless at from 250,000 to 350,000, a figure drastically below previous estimates (U.S. HUD, 1984b). Critics charged political motivations—the administration's desire to minimize the problem—and shoddy methodology. Among the more blatant methodological defects were frequent reliance on patently unreliable local estimates; use of doubtful assumptions and extrapolation techniques; concentration on estimating the number of homeless seeking or using shelter facilities on a given night, instead of estimating the number homeless throughout the year; difficulties in counting the number of homeless who do not seek out formal shelter facilities; inadequate attention to "pre-homelessness" such as temporary doubling up; and use of a "metropolitan area" definition that skewed results to minimize the final figure. [*See also note 1 to Chapter 2 by Kim Hopper and Jill Hamberg.*] The House Subcommittee on Housing and Community Development held hearings on the HUD report on May 24, 1984.

4. The Mortgage Bankers Association of America began keeping such records in 1953, but it is doubtful that the rate was higher in the postwar or war periods.

---

*In October 1984, a sixty-six-year-old black woman, Eleanor Bumpurs, was shot to death in her New York City public housing apartment by a police officer who was attempting to restrain her while Housing Authority officials evicted her for nonpayment of rent. The incident raised many questions and considerable controversy regarding the appropriateness of police behavior and procedures, underlying racial dynamics, and the role of the city's social service agencies in handling Mrs. Bumpurs's case prior to the eviction action. The following letter, by representatives of the Coalition for the Homeless, the Lower Manhattan Loft Tenants, the Metropolitan Council on Housing, and the New York State Tenant and Neighborhood Coalition, published in the* New York Times *(Nov. 25, 1984), offers a broader perspective on the incident.*

## MUST WE SHOOT SOCIETY'S LOSERS?

To the Editor:

Your Nov. 2 editorial ("Then, After the Killing . . .") concerning the fatal eviction of Mrs. Eleanor Bumpurs, a New York City Housing Authority tenant, raised important issues concerning the sensitivity with which our law-enforcement institutions handle such situations.

We commend you for suggesting that more thoughtful, sympathetic procedures should be developed to avoid adding still "more unstable people to the city's growing homeless population." Certainly, it is not cost effective to add another bed to a public shelter at $29 a night when this woman was already sheltered at city expense for $2.98 a night

($89.44 monthly rent) in her own home! Not to mention humane.

However, in view of the alarming increase in homelessness now occurring in New York and of the hundreds of thousands of middle- and low-income tenants barely winning the struggle to hang onto their homes, an essential vein of questions raised by this savage episode must be addressed.

Should a human being who cannot pay his or her rent be ordered, forcibly or not, from his or her home? Is eviction from one's home an appropriate response to that person's economic failure? Should we continue to inflict homelessness, and the malnutrition and sickness that accompany it, upon those of us who fail to succeed in the financial arena?

To go a step farther, is the economic arena we have devised to organize our society so odious that we need dire consequences to insure that it won't be avoided? If masses of people would indeed shun the economic thrall encompassing our society unless pain of suffering and death are promised for doing so, isn't it appropriate to rethink at least some aspects of our social organization?

There is something profoundly wrong with a system that legally allows an armed force to break down the door, invade someone's home and throw that person into the street at gunpoint—for money. This is precisely what our eviction laws permit.

Resisting being torn from her shelter, Mrs. Bumpurs's naked terror at the siege of her sanctuary shames us into facing at this late date how inextricably shelter and survival are bound; how instinctively we feel their connection. So basic a need must be recognized by all as a right and so reflected in our laws. We must find solutions other than eviction—the stripping away of one's home—for economic hardship.

We have already decided (at least, in law) that racial, religious, ethnic and gender discrimination are not tolerable. Only until we reject that last bastion of cruelty and incivility, economic discrimination, and then actually practice what we have codified, will we be able to call our human species civilized. Until then, we will continue to mortgage our lives to buy the fictitious security that weapons provide, leaving our priorities in the miserable state where warheads and profits precede housing and human compassion.

*Fred Greisbach*
*Adrienne Leban*
*Jane Benedict*
*William Rowen*

---

This letter to the *New York Times* is reprinted here with the permission of the writers.

*Critical Perspectives on Housing*

# Part I

# The Workings of the Private Housing Market

# 1

# The Causes of the Housing Problem

*Emily Paradise Achtenberg*
*Peter Marcuse*

*The housing problem in the United States, as outlined in the Editors' Introduction, has several distinct aspects: availability, affordability, quality, security, and inequality. The treatment of housing as a commodity and its subservience to the maintenance of profitability are seen as the root causes of the nation's housing problems, in conjunction with vast inequalities of income and wealth and the roles of racism and sexism in perpetuating these inequalities. Far from limiting or constraining the commodification of housing, government, both historically and in the present, has actively assisted in the process of capital accumulation by the private sector and has provided whatever was deemed necessary to maintain the social peace in the face of vast inequality. Now, with declining economic growth and cyclical inflation, increasing foreign competition, and Third World resistance to U.S. domination, housing problems are increasing, and the ability of both the private sector and government to contain the conflicts around housing issues is sharply reduced.*

## The Commodity Treatment of Housing

Why is the housing problem so bad, and why is it getting worse? There are many contributing factors, but the principal reason is that housing in our society is produced, financed, owned, operated, and sold in ways designed to serve the interests of private capital. Housing—a necessity of life—is treated not as a social good but as a source of private profit, as a commodity [*for a discussion of the meaning and limitations of this term, see our Chapter 28*]. Government policies affecting housing, which supposedly serve the common good, systematically operate to reinforce the profitability of the housing sector and of the business community as a whole [*see Chapter 14 by Peter Marcuse*]. Such improvement in housing as has occurred historically

Originally published as "Towards the Decommodification of Housing: A Political Analysis and a Progressive Program," in *America's Housing Crisis: What Is to Be Done?* ed. Chester Hartman (Boston: Routledge & Kegan Paul, 1983), 202–18, 231. Reprinted by permission of the Institute for Policy Studies.

has come about only when it has served the interests of private capital, or when pressures from below (both political and economic) have forced it to occur.

## The Private Housing Sector and Private Profit

In the most immediate sense, the supply, cost, quality, location, and use patterns of housing in our society reflect the market activities of the private housing sector, which is itself comprised of multiple interests. These include real estate developers, builders, materials producers, mortgage lenders and other providers of housing credit, investors, speculators, landlords, and homeowners. [*See Chapter 4 by Ann Meyerson, Chapter 5 by Joe R. Feagin, Chapter 6 by Barry Checkoway, and Chapter 7 by Tom Schlesinger and Mark Erlich.*] While each of these "actors" makes money from housing in a different way, they share a common interest in housing as a profitable commodity. (Homeowners, of course, have a contradictory relationship to their housing as both shelter and investment, a matter of significance for this analysis.)

For housing consumers, the consequences are manifold. First, the high and rising cost of housing in the marketplace reflects, in part, profits made during the initial production or development stage. Land and construction loan interest (including profits to speculators and private lenders) are by far the most rapidly rising elements of housing production costs (President's Commission on Housing, 1982, 181). Further, most materials used in the construction of housing are produced by giant corporations with few incentives for cost control.

Once a house or apartment building is completed, its cost to the consumer also reflects the speculative gain generally made by each successive owner who trades it for profit in the marketplace (housing is perhaps the only common commodity whose market value increases with age). And since virtually every real estate purchase is financed with borrowed funds, added to that is the cost of mortgage interest, which has skyrocketed in recent years. For tenants and homeowners alike, mortgage payments—reflecting both the market price of housing and the interest on the permanent loan—constitute the single largest element of monthly housing costs (40–65 percent). Other significant cost elements are the property tax—a regressive tax on real estate as a form of private wealth—and utilities, with their substantial profit component.

The quest for profits also limits the production of housing because the privately controlled resources required for its production are allocated to housing only when it is profitable for developers, land speculators, materials producers, and mortgage lenders to do so. For example, at the peak of economic booms when business is expanding, commercial banks traditionally cut back on housing loans in favor of more profitable, short-term lending to government and corporate borrowers. And savings and loans, which traditionally make their funds available to housing, have less money to lend because their depositors seek more profitable investment outlets elsewhere. Similarly, scarce urban land is available for housing only when housing is its "highest and best" (most profitable) use; and even basic construction materials are diverted from the housing sector when they can be sold more profitably elsewhere. The result is an extremely cyclical pattern of housing construction, which has significantly inhibited the productive capacity of the housing industry (President's Commission on Housing, 1982, xxi, 182; Solomon, 1981, 200).

In addition, because housing is adequately maintained only when it yields a profit, real estate owners and lenders "disinvest" from poor or "high-risk" neighborhoods through undermaintenance, tax delinquency, arson, abandonment, and redlining, accompanied by the withdrawal of public services (Marcuse, 1979a, 1981a). At the same time, housing capital and credit are reinvested in the speculative purchase and refinancing of existing buildings in profitable "upscale" neighborhoods, without adding to the housing stock or improving its quality. Finally, discriminatory practices persist in the housing market, in part because they benefit certain segments of the housing industry. For example, blockbusting tactics enable real estate speculators to buy cheap and sell dear, while mortgage lenders can convert their old loans to higher-yield investments in both the newly segregated black and resegregated white neighborhoods (U.S. Commission on Civil Rights, 1975).

## The Housing Sector and Capital as a Whole

At the same time, the private housing sector operates within the broader context of an economic, social, and political system that serves the interests of private capital (business) more generally (Offe, 1975). The way in which the organization of production and the relationship between different economic and social groups interacts with the commodity nature of housing and is in turn reinforced by the private housing system is basic to understanding—and addressing—the root causes of our housing problems.

For example, as noted above, the cyclical nature of economic activity in our profit-oriented system shapes the flow of capital and credit to the housing sector and structures opportunities for profit in housing development, finance, and ownership. Thus, while housing is crowded out on the upswing of the business cycle, it has traditionally led the way out of recession as business demand slackens. In turn, this countercyclical pattern of housing activity has played an important role in stabilizing the economy, and in restoring conditions for more profitable business growth (Solomon, 1981). In recent years, however, fluctuations in both the housing and business cycles have tended to be more extreme and mutually reinforcing. This has led to some prolonged periods of "stagflation," which has significantly intensified the housing crisis and the problems of the economy as a whole.

At the same time, the unequal distribution of income and wealth created by our profit-motivated production system leaves many people with jobs and incomes that are inadequate to meet the rising cost of housing, while others are quite well off. The movement of business capital in recent years from manufacturing to the more profitable service sector (and from Frost-belt to Sunbelt) has exacerbated these disparities, through the transformation of both the labor market and the housing market. Thus, in some cities, plants shut down, blue-collar workers lose jobs, real estate owners and lenders disinvest, and the housing market collapses. In others, well-paid technicians, managers, and professionals attracted by revitalized service industries compete with low-paid workers for scarce housing, creating profitable opportunities for real estate speculation and gentrification. The net result is a loss of affordable housing at both ends, while communities and cities are transformed to meet the changing requirements of profit-oriented production.

Similarly, racism and sexism in the society as a whole help to structure patterns of housing use that serve the interests of capital at the expense of disadvantaged groups. Racial discrimination in employment makes housing less available to and affordable by minorities, while discriminatory housing practices foster the creation of segregated, disenfranchised communities that either become ripe targets for profitable business redevelopment or are abandoned by the public as well as by the private sector. Housing options for female-headed households are similarly restricted by women's inferior employment status. At the same time, housing design and development patterns isolate and tie women to the home and increase profit opportunities, not just for the real estate industry, but also for the producers of a vast array of household consumption goods. Finally, the social and economic inequalities perpetuated by the housing market reinforce stratification within the labor market, which supports the profitability of business and the tractability of labor in general.

## The Role of Government

While government policies have led to some improvements in housing, they have not solved the housing problem. Indeed, in some respects they have operated to intensify the housing problem, especially for low-income and minority groups. In any case, government actions affecting housing have not stemmed primarily from a benevolent desire to assist the ill-housed, but have tended to serve two major functions.[1]

ACCUMULATION. Enhancing opportunities for private profit, both within the housing sector and, more important, for the business community as a whole. This includes actions taken to assure that the minimal housing requirements of the workforce are met in a manner consistent with the needs of profit-oriented production. It also includes housing-related measures geared to promoting more profitable economic growth—for example, by stimulating housing production to restart the economy in a recession, or by choking off housing credit to curb inflation.

LEGITIMATION. Preserving "social peace" against the threat of disruption (real or perceived) from disaffected social groups, through measures that stabilize and reinforce the existing social and economic order. These include housing concessions granted in order to integrate subordinate groups within the dominant system, as well as the use of housing for purposes of repression, oppression, and exploitation.

Particular housing policies may serve both of these functions, and will reflect the political, economic, and social situation (and balance of forces) at a given time. Neither the business community nor the government acts monolithically in relation to housing; even within the housing sector, different interests may have conflicting needs for government support (e.g., mortgage lenders want to raise interest rates, developers want to lower them). Moreover, the requirements of the housing industry may be incompatible with those of business or of the economy as a whole at certain times, as during inflationary periods when continued housing expansion cannot be supported. In general, the government acts to mediate or manage these conflicts—as well as those resulting from the political pressures exerted by organized housing consumers—in ways that best support the accumulation and legitimation needs of the system as a whole.

These patterns are illustrated by the history of federal efforts to promote homeownership in the postwar period. [*See related discussion in Chapter 3 by Michael E. Stone and Chapter 14 by Peter Marcuse.*] After World War II, the pent-up need for housing, coupled with war-induced prosperity and the increased productive capacity of the economy, stimulated a huge housing construction boom. With expanded federal mortgage insurance and tax incentives for homeownership, the suburban single-family tract house became the vehicle for this explosive growth, supported by the development of federally assisted infrastructure and highways.

While the postwar homeownership boom helped many Americans to improve their living standards, it also provided vast new outlets for profitable investment by real estate developers, mortgage lenders, and other segments of the housing industry. The creation of new demand not just for housing but for a wide variety of household consumption goods was profitable for business as a whole. And with long-term mortgages (and other forms of household credit), consumer buying power could be expanded without creating new pressures on business for higher wages.

At the same time, federal promotion of homeownership gave working families an economic and social "stake in the system," at the price of reduced mobility (and hence more limited bargaining power with employers). It provided housing consumers with the illusion of control but the reality of burdensome long-term debt. And it channeled their legitimate shelter needs into concerns with investment risk and profitability. Federal homeownership policies also fostered racial exclusion, reinforced the oppression of women, and increased the housing problems of the poor by eroding the central-city tax base.

In recent years, the growing problems of the economy and of the housing industry have significantly altered the functions of homeownership. Unprecedented inflation (fueled in part by the tremendous increase in residential mortgage debt) and the lack of new housing construction have driven up the value of existing homes and encouraged the use of homeownership as an investment vehicle, especially by those in upper-income tax brackets. Today, the same tax incentives that fostered the growth of the suburbs are stimulating housing speculation and displacement of the poor from the inner city, as affluent condo converters bid up the price of scarce housing resources (Goetze, 1981; *Boston Globe*, June 20, 1982).

While buying a home has now become a privilege reserved for the wealthy, the supposed benefits of homeownership for many others are gradually being undermined. With today's variable-rate mortgages and rising property-tax bills, few moderate-income homeowners can count on stability of costs or liquidity for their investments. And a growing number who live a paycheck or two ahead of the bank risk the loss of their equities—as well as their homes—to foreclosure. . . .

Public housing—the only government program that has over the long run directly addressed the housing needs of the poor—was originally designed for other purposes. The earliest government-sponsored projects were built to ease housing shortages for munitions and defense workers during World War I, thereby aiding the U.S. war production effort. The National Housing Act of 1937 was primarily a public works program, intended to stimulate the depressed economy and to stem the tide of social unrest by providing jobs for temporarily unemployed city workers. After World War II, more public housing was built to appease the discontent of returning veterans. Locally, public housing often provided a vehicle through which politicians could dispense patronage.

In the 1950s, as government slum clearance uprooted the poor from central cities and the upwardly mobile left the projects for the suburbs, public housing was increasingly occupied by lower-income households and in many large cities by minorities. Political pressures generated by the ghetto rebellions and by the civil rights and welfare rights movements of the 1960s led to significant reforms, including rent reductions, liberalized admission criteria, and protection against arbitrary eviction. Ultimately, many large projects became the "housing of last resort" for those left behind by the restructured economy (primarily elderly and female-headed households on fixed incomes).

Today, public housing suffers from official neglect, chronic underfunding and undermaintenance, and often inefficient and bureaucratic management. It has become an oppressive device for stigmatizing the poor, for maintaining racial and class divisions, and for discrediting the concept of public enterprise in our society. Together with the other lower-income housing production programs of the 1960s and 1970s—which provided lucrative tax shelter benefits and direct subsidies to the private housing and mortgage lending industries—public housing has met only a fraction of the existing need. [*For further discussion of the public housing program, see Chapter 20 by Rachel G. Bratt.*] And as the programs for providing lower-income housing have become increasingly dependent on the system of private housing development, finance, and ownership, their costs have risen dramatically. As of 1982, the direct subsidy cost for a new unit of Section 8 housing was $4,000–5,500 per year (U.S. HUD, 1982b).

As for neighborhood policies, the federal role is well known. Urban renewal enhanced opportunities for profit in the development of prime inner-city real estate while fostering business and institutional expansion. In the process, at least 1 million lower-income and minority households were uprooted and their communities destroyed (Gans, 1982, 385–86).

In the 1960s, with the growing threat of social disorder in the cities, outright "slum clearance" efforts were replaced with more muted attempts at housing rehabilitation and ultimately with the neighborhood-oriented Model Cities and Community Action programs of the Great Society. Then in the mid-1970s, as the problems of the economy worsened and the protest of the poor seemed to weaken, Community Development Block Grants provided the vehicle through which funds for neighborhood programs could be drastically cut, in exchange for increased local political control over resource allocation. Currently, block grants provide little more than a limited form of revenue sharing to offset the impact of local "fiscal crisis" cutbacks, and an arena in which local neighborhood groups are pitted against one another in the battle for diminishing resources.

Finally, the overall pattern of federal housing and neighborhood subsidies in the postwar period has been highly regressive, reinforcing the unequal distribution of income and wealth. Direct federal budget outlays for housing and community development, currently totaling about $11 billion, have barely kept up with inflation. But housing-related tax expenditures (revenues lost through homeowner and investor tax deductions) have more than doubled since 1979 and are now $40 billion (Dolbeare, 1985). Not included in this total is the loss of billions from accelerated depreciation of commercial and residential real estate, now the standard method for writing off the value of rental property (U.S. Office of Management and Budget, 1982, 7). These hidden subsidies primarily benefit those in the top 10 percent of the income distribution. [*For a more detailed discussion of tax expenditures for housing, see Chapter 15 by Cushing Dolbeare.*]

Today, federal policies affecting housing and neighborhoods are part of an explicit government strategy to bolster corporate profits. . . . The overall approach is one of income redistribution directly to business through tax cuts, deregulation, and other measures, combined with reduced social spending to offset the tax cuts and continued credit restrictions to curb inflation.

In support of this effort, all federal assistance for housing production and even federally supported housing credit activities will be drastically curtailed or eliminated. Limited demand-side subsidies are replacing existing production-oriented subsidies for assisted housing, assuring that the publicly aided stock will shrink as units are lost through deterioration, demolition, and private resale. Housing vouchers as currently proposed may aid private landlords but are unlikely to increase the housing supply or add to its quality. [*For further discussion of the administration's housing policies, see Chapter 21 by Chester Hartman.*] At the same time, continued credit stringency and reduced federal involvement in housing finance will diminish housing's share of resources in the economy as a whole. [*See Chapter 4 by Ann Meyerson.*]

These measures, coupled with the impact of income-maintenance cutbacks on consumer purchasing power, are guaranteed to make the housing crisis even worse, especially for the poor and increasingly for middle-income households also. But while it is tempting to view the current situation as a regressive departure from the mainstream of postwar housing policy, our analysis suggests that the basic accumulation and legitimation functions served by government have not changed. Rather, the underlying balance of economic, social, and political forces has shifted as the limits of postwar prosperity have been reached.

As long as the expanding economy provided room to increase living standards and sustain business growth at the same time, improvement in housing was possible. But today, as major U.S. corporations are increasingly threatened by foreign competition, Third World resistance to U.S. exploitation, and . . . inflation, business wants a larger share of the shrinking economic pie. Housing can be easily targeted for attack—precisely because of the wasteful way it has been produced, financed, and owned in our society.

Indeed, some segments of the housing industry will suffer as public and private resources are reallocated to bolster the profitability of more powerful corporate interests. Others—such as developers and investors who can shift their resources into downtown office, commercial, and retail construction or the luxury rehabilitation and conversion of well-located inner-city housing (aided by substantial tax incentives)—will continue to prosper. But housing consumers—especially lower-income and minority households—will pay the real price, in the form of reduced housing options, less stability, and higher costs. Moreover, the fundamental problems of the U.S. economy and the squeeze on corporate profits that are the root of today's housing crisis are likely to continue well beyond the Reagan administration. What is at stake politically is how the economy (including the housing sector) will be restructured in the long run to respond to these conditions, and in whose interest the restructuring will occur.

# Note

1. The terms adopted in the text stem from an extensive literature (and debate) about the role of the state, which has been very fruitful in many areas. For a more detailed discussion of their application, see Marcuse, 1980a. [*See also Chapter 14 by Peter Marcuse.*]

# 2

# The Making of America's Homeless: From Skid Row to New Poor, 1945–1984

*Kim Hopper*
*Jill Hamberg*

*Given the nature of the housing problem and its increasing intensity, it is not surprising that substantial numbers of people are now facing the most extreme form of housing deprivation—not simply inadequate shelter but homelessness. The homelessness phenomenon stems not only from changes taking place in the housing market but also from changes in the labor market (occupational structure, general economic decline, and household demography), in the structure of our urban areas, and in public policies designed for "dependent" populations. What we are witnessing in the 1980s is the culmination of structural trends developing over the previous decade that will continue to intensify even during cyclical periods of economic recovery.*

At first glance, it looked like a scene from the portfolio of Walker Evans or Dorothea Lange: a black-and-white photograph of a Galveston, Texas, family, grim-faced mother and two solemn youngsters posed against the rough-planked wall of a shack. But the year was 1984, not 1934. The photograph of the Reynolds family appeared—not in the archives of the Farm Security Administration—but on the cover of the January 2, 1984, issue of *Newsweek*, under the caption *Homeless in America*.

The echoes of the Great Depression may have been staged, but they are nonetheless telling. Who are these people if not tokens of mass dispossession of a sort not seen since the lean years of the 1930s? And what is their likely fate if this is their plight in the midst of an economic recovery?

Only in the past few years has a clumsy Victorian word, "homelessness," come back into prominence, snatched from oblivion by a public made increasingly uneasy by the presence of large numbers of fellow citizens living on the streets. The word succeeds a host of others, generally terms of derogation—words like "vagrant," "derelict," and "bum"—that only a scant decade ago were regularly used when describing this sector of the disenfranchised. The fact that such terms have faded (though not disappeared) from use suggests something about the scale of the transformation that the homeless have undergone. Grizzled veterans of the rails and flophouses have had to make way for unfamiliar cohorts of new arrivals:

men and women of all ages and colors, the hale and the disabled, the newly jobless and the never-employed. In some places, whole families on the road or in emergency accommodations outnumber the single homeless; many others are poised just short of homelessness, scraping by at a level few would grace with the term "decent." Still others slip periodically into homelessness as meager benefits meted out on a monthly or biweekly basis invariably give out before the next check's arrival. Indeed, the cautious imprecision of the word itself suggests a reluctance to categorize, a prudent reminder that the only sure thing these people have in common is the one thing they all lack.

This nascent distrust of the traditional categories of dereliction may signal another change as well, for it has become increasingly apparent that the problem of homelessness has less to do with personal inadequacy than it does with resource scarcity. Accordingly, it makes little sense to confine analysis of the problem to a scrutiny of those who are its victims. To state only the obvious, to understand homelessness today one must understand not only why people are poor but why their poverty takes the distinctive form of having no place to live. Homelessness must be approached as one manifestation of the housing crisis at large.

## The Emergence of Widespread Homelessness

Locating the precise moment at which a "crisis" emerges is a hazardous and perhaps unrealistic undertaking. Declarations of crises—official or otherwise—are as much political pronouncements made in the interest of provoking corrective action as they are statements about the gravity or urgency of the issues at stake. The available evidence suggests, however, that it was in the period from the early to the late 1970s that the relevant factors fell into place and their combined force gathered momentum. In the early 1980s, as the economy worsened and the housing market tightened even more, the limits of tolerance were reached, and widespread homelessness resulted. To be sure, the effects were differentially distributed. Groups whose hold on a settled mode of life was already tenuous were the first to be affected: Thus the arrival of ex-psychiatric patients and of young, jobless minority men on the streets and in the shelters was apparent in some areas by the mid-1970s. As the decade progressed and the forces responsible for homelessness intensified, the numbers of the homeless grew, and their composition diversified.

Displacement by itself does not make for sustained homelessness. If affordable replacement housing can be located, families and individuals resettle; their homelessness becomes a transient dislocation. But when the option of relocation is foreclosed or postponed into the dim future, it becomes misleading to speak of homelessness as a transient phenomenon. Today, as more and more individuals and families find themselves living in emergency quarters for extended periods, homelessness has taken on the character of a captive state. Consignment to shelters and hotel placements is fast becoming routinized as a makeshift way of life for many of those displaced from their homes.

Briefly, we shall argue that decisive changes have occurred in the economy at large, in the housing market, and in government programs providing for the disabled and dependent, and that these changes have made the course of everyday life an increasingly tenuous affair for growing numbers of Americans. Homelessness is but one extreme instance of this process. The driving dynamic behind it is a widening gap for many households between the cost of their subsistence needs and the resources available to meet them. The growing scarcity of affordable housing operates in reciprocal fashion with the progressively deteriorating situation of individual households. The upshot is the dearth of housing as a procurable good.

## The Magnitude of Need

Images and observations of contemporary homelessness abound, but they cannot substitute for a thoroughgoing review of the subject. Efforts to go further, to take the measure of the causes and consequences that would adequately capture the dimensions of the problem today, bristle with difficulties. To begin with, there is scant information—primarily the yield from local studies and anecdotal testimony on the part of shelter and soup-kitchen workers—on the scale of the problem. Homeless people cannot be tagged like geese and their patterns of migration charted.

Something is known, however, about the dimensions of need and the likelihood of its persisting. In November 1983, the Department of Health and Human Services reported (on the basis of estimates provided by advocacy groups) that as many as 2 million people may be homeless nationwide (*HHS News*, Nov. 25, 1983; *New York Times*, Dec. 4, 1983). Shortly thereafter, this figure was revised downward by the Department of Housing and Urban Development in a report that concluded the "most reliable" range for the total number of homeless on a given night was between 250,000 and 350,000 (U.S. HUD, 1984b). Serious questions have been raised about the methods employed to arrive at such an estimate, however.[1] Estimates of those tottering on the brink of homelessness are even more difficult to obtain. Nonetheless, there is ample reason to believe that significant numbers of people are making do under barely tolerable circumstances: doubling up, squatting in abandoned buildings, living in dwellings without heat, taking up permanent residence in flophouses.

## Behind the Present Crisis

Recent studies of homelessness typically cite four main causes of the explosive increase in numbers: (1) rising rates of unemployment (especially among the young and minorities), (2) a dire shortage of affordable housing, (3) the deinstitutionalization of patients from psychiatric hospitals, and

(4) intensive reviews of disability-benefit recipients coupled with tighter eligibility restrictions (Baxter and Hopper, 1981; Cuomo, 1983; Hombs and Snyder, 1982; Hopper et al., 1982; Salerno et al., 1984; U.S. Conference of Mayors, 1984b). These factors point to the relevant developments behind the precipitating events (eviction or the threat of it, loss of income, personal crisis, among others) that may propel someone onto the streets. But the dynamics behind such developments remain mysterious. Insofar as such factors are put forward as "explanations," then, they themselves are in need of explaining.

One clue is the fact that most of the causes identified above, and phenomena closely allied with them, have occurred at various times in the postwar era and yet did not produce the level of homelessness we see today. Indeed, if widespread poverty, hunger, unemployment, deinstitutionalization, and migration were invariably linked with homelessness, we would expect to have seen much more of it at other times during the postwar period. The proportion of the population living below the federal poverty level has been increasing steadily since 1978. By 1983, some 35.3 million people, representing 15.2 percent of the population, were considered poor; this compares with approximately 11 percent in the 1968–1978 period. Yet, in 1959, 39.5 million people, or 22.4 percent of the population, were considered poor, and welfare benefits reached far fewer people (U.S. Bureau of the Census, 1982e, 1984d). Similarly, hunger and malnutrition were "rediscovered" in the early 1980s (Citizens' Commission on Hunger in New England, 1984; Community for Creative Non-Violence, 1983). But they were much more prevalent well into the late 1960s, before massive federally funded food programs made great headway toward eradicating such disorders of the poor by the late 1970s. Unemployment peaked at 10.8 percent in late 1982, but it had climbed above 9.0 percent during the 1974–1975 recession (*Dollars and Sense*, Oct. 1979, Feb. 1983). Not until the late 1970s did the sidewalk psychotic become a commonplace feature of the urban landscape, yet most deinstitutionalization occurred in the late 1960s and early 1970s (Scull, 1977). And only in the last few years have tent cities, mimicking the Hoovervilles of the 1930s, sprung up in the Sunbelt, although massive migration to the region has been occurring for decades.

The suspicion is unavoidable that boundary conditions have changed, that the operating set of limits and tolerances that determines a social order's capacity to absorb surplus populations has been materially altered. Somewhere a threshold was crossed.

The notion of a threshold is a crude one, meant in a figurative, not an analytic, sense. There is no charmed point at which the numbers of the disenfranchised suddenly attain crisis proportions. What we are reaching for is a means of describing a qualitative change in the experience of poverty in this country. How is it that the proximate causes of dispossession, documented in a raft of recent studies, eventuate in outright homelessness today, rather than in mere hardship and penury? Our contention is that closer scrutiny of the trajectories of the economy, demography, and relevant public policy will show how these developments have converged to create one peculiar form of marginalization—widespread homelessness—in this decade.

This will become clear if we compare the dynamics and causes of contemporary homelessness with those prevailing in two previous periods.

# 1945 to 1970: Prosperity and Its Discontents

The long period of postwar prosperity—when homelessness seemed to be on the verge of extinction—saw an unparalleled improvement in both real household income and housing conditions. The most pressing housing problem in the first decades after the war was considered to be substandard housing conditions. In 1940, 45 percent of all units lacked complete plumbing, but this had dropped to 7 percent by 1970. Similarly, poor structural conditions declined from 18 percent in 1940 to 5 percent in 1970 (Nenno, 1984). Old and obsolete dwellings were removed from the housing stock during this period for several reasons. Massive rural-to-urban migration effectively eliminated many of the worst shacks in the countryside. Large-scale urban renewal and highway programs cleared extensive sections of central cities, resulting in considerable displacement. But massive suburbanization had sufficiently opened up the housing stock in the central cities so that it could serve as a resource not only for those displaced by public action but for the large influx of rural migrants as well.

The starkest images of "the housing problem" were the cold-water slum tenement and the coal miner's or sharecropper's shack. The "homeless" skid-row "derelicts" were relegated to the charge of the missions, detoxification units, flophouses, landlords, jails, and social workers. In fact, except for the elderly and the disabled, government housing programs at that time explicitly excluded "nonfamily households" from eligibility—a policy, except for rare demonstration projects, still in effect today.

## The Rise and Fall of Skid Row

Skid row was essentially a residual product of the depression and the subsequent recovery. New federal relief and work programs, a revived economy, and the demands of the war effort all contributed to a marked reduction in the ranks of the homeless. Out of the remainder there emerged after the war the classic profile of skid row, subject of scores of sociological treatises and object of generalized contempt. It was a place populated almost exclusively by men, usually older white men, many of whom had long resided at the margins of polite society and a good proportion of whom suffered from chronic ailments, especially alcoholism. Depending on local economic conditions, between one-third and one-half of skid-row men worked, typically at menial jobs (Bahr, 1973). The rest relied on charity, missions, public agencies, or pensions. With rare exception (see O'Connor, 1963), and whether describing the geography of an urban niche or the ethnography of a culture, the studies of this period found not community but exile—a listless, aimless world, void of ambition or bonds, populated by casualties of poverty, pathology, old age, character deficiencies, or alcohol dependency. Victims rather than veterans of a chosen way of life, theirs was a world whose watchword could be found in the title of Tom Kromer's depression-era memoir of life on the skids, *Waiting for Nothing* (1935).

If there was one thing notable about the skid-row way of life as the 1960s drew to a close, it was the prospect of its imminent demise (Bahr, 1967). Urban renewal had already removed many of the more dilapidated regions, and the planned revitalization of other inner-city sections did not augur well for the future of remaining skid rows. At the same time, new additions to its population were on the decline. The future of skid row, observed one sociologist in 1970, hinged on the likelihood of its becoming an "open asylum" for the psychiatrically impaired and alcoholic (Rooney, 1970). Events in the following decade would confirm the partial truth of the prediction even as they would challenge the narrowness of the vision.

Note, however, that for the most part, skid-row men were *housed*—wretchedly, to be sure—but quartered nonetheless, in the missions, flop-houses, jails, and municipal lodging houses that catered to their numbers. They were not, in significant numbers, a street-dwelling population. Exceptional habitats were discovered—as when George Nash stumbled on a colony of homeless men living in a cache of sewer pipes in lower Manhattan (Nash, 1964)—but these were few and far between. Nothing like the organized squatting of the 1930s took place. Those on the skids hit the flops; the other poor remained in the urban slums and rural shacks.

## 1970 to 1979: A Gathering Storm

During the 1970s, the distinctive forces making for contemporary homelessness took shape, and the first signs of a nascent crisis surfaced. The decade was characterized by bouts of economic stagnation, with persistently high unemployment levels, rising inflation, declining real wages, and stagnant household incomes. Rapidly rising prices for houses barred many potential first-time buyers from the market, thereby increasing the demand for rental units. Urban displacement as the result of direct public action continued, but it was joined increasingly by housing abandonment and gentrification, encouraged by government policies. Instead of disappearing, the homeless population started to multiply and diversify; the deinstitutionalized mentally disabled were pushed out of whatever dwellings they had been able to find, unemployment soared, families broke up, and more and more households sought refuge after fires, vacate orders, and evictions.

### Income

In contrast to the 1950–1970 period—when median family income, in real terms, almost doubled—real wages in the 1970s declined 7.4 percent. Adjusted for inflation, median household income was the same at the end of the decade as at the beginning, but this was because an increasing number of households had more than one wage earner to compensate for the declining buying power of wages (U.S. Bureau of the Census, 1982e, 401, 432). Moreover, the relative stability of the median obscures another development: the growing polarization of the income distribution, reversing what had been the trend up to the early 1970s (*Dollars and Sense*, Apr. 1984). The middle began to shrink, while the top and especially the bottom started to expand. There were four primary reasons for this shift in the 1970s: (1) the changing occupational composition of the U.S. labor force; (2) the rising divorce rate and the growth of female-headed households; (3) high levels of unemployment; and (4) the erosion of the real value of benefits in means-tested income maintenance programs. These trends were intensified in the 1980s by the Reagan administration's tax and budget policies.

The shift in the occupational structure is the main and most enduring structural factor producing an increasingly bipolar income distribution. From 1960 to 1980, the percentage of the labor force employed in manufacturing fell by 20 percent. New private-sector jobs in the 1970s were overwhelmingly low-paid ones, principally in the retail and service areas. Traditional "smokestack" industries like auto and steel actually saw a net loss of jobs by the end of the decade. And even the new manufacturing industries, such as electronics, tended to have low- and high-paying jobs—assemblers on the one hand, engineers and technicians on the other—but few jobs in the middle.

The Northeast and the Midwest have been especially hard hit by the loss of manufacturing jobs. Large numbers of people in urban areas of these regions have been rendered redundant to the productive process. A pool of residual, unneeded labor has been building in many northern cities—a surplus of experienced, skilled workers whose prospects for comparable employment are grim. Some have found niches in the low-wage service economy; ex-steelworkers can be found pushing brooms in McDonald's in Pittsburgh, displacing the unskilled labor that used to command such work. Many have migrated to other areas in search of jobs. During the 1970s, the Sunbelt was largely able to absorb these new migrants, but by the early 1980s, slow rates of growth in some parts of the South and West made jobs increasingly hard to come by.

The size and composition of households underwent significant transformations, and this in turn influenced the distribution of income. Suburbanization and economic expansion (with its attendant increase in geographic mobility) encouraged the extended family to give way to the nuclear family as the most typical household form in the postwar decades. Average household size dropped from 3.37 in 1950 to 3.14 in 1970 to 2.73 in 1980 (U.S. Bureau of the Census, 1982e, 43). For renters, average household size was a low 2.0 in 1980, with over one-third of such households consisting of only one person and nearly two-thirds of one or two people (Downs, 1983). Contributing to this trend was an unprecedented rise in the divorce rate, which more than doubled during the 1970s. By the early 1980s, half of all marriages ended in divorce (Hacker, 1983).

As households were disaggregating and getting smaller, it was increasingly the case that two incomes were needed to make ends meet. In 1950, 36 percent of husband–wife families had more than one breadwinner; 25 years later, 49 percent of such families had at least two members in the labor force (Women's Work Project, 1978). Not surprisingly, divorce is often devastating economically as well as emotionally. Financial hardship falls especially on the woman: There is a separate household to maintain; alimony and child support, when paid, are often skimpy; day care may be expensive and difficult to arrange; and on average women earn only 59 percent of what men earn.

Hence the trend toward the "feminization" of poverty: Half of all female-headed households lived below the federally defined poverty level by the late 1970s. Some 3.3 million, or more than a third of all families headed by women, received Aid to Families with Dependent Children (AFDC) benefits in 1979; about 2.6 million received food stamps (Ehrenreich and Piven, 1984). Such programs undoubtedly eased the hardship felt by female-headed households but made them especially vulnerable to cuts in these programs.

Persistently high levels of unemployment in the 1970s also contributed to the slow shrinkage of the middle class. Even when "only" 7 percent of the labor force is unemployed, some 15–20 percent of all households experience job loss during the year. And most middle-income households become at least temporarily low-income households if the principal earner loses his or her job.

Unemployment has been especially linked to the enormous growth in families headed by black and other minority women; half of all black families are headed by women, and three-fifths of them are poor. Nearly half of working-age black men are without regular employment (Joe and Yu, 1984). Many no doubt reside with wives, female companions, or relatives. But many others are dependent on the less-than-secure hospitality of friends or the precarious lodgings of roominghouses or single-room-occupancy (SRO) hotels. Still others are "housed" in jails, prisons, halfway houses, and rehabilitation programs.

Government social programs and the economic expansion during the Vietnam war brought the incidence of poverty to its lowest point by 1973, with 23 million people (or 11.1 percent of the population) below the federally defined "poverty level" (U.S. Bureau of the Census, 1982e, 440). The percentage hovered between 11 and 12 percent for the rest of the decade, but the relative position of the poor deteriorated. The "poverty line" was 54 percent of the median in 1960, but declined to 40 percent in 1970 and 38 percent in 1979 (Harrington, 1984a).

Nonetheless, the impression persists that a resilient support apparatus, typically referred to as a "safety net," is in place for the very young, the old, the disabled, the destitute, the homeless, and the hungry. Those sleeping on the streets or waiting on soup lines are merely "accidents" who "fall be-tween the cracks," people for whom proper referrals are indicated. But 42 percent of the 11 million households living under the poverty level in 1980 received no welfare, no food stamps, no Medicaid, no school lunches, and no public housing (U.S. Bureau of the Census, 1982e, 320).

Piven and Cloward (1971) have persuasively argued that societies have expanded relief programs, not in altruistic response to hard times, but to ward off social unrest. Not need but demand, not the deserving but the unruly poor, not misery but the unwillingness to put up with it any longer—historically these have been the moving forces in liberalizing welfare ben-efits. When stability has been restored, the relief system, typically in con-tracted form, remains in place but is administered in adherence to the principle of "less eligibility." Relief must be made so onerous and demean-ing that any and all other resources will be resorted to before the state's grudging bounty is tested.

During the 1970s, in the absence of disruptive social unrest, there were gradual—and in the early 1980s, abrupt—reductions in the levels of benefits and numbers of beneficiaries in many social programs. This occurred in tandem with the worst unemployment levels since the 1930s, reaching depression dimensions in certain industries and sectors of the population. Under these circumstances, the main effect of contracting assistance pro-grams was not to channel people into the work force, for there were few jobs to be had, but to lower real wages and living standards for those working and to diminish the power of unions.

It is not surprising, then, to find that even before the Reagan administra-tion's assault on welfare benefits, there had been a steady erosion. The number of families receiving AFDC benefits tripled in the 1960s and con-tinued to rise steadily until 1976, then leveled off for the rest of the decade. But the real value of AFDC benefits declined by 28 percent between 1970 and 1980 (U.S. Bureau of the Census, 1982e, 340, 361).

More than half the states do not make AFDC payments to families when both parents are present in the home. These families, along with single adults not eligible for the Supplemental Security Income (SSI) program for the blind, the disabled, and the aged, find themselves relegated to locally funded General Assistance (GA, also known as Home Relief)—assuming they live in states and counties where it is available. Compared with other income-maintenance payments, GA benefits are invariably lower, some-times woefully so. Moreover, the real value of these benefits fell 32 percent during the 1970s (U.S. Bureau of the Census, 1982e, 340, 361).

## Housing

The growing polarization of the income distribution and the relative de-terioration of the situation of the very poor, when combined with related trends in the housing market, had two important effects: (1) It set the stage for both housing abandonment and gentrification; and (2) it brought an ever-larger number of households to the brink of a new level of shelter poverty.

The 1970s experienced an unprecedented wave of residential construction, particularly in the early part of the decade. More than 20 million units were added to the housing stock, equal to what it had taken the two previous decades to produce. The annual average of 2.1 million new units (including mobile homes) more than outpaced the rate of household formation, which averaged only 1.7 million a year (Downs, 1983).

There were two separate trends in terms of housing quality. New single-family houses were spacious—averaging 1,650 square feet by 1978—and relatively luxurious. Meanwhile, overall improvement in substandard housing halted, with the percentage of structurally deficient units roughly the same at the end of the decade as at the beginning (Nenno, 1984). And, as expected, the prevalence of substandard housing was concentrated among low-income and minority residents. Moreover, neighborhood quality—as measured by environmental conditions and local services—worsened in many areas during the decade.

Both purchase prices and monthly costs of homeownership increased much more rapidly than prices as a whole. Families that had purchased houses before 1975 benefited from the increase in value of their dwellings and enjoyed fixed-rate, low-interest mortgages. But while in 1950 roughly two-thirds of all families could have afforded to purchase a house, by 1976 that proportion had fallen to one-quarter (Stone, 1983). The proportion of all households owning a house grew only slightly from 62.9 percent in 1970 to 65.2 percent in 1979, despite the high rate of new single-family house construction (U.S. Bureau of the Census, 1984a, 1984b).

Although the proportion of homeowners did not change substantially, there was a shift in the characteristics of renter and owner households. In 1970 the median income of renters was 65 percent of that of homeowners, but by 1979 it had dropped to 55 percent (Dolbeare, 1983a). In 1970, less than half of renter households consisted of single men or female-headed families; in 1980, almost two-thirds were so constituted (Downs, 1983).

Rents increased more slowly than the Consumer Price Index (Downs, 1983), but still somewhat faster than tenant incomes—nearly double the rate, according to some estimates (Dolbeare, 1983a). The result was a dramatic increase in the proportion of income paid in rent, which jumped from a median of 20 percent—where it had hovered from 1950 to 1970—to 27 percent in 1980 (LeGates and Murphy, 1984; U.S. Bureau of the Census, 1981a, 7). Seven million households, mostly low-income renters, were paying more than 50 percent of their incomes for housing. For the very poor, the 2.7 million renter households with incomes below $3,000, the situation became catastrophic: Half were paying over 72 percent of their incomes for rent, leaving $71 a month for all other needs (Dolbeare, 1983a).

It should be clear by now that we are facing a qualitatively different level of shelter poverty from that described by Michael E. Stone in Chapter 3. According to Stone, approximately one-third of the nation's households were "shelter poor" in 1980; that is, they were unable to pay for nonhousing necessities and still cover their housing costs. But clearly only a portion of this one-third were homeless or near homeless. It is the very low-income households, paying more than half their incomes for rent, that literally must choose between housing and the other vital areas of sustenance.

Extremely high rent-to-income ratios are but one factor pushing people toward the edge of homelessness. Each year, some 2.5 million Americans are displaced from their homes. Moreover, approximately half a million low-rent units disappear annually through the combined efforts of conversion, arson, abandonment, inflation, and demolition (Hartman, Keating, and LeGates, 1982). Until the late 1970s, the vast majority of those displaced found alternative residences, often in the same neighborhoods. Studies of the fate of people forced to move have found that their new accommodations were usually more crowded, in poorer condition, and demanded higher rents than the housing they were forced to quit (LeGates and Hartman, 1981). But despite these worsened conditions, filtering down of a sort did operate. By the late 1970s, however, some of the displaced were not simply filtering down through the housing market; they were being winnowed out of it.

The polarization of income distribution and the relative deterioration of the economic situation of the poor, especially the dependent poor, were important factors in creating the conditions for both abandonment and gentrification (see Smith and Williams, 1986; Marcuse, 1981a, 1985a). Unlike the Great Depression, when households doubled up and owners boarded up vacant units awaiting the return of prosperity, in the 1970s landlords and financial institutions gave up on the "bottom" of the market—both on the buildings and on the people. At the same time, a growing number of young professional and managerial people, increasingly locked out of the first-time homebuyer market, began to outbid moderate-income tenants in a pinched rental market. The result is a situation in which people—rather than buildings—filter down through the market. Thus, while there is a growing surplus of people and buildings at the bottom, rents and incomes do not match up. Hence there is abandonment—often of sound housing—and homelessness.

One factor that has acted as a catalyst during the crisis of homelessness has been the steady disappearance of what had been housing of choice for some, housing of last resort for others—roominghouses, lodging houses, and "single-room-occupancy" (SRO) hotels. Such places provided affordable housing for a wide range of persons, from the elderly and younger working adults to the recently deinstitutionalized and the unemployed. The conversion of single- and multifamily housing to roominghouses in an earlier period reflected the adaptation of the housing market to this demand. But as the number of single-person households reached record levels in the 1970s, the supply of low-income, single-room housing became seriously depleted.

The first wave of urban renewal and highway-related displacement eliminated much of this housing in some downtown areas. A second wave of displacement, chiefly the result of abandonment and gentrification, as well as publicly sponsored urban-renewal projects in some cities, wiped out much of what remained.

From 1970 to 1982, 1,116,000 single-room units, nearly half of the total stock, disappeared nationwide. Many cities lost more than two-thirds of their rooming units (Green, 1982; Paul, 1981; Werner and Bryson, 1982). Residential hotels not facing demolition or slated for conversion are unusually susceptible to the ravages of inflation, owing to the labor-intensive nature of the service they offer.

By 1980, the economy was in a period of record-high interest rates and near-record-low residential construction, conditions that increased the demand for rental housing. During the late 1970s, "non-new creation" of rental units (i.e., conversion of nonresidential structures, retrieval of units temporarily off the market, and subdivision of existing units) exceeded new construction, reflecting elevated demand (Downs, 1983). Between 1975 and 1979, the rental vacancy rate dropped nationally from 6 percent to 5 percent, and in regions like the Northeast it fell well below the 5 percent usually considered necessary to accommodate normal mobility in the system (Sternlieb and Hughes, 1981).

## Deinstitutionalization

Early in the 1970s, the first reports surfaced of the failure of a "bold new reform" in community psychiatry launched in 1963 with the Community Mental Health Act. Actually, the policy of emptying out the state hospitals had begun in the mid-1950s, when asylum populations and costs were at record levels. It accelerated in the 1960s, prodded by a raft of patient-rights lawsuits, mounting evidence of the deleterious effects of hospitalization on long-term patients, widespread use of "antipsychotic" medication to quell the more disturbing overt symptoms of psychiatric disorders, and the lure of cost-savings that community-based treatment promised (Rose, 1979; Scull, 1977).

It should be stressed that deinstitutionalization was not, at its inception, a bad idea—quite the contrary. Its architects were thoroughly acquainted with the hazards of the hospital and well versed in the humane rhetoric of community-based care. But the reality bore little resemblance to the ideal. The depopulation of mental hospitals—from 559,000 patients in 1956 to 133,550 by 1980 (U.S. Bureau of the Census, 1984f, 120)—was never complemented by the mobilization of the resources needed to make community placement a workable reality. Specifically, the network of appropriate housing and support services failed to materialize (Baxter and Hopper, 1980).

In most instances, the route from hospital to homelessness was a circuitous one. Although direct discharges from the hospitals to the streets or shelters were not unknown, they were by no means typical. Most ex-patients were transferred to nursing homes (where the chronic mentally disabled now constitute the majority of the resident population), returned to families, or found their way to any of a variety of residential settings (board-and-care facilities, adult homes, SROs, congregate care). What is important to note is that the vast majority were housed, if poorly, outside the asylums. Only when such arrangements were disrupted, as happened frequently among a population unused to living on its own and often subject to harassment by landlords seeking to attract more "desirable" tenants, was the threat of homelessness posed. Displacement was not uncommon—owing to a check's failure to arrive on time, inability to manage budgeting on one's own, progressively deteriorating conditions within one's residence, the threat of eviction, or the slow unraveling of whatever precarious stability one had managed to achieve. Once lost, housing proved increasingly difficult to replace. As the number of residential hotels declined precipitously, even housing of last resort became scarce.

As the decade progressed, the second face of deinstitutionalization—the tightened admitting criteria in effect in most psychiatric facilities—assumed greater importance. Disturbed individuals who formerly would have been hospitalized now found themselves turned away, often without any other recourse or refuge. Others were admitted for brief hospital stays or referred to outpatient clinics, often with scant regard for their day-to-day living arrangements.

*The New Homeless*

The 1970s played host to a momentous transformation in the ranks of skid row. In the first place, skid row was no longer a geographically well-demarcated section of the inner city. As the old flophouses and bars were torn down, their clientele simply dispersed throughout the city. Moreover, as the old institutions were disappearing, a demand for the services they had provided was growing—a fact that contributed to the increasingly visible profile the homeless assumed throughout the 1970s. The new arrivals tended to be younger than their counterparts of the 1960s, and they were no longer exclusively male; homeless women began to appear on the streets in the early 1970s, and their numbers climbed steadily throughout the decade (Besser, 1975). Blacks and other minorities—rarely seen in the skid rows of the 1960s—were increasingly counted among the homeless. And, finally, the presence of obviously disturbed street-dwellers slowly took on the character of an urban cliché, startling only to the newcomer.

# 1980 to 1984: The Threshold Is Crossed

By 1981, advocates for the homeless had noticed a rapid increase in the number of people seeking shelter. As we have seen, by the end of the 1970s a significant number of households had been brought to the brink of destitution, but most of them were still managing to scrape by at the margins. In retrospect, early warning signals may be detected in 1978–1979, when the rates of those doubling up and those officially classified as poor reversed what had been long-standing trends of decline. The particular severity and characteristics of the twin recessions of 1979–1982—unusually high and protracted unemployment coupled with high real and nominal interest rates—intensified by the Reagan administration's drastic budget cuts and regressive tax policies, pushed increasing numbers of people over the edge. That homelessness, instead of receding with the 1983 economic upturn continued to rise, is an indication not only of the impact of the cuts in social spending but also of the unevenness of the recovery and of the deep structural roots of the problem.

## Income

The Reagan administration's tax policies and social spending cutbacks reinforced the broader structural tendencies toward income polarization and increasing poverty. Between 1978 and 1983, the number of households with annual incomes in the "intermediate" range fell by nearly 24 percent; most of them dropped to lower income brackets (Rose, 1983). The situation of the poorest fifth of the U.S. population became especially bleak. From 1980 to 1984, it is estimated that their average tax burden rose 24 percent, cash welfare benefits declined 17 percent, and food stamp benefits fell 14 percent. In the same period, average disposable income of families in the poorest fifth declined by nearly 8 percent, while that of the most affluent fifth rose by nearly 9 percent (Moon and Sawhill, 1984). Income disparities grew wider than at any time since 1947 (Ridgeway, 1984b). Moreover, the number of people living below the poverty line increased more than 40 percent between 1978 and 1983 (U.S. Bureau of the Census, 1982e, 1984d).

Unemployment has been perhaps the factor contributing most to the higher incidence of poverty, not only during the recession itself but afterward. In July 1984, the Congressional Research Service reported that nearly three-fourths of the 2.2 million individuals who had fallen below the poverty level between October 1981 and October 1982 were victims of the recession; slightly over a quarter of the new additions were casualties of the budget cuts (U.S. Congress, House Subcommittee on Oversight, 1984). Job loss and the unusually precarious situation of the newly unemployed produced what has come to be known as the "new poor"—destitute, sometimes homeless, former workers and their families. More precisely, the peculiar character of unemployment generated by the last recession, coupled with reductions in benefit programs for those who lose jobs, helps to account for some of the homelessness witnessed in the 1980s and for its continued growth during the recovery.

In the first place, more of the newly unemployed in the last recession were permanently separated from their last jobs than is typically the case. Over half (53.1 percent) of those rendered jobless in the 1981–1982 recession were permanently dismissed and forced to seek employment elsewhere; the average figure in the three previous recessions was 36 percent (Bednarzik, 1983).

Second, once out of work, today's unemployed are more likely to stay jobless for extended periods. At the low point of the 1973–1975 recession, the average duration of unemployment was 15 weeks; in June 1983, well after the recovery began, it was 22 weeks (*Dollars and Sense*, Oct. 1983).

Third, while the market produced a larger and longer-lasting need, government responded by curtailing unemployment benefit programs for the jobless. Fewer than half of newly jobless workers in 1982 received unemployment benefits, compared with over 78 percent in the last fiscal year of the 1973–1975 recession (Burtless, 1983). In September 1983, with over 9.8 million still officially unemployed, only 32.8 percent were collecting unemployment benefits of any kind—at that time the lowest percentage on record (Center on Budget and Policy Priorities, 1983b).

Other factors were at work as well. In the recent recovery, a far smaller proportion of discouraged workers returned to the labor force, when compared to previous postrecessionary periods, thus resulting in a deceptively rapid drop in the unemployment rate. Moreover, many of those who returned to the labor force and were able to find employment are working at lower paying and often part-time jobs. And in many states double-digit unemployment rates persisted well into the recovery (*New York Times*, Aug. 14, 1983, Mar. 3 and June 2, 1984).

These phenomena help account for the apparent discrepancy between declining unemployment rates and rising numbers of the hungry and homeless. The U.S. Conference of Mayors reported in January 1984 that even with lowered unemployment rates, demand for emergency food, shelter, and energy assistance in 1983 had risen substantially in most of the cities it surveyed (U.S. Conference of Mayors, 1984a).

Undoubtedly, some portion of the new poor escaped destitution, either because they had other sources of income or because they lived in households in which other members were working. But just as surely, many were forced to seek assistance elsewhere, often resorting to food stamps, surplus food distribution, and welfare; others simply picked up and sought work elsewhere.

Population flow from the industrial heartland to the Sunbelt seems to have accelerated in recent years (*New York Times*, May 19, 1984). The more recent migrants, often traveling with meager resources, arrive to find a job market quite at odds with their expectations. Some of the jobless resort to "dirty work" in what are essentially indentured labor camps operating with relative impunity in backwater regions of the South. Others pick up spot work, sell blood plasma, and try to hold out until the recovery arrives. The same "right-to-work" laws and low taxes that account in part for the Sunbelt's attractiveness to industry spell hardship for its castoffs. New migrants find themselves in less than hospitable circumstances when their savings run out. Where labor demand is already low, an influx of job seekers not only increases competition for the local unemployed but also threatens to displace those marginally employed.

Others among the homeless and hungry were part of the dependent, nonworking poor, a population largely unaffected by the recovery. For them, the 1980s has meant a further unraveling of the safety net, due to inflation and Reagan administration budget cuts. From 1980 through early 1984, means-tested programs—such as welfare, energy assistance, and food stamps—were reduced 16.4 percent, while non-means-tested human service programs increased by 24.5 percent (Ridgeway, 1984a).

AID TO FAMILIES WITH DEPENDENT CHILDREN (AFDC).   The real value of AFDC benefits continued to erode, declining by 7 percent from 1981 to 1983 (U.S. Congress, House Subcommittee on Oversight, 1983). As the result of 1981 regulations, 50 percent of the nearly half a million working families receiving AFDC lost eligibility and another 40 percent had benefits reduced. These new regulations mean that in 40 states a working mother of three is ineligible for benefits if her monthly income exceeds $479—roughly 58 percent of the poverty level (Citizens' Commission on Hunger in New England, 1984). Moreover, those on welfare may find themselves suddenly removed from the rolls for reasons unrelated to their actual need or the new eligibility standards—a practice that the New York City welfare department has called "churning" (Downtown Welfare Advocate Center, 1983). Most of those dropped from the rolls are reinstated on reapplication, although this does little to compensate for the months of disruption in the interim (New York State Department of Social Services, 1984).

DISABILITY BENEFITS.   In late 1983, in the wake of widespread protests, the Social Security Administration curtailed its practice of terminating disability benefits to those it considered able to work, but not before almost half a million of the disabled (nearly a sixth of the total) had been dropped from the rolls (*New York Times*, Dec. 10, 1983). Studies of those whose benefits were ended show that, most often, the loss of benefits was due to the impaired ability of the recipient to challenge the ruling, not to a legitimate weeding out of those who had recovered (Mental Health Law Project, 1982). Equally noteworthy, the mentally disabled, who represent roughly 11 percent of those receiving disability benefits, were overrepresented among the terminated by a factor of three. About half of those who managed to mount appeals of their discontinuations were reinstated. Indeed, so capricious was the government's performance in executing its reviews that one federal judge was prompted to denounce the Department of Health and Human Services as "a heartless and indifferent bureaucratic monster" (*Merli* v. *Heckler*, Civ. No. 83-189, Slip op., p. 2; D.N.J. June 7, 1984).

LOCAL ASSISTANCE.   About the only alternative for those dropped from the AFDC and disability rolls is General Assistance. But, as noted earlier, this alternative is not found throughout the country. A number of states—concentrated in the Sunbelt—do not fund such assistance, and even in states where it is available, many local authorities refuse to participate. Of the more than a million reported recipients of General Assistance in March

1982, 80 percent were concentrated in seven mid-Atlantic and midwestern states: Illinois, Michigan, Ohio, Indiana, Pennsylvania, New Jersey, and New York (*Social Security Bulletin*, Apr. 1984, 43).

The dependent poor thrown onto local relief face a more precarious future than those receiving federal benefits. Not only has there been continuing erosion in the real value of payments, but attempts have been made to deny or curtail this benefit of last resort in some of the states and counties where it is available.[2]

FOOD PROGRAMS.    It is projected that the cumulative effect of legislative changes enacted in 1981 will amount to a reduction of $7 billion from food stamps and $5.2 billion from child nutrition programs from 1982 to 1985 (U.S. Congress, Congressional Budget Office, 1983b). By the end of fiscal year 1983, the average monthly benefit per person was only $43, or 48 cents a meal (*New York Times*, Oct. 31, 1983). Little wonder, as even the President's Task Force on Food Assistance (1984) implicitly recognized, that food pantries and soup kitchens across the country report a surge in the numbers of people seeking assistance in the latter part of each month. This occurs, as a study commissioned by the Department of Agriculture put it, "because food stamp benefits are insufficient, delayed or had been reduced, and available cash has been allocated to meet other necessities" (*New York Times*, Dec. 19, 1983). Hunger may thus be viewed as the flip side of homelessness: For many sorely strapped households, the end of each month poses the choice of eating or paying the rent.

Nationwide, according to a survey of 181 food pantries and soup kitchens in 12 states, over half of these emergency food programs increased their outlay by at least 50 percent from 1982 to 1983; a third of the programs doubled in size. A significant portion of those seeking assistance were recently employed; many are families with children; and many, it is commonly reported, are in need of help for the first time in their lives (Center on Budget and Policy Priorities, 1983a; Kaufman and Harris, 1983).

## Housing

Record-high interest rates and two recessions sent the rate of construction of new housing plummeting. Housing starts averaged only 1.2 million in the three years ending with 1982 (U.S. Bureau of the Census, 1984a). That total, plus mobile-home deliveries, barely kept pace with the 1.3 million average annual increase in households for those three years, not to mention replacing units lost from the inventory (U.S. Bureau of the Census, 1984b). Elevated interest rates placed a house out of the reach of a significant segment of likely homebuyers. In 1983, only 30 percent of "typical" homebuying households—a married couple under age thirty-five with two children—could afford to purchase a mid-priced house (National Housing Conference, 1984). In previous decades, 65 percent of this group could afford a house. Thus, an estimated 35 percent of potential buyers, or about 4 million households, remained in the rental market in 1983. The proportion of the population owning houses declined for the first time since the Great Depression (U.S. Bureau of the Census, 1984b).

The consequences of this squeeze in the homebuying market have been severe. Despite the 1983 increase in new construction and the larger numbers of people in the prime homebuying ages of twenty-five to forty-four, only 833,000 households were formed in that year, nearly half of which ended up as renters (U.S. Bureau of the Census, 1984b). In a reversal of the postwar trend, doubling up also began to increase. The number of families living with others as "subfamilies" doubled, from a low of 1.3 million in 1978 to 2.6 million in 1983. Similarly, the number of unrelated individuals living with others went from 23.4 million in 1978 to 28.1 million in 1983 (Schechter, 1984). Young singles are increasingly compelled to live with parents or to pool resources with others in like circumstances in order to afford housing. Their plight is, however, far less serious than that of low-income families forced together in overcrowded quarters in what is essentially a form of borderline homelessness. The New York City Housing Authority has estimated that 1 out of every 10 households officially living in public housing projects is doubled up (*New York Times*, Apr. 21, 1983).

At the same time, the rental market tightened even more. Annual vacancy rates hovered nationally between 5.0 percent and 5.4 percent from 1979 to 1982 (U.S. Bureau of the Census, 1984c), far below the rates that are typical during recessions (U.S. Department of Commerce, 1983). By the end of 1983, rental vacancy rates were 3.7 percent in the Northeast and 4.4 percent in the West. In local markets, vacancies were even scarcer, with rates averaging between 1 and 2 percent in New York, San Francisco, and Boston. Landlords took advantage of this sellers' market by raising rents. In the 12 months ending July 1983, the rent component of the Consumer Price Index increased 5.4 percent, as compared with 2.2 percent for prices generally (Schechter, 1984).

Even in regions where rental vacancy rates were high, such as the North Central states (6.1 percent) and the South (7.3 percent), homelessness was widespread (U.S. Bureau of the Census, 1984c). In late 1982, for instance, Houston's tent city attracted international attention; less often pointed out was Houston's 20 percent rental vacancy rate, concentrated in the high-rent market.

As affordable vacancies grew scarcer, evictions—one of the most frequent precipitants leading to homelessness—increased in the early 1980s. Evictions include both formal court-ordered removals and informal evictions by primary tenants or the landlord. Often tenants move out before the sheriff comes to put them out, but usually not until a nonpayment action has been brought. In New York City, with a total of nearly 2 million rental units, there were nearly half a million such actions in 1983 (Stegman, 1982a). Many of these actions were taken against public assistance recipients, and a good percentage of them involved tenants paying rents above the maximum housing allowance. Welfare rent ceilings had not been increased since 1975, while rents had nearly doubled (*New York Times*, Sept. 4, 1983). Housing allowance increases of 25 percent finally went into effect statewide in early 1984 in New York.[3] Elsewhere in the nation, the amount a public assistance recipient was allotted for rent in 1981—whether as a separate "shelter allowance" or as part of a flat grant—ranged from 20 percent to 60 percent of local "fair market rent," depending on the state (Nenno, 1984).

Faced with what is widely recognized to be a severe housing crisis, the federal response has been one of studied neglect. Inaction has been coupled with the undoing of past actions. Instead of increasing federal housing subsidies and new construction to keep up with the rise in housing distress, these programs have been drastically reduced. The total annual commitment to additional subsidized units in the 1984 budget covered 100,000 units, about a third of the amount for which budgetary commitments were made in the mid-1970s (*New York Times*, Dec. 12, 1983). Moreover, the share of this total devoted to new construction and rehabilitation shrank. In 1979, there were 200,000 publicly subsidized housing starts and renovations. This was reduced to 55,000 in 1983, and the $615 million allocated for new construction in fiscal year 1984 was enough to build only 30,000 units nationally (*Guardian*, Jan 25, 1984). [*See also Chapter 21 by Chester Hartman.*] The existing stock of public housing is being eroded as cuts in operating and maintenance subsidies contribute to the removal of units from the publicly owned stock—in some cities up to 25 percent of these units (*Time*, Feb. 13, 1984). [*See also Chapter 20 by Rachel G. Bratt.*]

## *". . . and the poor get shelters"*

The 1980s have seen the intensification of the trends in homelessness first apparent in the mid-to-late 1970s and the emergence of new ones. The homeless have become much more visible as increasing numbers of people take up semipermanent life on the streets, repelled by the often unsafe and demeaning conditions in many public and some private shelters, or turned away because of lack of space. The single population today in the streets and shelters is younger than it was a decade ago; according to HUD's national shelter study, the average age of homeless adults in 1984 was estimated to be thirty-four (U.S. HUD, 1984b). The study also reported that nearly half of those in shelters nationwide are there for the first time.

In the course of its research, HUD conducted a telephone survey of 184 shelters nationwide, the results of which confirmed the progressive transformation of skid row begun in the 1970s. To take but one indicator: The survey found that roughly a third of the homeless today consist of women and family members (U.S. HUD, 1984b). This is undoubtedly an underestimate, since the sample explicitly excluded families "vouchered" into hotels and motels on an emergency basis. The survey also showed that the representation of minority groups is disproportionately higher among the homeless than in the population at large.

Not surprisingly, western and Sunbelt communities report that a majority of the homeless seen in local shelters are recent arrivals, lured by the hospitable climate and the rumor of jobs. Families make up the bulk of those living in tents and trailers in state parks and private campgrounds in the Southwest.

It appears that many, if not most, of the homeless families in the Northeast are headed by females, at least for those eligible to be lodged temporarily with Emergency Assistance to Families vouchers. Existing statistics miss many cases that should be counted: In some instances, children have been taken away from their parents and placed in foster care, inability on the part of the mother or father to provide stable housing being taken as prima facie evidence of poor parenting. Ironically, the parents in these cases may then lose their AFDC benefits and, with them, any hope of finding replacement housing. To complete the vicious circle, state social service departments may refuse to return the children until housing has been secured (Kaufman and Harris, 1983).

The number of New York City families seeking shelter increased by 24 percent between July 1981 and July 1982—and then doubled in the following year. As of October 1984, over 3,100 families were being quartered each night. The average length of stay increased from 2.0 months in 1981 to 4.3 months at the beginning of 1983 and to 7.8 months by October 1984 (Citizens' Committee for Children, 1983; New York City, Human Resources Administration, 1984). Over half of the families applying for shelter are there because they have been turned out by primary tenants with whom they have been doubling up (Brantley, 1983; New York City, Human Resources Administration, 1984).

Throughout the 1970s and into the 1980s, the highly visible presence of mentally disturbed people on the streets has contributed to the prevailing picture of the homeless in the popular press as addled nomads, victims of their own eccentricity or pathology. To be sure, studies of the single, "unattached" homeless population have consistently found evidence of a significant proportion of mentally disabled. Typically, estimates have ranged from 20 percent to 50 percent or higher, depending on the population surveyed, methods employed, and clinical evaluation criteria used (Bassuk, 1984; Baxter and Hopper, 1984). But despite widely reported evidence to the contrary, the impression lingers that, as one news story put it, the "vast majority" of the homeless poor are psychiatric casualties (*New York Times*, Oct. 2, 1983).

Again, the problem is not primarily one of personal inadequacy. As discussed above, deinstitutionalization as an alternative to hospitalization ran into problems early on. But the faltering program crashed once the linchpin of affordable housing—however indecent it may have been—was pulled. The decisive factor that transformed the wretchedly quartered deinstitutionalized into the wandering deranged was—and remains—the depletion of the low-income housing stock. For that reason, not only do the disabled homeless seek refuge on city streets and in shelters, but their counterparts drive up hospital censuses, languishing in wards for want of alternative housing.

With respect to the rise in the numbers of homeless youth and battered spouses seeking shelter, it cannot be said that declining incomes and a dwindling low-rent housing supply are *directly* responsible for their plight. Still, it would not be unreasonable to count at least a portion of the reported recent rise in spouse and child abuse, which often leads to homelessness, among the indirect costs of unemployment and plummeting incomes, given the toll on family stability, self-esteem, sexual relationships, and the simple tolerance of day-to-day mishaps.

# Conclusion

At this juncture, the yield of our inquiry may be summarized in the form of a general conclusion, an interpretation, and a guideline for further action. Respectively, these are as follows:

1. If the foregoing analysis is accurate, the present "crisis" is one that is likely to persist.

2. The pace, form, and vagaries of contemporary relief efforts—their reputed "failures," in short—may be read as signaling the reemergence of an older disciplinary agenda. Specifically, they portend the return to a style of assistance that, while alleviating some distress, accepts humiliation as the price of relief and upholds the example of its labors as a deterrent to potential applicants for help.

3. When devising corrective strategy, therefore, we should not allow the urgent need for immediate relief to obscure the necessity of far-reaching structural reform if present misery is to be abated and the forces that generate it are to be contained.

Let us take each item in turn.

## *The Crisis Will Endure*

What is now fitfully acknowledged to be a temporary aberration in the machinery of affluence may well be the telltale indicator of its new setting. The 1980s have so far confirmed that the troubles of the 1970s were but a sign of things to come. Nor are emergency measures likely to arrest the growth of homelessness or to ease significantly the lot of the dispossessed. Instead, a permanently dislocated class of the absolutely shelter-poor, forced to resort to emergency accommodations or to double up for periods of indefinite duration, seems the probable prospect.

While parallels with the Great Depression are revealing, they should not be overdrawn. The most striking thing about the present is not a drastic lowering of living standards generally, but the growing polarization of such standards. More precisely, the steady widening of income differentials coupled with its related development, the depletion of low-rent housing, makes for the driving dynamic behind homelessness today.

The decisive issue is whether homelessness should be understood as something confined to "problem populations" or as a surface manifestation of deeper difficulties. In this regard, the thrust of our argument should be clear. Homelessness on the scale we see today reveals serious deficiencies in the mechanisms available in this society to meet basic needs, deficiencies that have notably worsened and taken on a distinctive cast over the past few years. Paramount among such deficiencies is the failure to provide sufficient affordable housing.

During the early postwar period, there was little or no homelessness as we know it today—that is, it was limited to skid-row populations—when poverty and hunger were more prevalent and benefit levels lower. The problem of the deinstitutionalized could be confined to the service-delivery sector as long as ex-patients were housed, however miserably. The problem of unemployment remained one of manpower deployment, retraining, and proposed "full employment" programs as long as the jobless were not on the streets. The problem of inadequate public assistance benefits could be safely relegated to the thickets of "welfare reform" as long as recipients could still find housing and make rent. But once the supply of even poor-quality, affordable housing was depleted, these and related problems quit their assigned places and found common expression in homelessness. Conversely, whereas once the "housing crisis" was characterized by overcrowding, poor-quality dwellings, and a lack of plumbing or heat, what we face today has taken on the ruder dimensions of people with no place to live.

Again, our argument is not that homelessness is simply a housing problem. Rather, in the absence of housing, living circumstances that had been tenable—if but marginally so—become desperate. The causes of contemporary homelessness, as we have shown, are multiple. But the determinant factor that gives this form of impoverishment its distinctive imprint is the inability to secure housing.

Contrast such a perspective with the one offered by then Secretary of Health and Human Services Margaret Heckler (and no doubt shared by many of the public at large):

> The problem of homelessness is not a new problem. It is correlated to the problem of alcohol or drug dependency. And there have been a number of alcoholics who become homeless throughout the years, maybe centuries. They are still there. . . . I see the mentally handicapped as the latest group of the homeless. But, the problem is as old as time and with this new dimension complicating it, it's a serious problem, but it always has been. (Heckler, 1984)

Of the various mechanisms of accommodation the Reagan administration has resorted to,[4] this is perhaps the most ingenious. For here the problem is acknowledged only to be reduced to the familiar dimensions of vice and disease, worrisome, to be sure, but hardly cause for general anxiety.

## Homelessness as Part of a Disciplinary Agenda

Heckler's remarks, willfully uninformed as they may be—and, indeed, in part because of the distortions they contain—serve to exemplify how a presiding administration will recognize a potentially explosive issue in such a way as to domesticate it, render it harmless, even pathetic. Thus it grants legitimacy to the problem while restricting the range of remedial efforts that ought to be considered in correcting it. The point has broader implications as well. As one commentator has noted, the net effect of all the recent attention and effort devoted to homelessness has been to take the issue of the dependent poor from the vexing arena of "welfare rights" and return it to the safer confines of Victorian charity (Stern, 1984). The offer of assistance is hedged by the requirement of appropriate behavior (gratitude) on the part of the recipient; humiliation is the modality of acceptance. Homelessness becomes the contemporary paradigm of misfortune; and privately organized relief efforts, personalized giving, a revitalized rhetoric of compassion, and, we might add, confinement as necessary, become the appropriate avenues of response.

Unwittingly, some advocacy efforts have been party to this transformation. Most such efforts (at least until quite recently) have focused chiefly on obtaining decent shelter; the larger implications of how the plea is pitched or the relief secured have remained of peripheral concern. Many advocates, for example, point to the existence of a large and growing population of the homeless poor as an indictment of this society's claims to justice and decency. The stance of such criticism is moral, its animating force is indignation at gratuitous misery, and its objective is to shame a responsible citizenry into corrective action. The demand for relief is thus bracketed, much to the dismay of some advocates, in a way that discourages inquiry into the origins or complexities of the need to be met.

Other critics, while mindful of the moral dimensions of the issue, locate the problem at a deeper level than consciousness or will, a move that calls into question the ground rules of the system itself. Witness the query raised by *New York Times* columnist Russell Baker (1982). Reacting to a TV newscast of homeless women sleeping on the floor of New York's Pennsylvania Station, a story wedged between ads for mink coats and watches fashioned from gold coins, Baker wondered:

> If we had film of this sort of thing from Moscow, wouldn't it be widely screened as evidence of the failure of Communism? Does the juxtaposition on television of stone beds and gold coins for wrist decoration tell us something depressing about the failure of capitalism?

Perhaps so—but the acute visibility of the problem, the glacial pace at which remedial efforts have been mounted, and the government's failure to recognize the different needs of various subgroups among the single homeless,[5] may be reason enough to offer a different reading. Recall Piven and Cloward's (1971) observation that straitened, even punitive, welfare measures tend to be initiated during times of relative prosperity and persist even into times of widespread unemployment, unless challenged by disruptive protest. Obviously, in this way direct costs to the state are kept down. But the practice has a larger disciplinary function as well. The prospect of a degraded life on the dole serves to steel otherwise recalcitrant workers to the rigors of the laboring world, to stifle demands for higher wages or better working conditions, and to cause those who do fall on hard times to seek assistance elsewhere. Among the dependent poor, harassment and the threat that benefits may be withdrawn altogether work to suppress complaints about arbitrary practices.

One may conjecture, then, that the desultory character of contemporary relief efforts betrays something more than bureaucratic bungling, weary disinterest, or a willful refusal to care. Persistent homelessness may well figure as an accessory to the straitened measures instituted throughout the safety net apparatus: an unanticipated, but not entirely unwelcome, adjunct to reduced benefits, restricted eligibility rules, arbitrary dismissals, and workfare requirements. Moreover, the threat of such abject penury dovetails with industry's efforts to hold down labor costs.[6] Homelessness, as it exists today, may say as much about how the system currently "works" as it does about how it "fails."

We are not suggesting that homelessness was a planned crisis. Our contention addresses not the causes of homelessness but the uses to which the crisis and efforts to alleviate it may be put. Social policy in practice may serve "latent" objectives that are quite removed from its "manifest" purposes, as classical sociology has long supposed. This, of course, does not mean that those who participate in relief efforts share these latent objectives.

The contemporary approach to homelessness also reveals that, under certain circumstances, the disciplinary function of relief that Piven and Cloward have identified takes on contradictory aspects. On the one hand, the theater of welfare—the humiliation and hardship that are part and parcel of life on the dole—is staged for the edification of working people at large. On the other hand, relief does perform positive services: It alleviates real suffering and the onus of care that would otherwise fall on friends or family, and it helps to quell the potential threat of discontent. Moreover, it serves to enhance the legitimacy of the established order. Civil society, after all, is ill served by random and visible evidence of hardship; one of the fruits of "civilization," John Stuart Mill once observed, is that privileged classes are spared forced confrontation with the spectacle of pain.

A judicious measure of deterrence is thus one that keeps alive the example of the wages of failure while not letting the exhibit get out of hand. Containment of the deviant and discarded cannot be allowed either to bankrupt the public fisc or to erase their image from the public consciousness. At the same time, the display of discredited ways of life cannot go so far as to contaminate the public spaces that play host to normal social intercourse. Hence the contemporary dilemma to the state of devising appropriate forms of relief for a population—the homeless—who "continue to consume tax dollars and demoralize society" (*New York Times*, Editorial, Apr. 9, 1984).

If such an interpretation is correct, no consistent, rationalized approach to the problem of homelessness will be forthcoming. Instead, a patchwork amalgam of piecemeal relief, demonstration programs, and scattered repression can be predicted.

## Toward a Strategy of Reform

Any attempt to address the issue of "solutions" to homelessness must bear in mind the various antecedents to dispossession, the peculiar features of homelessness itself, and the larger functions that it appears to be playing. Although Reagan's policies have undoubtedly intensified it, the distinctive dynamic behind contemporary homelessness was in force before his administration assumed office. Accordingly, proposals must be formulated at several levels and with the longer view in mind.

Decent, emergency respite remains the unavoidable first step, one that "right-to-shelter" litigation and legislation—perhaps leading to a national homeless relief program—may well help to secure.[7] Where repressive practices have resurfaced, such as the forced "moving on" of homeless individuals now occurring in many communities, anti-harassment measures are needed. Careful outreach efforts must reach many of those who would otherwise fail to avail themselves of a safe haven, given the wariness that survival on the street exacts of even its ablest practitioners.

But beyond emergency relief looms the need for massive housing, retraining, and reemployment programs, and enhanced levels of benefits to public assistance recipients. Without these measures, even the most dignified refuges take on a dead-end character.

The basic demands of a progressive agenda are clearly relevant here, although this is not the place to argue in detail for the entire array of items that constitute such as agenda. A partial listing of such items would include full employment, decent jobs at living wages, and measures taken to cushion the regional impact of broader economic restructuring. Suffice it to state the obvious: As part of the momentous restructuring currently under way in our late capitalist economy, nationally as well as internationally, the state's role in insuring acceptable standards of subsistence is shrinking when—if measured by the need—it should be expanding. For purposes of this discussion, a number of key areas of intervention can be specified.

For housing to be maintained and other necessities insured, benefit levels for public assistance recipients must first be raised and then indexed to local cost-of-living trends. Moreover, ways must be sought to destigmatize the lot of the dependent poor—symbolized in the phrase "welfare handout"—and to make "social security" a term descriptive of a guaranteed level of decent subsistence available to all.

At the same time, it is one of the chief contentions of this analysis that the housing crisis today is not merely one of insufficient income but also, and working in reciprocal fashion, one of a restructured housing market—in particular, the declining number of low- and moderate-rent units. Thus it is difficult to conceive of anything short of a massive publicly subsidized housing effort making a substantive difference. Funds for construction, rehabilitation, and rent subsidy are needed. Under present circumstances it is only if housing is recognized as a social good, provided as of right to specific groups under certain conditions, that adequate action will be taken. [*See Chapter 28 by Emily Paradise Achtenberg and Peter Marcuse.*][8] A "right to shelter" is not the same thing as a "right to housing"—much less a "right to appropriate housing"—although it may be an opening wedge. And unless more permanent measures are enacted, including housing with social support services built in where indicated, shelters bid fair to become the housing solution for the very poor in the 1980s.

Effective reform will be an arduous undertaking, one in which advocacy efforts, for all their present limitations, will play a necessary part. There is, after all, little to be lost in denouncing widespread homelessness for the obscenity it is in this land of conspicuous bounty. There is also no guarantee that such action will much advance the cause for its eradication. Advocates for the homeless will need to press beyond the narrow bounds within which they have traditionally worked, to begin to establish linkages with other groups whose living circumstances are increasingly tenuous. If, as we have argued, the plight of the homeless is but an extreme instance of a more general distress, then one political task is to forge a constituency from those who experience that distress. The jobless, the marginally employed, the dependent poor, the sorely strapped working poor, and the elderly—members of all these groups (and minority populations especially) have become part of the homeless poor in recent years. Many others have edged closer to the brink of destitution. The existential fact of their common insecurity is fertile ground for cooperative organizing.

But the threat of homelessness, we have suggested, is not limited to the already disenfranchised or marginally situated. By virtue of the disciplinary power of its example, homelessness figures indirectly in the struggles of organized and unorganized labor at large to improve wages and working conditions. Mutual interest, no less than simple justice, could be appealed to in an effort to enlist their support for reform measures.

In any event, unless advocates for the homeless make common cause with other aggrieved groups and take on the larger issues implicated in the production of homelessness, their endeavors can expect only limited success. And unless the effort is made to secure these linkages, theirs will be the ironic lot to serve—even as they oppose—the spectacle of homelessness.

To arrest and reverse the course of present developments will require an oppositional movement of daunting proportions. Obviously, such an effort will be fueled not by the lure of easy accomplishment but by a foreboding of what the costs of failure will be. For the alternative is the prospect that our communities will become laboratories for a new venture in social Darwinism.

# Acknowledgments

A longer, more closely documented version of this chapter is available under the same title from Community Service Society, 105 East 22nd Street, New York, NY 10010 (Working Papers on Social Policy Series). Mr. Hopper's work was supported by grants from the Ittleson and van Ameringen Foundations.

We would like to thank the following people for comments, often painstaking and always instructive, on earlier drafts: Victor Bach, Frank Caro, Matthew and Kim Edel, Fred Griesbach, Bob Huneau, Jacqueline Leavitt, Peter Marcuse, Harriet Putterman, Fred Rosen, Terry Rosenberg, Dan Salerno, Roger Sanjek, Alvin Schorr, Tony Schuman, Ron and Yvette Shiffman, Elliott Sclar, Bill Tabb, and the editors of this book. A special thanks to Marg Hainer for editorial assistance.

# Notes

1. HUD addressed the numbers question through literature reviews, interviews with local experts and shelter providers, street counts, and site visits to selected cities. When informants were reluctant to offer estimates, HUD pressed for "best guesses." Some are of doubtful quality; in other instances, the fidelity of the reporting or the competence of informants is questionable. To take but one local example, the lowest, apparently "reliable" estimate given for New York City is 12,000, when on the night in question (in January 1984), over 16,000 people were actually listed on the city's shelter rolls.

More worrisome is the fact that, as Richard Appelbaum has noted in congressional testimony, the HUD researchers, in compiling the estimates of local experts, used a definition of metropolitan areas—the "Rand-McNally trade areas"—that is much larger than commonly used definitions. When extrapolated to the national population, this resulted in an artificial deflation of the total number of the homeless. Moreover, the HUD count explicitly excluded homeless youth, families and individuals "vouchered" into hotels and motels on an emergency basis, and the institutionalized population—in such places as jails and hospitals—that would otherwise be homeless. Finally, it is not apparent that HUD's use of a point-prevalence count—how many are homeless on a given night—is a more useful measure of the true magnitude of the problem than an estimate of the total number of people who are or become homeless in the course of a year. It cannot simply be assumed that those who leave emergency accommodation do so because permanent quarters await them.

For further criticisms, see the record of the May 24, 1984, hearings, available from the House Subcommittee on Housing and Community Development.

2. One striking example is the 1982 revision of the Pennsylvania Public Welfare Code. The new regulations classified able-bodied men and women between the ages of eighteen and forty-five as "transitionally needy" and ruled, with certain exceptions, that they were entitled to benefits for only three months in any calendar year. More than 68,000 people were removed from the state's rolls before a court challenge succeeded—for a four-month period, until being overturned on appeal—in blocking implementation of the new regulations. A fifth of those sheltered in Philadelphia's refuges are estimated to be casualties of the new regulations (*New York Times*, Sept. 18, 1983).

Equally extreme is the case of Sacramento, California, where regulations designed to discourage applications for local relief in some instances actually resulted in creating homelessness. From October 1982 until June 1983—when the California Supreme Court ordered a halt to the new system—the county welfare department required all employable new applicants for General Assistance to take up residence in its Bannon Street Shelter, the first "poorhouse" to be established in the United States in half a century (*Sacramento Bee*, July 1, 1983).

3. Recipients do not receive the full benefit of this increase. For every $3 of increased shelter allowance, they lose $1 in food stamp benefits, since the increased rent allowance is counted as income by the Department of Agriculture (*New York Times*, Dec. 3, 1983).

4. The Reagan administration's handling of the homelessness issue has coupled dissembling with outlandish dodges. In June 1982, HUD Assistant Secretary Philip Abrams told a Boston audience that "no one is living in the streets" (*Boston Globe*, June 17, 1982). Presidential adviser Edwin Meese chose the Yule season of 1983 as the setting for dismissing reports of hunger as anecdotal and voicing his opinion that soup-kitchen patrons were there "because the food is free and . . . that's easier than paying for it" (*New York Times*, Dec. 10, 1983). On January 31, 1984, President Reagan let it be known that some of those on the street were there, "you might say, by their own choice" (*New York Times*, Feb. 1, 1984). In May, HUD released a report purporting to show that previous estimates had vastly overstated the scale of the problem (U.S. HUD, 1984b). And in June, Philip Abrams allowed as how overcrowding in Hispanic households was an expression of a cultural preference (*New York Times*, June 15, 1984).

5. It is easy to construe skid row in its classic form (i.e., as it appeared in the 1950s and early 1960s) as part of the theater of welfare. Less often noticed is the fact that even today, the single homeless tend to be lumped indiscriminately in shelters—young and old, sane and less-than-so, hale and decrepit. This mixing arguably serves to amplify the repellent character of homelessness for those who are still housed, however precariously. Moreover, the insufficient supply of beds and the conditions in many existing shelters make it inevitable that many of the homeless will remain on the streets. These are but two clues leading us to the more general observation that one function of the plight of the homeless is the deterrent spectacle it provides to those still in the labor market or relying on informal support (friends or family) to survive. Curiously, the policy of indiscriminate lumping represents a return to the nineteenth-century notion of the almshouse, a move that runs counter to the modern tendency of the welfare state to "disaggregate" categories of deviance (Scull, 1977, chap. 2).

6. In 1983, unit labor costs declined throughout the manufacturing sector for the first time in 20 years (Harrington, 1984b), and average annual wage increases negotiated in labor contracts were the lowest on record (Ruben, 1984).

7. The first right-to-shelter lawsuit was filed in behalf of homeless men on October 1, 1979, in New York City. After a preliminary ruling in favor of the plaintiffs was obtained in December of that year, the case went to trial. It was settled by means of a negotiated consent decree, signed on August 26, 1981, which reaffirmed the initial ruling of a right to shelter and established minimally acceptable standards that public shelter would henceforth have to meet. Lawyers for the plaintiffs repeatedly have had to return to court for judicial enforcement of the provisions of the consent agreement regarding the adequacy of public shelter offered.

Subsequently, suits have been filed in New York in behalf of homeless women, homeless families, and the homeless mentally ill. Similar suits have been filed in West Virginia, New Jersey, Connecticut, and California. Favorable rulings, negotiated settlements, or both have been obtained in a number of these suits, although most remain in litigation. Notably, too, all of them—with the exception of one in New York (which seeks to secure the right to appropriate permanent housing for ex-state psychiatric patients)— are concerned only with the right to, and appropriate conditions of, emergency shelters.

A different tack has been taken in Washington, D.C., where in November 1984 local citizens voted 72 to 28 percent in favor of a ballot initiative establishing a right to shelter for homeless people. The city has challenged the constitutionality of the result in court and as of this writing (July 1985) the practical consequences of the initiative remain unsettled.

8. Such a vision receives qualified recognition in the British Housing (Homeless Persons) Act of 1977, at least with respect to homeless families (Donnison and Ungerson, 1982; U.S. Congress, House Subcommittee on Housing and Community Development, 1984, 549–66). [*See also Chapter 30 by Steve Schifferes.*]

# 3

# Housing and the Dynamics of U.S. Capitalism

## Michael E. Stone

*Complementing the work of Achtenberg and Marcuse in Chapter 1, this landmark chapter by Michael E. Stone comprehensively sketches the dimensions of the current U.S. housing problem, specifically focusing on the primacy of the mortgage lending system. In tracing the origins and development of that system and how it has been used to resolve certain built-in contradictions in the provision of housing in the United States, Stone argues that we are facing truly insoluble difficulties not only for the housing sector but also for the nation's financial structure. The strategic implications of this analysis are of great importance: They elevate housing struggles to a central position in the overall movement to produce a society in which wealth and income are distributed more equitably.*

Struggles around housing have been second only to workplace and job-related conflicts as a focus for organizing and mass action by working-class people in most capitalist countries [*see Chapter 23 by John Cowley*]. At the local level, and within the sphere of consumption—or, more properly, "reproduction of labor power"—there has been no more active arena.

There have been innumerable fights against the physical destruction of working-class housing by urban renewal, highway construction, and institutional expansion by universities, hospitals, and so forth. Tenants have organized to restrict or remove landlords' control over rents and evictions, to force repairs to be made, and even to drive landlords out of business. Working-class people have attempted to defend their communities against destruction by less overt forces as well, such as real estate speculation or "gentrification," where an influx of higher-income people drives up rents and sales prices; "redlining," where banks and insurance companies refuse

This chapter is an updated and consolidated version of portions of "The Housing Problem in the United States: Origins and Prospects," reprinted, with permission, from *Socialist Review* 52, July–August 1980, and of portions of "Housing and the Economic Crisis: An Analysis and Emergency Program," in *America's Housing Crisis: What Is to Be Done?* ed. Chester Hartman (Boston: Routledge & Kegan Paul, 1983), reprinted by permission of the Institute for Policy Studies.

to make loans or provide insurance; "blockbusting," where realtors play upon racism to acquire property cheaply from whites and sell dearly to black or other minority people; "abandonment," where owners walk away from buildings after letting them run down; and arson, where owners burn buildings in order to collect on inflated insurance policies. Furthermore, battles around such housing issues have often served as the starting point for multi-issue organizations in working-class communities.

People are obviously going to continue to try to defend and improve their homes and living standards, and to some extent these struggles are teaching them the ultimate sources of their housing problems. However, people do not automatically come to assign responsibility to the institutions of capitalism. And even if their experience and their organizations lead them to want a revolutionary transformation of capitalism, they also need to understand that not all strategies, struggles, and issues are equally likely to contribute to bringing about such a transformation. Some may be dead ends; some may divide the working class; some may be deflected or coopted [*see Chapter 24 by Kathy McAfee*].

How can housing struggles help build a successful socialist movement? In part the answer to this question depends upon analysis of actual political practice and strategies. But it also requires a precise analysis of the contradictions within capitalism that have generated housing problems, the responses to these problems, and the further contradictions generated by these responses. It is only through such an analysis that we can hope to identify the opportunities and constraints that history provides.

Until recently radicals in general and Marxists in particular have made remarkably little systematic, theoretical analysis of the underlying processes that have spawned housing problems and conflicts, and they have made little effort to understand these kinds of issues and their strategic potential. To some extent this is due to a traditional argument, which may be stated simplistically as follows: The essential social relationship of capitalism is the wage contract, which permits capitalists to extract surplus (i.e., uncompensated) labor from workers in the process of production. The inevitable antagonism between capitalists and workers is therefore the primary contradiction of capitalism, and the housing problem must be a "structurally secondary contradiction." From this it allegedly follows that struggles around housing and other consumption issues are *strategically* secondary.

In fact, the only valid conclusion about housing that can be drawn from the basic premise is that the housing problem cannot be solved within capitalism. The significance of housing struggles depends upon the relationship of housing to the structure and dynamics of capitalism as a whole, as well as the particular forms of class conflict arising from contradictions in this relationship. There is a dialectical relationship between the spheres of production and consumption—in this case between the labor market and the housing market—and "structurally secondary contradiction" is an undialectical and ahistorical category.

While the analysis presented in this chapter suggests that housing has acquired extraordinary strategic potential, an examination of past and present organizing reveals that such organizing has barely begun to realize this potential. Furthermore, it has become increasingly clear that the meaning of housing organizing is tied to the fact that housing is not just a major consumption item, but is indeed the principal locus of reproduction and domestic production. This is a realm in which women have of course had a particularly profound role and have been especially involved in organized (as well as unorganized) struggles. Housing organizing thus needs to be examined and guided also by an understanding of these aspects of housing, which are not explored in this chapter. Finally, housing organizing needs to be considered in relation to other struggles, for as important as housing struggles can be, their effectiveness will necessarily be limited if they are not part of a larger political strategy and movement.

# The Structural Basis of the Housing Problem

Under capitalism human labor power is a commodity. That is, most people need to sell their labor power for a wage in order to be able to obtain housing and other necessities, which are, for the most part, commodities as well. In the long run the minimum level of wages certainly must be at least sufficient for the working class to maintain and reproduce itself at the level of subsistence. It is in the immediate interest of capitalists, though, to have wages at the lowest possible level that will assure them of the quantity and quality of workers they wish to employ—a level that may be above or below bare subsistence. In industrialized capitalist countries like the United States, the history of class struggle, the demand for various kinds of skilled labor, the intensive exploitation of other parts of the world, and the need of capitalists to have buyers for their products have enabled most people to achieve incomes above the level of subsistence. Nevertheless, the labor market continues to exert a downward pressure on working-class incomes, and hence on working-class living standards.

On the other side, under capitalism the price of housing is determined primarily by the structure of the housing market—which includes not only the retail market for homes and apartments but also much of the land market, the construction industry, the materials industry, and finance capital. However, since housing is both a necessity and a commodity, its price is also greatly influenced by people's ability to pay, which interacts with the profit expectations of the various housing capitalists. That is, if the price of housing rises, people generally have to pay, but they obviously cannot pay more than they have. If the price of existing housing is much lower than the cost of producing new housing, it will not be profitable for capitalists to produce new housing. Indeed it may not be profitable to keep some existing

housing on the market. The shortage may force some people to double up and may eventually drive the price of existing housing up toward the cost of producing new housing, but the price is ultimately limited by people's incomes. The labor market can thus restrict the profitability, and hence the quantity and quality, of available housing.[1]

While the squeeze between high housing costs and limited incomes has a depressing effect on the housing market, it also exerts an upward pressure on wages. Capitalists in the housing market may be indifferent about whether the price of housing leaves households with enough income to pay for other necessities, but they do want buyers who can pay the price. Workers, in turn, struggle for higher wages to pay the price required to produce and provide their shelter and also meet their families' other needs. The price of housing thus enters into the determination of the level of wages, as the interests of capitalists in the housing market are advanced by higher wages, while the interests of capitalists as employers are served by lower wages.

At first glance, the relationship of housing costs to wages and living conditions might appear to be no different than the cost of food, clothing, or other necessities that enter into the reproduction of labor power. It might also seem that there can be no inherent conflict between the requirements of the labor market and the housing market: Since housing is itself a product of labor, the level of wages should simultaneously and consistently determine both the cost of producing housing and the level of working-class incomes. In fact, housing possesses a number of distinctive characteristics, which distinguish it both socially and economically from other commodities, which give it a fundamental and pivotal role in determining working-class living standards, and which make it unusually problematic for capitalism.

Housing is a bulky, immobile, and durable good that rarely can be purchased in amounts other than whole dwelling units and usually is used over a considerable period of time. These characteristics make it extremely difficult, at least in the short run, for a family to alter the quantity, quality, or amount spent for the housing they consume. Sudden changes in the income of a household, especially downward changes, are generally reflected immediately in other expenditures, including food, but not in the amount spent for shelter. Increases in housing costs usually must be offset by reductions in other expenditures, rather than reductions or substitutions in housing consumption. When the rent or property taxes go up, a family cannot readily give up its living room or switch to a cheaper brand of bathroom to offset the increase.

Obviously, in extreme financial emergencies people will normally buy the food they need to survive even if it means not paying the rent. But above this starvation level, food consumption patterns and expenditures can and do vary from day to day and week to week. They vary because, unlike housing, food products are quickly consumed and must be purchased anew, and because each purchase involves a mix of distinct items rather than a single, costly item.

The second way in which the cost of housing uniquely affects the overall standard of living of a family is through its determination of where they can live. This relationship influences the physical quality of the housing people are able to obtain, the amount of dwelling space they have, and the type of community and neighborhood they live in. The influence over locational choice means that the amount a household can pay for housing affects its access to commercial facilities, the quality of schools and other social services, the character of the immediate physical and social environment, and the availability of transportation networks to jobs and other services elsewhere in the metropolitan area. No other consumption item is nearly as pervasive in its effects.

Furthermore, because housing is so durable, in an economy where housing is a commodity it is generally bought and sold many times during its useful life. This means that at every point subsequent to its initial production and sale, the market value of a residential structure is determined not by its actual cost of production but by its *replacement* cost adjusted for depreciation. In addition, because housing is tied to land, its market value includes the "value" of the land (i.e., the rent-generating potential of the particular location). At the time that housing is initially built, the "value" of the land amounts to simply a fraction of the total value created in producing the building—in formal Marxist terms, a fraction of the surplus value created by the workers who built the house is appropriated by the provider of the land. Subsequent to the initial production and sale of the housing, though, the "value" of the land can and does change quite considerably as the rent-producing potential of the location changes.

Finally, the actual shelter costs for a particular housing unit do not involve the direct payment of the sales price or market value to the seller in one lump sum, but incremental payment to the investors or financiers over time. On top of this incremental payment there is, of course, the payment of interest or profit—a form of rent—to the investors. Then there are property taxes and operating expenses. Thus, the actual cost of shelter, as determined by the structure of the capitalist housing market, bears only a tenuous relationship to the general level of wages—and even to the wages of the workers who produce and service housing.

Because shelter costs generally represent the first claim on a household's income, to say that people are paying more than they can afford for shelter means that after paying for their shelter they have insufficient resources left to meet their other needs at some minimum level of adequacy. That is, it is not merely insufficient income that limits a household's capacity to meet its other needs adequately; it is also their housing cost, through its determination of residual resources and through its locational restrictions.

A rational standard for determining how much a household can afford for shelter thus has to reflect differences in income, on the one hand, and variations in the cost of nonshelter necessities, such as food, clothing, and medical care, plus taxes, on the other. Although every household faces distinctive expenses and conditions of life, the standard budgets computed annually by the U.S. Bureau of Labor Statistics (BLS) provide a set of typical living costs for households of various sizes and composition. The "lower budget" in this series defines a minimum adequate standard of living.

The BLS lower budget can be used to determine the maximum amount, on average, a household of a given income and size can afford for shelter and still meet its other needs at this minimum adequate level. For each household size and income level, the calculation involves subtracting from income the sum of all nonshelter consumption expenditures in the BLS lower budget plus personal taxes corresponding to that income and household size.

This approach reveals that in 1980 a family of four needed an income of about $17,500 to be able to afford 25 percent of income for shelter. Indeed, if their income was about $11,000 or less, they could not afford to pay anything for shelter and be able to meet their other needs at the minimum level of adequacy. Clearly the conventional standard of 25 percent of income hides the actual hardship faced by low-income and even middle-income working-class families who may be paying less than 25 percent of their income for shelter, but who are still "shelter poor" because the squeeze between their housing costs and incomes leaves them insufficient resources for meeting their other needs at even a minimally adequate level.

The extent of shelter poverty, based upon the income-dependent standard just described, has been estimated from Annual Housing Survey and census data. In 1980, more than 25 million households in the United States were shelter poor—32 percent of all households (see Table 3.1). This included 11.6 million renter households—43 percent of all renters—and 13.6 million homeowner households—about 26 percent of all homeowners. Nearly 90 percent of all shelter-poor households in 1976 had incomes below $10,000, and virtually 100 percent had incomes below $15,000. Between 1970 and 1980 the total number of shelter-poor households increased by 33 percent.

Shelter poverty is a pervasive and growing problem in the United States, a problem that cannot be eliminated simply through growth in the economy or government subsidies. To eliminate shelter poverty and thereby prop up the housing market, every household would have to be guaranteed an income sufficient to pay their housing costs, meet their other needs at a minimum level of adequacy, and also pay their taxes. Labor would then take a bigger share of the nation's productive output; profits would decline, leading to reduced investment and cutbacks in production. At least as important, with the working class no longer manacled to low-wage jobs by the threat of unemployment, capital would lose much of its power over labor.

On the other hand, if a large proportion of American families continue to have insufficient incomes, the housing market will collapse, as it already has in many urban neighborhoods where housing stands abandoned. More generally, to eliminate shelter poverty without disturbing the labor market, the price of housing would have to be set at a level the occupants realistically could afford after paying for their other necessities. Housing prices would be

TABLE 3.1
SHELTER POVERTY IN THE UNITED STATES, 1980
(numbers in millions)

| | SHELTER POOR | | | | | | 25% + OF INCOME FOR SHELTER | | | | | |
| | 1-3 Person Households | | 4 + Person Households | | Total | | 1-3 Person Households | | 4 + Person Households | | Total | |
| | N | % | N | % | N | % | N | % | N | % | N | % |
|---|---|---|---|---|---|---|---|---|---|---|---|---|
| *Renters* | | | | | | | | | | | | |
| Under $10,000 | 7.3 | 67.7 | 1.9 | 93.2 | 9.1 | 71.8 | 8.1 | 75.7 | 1.5 | 75.7 | 9.7 | 75.7 |
| Under $15,000 | 8.1 | 47.3 | 2.9 | 93.7 | 11.0 | 60.6 | 10.1 | 67.4 | 2.1 | 67.9 | 12.3 | 67.5 |
| Total | 8.1 | 37.5 | 3.5 | 66.9 | 11.6 | 43.2 | 10.9 | 50.4 | 2.4 | 46.9 | 13.4 | 49.7 |
| *One-family owners* | | | | | | | | | | | | |
| Under $10,000 | 4.4 | 66.0 | 1.0 | 100.0 | 5.4 | 70.0 | 4.3 | 64.7 | 0.2 | 23.8 | 4.5 | 59.2 |
| Under $15,000 | 5.0 | 49.4 | 2.2 | 95.0 | 7.3 | 58.0 | 5.5 | 54.3 | 0.7 | 28.0 | 6.2 | 49.3 |
| Total | 5.2 | 21.7 | 3.8 | 27.6 | 9.0 | 23.9 | 7.5 | 31.5 | 2.3 | 16.7 | 9.9 | 26.1 |
| *All homeowners*[a] | | | | | | | | | | | | |
| Under $10,000 | 7.0 | 66.1 | 1.7 | 100.0 | 8.7 | 70.6 | 6.9 | 65.3 | 0.4 | 26.0 | 7.4 | 59.9 |
| Under $15,000 | 7.9 | 49.8 | 3.4 | 95.4 | 11.3 | 58.1 | 8.8 | 55.0 | 1.0 | 28.7 | 9.8 | 50.2 |
| Total | 8.2 | 23.6 | 5.4 | 30.1 | 13.6 | 25.8 | 11.5 | 33.3 | 3.1 | 17.3 | 14.6 | 27.8 |
| *Total* | | | | | | | | | | | | |
| Under $10,000 | 14.2 | 66.9 | 3.6 | 96.3 | 17.8 | 71.3 | 15.0 | 70.6 | 2.0 | 53.1 | 17.0 | 68.0 |
| Under $15,000 | 16.0 | 51.7 | 6.3 | 94.6 | 22.3 | 59.3 | 18.9 | 61.0 | 3.1 | 47.1 | 22.0 | 58.5 |
| Total | 16.3 | 29.0 | 8.9 | 38.3 | 25.2 | 31.7 | 22.4 | 39.9 | 5.7 | 23.9 | 28.0 | 35.3 |

[a] Estimate based on projections from one-family homeowners.

driven down, in many cases to zero. Property values would collapse, and private investment in housing would cease. Mortgage payments would stop on many buildings, leading to collapse of the mortgage system, and with it much of the financial structure. While such a collapse would wipe out a portion of real estate values and mortgage debt (as it did in the 1930s), it would also bring production to a halt. Vast unemployment obviously would not resolve the conflict between incomes and housing costs.

The experience of Western European countries might seem to indicate that the problem is not insoluble; that is, that the private housing market can be substantially eliminated without undermining the basic institutions of the existing system. Actually, the European situation reveals that control or elimination of much of the entrepreneurial element in housing does not get at the essence of the capitalist housing market.[2]

After World War II, most Western European governments maintained strict control of rents and security against eviction to protect tenants from landlord exploitation amid a severe housing shortage. Other prices were not similarly controlled, so the costs of operating existing housing and building new housing rose, with no compensating increase in the price of existing housing. As a result, private housing investment dried up, as landlords, bankers, and developers had predicted would happen. Instead of returning control to the private market, though, the state increasingly became a major developer and owner of housing; and unlike public housing in this country [*see Chapter 20 by Rachel G. Bratt*], what has been produced is at least as desirable as most private housing.

However, the governments generally buy land in the marketplace and pay private builders to construct the housing. They still raise funds for housing by borrowing from financial institutions and wealthy individuals, and this money must be repaid with interest out of rents and taxes. In other words, housing continues to be quite expensive; bankers, builders, and land speculators continue to profit from it; and the working class continues to pay for it, partially through its direct housing expenditures and partly through its taxes. In a pinch the landlords are expendable; but their demise does not really get at the roots of the housing problem.

## The Historical Roots of the Housing Affordability Crisis

The conflict between incomes and housing costs is by no means new, but has evolved through a number of phases that can appropriately be characterized as "medieval," "classical," "baroque," and "rococo." With the rise of industrial capitalism and the attendant growth of cities in the middle of the nineteenth century, housing as well as human labor became commodities to be bought and sold for money. Relatively few urban residents, apart from the poorest shanty dwellers, built their own housing, and only the well-to-do could afford to buy their own housing. This, then, was the heyday of the urban landlord and housing entrepreneur—the "medieval" period of housing. Most housing construction, particularly rental housing, was financed with entrepreneurial capital and private borrowing. Mortgage lending institutions (mainly savings banks and savings and loan associations) existed, but were less important than other sources of financing and primarily loaned to people well enough off to have saved some money for a house of their own. In this period, the conflict between incomes and housing costs appeared principally via the squalid and overcrowded living conditions of the rapidly growing urban working class. Within the constraints of low wages, the housing provided was of low quality to begin with, with few if any services and amenities, and packed full of people in order to generate an acceptable return for the landlords.

As long as the flow of immigrants into the cities provided employers with an adequate supply of cheap labor, the conflict between incomes and housing costs posed problems for the system only when tenants organized rent strikes or rioted and, more significantly, when disease and fire threatened both wealthier neighborhoods and the reproduction of an adequate labor force. The resulting codes and ordinances halted new construction of the worst types of tenements but did not eliminate many that already existed and certainly did not result in new and better-quality affordable housing for the poor. Rather, urban building turned more toward housing for the emerging middle class, housing that only gradually filtered down to the poor over succeeding generations, with inevitable decline in the quality of the housing. With this transition, entrepreneurial dominance was gradually replaced by the growing power of institutional mortgage lenders, as the "medieval" period gave way to the "classical."

Emerging out of both the successes and failures of nineteenth-century capitalism, financial institutions provided a way of relieving some of the squeeze between incomes and housing costs by stretching out payment of the initial construction cost. Their ability to channel billions of dollars into housing indeed defined the dominant form that consumption has taken throughout this century, namely debt-financed suburbanization.

In the latter part of the nineteenth century, rapid technological progress and the rise of large corporations led to the growth of a new technical and managerial middle class. These people had enough income to maintain some savings, which they put primarily into savings accounts and life insurance policies. Seeking outlets to invest these rapidly accumulating funds, around the turn of the century the banks and insurance companies began to finance large amounts of housing construction, and over the next three decades institutional mortgage lenders came to dominate the housing industry, largely financing the pre–World War I streetcar suburbs, the first wave of auto suburbs in the 1920s, and modern apartments in the central cities.

Between 1900 and 1930, nonfarm residential mortgage debt grew from under $3 billion to over $30 billion.[3] This investment contributed significantly to economic growth over the period, but because it was debt financing that rested upon the expectation of future repayment, the mortgage system was very dependent upon continuous economic growth and prosperity. Furthermore, since lenders required a large downpayment and sufficiently large and secure income from each borrower in order to minimize risk, the growth of the mortgage and homeownership markets was still limited by the income–housing cost squeeze. Thus, when housing construction slackened after the mid-1920s, lenders increasingly financed housing speculation and cost inflation, which sustained the illusion of prosperity, but only for a while. The net result was that mortgage debt grew in the 1920s four times faster than the overall economy (i.e., much faster than the ability to repay it). So when the economy collapsed at the end of the decade, the mortgage system was a big part of the debacle. Millions of people lost their homes to foreclosure because they did not have the incomes to pay off their mortgages. Millions lost their savings because the banks had invested in home loans that could not be repaid. Savings deposits failed to grow again until the start of World War II; with no new funds available for investment, private residential construction practically came to a halt and the private housing market nearly ceased functioning.

While the "classical" period of U.S. housing ended with the depression, the new institutional framework for housing finance that was erected in the 1930s was still built around the central feature of the classical system—mortgage lending by private financial institutions—reflecting the power these institutions continued to wield and the general philosophical commitment to have the government assist rather than replace private investment. Thus the major and ultimately most profound and pervasive forms of federal intervention in housing were the system of central banking and deposit insurance provided by the Federal Home Loan Bank System, the mortgage insurance programs of the Federal Housing Administration, and, a decade later, the mortgage guarantees of the Veterans Administration, and the secondary mortgage market facilities of the Federal National Mortgage Association. All were designed to stimulate and protect private institutional mortgage lending and hence can be seen as a "baroque" extension, elaboration, and enhancement of the classical form of housing finance.

Strategically, the rebuilt mortgage system was built around the much wider promotion of debt-encumbered homeownership through the creation of the low downpayment, long-term loan to replace the earlier type of large-downpayment, short-term mortgages that had restricted the market to the relatively well off groups in the population. The new type of loan was designed to undercut the affordability problem in several ways: economically, by both lessening monthly payments for a given loan and reducing the personal savings needed to buy; politically, by promoting the illusion of ownership through the reality of debt. Furthermore, by making loans more easily available, the effective demand for houses was expected to increase, which in turn would contribute to overall economic growth as well as benefit the construction and lending industries in particular.

Of course it took World War II to restart the economy and generate the savings needed to get the reconstructed mortgage system into operation.

Savings that had accumulated during the war, along with housing needs virtually unmet since the start of the depression, provided the impetus for what indeed became the postwar housing boom, facilitated by federal support for financial institutions to provide the new long-term, low-downpayment loans. The suburban boom produced about 30 million new housing units in two decades, increasing homeownership from about 40 percent at the end of the war to over 60 percent by the 1960s. Housing construction accounted for one-third of all private investment and nearly one-half of all public and private construction during this period. And housing debt represented the biggest single component of a vast explosion of private borrowing, as Table 3.2 shows. Yet, despite the success of the new mortgage system in dealing with the housing affordability problem for the majority of Americans and contributing to the postwar prosperity, the edifice contained some inherent flaws and weaknesses that began to emerge in the late 1960s, bringing forth the crisis that seems only to worsen, and with

TABLE 3.2
DEBT OUTSTANDING IN THE U.S. ECONOMY
($ in billions)

|  | 1946 | 1965 | 1970 | 1975 | 1980 |
|---|---|---|---|---|---|
| Total debt | $353.2 | $1,107.2 | $1,600.1 | $2,620.4 | $4,651.7 |
| U.S. government | 228.0 | 260.6 | 300.8 | 446.3 | 742.8 |
| Federally sponsored housing agencies | 0.3 | 8.7 | 29.6 | 81.7 | 226.6 |
| Other federally sponsored agencies | 0.9 | 6.0 | 14.0 | 25.6 | 47.3 |
| State and local governments | 14.9 | 100.3 | 144.4 | 223.8 | 336.1 |
| Total private debt | 109.1 | 731.6 | 1,111.6 | 1,837.3 | 3,299.5 |
| Residential mortgages | 28.3 | 258.7 | 357.8 | 591.4 | 1,086.8 |
| Commercial mortgages | 8.8 | 55.5 | 85.2 | 157.9 | 256.7 |
| Consumer credit | 8.4 | 89.9 | 143.1 | 223.2 | 385.0 |
| Corporate and foreign bonds | 27.7 | 123.0 | 202.4 | 323.4 | 503.8 |
| Other private credit | 36.1 | 204.6 | 323.8 | 546.3 | 1,067.2 |
| Gross National Product | 209.6 | 688.1 | 982.4 | 1,516.3 | 2,626.5 |
| Disposable personal income | 158.6 | 472.2 | 685.9 | 1,084.4 | 1,822.2 |
| Residential mortgage debt as percentage of GNP | 13.5 | 37.6 | 36.4 | 39.0 | 41.4 |
| Residential mortgage debt as percentage of disposable personal income | 17.8 | 54.8 | 52.2 | 54.4 | 59.6 |
| Residential mortgage interest rate | 4.5[a] | 5.8 | 8.5 | 9.0 | 12.9 |

*Sources:* Federal Reserve Board, *Flow of Funds Accounts: Assets and Liabilities Outstanding*; U.S. Department of Commerce, *Survey of Current Business*; and Federal Home Loan Bank Board, *Journal*, various issues.
[a]Approximate.

it the transition from the "baroque" to a truly "rococo" period of housing finance.

First, even as mortgage lending contributed to expansion it grew much faster than the overall economy, and hence faster than the ability to repay this debt, just as it had during the 1920s. As Table 3.2 shows, between 1946 and 1965 residential mortgage debt grew about three times as fast as GNP and disposable personal income, so that once again the debt that was essential to prosperity was placing an increasingly heavy burden on the future.

Second, while the expansion of mortgage credit contributed immensely to the growth and profitability of the entire housing industry, increasing dependence on credit made the production of new housing and the cost of buying and occupying both new and used housing increasingly sensitive to the supply and cost of mortgage money. No other major industry is as dependent on borrowed funds, and the price of no other major item of consumption as sensitive to interest rates as is housing.

The increased vulnerability of housing to credit conditions has led to ups and downs in housing production as interest rates, the total supply of credit, and housing's share of credit have all varied with the business cycle. Although the business cycle was relatively mild for two decades after World War II, housing production fell an average of 30 percent during each of the three major periods of restricted mortgage credit that occurred prior to the mid-1960s. Thus, while the mortgage system facilitated large amounts of housing production over this postwar period as a whole, the year-to-year instability left the construction industry permeated with small, labor-intensive firms that could easily enter and leave, but that, for the most part, could never develop factory technology and achieve significant economies of scale. Even more important, because the evolution of the mortgage system has caused housing production to overreact to the business cycle, there arose the danger that a worsening of the cycle could lead not only to wilder swings in housing construction but also to larger economic problems if the inability of buyers to obtain and afford long-term mortgages left developers with houses they could not sell, and thus left lenders with uncollectable construction loans.

The third major weakness built into the new mortgage system was the financial vulnerability of the so-called thrift institutions—savings and loan associations and mutual savings banks—which have been the mainstays of residential lending. Since they have put nearly all their funds into long-term mortgages, as long as interest rates on these loans were fixed such lenders have received a fairly constant rate of return year after year regardless of what has happened to rates since the loans were made. The thrifts obtained most of the funds they loaned, though, from savings deposits that could be withdrawn with little or no notice. Until the late 1960s, interest rates on savings accounts were generally competitive with other investments and were substantially higher than the rate of inflation, so the imbalance in "borrowing short and lending long" was not yet a problem. Thrift institutions were thus fairly successful at sustaining a steady inflow of funds and using them to support their own growth and a large fraction of the expansion of mortgage credit. In periods of tight money, housing funds were restricted primarily because the other major types of lenders—commercial banks and insurance companies—reduced their housing lending; as the major suppliers of housing credit, the thrifts were for a while relatively insulated from the rest of the capital markets and not dramatically affected by economic fluctuations, although their financial structure was inherently flawed.

The fourth major difficulty in the new mortgage system has grown out of the promotion of homeownership and perhaps has more obvious political implications than the other three tensions, as profound as they are. The overwhelming majority of Americans have of course aspired to be homeowners, and for many years the new mortgage system made the dream available to most (though not most with low incomes or dark complexions) who pursued it, even though this mortgage system saddled people with immense debts. Homeownership became the mark of full citizenship, the symbol of status, almost a civil right to anyone who saved up a little for the downpayment, as well as providing a hedge against inflation and the means to accumulate a little wealth for retirement or one's heirs. Having created the expectation, fostered the hope, promoted the dream, what would be the consequences if the system could no longer deliver the goods?

## Housing and the Economic Crisis

During the 1960s the postwar prosperity began to crumble. Third World insurgency, especially in Southeast Asia, forced the government to increase military spending. Militant social movements plus domestic opposition to the war in Vietnam forced increases in spending for social programs while restricting tax increases. The federal budget thus had a growing deficit in the late 1960s, which had to be financed by borrowing. At the same time, growing competition from Europe and Japan posed an additional economic challenge. These foreign pressures, along with decreasing unemployment and rising wages at home, resulted in a sharp decline in corporate profits in the late 1960s. In response, the corporations began to borrow more money to finance moveouts and mergers that they hoped would restore profits.

The new demands for credit have come on top of the continuing needs of other sectors of the economy, including housing, as Table 3.2 shows. This process has increasingly exposed a basic contradiction in the whole system of debt financing. On the one hand, if the Federal Reserve allows the money supply to increase to meet all the needs for borrowed funds, this contributes to price increases in the economy, since the amount of borrowed money being spent goes up faster than the amount of goods and services being produced. Inflation leads to higher interest rates and more borrowing in anticipation of further price increases. Debt accelerates far ahead of the ability to repay it, leading toward a financial crisis.

On the other hand, if the government tries to restrict the growth of credit to prevent or limit inflation, then some borrowers get squeezed out. Previously accumulated debts eventually have to be paid, and many individuals, businesses, and governments are totally dependent on new loans to pay off the old ones. Without continued access to credit to pay their bills, they may go bankrupt. Since the banks and other creditors have also borrowed heavily to expand their lending and stimulate the economy, a chain of defaults can ensue when they do not get paid. Thus a credit squeeze can bring the financial system to the brink of collapse.

Since the late 1960s, the economy has swung more and more violently between the poles of this contradiction. Housing has been at the center of the crisis because of the spread of long-term mortgages and the associated growth of mortgage debt. Since 1966, increased competition for borrowed funds has caused a long-term rise in interest rates on top of ever-sharper short-term fluctuations. Periods of tight money have been increasingly severe, with interest rates soaring higher each time and housing credit being ever more drastically curtailed.

As interest rates on savings accounts have become less competitive and even lagged behind the rate of inflation, many depositors have withdrawn savings to invest directly—and more recently indirectly through money market mutual funds—in more profitable instruments offered by commercial banks, governments, and industrial corporations. Thrift institutions have experienced such periods of "disintermediation" four times since 1966, with obvious consequences for their ability to channel savings into residential mortgages and for their ability to survive.

In addition to the problems of thrift institutions, increased corporate and government borrowing has left more diversified lenders with less inclination and ability to finance housing construction whenever credit has been restricted and short-term interest rates have risen. Thus, in the tight money crunch of 1966, housing starts plunged 30 percent in just six months, to the lowest level since 1946.[4] As the credit supply was allowed to expand again to avoid a more severe financial crisis, housing production recovered in the late 1960s and declined somewhat less severely in the recession of 1969–70 due to some interventions discussed below. Housing then led the credit boom of the early 1970s, as production reached the highest level in history in 1972. But by 1974, when the economy entered what was (until the 1980s) the worst recession since the 1930s, the bottom fell out. In 1975 housing starts were more than 50 percent below the 1972 peak, and the low point was a postwar record below even the 1966 trough. Half a million new homes stood vacant and thousands of apartment buildings were left unfinished as mortgage credit evaporated. Housing production had traditionally led the economy out of a recession, but at the beginning of 1977, nearly a year and a half after the recession had supposedly hit bottom, housing starts were still 30 percent below what they had been in 1972. By mid-1977, after three and a half years of depression in the housing industry, a new speculative boom finally brought housing production up to an annual rate of about 2 million units, where it remained until the end of 1978.

As in the past, the expansion of the late 1970s was fueled by the credit expansion policies of the Federal Reserve Board, plus special government efforts in housing finance that prop up the housing industry and use housing as a stimulus to the overall economy. But with inflation accelerating out of control, stimulated in part by the continued availability of high-cost credit, toward late 1978 the end of the miniboom was in sight. Sales of new and existing housing peaked in the fall of 1978; mortgage interest rates passed 10 percent by the end of the year, signs of overbuilding appeared in some parts of the country, and housing starts dropped about 30 percent during the first two months of 1979. With the spring of 1979 things picked up a little, and many economists and housing industry forecasters naively and wishfully predicted there would not be a severe housing decline. But with interest rates continuing to rise, billions of dollars began to leave thrift institutions as savers sought even greater returns than they could get on newly created high-interest savings certificates. In the fall the Federal Reserve administered the traditional medicine for an overheated economy: raising interest rates still higher and severely tightening the money supply. The mortgage industry responded desperately, charging more for mortgages in order to be able to pay higher rates to keep and obtain some funds to lend. Mortgage interest rates passed 12 percent late in 1979 and reached 16–17 percent early in 1980, but there was very little mortgage money available even for those borrowers willing and able to pay such rates. New construction plummeted nearly 50 percent between the fall of 1979 and spring of 1980, dipping again below the 1 million level. Fears about the impact of the crunch, and the traditional willingness of the Federal Reserve Board to accommodate incumbent presidents in election years, led to an easing of the monetary reins, and housing construction took off until the start of 1981, when there was a new administration and a new resolve at the Federal Reserve to control inflation at any cost. Housing production again collapsed, plummeting 50 percent between winter and fall of 1981, setting another postwar record low of about 850,000 units at an annual rate, and remaining well below the 1 million level from the summer of 1981 until nearly the middle of 1982, as most commentators ran out of adjectives trying to describe how much worse this depression was than the last worst housing depression.

In addition to its impact on housing production, the crisis has of course also had a devastating effect on the cost of housing. Because of the dependence on credit and the sensitivity of housing costs to interest rates, the cost of shelter reflects a piggyback effect of rising interest rates on top of rising house prices. Thus between 1970 and 1976, while median family income was rising 47 percent and the overall Consumer Price Index went up 46 percent, median sales prices for new houses rose 90 percent, and the monthly ownership cost for a median-priced new house rose 100 percent, while the monthly ownership cost for a median-priced existing house rose 65 percent. Between the end of 1976 and the end of 1981, the median price of a new house rose another 50 percent, while prices of existing houses rose by over 70 percent, and mortgage interest rates increased from about 9 percent at the earlier point to about 16 percent at the end of 1981; so buyers entering the market had to pay over 200 percent more for their mortgage payments than did the typical new buyer just five years before. To be sure, first-time homebuyers, who represented 36 percent of all buyers in 1977, had decreased to under 14 percent of all buyers in 1981. During the 1950s, about two-thirds of all families could have afforded the typical new house; by 1970 the proportion had declined to one-half, by 1976 to just one-fourth (Frieden and Solomon, 1977), and by 1981 to less than one-tenth.[5]

Housing has clearly been one of the disaster areas of the past decade. However, the housing sector has not been merely a passive victim of the pervasive crisis. The housing and lending industries, with the aid of the government, have tried to deal with the increasingly weakened and unstable mortgage system, but these attempts have ultimately only exacerbated the difficulties of the overall economy without solving the housing affordability and financing problems. All sorts of new programs, institutions, and techniques have been created, but they truly represent just rococo adornment on the facade of a structure that had flaws from the start and has been decaying from within. No amount of superficial decoration can be expected to prop up an unsound structure; indeed, it only adds more weight, thereby increasing the likelihood of collapse.

The list of additions to the mortgage lending system since the late 1960s is a long one, with new variations appearing almost monthly, and no attempt will be made to describe and evaluate each one. A listing of some of the major elements, though, will serve to indicate the scope of the changes. In the late 1960s and early 1970s the Federal National Mortgage Association was reorganized and privatized, a new, federally backed Government National Mortgage Association was created, and a Federal Home Loan Mortgage Corporation was established, all to create a national money market for housing and to tap new sources of funds for residential mortgages. In addition, private mortgage insurance opened up secondary mortgage markets for raising money and trading mortgages without involvement of government-created agencies, and more recently some private lenders have been issuing mortgage-backed securities without government guarantees. The Federal Home Loan Bank Board has in times of tight money provided huge advances, raised by selling securities in the bond market, to member institutions losing deposits. State and local housing finance and development agencies have raised housing funds by selling tax-exempt bonds; real estate investment trusts have also raised money by using certain tax advantages. In addition to such devices designed to tap the national capital markets and reduce mortgage loan dependence on savings accounts, the thrift institutions themselves have been allowed to try to hold on to savings by issuing various long-term certificates, money market certificates, All-Savers Certificates, and so forth that pay higher rates than traditional passbook savings accounts. There are also alternative mortgage instruments designed to try to protect thrift institutions from interest-rate fluctuations and overcome (hopefully only) initial affordability problems of homebuyers, ranging from adjustable-rate and variable-rate mortgages to graduated-payment and shared-appreciation mortgages, with a whole alphabet soup of abbreviations for the various types of mortgages to match the alphabet soup of agencies and programs.

The development of these new institutions and devices to raise and allocate mortgage credit has not been entirely successful, as revealed by the production crashes of 1973–1975 and 1980–1982. They have, however, had two very significant consequences for the overall economy, as well as for the housing and lending industries.

First, they have increased the total demand for credit in the economy. When the supply of credit has been plentiful, the result has been a more rapid growth in the total amount of debt and a relatively larger share allocated to real estate in general and housing in particular. For example, during the late 1960s, before the new mortgage institutions reached their maturity, the growth of mortgage debt slipped relative to corporate and government borrowing, as Table 3.2 reveals: From 1946 through 1965 residential mortgages accounted for 31 percent of the total increase in debt; in the following five years the increase in housing debt was only 20 percent of the total. However, during the boom of the early 1970s, despite the massive increase in corporate and government borrowing, the new institutions enabled housing debt to increase its share to 23 percent of the total increase in debt. In the late 1970s, even with continued growth of corporate and government borrowing, residential debt accounted for 24 percent of the total increase in debt in the economy, 34 percent of the increase in private debt; and residential mortgages plus federally sponsored housing credit accounted for 32 percent of all public and private borrowing during this period. Indeed, by 1980 over 22 percent of the total debt (direct plus sponsored) of the federal government was housing related.

The changes in mortgage financing over the past decade and a half thus gave a tremendous boost to real growth in the economy, but also to the unprecedented inflation and the overblown credit bubble. On the other hand, when monetary policy has sought to contain inflation by reducing the supply of credit, the new mortgage institutions, especially the federally created and federally backed agencies, have only intensified competition for scarce credit, leading to even higher interest rates throughout the system. Higher interest rates not only have added to inflation but also have led to further withdrawals of savings deposits as savers have pursued the higher returns available elsewhere. Increased withdrawals from thrift institutions have substantially offset the additional housing funds raised through the capital markets and so weakened a number of thrifts that they have been saved only by being absorbed (with federal financial assistance) by larger and stronger financial institutions. Thus, the attempts of mortgage lenders and others in the housing industry to compete more effectively for funds have not been fully successful, but they have contributed to higher housing costs, higher interest rates generally, and greater concentration in the mortgage industry. [*See Chapter 4 by Ann Meyerson*].

The second major consequence of the new institutions and financing techniques is that residential finance is no longer a relatively separate and insulated component of the credit system. Many investors other than thrift institutions and small savers now have hundreds of billions of dollars tied up with the mortgage system. The stability of the structure of residential debt is thus increasingly vital for the stability of the entire financial structure of American capitalism. But the stability of the housing debt system depends upon continued mortgage payments from people in existing housing and on the ability of prospective buyers to obtain long-term loans for new housing being built with short-term construction loans. The ratio of mortgage debt to disposable personal income climbed from 18 percent in 1946 to 55 percent in 1965. Between the mid-1960s and mid-1970s this ratio did not rise, but the ratio does not reflect rising interest rates, so mortgage payments actually grew faster than income even over this period. During the 1960s, the number of mortgage foreclosures per year doubled from about 50,000 to about 100,000, and by 1975 had increased to over 140,000.[6]

In the five years after 1975, residential mortgage debt increased by about $500 billion (see Table 3.2), an increase of nearly 84 percent. This increase does not even include all the debt that was refinanced by homeowners cashing in on rising property values. With all of the selling and refinancing of existing homes and apartments, probably over $300 billion of the nearly $600 billion in mortgage debt outstanding at the end of 1975 was paid off over the next five years.[7] This means that over 70 percent of $1.1 trillion in residential mortgage debt at the end of 1980 consisted of loans that had been taken out just since 1975 and at the highest interest rates in history! Mortgage debt thus reached 60 percent of disposable personal income in 1980. Coupling the immense growth of mortgage debt with the higher-than-ever interest rates at which it has been borrowed, the amount of money tenants and homeowners have to lay out for mortgage payments has more than doubled since 1975, while disposable income, out of which mortgage payments (and everything else but personal income taxes) have to be made, has gone up little more than 50 percent—suggesting more starkly than ever the danger for the financial system posed by the conflict between housing costs and incomes. In 1982 the Mortgage Bankers Association reported that home mortgage foreclosures were at the highest level since they began keeping records 30 years before and nearly 66 percent higher than the year before. Furthermore, during the first half of 1982, bank failures reached the highest level since the start of World War II (*Boston Globe*, June 17, 1982; Brooks, 1982, 68).

The present situation is really quite desperate. Despite the relative prosperity of 1983–1985, it is very likely that in the next few years the number of people unable to pay for their housing will again dramatically increase—especially of those who bought homes in recent years at inflated prices and interest rates and now pay 40, 50, or even 60 percent of their (sometimes combined) incomes. Widespread mortgage defaults will again send shock waves through the unstable financial system and result in many people losing their homes. It is a terrifying prospect, since people are at present unprepared and defenseless, and they lack a credible alternative to the present chaos in the housing market. What are the possibilities? The fact that tenants do not generally share homeowners' direct interest in maintaining mortgage payments on their housing is important. Only about one-third of American households are renters, and many of these households understandably want to "move up" to homeownership as quickly as they can. Nonetheless, the growing housing problem in the United States seems to be giving rise to a process of "tenantization" that is reducing the possibility and meaning of homeownership, especially for working-class people, and may widen the prospects for progressive housing organizing. [*For a fuller discussion of progressive housing organizing strategies, see the chapters in Part 3.*]

There are four discernible threads to the tenantization process so far. First, many families, especially young families, who in the past could have expected to buy a home, have been finding it impossible. Most first-time buyers are either high-salaried professionals or families depending on two incomes, and even then the burden of housing costs is staggering while the benefits are often illusory. Most first-time buyers with incomes under $30,000 have little choice other than mobile homes or old, two-to-four unit houses in urban neighborhoods where "gentrification" has not yet led to spiraling property values. In many areas and for most young working-class families these options are not even available, for the banks will not make loans to them, or will not do so in the neighborhoods they could afford, and thus they remain caught in the rental market.

Second, despite all the publicity about the "back to the cities" movement, in most working-class neighborhoods in most cities property values are rising little if at all, and those homeowners who want to sell are often unable to do so. "Redlining" practices—the refusal by banks to lend and insurance companies to issue fire insurance—declining city services, deterioration, arson-for-profit by absentee landlords who want to bail out, and inadequate incomes among both homeowners and tenants have led to the virtual collapse of the housing market in these areas. In some instances, real and imagined dangers have caused people to abandon their homes and move into apartments elsewhere. In most cases, though, residents remain and continue to pay their mortgages and property taxes, even though the market value of their investment may be negligible. They may have a deed, but they are in effect tenants.

Third, in those urban neighborhoods where higher-income people are moving in, existing homeowners are often experiencing rapid increases in the market value of their houses—rather than stagnation or decline as in other neighborhoods. If they sell and reap the windfall, however, they will frequently be unable to buy another house elsewhere, since the money from their old house may be insufficient or partially used for other necessities, and they cannot afford a mortgage. And if they do not sell, they will generally feel the cost pressures of rising property-tax assessments plus official and unofficial demands to "upgrade" their property. Furthermore, there are the social and psychological pressures to move when the neighborhood is invaded by Porsches, boutiques, and their patrons. While tenants are generally the first to be displaced by such "gentrification," some working-class homeowners are clearly being "tenantized" by the process.

Finally, many families who have bought homes during the past decade are losing their homes (and their investments) through foreclosure and are being forced back into the rental market. As already indicated, this process will surely increase dramatically in coming years, but since the 1960s the rate of foreclosures has already tripled. Most of the victims so far have been working-class families, a large proportion black, who bought homes in older urban areas. The residents have found it impossible to keep up on their mortgage payments, property taxes, and fuel bills, and provide the maintenance and repairs necessary to make and keep their homes livable. As unemployment comes on top of continuing inflation, foreclosures will spread rapidly.

While one should never underestimate the capacity of capitalism to find imaginative ways of coping with its problems, the powerful spread of tenantization will surely begin to undermine the myth of homeownership. The first result undoubtedly will be frustration at being deprived of the opportunity to realize or sustain the American dream of a home of one's own. The second result could be increasing recognition and acknowledgment of the objective reality of tenantization, and with it a declining commitment to the protection of property values and the payment of mortgage debts, especially as they are seen to conflict with the need for adequate shelter, as well as with the need for food, clothing, and medical care. The most progressive housing struggles have generally been those of tenants. Because they do not have a direct stake in their housing as an investment, tenants have most frequently become mobilized to restrict increases in their rents—and (often in conjunction with rent struggles) to restrict evictions and get physical improvements in their housing—even though this has brought them into direct conflict with the interests of landlords and lenders. Indeed, there have been situations where well-organized tenants have tried to force their buildings into foreclosure, and then prevent evictions and resale of the property, in order to wipe out the mortgage payments. While such militancy obviously encounters considerable resistance, it certainly suggests the potential of tenant organizing, especially if this type of consciousness and solidarity can encompass homeowners who are being tenantized (e.g., organizing homeowners who are facing foreclosure, helping them resist eviction).[8]

Since the late 1960s, struggles to enact, defend, and strengthen rent control have certainly been the most widespread manifestation of tenant militancy in this country [*see Chapter 22 by John Atlas and Peter Dreier*]. Obviously the demand for rent control has grown directly out of the squeeze between housing costs and incomes. Where successful, it has extended social control over housing profits, and in this sense it has been progressive, as well as being an important vehicle for organizing and political education. Yet in practice rent control advocates have been at pains to endorse the concept of "fair return" for landlords over "fair rent" for tenants and to argue that rent control does not have to lead to reduced private housing investment (Dreier, Gilderbloom, and Appelbaum, 1980). Not surprisingly, where such rent control programs have been adopted, they have not made much of a dent in the affordability problem, especially for lower-income working-class tenants. Indeed, the greatest concentration of rent control organizing in recent years— in New Jersey and California—has had its principal bases among middle-class tenants. Strict rent control, which would move toward a tenant affordability standard for rents rather than a landlord profitability standard, would certainly be much harder to win politically, but also might be more successful in mobilizing lower-income tenants. Such a program would and should drive down profits and hence reduce property values and threaten mortgages; it would of necessity have to be presented as just the first step of a program moving from increasing social control toward social ownership of housing. Rent control in some European countries has had this more radical character, despite the limitations noted near the beginning of this chapter. In this country, few organizers have yet acknowledged to themselves—let alone publicly—that such a program is not only what is required to deal with the affordability problem of tenants but increasingly might have considerable organizing potential.

Although tenant organizing has largely grown out of the housing affordability squeeze, it has rarely focused on or even identified the crucial role of mortgage lenders and mortgage payments in the housing cost problem. This weakness cannot in general be due to political reluctance, since rent strikes in most instances directly undermine landlords' capacity to keep up their mortgage payments. Rather, it is largely due to the limited understanding of the political economy of housing by most tenant activists. Only a few of the most sophisticated and militant rent strikes have consciously used the threat of mortgage default as a political tool. It is fair to conclude, then, that despite its positive accomplishments, tenant organizing has not yet gone very far toward striking at the heart of the housing problem. Tenantization may be broadening the base for progressive housing action, but such action certainly cannot be expected to arise spontaneously.

Homeowner organizing, on the other hand, is inherently more problematic. While it has often included concerns about housing as shelter (especially cost and housing-related municipal services), in most instances it has also included substantial concern about property values. Concern with housing as an investment is understandable within the context of the American housing dream, but when homeowners have organized around housing issues, the results have frequently been detrimental to tenants, especially low-income tenants, and often have been more beneficial to capitalists than to the homeowners themselves. Certainly Proposition 13 in California is the most familiar example of this phenomenon. The housing speculation of the 1970s was especially wild in California, but homeowners were finding that their property-tax assessments were going up with their property values. The response reflected not only a concern with rising shelter costs, though, but an unwillingness to control the speculation. The benefits of Proposition

13 flowed, of course, disproportionately to the largest property owners; landlords generally refused to pass the tax breaks on to tenants; and the service cuts, which will come eventually, fall especially hard on lower-income people.

Nor is Proposition 13 a unique example of the pitfalls of homeowner organizing. A major homeowner issue of the past decade has been "redlining," the failure of mortgage lenders to provide loans in certain neighborhoods for buying and fixing housing. This has been a classic populist issue, focusing on the power of the banks to decide the fate of whole communities, and the struggles against redlining have been assumed to be inherently and inevitably progressive by many activists and analysts. Yet virtually all of the organizing has focused exclusively on the *availability* of loans, choosing to ignore the problem of the *affordability* of such loans, despite the implications of high interest rates. Thus even the most progressive proposals to require lenders to make loans to areas on the basis of social rather than economic criteria have failed to recognize the entirely predictable consequences (Marcuse, 1979a); When loans become available, the only people who can afford them have been relatively higher-income existing homeowners and newly arriving "gentry." Lower-income tenants have rarely been able to become homeowners and have often been forced out by the rising rents charged by the owners to pay for home improvement loans. The principal beneficiaries have been the homeowners who could afford to buy in or to stay, the realtors and rehabilitators who live off the transformation, and the lenders who stimulate profitable new investments for themselves and often receive praise for their sudden enlightenment.

This analysis is not meant to suggest that there is an inescapable cleavage between the interests of working-class homeowners and tenants. It does suggest, though, the need for more careful evaluation of the class basis of actual housing issues and strategies. Certainly tenure differences do not correspond to class differences, especially since so many working-class people have become homeowners. The tenantization process may tend to bring tenure distinctions into closer correspondence with class position. More specifically, working-class homeowners frequently live in neighborhoods where there is a substantial proportion of tenants. There may thus arise the possibility of progressive unity with tenants where the squeeze between their incomes and housing costs is creating a conflict between their housing as shelter and as an investment: for example, where continuing to make mortgage payments means being unable to afford to buy fuel or make necessary repairs, or where the increased value of homeowners' property due to speculation or gentrification in the area has lower priority than keeping down costs and preserving the social fabric of the community. Under such circumstances, it may be possible to generate homeowner support for, say, rent control, a speculation tax, a ban on condominium conversions, and so forth, but these tenant-oriented demands should be combined—as they have not yet been—with such demands as eviction protection for homeowners in the event of foreclosure. Furthermore, these types of defensive organizing objectives have to be coupled with well-developed affirmative programs. Such programs should demonstrate the necessity and possibility of moving toward social ownership of housing and reduction of dependence on the mortgage finance system in ways that acknowledge people's legitimate desire for secure tenure, decent housing, safe and congenial communities, and for an economic cushion, which so much of the dream of homeownership rests upon.

Some housing activists have been working on trying to develop such socialist housing programs in response to the growing national housing problems and their various local manifestations. While there is always the danger of utopianism in such efforts, there also seems to be increasing recognition of the need for strategies and programs that go beyond the immediate defensive actions that inevitably predominate. Locally the efforts are focused primarily on expanding social ownership of housing—removing and keeping housing out of the private, speculative market, thereby trying both to alter control over the housing and to contain cost increases due to speculative resale and associated mortgage increases.[9] There are some attempts to preserve, revitalize, and expand public housing, in the face of a history of abuse and neglect in many cities followed by current government and private efforts to demolish or sell off much of the existing public housing [*see Chapter 20 by Rachel G. Bratt*]. There are also some efforts to prevent the sale of housing that local governments have acquired through tax foreclosure or the federal government acquired through foreclosure on FHA-insured mortgages; or if it is to be disposed of, there are demands that it be fixed up and then turned over to the tenants or a community organization for a nominal sum and debt free. Finally, various examples of nonpublic social ownership are being used, such as low-equity cooperatives and ownership by community organizations.

There are debates about the political and economic implications of the various approaches to social ownership. The analysis developed here and the experience of Western Europe suggest that while struggles for social ownership can be progressive and important, as long as there are mortgages to be paid, there will be neither substantial reduction in housing costs nor significant challenge to other fundamental features of the capitalist housing market. In this regard, struggles for public ownership do seem to offer greater long-term strategic potential than community ownership, even though resident or community ownership may be easier to achieve in the short run. Public ownership places the housing directly in the political arena, where struggles over affordability and financing of housing can be waged along with other struggles. Resident or community ownership, unless the housing can be acquired mortgage free and with guaranteed subsidies for operating expenses, still must contend with the mortgage payments, unless there is a sophisticated strategy to default eventually on the mortgage and fight to hold on to the housing. Also, organizations that have become involved with community housing development and ownership have almost always become so involved with the technical and operational aspects of the housing that they have been unable to sustain mass participation and move on to other issues. There is a tremendous burden on the organizational leadership when rents have to be collected from people who still cannot afford to pay. Under capitalism, community or resident ownership can mean that working-class people are just administering their own dependency, since they still have no control over their incomes and most of the costs of their housing [*see Chapter 26 by Robert Kolodny and Chapter 27 by Tony Schuman*].

Finally, considerable work has been done on developing a national housing program, emphasizing the replacement of the mortgage system, as well as changes in ownership and tenure. The program has been developed in considerable detail, including cost estimates, demonstrating that it would be quite feasible economically to move toward replacing the private housing and mortgage markets [*see Chapter 29 by Chester Hartman and Michael E. Stone*].

## Conclusion

Despite the tremendous growth of the forces of production in the United States, a large proportion of the population has always been unable to afford the official national goal of "a decent home and a suitable living environment for every American family" (42 U.S.C.A. § 1441). The problem is partly caused by the extremely high cost of housing generated by the various elements of the housing market. But it is also the result of the extremely unequal distribution of income produced by the labor market.

The problem of incomes and housing costs cannot be solved within capitalism because the required redistribution of income would lead to the collapse of the labor market, while the required reduction of housing costs would lead to the collapse of the private housing market. Yet the problem cannot be ignored because inadequate incomes undermine the profitability of the housing market, high housing costs add to the wage costs of employers, and this squeeze is a potential source of political disruption. Seen in these terms, the evolution of the housing sector in the twentieth century—particularly the growth of the mortgage system and the extensive intervention of the government—can be understood as attempts to manage the conflict between the housing and labor markets in the interests of capital.

On the one hand, these efforts have been defensive. Mortgage lenders and the state—primarily through the promotion of mortgaged homeownership—have attempted to relieve some of the pressure on the housing and labor markets and defuse the problem socially and ideologically so that it does not become a source of radical political consciousness and action. At the same time, state action has also sought to serve the interests of capitalists offensively—stimulating profits and capital accumulation in housing and mortgage lending in order to counteract the depressing effect of inadequate income on the housing market, the construction industry, and thus the overall economy.

In the long run these attempts have not ony failed to solve the housing problem but have actually generated some very serious economic and political problems. First, the stability of the entire financial structure has become interwoven with the stability of the huge residential mortgage debt created by the evolution of the mortgage system. Since the mortgage payments on this debt constitute the biggest single component of most families' housing costs, the increasing difficulty in paying for the high cost of housing threatens the mortgage system—and the rest of the financial system—with collapse. This linkage has made housing a significant contributor to the ongoing economic crisis, and has made the housing sector especially vulnerable to the crisis.

Second, the growing sensitivity of the economy to the ability and willingness of people to continue to pay the mortgage debt service costs—directly as homeowners and through rents as tenants—has given housing unprecedented political significance. That is, the working class has acquired a tremendously powerful weapon, which might be used quite effectively as part of a revolutionary strategy. However, if housing struggles either consciously or unwittingly come to threaten the mortgage system, there is the danger of swift and heavy repression. The potential of housing struggles can therefore be realized only through a powerful, broad-based movement that is able to defend itself while it takes advantage of the vulnerable financial structure of American capitalism.

## Notes

1. The housing market is far more complex than suggested by the simple line of analysis in this paragraph; the significance of some of this complexity is discussed below. By way of clarification at this point, though, because of its durability, most housing is not new, and most older housing is comparable to new housing in both quality and price. On the other hand, because housing is immobile and does vary in quality, the housing market is not homogeneous, and the price certainly does vary over a considerable range. Nevertheless, housing submarkets are fairly easily identifiable, and within each submarket the price, the quality, and rate and type of construction of housing are closely correlated with and indeed to a considerable degree determined by the prevailing level of residents' incomes.

2. Various perspectives on Western European housing issues are represented by the following: Community Development Project Information and Intelligence Unit, 1976; Donnison, 1967; Housing Workshop of the Conference of Socialist Economists, 1975; Mandleker, 1973; Marcuse, 1978b; OECD Financial Markets Committee's Working Party on Housing Finance, 1974; Services to Community Action and Tenants and NUPE, n.d..

3. The quantitative data included throughout the rest of this section are from U.S. Bureau of the Census, 1976; for more detail and page references in this source, see Stone, 1980a, 1980b.

4. Figures on housing starts are published monthly in U.S. Bureau of the Census, *Construction Reports*, Series C20. Mortgage interest rates are published monthly in the *Federal Home Loan Bank Board Journal*, which also presents sales prices for new and existing homes financed by member institutions of the Federal Home Loan Bank System. Another source on existing home sales prices and volume is National Association of Realtors, "Existing Home Sales," monthly. Also, U.S. Bureau of the Census, *Construction Reports*, Series C25, monthly, presents data on new homes.

5. Since the mid-1970s the mass media have been filled with stories on homeownership costs, most echoing the argument of this paragraph, but some industry sources claiming that the use of median prices and the emphasis on new housing gives a misleading picture. The principal industry response has been by the U.S. League of Savings Associations, 1978a, 1978b, 1980, 1982, 1984. The earlier of these reports argued that many homebuyers are still of modest income and buying their first home; yet their data, plus other sources, reveal a pronounced shift of homebuying up the income distribution, a significant decline in the proportion of first-time buyers, and a steady rise in housing cost–income ratios for homeowners.

6. U.S. Bureau of the Census, 1976, 751. These figures are for nonfarm real estate, most but not all of which consists of housing. This particular series has not been published for years after 1975.

7. In the five years from 1976 through 1980, repayments on long-term residential mortgage loans totaled almost exactly $400 billion (U.S. HUD, 1980c, 177–80; 1981c, 2).

While some portion of this $400 billion represents repayments on loans originated during these five years and thus was not part of the $600 billion outstanding at the end of 1975, it is reasonable to conclude that most of the repayments were on loans outstanding at the end of 1975, for several reasons. First, the newer the loan and the higher the interest rate, the smaller the fraction of each monthly payment that goes toward repayment of principal; thus monthly payments on loans made after 1975 will on average include smaller repayments of principal than loans made earlier. Second, the longer a loan is outstanding, the greater likelihood that the loan balance will be repaid through sale of the property or refinancing; the normal life of a long-term mortgage is 10 to 12 years, and few are discharged in less than 5 years. It is therefore likely that the rate of resale and refinancing was substantially higher for mortgages taken out before 1976 than in later years. On the basis of these two factors, probably at least three-quarters of total loan repayments from 1976 through 1980, or more than $300 billion, were on mortgage loans outstanding at the end of 1975.

8. For a discussion of the strategy, see Achtenberg and Stone (1974, 108–14); Brodsky (1975, 37–46). For the response, see "Major Conspiracy Suit Threatens Tenants' Right to Organize Union," Civil Liberties Union of Massachusetts, *Docket* (Dec. 1976); and "An Historical Analysis of Tenants First Coalition," *Shelterforce* (Summer 1977), 8–9.

9. In Boston, for example, a number of groups have been promoting a set of progressive housing policies for the city, under these five broad goals (see Stone, 1985):

*1. To maintain and enhance the affordability of existing unsubsidized housing:* enact permanent rent, eviction, and condominium conversion controls; enact a tax on the speculative turnover of housing; require owners of rental housing to use fire insurance proceeds to restore fire-damaged buildings for present residents; increase grants and low-interest loans for low- and moderate-income homeowners to pay for repairs and weatherization; establish municipally capitalized reverse-annuity mortgages for low-income elderly homeowners; support and provide foreclosure relief for low- and moderate-income homeowners; and reduce property taxes for low-income homeowners through the use of existing legal mechanisms for abatement due to financial hardship.

*2. To facilitate the transfer of existing housing to forms of nonspeculative ownership*: transfer city-owned property, tax-foreclosed, condemned, or surplus, to the Boston Citywide Land Trust (BCLT), rather than auction it off back into the speculative market; provide city and/or CDBG funds to help cover the overhead costs of the BCLT and other nonprofit entities that acquire and manage housing for nonspeculative ownership; link homeowner relief programs to future acquisition by the BCLT; make greater use of condemnation and receivership provisions of the Sanitary Code as mechanisms to transfer housing from owners who cannot responsibly manage it to nonspeculative resident or community owners; and support acquisition by the Boston Housing Authority (BHA) of some existing one- to-four-family homes on a scattered-site basis to house large low-income families, with emphasis on community assistance and resident self-help to reduce housing costs and promote other social objectives.

    3. *To preserve existing public and subsidized housing and enhance its affordability:* support upgrading and preservation of existing public housing as housing for low-income people; resist the sale of HUD-foreclosed housing developments except to nonprofit or nonspeculative resident ownership; and advocate and support changes in the rent formulas for public and subsidized housing in order to make the housing truly affordable, along with adequate operating subsidies for such housing.

    4. *To support production of more housing for nonspeculative ownership:* strengthen the linkage formula with the funds targeted for development of nonspeculative housing; support development of new public housing; use CDBG funds for seed money and technical assistance for community-based developers, and, resources permitting, for capital grants and low-interest loans; explore the use of municipal borrowing and the use of a portion of municipal pension funds for financing new construction and substantial rehabilitation of housing; and earmark receipts from the tax on speculative turnover of housing for community-based development for nonspeculative ownership.

    5. *To establish a local housing Bill of Rights:* enact statutory life tenure for tenants who continue to pay their legally established rent and do not interfere with the rights of other tenants; establish life estate security for homeowners under the reverse-annuity and foreclosure-relief programs; strictly enforce the Sanitary Code, with community and resident participation, use condemnation where appropriate, and encourage the Housing Court to use the Boston Citywide Land Trust as receiver; legislatively recognize the right of tenants to form unions and bargain collectively; strengthen the enforcement powers of the Fair Housing Commission; and provide public education, outreach, publicity, and technical assistance to housing residents and groups on their housing rights and the exercise of them individually and collectively.

# 4

# Deregulation and the Restructuring of the Housing Finance System

*Ann Meyerson*

*The most far-reaching developments in the mortgage lending system in the half century since the Great Depression were triggered in the early 1980s by the near collapse of the nation's thrift institutions—the savings and loan associations and savings banks. The financial viability of these traditional suppliers of mortgage funds was threatened by an unprecedented period of rising interest rates. Efforts to rescue the ailing thrifts resulted in increased deregulation and homogenization of the banking system, profoundly altering the nation's housing situation and financial structure. Just as the housing finance developments described by Michael E. Stone sharpened the contradictions for working-class housing consumers, so will these more recent changes exacerbate the affordability problem, increase concentration in the financial industry, and produce a more fragile financial system.*

In Chapter 3, "Housing and the Dynamics of U.S. Capitalism," Michael E. Stone describes the emergence of unresolved contradictions in the housing sector as a result of the new mortgage system established after the financial collapse of the 1930s. He foresees an increased risk of general financial collapse as "all capitalism has to offer is higher-priced houses and more debt" and as households become less able and/or willing to continue to repay their mortgage indebtedness.

Indeed, delinquencies, defaults, and actual mortgage foreclosures increased dramatically in the early 1980s as the economy went into deep depression. In May 1983, the House of Representatives was considering emergency mortgage-assistance legislation to rescue families from imminent foreclosure (Shribman, 1983). But although the housing affordability squeeze (and the threat of widespread mortgage default) has been exacerbated and continues to be a major tension in the housing finance system, it has not been the major pressure forcing a far-reaching restructuring of the financial system, on the scale of changes enacted a half-century ago.

Instead, the problems of the nation's thrift institutions—their inability to attract savings and simply stay in business—reached crisis proportions in the early 1980s and precipitated a restructuring of the financial system that will have a severe impact on housing and will contribute to the vulnerability of that system. Because of their historic dependence on short-term deposits with regulated interest rates and their predominant investment in long-term, fixed-rate mortgages, thrift institutions have been particularly vulnerable to steeply rising interest rates, such as began to occur in an unprecedented manner in 1966. During such periods of "tight money," thrift institutions suffer as rate-conscious depositors withdraw their savings in favor of less-regulated investments, as well as from low earnings as deposit rates rise above returns on mortgage portfolios. To accommodate these deposit losses and low earnings, thrifts are forced to dip into surplus funds, sell relatively nonliquid assets at a loss, merge with healthier institutions, or do all three.

Although Stone observed these thrift problems, he did not foresee that the near collapse of the thrift industry would lead to widespread deregulation and homogenization of the financial system. This deregulation—brought about by the federal legislative enactments of 1980 (the Depository Institutions Deregulation and Monetary Control Act) and 1982 (the Garn–St Germain Depository Institutions Act), together with other regulatory changes on federal and state levels—has helped produce the profound restructuring of the mortgage finance system that is the subject of this chapter. As housing has long been dependent on the thrifts, with the industry first in a state of collapse and subsequently altered by the reorganization of the financial system, we can predict a dramatically changed housing and mortgage market, with implications for homebuyers, renters, landlords, and housing conditions in general.

Almost all of the mainstream analyses of the changes taking place in the housing finance system make the assumption that the earlier housing finance system was untenable, government overregulation together with high interest rates was the key culprit, and thus deregulation was necessary to save the financial services industry and benefit the public (Baer, 1983; Colton, 1983; Kaplan, 1983; Seiders, 1982, 1983; Tuccillo with Goodman, 1983; Vartanian, 1983a, 1983b). Almost all take for granted that the public will benefit greatly from this shift to a "free market" approach and that the housing finance system will become much more efficient.

As the following analysis indicates, however, the future will not be all that rosy for housing or for the nation's financial structure generally. The deregulation and restructuring of the housing finance system will not resolve the system's problems in the interest of low- to moderate-income consumers, nor will it help solve "the housing problem." Moreover, as yet another mechanism to shore up the financial system, deregulation appears to be failing. The institutional structure of housing finance has been altered, with a reduced role for the thrifts, an increased role for mortgage bankers, and much greater reliance on secondary-mortgage-market activity. Housing has lost its specialized and locally oriented financial institutions; its cheap pool of money for mortgages (as a result of deposit-rate deregulation); and its overwhelming reliance on the long-term, fixed-rate mortgage instrument (as a result of the increasing predominance of adjustable-rate mortgages). Although the thrifts could no longer perform their historic role, little effort has been made during the restructuring to find a new way to channel low-cost funds into housing. Consumers will now have to compete with the giants of industry, losing out as housing consumers and as savers. Housing will become more expensive and less secure, and banking for low-balance depositors will become more expensive and onerous.

Deregulation of the financial system thus represents a significant departure in government housing policy. The financial restructuring of the 1930s gave the housing sector a protected status and a substantial amount of government support, which the recent restructuring is eliminating. Today, as in the 1930s, the government is intervening to strengthen the financial institutions per se, but unlike the 1930s, requirements and incentives for those institutions to specialize in mortgage lending are being reduced. It is not at all clear that these thrift institutions will be replaced by adequate and stable alternative sources of mortgage credit. It seems there is no longer the same interest there once was in stimulating housing—in using construction as a lever of economic stimulation or in continuing the absorption of capital resources by housing as opposed to other economic sectors.

This chapter departs from the question addressed by many of the mainstream analysts cited above in that it looks at the broader context of financial deregulation rather than at housing finance alone. In fact, much of the impetus behind the changes in the financial structure, including those affecting housing, came from institutions outside the traditional mortgage lending sector, most particularly the large commercial banks. Thus, although the thrifts were in an untenable position and the deregulation legislation was ostensibly an effort to resolve their difficulties, the legislation represented, in reality, the institutionalization of a broader process of restructuring the financial system. In this restructuring, it was not the thrifts but the large commercial banks that primarily benefited, as they too had been experiencing difficulties over the years, although of a different kind and a lesser magnitude than those of the thrifts. To understand the future of housing finance, then—its institutional framework, the sources of housing credit, and the manner in which funds will flow into housing—one must define a wider perspective, viewing all the interrelated changes taking place at the same time. In so doing, one sees, for example, that the general deregulation of deposit rates becomes as important to the future of housing finance as the deregulation of the asset structure of thrifts. And the increased concentration of the financial industry as a whole, as a result of deregulation, with its implications of risk to the entire system, also becomes critical to examine.

# The Thrift Crisis and the Restructured World of Housing Finance

The year 1981 and the first half of 1982 was the worst period in savings banking history since the great depression. Against a background of national economic recession, depressed personal savings and generally high interest rates, industry earnings in 1981 plummeted for the second consecutive year and continued to falter during the January—June 1982 period. . . . At the same time, deposit outflows continued massively and overall asset growth remained far below recent experience. As a result, savings bank investments strategy was once again forced to emphasize the maintenance of strong liquidity positions and further reductions in longer term investments. (National Association of Mutual Savings Banks, 1982, 2)

For much of the post–World War II period, thrifts, armed with the Federal Reserve Board's Regulation Q—which set a ceiling on the amount of interest financial institutions could pay to depositors, with thrifts allowed to pay ¼ percent more than commercial banks—were able to charge borrowers a lucrative two to three points more than the deposit-rate ceiling and still offer a reasonable mortgage rate. Hence, *Newsweek* (Mar. 15, 1982) described running a thrift in the postwar years as "almost a license to print money." Moreover, housing credit was greatly expanded and mass homeownership facilitated by federally initiated housing finance programs: the Federal Home Loan Bank system of reserve banks for savings and loan associations; the Federal Deposit Insurance Corporation (FDIC) and Federal Savings and Loan Insurance Corporation (FSLIC) deposit insurance programs; the Federal Housing Administration (FHA) and later Veterans Administration (VA) mortgage insurance programs (and a new fixed-rate, level payment, self-amortizing mortgage instrument); a national secondary-mortgage market with "national mortgage associations" (the Federal National Mortgage Association [FNMA] in 1938, Government National Mortgage Association [GNMA] in 1968, and Federal Home Loan Mortgage Corporation [FHLMC] in 1970); and by tax incentives for thrifts to specialize in mortgage lending.[1] These programs essentially shored up the failed institutions after the Great Depression and shifted a substantial amount of the risk involved in mortgage lending to the government and, to a lesser extent, to the mortgage borrower. However, when economic conditions changed, namely when interest rates began to rise in 1966, none of the mechanisms at hand—infusions of funds from Federal Home Loan banks, FDIC and FSLIC actions, secondary-mortgage-market activity, and so on— was able to ease substantially the situation for thrifts and allow mortgage lending to continue as usual.[2]

It was the Garn–St Germain Depository Institutions Act of 1982 that came to the rescue of the ailing thrifts. But that legislation also represented the culmination of many years' efforts at "reform" or change of the financial system. Dating back to the 1958 Commission on Money and Credit and the 1971 Hunt Commission that first advocated increasing the flexibility of the system, "free competition, financial deregulation" advocates have been battling "housing protection, government-involvement-in-the-allocation-of-credit" advocates. The debate continued back and forth until the decisive 1980 Depository Institutions Deregulation and Monetary Control Act[3] and the Garn–St Germain Act. But these two were also preceded by earlier regulatory changes, such as (1) the introduction of money market and other deposit certificates in 1978; (2) the introduction of alternative mortgage instruments,[4] which were being offered widely by state initiation by 1976 (Colton, 1980, 105) and in 1979 were authorized for federally chartered savings and loan associations; and (3) the expansion of the mortgage-backed securities market by the federally related secondary-mortgage-market agencies, FNMA, GNMA and FHLMC.[5] The thrift crisis in the early 1980s became the occasion to pass a bill that went way beyond bailing out the thrifts. The Garn—St Germain Act represented a dramatic shift toward deregulation and homogenization of the entire financial structure.

## The Garn–St Germain Act of 1982

This act basically provided emergency assistance and expanded investment authority to thrift institutions and further deregulated deposit rates at all depository institutions. Not only were the thrifts subsidized, thereby rescuing many of them and slowing down an intense period of merger activity, but they were given broad new lending powers, similar to those of commercial banks.

CAPITAL ASSISTANCE. Federal regulators (the FDIC and the FSLIC) were authorized to increase temporarily the net worth (assets minus liabilities) of thrifts that have at least 20 percent of their loans in mortgages, through government-backed promissory notes. Institutions that are troubled but that are seen to have a good chance of surviving can issue instruments called "net worth certificates" and swap them with the federal insurance agencies for promissory notes. The government pays off the notes to a thrift institution's creditors only if the thrift fails. No direct government appropriations are required for these notes because they are backed by funds that exist in the federal depository insuring agencies.

The capital assistance provisions of the Garn–St Germain Act were quickly utilized. By January 1983, $175 million had been pumped into 15 troubled savings banks, mostly in New York City (Bennett, 1983a). In addition, savings banks receiving the capital note assistance are exempt from city and state franchise taxes. Thus, these 15 banks, which otherwise would have been merged, were bailed out by the new legislation.

On the other hand, the act eased future merger activity by giving federal regulators wider latitude in selecting merger partners. There is now a procedure and order of priority for certain interstate and interindustry acquisitions. Intrastate mergers between thrifts are the top priority; if these are not possible, then interstate mergers between thrifts; then intrastate cross-industry mergers; and finally interstate cross-industry mergers. Furthermore, the act supplements and broadens the Federal Home Loan Bank Board's power to approve interstate acquisitions, by allowing the FSLIC to override any law that would interfere with a financially troubled FSLIC-insured bank merging with any other insured bank or an FDIC-insured bank, or being acquired by any person or company (Vartanian, 1983a, 169).

NEW INVESTMENT POWERS. The key provision allowed federally chartered thrifts for the first time to put up to 10 percent of their assets into corporate, commercial, and agricultural loans, areas dominated by commercial banks. In addition thrifts were given the opportunity to increase consumer loans from 20 to 30 percent of assets and nonresidential mortgage loans from 20 to 40 percent of assets. Previous asset limitations on investments in state and local obligations were also removed. And thrifts were given authority to invest up to 10 percent of their assets in tangible personal property and engage in equipment leasing, an activity found very profitable by commercial banks. In summary, "the Act provides a federal thrift with the ability to place up to 90 percent of its assets in commercial-type investments" (Vartanian, 1983a, 173).

Another key provision that enhanced the asset side of the thrift problem concerned the liberalization of mortgage loan terms. State regulation of "due-upon-sale" clauses, restricting financial institutions from calling in a home mortgage whenever a home is sold, were overridden. This means that lenders can now issue new loans at current market rates.

The act also enhanced the financial viability of these institutions by expanding federal chartering options for both savings banks and savings and loans. Since some states preclude mutual savings banks from converting to stock ownership—a form that allows the institutions to raise capital by issuing stock—and federal chartering does not, this allowed an easier conversion from the mutual to stock ownership form. Since the legislation has been passed, many thrifts have successfully "gone public" and rapidly increased their prosperity (Bennett, 1983c).

On the liability side, the act directed federal regulators to devise a new federally insured, high-interest-rate account, to be offered by commercial banks and thrifts, equivalent to and competitive with the high-yielding money market mutual funds. These new accounts, first available in December 1982, are free from interest-rate ceilings, and, as such, represent a considerable leap in the direction of deposit-rate deregulation. Further, unlike the money market mutual funds, they are federally insured. Thus they have contributed to the winning away of deposits from the money market mutual funds. Commercial banks, too, gained a great deal from this provision, as the chief cause of their deposit losses had been the money market funds. But there are fears that the new accounts may also attract a lot of depositors who will simply shift their money out of 5 1/2 percent accounts at the same savings institution. This will produce a negative earnings effect. In fact, there is some concern that thrifts may suffer in the short run, for they will have to pay out higher rates to depositors, and it may take some time for them to make the transition to commercial lending.

The act also eliminated the Regulation Q advantage thrifts have enjoyed over commercial banks. As of January 1, 1984, they are no longer able to pay ¼ percent more on certain deposit accounts. (On the other hand, thrifts may now offer demand accounts to persons and organizations that develop a business or commercial-loan relationship with them.)

As a result of this legislation, then, the thrifts received emergency assistance, they were allowed to diversify their portfolios substantially, and the financial structure became considerably deregulated and homogenized. The lines between commercial banks and thrifts will become increasingly blurred, and the two will be in greater competition with one another. Interest-rate ceilings on deposits are, to a large extent, removed, leaving everyone—banks, thrifts, money market mutual funds, and so forth—freer to compete.

In addition, since passage of this federal legislation, some states have been enacting banking laws that are more permissive than the federal law. In mid-1984, New York State enacted a broad omnibus banking law that moves deregulation to new heights. And given New York's prominence as a financial center, its move will undoubtedly be widely copied. The New York law, for example, allows savings banks to use an unlimited percentage of their assets for commercial loans and to invest in stocks and bonds unrestrictedly. All state-chartered banks including commercial banks will be allowed to invest in real estate development and ownership and to engage directly in leasing activities, without the need of separate subsidiaries; and restrictions will be removed on where banks can invest their assets (no longer confining them to a 75-mile radius of their headquarters). What is particularly noteworthy in terms of thrift support of local mortgage markets is that the current 20 percent limit will be removed on the portion of savings bank assets that can be invested in conventional mortgages *outside* New York State. With this more permissive state legislation, then, New York is better able to stem the conversion of state-chartered banks to federal charter that had been occurring as a result of the Garn–St Germain Act.

## Housing Sector Loses Support

The "protected" status that residential finance had enjoyed since the 1930s was substantially ended in 1982. With the liberalization of thrift asset restrictions, the special link between the thrifts and the housing sector, formed and fostered over the years to stimulate housing production and, in turn, the economy, was largely severed. With the deregulation of deposit rates, especially the end of the Regulation Q protection, housing will permanently suffer the loss of a cheap pool of money for mortgages. With due-upon-sale clauses and alternative mortgage instruments, housing consumers will lose a certain amount of security in their housing and potentially suffer higher mortgage rates. And in an environment of intense intermediary competition resulting from deregulation, thrifts will be driven to the highest-yielding investments possible, housing or not.

Housing finance still retains mortgage insurance, deposit insurance, a tax exemption for mortgage specialization by thrifts (but this is less effective given asset diversification possibilities—see below), federally related secondary-mortgage-market agencies—all established in the 1930s. Nevertheless, a definite shift in housing finance policy and in housing policy itself is taking place. The government's commitment to intervene in credit allocation on behalf of housing is no longer there.

In part, previous governmental support for housing reflected the strong housing lobby in the postwar period, the interests of which have usually been tied to those of the thrift industry, and both have historically presented a more or less unified position. But this solidarity broke down with the 1982 act, as shown by the thrifts' move toward expanded nonhousing investment powers. The National Association of Home Builders was, however, in favor of capital assistance for the thrifts even with the expanded investment powers. As a NAHB legislative counsel put it when interviewed, "We felt that half a thrift was better than no thrift at all." The housing lobby did push for the 10 percent cap on new asset powers when a higher percentage was requested by the thrift industry. It also won protections against encroachment on its construction turf by savings and loan subsidiary service corporations.[6] But it seems quite clear that the housing lobby has lost a lot of clout. As Colton observed in 1980:

> Congress has shifted in its outlook concerning housing interests. A few years ago the housing lobby was able to work against financial reform on the grounds that the impact on housing was uncertain. It is no longer clear that they have such power; as one congressional staff person noted, "People are tired of hearing about more assistance for housing. Housing subsidies have been substantial over the years, and they will continue. But Congress is also interested in finding somebody new who they can assist." (Colton, 1980, 107)

Michael Harloe adds an important dimension to this shift in government support of housing, particularly housing finance, by pointing to the problem of the housing sector's competition with other economic sectors. He says:

> In several countries concern has been expressed at the effects that a rapidly growing housing sector has had in diverting possible investment from other "more productive" sectors of the economy. . . . in Britain and the United States, for example, there has been criticism of the privileged position of the arrangements for housing finance which have often served to make it an attractive alternative to investment in other sectors. . . . Such a conflict only becomes apparent at a time when investment in these other sectors sags and yet investment continues to flow, aided by government support, into housing. . . . So perhaps the continued development of the private market in housing, at the very time when it seemed as if its dominance was generally established, is becoming ever more problematic, and clear divisions may be beginning to emerge between the interests of those active in this sector and those of capitalist enterprise more generally. (Harloe, 1983)

Thus, not only is housing no longer seen as an important lever of economic stimulation, but a movement toward reindustrialization is afoot, demanding that capital formation be shifted from housing to other "sagging" economic sectors.[7] (See also Grebler, 1983; Sternlieb and Hughes, 1984.)

Whether this departure in government housing finance policy will bring about greater "efficiency" and benefit the public, particularly housing consumers, is a controversial question. But before examining the implications of the financial restructuring for housing in further detail (e.g., questions such as how much will thrifts diversify?, will the cost of mortgage money go up?, will the supply of mortgage credit be adequate?), it is important to look at the implications of the restructuring for the financial industry as a whole. The impact of deregulation on the various sectors of the financial industry has considerable bearing on housing, as well as on the future of the financial system. The problems that housing will face stem in part from the shifting balance of power within the financial structure, on which housing is so dependent.

## Financial Institutions Strengthened

What is particularly striking about the financial restructuring of the 1930s and 1980s is the extent to which, at both times, the government's overriding aim seemed to be to support the interests of the nation's private financial institutions. In the 1930s, the thrifts received mortgage insurance, deposit insurance, a regional banking system, and so on. In 1982, the failing thrifts were rescued with capital assistance and were granted expanded investment powers and deregulated deposit-rate ceilings. The commercial banks (as well as the thrifts) were authorized to offer money market fund accounts. They benefited from the regulators' greater flexibility in assisting mergers of troubled institutions. They got Regulation Q rescinded. They lost their edge over thrifts in terms of asset powers, however, although thrifts can invest no more than 10 percent of their assets in the expanded forms.

In having to support, to some extent, both thrifts and commercial banks, the 1982 restructuring will open the door to further homogenization down the road, benefiting both groups.

> If you give savings and loans commercial lending powers and in a sense allow them to become like commercial banks, then obviously the ABA [American Bankers Association] and the IBAA [Independent Bankers Association of America], probably to a lesser extent, will say wait a minute, if they can do everything we can do and even more, then give us the same non-bank powers that they have. Then you get a sort of ratcheting process that ratchets you down to the lowest common denominator.... (U.S. Congress, House, Committee on Banking, Finance and Urban Affairs, 1982, 553–54)

Lane Kirkland, then secretary-treasurer of the AFL–CIO, in a strong dissent from the Hunt Commission's 1971 report, which, like Garn–St Germain, favored free competition and a non-public-purpose oriented system, points out the fundamental bias of financial "reform" toward serving the interests of private financial institutions:

> I am persuaded that the basic thrust of these recommendations is designed to promote the interests of private financial institutions without any genuine regard for the most urgent problems and needs of the nation. . . . Unfortunately, the Commission, while giving lip service to the broad public interest, washes its hands of the problems and disclaims any responsibility for seeing to it that a fair share of the financial resources are allocated for social priorities. . . . Besides avoiding the social priority area, it would appear that the net effect of the Commission recommendations would be to channel funds out of the housing market as well as to raise the cost of mortgage money—especially during a

tight credit market. . . . These recommendations [wider investment powers] would make the savings and loan associations and mutual savings banks more nearly like commercial banks. It would probably increase their profitability, but it would not generate any additional funds for the mortgage market. In fact, in periods of tight money, the mortgage market would be hard hit. (President's Commission on Financial Structure and Regulation, 1971, 129–31)

The 1982 restructuring did not simply promote the interests of financial institutions at the expense of social priorities, however. It promoted those interests differentially, thereby affecting (and reflecting) the balance of power among the financial institutions concerned. It also increased concentration in the financial industry as a whole.

## Commercial Banks Gain; Financial Industry Becomes Concentrated

Although the restructuring was designed to, and did, temporarily strengthen the thrifts, the large commercial banks have become the major beneficiaries. As a result of their ability to exploit deposit-rate deregulation, they have increased substantially their share of the savings market. They also are increasingly able to acquire smaller institutions, as a result of new merger procedures, the liberalization of thrift asset powers (paradoxically), and the highly competitive deregulatory environment in general.

It is apparent, particularly from the 1982 House hearings, that the more powerful push for the legislative changes came primarily from the large commercial banks, which had been increasingly losing deposits to the money market mutual funds, on top of more long-standing difficulty in holding on to their corporate deposit and loan business and competing with nonbanking "predators."[8] The tone of the American Bankers Association's "Banking Leaders' Consensus" report reflects the prevailing power relations:

> Regarding action on expansion of depositories' powers, the determinant is whether the Congress, the DIDC [Depository Institutions Deregulation Committee] and the thrift industry show by their actions a bona fide interest in working with banking for our agenda for change. A key measurement of this commitment will be the DIDC's March 22 decisions [concerning deregulation of Regulation Q and the establishment of the new money market accounts]. If this commitment is evident, banking is prepared to reciprocate by considering a fiscally responsible program for dealing with the low-yielding mortgage situation of all depositories and by agreeing to the plan described above for thrift asset powers. (U.S. Congress, House, Committee on Banking, Finance, and Urban Affairs, 1982, 512)

This view is further supported by Hendershott and Villani's observation that "commercial banks have several powerful lobby organizations and have the strongest political clout among parties interested in housing finance reform; their stand is pivotal to the success or failure of reform legislation" (Hendershott and Villani, 1977, 126).

An examination of how financial institutions operate illustrates how the large commercial banks will especially benefit from the deposit-rate deregulation instituted by the Garn–St Germain Act. In an environment without rate ceilings on deposits, all institutions will simply be able to gain savings on the basis of how much they are willing to pay. But in the long run, that amount is limited by how profitably the institution can invest the funds acquired.

The nation's big commercial banks have clear advantages in this environment. Unlike thrifts, few of the commercial banks' funds come from small consumer passbook accounts; in fact they get most of their deposits from markets where rate ceilings never existed. Thus they will experience little shifting of passbook balances to the higher-yielding accounts and, hence, no significant added costs. More important, large commercial banks invest their funds largely in an international market earning very high rates of return. For example, at the end of 1981, only 40 percent of Citicorp's $116 billion in assets was invested in the United States (*Savings and Loan News*, Nov. 1982, 30).

> The point is that under today's rules [Financial Accounting Standards Board Ruling No. 15—the special treatment of sovereign loans and lack of disclosure requirements] Citicorp will be able to make high-risk loans and gain large returns with relatively little fear that its bad loans will come back to haunt it. As a result, it will be able to pay depositors more than its conservative competitors.
>
> Commercial banks that take less loan risks will be disadvantaged. Savings associations with low-risk mortgages or anything similar will find it difficult if not impossible to match Citicorp's savings rates. (*Savings and Loan News*, Nov. 1982, 31)

The theory behind deregulation is that free competition will allocate capital most efficiently. Institutions will compete for funds, paying depositors based on the profitability of their investments, and the market will "discipline" those institutions that take too much risk. According to this view:

> Depositors will assess the risk of loss associated with the assets of various financial institutions and require large interest premiums from those facing possible losses. If conditions deteriorate, savers may flee, a liquidity crisis could develop and the institution might fold. Of course, to monitor the condition of institutions effectively, savers must have detailed and accurate information concerning the financial institutions bidding for their funds.
>
> In the real world, however, depositors cannot be expected to measure financial institution risks. For one thing, the saver has very little information concerning financial institution performance. . . . Most depositors in the 1980s depend on federal insurance of accounts to protect them from loss. . . . In the normal course of events, regulator and regulated are in a perpetual tug of war over how aggressive a financial institution's lending practices may be. But the global scope of giant banks' activities makes it impossible for regulators to find out what is really going on. . . . Federal regulators have been unwilling or unable

to limit institutions to what would appear to be prudent loans. (*Savings and Loans News*, Nov. 1982, 31)

So there is little impeding the large commercial banks from investing in increasingly risky loans at high returns to pay savings rates higher than other institutions, especially thrifts, can afford. This obviously has implications for the growth and expansion of large commercial banks at the expense of the thrifts and small commercial banks and tends to lead to greater concentration in the banking industry as a whole. It also has implications for the health and security of the financial system as it becomes dominated by institutions that accept an ever-increasing level of risk. If these loans go bad, the whole system is put at risk.[9]

In addition to deposit-rate deregulation, the large commercial banks benefited from the 1982 legislation's new procedure and priorities for federal regulators in arranging mergers. Now there is some official opening to interstate banking, which technically is restricted by the 1927 McFadden Act and later Douglas Amendment.[10] Commercial banks can now undertake interstate acquisitions of thrifts, something they have long sought in their drive to capture new markets, diversify, and compete with the substantial branching advantage of federal savings and loans.[11] Moreover, the larger commercial banks will now be able to manipulate the regulators in arranging these mergers and, as the Public Interest Research Group (PIRG) testified at the House hearings: "There is a very serious danger that the agencies will abuse their discretion and in fact take advantage of the current crisis to implement their own version of how the industry should be structured. . ." (U.S. Congress, House, Committee on Banking, Finance, and Urban Affairs, 1982, 535). The agencies (e.g., the Federal Home Loan Bank Board) are headed by "deregulation advocates," according to the PIRG, who are interested in arranging cross-industry, interstate supervisory mergers.

Citicorp's takeover of Fidelity Federal Savings and Loan in San Francisco illustrates both what large commercial banks can gain in a merger and what this maneuvering by one of the federal regulators looks like. Citicorp took over Fidelity in the fall of 1982, adding $2.9 billion to Citicorp's $120 billion in assets, putting it ahead of BankAmerica Corporation as the largest bank holding company and giving Citicorp "a long sought outlet for gathering consumer deposits in the most populous state, California" (*Business Week*, Aug. 30, 1982). There was considerable opposition to "this use of serious thrift industry problems to restructure the financial system of the United States," according to Kenneth Guenther, Director of the Independent Bankers Association of America (IBAA) (*Business Week*, Aug. 30, 1982). Critics felt Citicorp had circumvented federal and state laws prohibiting interstate banking. And many savings and loans were angry that their insurance premiums were going to install a powerful rival in their neighborhoods. While the FHLBB said that Citicorp's bid was substantially better than the second one, Jonathan Brown of the Public Interest Research Group disagreed, citing a bid from a California federal savings and loan that would have cost the FHLBB $20 billion less than Citicorp's. Overall, he testified:

> Many worry that Citicorp, like a giant vacuum cleaner, will be able to suck massive amounts of money out of California to fund its foreign and other operations. The implications, says [Kenneth] Guenther [director of IBAA], could be "far less funds available for small businesses, small farmers, and small states" and the situation could become even more serious if thrifts gain some commercial lending powers, as a financial reform bill now languishing in Congress [the Garn–St Germain Act] has proposed. This would allow savings and loans to look more like banks—which would suit Citicorp just fine. (U.S. Congress, House, Committee on Banking, Finance, and Urban Affairs, 1982, 545)

The granting of commercial lending powers to thrifts, as well as the deregulation of deposit rates and new merger procedures, thus contributes to the growth and hegemony of the large commercial banks. Rather than create more competition for large commercial banks, the expanded investment powers make thrifts more attractive to takeover and thereby achieve interstate banking.[12]

Through deregulation, then, the large commercial banks gain, but more important, the financial industry as a whole becomes more concentrated. Large commercial banks gain an increased share of the savings market; commercial banks but also strong thrifts (see Marcis, 1980, 153), nonbanks, securities/brokerage houses and nonfinancial corporations take over troubled thrifts; institutions merge as curbs against interstate banking are relaxed, and stronger institutions in general acquire weaker ones in the intense competition generated by deregulation.[13] To be sure, the unprecedented period of rising interest rates beginning in the mid-1960s caused the failure of many thrifts and led to a considerable amount of concentration in the industry.[14] But the new structure established in 1982 brought this development to another, more far-reaching stage. Now it is no longer simply market forces encouraging concentration but explicit government policy as well.

As the industry becomes more concentrated (particularly with the acquisition of failing thrifts), the nationally and internationally oriented institutions that become dominant, like Citicorp, take the place of the formerly locally oriented thrifts. Their priorities could very well be overseas investments; or they could be luxury housing, second homes, large-scale real estate development, or land speculation in fast-growing areas; or they could be investment in a powerful corporation, "such as the Standard Oil Company of California, which recently raised a $14 billion credit in just a few days" (Bennett, 1984c); or even all these things. They are highly unlikely to be local mortgages or small business loans. Concentration itself can lead to less local lending and monopoly pricing on interest rates. For example, the Independent Bankers Association of America provided evidence during the 1982 House hearings that loans to farmers in local communities went down when lending was done by a large bank holding company (U.S. Congress, House, Committee on Banking, Finance, and Urban Affairs, 1982, 556). Bank concentration also was associated with higher interest rates charged on business loans, consumer loans, and mortgages and lower interest rates paid on time and savings deposits (U.S. Congress, House, Committee on Banking, Finance, and Urban Affairs, 1982, 567). Increased earnings pressures from the intensified competition and the higher cost of deposits are also causing banks to cut costs by reducing their full-service branches. This not only causes inconvenience to the elderly and shopkeepers but can reduce local mortgage lending (i.e., exacerbate redlining). "When the Philadelphia National Bank closed one branch in the West Oak Lane section in 1980, mortgage lending in the neighborhood decreased by 62 percent, while the bank's overall mortgage lending increased by 40 percent" (Kerr, 1983).

## The Role of the State

It seems clear, then, that the changes outlined above were aimed at more than temporarily bailing out the thrifts and simply creating an efficient and equitable financial structure. The state's (government's) role appears as one of facilitating the capital accumulation process (e.g., of the big banks), and at the same time making some attempt at legitimating itself in the eyes of the public, to use O'Connor's model.

> Our first premise is that the capitalistic state must try to fulfill two basic and often mutually contradictory functions—accumulation and legitimization. This means that the state must try to maintain or create the conditions in which profitable capital accumulation is possible. However, the state also must try to maintain or create the conditions for social harmony. A capitalist state that openly uses its coercive forces to help one class accumulate capital at the expense of other classes loses its legitimacy and hence undermines the basis of its loyalty and support. . . . The state must involve itself in the accumulation process, but it must either mystify its policies by calling them something that they are not, or it must try to conceal them (e.g., by making them into administrative, not political, issues). (O'Connor, 1973, 6)

O'Connor was analyzing the role of state tax policy and budgetary expenditures (e.g., expenditures on highways, social security insurance, Medicaid) in benefiting monopoly (industrial) capital. Although this chapter has been analyzing state administrative and regulatory intervention on behalf of finance capital, the model still applies.

In the financial deregulation and restructuring, the state is clearly intervening to aid in the private appropriation of profit, directly in the case of the thrifts, through the capital assistance plan, and less directly in the case of the large commercial banks, which gain a hegemonic position as a result of the legislation's provisions. Deregulation, furthermore, helps the institutions at the expense of consumers—for example, variable-rate mortgages, which shift inflation risk to the borrower, and higher borrowing rates in general to cover the increased cost of funds. Moreover, the costs of this state aid get shifted onto taxpayers, hence "socialized"—e.g., capital assistance, costs incurred in regulator-assisted mergers, government insurance of money market accounts—although the costs, by and large, do not take the form of actual budgetary outlays so much as government guarantees. Expansion of the federally related secondary-mortgage-market credit agencies (FNMA, GNMA, FHLMC), which are an important piece of the restructuring of the mortgage finance system, also involves the state (or taxpayer) underwriting risk. For example, GNMA, or government-guaranteed mortgage-backed securities provide a relatively riskless, lucrative investment opportunity for private institutions and investors. Here, the state not only is rationalizing and broadening the supply of credit for housing but also promoting capital accumulation. As the *New York Times* reported in January 1984, the rise in this secondary-mortgage-market activity "has produced a bonanza for Wall Street. Nearly every major house has expanded its mortgage-trading activity, generating countless dollars in new commissions and trading profits" (Berg, 1984).

The state's "legitimation role" is relatively weak in this financial restructuring process. Some attempt has been made to argue that the recent deregulation promotes "efficiency and equity" (see President's Commission on Housing, 1982; U.S. Congress, House, Committee on Banking, Finance, and Urban Affairs, 1982). For example, small savers are said to benefit from deregulation; in fact, prior discrimination against them, some say, was one of the most important factors behind the deregulation. With deposit-rate regulation, small savers in thrift institutions had been precluded from taking advantage of rising interest rates. Now, their savings will earn more competitive yields, and supposedly equity will be returned to the financial system. However, it turns out that for low-balance depositors, representing as much as four-fifths of the population, the increased interest they get does not offset the higher fees charged by the banks as they pass along the increased costs of consumer deposits and the stepped-up competition. Many banks have imposed monthly or quarterly fees on savings accounts with small balances.[15] High-balance depositors, on the other hand, do quite well. The problem of higher fees (and of bank branch closings, see below) is becoming so great that the New York State Legislature is considering "lifeline banking services," that is, new community-oriented institutions providing basic banking services for the poor (Bennett, 1984a).

In this restructuring, then, there seems little interest by the state in promoting the appearance of being above class interest. The promotion of financial industry concentration (the capital accumulation of the big banks) and the lack of real equity for the small saver, coupled with the uncertain provisions to channel funds into housing (discussed below), starkly reveal the class bias of the restructuring scheme. The state is thus exhibiting conservative tendencies typical of the 1980s. It is clear that the political climate is radically different from the 1930s, a time of considerable insurgency and leftist political activity.

# Implications of the Restructuring for Housing and Urbanization

The restructuring scheme seems to be an attempt to resolve certain crisis-level contradictions of the financial system in the interest of some private financial institutions. The question remains, What impact will this have on mortgage lending, the housing sector, and housing consumers? What will the restructured system of housing finance look like?

## Thrift Diversification

One of the most important questions concerns the institutional framework of mortgage lending: Will the thrifts continue as an important source of mortgage originations, or will they diversify? Opinion is divided here. Some analysts say that the new investment powers will enable thrifts to compete in rapidly changing financial markets and allow them to stay in housing as long as they can earn a competitive profit in mortgage loans. They do not foresee a large-scale shift out of mortgage assets by thrifts (Colton, 1983; Kaplan, 1983; Vartanian, 1983a, 1983b). Others predict the possibility of substantial diversification (Baer, 1983; Seiders, 1982). Still others find the situation unpredictable (Tuccillo with Goodman, 1983).

One of the elements in this debate is the extent to which the preferential tax treatment thrifts receive for investing in mortgages (the bad-debt reserve requirement) will continue to provide a strong incentive to invest in mortgages despite the ability to diversify into more lucrative assets. Seiders's and Baer's analyses are compelling here: that the mortgage investment incentive of the bad-debt provision has been scaled down over time, and more important, that the availability of new tax-avoidance devices—such as the ability to invest in equipment leasing and tax-exempt securities—strongly counters the mortgage investment incentive.

Thus the 1982 changes will likely exacerbate a process already underway in which other institutions have increasingly become as important as, or more important than, thrifts as sources for housing credit—state and local housing finance agencies, mortgage bankers, secondary-mortgage-market agencies, and householders, through "creative financing" (see below). It is likely that thrift savings will increasingly be channeled away from direct, long-term residential mortgage investment, given expanded thrift investment powers, as well as numerous commercial bank and nonbank takeovers of thrifts, generating their own sets of priorities. With asset diversification, thrifts will have greater control over interest-rate risk, the key problem from which they had been suffering for so many years. And given the intense competitive pressures on returns in a deregulated market, they will be powerfully driven to higher yielding and shorter-term, nonmortgage uses of funds.[16]

Although most analysts agree that asset diversification at thrifts will be slow and cautious—they need time and money to hire the expertise required in this area to compete with the large commercial banks, and they also lack sophisticated cash-management services and experience in international transactions that business customers require—their commercial lending will grow. Commercial lending has a small overall market relative to that of mortgage loans ($392 billion compared to $1.64 trillion in 1982), but it is very lucrative. The Dime Savings Bank, for example, has aggressively begun pursuing small and medium-sized businesses as loan customers and is doing quite well (*New York Times*, May 23, 1983). Other thrift institutions are forming syndicates of like institutions to offer long-term loan packages to industrial borrowers (Noble, 1983). The Gold Dome Bank for Savings in New York is now using its explosion in deposits from the new money market accounts to lease computer equipment and finance company buyouts by management and employees (Williams, 1983). Thrifts are also increasingly getting involved as equity partners in real estate development—doing primary construction financing, rehabilitation, and land development of both commercial and residential projects (*New York Times*, July 20, 1983). And the new kinds of investments that thrifts are getting into not only will be different from long-term residential mortgages but increasingly risky, in order to earn the higher returns necessary to cover the higher cost of deposits and other overhead costs, such as sustaining large branch networks. This most likely will be particularly true of thrifts taken over by commercial banks or other nonbanks where the thrifts' priorities will be shaped by the parent institution.

The thrifts are not only being permitted to move away from long-term residential mortgage lending but they are being given the wherewithal to plunge into the new businesses described above and compete with commercial banks due to their ability to sell off old mortgages on the expanded secondary-mortgage market, to an influx of funds from the new money market accounts, and to the issuance of new stock.

Thus the movement away from residential mortgage lending begun in the mid-1960s by the thrifts when they were hit with liquidity and solvency problems will continue despite the current resolution of their financial difficulties.[17] Hence, the housing sector loses its specialized, primary financial institutions.[18] The repercussions of this can be serious. As Jonathan Brown of the Public Interest Research Group stated:

> There is still a broad public benefit in maintaining a system of savings institutions that are mortgage specialists. Depository institutions that specialize in mortgage lending are needed to assure the broadest possible availability of mortgage credit and accountability to local community housing needs. Savings institutions that specialize in mortgage lending are in a position to adopt more flexible mortgage lending criteria than capital market investors. They also have

a clearly defined mandate to serve local community housing needs, which commercial banks do not do. (U.S. Congress, House, Committee on Banking, Finance and Urban Affairs, 1982, 543)

## New Sources of Mortgage Credit

Less controversial than the question whether the thrifts will pull out of housing is the question of which other institutions will enter the mortgage market. Here we can expect increased participation by mortgage bankers[19] (who have grown from originating 2 percent of conventional one-to-four family mortgages in 1970 to 17 percent in 1982 [Colton, 1983, 141]), and perhaps commercial banks, and greater reliance on secondary-mortgage-market institutions (although Seiders [1983] doubts the widespread expansion of mortgage-backed securities).[20] It is becoming common practice for lenders to originate (and continue to service) rather than hold mortgages as the secondary markets expand. Sales of conventional mortgages as a percentage of conventional originations have increased dramatically in recent years. Colton (1983) foresees two-thirds to three-quarters of all mortgages flowing through the secondary market. New conduits besides FHLMC, FNMA, and GNMA are being developed as well (Colton, 1983, 142–43, and table, 152).

How involved commercial banks will become in the mortgage market is uncertain. As mentioned above, they have been interested in decreasing reliance on their declining corporate loan market and expanding their consumer market. Since the thrift industry is in a very different position now from that of the commercial bank industry, investments, such as mortgage loans, that are unattractive to one can be very attractive to the other. The thrift industry needs to diversify now in order to build up net worth and be better able to compete in the long run.

The recent regulatory and legislative changes in mortgage lending—for example, variable-rate mortgages that better keep pace with the bank's cost of funds than the rate paid on consumer loans; the national usury preemption law; the preemption of restrictions on due-upon-sale clauses; and the expansion of the secondary-mortgage market—enhance the attractiveness of mortgages to commercial banks. Residential mortgage lending may be seen as a potentially lucrative investment opportunity for commercial banks, especially as the thrifts leave that market (giving commercial banks a competitive edge) and as overall mortgage rates go up.[21] Commercial banks additionally anticipate expanded demand for housing finance because of demographic changes (Van Bogan, 1982b).

Additionally, commercial banks may see mortgage loans as a way to cultivate relationships with their best customers and build a strong customer base, later tapping into savings and checking accounts, certificates of deposit, trusts, bank cards, and personal loans (Lacy, 1982, 118). Moreover, although large commercial banks like Citicorp heavily invest in overseas loans, they have also embarked on a strategy to reduce reliance on foreign activities as foreign countries have increasingly experienced difficulties paying their debts. Diversifying its portfolio through mortgage investments at home is thus an important part of Citicorp's current diversification strategy. How far this portfolio diversification will go, given the substantial profits of overseas investments, is unclear.

The loss of the specialized housing finance institutions and the reliance on the secondary-mortgage market may very well lead to an inflexibility in mortgage lending and an abandonment of those properties that do not conform to a uniform type, such as older, inner-city, multifamily properties with balloon mortgages in need of refinancing; limited equity cooperative housing; and so on. These properties traditionally have been served by the thrifts, although they may not have been serving them well for some time due to alleged redlining practices. Nevertheless, it is questionable whether mortgage bankers or commercial banks will take their place and the second-ary-mortgage market will accept such properties. Mortgages, especially those pooled for the pass-through securities market, will increasingly become uniform, standardized, interchangeable investment instruments, an alternative to government bonds or triple-A corporate bonds, and thus further removed from individual buildings or homes, which are considered too risky to invest in per se. It may be that only the most secure, traditional, standard, and profitably located housing will be considered. Thus, the secondary-mortgage market (and its agencies) will increasingly be calling the shots in the overall mortgage market.

## The Adequacy of the Supply of Mortgage Credit

What effect will deregulation and restructuring have on the overall supply of mortgage credit? Will there be enough to meet the current and future needs–demands for mortgage credit?

It is not altogether clear whether the restructuring will reduce the volume of mortgage lending. The President's Commission on Housing says no, "as long as funds could flow freely through financial markets to meet the underlying demands for capital in the economy" (1982, 120). Likewise, Colton (1983) predicts that the level of investment in mortgages will be adequate, as do Vartanian (1983a) and Tuccillo with Goodman (1983). Seiders (1983) takes the unusual view that mortgage pass-through securities are unlikely to expand greatly in the future, but he believes that mortgage credit gaps necessitating such expansion are also unlikely to develop. In addition, a recent *New York Times* article reported increased mortgage lending and the rise of a national mortgage market as a result of the booming secondary-mortgage market (Berg, 1984). To some extent this secondary-market activity will allow local thrifts and banks to extend mortgage credit even when their costs of deposits exceed mortgage interest rates because they can immediately sell the mortgages.[22]

Others are much more skeptical about the ability of the restructured system to meet mortgage credit needs. For example, Grebler (1983, 169) expresses doubt as to whether pension funds, given their meager participation in the past, will get involved substantially in the residential mortgage market. He also sees expansion of mortgage credit through the securities market occurring in intense competition with huge credit needs created by the federal budget deficit and nonfinancial corporations (the latter, as they increasingly engage in leveraged buyouts, takeovers, mergers, etc.). In addition, the expansion of the securities market backed by conventional loans, which is likely to be the future direction, will take considerable time, according to Grebler. In sum, he states:

> Thrifts, FNMA, and FHLMC together accounted for about two-thirds of the total amount of housing loans held by all financial institutions and federal agencies or in the form of mortgage pools in the second half of the 1970's. It seems highly questionable that pension funds and buyers of mortgage securities can compensate for the reduction of residential mortgage portfolios of thrifts if the latter are indeed "to serve the credit needs of all sectors of the economy." In the probable event of the shift falling short of the Commission's [President's Commission on Housing] expectations, there will be adverse effects on the flow of funds into housing or on the cost of funds to borrowers. (Grebler, 1983, 176)

Robert Lindsay's research on trends in the mortgage market during the 1970s also raises doubts about the future adequacy of the supply of mortgage credit. He sees pressures on the mortgage finance system coming not only from demographic factors (e.g., increasing household formation) but from "(a) demands to refinance the existing as well as new housing stock, and (b) a persistent and possibly widening gap between these gross new demands and the repayment flows from earlier loans" (Lindsay, 1980, 146). He notes that sales in the used-home market vastly overwhelmed sales in the new-home market. Overall residential mortgage debt in the postwar period soared relative to GNP but spending for new residential construction lagged behind, relatively. In an inflationary period, homeowners use mortgage financing to "cash in" on the equity in their homes in order to purchase other things. (Additionally, in recent years homeowners have resorted to "creative financing" techniques that result in short-term debt, which must now be refinanced.) This contributes to increased total mortgage debt, but it does not produce new housing units. If we can assume that this "weak housing bang for the mortgage buck" (Lindsay, 1980, 118) is a feature of the housing finance system, there is additional reason to feel that the restructured housing finance system will be somewhat ill equipped to meet housing needs–demands.

> What. . . has been driving the new mortgage demand at so much faster a rate than the new housing demand? If these or similar forces are also our destiny in the 80's, they will create the same additional burden for mortgage lenders as in the recent past, even to achieve the same flow of new housing, and a greater burden if still more housing is required. (Lindsay, 1980, 134)

And it is estimated that 16 million new households will be formed in the 1980s—25 percent more than were formed in the previous decade (Van Bogan, 1982a, 113; see also Treadway, 1982, 102–4).[23]

## The Cost of Mortgage Credit

A more important question is what the restructuring will do to the cost of mortgage credit. Some analysts hold to the belief that deregulation will create greater competition among financial institutions for consumer business, which will, in itself, benefit mortgage borrowers (Kaplan, 1983; Vartanian, 1983a). More convincing is the prediction that the cost of mortgage credit will remain high, although rates may become more uniform throughout the country. Even if the supply of mortgage money vastly increases, this would not lower mortgage rates. These rates are not determined by the supply and demand for mortgage credit but by the supply and demand for credit in the capital markets in general.[24] Thus, as the banks' cost of funds will stay high, so will the cost of lending money out. With deposit-rate deregulation, commercial banks and thrifts no longer have a cheap pool of funds to draw upon for low-cost mortgages. In addition, mortgage rates will become higher and more volatile as they have to compete more aggressively in the credit markets. "The AAA bonds have become the 'Pied Piper' of the mortgage rates. Home buyers and major corporations are thus competing for the same investment dollars" (Wald, 1983). This linkage of mortgage interest rates with conditions in the corporate and government bond markets can only make mortgage rates more unsteady (Marcis, 1980). The secondary-mortgage market itself additionally increases costs as more intermediary levels and servicing–brokerage fees are added.

## Impact on Housing Consumers

Thus, buying a home or financing a rental property will most likely be more expensive, increasingly influenced by locational factors, and less secure. Due-upon-sale clauses, greater bank discretion in setting loan-to-value ratios, and new mortgage instruments all make mortgage borrowing riskier and more onerous. Loss of the predominance of the long-term, fixed-rate mortgage is particularly significant. This mortgage instrument has represented the long-term financial security that middle-class families traditionally have looked to and a shield against inflation relative to other conventional investments. Thus, although in the short term adjustable-rate mortgages may lower interest rates and make housing more affordable to some, shifting the interest-rate risk onto borrowers represents an erosion of the middle-class standard of living. And adjustable-rate mortgages have been proliferating: In December 1983, such mortgages represented 55 percent of all mortgages granted, up from 36 percent in January 1983 (Kilborn, 1984).

We are faced with a paradox: Just as housing need is expanding, the housing finance system is moving in a higher-priced direction, perhaps preventing this need from being translated into effective demand. "The basic reality," as George Sternlieb states, "is that the housing buying power of Americans has gone down. . . . The average worker's pay check minus the buying power lost to inflation has fallen 9.7 percent since its peak in 1973, meaning that most potential home buyers have less to spend" (Wald, 1983). On the one hand, new types of mortgage instruments will be increasingly used to cope with the affordability problem, and the many middle- and low-income families who get priced out of the market will scale down their housing expectations by doubling up, moving in with parents, and remaining as tenants [*see Chapter 3 by Michael E. Stone*]. On the other hand, it is likely that these "solutions" will work only in a limited way and hence may result in some degree of political unrest.

Interestingly, in response to the affordability problem, in 1980 the Mortgage Guarantee Insurance Corporation lifted its permissible levels for basic housing debt to 33 percent of income instead of the general 25 percent rule of thumb. "There is an acute need for this increase," said Max H. Karl, the organization's chairman. "In the last 15 years," he added, "the median family income had risen only about half as quickly as housing costs, a situation that had been particularly tough on first time buyers" (Brooks, 1980). Around the same time, FHLMC also decided to rely less on the 25 percent of income criterion. These moves demonstrated the "recognition that people have to devote more of their income to shelter" (Brooks, 1980).

These decisions encouraged banks to extend more mortgage loans and helped the sagging mortgage market slightly, but clearly both the decision to allow higher housing cost–income ratios and to offer new mortgage instruments have grave implications for consumers' "shelter poverty," the inability to afford other basic needs such as food and clothing after paying shelter costs [*see Chapter 3 by Michael E. Stone*] and for the stability of the financial system as a whole. As Stone has pointed out, our economic system contains an inherent contradiction between people's incomes and housing costs. There is a need both to keep incomes as low as possible to satisfy employers in the labor market and a need to keep incomes high enough to satisfy housing producers in the housing market. This contradiction is fundamentally insoluble. At best, it has been "managed" historically through state intervention—for example, stretching out the housing costs of consumers by long-term, low-down-payment mortgages, thereby keeping wage demands down and at the same time saving the housing sector from collapse. The events described above are the most recent attempts to manage the insoluble conflict in this way, but they are likely to be less effective than in the past.

Moreover, the mechanisms selected may create additional problems for housing and the whole economy. The new mortgage instruments (and the expanded secondary-mortgage market) increase residential mortgage debt, which was one of the key factors leading to the creation of a huge national debt, which in turn contributed to an increased competition for capital and to higher interest rates. Rising interest rates (also the result of deregulation) lead to reduced rates of principal repayment (especially with adjustable-rate and other new mortgage forms), which adds to the need for new funds to finance additional mortgages, increasing competition for funds even further and adding more to interest rates in a self-reinforcing cycle. The mortgage finance system thus becomes more and more central to the overall financial structure as residential mortgage debt continues to grow. But at the same time, at the base of this system are increasingly strapped housing consumers. As they become less able to shoulder the repayment costs, they threaten the mortgage finance system and, as Stone shows in Chapter 3, the larger economic system as well.

The likelihood of increased shelter poverty and the risk of delinquency and foreclosure are also being articulated by leaders in the housing finance industry. They seem to be unworried, however, seeing mortgage lenders as able to adjust to increased delinquency rates, people as generally capable of paying off in the end, and capital appreciation of homes as cushioning any added risk.

> Leaders of these large mortgage organizations dismissed the potential added risk factor in allowing these [higher mortgage cost–income] loans. "We feel that if people are allowed to spend one-third or more of their income on housing then they will be willing to tighten their belts and make some sacrifices in other places. . . ." Most of today's buyers have no choice. . . . These industry leaders also dismissed the notion that to become more liberal might seem imprudent at a time when the delinquency rate on mortgages was at an all-time high. (Brooks, 1980)

One could argue convincingly that short-term self-interest blinds them to more pessimistic but realistic conclusions.

## The Impact on Urbanization

Just as the financial restructuring will in general exacerbate shelter poverty and potentially weaken the system, so will it have a significant impact from a spatial point of view on cities and the urbanization process. Financial institutions have traditionally played a crucial mediating role, mobilizing the surplus that investment in urban infrastructure represents (housing, transport facilities, community facilities) for national economic growth (Harvey, 1975). They have channeled mortgage investment away from one area and into another in the postwar period, away from inner cities and toward the suburban periphery. This was part of the policy of stimulating effective demand, Harvey argues, begun in the 1930s to deal with the effects of underconsumption crises.

It is clear that financial deregulation and restructuring will exacerbate current processes of neighborhood change. The increasingly competitive drive for funds to flow where the rate of return is highest means that mortgage disinvestment in inner city housing will only continue at a more rapid pace [*see Chapter 10 by Ann Meyerson*]. But whether funds will be channeled into suburban development as in the past is a different matter. It seems that, compared with the post–World War II period, we are now in an era in which housing production, particularly suburban housing production, is not being used to resolve underconsumption crises. Financial institutions' deposits go into a variety of investments—real estate development projects in distant states, downtown redevelopment as part of "gentrification," overseas loans, and so forth. This, as well as the shift to a more national mortgage market, allowing greater geographic flexibility in the flow of funds, is consistent with current urbanization changes. We are moving away from major metropolitan centers ringed by appended suburban communities to the growth of nonmetropolitan, small and medium-sized cities and heretofore rural areas beyond the suburban ring. These urbanization shifts are being facilitated by the changes taking place in the financial structure, and thus the latter have even greater significance than indicated previously. The magnitude of the effects of displacement and population shifts from these changes can only be speculated upon at this point.

## Conclusions

This chapter concludes that the altered institutional framework of housing finance, the competition and concentration within the financial industry and consequent domination by the large commercial banks, the questionable adequacy of the supply of mortgage credit, the higher cost of mortgage credit, and the changed mortgage lending process all will lead to adverse effects on housing and housing consumers, and shifts in the urbanization process.

The earlier system of housing finance clearly was no longer functioning properly to facilitate the flow of credit to housing. But these new developments resolve those problems in the interest of financial institutions primarily (particularly the large commercial banks) and not in the interest of low-cost and community-responsive housing provision. Moreover, although some financial institutions get strengthened in this restructuring, the financial structure itself may become considerably weakened.

We thus see a further exacerbation of some of the weaknesses in the housing finance system that emerged in the 1960s and 1970s. Then, the tremendous growth of residential mortgage debt became apparent, contributing (among other things) to higher interest rates generally, thereby exacerbating housing affordability problems. And, in the early 1980s, deregulation of the financial system has contributed to higher interest rates and further aggravated the housing affordability crisis.[25] Ironically, both the increase in mortgage debt—originally through the low-down-payment, long-term mortgage instrument, later through the adjustable-rate mortgage and mortgage-backed securities—and the deregulation of interest rates were supposed to ease the conflict between housing costs and incomes, but, by increasing interest rates, failed to do so.

In addition, as Michael E. Stone indicated in Chapter 3, the new institutions and financing techniques developed since the late 1960s to deal with the weakened mortgage system (the secondary-mortgage markets, tax-exempt bond financing, mortgage-backed securities, etc.) made not just savings institutions but the overall financial structure vulnerable to people's failure to make their mortgage payments. Likewise, deregulation—particularly the blurring of lines between thrifts, banks, and "nonbanks" in terms of assets and deposits—further contributes to this merging of residential finance with the general financial structure, and hence the dependence of the latter on the system's ability to manage the conflict between incomes and housing costs.

Deregulation additionally has led to a shakier financial system in that the fierce competition it generates gives rise to risky, high-yield bank investment strategies. For example, as a result of a new round of high interest rates recently, many thrifts, despite deregulation, were again caught in their "borrowing short, lending long" bind and were forced to engage in high-risk lending to prevent failure. Highly risky real estate construction and development is thus becoming quite popular with the thrifts, with construction loans at savings and loan associations rising from 4.1 percent of all outstanding loans in 1980 to 10.2 percent in 1984. As one savings and loan president was quoted:

> You can't be a traditional thrift anymore, there's no earnings in the balance sheet . . . you have to go outside the traditional lines of business, into such fields as loan development, high volume mortgage banking, things that will bring abnormal fee income or returns. (Bennett, 1984d)

The risk factor is further exacerbated by the extension of government insurance. If banks are assured that monies raised through their money market accounts are guaranteed by the federal government, they have even less incentive to be prudent when investing. If the investments go bad, the FDIC promises to pay back depositors, but, unfortunately, FDIC resources are finite and could not possibly accommodate widespread failures.[26] Thus, government insurance provides the opportunity for more and more lucrative investment outlets and, at the same time, strains the system.

As deregulation takes hold, the financial system is becoming more concentrated, and banks are expanding into all kinds of fields. For example, the Bank of America recently announced it would begin offering insurance at its California branches; Citicorp is operating a convention center in Westchester County and offering customers a discount shopping service; Chemical Bank is offering cut-rate merchandise to its customers through a catalogue; and banks, nationwide, have begun selling stocks. Sears Roebuck and Company, a nonbank, now earns as much from its financial services as from selling merchandise; money market mutual funds, for the most part operated by securities firms, have begun to look remarkably like banks; and, of course, thrifts will increasingly diversify away from long-term mortgage investments (Bennett, 1984b). With this greater homogenization of the financial system, many kinds of institutions—thrifts, commercial banks, insurance companies, mortgage banks, corporations, securities–brokerage houses—will be undertaking a wide (and overlapping) variety of activities. Thus, the difficulties that inevitably arise, especially given higher risk investment strategies, will be increasingly impossible to contain and treat. As Securities and Exchange Commissioner Bevis Longstreth said, "The difficulties of a single financial institution threaten to trigger a chain reaction" (Heineman, 1983).

Against the background of the developments of the 1960s and 1970s, the contribution of the 1980s financial deregulation and restructuring to both housing affordability problems and the vulnerability of the entire financial structure looms large indeed. Like earlier mechanisms to shore up the financial system, deregulation has thus far failed. Specific institutions get strengthened, but the entire system is placed at greater risk. Thus, capitalism again reveals its penchant for private, short-term gain at the expense of the wider good.[27]

# Acknowledgments

The author wishes to thank Rachel G. Bratt, Jill Hamberg, Chester Hartman, and Michael E. Stone for their helpful comments on an earlier draft of this chapter.

# Notes

1. Unlike other financial institutions, thrifts receive tax benefits that encourage them to invest heavily in mortgages. Section 593 of the Internal Revenue Code allows thrifts a special 40 percent bad debt reserve deduction if a minimum percentage (82 percent for savings and loans and 72 percent for mutual savings banks) of their assets is invested in mortgages or other qualifying assets. This provision can present a considerable barrier to asset diversification at thrifts. Nonqualifying investments would have to provide considerably higher net tax yields than those available in qualifying assets to offset the additional taxes from diversifying. It is interesting to note that, according to the President's Commission on Housing, the benefits of this tax break accrue to thrift institutions but have had little impact on mortgage rates paid by borrowers (1982, 138).

2. At the end of 1981, for example, 801 institutions, representing $167 billion in assets, were at or below the minimum statutory level of 3 percent net worth. Also in 1981, there were 296 mergers, more than double the number in 1980; in dollar terms the industry suffered record losses and its collective net worth eroded by 15 percent (see U.S. Congress, House, Committee on Banking, Finance and Urban Affairs, 1982, 593–94).

3. The act phased out over six years the interest ceilings on passbook accounts (later shortened by Garn–St Germain); authorized interest on checking accounts (NOW accounts); permanently overrode state-imposed usury ceilings on mortgage rates (unless states acted within three years to reenact them); required, over an eight-year phase-in period, all depository institutions to post reserves at the Federal Reserve Bank; allowed federal savings and loan associations to expand their consumer-loan and credit-card operations, make second mortgages and originate residential mortgage loans without geographic restrictions; and permitted federal mutual savings banks to invest 5 percent of their assets in commercial, corporate, and business loans made within their state or a

75-mile radius of their home office. As a result of the act, a Depository Institutions Deregulation Committee was set up to oversee and plan for the eventual deregulation of deposit rates.

4. New mortgage instruments have been developed that essentially shift the interest-rate fluctuation risk from the lender to the borrower. With the adjustable-rate mortgage, for example, the lender moves the interest rate up or down at specified intervals. With the graduated-payment mortgage, the interest rate remains constant but monthly payments are lower than average during the first few years of the mortgage, higher than average after that. With the negative-amortization mortgage, monthly payments remain constant but the interest rate may rise, with the additional cost added to the principal. With the zero-rate mortgage, no interest is paid, just principal, but the price of the housing is set higher to compensate the lender. Balloon mortgages are also being offered, requiring the payment of interest only or partial principal payments that will not retire the mortgage over its full term, leaving a balance or balloon at the end. Longer terms—40 years or more—are also being offered to stretch out the payments. And "equity stakes" are being used, which involve lowering the interest rate in return for a percentage of the profits when the property is sold.

5. See also Vartanian, 1983b, 162–66, for discussion of the Federal Home Loan Bank Board deregulation initiatives beginning in 1981.

6. Savings and loan associations wanted to enhance their profits by doing more direct housing development and construction. The housing sector (e.g., developers) was able to contain this demand in the final legislation.

7. Many see this as a positive effect of deregulation of the housing finance system. See P. H. Hendershott and S. C. Hu article referred to in Grebler, 1983. See also Sternlieb and Hughes, 1984, 32.

8. An American Bankers Association report, dated September 9, 1981, on "Activities in the Financial Institution Marketplace 1981," lists "non-banks offering near bank or partial bank services": (1) American Express and Provident to offer cash-management service with Hutton, Shearson, and Bache; Provident is adviser to certain Shearson money market funds; (2) E. F. Hutton acquired International Paper Credit Corporation to do commercial financing and correspondent banking; (3) Gulf and Western owns Associates First Capital Corporation, which owns Fidelity National Bank of Concord, which spun off commercial-loan portfolio; (4) Sears (savings and loan holding company) to establish money market mutual fund; (5) three major savings and loans—Citizens of California, West Side of New York, and Washington of Florida—merged; the resulting savings and loan, Citizens Savings and Loan, owned by holding company, United Financial Corporation, owned by National Steel Corporation (U.S. Congress, House, Committee on Banking, Finance, and Urban Affairs, 1982, 487). Also see Bennett 1983b, 15–46.

9. This concern relates specifically to the problems of Third World debt involvement by the large U.S. commercial banks. Loans by these banks to countries like Argentina, Mexico, Brazil, and Colombia are continually being threatened with default and are frequently restructured.

10. The McFadden Act prohibits interstate branching by a bank; the Douglas Amendment to the 1956 Bank Holding Company Act prohibits bank holding companies from acquiring a bank in another state unless the state in which the bank is to be acquired

Thrift acquisition is not the only entree into interstate banking. Many banking companies are setting up "nonbank banks," which accept deposits and provide a range of services but do not make commercial loans. These institutions are technically permitted across state lines. Many small banks fear the competition from these big banks and argue that the latter do not lend in the community but to big corporations and foreign governments (Noble, 1983).

11. After World War II, commercial banks began to realize that their sole reliance

on demand deposits limited their growth: During the 1950s, demand deposits grew by only 3 percent per year, and the commercial banks' share of the total assets of depository institutions declined between 1945 and 1960. The banks began to enter the market affirmatively for time and savings deposits, aggressively bidding for time certificates of deposit, Eurodollars, and federal funds (see Cutler, 1974, 55).

Also, after World War II, commercial banks had less of a business-loan role to play as U.S. corporations increasingly were able to finance their cash requirements internally, lend to one another through the commercial paper market, or both. Commercial banks also lost out to the Eurodollar market in London, where corporations could take advantage of cheap loans and high deposit rates from international banks. This pushed them into the consumer business, but there they found competition from the money market mutual funds as well as the thrifts.

Most recently, the drive of commercial banks to expand into consumer markets is demonstrated by Citicorp's appointment of John Reed, head of consumer banking, to succeed Walter Wriston as chair. The acquisition of savings and loans, together with the chartering of industrial banks and the expansion of credit-card operations, represents Citicorp's present thrust in this direction (Wayne, 1984).

12. In January 1984, Citicorp was given permission to take over Biscayne Federal Savings and Loan and First Federal Savings and Loan Association of Chicago, which resulted in considerable controversy and bitter local opposition. With these acquisitions, Citicorp is now by far the largest commercial bank holding company and one of the nation's largest operators of savings and loan associations. Citicorp's intense drive for interstate banking was also recently indicated by a lawsuit it filed against regional banking compact laws that allow banks in one New England state, for example, to acquire banks in other New England states while prohibiting banks outside the region from doing so. The Bank of Boston has been acquiring banks in Connecticut, Rhode Island, and Maine under these laws to get an edge over banks like Citicorp before full-scale interstate banking takes over. Citicorp does not want to be kept out. See Bennett, 1983e, and *New York Times* (Dec. 8, 1983).

It is interesting to note that in the course of the legislative battles, the thrifts expressed fear that they would be liquidated or merged away by Congress (U.S. Congress, House, Committee on Banking, Finance, and Urban Affairs, 1981). Thrift representatives spoke out against attempts by the Treasury Secretary to "organize this country into a series of financial conglomerates" (U.S. Congress, House, Committee on Banking, Finance, and Urban Affairs, 1981, 140). Commercial bank takeovers were seen as efforts to consolidate and centralize financial institution power in the country (U.S. Congress, House, Committee on Banking, Finance, and Urban Affairs, 1981, 147).

13. The greater concentration in the banking industry predicted here has a basis in the experience of other industries that have been deregulated. In a study of the impact of deregulation on five recently deregulated industries—securities brokerage, business terminal equipment (telephone systems for offices), airlines, trucking, and railroads—three phases of merger and acquisition activity were noted. Stage 1, consolidation among the weak (two to three years after deregulation); Stage 2, selective acquisition by the strong (three to five years following deregulation); and Stage 3, interindustry acquisition (more than three years following deregulation). "In the banking industry, a wave of consolidations among banks in the second tier will likely occur, although few mergers will produce the hoped-for economies of integration. Firms in the second tier will generally not be successful in becoming first-tier firms unless they merge with one. Many national commercial accounts will gravitate toward a small number of first tier banks that offer operating integration over a broad geographic area. This migration will be primarily at the expense of second tier banks" (Waite, 1981, 30).

14. For example, at the end of 1981 there were 233 fewer savings and loan associations in the United States than there were at the end of 1980 (4,380 vs. 4,613), but the total

assets of savings and loans were up $32 billion (from $630 billion to $662 billion). Over that same period, the number of mutual savings banks decreased by 14 (from 462 to 448), while the total assets of these institutions rose $4 billion (from $172 billion to $176 billion) (data supplied by the FHLBB and the National Association of Mutual Savings Banks in President's Commission on Housing, 1982, 134). The policy of the regulators—the FDIC and FSLIC—encouraged mergers as opposed to their taking over banks' assets themselves and paying off insured depositors. As a result, many stronger merger partners were subsidized to expand—something many institutions wanted to do, given the increasingly competitive nature of the financial industry.

15. For example, the Manufacturers Hanover Trust Company recently raised consumer fees dramatically. Now, unless a customer keeps a substantial amount of money in accounts at the bank, the customer must pay a monthly fee of $8 for a checking account, plus 50 cents a check. The California-based First Nationwide Savings, which has offices in New York and Florida, recently imposed an annual fee of $8 on its Individual Retirement Accounts. The fee is waived if there is at least $5,000 in the account, or if the customer adds at least $1,000 to it a year, or maintains at least $10,000 in accounts at First Nationwide (Bennett, 1984c).

Likewise, on passbook accounts with less than $500, the Dime Savings Bank of New York charges $1 a month. "So a family with $100 in such an account would wind up the year with only $88 of principal" (Bennett, 1983d). The *New York Times* reported the situation of an elevator operator in New York whose bank refused to pay interest on his opening deposit of $100 and asked for monthly service fees for keeping it. This led the reporter to conclude: "Even while the Government continues to maintain a safety net under the banks themselves, the poor and those with only moderate incomes are expected to pay their own way" (Bennett, 1984b).

16. Even the President's Commission on Housing (1982, 120), which argues that the thrifts will remain significant in the future housing finance system, states that "many thrift institutions probably would choose to reduce the asymmetry in the maturity structure of assets and liabilities partly by moving into assets that are, by their nature, shorter in term than residential mortgages."

17. In the case of New York City–headquartered savings banks, one can document the shift in the volume and composition of mortgage lending portfolios occurring in the mid-1960s. They reduced mortgage loans in favor of nonmortgage assets such as corporate stocks, short-term paper, and obligations of states. In addition, they shifted their mortgage portfolios into loans on out-of-state property, nonresidential property, and larger as opposed to smaller loans. These mortgage loans were more profitable—especially those utilizing higher out-of-state mortgage rates—than the ones they had been accustomed to offering (e.g., those on local, residential and often multifamily property). The withdrawal of these institutions, particularly the urban-centered mutual savings banks, from their historic mortgage markets had much to do with the steadily worsening situation of the multifamily housing stock in the older cities of the Northeast (i.e., widespread landlord abandonment, as well as with the more recent phenomenon of cooperative and condominium conversion of rental property). [*See Chapter 9 by Ann Meyerson.*]

18. There is also the question of how profitable the thrifts will remain. Vartanian (1983a, 1983b) predicts great prosperity for the thrifts from deregulation, whereas Kaplan (1983), Tuccillo with Goodman (1983), and Grebler (1983) are less sanguine. According to Kaplan, thrifts could reduce interest-rate risk through diversification, but long-term profitability may not be improved because there is nothing inherently more profitable about nonmortgage assets or variable-rate mortgages. Tuccillo and Goodman foresee considerable solvency problems for thrifts. Grebler (1983, 169) points to problems that the thrifts will undoubtedly experience as they diversify—greater risks, management and

training difficulties, the fact that "new competitors usually find it difficult to invade established markets without compromising investment standards."

19. Mortgage bankers originate mortgage loans and then, in almost all cases, immediately sell them to other institutions, while continuing to service the loans.

20. A relatively recent development in government support of housing finance concerns the issuance and guarantee of pass-through mortgage-backed securities by GNMA and FHLMC (and more recently by FNMA). These pass-through securities are designed to aggregate individual mortgages and convert them into investments that can be marketed on the private capital market to attract more funds into the intermediation market.

Usually a mortgage banking company issues a liquid, fully transferable investment instrument called a mortgage-backed security, which is backed by a homogeneous pool of conventional or FHA/VA mortgages. As these securities involve not simply the buying and selling of individual mortgages but a liquid trading market much like that for stocks and bonds, they represent a significant shift in the secondary-mortgage market. GNMA (dealing mainly with FHA/VA mortgages) guarantees the interest and principal on the security, which passes through from the homeowner to the investor. FHLMC's securities are backed by conventional mortgages. These mortgage-backed securities have become an important piece of the post-thrift-crisis restructuring. They are currently proliferating because they serve as a vehicle for thrifts to sell off their low-yield, fixed-rate mortgages.

21. Citicorp, for example, recouped its losses on consumer loans in 1979 and 1980 by invading the mortgage business—first and second mortgages, home improvement loans, and loans on coop apartments and condominiums. This portfolio soared from $3.2 billion in 1979 to $9.3 billion in 1982 (Bennett, 1983b).

22. And, according to HUD Secretary Samuel R. Pierce, Jr., who was recently reported marketing GNMA mortgage-backed securities in Japan, each additional $1 billion invested means 20,000 additional housing starts (Lohr, 1984).

23. A corollary question to that of the adequacy of the supply of mortgage credit concerns the cyclical stability of mortgage credit. Many predict that with deposit-rate deregulation and asset diversification, disintermediation crises will be avoided and available funds will flow freely if the demand is present. Grebler (1983, 179), however, makes the interesting observation from history that deregulation does *not* reduce instability; the housing credit cycles prior to the 1920s and the boom cycle of the 1920s showed great instability during a period of little government regulation.

24. Hendershott and Villani (1980), however, state that an expansion of the mortgage supply, especially through federal credit agencies, has caused the mortgage rate to decline relative to other market rates, although the impact of this growth was offset in the late 1970s by an explosion in demand for mortgage credit.

25. See Sweezy and Magdoff, 1984, for an excellent discussion of the role of the expansion of the nation's financial sector during the 1960s and of deregulation in the early 1980s in creating out-of-control interest rates.

26. This issue has recently become more complicated. It is not simply the banks that are potentially straining the resources of the government insurance funds. The banks' insured money market fund accounts, having initially wooed funds away from the money market mutual funds, have now spawned new activity on the part of securities houses, which are packaging customers' funds and depositing them in insured money market fund accounts at banks and thrifts. The securities houses continue to control the funds, maintain the same relationship with their customers, and collect a brokerage fee from the banks for bringing in the deposits, while their customers get the ease of withdrawal as well as deposit insurance. The problem with this is that securities houses, seeking only the highest interest rates, might very well not scrutinize the stability of these banks, which in turn may make risky investments on the basis of the relatively secure deposit inflow and

deposit insurance. If these banks fail, the FDIC must make good on the deposits. Thus, government insurance on these accounts again opens the way for greater bank instability. Also, this new money brokering gives the brokerage houses a great deal of power over banks and thrifts; the threat of their withdrawal of deposits can put pressure on fees, types of investments, and the like, and if they should withdraw large blocks of funds, instability could again result.

27.  For empirical data on the impact of financial deregulation from 1982 to 1984 on the mortgage market, see a forthcoming article by the author in the *International Journal of Urban and Regional Research*.

# 5

# Urban Real Estate Speculation in the United States: Implications for Social Science and Urban Planning

*Joe R. Feagin*

*The private housing market consists of many important actors. Each of the next three chapters explores a key player in the complex process of getting housing produced in the United States: real estate–land speculators, homebuilders and developers (specifically suburban ones), and the construction industry. In each instance, layers of profit making add substantially to the final cost of the housing; decisions often are made that conflict with the needs of consumers and the population in general; and government policy aids and supports private-sector objectives.*

*Real estate speculators have played a major role, historically and currently, in shaping urban areas and the rules by which the market system operates. In this, they have powerful allies among financial institutions, other actors in the real estate game, and in government. While the conventional literature has held out "consumer sovereignty" as the principal explanatory factor in housing choice and urban form, this chapter puts forth a more power-class perspective for understanding these issues. From the original location of cities to their internal development patterns (including slum and ghetto formation and the more recent phenomena of gentrification and the conversion of rental apartments to condominiums) to suburban development patterns, the role of real estate speculation and speculators—which in recent times include in their ranks large corporations—has been central.*

U.S. social scientists have written extensively about the city since the pioneering work of the Chicago school in the 1920s. With the research of U.S. sociologists like Park, Burgess, and McKenzie arose a research tradition with a central focus on urban land use and land patterning. Since the 1920s a considerable urban ecology literature has emerged. Yet, with brief exceptions, nowhere in this extensive U.S. literature on land use and urban patterning is there a serious concern with the ways in which the inequality of the urban structure of power or the class structure shapes the decisions that originate and arrange the physical face of cities.

An earlier version of this chapter appeared in the *International Journal of Urban and Regional Research* 6, no. 1 (March 1982): 35–59, and is reprinted by permission of the journal and its publisher, Edward Arnold, London.

It is the purpose of this chapter to examine a central figure in urban land patterning decisions—the real estate and land speculator. Such a focus is linked to my concern to contribute to an alternative theory of urban ecology that accents the role of class structure, the role of powerful, land-oriented, capitalist actors in shaping the location, development, and decline of American cities. A first step toward an alternative theoretical framework for urban ecology, as well as for urban planning, is an intensive focus on these powerful capitalistic land-interested actors. . . .

## An Alternative Perspective

A close examination of the U.S. urban sociology literature reveals that there is only one brief paper that has developed the idea that the actions of specific, powerful land-use actors, an array of capitalist-class actors, might be major factors shaping urban land use and development.[1] This unique, pioneering paper was prepared by William Form and appeared in the 1950s in *Social Forces*. Form (1954, 528) suggests there that the Adam Smith model of a free and unorganized urban land market must be discarded, for that market is very organized and that powerful actors operate in self-conscious and purposeful ways. Form notes four main groups: (1) the real estate and building business, (2) industries and utilities, (3) homeowners, and (4) local government agencies. After briefly sketching the important interrelationships between these groups, Form examines their impact on a few zoning decisions in Lansing, Michigan. The bottom line in Form's analysis is that social structure must be examined in order to understand land use and changes therein. He calls for a shift in urban ecological research that would place heavy emphasis on "isolating the important and powerful land-interested groupings in the city." This provocative suggestion has not been followed by most U.S. sociologists as yet.

However, clues for a thoroughgoing, class-based theoretical framework have been provided by a British urban geographer (David Harvey) and a few European Marxist social scientists, who have begun to criticize both conventional urban ecology and urban planning from a power-conflict perspective. Thus Manuel Castells (1976a, 55) has argued that the Burgess concentric-zone pattern (Park, Burgess, and McKenzie, 1925) is limited historically and geographically to certain types of cities; in a general analysis he demonstrates that modern capitalist cities are shaped by capitalist investment patterns. Another European, Lamarche (1976, 117), notes that the city is in the image of the larger capitalist society around it: "Subjectively, this means that urban advantages are appropriated by the same people who monopolize social wealth objectively, that the development of the city can only be determined by the development of capital." According to David Harvey (1973, 133), the power-class approach to urban zones in industrial cities taken by Engels in his *Condition of the Working Class in England in 1844* is "far more consistent with hard economic and social realities than. . .

the essentially cultural approach of Park and Burgess." The integration of the city, from Engels's point of view, was not the moral order of impersonal market equilibrium of ordinary consumers but rather the exploitative realities of a capitalist-dominated system of urban land development.

## The Producers of the Built Environment

If ordinary consumers play a secondary part in the shaping of cities, who is it that plays the primary part? The primary decision-makers who shape cities are the producers. Who are these producers? In the United States land-use and development decisions are governed by a capitalistic political–economic system. The conventional view sees urban land use and development as resulting from individual self-maximizing behavior in a market context. Yet power and wealth inequality means that the decisions of some are far more important than those of others. Rank-and-file homeowners, or renters, often give way before the preferences of the powerful. Conventional thinking about cities assumes that there is a free market in land relatively unfettered by the actions of organized elite interests. Urban commercial and residential land markets are seen as determined by free competitive bidding. Actors in this competitive bidding for land are recognized as having different interests, even different incomes, which affect the bidding process. But the fact that the small group of most powerful and wealthy actors can do far more than simply outbid their competitors is not analyzed. Powerful actors such as wealthy speculators and industrial capitalists can and do shape the *rules* of the market system within which the ostensibly free land competition is taking place.

U.S. business leaders tend to see themselves as dependent, as following the lead of consumer values in building cities or as dependent on government action. Yet occasionally they admit their independence. Thus one recent analysis in a 1980 real estate journal, *Buildings*, candidly notes that "the building industry has always played a major role in determining quality of life and social groupings, whether it's in the work sector or in the provision of adequate housing." And profits are the major goal of this building industry. As Lorimer (1978, 79) put it, "The consequence of this arrangement, however, is that the corporate city and its interlocking pieces are designed not to provide a humane and livable city, but rather to maximize the profits to be made from urban land and to capture as much control over the process of urban growth as possible for the development of industry." The corporate capitalist city is a machine to make money.

## Modern Real Estate Capitalism

Today real estate capitalism is organized around a complicated network of corporations and companies of varying sizes and functions. One way to list the critical corporate actors in urban development is in terms of the development decisions they take part in:[2]

1. Industrial and commercial location decisions
    Industrial companies (including service industries)
    Commercial companies
2. Development decisions
    Development companies (developers)
    Land speculators
    Landlords and landowners
3. Financial decisions
    Commercial banks (including trust and pension funds)
    Savings and loan associations
    Insurance companies
    Mortgage companies
    Real estate investment trusts
4. Construction decisions
    Architectural firms
    Engineering firms
    Construction companies (contractors and builders)
    Building materials companies
5. Support decisions
    Chamber of Commerce
    Business associations
    Real estate brokers
    Leasing companies

Such a listing can be misleading in a number of ways. In the first place, one modern capitalist corporation can include within it a development subdivision (which not only develops projects but engages in land speculation), a real estate brokerage subsidiary, and an architectural department. Or a major insurance company may have a financial department as well as its own urban land development subsidiary. Thus the various decisions listed above can be distributed among certain companies or concentrated within one large corporation. Second, there is the issue of scale and region. These land-use decisions are often made not just by local real estate companies but also by powerful regional and national companies. Powerful interests of regional and national scope now determine the shape of U.S. cities. There are complex interconnections between those powerful interests external to cities and those that are intricately interwoven into the internal structure of any particular city. An example of this would be Prudential Life Insurance Company, which now finances and owns real estate projects and development projects in many cities across the United States. There is indeed a complex urban puzzle lying behind the development and ownership of the modern American city—involving development companies, banks and contractors, and supportive government agencies.

A third feature of this modern land development is its capital banking aspect. Land and buildings are always important investments, but when economic growth slows in other industrial sectors, capital will often flow in increased amounts to the real estate sector. Suburbanization has been linked closely to heavy capital flows into suburban land speculation and the construction of residential housing.

Thus the tabulation of powerful land-interested actors in the list above is only a first step toward identifying the critical decision-makers whose land-use and development decisions disproportionately shape cities. In the rest of this chapter I focus primarily on the category of land speculation decisions and on closely related development decisions as they have affected U.S. cities.

## Land Speculation

A major figure in urban land use and development is the real estate specula-tor. Yet the central role of land speculation decisions has not been seriously discussed in the U.S. sociological literature centering on the patterning of cities. Form's pioneering article omits speculators, as does the work of the geographer Harvey and the social scientist Castells. One of the few theo-retical discussions of these speculators in the American literature dealing with land use appears in the book *Progress and Poverty*, written by the nineteenth-century reformer Henry George. This provocative analysis has been neglected by urban social scientists, yet it provides an excellent starting point for a new urban ecology, one directed toward those powerful land-interested actors that Form urged researchers to study. George argued that it is the work and effort of an entire community that brings a steady advance in land values. George (1962 ed., 264) notes that "this steady increase naturally leads to speculation in which future increase is anticipated." The land speculator thus secures, unjustly and without productive effort on the land, the increased value generated by community effort. By control of land, the speculator secures hard-earned dollars from working people who must rent or buy.

Speculation in real estate—including land and the buildings on that land—is a different sort of capital venture than investment in machinery. Real estate speculation is not productive, that is, it does not increase the goods and services available in the society. Yet great amounts of money are realized in landholding, buying and selling. Land is a unique commodity, for it is finite. Occupying space is a fundamental requirement of existence; to live, to work, to be housed—human beings must occupy land. The "created value" of land is the explicit concern of the large-scale real estate industry, of bankers, speculators, developers, and builders. "Creation of value," often on paper, occurs as urban land changes hands many times in its life span. Land speculators are at the heart of this processing of land. A real estate speculator can be defined as an entrepreneur or corporate entity that purchases (or purchases and develops) real estate with the hope of a profit from rising land and property values. Major speculators are, broadly speaking, capitalists, since they are investors who buy and sell for a profit in a capitalist market system. Such speculators can be individuals or corporations, but they are by definition owners seeking to become sellers for a profit. Of great interest in real estate speculation is the ability of these capitalists to shift capital not only from one real estate sector to another—as from slums to suburbs—but also to "bank" capital from commercial or industrial sources in the form of landholdings, banked wealth that is perhaps to be returned to commercial or industrial activities when future profitability dictates that shift.

I now examine a number of activities that illustrate the central role of speculative land decisions in urban development:

1. The site selection of cities
2. Shaping the internal structure of cities, including slums and business districts
3. Suburban development.

## Speculators and City Site Selection

In the urban sociological literature, geographical and communication factors are usually cited as major reasons for the original siting of cities. There is truth to this argument. Yet real estate speculators have had their hand in determining just which promising geographical locations actually become city sites.

Real estate speculation is an old enterprise in North America, coming into its own in the late eighteenth century. Many of the oldest fortunes in the United States have grown up out of land dealings. In the first centuries of development real estate speculators, especially men with wealth and means, launched city development from Washington to San Francisco, often setting the pattern for future growth. Acting legally and illegally, they bought land, advertised to settlers, pressured legislatures, and bribed officials in their quest for land profits. Colonial real estate speculators included the U.S. founding fathers. Indeed, the large-scale real estate speculation of George Washington and Patrick Henry in western lands brought them into direct conflict with King George III (Sakolski, 1957, 53–55). After the American Revolution, numerous cities, from Boston to Yorktown, put in a bid for the site of the capital of the new nation. Thomas Jefferson's desire to have the capital near Virginia won out in the political struggle, and George Washington had Major Charles L'Enfant survey a large area on the Potomac River. The land was then in the possession of wealthy speculators. Since the new government had no money, a deal was worked whereby a large part of the surveyed area remained in the hands of the speculators. Part of the tract was put up for sale to the public at a tavern auction in Georgetown in 1791, presided over by Washington and Jefferson. But few people came to buy lots in what was then considered a desolate area. Washington himself bought a number of lots, for speculative purposes. Thus Washington's promotion of the city to American and European investors was not financially disinterested. Vigorous attempts were made to promote Washington, D.C., real estate for European investment, and the President had his secretary work up a pamphlet for London investors (Sakolski, 1932).

Moreover, Cincinnati came to be located where it is because of an offhand decision of a trapper-turned-land-speculator. In pursuit of thieves, this trapper traveled in the Northwest Territory. Impressed by the fertility of the land and the river location, he petitioned Congress to sell him millions of acres on the Big Miami River. Soon, two real estate syndicates bought land in the region because of this new activity, and on one of these tracts Cincinnati was located. The location of Omaha, Nebraska, similarly reflected the profit-oriented activity of speculators. A financier, George Francis Train, had inside information that a terminus of the Union Pacific Railroad would be at a certain place (Omaha), so a real estate syndicate headed by Train bought up large amounts of acreage. Another syndicate fought to locate the terminus 50 miles to the south, but lost. According to Thomas (1977, 70–87) no less a figure than President Abraham Lincoln was one of these competing speculators. In the development of western areas cheap government land meant, in numerous cases, that wealthy agricultural, commercial, and industrial capitalists could buy up very large amounts of potentially valuable land; later, they could sell land and lend money, sometimes at exorbitant rates, to the farmers and town dwellers settling in the area. Thus "men in the East with surplus capital scanned maps looking for likely spots to establish a town" (Wade, 1959, 30). Some such city speculators made no profit, but their speculative action shaped urban site locations nonetheless. Advertisements for these towns played an important role in generating the migration west of the Appalachians.

Actions by U.S. railroad capitalists had a significant effect on land use and development, rural and urban, as the westward movement took place. Two major effects can be noted. Many railroad lines were extended into relatively unoccupied territory primarily for land speculation reasons. Railroad capitalists received huge government subsidies, the most significant of which, in the long run, were the large grants of government land along the railroads. These lands rose in value with the railroads and towns along the railroads, leading to large real estate profits. In addition, railroad capitalists sometimes shaped where and whether towns and cities grew and prospered. The growth of some midwestern and western cities was significantly accelerated or depressed by the actions of these men. Because the placement of railroads heavily shapes land values, many railroad companies sought private bribes from towns in return for putting the towns on a railroad line (George, 1962 ed., 192; Sakolski, 1932, 1957, 163–74). Towns and cities often had to pay or face serious economic troubles.

## Speculation Within and Around Cities

Land speculation within and around U.S. cities has greatly shaped urban development. The practice of buying and holding land until nearby urban development pushes the price up has a long history in the United States. In the early 1800s land speculation within and around cities such as Louisville and St. Louis increased as real estate speculators drove up land prices. A considerable amount of the surplus commercial capital went into land speculation around cities, rather than into industrial development within these cities. In some nineteenth-century cities publicly chartered transit or utility companies secured considerable blocks of urban land, then held them off the market, driving land prices upward to very high profit levels (Edel, 1976, 114). Great fortunes were made in urban real estate, speculation that frequently charted the course for specific lines of urban growth. A German immigrant who first made money in the fur trade, John Jacob Astor, went on to found one of the great landed fortunes. Making his first million in commercial enterprises, Astor put his money into long-term real estate speculation. In the early 1800s Astor bought up large areas of farmland just outside central Manhattan, and lots in central Manhattan as well. His speculative actions generated a number of the developmental surges around Manhattan Island. By 1920 the Astor family real estate in New York made them the biggest landlords there, worth $1 billion (Sakolski, 1957, 235–36; Thomas, 1977, 40–46).

A good example of the influences of powerful real estate interests, including major speculators, in shaping the internal structure of cities can be seen in certain key units of urban space. The basic land unit selected was often the one best suited to business purposes in a capitalist system—individual lots set into a grid pattern of lot and block development. Lots narrow at the front and long at the side—such dimensions reflected land values calculated in terms of front footage (Sakolski, 1957). New towns and cities could be planned into standardized lots and blocks without any special surveying skills. Such lot-block rectangularism was appropriate for division and sale of land for profit. Cities would sprawl out along traffic arteries, and the gridiron plan forced utility lines and streets to follow along (Mumford, 1961, 422–23). In nineteenth-century America the gridiron pattern was logically extended along the expanding transportation lines. Traffic lines were sometimes laid out with speculative profit specifically in mind. Thus engineers of New York's Public Service Commission in the early 1900s described the growing subway system this way: "All lines must necessarily be laid to the objective point—Manhattan. Every transit line that brings people to Manhattan adds to its real estate value" (quoted in Mumford, 1961, 425). A few government reports have recognized the role of land speculators. In England, for example, one government report noted that "the artificial causes of the extension of the town are the speculations of builders encouraged and promoted by merchants dealing in the material of building, and attorneys with monied clients, facilitating, and indeed putting into motion, the whole system" (quoted in Mumford, 1961, 428).

Some land-oriented capitalists have been so powerful that they have actually shifted the business center of cities, profiting on the side from the rising real estate values this shift resulted in. Take, for example, the two powerful landed capitalists Marshall Field and Potter Palmer, whose real estate operations remade the face of Chicago. At the end of the Civil War, the Lake Street area there was the central retail and financial district. However, Potter Palmer single-handedly rechanneled this business growth to another section of Chicago. The area he chose, the State Street area, was a rundown area then viewed as a "slum." Palmer quietly bought up much of the property in the area, pushed for and got a wide street heading into the area, and then built a plush hotel to entice other businesses there. He eventually succeeded in relocating the center of Chicago business activity, a result signaled by the rise of property values from $300 a front foot in 1860 to $2,000 a front foot in 1869. This speculative venture was dramatically successful. Moreover, after the great Chicago fire in 1871, Marshall Field made decisions that relocated substantial business activity in Chicago. As with Palmer, Field avoided former business centers and chose another dilapidated area inhabited by the poor. Field rebuilt his large retail store in a poor Irish area. Numerous major businesses followed his lead, a clear indication of the importance of one powerful capitalist in reshaping urban areas. Together with a partner, Field became the largest real estate speculator and landowner in Chicago; his speculation came to be more profitable than the retail business operations (Thomas, 1977, 145).

Speculation in central-city areas remains of great importance today. Central-city land in major cities, particularly that useful for office buildings, is very expensive, in part because of land speculation. One survey found that average acre values for prime office space ran in the $2 million to $9 million range, with figures up to $17 million in New York City (Meyer, 1979, 52). Much of the land in central areas already has older built structures on it. Many powerful speculators have gone into land buying for new building construction. Old buildings, including those in good condition, are torn down and replaced with new construction, since there is more profit to be made, given the high depreciation allowed, in new buildings. Freeways, parking lots, and high-rise buildings come to dominate areas where such speculators operate in conjunction with other powerful actors. The diversity of housing and life there previously disappears; cities increasingly look alike. Note that skyscrapers have emerged with monopoly capitalism, the domination of industries by a few firms. Earlier, competitive capitalism did not require such highly concentrated office facilities (Sawers, 1975, 65). With the rise of monopoly capitalism major administrative centers were necessary in order to control these economic empires. Numerous central districts became administrative centers. Government-funded urban renewal has been used to facilitate these developments.

Speculators play an important role in pulling together smaller parcels, hoping that the large land package can be used, for example, by a big corporation interested in an office building. Once speculators have finished their packaging of land, sometimes with the aid of urban renewal, profitable insurance companies and real estate syndicates have been used to generate the money to put up office skyscrapers, the depreciation on which attracts highly paid professionals (such as doctors and lawyers) and other outside investors seeking tax shelters. Downie (1974) notes that in 1972 these real estate syndicates were one-tenth of new security arrangements on Wall Street. Two results frequently follow from this office-oriented speculation— too much unrented office space and cheaply built office buildings, which may become the "slums" of tomorrow. This process has become common in some European cities as well (Downie, 1974, 72, 211).

In addition, speculative real estate operations create or contribute significantly to contemporary slums in central cities. Ghettos and slums with slowly or rapidly deteriorating housing are sometimes seen by urban sociologists as the result of (1) disorganized poor people without the means to keep up the property or (2) the inevitable invasion and succession process whereby as one group of people becomes more affluent, another moves in behind them. Yet there is another view of this slum-making process: that this degradation of central cities is the natural result of intentional profit making on the part of those who invest in slum real estate, and that for most such speculative investors the investments are very profitable. While most slumlords are small-scale operators (Sternlieb, 1966, 123), there is a significant minority engaged in buying slum property for depreciation and speculation purposes, which activity helps create dilapidated, later even abandoned, residential areas. There are profits to be made in this speculation. Thus one Washington, D.C., savings and loan association grew from $30,000 in assets in 1952 to $57 million in 1967 in part by loaning money to speculators working Washington slums (Downie, 1974, 32). Slum speculation can involve outside speculators by means of real estate syndicates. Doctors, lawyers, and business executives buy into a slum investment scheme because the very large depreciation allowed on such buildings can sharply reduce their income taxes. Slums are created by this profit-centered activity, as upkeep on the purchased buildings is kept low to keep profits high. As Downie notes, "far from being the pitiful victims of unavoidable deterioration of inner-city housing, as they so often represent themselves to be, the slum speculators are cunning actors in a sophisticated real estate industry conspiracy aided and abetted by large, respected financial institutions [*see Chapter 10 by Ann Meyerson*] and agencies of the federal government" (Downie, 1974, 39–40). The quality of the housing can be irrelevant to this speculation. Rundown poverty-area tenements can bring in as much profit, because of depreciation and mortgage advantages, as better-quality housing elsewhere.

## Gentrification

In the last decade or so a considerable amount of urban revitalization has occurred in the central cities of the United States. One type of revitalization has involved the displacement of lower-income urbanites by higher-income urbanites, often returning to the central city from outlying city areas, or from suburban backgrounds, or, in the case of young people, opting for the central city instead of the suburbs. Often called "renaissance," this process has taken two major forms: (1) incumbent upgrading, where local residents together with newcomers of the same socioeconomic background upgrade a central-city area; and (2) speculator–developer upgrading, where land speculators and developers buy up low-income housing, rebuild or replace it, and then sell it to white, affluent, often young, families with professional, technical, or managerial workers (gentrification). Poorer, local residents are pushed out. Displacement resulting from private urban renewal has been documented in various U.S. cities, including Atlanta, Baltimore, Boston, and Houston, to name just a few.

## Gentrification and Capitalism

Gentrification is associated with two aspects of modern capitalism. One aspect is continuing and constant; the other is cyclical. The continuing aspect is the importance of cities as headquarters for large corporations. The city is the symbolic center of American capitalism. It is the center for political, cultural, and economic dominance by the ruling class. Decline there has a tremendous negative symbolism for the ruling class. So decline can be tolerated for a period, but then new pressures arise from the cyclical aspect, the investment aspect. Capitalists must decide whether to abandon the capital already in built environments or to rehabilitate that investment.

There is today an urban renaissance in many U.S. cities. The new hotels, exclusive neighborhoods of historic houses, marinas, and speciality shops signal the return of well-off people to central cities. But this is only the superficial face. Beneath is the long-term urban process of uneven development. Cities under capitalism grow and decline as part of this process of uneven development. The spatial seesawing of capital, from central cities to suburbs, then from suburbs to central cities, is to be expected. It is rational in terms of profit seeking by land-oriented capitalists. Gentrification is only a small part of the larger economic restructuring going on in the society. But it does signal the fact that central cities are now the locations for a new round of capital accumulation in residential housing. Once central-city housing and land prices have declined sharply as a result of the earlier withdrawal of capital, as in the undermaintenance of older rented buildings by landlords, then there is a renewed opportunity for redevelopment and a new round of profitmaking in central cities (Smith, 1981, 20–21).

Absentee investment is often a part of the gentrification process. Speculators buy property, often in large amounts, in areas potentially attractive to better-off white-collar families. Existing tenants are forced out by eviction or rising rents. "These properties are purchased at a low price, and may be sold quickly at a substantial profit (sometimes after renovation but often without any additional investment" (U.S. HUD, 1979b, 23). Many speculators look at the gentrifying and nearby areas in terms of their investment potential.

A 1978 National Urban Coalition report found significant speculative activity in the 44 U.S. cities surveyed. The more extensive the citywide rehabilitation, the more speculation was reported as a threat to existing neighborhoods. The threat occurs because "speculative activity is impersonal; monied forces appear to manipulate the lives of those with little money who have lived in the neighborhood and yet have no control over their future there" (National Urban Coalition, 1978, 21). Speculators and developers usually play a critical role in the gentrification process as it proceeds. One study of Washington, D.C., found speculators combing "neighborhoods on foot and by telephone just ahead of the restoration movement, making attractive cash offers to owners" (Richards and Rowe, 1977, 54–61). If owners do not wish to sell, building inspectors may be called in; and they may order expensive repairs, forcing a sale. Between 1972 and 1974 a fifth of all recorded sales in Washington, D.C., involved two or more sales of the same property; most of these were located in five neighborhoods (Richards and Rowe, 1977).

Gentrification has been important in the District of Columbia, in both the Georgetown and in the Capitol Hill areas. Zeitz (1979) has documented the role of speculators and developers, who have bought up blocks of rental housing for conversion to owner occupation. In one block houses selling for $7,000 to $15,000 in 1973 were bought up and resold for $100,000 in 1978. Zeitz further notes a typical transaction in the Adams–Morgan area: "A row of houses on one particular block were sold fully tenanted and unremodeled for $26,000 per house. These houses were sold only weeks later for $65,000 per house. Remodelers are now working on these houses and sales are expected to be in excess of $125,000" (Zeitz, 1979, 78). Clearly, the displaced black renters cannot afford the new housing, and the amount of available, livable housing for working-class renters in a low-vacancy-rate area such as D.C. is gradually reduced. White middle-income and upper-income families replace the poorer black families. Political discontent in D.C.'s black areas facing gentrification has even led to the passage of a city ordinance, called the 1975 "Speculator's Bill," designed to limit speculation and tenant evictions for the purpose of gentrification. Watered down considerably, it became law in the summer of 1978; several loopholes protected most real estate speculation and gentrification development (Zeitz, 1979, 82). Well-organized speculators and developers had successfully lobbied the city council. [*For further discussion of the connections between private developers and government officials, see Chapter 17 by Robert Schur and Tom Robbins.*]

In her research on a half dozen areas in D.C., Zeitz (1979, 101–2) noted several steps in the gentrification renewal process:

1. Pioneers call attention to a new area.
2. Real estate agents become interested in sales there.
3. Speculators and builders move in, with the assistance of banking institutions.

This research suggests one common pattern of powerful actors' intervention: Realtors follow a few (white) pioneer families and publicize the virtues of a new area. Speculators and builders expand the area beyond the pioneers and make much more housing available for higher-income families, usually at prices even the pioneers could not afford. Realtors, speculators, and developers require lending institutions, with which they usually have close ties from previous land projects.

In their research, Pattison (1977) and Clay (1979) found two somewhat different patterns in many gentrifying neighborhoods. Clay's study of 105 neighborhoods in 30 cities found 57 examples of gentrification and 48 examples of incumbent upgrading (Clay, 1979, 17–21, 105). In many cases of gentrification the first stage involved the "sweat equity" and personal savings of pioneer families, who were followed at first by small then by larger speculators and developer–speculators. In other cases, a few capitalist speculators or developer–speculators (usually small companies) were found to have actually begun the gentrification in some central-city areas without pioneer families showing them the way. Most of the neighborhoods had previously housed the elderly poor, nonwhite families, or poor white (blue-collar) families prior to gentrification. Afterward, more than 80 percent of the gentrified neighborhoods were dominated by whites, mostly by professional and other white-collar white families. Most gentrified neighborhoods possessed attractive city features such as "high elevation and proximity to water, public spaces, parks, landmarks" (Clay, 1979, 21). Because of professional whites' demand and speculation, most gentrified housing has sold for relatively high prices, often over $100,000 by the late 1970s.

Clay (1979, 26) found neighborhood observers complaining that developer–speculators frequently did not carefully restore the housing, but rather modernized it. They "butcher" fine old buildings, as some local critics have phrased it. Developer–speculators often have not been sensitive to the distinctive architectural features of an area and have ignored the negative effects of their actions on incumbent residents. Yet many of these have been small or new developers whose speculative interest in seeing risky investments pay off in substantial profits was coupled with the courage and imagination to work in older central-city areas without massive bulldozing. Clay also got complaints that the actions of speculators and developers were uncontrolled, that they cut too many corners to make a profit. In most gentrifying areas concerned officials and incumbent residents were at the mercy of a capitalist housing market. Thus Clay (1979, 27) notes that "in almost all cities developers who have access to capital and who can identify a market for their products can operate at will."

Realtors also play a role in gentrification, sometimes as brokers and sometimes as land and housing speculators themselves. In addition, city governments have frequently cooperated with the capitalist actors by improving local facilities in gentrifying areas, such as parks and streets, by subsidizing gentrification with below-market interest-rate loans, and by selling government-owned structures at low cost, and even by helping to market and actively publicize the gentrified areas with home tours, fairs, and media campaigns (Clay, 1979, 26–29).

This cooperative action by developers, speculators, realtors, governments, and banks has displaced low-income and moderate-income families in most gentrified areas. These families, often black or other nonwhite families, must move to other areas and there compete with other families of modest incomes in what is usually a declining number of decent housing areas in the central city. Here we see a small group of powerful capitalist actors again rearranging the face of cities for private profit, with little input into the process from those most directly affected, the incumbent residents. By seeking profit, they can shift poor areas and change the racial composition of large neighborhoods, a type of "reverse blockbusting."

## Condominium Conversions

Condominium conversions may or may not involve housing renovation, but they are often similar to gentrification in the housing problems they create. For example, a Denver study (Flahive and Gordon, 1979, 6–10) found that in 1973–1978, 5,500 apartments and multifamily structures were converted to condominiums, most of which were sold to affluent households. A significant number of low- and moderate-income households were thus displaced. Looking at 85,000 households in a large U.S. central-city area for 1978, the Denver study estimated that 2,000 households were displaced in that year alone, with demolitions, condo conversions, and houses going from renter to owner accounting for most of the displacement.

In recent years a number of corporations have become involved in the conversion of existing apartment buildings into condominiums. Large, if not huge, speculative profits are being made in this process. In a typical case in Philadelphia, an apartment building worth only $25 million was sold to a development corporation for $50 million.[3] The development corporation then, with little renovation, converted the rental apartments into condominium apartments for sale. Reportedly, a typical rental charge was about $560 a month prior to conversion, but after conversion the total payment (for mortgage and interest, etc.) was $1,200 a month, plus several thousand dollars in a down payment on the unit. As a result, most existing households had to leave such a building because they could not afford the greatly increased cost for the same housing unit. And in most cases low-income and low-middle-income families will never again be able to afford housing in such apartment buildings, forcing them to look elsewhere, often for less than adequate housing.

## Suburban Speculation

Obvious gridiron-block extensions in the twentieth century can be seen in the suburban patchwork quilt sprawling out from the edges of central areas in American cities. So far, the great suburban migration has involved more than 50 million people. The area currently used for urban use in the United States is over 10 million acres, although twice as much land is withdrawn from other uses because of the leapfrogging that characterizes much suburban growth. Such idled land, one land-use report notes, is "ripening for active urban use" (Ackerman et al., 1962, 9). By A.D. 2000, perhaps 40 million acres of U.S. land will be withdrawn from other use for urban development, mostly for suburban growth. Clawson (1971) has estimated that as of 1970 the rise in land prices each year, for land moved from rural to suburban use, is about $14 billion. Like cities, suburbs are usually seen by urban sociologists as spontaneous, disorganized developments, the result of an unpredictable, freewheeling market system. This is part of the usual explanation of suburbanization, which touches on other explanations, such as rising affluence leading to demand for single-family housing and government subsidization of mortgages and utilities. But in reality the growth has involved considerably more planning and purpose than the traditional view suggests. Here too the role of profit making on the part of real estate speculators and their partners, developers and bankers, has radically shaped urban development. This applies as well to suburban growth.

Suburban real estate speculators often have been seen in the real estate literature as a critical group of capitalists who fill the ownership gap between agricultural users and developers, with the former selling out to speculators willing to hold the land for later development (Lindeman, 1976). In urban fringes land will often go through a series of speculators before it becomes a suburban development. A number of studies have illustrated the profits made by speculators buying up such farmland. In areas like California land speculators have bought out farmers by offering $200–$6,000 more an acre than they paid for it. Such sales push up the property taxes on surrounding farmlands not yet sold to speculators. Tax pressures, coupled with the water runoff and pollution problems of suburban development, eventually force even the most obstinate farmer to sell out to speculators. As a result, residential land prices, particularly in suburban areas, have risen 200 to 400 percent faster than the price of housing in the same areas (Downie, 1974, 88). In some areas, such as Los Angeles, the price of residential land went up at the rate of 40 percent a year in the late 1970s, in part the result of speculative activity.

In some cases, suburban development at the rim of major cities had been generated by the profit objectives of only one or two real estate speculators, as can be seen in the operations of two brothers in Cleveland after World War I. Using speculative options and large-scale leveraging, they generated a surge of suburban development in the Shaker Heights area of Cleveland. Then, to reinforce their highly influential suburban real estate activities, they got into trolley-line operations as well (Thomas, 1977, 255–56). In other cities, a number of speculators triggered suburban development. Downie has shown that real estate people in Los Angeles admit that sprawl development there was heavily shaped by the quest for private profit, that the sprawl pattern was "merely the easiest, fastest, most lucrative way to cash in on the motor-age California land rush: buy a tract of vacant land, wait a short time for the population and roads to move toward it, subdivide it into lots for cheaply built single-family homes, and sell them to builders at prices that total several times the land's original cost" (Downie, 1974, 10). This drive toward profit created the sprawling freeway system as well.

Speculation is regarded in the conventional literature as a positive bridging force, as a brokerage operation between the farmer and the builder, but as we have seen it has numerous negative effects. There are others yet to mention. Illegal and unethical activity is, according to one researcher, commonplace among speculators, developers, and their financiers. Downie notes that "land speculators push farmers off their land and employ deceit and bribery to rezone and subdivide it" (Downie, 1974, 6). Moreover, Lindeman (1976, 150–51) argues that real estate speculation activities actually alter the nature of the land commodity primarily by restricting the supply of available land and by forcing prices up above what they would have been without the speculative activity. Higher-than-necessary prices come in part from the expensive, usually high-leveraged, financial arrangements that speculators get into, as well as from the speculative pricing process itself. Both costs are passed on in the form of higher prices for actual land users. Restrictions on land supply sometimes arise because of the complex legal arrangements a series of speculators bring to a parcel of land, legalities that can later hamper the sale of land to builders: Encumbered by mortgages, land changes its character as a commodity. One result of this is an acceleration of sprawl, as builders try to leapfrog land that is too tied up or held by speculators holding out for very high profits. The characteristic pattern of urban sprawl is often defined by the flight of speculators and developers to cheaper land farther out.

## Financing Speculation

A complex social structure is woven around the operations of city and suburban speculators, including government officials (as in the case of urban renewal) and banking organizations. Speculators nearly always rely on lenders for their leveraging operations. Leverage is the mechanism that allows the pyramiding of a large investment operation on a small initial investment. Since the property bought serves as collateral, real estate speculators need far less of their own money to get into the real estate business. They can borrow far more (80 to 90 percent) of the purchasing price from banking institutions than if they purchase industrial equipment. And for those who buy land and older buildings, build new apartment and commercial buildings, and rent them out, there are several ways to profit. "For here there is not only the prospect of leverage at a high ratio but also of shielding the resultant profits through the liberal tax shelter permitted to owners of income-producing property in the form of depreciation allowances, as well as other expense deductions associated with development and ownership" (Goodkin, 1974, 6).

## Large-scale Corporate Intervention in Speculation

In the last two decades very large multinational corporations have moved into real estate banking speculation, construction, and development. Until the 1950s, the land and housing industries were dominated by relatively small capitalist entrepreneurs, some of whom were involved only in real estate operations. When there are distinct landowning and industrial capital groups within the top capitalist class, there can be conflict. Excessive land costs may mean increased worker demands for higher wages, which can generate industrial capitalist support for holding down land and housing costs. However, the growing corporate and conglomerate involvement in land and housing development makes this distinction among capitalists less significant. Corporate intervention, into a real estate industry once dominated by relatively smaller capitalists, has developed rapidly. In the 1960–1975 period 300 of the top 1,000 corporations developed real estate departments; particularly active in this area have been the oil, food, chemical, paper, and machinery industries. Profit making ("equity participation and diversification") was the major reason given for land activities by corporations in a 1971 survey by the Society of Real Estate Appraisers (Goodkin, 1974, xv). The 250 corporations replying to that survey held $25 billion in real estate in 1971. While the recessions of the 1970s forced some companies to get out of real estate, many still remain.

Certain rationalizations for the activities of monopoly- or oligopoly-oriented corporations have appeared to defend the growing domination of fewer and fewer corporations in most major American industries. Now these rationalizations are being extended to oligopoly trends in the housing industry and land markets. One capitalist rationalization of monopoly-corporate involvement in real estate operations in cities is that corporations provide larger-scale planned developments. Thus Goodkin (1974, 20) notes that the smaller "entrepreneurial builder, short on bankroll and long on leverage" has to follow a hedgehopping pattern of suburban development, so large-scale development can mean less hedgehopping and less sprawl. Large corporations have now built a number of major suburbs, including many in California. The Chrysler Corporation set up a real estate department in 1967, with holdings of over $300 million by 1970. Chrysler was into "a whole string of projects around the country, including townhouses, office buildings, student housing in California and Arizona, shopping centers, condominiums, and a ski resort in Montana headed by the late television newsman Chet Huntley" (Goodkin, 1974, 22). Aerospace companies (e.g., McDonnell–Douglas), major utility companies (e.g., Mississippi Power and Light), timber corporations (e.g., Weyerhaeuser) and oil companies (e.g., Exxon) have expanded into the land, residential, and recreation development business. Today the trend in the land and housing industry is in the direction of accelerated monopoly control. [*See Chapter 7 by Tom Schlesinger and Mark Erlich.*] Inflation creates tighter profit margins, forcing smaller developers and builders out of business. Soon 200 major developers may be in control of a majority of the U.S. housing business; one informed estimate sees that figure as dwindling to 25 large firms by the year 2000.

## Conclusion

The purpose of this chapter has been twofold. First, I have illuminated the role of real estate speculation in shaping urban and suburban land and building development. At best shadowy in the existing social science literature, real estate speculation has not been systematically studied by urban analysts in the United States. The materials presented here show that real estate speculators are in fact powerful land-interested actors, as individual entrepreneurs or as corporations, who buy, bank, and sell land in a quest for forever renewed profit.

Real estate speculators have shaped the sites for numerous American cities, using legal and illegal means to secure their goals. Powerful land-interested capitalists have contributed substantially to the internal physical structure and patterning of cities themselves. The central areas of cities such as San Francisco have been intentionally remade, in the name of private profit, by combinations of speculators and other capitalists such as developers.

Slums too have often seen the intervening hand of the real estate speculator. The theories that focus on the values of the poor or the inevitable invasion–succession process—fairly common in conventional urban sociological treatments of slums—need to be supplemented with a theory of real estate speculation. In this process, speculators can create or accelerate increased dilapidation in central cities. They can help create that area Burgess called the "zone of transition." Later, they can help gentrify such areas. Burgess's commuter zone emerges in part because of the activities of land speculators. The hedgehopping look to suburbia reflects in part the planned profit of real estate speculators and their associates.

Tracking speculators through site selection, central-city decisions, and suburban sprawl, we see the planned, organized activities of these powerful land-interested actors—which brings us to the second purpose of this chapter. It is very important for urban analysts in the United States and Europe to develop an alternative framework to deal with urban land use and land patterning, topics that have been at the heart of both urban ecological theory and urban planning theory for more than half a century. I have here emphasized that a class-oriented theory of urban land use provides significant insight into the internal dynamics of urban land use, development, and change, which traditional ecological and planning theories do not offer. In this chapter I have illustrated this point by cataloguing major groups of capitalist actors that deserve systematic, detailed research on how and where they operate in shaping and reshaping the land uses and built environments of cities. Even the challenging theoretical discussions of Europeans such as Harvey and Castells tend to be vague when it comes to identifying the exact role of specific capitalist land-use actors. Here I have gathered together scattered data to document in specific detail one major category of land-use decision-making by capitalist actors. If urban ecologists are to understand the how, when, and where of urban land-use change and development, they must begin with a systematic analysis not only of complex demographic patterns but also of the character and operations of powerful land-interested actors.

Moreover, the practical field of urban planning has traditionally operated with a theoretical framework closely allied to that of traditional urban ecology. Both have assumed a free market in land without much analysis of that market. Indeed, in recent years both urban ecology and urban planning have placed emphasis on demographic analyses, computerized analytical techniques, and cost–benefit procedures. Sophisticated technical analysis of data for the clients at hand often seems to have replaced a concern for a broader theoretical understanding of urban structure and process. This is not to say that both fields have totally ignored the need for new urban theory, but they have neglected such a task. Careful analysis of all categories of powerful land-interested actors would provide a more realistic framework not only for understanding how cities actually work but also for understanding why idealistic urban planning often ends in problems and frustration.

Planning that attempts to meet idealistic goals such as the "decent home for every American family" proposed in the 1949 U.S. Housing Act or environmental quality often founders on the day-to-day realities of adapting planning to the needs of capitalist actors. Thus in a study of a massive commercial mall development in a southwestern city McAdams (1979) found that urban planners entered into the development process in two ways, as private consultants for the developer and as staff planners for the city's Planning Commission. The first phase of development was hidden from the general public, and a private planner helped the developer prepare a profitable development plan in secret. When the city's staff planners finally saw the plan, several raised idealistic objections to the plan's environmental impact. In spite of their misgivings, however, and surrounded by pressures to improve the "business climate" of the city, the planners recommended approval of zoning changes with a plea that the "applicant continue to recognize" the environmental impact of the project. A start toward coping with this planning dilemma would be to develop a class-based planning theory coupled with power structure research that would clearly explicate the way planners relate to and serve the powerful land-interested actors.

A move toward more democratic urban planning in the United States requires more than new developments in planning theory. It requires implementation of theory in actual planner-aided efforts on behalf of working-class people in cities to help them express their values in their struggles with speculators and developers. A few "advocacy" planners have already made attempts to provide planning skills for "have nots" in the urban revitalization process. One prominent planner, Chester Hartman, provided aid to the residents in San Francisco's South-of-the-Market area, where a tenant's association successfully forced capitalist leaders, including developers, speculators, and builders, to revise their commercial plans for the area to include a significant number of low-income residential units (Hartman, 1974). In this case the advocacy planner and the tenants' association came in too late to stop the revitalization process, but they did force significant changes in the original project. In two more recent struggles in San Francisco, social advocacy planners have developed the information and financial plans for incumbent residents attempting to fight the bulldozing of two major buildings in areas developer–speculators wish to redevelop (Hartman, 1980, 78–79).

Hartman (1980, 76–77) has suggested to a planners' conference that planning from the bottom up will require recognition of the skewed power structure shaping urban land use and the development of mechanisms that provide for democratic control over land-use decisions. With regard to speculators and developer-speculators, in 1974 one community-based group in Washington, D.C., the Capital East Community Organization, made an aggressive attempt to halt gentrification and the displacement of low-income renters. Trying to stem the tide of what they termed "reverse blockbusting" in D.C., they pressured the city council to pass a bill called the "Real Estate Transaction Tax," which would have restricted speculative buying and selling by imposing a stiff transaction tax. Yet developers and speculators organized to resist what was popularly called the "Speculator's Bill." They succeeded first in delaying the bill's passage until 1978 and then in watering it down so that developer–speculators were effectively exempt from the law. In this case, in part because of a lack of effective planning assistance and of adequate resources, a community-based group was not ultimately successful in its attempt to bring developers and speculators under democratic popular control. Still, increasingly, speculators, developer–speculators, and bankers seem to be targeted by community groups for more democratic control. A class-based planning theory and expanded advocacy planning might assist such community groups to be more successful in their struggles with powerful capitalist land-oriented actors.

## Notes

1. A partial exception to this statement is the work of Harvey Molotch (1976).

2. An earlier version of this typology appeared in a joint paper (McAdams and Feagin, 1980) with D. Claire McAdams. McAdams has done pioneering work on shopping center development in the United States.

3. This discussion is based on information presented in a "60 Minutes" news report, CBS News, March 29, 1981.

# 6 | Large Builders, Federal Housing Programs, and Postwar Suburbanization

### Barry Checkoway

*Homebuilders and developers obviously play crucial roles in the housing market. Nevertheless, they do not operate without substantial support from the federal government. This chapter explores the relationship between large merchant builders (like Levitt and Sons) and the federal government, traces how the growth of the suburbs resulted from explicit needs and goals of each, and rejects the popularly held belief that suburbia resulted primarily from consumer preferences. The chapter's focus on the institutional context of suburbanization provides a clear picture of how private interests and public policies often are meshed in relation to housing. The* Washington Post *article reprinted at the end of the chapter provides an example of the political power and influence that merchant builders wield on state government (in this case, Virginia) as they shape metropolitan areas. But they are by no means the only well-organized interest group in the private housing sector. Realtor PAC, representing local real estate agents, ranked first among political action committees in contributions to federal candidates during the 1981–1982 election cycle, giving $2.1 million (see* Washington Post, *Mar. 10, 1984.)*

## I

It is customary in the literature on postwar American suburbanization to neglect the decision process and institutional context by which suburban places were established and developed. In one popular image, for example, postwar residential suburbs "exploded" on the American landscape or appeared as the sudden product of unspecified or invisible hands. Once there were rural farmlands and small villages at the edge of the city, then suddenly there were Levittown, Park Forest, and even Los Angeles, all the overnight work of get-rich-quick developers or families in flight (Editors of *Fortune*, 1958). In another image, postwar suburbs resulted from a virtual "tidal wave of metropolitan expansion." Suburbanization was no overnight

Reprinted from the *International Journal of Urban and Regional Research* 4:1 (1980) with the permission of the journal and its publisher, Edward Arnold, London.

explosion at all, but only the latest episode in a secular shift of metropolitan population from center to periphery and an ad hoc decision process fragmented and diffused among a large number of separate decision-makers (Blumenfeld, 1954; an earlier example is given in Warner, 1962). In yet another image, postwar suburbs resulted from the shifting preferences of consumers. Suburban development prevailed because the public demanded it, directed government to provide incentives for suburban production and consumption, and fueled a revolution in the residential construction industry (Dobriner, 1958; Donaldson, 1969; Masotti and Hadden, 1973). Suburbanization appears as a product of "forces" originating elsewhere. It has an uncanny, dramaturgical quality. It appears irreversible.

In all this, there has been little effort to conceptualize postwar suburbanization as a product of decisions and institutional interactions. Yet there was no magic in the appearance of postwar suburbs. On the contrary, at any moment metropolitan form is the product of understandable processes put in motion and perpetuated by its key decision-makers. But there are few accounts that approach suburbanization as a process rather than as something to be taken for granted, and little is known about its principal postwar participants, their interests and aims, their partners and handmaidens. There *are* studies of the decision behavior of homebuying consumers, but few examine the prior, precipitating decisions in this period (an exception is Clawson, 1971; see also Harvey, 1973).

This chapter reports a search for the historical background of the decisions and institutions that together "built the suburbs." Who were the key actors? What factors influenced their decisions? What interests and values were involved? Who participated in—and who was excluded from—the process? And what are the lessons of this history? The focus is on large residential builders and how they were supported by the federal government. They do not comprise all those who participated in postwar suburban development, but they are among the most important. They have been selected for their importance in postwar suburban *residential* development.[1]

My own belief is that the key decisions in postwar suburbanization were made by large operators and powerful economic institutions supported by federal government programs and that ordinary consumers had little real choice in the basic pattern that resulted. . . .

## II

The growth of many postwar suburbs was precipitated by decisions of large residential builders to select and develop suburban locations. There was nothing new about suburban development in America. What was new in this period was the developed capacity of large builders to take raw suburban land, divide it into parcels and streets, install needed services, apply mass production methods to residential construction, and sell the finished product to unprecedented numbers of consumers. These decisions are best explained in terms of the changing market conditions of housing and developed technological capacity of housebuilding itself.

There was a shortage of adequate housing in postwar America. In 1947 it was estimated that between 2.75 million and 4.4 million families were living with other families and 500,000 more were occupying transient or nonfamily quarters. Although estimates of the quantity of housing required to replace deteriorated structures and stay abreast of population and family increases ranged between 1 million and 1.5 million units per year, the building industry was unable to construct more than 500,000 units per year. Housing surveys in 1947 found more than 6 million low-income urban families either searching for better housing or planning to do so (Bauer, 1948; Hauser and Jaffe, 1947; Newcomb and Kyle, 1947; Rosenman, 1946).

Several factors were cited to explain the housing shortage. Some analysts attributed it to wartime conditions and military priorities that had virtually stopped civilian residential construction and created shortages among postwar consumers (Abrams, 1948). Others attributed it to increases in family formation and birth rates that had resulted in a population that was eager for better housing (Glick, 1957; Taeuber and Taeuber, 1958). Others attributed it to postwar prosperity and a rising standard of living that had resulted in a growing demand for more products and consumers with purchasing power to back up demand (Haar, 1960; Miller, 1965; Saulnier et al., 1958). Yet others attributed it to the shortcomings of the residential construction industry. Housebuilding was dominated by small and local firms lacking the capacity to reduce shortages and reach demand. The typical small builder could not employ a permanent labor force, develop a research staff, bargain for materials in volume at lower cost, or buy a substantial area of land for large-scale development.[2] Housebuilding was, in a popular contemporary image, the "industry capitalism forgot" (*Fortune*, Aug. 1947, 61–67). [*See also Chapter 7 by Tom Schlesinger and Mark Erlich.*]

The national production of housing increased significantly in the period that followed. In the decade after 1950 more than 15 million new housing units were started. The rate of new residential construction in 1950–1959 was approximately twice that in 1940–1949, six times that in 1930–1939 (see Table 6.1). The number of new housing units started was 515,000 in 1939, 1,466,000 in 1949, and 1,554,000 in 1959. In 1946, housing production almost quadrupled; in 1950 the housebuilding industry produced more houses than in any one year in history. Although the shortage remained, production advances were nonetheless significant (Maisel, 1953, 11ff).

Important in postwar production advances were basic changes in the residential construction industry. What distinguished the period was an increase in the number, size, and importance of large residential builders (see Table 6.2). Postwar studies by Sherman Maisel in the San Francisco Bay Area documented the primacy of these builders. Maisel examined all Bay Area residential builders in 1949–1950 and identified four basic types by size. A builder was classified as large if he annually completed 100 or more houses, had a volume of more than $1 million and more than $600,000 in total assets, and employed 100 or more workers and a large overhead staff. Maisel found that although small builders were the most numerous type, they were of less overall importance than the small number of larger builders that built most of the houses and dominated the market. In 1949, large and medium builders constituted only 2 percent of the local total but accounted for 55 percent of the houses produced. Follow-up studies showed that between 1950 and 1960 large builders increased their share to 74 percent of all houses produced. By 1960 large builders built three out of every four houses in this area (Maisel, 1953; follow-up studies include Herzog, 1963, 19–32).

The Bay Area findings typified the national pattern. Several builders had developed gradually and grown before 1940, and others were born of the defense programs that followed. In 1939 it was estimated that there were 480 large and medium builders that together accounted for less than 20 percent of the houses produced nationally. In 1949 there were 3,750 builders of this size and they accounted for 45 percent of the total number of units built. This was more than six times greater in 1949 than in 1939 (Maisel, 1953, chap. 2). Fully 70 percent of the houses built in 1949 were built by only 10 percent of the builders. Large builders alone accounted for 5 percent of all houses built in 1938, 24 percent in 1949, and 64 percent in 1959. This period thus saw a significant increase both in the number of large builders and in the number of houses built by them.

The large builder was distinguished by his size, scale, and operating structure. These were not small and local craftsmen but large, often national operators identified more with automobile industrialists than with small operators of their own field. The typical large builder reduced costs through direct buying of materials, purchased in carload lots, maintained large inventories, developed new and more efficient subcontractual relationships, and specialized his labor force. He applied government financial aids and housing research to his work. Government research laboratories cooperated with large builders to make advances in materials and equipment (Dietz et al., 1959; *Housing*, 1954, 42–56), in land development and site planning (Spring, 1959), and in faster, less costly methods (Sasaki, 1959; Whyte, 1958). Mass production and prefabrication promised factory en-

TABLE 6.1

NEW HOUSING UNITS STARTED IN THE UNITED STATES, BY DECADE, 1930–1959

| | New Housing Units Started |
|---|---|
| 1950–1959 | 15,068,000 |
| 1940–1949 | 7,443,000 |
| 1930–1939 | 2,734,000 |

*Source:* U.S. Bureau of the Census, 1966, 18.

gineering, standardized dimensions, preassembled units and prefitted systems.[3] It also promised more rapid construction and higher production.

The large builder also was distinguished by his suburban orientation. Mass production required large tracts of land typically found near the city limits or in suburban areas beyond. In the suburbs was open and available land at the right price and without restriction, and the promise of excellent transportation by automobile and expressways. Retail, manufacturing, wholesale, office, and service establishments all sought suburban locations in the postwar period. Given the orthodox market assumptions and locational principles, postwar suburbanization was a logical alternative to investment in the central city.[4]

The overall result was a significant increase in postwar American suburban development. In 1950 the growth rate of suburbs was more than ten times that of central cities. Between 1950 and 1955 the total metropolitan population increased by 11.6 million people, 9.2 million of whom were suburban. Between 1950 and 1956, 64 percent of the net national increase in housing was in metropolitan areas. Of this, 19.4 percent was in central cities, 80.6 percent was in suburbs. New residential construction was by far the most important single factor of change. The total volume of new construction in suburbs was almost three times that in central cities in this period (U.S. Bureau of the Census, 1958, 1966; U.S. Department of Labor, 1959). It was among the great population migrations in American history.

Large-scale residential development spearheaded and symbolized the movement. Orange County, California, increased in population by 65 percent between 1940 and 1950. The increments outside Los Angeles alone were phenomenal. Torrance increased by 124 percent, Lynwood by 133 percent, Monterey Park by 140 percent, Arcadia by 154 percent, Montebello by 171 percent, Manhattan Beach by 175 percent, Compton by 198 percent, and Hawthorne Covina by 350 percent. Levittown, New York, had more than 51,000 people living in 15,000 identical houses by 1950. Park Forest, Illinois, housed 30,000 on 2,400 acres 30 miles south of Chicago by 1956. In 1957 the editors of *Fortune* estimated that suburban land was being

TABLE 6.2
NUMBER OF NEW HOUSING UNITS STARTED AND PERCENTAGE BUILT BY
LARGE BUILDERS, 1938–1959

|  | New Housing Units Started | Percentage of Houses Built by Large Builders |
|---|---|---|
| 1959 | 1,554,000 | 64 |
| 1949 | 1,466,000 | 24 |
| 1938 | 406,000 | 5 |

*Sources:* 1938 data from U.S. Bureau of Labor Statistics (1940); 1949 data from U.S. Department of Labor (1954); 1959 data from National Association of Homebuilders (1960, 17). Data on the homebuilding industry in this period are generally unavailable. On this point, see Maisel, 1953, 3–9.

bulldozed at a rate of 3,000 acres per day. It was a triumph for the suburbs and the large builders who built them.

## III

Levitt and Sons exemplified the growing potential of large residential builders in postwar suburbanization. The firm had been founded in 1929 by Abraham Levitt, whose early background in real estate helped him to recognize the profitability of large-scale housebuilding operations, and by his two sons, Abraham and William. In the 1930s, Levitt had built custom homes for affluent families in suburban Long Island and Westchester County, New York, and the company continued to build by conventional methods until World War II. A wartime ban on most civilian construction forced Levitt to build low-cost housing in government defense areas. This experience gave Levitt an opportunity to experiment with prefabrication, to grasp the principles of mass production, and to imagine a housebuilding scheme of unprecedented scale. By the end of the war, Levitt had grown in size, developed in capital, and was ready to expand (Gans, 1967; Larrabee, 1948; Levitt, 1951, 1969; Liell, 1952).

In 1947 Levitt acquired 1,400 acres of Long Island farmland about 30 miles from New York City and proceeded to revolutionize the housebuilding industry. By 1948 Levitt was completing more than 35 houses per day and 150 houses per week and rapidly selling the low-cost product. More than 17,000 identical houses for over 70,000 people were finally built side-by-side in uniform rows and sold for the same price of $7,990. By 1950 "Levittown" was praised as "an accomplishment of heroic proportions," and the Levitt house was known as "the best house for the money in the United States."[5]

How did Levitt do it? Levitt adapted assembly-line techniques to the mass production of housing. An army of trucks speeding along new-laid roads stopped and delivered neatly packaged bundles of materials at exact 100-foot intervals. Giant machines followed the trucks, digging rectangular foundations in which heating pipes were embedded. Each site then became an assembly line on which houses were built. Men, material, and machines moved past each site in teams, each performing one of 26 operations over and over again from site to site according to standards derived from systematic studies of time and motion. Every possible part and system was preassembled, prefabricated, or precut to specification and size in the factory and then brought to the site ready to assemble with machinery developed just for the purpose. As operations were shifted from site to shop, scheduling and delivery grew in importance. Materials reached the site only minutes before a team would arrive to perform its particular operation. Mechanization and labor-saving machinery, forbidden or prohibitive in traditional operations, were everywhere evident in Levittown. Levitt was less a builder, more a manufacturer of houses.[6]

Each Levittown house was controlled by Levitt from start to finish. Over several years Levitt had recruited executives with specialized competence in all aspects of housebuilding. Levitt also had developed a construction crew that was thoroughly familiar with company techniques and capable of any construction task. Construction workers were nonunionized and assured of steady employment. Such stability and permanence were atypical of the housebuilding industry.

Levitt applied vertical organization and rationalization as rigorously as housebuilding would allow. He altered traditional distribution channels and reduced costs. Lumber, for example, came from Levitt's own company and was cut from his own timber on his own equipment to the exact specification and size at which it later was used in assembling the house, enabling further savings in handling and freight. Nails and concrete blocks were made in Levitt's own factory by contractors working only for him. Those few materials not produced by Levitt were bought in carload quantities directly from manufacturers by Levitt's own wholesaler, eliminating middlemen and markups. The typical builder was entangled in a costly distribution web. Levitt in comparison eliminated charges and even influenced product design to suit his own needs.[7]

Levitt also had an enviable capital position and a profitable partnership with government. In addition to personal resources, he boasted the largest line of credit ever offered a privately owned American housebuilding firm. This proved an important competitive advantage at every stage. He had easy access to government credit and financial aids. For large builders like Levitt, the federal government offered billions of dollars of credit and insured loans up to 95 percent of the value of the house. Such builders easily received FHA "production advances" before purchases were made. Levitt was able to get FHA commitments to finance 4,000 houses before clearing the land. Veterans using the G.I. Bill of Rights could buy in Levittown with no down payment and installments of only $56 a month.

The completed Levitt house was attractive to consumers. Levitt spent more money on consumer research than any builder of small houses in history. The Levitt house—and Levittown itself—was meticulously designed to match consumer preferences. Each house was small, detached, single family, Cape Cod in style, and centrally located on a small lot in a development in the suburbs. To insure the sale, each house came complete with radiant heating, fireplace, electric range and refrigerator, washer, built-in television, and landscaped grounds. All were included at no added cost. For middle-income consumers, Levittown offered a virtual dream house, and Levitt was the dream's entrepreneur.[8]

Levitt also rationalized and simplified his marketing and merchandising. Full-page advertisements directed customers to a display building adjacent to Levittown. Inside were carefully decorated model rooms and all the appliances, design innovations, and gadgets for which Levitt was known; a scale model of the completed development; and several salespeople to answer questions, offer advice, and take deposits. The entire financing and titling transaction was reduced to two half-hour steps, one to purchase and another to clear title. Contract forms already stamped with fixed title enabled clerks to sign up to 350 buyers per day. In minutes customers could be assured of a completed transaction. Levitt could get three banks, a mortgage broker, and the construction superintendent on a single telephone to arrange several thousand FHA and VA mortgages for veterans. Levitt handled all legal and real estate details and charged $10 flat for closing costs. For an inexperienced buyer entering the market for the first time and looking for investment security, Levitt offered a creditable commodity and proven reliability. In 1947 Levitt undersold his nearest competitor by $1,500 and still earned $1,000 profit on each $7,990 house.[9]

In 1950 Levitt sought to expand further and to create an entire community somewhere on the eastern seaboard. Levittown, New York, was the largest housing development ever built by a single builder, but now he wanted to build more than houses alone. The scheme was detailed by Alfred Levitt in the *Journal of the American Institute of Planners* in 1951. The proposed community could incorporate past Levitt experiences and "the principles of good planning laid down by leaders in the field." It would include neighborhood residential areas divided by parks, playgrounds, and schools; an industrial area separated by a green-wooded shelter belt; and an interior expressway connecting the neighborhoods and on which commercial facilities would be located. Because all land would be owned in advance, it would be possible "to plan right down to the last tree and shrub" (Levitt, 1969).

Construction originally was intended for Long Island, and several hundred New Yorkers had made cash deposits before examining the proposed plans or the model house. But the Korean national emergency forced postponement of construction, and Levitt instead proposed to adapt the plan to one of several critical defense areas around the country. He sought a large area of land requiring little modification and easily converted to large-scale use. He also sought an active housing market, assurances of consumer demand, and access to government financial aids aimed at large builders. Several sites were considered; all were suburbs.

Levitt decided to locate outside Philadelphia in Lower Bucks County, Pennsylvania. This area offered agricultural land on the suburban fringe of a large city which shared strongly in the postwar housing shortages. It also offered assurances of government financial aids. A prior decision by United States Steel to construct a major defense-related steel plant had made the area eligible for designation as a critical defense area. But the particular location was not key. It is fair to assume that any of several similar suburban sites also would have been acceptable. (These decisions are described in detail in Checkoway, 1977a, chap. 3.)

Levitt was the largest but not the only builder of his kind. Large builders were increasing in number and production outside every major city. . . . They symbolized a revolution in housebuilding and were instrumental in postwar suburbanization. Maisel said of them: "These are the new giants in an industry once populated by pygmies. Here, at the very peak of their housebuilding pyramid, are the leaders of construction who are not content merely to build houses. They construct communities" (Maisel, 1953, 95).

## IV

State support of large residential builders by federal government programs was crucial in postwar suburban development. For, in addition to the changing market conditions of housing and the developed technological capacity of large builders, some measures were required to guarantee the mortgage money, share the risk, and insure the profitability of the suburban enterprise. Although there was nothing new about government aids to private industry in America, postwar conditions combined to enlarge the federal role in the housing field.

The shortage of housing was viewed by some as a problem of industrial production. Wartime conditions had resulted in record rates of production, had depleted supplies of many materials, and had reduced the capacity of industry. The war effort had virtually exhausted America's plants, and facilities were too small, strained, and inadequate to meet the growing demands of a heavily consuming economy. Production backlogs in excess of six months were common. Shortages of some nonmilitary goods had accumulated to alarming proportions. Postwar supply fell short of demand. Postwar industry thus found itself searching to install capacity and increase production.

Residential construction was only one of several industries with postwar production problems, but it was considered among the most important. The housing shortage was commonly identified as a failure of residential construction. Legislators and analysts generally agreed that federal intervention would benefit both the housebuilding industry and the entire economy. Residential construction is considered a bellwether of the economy, an effective pump-primer in an economic slump (Abrams, 1950; Meyerson et al., 1962, 18–31).

The federal housing policy that followed was mostly suburban in its orientation.[10] FHA, a profit-making enterprise based upon bankers' standards, encouraged new building in the suburbs and discouraged development in the central city. Its overall concern for "economic soundness" shaped a belief that poor and minority neighborhoods were bad credit risks and placed further emphasis on suburban development [*see Chapter 18 by Citizens Commission on Civil Rights*]. Mark Gelfand (1975) documents how builders and buyers generally could take advantage of FHA home mortgage insurance programs only if they located themselves beyond the inner city.[11] The result was that the vast majority of FHA houses were built in the suburbs, and the suburbs could not have expanded as they did in the postwar years without FHA.[12]

The Housing Act of 1949 also increased the amount that could be insured under the FHA home mortgage program to $6 billion. In 1950 Congress increased the FHA mortgage insurance authorization by $2.25 billion, amended FHA sales housing programs to provide incentives for production of three- and four-bedroom houses, liberalized FHA terms on loans for manufactured houses and large-scale residential construction, established a new FHA program for homes in suburban and outlying areas, and reduced the low-rent public housing authorization to 75,000 units for the year. In 1951 Congress increased the FHA mortgage insurance authorization by $1.5 billion, authorized loans to facilitate the production of prefabricated houses and major components for new houses, authorized $60 million for loans and grants for facilities and services in critical defense areas, and further reduced the public housing authorization to 50,000 units for the year. In 1953 Congress increased the FHA mortgage insurance authorization by $1.5 billion, liberalized FHA terms on loans for new owner-occupied homes and in suburban areas, and further reduced the public housing authorization to 35,000 units for the year and subsequent years. Early in 1954 Congress again reduced the public housing authorization to 20,000 units and added the condition that unwanted public housing under construction could be stopped by the locality. The Housing Act of 1954 increased all FHA mortgage insurance authorizations by another $1.5 billion, liberalized the amounts and terms of FHA sales housing mortgages, and established another FHA mortgage insurance program for single-family dwellings in suburban and outlying areas (U.S. Congress, Subcommittee on Housing and Urban Development, 1975; see also the various works of Charles Abrams). The 1954 act was hailed by large builders as "an aid to private enterprise." Public policy is not what is stated or intended but what is actually done [*see Chapter 14 by Peter Marcuse*]. Federal housing policy was mostly suburban in its orientation.

Other federal programs also promoted suburbanization. The federal highway program made possible the roads that made large tracts of suburban land more accessible for development. The roads and highways that resulted laced metropolitan areas and transformed farmlands and old villages into real estate for suburban developers (Gelfand, 1975, 222–35; Howard, 1957, 38–39; 1959; Leavitt, 1970; Muller, 1976; Mumford, 1968; Rae, 1971). Federal tax policies also promoted suburban construction. Federal income tax deductions on owner-occupied houses made government contribute a fifth or more of costs of homeownership [*see Chapter 15 by Cushing Dolbeare*] and virtually subsidized the new suburban houses (Meyerson et al., 1962, 236–37; other federal suburban programs are described in Arnold, 1971).

An explicit focus of federal housing programs has been on homeownership and new construction. FHA was designed to make homeownership possible for more people by bringing carrying charges within reach of a mass market through long-term indebtedness. The agency joined with local chambers of commerce, real estate operators, and large builders to promote homeownership actively, putting hundreds of government salesmen in the field to organize local drives, circulate promotional literature, and sponsor "better selling meetings" and expositions. Local realtors and builders advertised the virtues of homeownership by using the FHA seal as a symbol of government approval (Dean, 1945, chaps. 3 and 4).

A class of consumers was ready to purchase these new houses, and the federal government sought to effectuate their demands through special incentives and financial aids to large suburban builders. In addition to the FHA, a Veteran's Emergency Housing Program was enacted in 1946 to facilitate the financing of priority housing for returning veterans. The prefabrication industry got an important boost under this program, as government contracts were offered to all prefabrication firms and several hundred thousand dwellings were finally built. The Housing and Home Finance Agency was established in 1947 and soon began cooperating with government laboratories, universities, and the largest builders to develop products, methods, and ideas for housing. The emphasis was on new single-family suburban houses. New construction was by far the most important factor of change in the national housing inventory in this period (U.S. Bureau of the Census, 1958, 14).

Another focus was on large builders. The federal government encouraged small builders to grow large and large builders to further grow to a size that would be economically more meaningful. To the builder ignored by past federal programs, noted Charles Abrams, "FHA brought a rare prize." And the larger the builder, the larger the prize. Large builders more easily received credit advances and more easily negotiated with the FHA. Large operators and powerful economic institutions were among the principal beneficiaries of federal programs. Small operators were either excluded, penalized, or driven from the market. Any builder who could promise a large quantity of mortgages was eagerly sought after by a federal program (Abrams, 1946, 232; Eichler and Kaplan, 1967; Stone, 1973).

The suburban orientation of federal housing policy was the direct result of the effort to stimulate production in the housing field and the national economy. The focus on homeownership and new construction stimulated the production and consumption of house-related goods in the marketplace and the flow of capital in the entire economy. It allowed for capital outlays in public works, physical facilities, social services, transportation systems, and more. It offered incentives to realtors, large builders, bankers, lumber dealers, highway contractors, automobile manufacturers, and others. Postwar suburbanization was a "built form" and an economic instrument for production, and federal legislators were predisposed to facilitate the process.

# V

Large builders also organized to determine the direction of the programs that benefited them. There was nothing new about their efforts. The National Association of Real Estate Boards (NAREB, changing its name later to the National Association of Realtors) from its inception had a standing committee concerned with federal legislation and was instrumental in the housing acts of the 1930s. (The standard work on NAREB is Davis, 1958. On NAREB influence in the 1930s, see McDonnell, 1957.) The National Association of Home Builders (NAHB) originated in NAREB and then developed as an independent organization concerned primarily with large builders and new suburban houses (Lilley, 1973; Mason, n.d.). Postwar shortages and the promise of federal intervention necessitated more active involvement in legislation. In 1942, the Realtor's Washington Committee was formed to represent, promote, and protect the industry's position in Congress. This committee was led by NAREB and NAHB and was backed by the U.S. Savings and Loan League, the U.S. Chamber of Commerce, the American Bankers Association, the Mortgage Bankers Association of America, the Building Products Institute, the National Retail Lumber Dealers Association, the Associated General Contractors, the National Association of Retail Lumber Dealers Association, the National Clay Products Association, the Producers Council, and other trade associations representing apartment house owners, building materials manufacturers, lumber industrialists, subcontractors, prefabricators, and others. (The formation of the Realtor's Washington Committee is described in R. O. Davies, 1966, chap. 2.)

The housebuilding lobby became one of the most powerful political groups in Congress. It operated from a well-defined, although not singular, position. It sought to facilitate the production and sales of new suburban houses. It favored FHA, VA, and other programs to remove risks and insure profits of residential construction, and opposed public housing as a "socialistic" threat to private enterprise [see Chapter 20 by Rachel G. Bratt]. It employed pressure tactics that were fundamentally grass roots in nature. NAREB alone reported 44,000 members in 1,100 communities, NAHB 16,000 members in 130 local chapters. Local affiliates placed congressmen on boards of directors, thus contributing to congressional understanding of, and responsiveness to, their position. On any given day the lobby could flood Congress with letters, telegrams, and telephone calls from influential constituents in every part of the country. Local leaders were also major advertisers in local media, thus contributing to media willingness to report their position and lend editorial support. A full-time, well-paid Washington staff prepared leaders for participation in hearings and meetings, produced form letters for constituents to mail, conducted active public information programs, sponsored homeownership fairs and displays, maintained a constant flow of press releases and news feature stories, and wrote model curricula for school teachers. Large sums of money were spent on advertising to persuade consumers to prefer homeownership and new construction and to direct government to provide programs to facilitate these preferences.[13]

The housebuilding lobby influenced the legislation and programs that developed. It effectively delayed the Taft–Ellender–Wagner housing act for four years mainly out of opposition to the proposed public housing. When the bill finally reached the congressional floor as the Housing Act of 1949, the lobby worked to limit the number of public housing units authorized, to further aids to private housebuilding through expanded FHA and VA programs, and to assure inclusion as a national housing goal "that private enterprise shall be encouraged to serve as large a part of the total need as it can." It was estimated that more than $5 million was spent by homebuilders in the struggle over this act. So aggressive were their tactics that a full-scale congressional investigation was conducted.[14]

The housebuilding lobby also influenced policy through administrative action. Homebuilders gave sustained support to administrative agencies such as the FHA and VA, which in return tended to respond to the policy suggestions of their support groups. Homebuilders also worked to supply agencies with most of their personnel and guidelines.[15] At the national scale, Harry Truman appointed as head of the FHA Raymond Foley, who referred to himself as "a champion of free enterprise in housing" and said "the chief activity of government in housing should be to aid and stimulate private enterprise." Dwight Eisenhower replaced Foley with Albert Cole, a long-term opponent of public housing who labeled federal housing legislation as socialistic and voted against the Housing Act of 1949. Cole was later replaced by Norman Mason, who came to government after a career as a building supply and lumber retailer (Keith, 1973, chap. 6). It was no surprise that the FHA adopted guidelines consistent with the building and real estate industry and fully accepted the racial practices of the private society.

The homebuilders' lobby also influenced policy through local implementation. The FHA was relatively decentralized in its administration, permitting closer connections between field directors and local real estate operators, financial institutions, and homebuilders. When the Housing Act of 1949 was finally enacted and authorized public housing, the lobby immediately worked to amend the legislation and to defeat its implementation through local opposition and referenda. As a result, only 283,400 of 810,000 authorized units were actually produced in the scheduled period, and the number of authorized units was reduced in each successive legislative year after 1949 (R. O. Davies, 1966, 123–32). At the same time, programs benefiting homeownership, new construction, and large builders increased greatly.

The production of new single-family suburban houses was not the only focus of postwar federal housing practice, but others were minor in comparison. Urban renewal and public housing, for all of their clamor and controversy, were secondary to the houses whose mortgages were financed and guaranteed by federal housing programs. These programs operated as an economic instrument to stimulate production and large builders were influential in developing the programs which benefited them.

# VI

Most suburban studies attribute postwar suburbanization to the shifting preferences of consumers. Indeed, so common is the focus on suburban consumers that they are pictured as independent actors in a process in which they chose to participate. In this image, postwar suburbanization followed from the selective migration of individuals with unprecedented preferences for social homogeneity and conformity, compulsory neighboring and membership in voluntary associations, a return to religion and a Republican Party switch, and other attributes of "the new suburbia" (Marshall, 1973). It was "a new way of life," "a new state of mind," and "one of the major social changes of the twentieth century." There was shaped a virtual "image of suburbia" in the American public mind, and so frequently have its attributes been addressed that when we think of suburbs we typically think of these attributes.

Later analysts argued instead that suburbanization resulted not from selective migration but from other more independent factors. In this image, postwar suburbanization was explained as an effort to achieve middle-class status and upward social mobility (Dobriner, 1963), or a "new bourgeois style" (Dobriner, 1963, chap. 1), or the homeownership ideal (Berger, 1960; Gans, 1967). Leo Schnore, for example, rejected the "social psychological approach" and argued that differential housing opportunities are the major determinants of growth differentials between subareas of the metropolitan community (Schnore, 1968, 162). Herbert Gans (1962a, 625–48) argued that there was little to distinguish the way of life in suburbs from cities, that those who sought suburbs mainly sought the best available house for the money (Gans, 1967, chap. 2), and that the nature of suburban community derived more from the consequent population mix than from selective migration (Gans, 1967, chap. 7). Postwar suburbanization was, in the revisionist image at least, "new homes for old values" (Ktsanes and Reissmann, 1959).

The problem in this analytic exchange is the assumption on which it is based. It is assumed by both the selective migration analysts and their revisionists alike that consumers were free to choose among several residential alternatives, that their choices reflected real preferences, and that their preferences were the independent factor in suburbanization. The only real point of dispute is whether the preferences resulted from "a new state of mind" or from middle-class mobility or from some other factor. *Not* in dispute is the assumption that consumers were the independent factor in the suburban pattern that evolved. This paper breaks with this assumption.

The customary view of the postwar consumer residential choice derives from a history that is well known and widely accepted (Checkoway, 1977b, chap. 4). It contends that the consumer decision and consequent federal programs were a response to urban decline and housing shortages. Central cities were surrounded by seas of deterioration in which housing quality and municipal facilities were allowed to decline. Studies of Philadelphia, for example, found central areas so blighted that they were wholly undesirable for business or residence; the majority of houses were grossly deficient and dilapidated; fully one-third of all dwelling units were labeled unfit for human habitation, and nothing short of demolition was recommended. Declining conditions were commonly identified with racially changing neighborhoods, lower property values, and an unsafe financial investment.

Suburban homeownership was believed more attractive. Consumers were turned away from conditions in the central city and toward the "suburban ideal." The suburbs offered a new, freestanding, well-equipped, carefully designed and attractively landscaped house, with ample yard space to play and garden. They also offered an escape from the city, a more wholesome environment, and a more neighborly community. The American predisposition to "suburbia" was confirmed by contemporary surveys of the subject.

The suburbs also offered the best available financial investment. The growing demand for suburban housing steadily increased its relative value. A slightly higher initial price seemed little to pay for a better product and investment security. Indeed, it probably confirmed the quality of the product and security of the investment in the minds of those purchasing their first house. And given the suburban orientation of FHA and other federal housing programs, suburban homeownership offered virtually the *only* sensible investment location.

Postwar consumers easily recognized the significance of any announced decision by a large builder to locate in a metropolitan suburb. For those turned away from central Philadelphia, for example, Levittown promised a planned alternative, a suburban oasis at a distance from the city, and a pioneering opportunity in a wholly new environment. It also promised a known commodity, a national reputation, and proven reliability. The advertised image—of a detached house with flower-filled windowboxes surrounded by grass, trees, shrubs, high clouds, and no other houses in sight—was hardly resistible. When the first model houses were opened for inspection in December 1951, more than 50,000 people filed through during the very first weekend. As salesmen on loudspeakers urged buyers to return on another day, police were needed to keep crowds in line. Several families squatted for days outside the salesroom waiting for the chance to put a deposit on a house that had not yet been built. On the first two days alone, more than $2 million worth of houses were sold. It was, as the national media reported, "the most spectacular buyers' stampede in the history of American housebuilding."[16] This is the customary view of the postwar consumer choice.

This chapter suggests something different about the postwar consumer residential choice. It does not question that growing families *were* justifiably turned away from conditions in the central city; or that suburban housing *was* more attractive and a better investment; or that residential suburbs *did* offer an escape from the city and a wholesome arena for family and child rearing; or that increased consumer demand *did* affect federal housing programs and residential construction decisions. Houses in suburbs like Levittown *were* a bargain and *did* offer a version of the suburban ideal to consumers who had never before been able to achieve it. All of these images are easily confirmed in the literature.

This chapter does question those studies that fail to explain the impossibility of inferring the spatial dynamics and decision behavior of large operators and government partners from the residential aspirations and satisfactions of the eventual suburban consumers, or which fail to specify the narrow range of alternatives actually available, or which fail to emphasize the fact that consumers were important but not decisive actors in the decisions which produced the choices they made. Consumers made a logical choice among alternatives developed elsewhere. The evidence that consumers aspired to, bought in, or expressed satisfaction with suburbs is not proof enough that they would have chosen to do so if a different set of alternatives had been available to them. The assumptions that consumers were free to choose among several residential alternatives, that their choices reflected real preferences, and that their preferences were the independent factor in postwar suburbanization, all ignore the fact that final decisions do not always reflect real preferences and that prior decisions may predetermine a narrow range of alternatives from which consumers can choose. (A general perspective on the fallacy of consumer sovereignty is given in Galbraith, 1971.)

It is wrong to believe that postwar American suburbanization prevailed because the public chose it and will continue to prevail until the public changes its preferences. Suburbanization prevailed because of the decisions of large operators and powerful economic institutions supported by federal government programs, and ordinary consumers had little real choice in the basic pattern that resulted. Postwar suburbanization resulted from a decision process and institutional context and the consequences and policy problems flow from the nature of the process. To alter the consequences, it is first necessary to alter the process.

## Acknowledgments

This paper was presented at the 1978 annual meeting of the American Political Science Association. Among those who commented on earlier versions are Bernard Frieden, Herbert Gans, Mark Gelfand, Chester Hartman, Seymour Mandelbaum, Roger Montgomery, Heywood Sanders, Allen Wakstein, Frederick Wirt, Michael Zuckerman, and colleagues at the Childhood and Government Project at the University of California at Berkeley.

## Notes

1. This is not to suggest that large residential builders were the only large operators in postwar suburban development. Other important actors—mortgage lending institutions and local suburban governments, for example—have not been selected for examination here but have been or will be treated elsewhere. I treat the role of large transportation and industrial operators in Checkoway, 1977c, and of local suburban government in Checkoway, 1977b. Michael Stone, 1973, examines the role of mortgage lenders. The literature on suburban economic development is massive.

2. Among the general studies are Abrams, 1950; Beyer, 1965; Foote et al., 1960; Maisel, 1953. On housebuilding operations and constraints, see Grebler, 1950; Kelly et al., 1959; and Meyerson et al., 1962. On local building practices, see Killingsworth, 1950, 538–80. On obstacles to production advances, see U.S. Congress, House, Subcommittee of the Joint Committee on Housing, 1946, especially 144–64.

3. Between 1948 and 1954, the number of manufactured homes produced in the United States increased from 30,000 to 77,000 (Beyer, 1965, 244). The development of prefabrication is explored in Bemis, 1936; Bruce and Sandbach, 1945; and Kelly, 1951. Prefabrication principles are described in Chapman, 1954; "Where Is Prefabrication?" *Fortune* 33 (April 1946): 12–32; "More Houses for Less Money," *Better Homes and Gardens* 28 (October 1949): 189–92; "Prefabrication," *Architectural Forum* 92 (April 1950): 160–64; "Prefabs Fill Special Needs," *House and Home* 2 (November 1952): 89–114.

4. It could be argued that economies of scale would have made large-scale development desirable in any given location. In this period, however, government programs were developed to bear the public costs of new residential construction, encourage homebuilders to grow larger, and give development a suburban orientation. This is discussed in Section IV of this chapter.

5. The construction of Levittown, New York, is described in Larrabee, 1948; Liell, 1952; and in "Up From the Potato Fields," *Time* 56 (July 3, 1950): 67–72.

6. See Larrabee, 1948; Liell, 1952; "4,000 Houses a Year," *Architectural Forum* 92 (April 1950): 20–22; "Levittown on the Assembly Line," *Business Week* 1172 (February 16, 1952): 26–27; "Biggest New City in the U.S.," *House and Home* 2 (December 1952): 80–91.

7. "A large company, in short, by its very size and prestige and integrity, can accomplish, can achieve, can perform, where individuals are helpless and disunited," wrote William J. Levitt (1948, 253–56).

8. The Levitt house and consumer research are described in Lader, "The Most Popular Builder's House"; and "Levitt Keeps Experimenting with . . .," *House and Home* 5 (February 1954): 118–23.

9. Lader, "Levittown on the Assembly Line." It is revealing to contrast Levitt practices with the more common practices described in Dean, 1945.

10. The evolution of federal housing policy is described in Gelfand, 1975; McKelvey, 1966; Wheaton, 1953. See also Checkoway, 1977c; Frieden, 1968, 170–225; Friedman, 1968; Hartman, 1975; National Commission on Urban Problems, 1968.

11. My debt to the work and prose of Gelfand, 1975, especially 216–22, is obvious.

12. La Guardia, 1935, 13–14; Bartholomew, 1939; 1940; "Rebuilding the Cities," *Business Week*, July 6, 1940, 38–39; U.S. FHA, 1942; "FHA Policies Said to Hinder Urban Rebuilding," *American City* 63 (March 1948): 120; Bauer, 1956; "FHA in Suburbia," *Architectural Forum* 57 (September 1957): 160–61; National Commission on Urban Problems, 1968, 99. See also Chatterjee et al., 1976.

13. The position of the housebuilding lobby is well described in testimony in U.S. Congress, House, Committee on Banking and Currency, 1954; and U.S. Congress, Senate, Committee on Banking and Currency, 1954. Lobbying activities and tactics are described in U.S. Congress, House, Select Committee on Lobbying Activities, 1949.

14. The influence and delaying tactics of the housebuilding lobby are described in Schriftgiesser, 1951, chap. 14. The political history of the Housing Act of 1949 is described in R. O. Davies, 1966, chap. 8; Keith, 1973, chaps. 2–5; Meyerson et al., 1962, 272–89; and *Congressional Quarterly Almanac* 4, 137–44.

15. Herbert V. Nelson, executive director of the Realtors' Washington Committee, told a U.S. Senate Committee in 1950: "We put several hundred of our people, whom we found and persuaded to go into government service, into positions where they could give their services" (quoted in Abrams, 1965, 61). But Nelson is probably best known for his

statement after passage of the Housing Act of 1949: "I do not believe in democracy. I think it stinks. I don't think women should be allowed to vote at all. Ever since they started, our public affairs have been in a worse mess than ever before" (U.S. Congress, House, Select Committee on Lobbying Activities, 1949).

16. On public affairs in Levittown in the 1950s, see Checkoway, 1977c, chaps. 4 and 5. On Levittown 20 years later, see Popenoe, 1977, chaps. 5 and 6.

---

"THEY OWN THE PLACE"

## VA. BUILDERS HAVE GRIP ON LEGISLATURE

*By Molly Moore*
*Washington Post Staff Writer*

RICHMOND—When Virginia State Sen. Joseph V. Gartlan decided to draft a law tying building rights to parks, sidewalks and other amenities in new subdivisions, he knew there was only one way he could push the bill through the General Assembly.

He didn't go to his colleagues for help. he went straight to the construction industry and spent two days on the telephone drawing the law under the tutelage of one of Northern Virginia's most powerful land developers, John T. (Til) Hazel.

"We talked on the phone and rewrote and rewrote and rewrote and he finally went along," said Gartlan, a Fairfax Democrat. With the endorsement of the home builders industry, the legislature went along, too.

And that is frequently how law is made in a capital in which some legislators say the home building industry maintains an almost viselike grip on the legislature. It is a broad-based influence that stretches from local county board rooms to the offices of Gov. Charles S. Robb.

Virginia's builders, says State Sen. Richard L. Saslaw (D-Fairfax), sometimes "have more clout than local governments."

The state's home builders are mavericks and self-made men whose fierce belief that government should keep out of their business and their profits is frequently matched by the legislators' belief in the same philosophy. The builders' political savvy and influence are fortified by their political action committees, which feed campaign coffers statewide and work the board rooms and legislative chambers of local and state governments.

In Northern Virginia, where political power often is diffuse, the Northern Virginia Builders Association and the individual giants of industry on its membership rolls are powerbrokers.

"They are the single most powerful group in Northern Virginia," asserts Fairfax County Supervisor Audrey Moore, whose wars against the builders have formed the centerpiece of her political career. "They are very powerful and they always have been."

The building industry has been the focus of disputes over growth, the longest-running political feud in Fairfax County. At times, the controversy has ripped apart the county board. And in those instances when county officials have tried to chip away at the industry's power base, the builders have turned to well-placed friends in the more sympathetic state legislature, aiming their biggest guns at the key committees that plod through Virginia's complex land-use law and building regulations.

"It would be almost impossible to get

a bill through the [House] Counties, Cities and Towns Committee if they were really against you," said Del. Gladys Keating (D-Fairfax), a member of the committee.

Each year the homebuilders have succeeded in convincing legislators to kill a bill proposed by Prince William County lawmakers that would require developers and builders to shoulder some of the costs for widening and improving roads leading to newly developed subdivisions. This year will be no exception, says Keating. "They will go to every one of my colleagues and say, 'Vote against it.'"

"More often than not, you go with them [builders]," said Saslaw, a likely Democratic candidate for Congress this fall and a politician homebuilders list as "one of our friends."

"But it's not like they come down here and get everything they want," said Saslaw. "They've won a lot and they've lost a lot." He pauses and adds: "They win more than they lose."

Mike Erkiletian, a Fairfax County builder and chairman of the state builders association's legislative committee for the past 11 years, dismisses the "power and influence" labels with a shrug and an emphatic wave of his cigar.

"If they think we're powerful, they're crazy," chortles Erkiletian, who retired this year from his legislative lobbying post to take over as finance chairman for Republican Rep. Stan Parris's bid for reelection. "The only power we have is if we can talk to people, if we can convey our point of view.

"Our view," he adds, taking a deep puff on the cigar, "always has been to help our friends."

That help frequently comes in the form of big bucks at election time, which some officials say is an important source of the builders' power. "They give heavily to the legislators—they own the place," said one Fairfax official.

"They contribute to people's campaigns," said Del. C. Richard Cranwell (D-Roanoke), who has been a strong patron of the homebuilder's causes in Richmond. "The contributions get him through the door, they get access. But nobody votes down here because of what somebody gave in the campaign."

Homebuilders in Cranwell's district gave him more than money in one recent campaign. He credited them with rounding up about fifty delegates to the Democratic primary caucus in Roanoke, where candidates can win a place on the general election ballot based on the number of people who turn out to vote for them.

In last fall's legislative campaigns, the Northern Virginia Builders Association's political action committee—the Affordable Shelter PAC—contributed $70,500 to the campaigns of state delegates and senators. In those elections few interest groups were more generous. In Robb's gubernatorial campaign in 1981, real estate and construction industries contributed $142,080.

That is only the tip of their financial giving, according to both politicians and builders' representatives.

"You will never see the results of campaign contributions of the builders," said Fairfax Supervisor Thomas M. Davis, a Republican. "They give to many state and local elections and it doesn't show. Each particular contributor can write you a $99 check. You will not be able to look at the record and see, but it's there."

State law requires candidates to report only individual contributions of more than $100.

Construction industry representative William Thomas of Alexandria, generally regarded as one of the most influential lobbyists in Richmond and a close political and personal confidant of Robb's, says he personally tapped clients and other friends in the Northern Virginia business community for "maybe $100,000, maybe $200,000" in Robb's gubernatorial campaign. . . .

The bond default controversy, during

which officials said Fairfax had the highest construction bond default rate in the nation, is only the latest in a decades-old battle between some county officials and the homebuilding industry, the single largest industry in the sprawling suburban county. . . .

[Fairfax] County officials note that some of the association's most prominent members have been among the builders who have repeatedly defaulted on subdivision projects. County records show that the association's 1980 president, Cecil M. Boyer, Jr., has defaulted on nine subdivision projects in the county since 1978.

Builder–lobbyist Erkiletian said it was what they perceived as the Packard board's [a rebellious, antidevelopment county board led by Jean Packard] no-growth policies that drove him and other builders to seek refuge in the [state] legislature and the state courts, whose judges are elected by the legislature.

"The builder's attitude has tended to be, 'If we can't make it work in Fairfax, we'll go to the legislature to override them,'" said [Fairfax] Supervisor [James M.] Scott. "And they've done that successfully.

It has become an almost annual rite that the builders turn to Richmond in an effort to undo the new zoning laws, or new condominium conversion laws, or new building regulations that Fairfax supervisors have imposed. Builders say the county board is too quick to impose restrictive regulations on all builders to correct the abuses caused by a small percentage of the businessmen. And in the world of zoning and building, one carefully placed word can mean thousands of dollars in losses—or profits—for the industry. . . .

And builders say they are usually treated more fairly in the statehouse than in the local board rooms. "The state legislature tends to be more enterprising, better balanced," said Finz.

Adds Saslaw: "There is a very pro-business bent in the state legislature. And that's good. . . ."

Just as important as campaign contributions and a business-oriented legislature, however, is the fact that changes in land use laws tend to attract little public attention.

"Land use is not the stuff by which glamour stories are made," said Keating. "It is exotic to most of our constituency. You don't hear that much from the opposition."

"If 1,000 people from the county showed up against the builders on these issues, they would not be as effective," said Saslaw.

# 7 Housing: The Industry Capitalism Didn't Forget

*Tom Schlesinger*
*Mark Erlich*

*Conventional wisdom has it that the housing industry has made less progress in terms of industrialization and innovation than is true of most other major sectors of our economy. But in fact there has been great concentration of activity and control in the industry in recent years, substantial technological change, and a considerable degree of vertical integration. The impacts of this transformation have led to the de-skilling and disempowering of construction workers and their unions, added workplace hazards, and, for the consumer, construction-quality problems, narrowed choices, and continuing high prices.*

At the end of World War II, Henry Luce's publishing empire confidently trumpeted the dawn of the American Century—supremacy abroad and unparalleled economic vigor at home. One hitch in the second part of the formula, however, was the homebuilding industry. Housing, Luce's *Fortune* sputtered, was "the one great sector of modern society that has remained largely unaffected by the industrial revolution." Its "feudal character" and "picayune scale" made the shelter industry "an unbelievably inefficient system for building houses." *Fortune*'s overwrought editors headlined this 1947 fusillade with the angriest epithet within reach. They called housing "The Industry Capitalism Forgot."

Henry Luce's crowd was not alone in this view. In 1948, the *Nation* disputed the very existence of a housing (as the magazine put it) "industry." A *Nation* writer described in hand-wringing detail the trials of hiring a carpenter, a plumber, an electrician, and a plasterer to build his house. Homebuilding's "antique ways," the writer complained, rendered it unable to "behave like a modern enterprise meeting modern needs."

> Karl (carpenter), Ed (heating contractor), and Joe (plumber) don't look like an industry to me. Each is a small entrepreneur, engaged in a continuous battle of wits with the unions, the lumber yards, the manufacturers of plumbing fixtures, the millwork people, the glaziers and all the rest . . . [they] are not, in fact, producers of housing. They are carpenters, plumbers, sheet-metal workers,

electricians, and cement men whose work happens—sometimes—to result in the completion of a house. (Lasch, 1948)

The left–liberal *Nation* concluded its analysis precisely where *Fortune*, the businessman's friend, had left off the preceding year:

The search for reform in the homebuilding industry becomes primarily a search for large-scale operations. . . . *If a housing industry really existed*, you could get a house by buying a certain number of standardized wall panels, roof panels and floor panels, together with pre-fabricated utility units and then hiring somebody to put them together. Or you could call the local agent for a prefabrication firm and have him ship a standard ready-made house to your site. (Lasch, 1948, *emphasis added*)

From the shelter-short days of the 1940s to the present, these critiques and images have dominated our understanding of homebuilding. Whether speaking in the name of capitalist efficiency, consumer satisfaction, or poor people's shelter needs, most housing analysts have fondled the touchstone of manufacturing and ritualistically pronounced the residential industry an anachronism whose structure and construction methods desperately need rationalization, centralization, bigness, and a grand technological fix.

The critics' passions stem from the centrality of housing in the domestic economy. In 1983, residential construction was a $113 billion business. Homebuilding generally accounts for about 4 percent of the GNP; directly employs 2 to 3 percent of the nation's labor force; triggers millions of jobs in lumber, appliances, and related industries; and has long been considered the "balance wheel" of the economy for its sensitivity to governmental monetary and fiscal tinkering (*Construction Review*, September 1984).

But for all the breast-beating and gnashing of teeth, neither capitalism nor modernism has passed American housing by. The industry's record of innovation in building materials, construction methods, and tools and equipment compares favorably with developments in any major industry. While small and medium-sized operations have characterized much of the shelter industry, significant large-scale operations and industrialized techniques have been commonplace since the nineteenth century.

In recent years, housing has become a more concentrated industry, defined increasingly by the actions of centralized contracting operations aimed at a national market. These organizations have achieved preeminence after years of experimentation in fitting residential construction ventures into horizontally and vertically integrated corporate plans and the development of elaborate financial strategems. Between 1973 and 1981, the 400 giants (representing less than .5 percent of all homebuilders) accounted for nearly a quarter of all housing starts and a third of all new shelter (conventionally built homes plus manufactured housing) (*Professional Builder*, July 1981).

In cities with rapidly expanding markets, concentration is particularly dramatic. A handful of national builders put up as much as 45 percent of new single-family housing in Dallas in 1983. The top 10 homebuilders *doubled* their share of the total U.S. market between 1977 and 1982, reaching a level of 12 percent. Smith Barney housing analyst Barbara Alexander predicts the top 400 will control more than half of the housing market by 1990 (*Wall Street Transcript*, Aug. 2, 1982).

Accelerating concentration has not eliminated the small builder. Vast numbers of contractors with an annual output of 5, 10, or 25 houses may well be a permanent feature of the business. In 1977, 91 percent of the general contractors who built single-family homes (one of the many census categories among residential builders) had fewer than 10 people on their payrolls. Yet these small firms employed over 60 percent of that category's work force (U.S. Bureau of the Census, 1981c). But those builders are moving to the periphery as their big-time brethren set the industry's terms. The total number of active builders has dwindled—from 100,000 in 1977 to 75,000 in 1982; and by 1976, contractors who built 25 or fewer homes a year had constructed only 13 percent of all single-family homes (Sumichrast, Ahluwalia, and Sheehan, 1979).

Karl, Ed, and Joe are still running around in their semiautonomous way, are still a personal and occupational mix of power and powerlessness. But today they are more likely to be working for one of the housing giants as a wage worker or a subcontractor than they would have been in 1948. Regardless of the name on the paycheck, they are apt to be installing factory-made components, not fabricating the units themselves; indeed, one of them may be building homes or shelter components *in* a factory.

Superficially, the industry retains some of the characteristics that made the *Fortune* editors' blood boil. The average tradesperson is still likely to work in small crews and know his or her employer. There are fewer general contractors; but more specialty subcontractors do a piece of the housing giants' total work—framing, roofing, wiring, or plumbing. In fact, the multimillon-dollar housing giants often have relatively few employees. "Craftsmen on our on-site homes are not U.S. Home employees," says Tina Scheibel about the first billion-dollar homebuilder. "We do usually use subcontractors."[1]

But the decentralization and disaggregation of employment patterns are not throwbacks to feudal times. They are logical responses of this increasingly concentrated sector. Rather than forgetting housing, capitalism has shaped the relationships between market, industry structure, technology, labor process, and work force to produce a dramatic transformation—albeit of an incremental and sometimes paradoxical nature.

# Concentration and Industrialization of the Construction Industry

World War II marked a watershed in federal housing policy and the shelter industry. As Washington's flirtation with public housing cooled, so did the possibilities for significant direct government production of housing. The private housing market blossomed when low-interest, long-term, low-down-payment VA and FHA mortgage loans to returning veterans detonated the explosive demand pent up during the Great Depression and the war. Federal highway legislation opened new areas for development and fueled the suburbanization of America [*see Chapter 6 by Barry Checkoway*]. An era of moderately priced, detached, single-family homes dawned in those suburbs, and builders positioned themselves to supply the expanding market by broadening their scale and employing quasi-industrial techniques.

Large builders, such as William Levitt and Sons of Long Island and the Byrne Organization of Baltimore, incorporated elementary principles of mass production into on-site construction. Using job-site minifactories, precut materials, preassembled components, labor-saving equipment, and direct-purchase contracts from suppliers, along with a tight rein on subcontractors and a lot of old-fashioned hucksterism, these builders offered two- and three-bedroom bungalows in the $8,000 range. In 1946, Bill Levitt, an immodest and incessant self promoter,[2] became the first private homebuilder to exceed an annual volume of 1,000 units. For the next several decades, Levitt and Sons ranked among the most successful builders, demonstrating that a system based on cheap materials, cornercutting, and aggressive marketing could hurdle the bumps of the business cycle as long as overall demand remained fairly strong (*Fortune*, Aug. 1947).

The postwar period also spawned a flurry of off-site industrialized homebuilding. In a widely publicized effort, Buckminster Fuller announced plans to mass-produce his metal, carousel-like Dymaxion House in a converted Wichita aircraft factory. But in the face of meager financing, the houses built in this putative "Kitty Hawk of housing" never flew past the prototype stage. In Ohio, engineer Carl Strandlund did manage to turn out the Lustron Home on a factory conveyor belt. But, unable to overcome monumental start-up costs and consumer skepticism about his porcelain and steel shelter, Strandlund went out of business after two years (Bender, 1973).

Less grandiose visions proved more successful. By the late 1940s the "trailer" industry had stabilized, producing roughly 50,000 units a year. Government support was the key; in 1951, the Pentagon purchased 93 percent of all mobile homes manufactured in the United States. As the industry demonstrated staying power, private markets flourished as well. Manufacturers increased trailer width size to 10, 12, and then 14 feet, sacrificing mobility for the appeal of an inexpensive permanent home (Center for Auto Safety, 1975).

While builders of conventional (or "stick-built") housing directed their appeal to middle-income buyers through the 1960s, the lower end of the shelter market fell almost exclusively to mobile-home manufacturers (soon to become one of the nation's glamour industries). Annual trailer sales jumped by a factor of eight between 1961 and 1972, peaking at 576,000 units. Mobile homes constituted one-third of all new, single-family housing; more important, they represented almost 90 percent of all housing under $20,000 (Schlesinger, 1980).

Both factory-based manufacturers and on-site builders went through a structural upheaval in the conglomeration-happy 1960s. Although conditioned by traditionally sharp cycles, the strong and persistent demand for new homes occasioned a flood of new corporate entrants in the shelter business. In 1965, International Telephone & Telegraph purchased Levitt and Sons. The following year, Levitt became the first residential contractor to sell $100 million worth of houses. ITT's success drew a flock of imitators. Between 1964 and 1967, Boise Cascade acquired three contracting firms and replaced ITT as the nation's largest homebuilder. Westinghouse entered the field in 1966, followed by Alcoa and Reynolds Industries. By the early 1970s, the roster of industrial corporations active in residential construction consisted largely of *Fortune* 500 firms.

For the most part, corporate acquisition departments hunted for the largest and most sophisticated builders. Parent corporations generally stayed out of their new subsidiaries' affairs, content to provide additional capital and count the profits as they rolled in. "It's expected we will see the $100 billion year in residential construction in the coming decade," ITT–Levitt President Richard Wasserman rhapsodized in 1970. "That's a pretty big pie and all of us want our slice" (Keating, 1973).

Corporate optimism stemmed, in no small measure, from the announced intentions of the Johnson and Nixon administrations to remedy the nation's housing shortages and overcome the shelter industry's alleged technological backwardness. Inspired by European efforts to replace war-damaged housing stock with modular components and other forms of industrialized housing, Illinois Senator Paul Douglas suggested that the government underwrite a five-year test program of six or seven major housing systems. Douglas, chairman of the 1968 National Commission on Urban Problems, asserted that proper cost evaluation would then show "how much there is to this question of prefabrication." Government-sponsored market aggregation would solve the problems that had plagued Lustron, the Dymaxion, and other failed efforts. "We can't have mass production without a mass demand," Douglas said. "I don't see how you can get mass demand in the present fragmented state of the building industry unless the Government steps in and helps to finance at least the experimental programs" (Keating 1973).

In May 1969, the social engineering opportunity of a lifetime was placed in the lap of George Romney, secretary of HUD and former president of American Motors. Romney and his assistant, former NASA official Harold Finger, dubbed their program of subsidized prototypes "Operation Breakthrough," and announced their plans to aggregate the market, "rationalize" construction methods, and bring the residential construction industry into the Space Age.

Romney promoted Operation Breakthrough fervently. He believed that industrialized housing and modular building systems would replace outmoded production methods, stabilize production volume, reform an antiquated collective bargaining structure, lower the cost of housing, boost productivity, solve the urban housing supply dilemma, initiate more efficient land-use patterns, and provide the necessary economic stimulus to offset the recessionary consequences of disengaging from Vietnam. Romney promised a "revolution in housing construction unmatched since men came out of the caves and started building dwellings with their hands" (*San Francisco Chronicle*, Jan. 24, 1971).

Like most industry critics, Romney assumed that organization and scale were the industry's gravest weaknesses. His program favored corporations with expertise in large-scale operations over firms with building experience. General Electric, Alcoa, 3M, Republic Steel, Westinghouse, Singer, CNA Insurance, American Cyanamid, McCulloch Oil, Borg-Warner, TRW, Hercules, and Boise Cascade all had their hands in "Breakthrough" at one time or another. With HUD's encouragement, 5 of America's 20 largest corporations were building and selling houses by 1969. The magazine of the New York Stock Exchange was certain that "by the mid-70s, nearly all housing produced for the mass market will bear the trademark of a major national corporation" (*The Exchange*, May 1969).

Romney thought that his success at American Motors offered a perfect model. A HUD report opined that the "mobile home industry of today may resemble the U.S. automobile industry prior to the full impact of Henry Ford" (Keating, 1973). Even the marketing structures were assumed to be transferable. Romney told *Newsweek* in 1970 that the future promised a "franchise setup analogous to that of the auto industry, in which local dealers would handle the houses built by major manufacturers" (*Newsweek*, June 22, 1970).

Despite the high hopes and fanciful rhetoric, Breakthrough broke down rapidly. As early as the end of 1969, field reports of cost overruns were arriving in Washington. After two years and $20 million, not a single dwelling unit had been erected. Undaunted, Romney and his colleagues blamed the slow start on poor marketing and unwarranted consumer leeriness. In August 1971, HUD awarded 22 contracts worth a total of $63 million for 2,796 units. Three months later, Romney buoyantly predicted that if financing problems were resolved, three-quarters of all housing in the United States would soon be industrialized (*Engineering News-Record*, Sept. 2, 1971, and Nov. 11, 1971).

By late 1972, some of the contract winners had gone under, and public support was fading. The program's administrators had not anticipated the high start-up costs and the long-term commitment required. Nor were they able to counteract significant forces outside their control, in particular the January 1973 federal freeze on all subsidized housing. The worst blow, from Breakthrough's standpoint, was that the housing market collapsed in 1973–1974. By 1976, only 5 of the 22 sponsored systems were even on the market (*Engineering News-Record*, Dec. 2, 1976).

Perhaps no innovative housing program could have overcome the building slump of the mid-1970s, but Romney, Finger, and Co. were particularly ill suited to the task. Critical of the supposedly backward and myopic perspective of construction insiders, they viewed their unfamiliarity with homebuilding as an advantage. Unfettered by industry customs, they planned to use their experience in auto and aerospace to turn shelter production inside out. In fact, their arrogance and ignorance blinded them to the vitality of the existing industry and the time and complexity involved in establishing a sound industrialized housing alternative.

The final epitaph to Breakthrough was written in 1980. In a minimally publicized action, HUD demolished a 147-unit housing project in New Haven, Connecticut, designed by the noted architect Philip Johnson as a model of systems building for Breakthrough. Constructed in 1972, the project had required constant repair. Eventually, HUD determined that the costs of continued maintenance outweighed the demolition and replacement costs. A conventionally built project now stands on the ashes of "Breakthrough's" dreams.

Breakthrough's failure as a construction project, industrial policy, and promotional venture sobered many advocates of industrialized housing. Shep Robinson, *Professional Builder*'s columnist on manufactured housing, lamented: "The consumer and financial press was one of the important constituencies that was burned in the failure of Operation Breakthrough. While that program was underway, you couldn't find a newspaper or magazine in the country that wasn't high on manufactured housing. Similarly, from 1972 on, you could hardly find one that had anything nice to say" (*Professional Builder*, Sept. 1982).

The industry that emerged from the most concerted federal initiative to "reform" it was a curious hybrid. Many of the corporations that dabbled in homebuilding during the merger and acquisition boom of the late 1960s departed as quickly as they had entered. But the boom left an enduring imprint. Some major industrial corporations stayed in the shelter business; and more and more residential contractors, regardless of their corporate provenance, now conduct their affairs in a markedly different way. Contrary to Romney's vision of an exclusively factory-based industry, most of the megabuilders of the late 1970s and early 1980s achieved their status either as stick builders or by combining on-site and factory techniques. And though the get-big-or-get-out dynamic slowly has made the homebuilding industry more concentrated, the megabuilders have increased their market share through adroit financing and marketing schemes rather than an ability to create the American Motors-like production capacity envisioned during the Romney era.

Today, four kinds of firms compose the upper crust of homebuilding: (1) major industrials, conglomerates, and multiproduct companies whose housing interests are only a small portion of their overall enterprise; (2) vertically integrated companies that participate in the shelter trade from forest to financing; (3) large merchant builders (also called operative builders); and (4) mobile-home manufacturers, whose ranks have been penetrated, to some degree, by all three previously mentioned categories of builders.

## Conglomerates

The 62 largest homebuilders in 1981 were subsidiaries of such companies as Penn Central (Arvida Corp., $270 millon in sales), Philip Morris (Mission Viejo Co., $164 million as the largest homebuilder in booming Orange County, California), Aetna Life and Casualty (Ponderosa Homes, $141 million), General Electric (Trafalgar Developers of Florida, $122 million), Inland Steel (Inland Steel Urban Development Corp., $117 million), INA (M. J. Brock & Sons, $94 million), Foremost-McKesson (Foremost-McKesson Property Co., $90 million), and Olin (Olin-American Inc., $87 million) (*Professional Builder*, July 1982).

City Investing Corporation, the nation's fifth leading producer of for-sale housing in 1981, is representative of this collection of tobacco, food, insurance, steel, and electrical firms. City Investing's housing divisions—General Development, Wood Brothers Homes, and Guerdon Industries—contributed $672 million to the $6 billion total revenues the New York-based conglomerate reported in 1981. General Development (with offices in Miami) and Wood Brothers (operating out of Denver) built 4,500 detached and attached single-family homes in Florida, Arizona, Colorado, Texas, and other states in 1981. Guerdon Industries, of Louisville, sold 10,800 mobile homes, making it the sixth biggest trailer manufacturer in the United States. In addition to its homebuilding operations, City Investing's farflung interests include restaurants, insurance, the country's largest magazine printer, water heaters, motels, and the leading military contractor in Alabama. City Investing's two principal stockholders—TAMCO and Sharon Steel—have similarly diversified interests (Moskowitz, Katz, and Levering, 1982; *Business Week*, Nov. 2, 1981).

## Vertically Integrated Companies

Alongside companies like City Investing are the corporations that engage in all aspects of the shelter process; they control substantial landholdings, produce and sell building materials (especially wood products), and finance houses. These vertically integrated companies include Weyerhaeuser (Weyerhaeuser Real Estate, $407 million in 1981 sales); Jim Walter (Jim Walter Homes, $200 million); Genstar (Genstar Ltd., $161 million); Evans Products (Capp Homes and Ridge Homes, $144 million); and Boise Cascade (Boise Corp.,[3] $84 million) (*Professional Builder*, July 1982).

Weyerhaeuser is the world's largest private owner of timberland and one of the nation's largest producers of lumber and plywood. (Boise Cascade and Evans Products also rank among top U.S. wood-products manufacturers.) Genstar and Jim Walter make other building products, ranging from cement to roofing to drywall. Genstar and the timber companies branched into homebuilding as part of acquisition or diversification campaigns. Jim Walter took another path that constitutes one of the great corporate success stories of the postwar South—built, as most of these stories are, on the backs of poor and working people in the nation's poorest region.

In 1946, Jim Walter, a twenty-three-year-old navy veteran and citrus hauler, effectively began the shell housing business in the United States. Until then, Walter's building experience consisted of buying a tiny unfinished house in Tampa and selling it at a one-third markup three days later. Walter proceeded to capitalize on the voracious postwar appetite for housing. Holding the house lot as collateral, Walter's company framed and enclosed hundreds of shells, leaving the rest of the job to the customer. The formula succeeded spectacularly among cash-starved southerners; they could invest hours, skills, and tools in the houses that Jim half-built. However, the key ingredient in Walter's success was the deceptively high mortgage rates he charged, enforced by a coldly efficient collections policy. If customers could not make the exorbitant interest payments, Walter still came out ahead; the company simply seized the collateralized land.

By the early 1960s, Walter's Mid-State Investment Company had enlarged the company coffers with enough finance charges to set off an acquisitions binge. Walter bought three building-materials companies—Celotex, the Barrett Division of Allied Chemical, and U.S. Pipe and Foundry. By the end of the 1970s, Jim Walter owned two dozen building-product firms and offered the largest line of materials for residential, nonresidential, and remodeling markets in the United States. Walter still sells shell homes through more than a hundred offices in 20 states. More than 230,000 sales have been completed since 1946, and the company is now exploring the vacation and second-home markets (Williams, 1980).

## Merchant builders

The merchant builders have a narrower focus than City Investing or Jim Walter. The generation that survived Operation Breakthrough and the 1970s has concentrated on site-built shelter, adapting their product to the cyclical winds swirling over housing markets. There is still no General Motors of housing. But in the last decade, two Texas companies, Centex and U.S. Home, have expanded their operations and revenues to levels previously unmatched in American homebuilding.

Centex, led by its subsidiary Fox and Jacobs, built $400 million worth of single-family units during the depths of the 1981 housing depression. During the late 1970s, Fox and Jacobs put up two-thirds of all the new houses purchased by lower- and middle-income families in Dallas, Fort Worth, and Houston's hot housing markets. In addition, Centex owns cement and oil and gas divisions and, unlike most other giant merchant builders, has a nonresidential construction capacity that rivals its residential side. The company has ranked among the top 25 commercial builders, and in 1981 its nonresidential contracts fetched more revenues than its housing work (*Centex Corporation Annual Report*, 1982; Mayer, 1978).

At the turn of the decade, Houston-based U.S. Home became the first merchant builder to tally over $1 billion in sales. More than any other firm, U.S. Home has succeeded in developing homes on a truly national scope. Despite a deep housing depression, U.S. Home stuck with its expansion goals, and grew from an 11-state to a 25-state operation between 1978 and 1982. In November 1982, the company capped the spurt with the purchase of Brigadier Industries, the nation's seventh largest mobile-home manufacturer (*U.S. Home Annual Report*, 1983).

## Mobile-Home Manufacturers

Brigadier and other trailer producers have become attractive takeover-buyout targets as the mobile-home industry undergoes a dramatic revival. In the mid-1970s, the bottom fell out of trailer production; annual output was chopped in half, dozens of manufacturers folded, and 130,000 trailers were repossessed. But the sector slowly recovered, benefiting from changes in FHA and VA loan policies and local tax and zoning laws, and developing a two-tier market composed of a more affluent clientele and the manufacturers' traditional low-income customers. Today, the top 10 manufacturers of mobile homes—including Fleetwood Enterprises in California, Skyline Homes of Indiana, and Detroit's Champion Home Builders—account for one-third to two-fifths of total industry production, most of which occurs in the Southeast (Schlesinger, 1980).

Why have these companies—without benefit of significant market aggregation—succeeded where previous efforts to jack up the scale of homebuilding failed? And what makes their market share grow? The distinctive (and destructive) housing depression of the early 1980s reveals part of the answer to those questions.

In the standard building-slump scenario, small contractors are forced out of business and reenter homebuilding once interest rates and demand return to acceptable levels. The housing depression of the early 1980s, however, was more severe and prolonged than most of its predecessors. According to Guy Nielsen of New York's Marine Midland Bank, "the infrastructure of the industry has been seriously damaged . . . something like 40 percent of the builders have been casualties" (*Wall Street Transcript*, Aug. 2, 1982).

The slump belied the scenario in other ways: Some big builders actually grew healthier. As a result, it is likely that the giants will achieve a permanent gain in market share instead of the cyclical increase that accompanies busts and disappears as small contractors surge back into booming markets. Some observers attribute this trend to fundamental shifts in demographics and demand patterns. With both population and household formation growth expected to slow between 1985 and 1995, Shearson Loeb broker

David Wilson notes that "the small builder who has either been forced out of business or is about to be forced out, will be a little more reluctant about coming back into the game" (*Wall Street Transcript*: Aug. 2, 1982). But the shift in who dominates homebuilding stems more from new megabuilder strategies and characteristics than from pessimistic demand projections.

*Fortune*, George Romney, and others called for a revolution in construction methods, scale, and ownership in order to eliminate the cyclical constraints on homebuilding's supply side. "Modernize" that supply side, they suggested, and the industry will respond to heavy demand in an even, noncyclical fashion. It will, in effect, symbiotically help smooth the demand side's curves.

That prescription never has been applied successfully; in fact, Operation Breakthrough and similar, smaller efforts cast a reasonable doubt on the value of the prescription. But what may be much more compelling than the abortive practice of such theories is the fact that today's giant contractors have achieved their unprecedented scale (in some cases, very nearly the scale that *Fortune* and Romney dreamed of) through sophisticated *adaptations to, rather than the overthrow of*, housing's troublesome cycles.

In the past, the perilous workings of the market shackled the industry and allowed for the persistence of small-scale enterprise. The wildly fluctuating demand for housing and the absence of stabilizing government programs served as a brake on contractors who might otherwise have been tempted by dreams of highly capitalized building empires. Until recently, there was little incentive for builders to invest large sums in fixed capital in the face of the inevitable short-term downturn. Similarly, builders were reluctant to develop mass-production capabilities and a uniform product line so long as the idiosyncratic single-family house remained the cultural definition of the American Dream.

Now, utilizing product variety, geographic diversification, economies of scale, and, above all, astute financial machinations, the giants have revised traditions associated with the industry's adaptive character. Many of the megabuilders finally have the flexibility to ride the industry's waves and increasingly can determine their fate at the expense of smaller competitors.

The acquisition of Brigadier, for example, means that U.S. Home now builds nearly every kind of shelter. Other firms, such as Ryland, have established modular-home factories to complement their site-building operations. Still other companies, like Lennar of Florida, have stretched condominiums into new market categories. Lennar builds "convertibles"— condos for sale or rent depending on the customer's ability to qualify for a mortgage. Apartments, townhouses, condos, attached or detached houses, single-family or multifamily units, rental or for-sale, factory-built (in whole or in part) or site-built—many megabuilders can and do offer it all as a hedge against fickle interest rates and changing demand patterns.

In the last 10 years, many large builders have sought to expand their geographical markets while varying their product mix. Invariably they have looked south. In the Southeast, housing stock is newer than elsewhere, and residential building constitutes a higher percentage of total construction. Thus Frostbelt builders have followed population shifts. In 1982, 33 of the 50 top builders had headquarters in Arizona, California, Florida, or Texas, the four states generally regarded as supporting the most vibrant housing markets. Florida officials estimate that 90 percent of the state's homebuilders have moved in from out of state during the past 30 years (Adams, 1981).

But a merchant builder who puts all his eggs into a Sunbelt basket may be disappointed. The Southeast still has the nation's lowest incomes, widest disparities in wealth, and a number of unemployment-shocked areas. When housing starts declined 2.5 percent nationally between 1981 and 1982, they plummeted 14.0 percent in the eight-state Southeast. Even Florida, long the bellwether of builders' southern fantasies, suffered a 39 percent decline in starts between 1980 and 1982 (Salter, 1983).

In any case, the giants now build any type of shelter in several regions and can effectively dance away from depressed communities or follow the long-term population exodus to exurban areas within various sections of the country. Increasingly, this mobility is not restricted to our shores. Los Angeles-based Kaufman and Broad builds in France; Tidwell Industries of Alabama has tapped the Middle East and South African markets for mobile homes.[4]

The internationalization of American homebuilding is a two-way phenomenon. Subsidiaries of Canadian (Genstar and Cadillac Fairview) and Australian (Lend Lease Corp.) firms ranked among the top 100 U.S. residential contractors in 1982. The single largest shareholder in mammoth U.S. Home is Société de Maisons Phenix, France's largest single-family homebuilder.

Big builders enjoy significant advantages in the four major cost areas of housing: land, materials, money, and labor. Able to buy building materials in massive quantities, they get favorable unit prices. The same holds true for land acquisitions. U.S. Home has a three-year supply of land, consisting of 44,000 finished lots and options on 25,000 undeveloped lots with a total value of $315 million. U.S. Home and other companies (sometimes called "land banking operations") have used their superior financial position to hold land during slow periods and sell at inflated prices in the ensuing upswings. U.S. Home further protects itself against the vagaries of the land market by spinning off huge chunks of holdings to subsidiaries while retaining options to repurchase after development (*Southern Exposure*, Spring 1980).

Ultimately, these economies of scale derive from the megabuilders' ready access to cheap money. Smaller contractors depend on local lending sources for construction financing or a floating interest rate that usually hovers a few points above prime. But the giants tap into national capital markets and can raise long-term debt at fixed rates. Most important, they can convert borrowing power to lending power—offering customers seductively priced and termed mortgages through their own mortgage banking subsidiaries.

Each of the 10 leading homebuilders has created at least one mortgage subsidiary (U.S. Home has three), founded on a well-placed faith in the appeal of one-stop homebuying. Contractors need no advertising to attract borrowers, salespeople fill out mortgage applications while showing houses, and buyers are spared long and complex bouts with third-party lenders. As a consequence, megabuilders' earnings have soared. In 1982, Weyerhaeuser Real Estate's subsidiary was the nation's second biggest mortgage company, with a bulging portfolio worth $7.8 billion (Breckenfeld, 1982).

Most of the builders' mortgage banking operations were initiated in the early 1970s to facilitate sales. Since then, they have acquired a much greater importance for overall corporate well-being. Wearing their financier's hat, the giants lend money to homebuyers, package those loans into mortgage-backed bonds, sell the bonds to secondary-mortgage-market investors, and service the loans by collecting monthly payments and delivering them to the noteholders. Servicing charges net .75 percent per year of the loans' outstanding balance. That seemingly negligible figure turns out to be the source of many of the greatest profits during housing recessions. During the early 1980s, some megabuilders' mortgage divisions effectively cross-subsidized the company's homebuilding operations. For instance, U.S. Home lost $1.1 million on its construction operations during the first half of 1982, but the firm's principal mortgage banking subsidiary turned a first-half profit of $1.4 million (Breckenfeld, 1982; Therrien, 1983).

The importance of these profits cannot be underestimated. As late as 1979, U.S. Home and other builders (e.g., Ryland and American Continental) derived less than 2 percent of their total profits from mortgage operations. During the first half of 1982, those paper proceeds accounted for 51 percent of U.S. Home's profits, 29 percent of Ryland's, and 42 percent of American Continental's (Breckenfeld, 1982).

Mortgage banking also confers huge tax breaks. Since IRS regulations treat revenues from mortgage-backed bonds as installment sales, the bulk of the capital gains are sheltered from immediate taxation. The tax bill is whittled down and deferred, freeing the giants to use these funds to finance yet more housing starts. Kenneth Leventhal and Co., a Los Angeles construction management consultant, estimates that a builder big enough to float $95 million of mortgage-backed bonds can shelter 75 percent of $10 million in taxable revenues. "It used to be that the winner was the guy who had the lowest manufacturing costs and construction costs," remarks one housing analyst. "Now the winner is the guy who is the most sophisticated in arranging financing" (*Wall Street Transcript*, Aug. 2, 1982).

Earning profits from financing is only one product of managerial transformations in homebuilding. Residential construction now boasts faddish management techniques to accompany computerized accounting systems, property management, scheduling, and estimating. More and more, the people who preside over these systems have graduated from schools of soft, rather than hard, knocks. "The most significant event in the last decade has been the entrance of the MBA into the real estate–community development business," says Anthony Ettore of Miami's Arvida Corp. "Graduate business schools have discovered that real estate is one of the last frontiers. The entrance of the MBAs into the development and building businesses has made it a more advanced and sophisticated one, whether it be in marketing techniques, financial planning, accounting, or technology in engineering and construction" (*Professional Builder*, July 1982).

Homebuilding is also changing at the lower management levels; the people actually responsible for putting up the houses no longer necessarily come out of the field. Centex, for example, hired its chief construction supervisor from an engineering job at Procter & Gamble. "I didn't know a hammer from a 2 by 4," he told the *Wall Street Journal* in 1978. "Fox and Jacobs asked me why I thought I could build houses and I said, 'You take men, materials and the right equipment, and if you put them together in the right quantities you get soap. I figure you do the same to get houses'" (Simison, 1978).

Toll Brothers is a large-volume Pennsylvania builder owned and run by a pair of siblings who got into housing from careers in law and accounting. "We are cloning our managers to be total developers," says President Robert Toll. "We want them to be able to run our entire operation if needed." The Tolls use managerial discipline and a book for their genetic engineering. Every Monday night, the company's executives and managers meet to discuss the state of the Tolls' nine homebuilding divisions and to update the manual that is central to the operation. "The manuals are complete to the point that a person with relatively little experience in the building process could come into the company and build a house simply by studying the manual's content," *Professional Builder* reported admiringly (*Professional Builder*, July 1982).

## The Impact on Housing Consumers

All this industrialization may or may not help homebuilding firms function like the well-oiled machines they apparently believe American industrial corporations to be. What is apparent is the strain placed on the total cost of housing by the extra padding—conglomerate-scale compensation for chief executive officers, the ever-present MBAs, and the computer hardware. Megabuilders, according to *Professional Builder*, help pay their bills by charging one and a half times more than small builders do for land development (Adams, 1979).

What are homebuyers getting for their money? The limited shreds of evidence, cropping up in analyses by private and public sources, indicate that consumer satisfaction may be swept aside in the rush to bigness. The Federal Trade Commission has launched several far-reaching investigations into alleged substandard building practices and misleading warranties among the nation's large homebuilders. The commission's complete findings have not been opened to the public as of this writing (December 1984), but preliminary charges have been leveled against Kaufman and Broad, Jim Walter, and a number of other major builders.

Jim Walter is no stranger to these kinds of accusations. In 1979, Kentucky filed suit against Jim Walter for violations of the state's usury law, claiming the company charged interest rates 38 percent above the ceiling established for home mortgages under $15,000. In a separate action in the same year, Kentucky's attorney general took Walter to court for shoddy construction on 900 of the 2,100 houses the company built in the state between 1972 and 1978 (Williams, 1980).

For Jim Walter, pricing chicanery exacerbates shoddy construction and excessive finance charges. "Jim Walter charges to put on plywood corners as an option," explains Alan Fell, a former construction superintendent for Jim Walter Homes in southern West Virginia. "For eight sheets of plywood, they charge $400. Jim Walter Homes has a 100 percent markup on everything they put into a house. If we don't build the foundation, we charge $500 to put a house on top of their foundation. I don't think we tell the customer. It's just plugged into the price."[5] In a cover story on the industry in late 1983, *Business Week* asked a number of new homebuyers about their purchases. "The paint job in our house was terrible," complained Tammy Wampler, who bought a Ryan home in a Pittsburgh suburb. "They only put a primer on. It comes off like chalk." But, like many other young couples, the Wamplers ruefully recognized that the big builders offered the only packages they could afford. "We shopped for quite a while, but the older homes were too expensive. The Ryan financing was good. Without it we never could have bought a home" (*Business Week*, Nov. 7, 1983).

The Wamplers faced a typical conundrum, choosing between an admittedly unattractive house or giving up the dream of owning their own home. With the megabuilders in the driver's seat, the scope of the American housing dream is shrinking along with standard room sizes, total square footage, and lot acreage.

## The Impact on the Labor Process

The restructuring of the industry has affected the men and women who swing the hammers in the shelter industry, as well as the consumers. As control of the industry passes into bigger and fewer hands, and as consumer choice dwindles, the nation's building producers face a "rationalized" future of eroding craft skills and work autonomy. Although the organizational and technological changes have been dramatic, the actual practice of housebuilding has undergone evolutionary rather than revolutionary transformation. Building production has never advanced through singularly pathbreaking innovations, as steel did with the Bessemer process. Nor has there ever been a single sudden transformation of the organization of work, as was true in the auto industry with the introduction of the assembly line. Synthetic materials have replaced wood and stone; power tools have supplanted hand tools; entire crafts have disappeared, while new trades have sprung up to handle new materials.

Even if dazzled by the labor-saving machinery, baffled by the petroleum-based products, and annoyed by the lack of precision required in much of the installation, a late-nineteenth-century tradesman would not be entirely lost on a contemporary site. He would still recognize the application of basic construction principles and the use of some of the appropriate, time-tested tools. The skills of the building trades have not been totally submerged by mass-production counterparts. Instead, slowly but surely, the building worker has been shorn of many fabricating abilities and refashioned as an *installer* of parts manufactured on a factory floor. As a result, labor costs have plummeted as a portion of the price tag on a new house; between 1949 and 1980, labor costs declined from 33 percent to 16 percent of the price of a new house (*Economic News Notes*, May 1983).

Prefabrication now affects every aspect of construction. About 85 percent of all homebuilding incorporates some manufactured components. It has been years since carpenters built doors and windows on the job. Factory-made window units and prehung doors are trucked to the job, installed in an opening, checked for level and plumb, and nailed. The art of cutting individual roof rafters is applied only in expensive, custom-built homes. Most multiunit buildings or tracts of single-family houses use factory-built roof and floor trusses. The carpenter just fastens the finished product.

Today, the plumbers' pipe, elbows, and Ts are frequently made of poly-vinyl chloride (PVC), and the careful joining of lead with solder is reduced to a single dab of cement on the plastic pipe. Kitchen walls arrive prefabricated from the factory with all the rough plumbing and wiring built right into the walls. Plumbers attach toilets and sinks at one end and the water source at the other; electricians screw in light fixtures and outlets to the wall and wire the other end to the main panel.

In some cases, complete rooms are prefabricated. Rick Yoder, a Boston electrician, worked in a Westinghouse plant during the appliance maker's short-lived foray into the world of industrialized housing. The workers were young and untrained, the work was monotonous, wages were low ($3 to $5 an hour), and, in Yoder's words, "In half a day almost anyone could learn to do most of the things in there." The two products, prefabricated bathrooms and kitchens (complete with Westinghouse appliances and fixtures), "moved down on rollers and the materials were on each side. A guy would have his station and he'd do the same job over and over." The units were designed for multiunit apartments or townhouses. On a big job, the carpenters would frame the structure, build a floor, and leave a cavity for the prefab package. Yoder says they would "lower the unit with a crane, unpack the plastic, and presto, you'd have a bathroom. All that was left was hooking up the wiring and the plumbing."[6]

The advantages to the employer are obvious, as Dave Fox of Fox & Jacobs stresses:

> We design our house and our process so you don't need real high skills. We

don't need a man who's learned how to cut roofs and joists, how to build a window and order wood and do all the things a journeyman carpenter needs to know. Same thing for paint—we don't need a painter who knows how to mix paint and stain. They don't need—because of the way the work is laid out—to ask a whole lot of questions. (Mayer, 1978)

For all the changes on the job site, the pinnacle of no-questions home-building is the factory. John Kupfer of the National Association of Home Builders describes manufactured housing as "idiot-proof." "All the worker has to do," says Kupfer, "is reach back and put the material on the line. It's almost impossible to get it wrong."[7]

Taylor Homes, in rural North Carolina, is a ramshackle, hangarlike factory that produces 600 mobile homes a year. Inside, the sidewall crew frames and panels walls for the five or six units that roll up the line every day. Whenever the trailer model changes, the foreman lays one-by-two strips—labeled with framing and paneling specifications, window and door dimensions and locations, and wiring cutouts—into a channel on one side of the long assembly table. None of the framing has a name; there are no studs, plates, cripples, cats, sills, headers, blocks, or jacks. Everything is a "board," differentiated only by length markings.

Builders of mobile homes could call the appropriate board a cripple as easily as a 14½. But the power to name and withhold names is central to "rationalized" building. The work crews at Taylor Homes understand very little about what happens to the trailer once it passes beyond their work territory. There is no bonus for learning about other stages—let alone the entire process—and there are powerful penalties for curious eyes and wandering feet.

As mobile-home managers prohibit craft knowledge, technical skills, and the pleasure of manipulating tools at a comfortable and rhythmic pace, they do more than simply expand their control over and centrality to the production process. They also cheat consumers of quality. For generations, carpenters have built uniformly planed walls by sighting down studs and laying their crown up prior to assembly. At Taylor Homes, because each stud has already been notched (for wiring), the notched edge must be turned down, crown or no crown. Trailer walls therefore curl in and out, *caveat emptor* (Schlesinger, 1980).

Unlike many manufacturing industries, the robot does not symbolize modernization of the residential construction process. Instead, the changing nature of homebuilding is tied to the inexorable march of component production from the muck of the construction site to the assembly line inside the plant gates, where the factory worker represents the wave of the future.

## The Impact on the Work Force

For building trades people, the wave of the past has been nomadism. From the Colonial era to the present, they have "tramped" from job site to job site. A typical work history might include half a dozen employers in different towns in the same year.

Presumably, the compensation for this travel was high wages. Residential construction workers, though paid less than their counterparts in commercial and large-scale building, earned an average wage of $9.68 per hour in 1982 (*Employment and Earnings Supplement*, June 1983). But the industry's chronic instability renders hourly pay a useless indicator of general well-being. Nationwide, construction unemployment has reached double digits every year since 1975. On top of that, on-site production slows dramatically in the winter (even in the southern states); the unemployment rate generally runs four to five times higher in February than in August. The industry's factory sectors are affected as well. Orders slide down with the thermometer because precut, panelized, and modular producers require outside workers to install the products. All these factors considered, on-site tradespeople earn an average annual income roughly equivalent to that of an industrial worker.[8]

Almost 9 of every 10 construction craft workers are white men. For all the recent hoopla about nontraditional blue-collar work, women still constitute less than 2 percent of the work force. Blacks and other racial minorities made slight gains during the affirmative action battles of the 1960s and 1970s and now represent nearly 10 percent of the trades; but they continue to be locked into laboring or crafts long associated with token minority participation such as bricklaying, plastering, and painting (U.S. Bureau of Labor Statistics, 1980a).

The nomadic nature of the work is more than geographic. Depending on the job market, tradespeople flow back and forth from residential to more lucrative commercial and industrial projects. Skilled workers often accept homebuilding jobs only as a last resort after exhausting better-paying options. Consequently, many residential contractors function on the fringes of the labor market, employing a few veteran workers to watch over young and inexperienced crews. When nonresidential work picks up, the housebuilder is left to recruit new workers to the industry. "Most men come to me," reported a Buffalo, New York, builder in a common observation, "to get experience and then they'll leave after a year for more money" (Foster, 1972).

They leave because they cannot make a living. In fact, many workers drift in and out of the industry altogether. A Department of Labor study of 79,000 construction workers showed that only half were able to support themselves on construction earnings. Seasonal variations forced a constant search for supplemental income—as factory hands, salesmen, or service workers (U.S. Department of Labor, 1980).

Finally, building-trade workers' self-images and interests are shaped by the mobility built into the industry. Construction offers its participants a puzzling menu of limits and opportunities, including the popular option of owner building (in 1978, almost one-fifth of all U.S. housing starts were owner built). A significant number of building-trade workers have been employed by others, self-employed, or employers.

In 1977, there were 720,000 construction firms without payrolls. These mom-and-pop builders are no threat to U.S. Home, but collectively they managed to erect $20 billion worth of construction (U.S. Bureau of the Census, 1981c). Self-employed builders neither define nor influence the fundamental direction of the industry. They slide through the cracks left unfilled by the giants. Nevertheless, they represent a tangible and attainable dream for those who aspire to escape the status of hired hand. That dream underpins a construction culture in which distinctions between employers and employees are blurred, and the common concerns of everyone who builds for a living are routinely exaggerated.

The vast majority of building-trade workers collect a paycheck. But within that culture, even tradespeople who will never start their own business still harbor smaller designs of independence. Frequently, they work on their own in the evenings and on weekends. At some point in their working lives, they probably accept pay on a piecework basis—making them, in essence, subcontractors. They bid on small jobs—to replace a neighbor's worn-out water heater, to install an outside light fixture, or to fasten store-bought kitchen cabinets. They may order building materials, possibly pay others, or fight to collect payment on an overdue bill. They face, from a worm's-eye view, some of the issues confronting their employers, facilitating a process of identification between worker and boss.

For tradespeople, the paths of upward mobility and reentry into the world of the worker both track the building cycle. From 1972 to 1977—a peak to a valley in the cycle—the number of self-employed builders rose 36 percent, while the number of wage employees grew by only 2 percent (U.S. Department of Labor, 1981). Slumps carry an opposite, if less powerful, dynamic; they push the small-time builder back to the weekly pay envelope. (Construction experiences more bankruptcies than any other industry.)

Construction spokesmen treasure images of their industry as a holdout against the dominant, numbing, bureaucratized work world. "Construction is the Nation's single greatest industry," boasted executive W. A. Klinger, "its finest example of free-enterprise, free-wheeling, devil-take-the-hindermost [*sic*], highly competitive business" (Rubey and Milner, 1966). The button-down world of U.S. Home, Centex, City Investing, and the other giants belie Klinger's claim, but the individualist, anyone-can-rise-to-the-top ethos lives on. That ethos combined with multiple forms of mobility and the double-edged implication of craft identity inhibit employees' conception of themselves as permanent wage workers, thereby making collective action and trade organization difficult to achieve and sustain.

## The Impact on Labor Organizing

Despite the barriers to cohesion among construction workers, the building trades have a long history of labor organization. Unlike union drives in basic industries or large public-sector workplaces, organizing in construction has rarely relied on numerical strength or the power of the collective. Instead, bargaining leverage originated at the traditional high-skill level of the craft worker.

Dependent on worker skills and vulnerable to any interruption of their limited cash flow, building employers of the 1880s and 1890s were unable to resist the growth of unionism the way that their industrial brethren did. Blacklists and summary firings were common, but in the long run, small and medium-sized contractors did not have the free rein and raw economic power systematically to suppress signs of budding unionism. In fact, enlightened employers recognized that unions could be more than an unavoidable nuisance; they could serve as a solution to the chronic problem of a guaranteed labor supply.

Contractors' needs for workers fluctuate over the course of a building project, a building season, or a building cycle. Catering to employer hopes for flexibility in hiring and layoffs, the early building-trade unions offered to act as labor contractors in exchange for union recognition and collective bargaining agreements. Unions established apprenticeship standards to insure adequate training and hiring halls to dispatch workers as needed. Contractors were under no obligation to retain tradesmen past their usefulness on a particular project, and the union took responsibility for directing the laid-off worker to the next employer.

As early as 1894, major builders like Otto Eidlitz in New York suggested that it was "not only the right but the duty of labor to thoroughly organize itself, and it . . . is a power for good in the trade" (Eidlitz, 1894). Ten years later, the Carpenters Union had over 161,000 members. Commercial and multi-unit builders like Eidlitz were the easiest to sign up. But the early methods of organizing, based on recruiting individual tradesmen, meant that even the smaller crews of residential builders were organized. A 1936 Bureau of Labor Statistics study claimed that 57 percent of all residential construction workers were union members, with the highest concentration in the larger cities of the Northeast and on the West Coast (Sanford, 1937). Subsequent studies questioned this optimistic estimate but generally accepted that houses in urban industrial areas were often built by unionized workers.

The feverish post–World War II housing activity strengthened the unions' hand and produced the apex of union representation in homebuilding. In 1950, 65 percent of the employees of firms belonging to the National Association of Home Builders (NAHB) were union members. As many as two-thirds of all new houses were union built, and in many areas union control was virtually complete (Foster, 1972; Haber and Levinson, 1956).

Paradoxically, the postwar building boom laid the groundwork for the ultimate loss of union control. The insatiable demand for housing prompted hired hands to strike out on their own and become independent contractors. Don Danielson of the Carpenters Union explains, "A carpenter would say, 'I'll frame 'em up for so much a piece, I'll take eight or ten houses.' Then anything goes: one guy and four cousins, anybody can throw 'em up and sell it" (Mayer, 1978).

The work changed for those who stayed in the union as well. Commercial jobs increased in number and duration. Wages skyrocketed on multimillion-dollar projects, while residential wages lagged behind. With most union locals enjoying full employment, members tended to forgo the lower-paying, short-term housebuilding options.

Today, organized labor is almost irrelevant in the homebuilding industry. As the locus of residential work shifted to the inhospitable organizing climate of the Sunbelt, the unions lost their already faltering bases of strength. The final blow came with the open-shop drive in the 1970s, orchestrated by powerful construction users in the Business Roundtable and the Associated Builders and Contractors, a nonunion trade association. Attempting to assert control over wages, work rules, hiring, and training, and introducing such innovations as the "double-breasted" firm (a contractor with both union and nonunion divisions), the open-shop assault focused mainly on industrial construction but managed to eradicate most vestiges of unionized residential work in its wake. Generous estimates now credit only 10 to 15 percent of all new houses to unionized contractors. The most recent NAHB survey reports that 92 percent of their members deal with no unions at all (Northrup and Foster, 1975; Sumichrast, Ahluwalia, and Sheehan, 1979).

Even the highly skilled trades, which historically parlayed craft knowledge into union power, have not been able to withstand the open-shop drive. Polls by the Mechanical Contractors Association of America demonstrate how the nonunion movement has overpowered subcontractors who once worked on a union basis. Almost two-thirds of the surveyed firms reported that owners or general contractors had barred them from bidding on work because of their unionized employees. In 1977, these formerly all-union employers of plumbers and pipefitters conducted 64 percent of their residential and garden apartment work on a nonunion basis. The figure leaped to 88 percent in 1982 and to 91 percent in 1983 (*Engineering News-Record*, Dec. 9, 1982, and Jan. 5, 1984).

Although they build shelter, the nation's 50,000 mobile-home assemblers function outside the culture of the on-site construction worker. Assemblers are poorly paid and eminently replaceable factory hands living with a regular diet of speed-up, unsafe conditions, and minimal rewards. In 1982, they averaged $6.61 in hourly wages, more than a dollar less than the national average for all production workers (U.S. Bureau of Labor Statistics, 1983).

Speed is king in factory-based housing. At the Schult Homes plant in Polkton, North Carolina, the production manager "was hollering at somebody all the time," recalls Schult worker Susan Leviner. "He was yelling over the intercom, yelling at people, 'Hurry up, hurry up, hurry up.'" Leviner's husband described management's willingness to waste for the sake of the clock. "If they got a wall that don't fit they tear that wall to pieces. They just take it down, don't try to save it. They just throw it away."

Health and safety are chronic problems in the mobile-home industry. Dangers posed by toxic chemicals in glues and finishes are frequently matched by minimal physical plant safety precautions. Schult Homes, the nation's oldest trailer manufacturer, offers a good example at its Polkton plant, which glided along for years without an electrical ground on one side of the facility. "They didn't do anything about it until there was a guy using an electric saw and a drop cord to cut off the metal roof," remembers Susan Leviner. "When he cut it off it started shocking him. He hung on to a metal chain—he couldn't turn it loose—and fell off the metal catwalk right flat on his back on that cement floor."

Leviner had her own brush with company contempt. "My screwgun didn't have a ground and I'd been getting shocked, but they were telling me that I wasn't. One day I turned it on when I was standing on one of those metal vents and it knocked me on the floor. I got up, I couldn't talk. I was just numb. When I could talk, I told them I'm not working no more. I wasn't leaving, but I wasn't working no more until they did something about it"[9] (Schlesinger, 1980).

The list of grievances is long—among them, low wages, lack of security, and physical danger—yet the men and women who factory-build homes remain largely unorganized. John Kupfer of the NAHB estimates that fewer than a third of the manufactured housing plants are unionized, and most of those are in the urban–industrial belts of Michigan, Ohio, and Indiana.[10] Industry expansion continues to center near its rural southern areas where union organizing is difficult at best.

Operation Breakthrough's architects voiced hopes for a federally endorsed spirit of labor–management cooperation in the manufactured-housing industry. Walter Reuther, then president of the United Auto Workers, announced his support for the program as consistent with two major goals of his social agenda—increasing the availability of low-cost housing and organizing the unorganized. The UAW did sign agreements with several firms, but the significance of these contracts expired along with Breakthrough.

The UAW still represents some manufactured-housing workers, as does the Teamsters. But the bulk of union membership lies in affiliates of the Building and Construction Trades Department of the AFL–CIO, such as the Carpenters, Operating Engineers, and Electricians. Traditionally representing on-site construction workers, these unions have made organizing attempts among factory-based building workers as a logical extension of their jurisdictional claims. For example, the Industrial Department of the Carpenters Union has won union recognition at over fifty plants of mobile, prefab, and modular-home builders, including several owned by Commodore and Boise.

Although organizing triumphs are few and far between, housing manufacturers take few chances. Recognizing that small work crews present obstacles to organizing, employers apply some of the principles of their on-site colleagues. Ryland Homes, for example, has brought the form of outside work organization into their factories. In their new modular plant at Windsor, Maryland, Ryland has, according to John Kupfer of the NAHB, "brought into the plant all of the subcontractors that they had working for them, and then renegotiated contracts with them. There are 225 people working at the plant and the number of Ryland employees is something in the neighborhood of 25."[11] The handful of Ryland's people work in the tool cages, sweep the floors, and inspect the work. Even foremen are paid by subcontractors.

We have now come full circle from *Fortune*'s anguished cry for "bigness" and "scale." Ryland has discovered the potential benefits of the old and the new: small, autonomous subcontractors carrying out assembly-line production. "The people working on that line have done that kind of work for some time," says Kupfer. "They're paid on a production basis, and they don't have any problems with work rules and speed-ups. They get five houses up and they get paid for five. And so they're looking for ways to speed up the line, develop the work rules, and set the standards."[12]

Ryland limits its role to overseeing a system that compels workers to establish faster and looser working conditions. Employers will continue to be many and small-scale; employees will identify with bosses that they can see and talk to. It is piecework writ large, encouraging workers to define their interests in harmony with employer production goals. Ryland has managed to have its cake and eat it. "It gets around the union," Kupfer notes, "because there are no employees to unionize. Two hundred in a factory makes a company suitable for organization, but you know unions don't go after one with 10 or 15 employees."[13]

If Ryland's Windsor plant becomes a model, organizing factory workers and on-site builders will pose similar problems. Reacting to the growth of the open shop, several unions have kicked off organizing projects such as the Carpenters Co-ordinated Housing Organizing Program (Operation CHOP) and the combined building-trade unions' well-financed and well-publicized joint efforts in Houston and Los Angeles. A number of proposals have emerged, such as establishing dual wage rates for residential and nonresidential work. But, by and large, only one strategy has been acted on consistently—granting more and more concessions. Tom Owens, director of organizing for the Building and Construction Trades Department, proclaims, "Our only hope is to keep union contractors competitive with the non-union companies" (*Carpenter*, May 1978). Since open-shop firms have always established their pay scales as some proportion of the union rate (usually anywhere from one-half to one-third lower), these efforts are likely to produce only a generalized lower standard of living for union *and* nonunion construction workers.

Some leaders have offered more daring suggestions. Michael Lucas, national organizer for the International Brotherhood of Electrical Workers (IBEW), has called on unionists to take "a look at what the people did who built our unions" when they organized, one at a time, every worker who was part of the industry (*Engineering News-Record*, Nov. 24, 1983). But this basic tenet of organizing contradicts the postwar strategies of American construction unions. Satisfied to reap the harvest of the commercial and industrial boom, union officers and staffers concentrated on convincing contractors of the value of a union agreement and forgot the art of organizing workers.

The challenge of changed circumstances has not been met. "So far, we have not demonstrated our ability to organize," says J. C. Turner, head of the Operating Engineers (*Engineering News-Record*, Mar. 5, 1981). Although there is widespread recognition of a crisis, many building-trade union officers seem surprisingly sanguine and lackadaisical. Phil Conti, a Massachusetts contractor who has sat across the table from union business agents at countless bargaining sessions, expresses surprise at the general apathy and the lack of sanctions against union members who work for nonunion firms. "When I was young and first starting out," he comments, "they would not tolerate anything like that, but today the idea is to keep the guy happy so he will come to union meetings and vote you in as business agent."[14]

Occasional organizing victories occur, and contracts are signed, but the reassertion of a formidable union presence in residential construction is unlikely in the near future. Mobilizing the work force will require a quantum leap in organizing skills and a major shift of political will on the part of the unions. Although the unions' general conservatism and orientation toward employer concerns may be understandable in the light of the industry's structure and past practices, it is useless in the prevailing employer atmosphere of antiunion sentiment. For now, residential workers must fight their own isolated battles.

## Conclusion

Since the days of *Fortune's* postwar plaint, changes in the homebuilding industry's structure, construction methods, and industrial relations have been dramatic. Using a potent combination of financing schemes, marketing flexibility, and mixed-production methods, a generation of shelter firms has achieved the scale, the apparent permanence, and the industry-wide influence that eluded past aspirants. Yet underpinning this transformation is a foundation of constancy manifested by the durability of such industry fixtures as small working units, unstable markets, and elementary designs, tools, and engineering methods.

Along with the new corporate pecking order, this mixture of change and constancy has produced some unappealing side effects: diminished opportunities and choices for small homebuilders; de-skilled and disempowered tradespeople, many of whose working lives are characterized by job and income insecurity and diminishing work satisfaction; the eclipse of building-trade unions as effective organizing and representational vehicles; a frequent decline in the quality of housing stock; continuing high prices and narrowed consumer choices; and severe workplace safety hazards, especially in mobile-home factories.

These conditions reflect a fundamental flaw in the conventional wisdom, which held that a fairly undifferentiated brand of structural, scale, and technological change was the "cure" for homebuilding's ills. In many ways this prescription bypassed or obscured the larger question of what a healthy housing supply side should look like.

We begin with the assumption that the residential construction industry must be judged and shaped by its ability to produce sound, durable, plentiful, and reasonably priced shelter, consistent with other major social objectives. The producers (the carpenters, plumbers, and electricians) must be able to count on a decent and secure income, entry opportunities, a chance to maintain their independence and develop their capacity for self-organization, and a voice in shaping building technology. Economic stability must be accompanied by equity among members of the work force and between employers and employees, homebuyers and sellers.

None of this can occur without public policies that protect workers, strike a socially productive balance between labor- and capital-intensive construction methods, and establish and preserve disaggregated production and decision-making units responsible to local housing needs.

Toward these ends, the government must redefine its far-reaching but currently fragmented roles as construction buyer, technology subsidizer, health and safety regulator, education and training promoter, development planner, and labor relations legislator in order to provide the residential construction work force a maximum amount of safe and stable employment. Public policy should also guarantee the same degree of access to tax benefits and inexpensive credits for small, independent contractors and megabuilders alike.

A reorientation of this magnitude is unlikely unless government's fragmented approach to implenting shelter policy is made whole. That feat will be impossible without pressure from the bottom. Those most deeply affected by the industry—housing producers and consumers—have rarely identified their interests in common and are without either organization or influence to lobby successfully for reform. The occasional proposal to harmonize interests—such as the use of building-trade unions' pension funds to finance high-quality, low-cost housing built by union labor—only point up how unusual such an alliance is—in theory or in practice. Yet it is exactly those alliances of tradespeople, homebuyers, independent contractors, housing and tenant groups, and local governments that will have to be formed to press for plentiful and affordable housing, job creation, and a public agenda that demands more of America's builders than big firms and big profits.

# Notes

1. Interview with Tina Scheibel of U.S. Home, June 1983.
2. Levitt once described his two-year stint with the Seabees as a chance for that "little branch of the Navy that had the pleasure of my company" to learn "much more about building from me than I did from them." (*Fortune*, Aug. 1947).
3. Developed as a division of Boise-Cascade, the Boise Corp. is now formally owned by Boise Cascade Housing Division Management.
4. The Federation of South African Trade Unions has accused Tidwell of paying black workers poverty wages, withholding benefits, and firing union activists. Tidwell, which established a plant in the South African homeland of KwaZulu in February 1984, declined to sign the Sullivan principles but asserts that it is full compliance with South African law as well as its own principles of "justness and fairness." (Ironically, Tidwell Industries is headquartered in Winston County, Alabama, which seceded from the Confederacy in order to fight on the Union's side during the Civil War.)
5. Interview with Alan Fell, November 1980.
6. Interview with Richard Yoder, September 1982.
7. Interview with John Kupfer, executive director, Home Manufacturers Council, National Association of Home Builders, June 1983.
8. A 1975 Department of Labor study of construction workers concluded that the median number of hours worked per year was 1,535. Using that as a base measurement (reasonably valid, since unemployment has held fairly stable), average annual income would be $14,858.80 for 1982.
9. Construction is a deadly force. Though employing only 5 percent of the total work force, the industry is nonetheless responsible for 20 percent of all job-related fatalities. In addition, construction workers have the highest rate of injuries and illnesses of any group of workers (U.S. Bureau of Labor Statistics, 1980b).
10. Interview with Kupfer, June 1983.
11. Ibid.
12. Ibid.
13. Ibid.
14. Interview with Phil Conti, March 1983, as part of the Massachusetts Carpenters History Project. This material is included in *From Woodshed to High-Rise: The Story of Carpenters in Massachusetts* by Mark Erlich, forthcoming from Temple University Press. For further information, contact Mark Erlich, Carpenters History Project, 253 Lamartine Street, Jamaica Plain, MA 02130.

# 8

# Supply-Side Economics and Rents: Are Rental Housing Markets Truly Competitive?

*Richard P. Appelbaum*
*John I. Gilderbloom*

*In addition to examining the role of individual actors in the housing system, it is important to look at how these various actors interact to create the dynamics of the private housing market. This is the focus of the next three chapters. In each, conventional views of the private housing market are critiqued and new explanations for observed patterns are suggested.*

*Chapter 8 examines the relationship between rental housing supply and rent levels. Do increases in the supply of rental housing result in lowered rents? The authors contradict conventional economic theory in answering (and proving) no. Housing markets do not operate competitively for inherent structural reasons. Therefore, lifting government restrictions on housing production and land development will not make housing more available and will not lower rents as "supply-side" economists would have us believe.*

Under the conventionally accepted assumptions of economic theory, the price of a commodity under perfectly competitive market conditions is a function of both supply and demand. When a good is in short supply relative to demand, its price rises. This, in turn, creates unusually high profits, encouraging additional production of the scarce commodity. Supply then increases, and prices are once again bid down to an equilibrium level.

This chapter tests that model with respect to rental housing. Specifically, it examines the extent to which increases in rental housing supply do in fact result in lowered rents. First, the chapter presents a model of the idealized competitive conditions under which prices are expected to respond to changes in supply. Insofar as actual housing markets depart from this ideal, one would expect rents to fail to respond to changes in supply. This leads to a consideration of evidence concerning the actual competitiveness of rental housing markets, before discussion turns to an empirical test of the supply-side thesis.

To state our conclusions briefly in advance: We do not believe that in many urban housing markets, new construction by itself will help reduce rents. We say this for two reasons. First, and probably more significant, rents and prices are determined in large part by factors that are extra-local in nature—primarily the state of the national construction industry, along with the availability and cost of housing credit. We return to this issue at the end of the chapter, but our principal focus is on a second set of factors: local conditions that impede market responsiveness to changes in supply. We seek to demonstrate that such impediments result largely from the *social relations* that characterize most housing markets—relations among landlords, and relations between landlords and tenants.

It is especially important to make this argument at the present time because of the widely held belief that housing inflation is caused by one type of restraint on local supply: "excessive" government restrictions on the "free" operation of housing markets. We argue that this form of restraint is relatively minor in significance, relative to other barriers to market competition. Our view is not widely held in either academic or policy circles. The prevailing belief is made most forcefully in Bernard Frieden's *The Environmental Protection Hustle* (1979), but it is echoed in diverse quarters. The President's Commission on Housing (1981, ii), for example, singles out "construction standards, environmental restrictions, Davis-Bacon wage requirements, the Federal Flood Insurance Program, municipal rent control and condominium/cooperative conversion laws, and local land-use policies" as major causes of the housing crisis. [*For a different view of rent control, see Chapter 9 by David Bartelt and Ronald Lawson.*] This diagnosis carries with it a simple prescription: Encourage a

> stable economic environment for homebuilding by reducing restrictions on the industry and terminating excessive regulation of land development and housing production. The free market would then be able to provide housing at lower prices and thereby make housing more widely available. These measures will enable the market to meet future housing demand. (1981, 3–4)

The National Association of Home Builders (1982a, 5) claims that "as much as 30 percent of the cost of a new home may result from unproductive and unnecessary government regulations and resultant delays"; the National Association of Realtors (n.d., i) pegs the figures at 20 percent. (Both figures are arbitrarily arrived at with no basis in systematic research.)

The Pacific Institute, a conservative think tank, has assembled an entire volume of articles that seek to demonstrate that growth controls, land-use planning, and even zoning are the villains (Johnson, 1982). Although the argument has strong bipartisan support (it was accepted by President Carter's Task Force on Housing—see U.S. HUD, 1979d), it is most consistent with the overall policies of the Reagan administration, which call for deregulation, urban enterprise zones, and dismantling all governmental controls over the private sector.

It is because we question the supply-side assumptions on which these policies are based and are concerned with their implications for local control that we are led to analyze the relationship between housing supply and rents.

# Rental Housing Markets Are Not Competitive

As noted, in order for increases in supply to result in lower rents, *ceteris paribus*, it is necessary for competitive market conditions to exist. Under such conditions, newly constructed housing, even if expensive, permits cheaper units to "filter down" as more expensive units are occupied by persons who would otherwise be living in less expensive ones. As cheaper units are vacated, they become available to consumers farther down the line—and so on, until housing trickles down to the poorest. As sellers compete with one another, so the reasoning goes, prices sink to a level that reflects costs, acceptable profit margins, and characteristics of the particular unit (e.g., location, quality, size, amenities). Other things being equal, as the relative supply increases, landlords are forced to compete with one another in a "buyers' market." Profit margins are squeezed, incentives mount to cut costs, and the savings are passed along to tenants in the form of lowered rents.

What competitive conditions are necessary for prices to respond freely to changes in supply? Olsen (1973, 228–29), in a frequently cited work, enumerates seven conditions that must be fulfilled. In discussing these factors, we are not interested in simply examining the extent to which actual housing markets are likely to depart from the perfectly competitive model, but, more specifically, in hypothesizing just how such departures are likely to influence rents.

1. *Both buyers and sellers of housing services are numerous.* Typically, renters (buyers) are numerous, unknown to one another, and compete fully with one another for housing. The ownership of rental housing, however, is often concentrated in a relatively small number of hands, affording the possibility of market control. Studies of Cambridge, Massachusetts (Mollenkopf and Pynoos, 1973), Santa Barbara, California (Appelbaum and Glasser, 1982; Linson, 1978), and Orange, New Jersey (Gilderbloom and Keating, 1982) have found that fewer than fifty owners typically account for over half the rental housing stock. Large owners are in a position to administer prices in oligopolistic fashion. That is, a relatively small number of owners may raise prices in order to increase their total revenues; since there is no significant competition, consumers have little choice but to pay the higher prices.

2. *Individual transactions are small relative to the total market.* If a significant proportion of available rental units are negotiated in a single transaction, such a transaction will have a substantial impact on the availability of units throughout the market and hence the average rental price. In fact, with a few unimportant exceptions,[1] this is unlikely to occur, since as a rule housing units are rented individually.

3. *Collusion is absent.* Here again, as with the first condition, the rela-

tionship between landlords and tenants is asymmetrical. Tenants are typically dispersed and unorganized, and do not speak with a unified voice in the
negotiation of rental agreements (Dreier and Atlas, 1980, 19; Heskin,
1981b, 95–106). There are very few instances of tenant unions playing an
active role in rent setting or even mediation. Rent strikes generally have
been unsuccessful in the United States (Lipsky, 1970; Marcuse, 1981b).
While the burgeoning tenants' movement may some day alter this situation,
at present rent controls, eviction protections, and habitability guarantees
are minimal to nonexistent in most places. Landlords, on the other hand, are
in a much more favorable position, passively or actively, to coordinate rent
structures. To the degree that ownership is concentrated, this may be
accomplished directly by tacit or even explicit agreement among the few
individuals who dominate the local housing market. Such actions are reinforced by a variety of social and professional mechanisms. For example,
local landlord associations routinely share informal norms for rent setting.
The process is often explicit, as when the trade journal *Real Estate Review*
urged annual increases of 15 percent for the period from 1979 to 1982
(Garrigan, 1978, 40–44). In Santa Barbara, California, the local Apartment
Owners' Association instructed members during a meeting on "where,
when, how, and by what dollar amount to raise rents" (Dreier, Gilderbloom, and Appelbaum, 1980, 169). In California, statewide apartment-
owner groups in the early 1980s urged landlords to raise rents according to
annual increases in the full Consumer Price Index, then running at 15 to 18
percent.

Nationally, such organizations as the National Association of Realtors'
Institute of Real Estate Management (IREM) help to educate landlords
through hundreds of publications, cassette tapes, and similar materials. An
examination of such materials is instructive. In one pamphlet, for example,
IREM (Kelley, 1975) criticizes owners for not raising rents sufficiently,
arguing that rents should "keep up with the economy . . . the most common accepted index [being] the Consumer Price Index." The pamphlet
further urges property managers to "act together," concluding with the
following advice:

> Here's a tip: when you raise rents, send a notice to your competition. It's the
> best mail they'll get all day. Everyone is afraid to be the first to increase rents.
> Once your competition sees you doing it, they'll very likely follow suit, thus
> making the rent increase a fact of life for all tenants.

Management companies, which operate units for many different owners,
are further able to reduce competition by administering uniform rent structures. Although few studies have examined the effects of management
companies on rents, those that have all find rents to be significantly higher in
managed versus nonmanaged units. Ipcar (1974, 11), for example, finds
rents in managed units to be from 6 percent to 14 percent higher in East
Lansing, Michigan, apartments. Dreier, Gilderbloom, and Appelbaum
(1980) report that five management companies, accounting for three-

quarters of all large (10-plus unit) apartment complexes in Isla Vista, California, met annually to discuss rent increases for their units. They further note (1980, 169) that large management firms in Boston were being sued for routinely colluding in the setting of rents. Appelbaum and Glasser (1982, 8–9) report that throughout much of the 1970s, rents in managed units in Isla Vista were higher than those in nonmanaged units. In a study of the same rental market, Gray (1979) estimates that managment companies charge $168 a year per unit more than it costs owners who manage their units themselves.

We are not arguing that housing markets are monopolistic, merely that ownership concentration and social networks permit a far greater degree of price coordination than is ordinarily assumed to exist. How does such concentration and networking influence rents? The answer to this question depends on the degree of vacancy in a particular market. In general, the higher the vacancy rate, the greater the amount of market control, price coordination, or both required to maintain high rents in the face of weak demand. At sufficiently high vacancy levels, presumably no amount of market control or price coordination would suffice to control prices effectively. Conversely, when vacancy rates are extremely low, very little formal coordination and control is necessary to maintain high rents.

In other words, a tradeoff occurs between scarcity, on the one hand, and the ability of landlords to administer prices, on the other. The greater the scarcity, the fewer formal mechanisms are required to maintain high rents. The greater the relative abundance of housing, the more extensive such formal mechanisms must be. The final sections of this chapter empirically examine this tradeoff, suggesting that housing markets do not actually behave "competitively" until vacancy rates of 9 percent or greater are achieved.

4. *Entry into and exit from the market are free for both producers and consumers.* Consumers of rental housing face many barriers to mobility. Most obvious are discriminatory practices of various sorts, which close off large segments of the housing market to families with children, racial minorities, the poor, or others deemed "undesirable" from the landlord's point of view. As a result, lower-income tenants pay proportionally more for their rental units, regardless of the quality of those units (see, e.g., Vaughan, 1968, 81–82).

Under competitive conditions, when the price of a commodity goes up, the consumer has the choice of either reducing consumption or switching to a substitute product. With a necessity such as housing, the former option implies a reduction in living standard, including overcrowding, fewer amenities, reduced maintenance, or some combination of the three. The latter option is seldom available: Few tenants are able to afford houses or condominiums; other solutions (conversion of garages, construction of backyard units) are outlawed on health and safety grounds. Even moving is seldom a viable option: Comparably priced units are likely to be scarce and, in addition to the economic costs, moving entails such noneconomic costs as broken social ties, lost neighborhood attachments, and the uprooting of children to different schools.

Landlords, however, are relatively free to move in and out of the rental housing business, responding directly to changes in market conditions. In most places, landlords retain the right to convert rental units to condominiums or nonresidential uses, to demolish units, to upgrade units out of the reach of low-income renters, to resell units at higher prices, to raise rents without restriction, to restrict rentals arbitrarily to particular categories of tenants, and to evict without just cause. As a result of this imbalance, tenants have very little leverage in the competitive determination of rents.

5. *Both producers and consumers possess perfect knowledge of the market and take advantage of every opportunity to increase profits and utility, respectively*. Tenants' knowledge of prevailing rents is usually based on fragmentary information obtained from newspaper advertisements and hearsay. Since tenants are seldom in a position to devote much time to systematic data gathering, they often "make do" with whatever is available to them, especially if rental units are scarce.[2] It is likely that a heavy reliance on newspaper ads imparts an upward bias to rentals, since less expensive units are often passed on by word of mouth. Most tenants therefore come to believe that average rents are higher than they actually are, and are therefore willing to pay more, in what becomes a self-fulfilling expectation of high rents.

Among owners, small landlords are often in a similar position to tenants.[3] As owners of only a few units, from which they derive long-term rental income, they are less likely to have full knowledge of market conditions. To the extent that they rely on newspaper ads for their general knowledge of the rental market, small landlords, like tenants, may acquire an upward bias in their expectations. Such landlords often develop personal relationships with their tenants (Krohn et al., 1977). To the extent this happens, they may be more willing to negotiate rents, and rents in their apartments may as a result be below market. Larger landlords are more likely to approach housing as short-term investors. Because of their financial stake, degree of market control, and overall professional orientation, they are usually well informed on market rent structures. Indeed, in some cases the largest landlords conduct market surveys to provide direction in the setting of rents (see Dreier, Gilderbloom, and Appelbaum, 1980, 169). Also, as noted, both formal and informal mechanisms facilitate the exchange of information among landlords.

In counterposing tenants as poorly informed (hence, weak) consumers to well-informed and well-organized professional landlords, we are again arguing that the former are at a competitive disadvantage vis-à-vis the latter. This, in turn, makes rents less responsive to changes in supply.

6. *Artificial constraints on supply and prices are absent*. Our earlier research indicates that local regulations are not a *major* factor in the determination of prices and rents (Appelbaum and Gilderbloom, 1983; Gilderbloom, 1980, 1981a, 1982). Although our views run counter to prevailing

opinions,[4] it is supported by the findings of one of the most thorough studies to date on the topic.[5] Based on our review of a number of studies,[6] we conclude that local land-use regulations, including growth controls, are responsible for no more than 15 percent of differences in price between areas, and probably considerably less.

Another form of artificial constraint on supply and price, *nonlocal* in nature, exerts a significant impact on prices and rents: National monetary and tax policies strongly influence the profitability of housing, the cost of construction and mortgage finance, and the rate at which property is resold for tax-sheltering purposes. From a purely local point of view, for example, high interest rates constitute an exogenous price constraint: Interest rates are unresponsive to local conditions, and will not come down if demand slackens as a result of the higher local prices. An increase in interest rates from 10 percent to 15 percent, for example, raises the monthly carrying costs of a conventional 30-year mortgage by 44 percent. Rising interest rates also raise the cost of construction, sales prices, and other consumer credit.[7] While high mortgage interest rates may reduce demand for owner-occupied dwellings, this demand is simply transferred on to the rental sector, where it helps to push rents still higher. People are limited in their ability to forgo housing consumption, and the demand for rental housing in particular is relatively price inelastic.

The effect of tax laws on high housing costs is equally significant, as the following summary from a recent study by the Congressional Budget Office (U.S. Congress, CBO, 1981, xii) makes clear:

> One study [Hendershott and Hu, 1980] suggests that as much as one-third of the owner-occupied housing in the United States as of 1976–1977 would not have been built if tax benefits had not lowered the after-tax cost of buying a house far below the cost of other investment assets. Other research [Hendershott and Schilling, 1980; Rosen, 1978; Rosen and Rosen, 1980] suggests that the fraction of homes that are owned by their occupants would be 4 to 5 percentage points less without the mortgage interest and property tax tax deductions, and without the exclusion of net imputed rental income. *Studies also indicate that households would buy less expensive houses in the absence of tax subsidies, and that housing prices might be lower.* [*Emphasis added.*]

Federal tax laws favoring homeownership indirectly affect the supply of rental housing as well. As inflation pushes households into higher tax brackets, homeowner deductions acquire increased importance, encouraging higher-income households to become homeowners. As a consequence, the remaining renters are of relatively lower income and therefore are unable to afford the rising rents necessary to induce investment in rental housing. Apartment owners respond with pressures to convert apartments to more profitable condominiums (U.S. Congress, Congressional Budget Office, 1981, 32–36).

7. *Housing is a homogeneous commodity*. Housing is not a homogeneous commodity, in which all units are equivalent substitutes. A house is unique

because of its amenities, size, architecture, age, quality, and neighborhood, as well as its location within a neighborhood. It would be difficult to find an exactly equal substitute for any particular house. As Olsen (1973, 229) concludes: "Most scholars would probably find [homogeneity] to be the least plausible assumption." He further notes that the attempt by housing economists to deal with this problem through redefining housing as a composite package of discretely commensurable attributes that yield a calculable "housing service" is also questionable (1973, 229).

In crucial respects rental housing markets are not perfectly competitive, and as a consequence, rents will not respond in any straightforward manner to changes in supply. The next section empirically examines the relationship between selected supply indicators and rents in an effort to determine just how much of a vacancy factor is necessary before markets in fact do begin to respond to increases in supply with lowered rents.

## Housing Supply, Vacancy, and Rents

The previous section listed seven reasons why rental housing markets are far from competitive. Therefore, new construction by itself will not necessarily result in lowered rents, or even lower rates of rent increase. Table 8.1 reports the results of an investigation into the relationship between rents and a number of characteristics of urbanized housing markets in 1970.[8] In this analysis, we examined all urbanized areas in the contiguous 48 states that satisfied two criteria: their central cities contained at least 50,000 residents, and they were located at least 20 miles from the nearest neighboring city of over 50,000. In this fashion we hoped to be able to examine relatively self-contained housing market areas—that is, markets relatively free from the disturbing effects of neighboring metropolitan areas. There are 134 such housing market areas in the 48 states; our analysis is based on the 115 areas for which we were able to acquire data on all the relevant variables.

Housing market analysts who stress the importance of supply predict that, other things being equal, rents are lower in housing market areas characterized by a relative abundance of rental housing. Accordingly, on the *supply side* we included the following indicators:[9]

1. *Rental housing vacancy rates*, a measure of scarcity
2. *New construction*, computed as the percentage of the rental housing stock built during the preceding five years (1965–1970)
3. *The proportion of housing stock in rental units*, intended as a measure of the degree of "professionalization" of the local housing markets (larger markets tend to be more professionalized)

On the *demand side*, a number of factors serve to bid up the price of rental housing.

1. *Urbanized area population*, since the greater number of amenities offered in larger places often serve to drive rents up (see Appelbaum, 1978, 29–37; Hoch, 1972)
2. *Median family income*, since rent levels are often determined by ability to pay (Anderson and Crocker, 1971; Appelbaum, 1978; Ball, 1973; Harvey, 1973; Stegman and Sumka, 1976; Vaughan, 1968; Witte, 1975)
3. *Population growth rate (1960–1970)*, since faster-growing places have higher demand for housing (Appelbaum, 1978, 37; King and Mieszcowski, 1973; Stegman and Sumka, 1976)
4. *Regional differences*, since numerous studies in the early 1970s found rents to be lower in the South
5. *Submarkets of blacks and Latinos*, since discriminatory practices and segregated housing markets may affect the rent structures confronted by minorities (Anderson and Crocker, 1971; Ridker and Henning, 1968; Stegman and Sumka, 1976; Susser, 1982)
6. *The quality of the housing stock*, as indexed by dilapidation (percentage rental units lacking adequate plumbing) and age (percentage built before 1940), since lower quality presumably is reflected in lower rents (see Anderson and Crocker, 1971; Cubbin, 1970; Kain and Quigley, 1970; Stegman and Sumka, 1976; Wilkinson, 1971)

We have estimated these effects through a linear multiple regression analysis. The results should be taken as provisional: A fully adequate analysis would examine intracity variation in rents over time, as a function of new construction and other local and nonlocal characteristics, such as regional construction trends, interest rates, and demographic conditions.[10] Table 8.1 presents the unstandardized beta (*b*) regression coefficients for all 115 places in the analysis. On the righthand side we utilize these coefficients to predict the *annual* change in rents associated with a 10 percent increase in each independent variable, computed at the mean for that variable. We present both the absolute (dollar) change in rents and the percentage this represents of the overall average rent for all cities ($100.83).[11]

Looking first at the indicators of *demand* for rental housing, we note that while five are statistically significant at *p* = .05, only two have a sizable impact: median income and location in the South. When all other indicators are taken into account, a 10 percent increase in median income between urbanized areas is associated with a nearly equivalent percentage increase in rent (8.6 percent) at the mean—an annual difference of $104.52. Rents in the South, on the other hand, are on the average $109.68 per year (or 9.1 percent) lower than elsewhere.[12] Growth, while highly significant statistically, only accounts for minor differences in rent once the other influences are considered (a 10 percent increase in growth rate is associated with a $4.20 annual increase in rents—about 0.3 percent). Similarly, while an older housing stock is significantly associated with lower rents, the difference again is small in absolute terms (−$8.16, or −0.7 percent). Interestingly, population size is of no significance in the equation.

TABLE 8.1
FACTORS AFFECTING MEDIAN RENTS, U.S. URBAN AREAS, 1970
(N = 115 areas)

| Indicator | REGRESSION STATISTICS | | AGGREGATE VALUES | | ANNUAL CHANGE IN RENTS ASSOCIATED WITH 10% INCREASE IN X (AT MEAN FOR X) | |
|---|---|---|---|---|---|---|
| | $b$ | $F$ | Mean | s.d. | Amount ($) | Percentage |
| *"Demand" indicators* | | | | | | |
| Population | -0.0000 | 0.8 | 310,039 | 330,467 | $ -0.96 | -0.1% |
| Median income | 0.0092$^c$ | 124.6 | $9,491 | $11,156 | 104.52 | 8.6 |
| % black, Latino | -0.0800 | 2.7 | 22.6% | 17.6% | -2.16 | -0.2 |
| South (1 = South, 0 = otherwise) | -9.1446$^c$ | 22.2 | 45.2% | 50.0% | -109.68 | -9.1 |
| % growth 1960-1970 | 0.1814$^c$ | 28.3 | 19.1% | 25.5% | 4.20 | 0.3 |
| % units 30+ years old | -0.1639$^b$ | 10.6 | 41.3% | 18.4% | -8.16 | -0.7 |
| % units without plumbing | 0.3391$^a$ | 6.2 | 5.2% | 7.8% | 2.16 | 0.2 |
| *"Supply" indicators* | | | | | | |
| % units vacant for rent | 0.4163 | 1.9 | 8.1% | 2.6% | 4.08 | 0.3 |
| % rentals built 1965-1970 | 0.6602$^c$ | 25.2 | 14.0% | 6.3% | 11.04 | 0.9 |
| % housing stock rental | 0.3541$^b$ | 9.4 | 38.4% | 6.4% | 16.32 | 1.3 |

Constant = -4.1104. Multiple $R^2$ (adj.) = .87. ($F$=77.5). Dependent variable: 1970 median rent (average for all 115 areas: $100.83).

$^a$ ≤ .05.
$^b$ ≤ .01.
$^c$ ≤ .001.

When we turn to the indicators of *supply*, however, the results are surprising. Counter to conventional economic expectations, rents are *not* found to be lower in places that have experienced relatively favorable supply conditions. On the contrary, vacancy rate is unrelated to rents, whereas rents are slightly higher ($11.04 per year, or 0.9 percent) in places with a large percentage of their rental housing stock recently constructed and with larger percentages of their housing stock for rent ($16.32, or 1.3 percent).[13] These results strongly suggest that policies simply aimed at increasing the rental housing stock will not guarantee lower rents.

How do we explain these findings? Although one would expect new construction to be highest in areas where rents are also high, our findings are consistent with a different conclusion: A large volume of new construction in these communities was apparently *followed* as well as preceded by *higher* rents. It is always risky to infer causal processes from cross-sectional analyses, but we are nonetheless led to this conclusion by the following reasoning: The relationship between rents at the beginning of the decade and new construction during the latter half is modest ($r = .28$), suggesting that the former in fact exerts a weak influence on the latter. Moreover, when we controlled for the effect of 1960 rents by including it in the regression equation, we found that the association between new construction and 1970 rents, far from being reduced, was in fact increased. This indicates that the impact of new construction on rent levels is strengthened, once prior differentials in rent among communities are controlled.

The relationship between vacancy rate and rent is ambiguous. High vacancy (an index of relatively favorable supply conditions) is not associated with lower rents, although there may be several reasons for this. It may indeed be the case that, under most conditions, the formal and informal ties among landlords serve to restrain competition, as we suggested earlier. It is also true that for certain classes of landlords, a low or zero vacancy rate may not be an economically optimal situation, and in fact some level of vacancy may be temporarily maintained as a matter of rational business strategy.[14] We merely note that to the extent landlords deliberately maintain vacancies in apartments, one would expect this variable to be unrelated to rents.

Why is there a positive relationship between new construction and rents? Although we have no hard data on this issue, we offer the following hypothesis: Rather than lower rents through increasing relative supply, new construction may often replace existing, cheaper units. In the short run, it is also possible that the construction of more expensive units has a price-leading or "ripple" effect, whereby existing landlords raise rents to match those being sought in the new housing.[15]

The final supply variable is the proportion of the housing stock that is available for rent. The higher this proportion, the higher the rent levels. Our hypothesis is that smaller markets may be less attractive to large, professional investors than larger ones, simply because fewer investment opportunities exist in the former. To the extent that this is true, this variable indexes the degree of "professionalization" of such investment in an area. The next section explores the significance of such "professionalization" for rents.

## Why Rents Rise, Despite Increases in Supply

We may represent the determinants of rents schematically as follows: To a large degree, rents are determined by institutional constraints that are extra-local in character and therefore constitute part of an *external environment* that is effectively beyond local control. This environment constitutes the general framework within which rents are set. It includes such factors as mortgage interest rates, credit availability, and federal income tax policy regarding deductions and depreciation allowances. In addition to having a direct impact on the landlord's costs and revenues, these factors contribute indirectly to costs by determining the relative attractiveness of real estate as an investment. In recent years, they have resulted in tremendous speculative pressures on land. Because credit and tax policies are nonlocal in character, they are, at least in the short run, perceived as given.[16] Additionally, local policies concerning property taxes and regulations of various sorts constitute a part of the framework. Since these policies are less distant and more direct in their impact, as well as subject to local influence, they are likely to be held responsible for local housing conditions, although their relative importance may in fact be small, as we have argued.

Counterposed to these institutional determinants is the *individual* element in the setting of rents.[17] This results from market imperfections of the sorts we have reviewed. Because housing is a necessity, the potential for price administration always exists, particularly in market areas where competition has been artificially reduced. Ownership concentration, management companies, professional associations, and informal networks among landlords all constitute mechanisms that interfere with the competitive operation of the marketplace, serving to maintain rents at higher levels than would be the case with perfect competition. While the bottom-line figure is largely given by the institutional constraints we have described, the latitude for individual discretion reflects these purely local conditions.

The individual landlord's response in turn reflects his or her own economic stake in rental housing. At one extreme are large (often professional) investors, for whom rental property is merely one possibility in a portfolio of investments. Such investors are largely interested in short-term returns, deriving maximum advantage from the tax-sheltering aspects of real estate investment. Generally, their rate of return must be relatively high, since alternative investments always beckon.[18] This pushes rents up, both through speculative pressures and the need to maintain a competitively profitable cash-flow picture. Such landlords are likely to be large in scale and therefore, in a strategic position to administer rents in a community.

At the other extreme are small landlords who are primarily interested in long term income potential, rather than short-term capital gains. These landlords are most likely to develop personal ties with their tenants, preferring a long-term relationship even if it means charging below-market rents. They are also under less pressure to raise rents frequently, both because their long-term property holdings result in relatively low monthly mortgage payments and because their alternative investment horizons are limited.

Within certain limits, landlords have a degree of latitude in determining rent levels. Under conditions of perfect competition, rents in the long run would settle towards the cost of supplying rental housing, with a sufficient profit margin to make rental housing attractive relative to other possible investments. But, for the reasons demonstrated above, conditions are far from competitive. As a result, rents do not reflect simple supply and demand. Monopoly profits may be the result.

It is important to reemphasize that the high cost of rental housing has little to do with local supply conditions. While a very high vacancy rate may help restore competition and drive rents down, we have shown that for vacancy rates well in excess of 5 percent (and possibly as high as 9 percent), rents do not respond to changes in supply. However much local building restrictions may appear to add to construction and maintenance costs, we seriously question the contention that they are a significant factor in escalating rents. To the extent that rents reflect local market imperfections, these are likely to result from *private* interventions rather than *public* interferences.

# Acknowledgments

Research for this chapter was supported by funds from the National Science Foundation, the Seed Fund, the Sunflower Foundation, and W. H. Ferry.

# Notes

1. One exception might occur when a large block of units is put on the market for a single "customer," as in the case of employee housing. Such instances are infrequent, however.

2. The difficulties of obtaining adequate information have been compounded in recent years by the proliferation of fee-for-service rent-search companies, which often replace private listings with ads that are outdated or otherwise misleading and cannot be confirmed without paying a membership fee to the company.

3. Krohn et al. (1977, 1–9) locate what they term a "dual economy" in rental housing, distinguishing between the "national professional" and "local amateur" sectors. Their discussion parallels our own, although they go further in tracing the characteristics and implications of such a split.

4. See, for example, Frech, 1982; Frech and Lafferty, 1976; Frieden, 1979; Gruen and Gruen, 1977; Johnston, Schwartz, and Klinkner, 1977; the Preface to the President's Commission on Housing, 1981; or the essays collected in Johnson (1982).

5. Schwartz et al. (1979, 54–59) conclude that housing prices in growth-controlled Petaluma, California, are only 7 to 8 percent higher than in neighboring communities,

once other factors are controlled. The authors further urge caution in generalizing from their results, since they acknowledge that unrelated market factors might account for the observed difference in prices.

6. See Keating (n.d.) for a recent annotated review of studies concerning the relationship between local land-use and environmental regulations and housing prices. Some two dozen studies are reviewed, with widely varying methodologies and assumptions. Not surprisingly, their conclusions vary considerably as well.

7. For a discussion of the effects of high interest rates on the housing sector, see Janczyk, 1980.

8. We are at present updating this analysis with 1980 census data. The 1970 data do provide an interesting test of our hypotheses, however, since that was a year of relative abundance in national rental housing: The overall national rental vacancy rate was 6.7 percent. We also note that none of the cities we examined had rent control, while growth controls were limited to large-lot zoning in residential suburbs. Thus, supply factors were strong during this period and local governmental restrictions minimal.

9. For a full discussion of the source and importance of all variables used in the analysis, see Appelbaum and Gilderbloom, 1984.

10. One of the authors (Appelbaum) is currently using time-series techniques to analyze quarterly changes between 1970 and 1981 in 20 California housing markets. We also note that in a cross-sectional analysis such as this, one cannot empirically determine whether the observed price differentials are the result of "permanent market phenomena or simply manifestations of adjustment lags" (Stegman and Sumka, 1976, 149).

11. The absolute dollar amount of change is simply the product of the unstandardized beta coefficient ($b$) and 10 percent of the mean value of the independent ($x$) variable, multiplied by 12 to annualize the result. Thus, for example, the mean value of median income for the 115 urbanized areas is $9,491. A 10 percent increase in median income is equal to $949.10. Multiplying this number times the beta ($b$) coefficient (.0092) yields a monthly rent increase of $8.71. Multiplying this figure in turn by 12 months gives an annual rent differential of $104.52. The same reasoning is applied where percentages are involved—that is, a 1.9 percent increase in the decennial growth rate (10 percent of 19.1 percent) is associated with a $4.20 annual increase in median rents (.1814 × 1.91 × 12).

12. The movement of industry to the Sunbelt during the past decade might well have attenuated this difference, since the South has been the recipient of considerable growth (and hence demand) in recent years.

13. Since our objective is to measure the effects of supply variables on self-contained housing markets at the aggregate level, we do not examine the interplay of supply and demand factors within urbanized areas. We can therefore draw no conclusions concerning the applicability of our findings to housing submarkets, such as those confronted by blacks or other minority groups.

14. Gilderbloom and Keating (1982), in their study of Orange, New Jersey, found that the owners of large apartments often temporarily maintained vacancies for two reasons: (1) to "test" the market (under the assumption that if all units are filled, their rents may be too low); and (2) to assure that all units were filled with "desirable" tenants (i.e., those with stable incomes and other preferred characteristics).

15. In the long run, presumably, market adjustments would eliminate this effect. When we included a variable in the regression equation that measured the percentage of apartment units built in the five years preceding 1965, for example, we found no significant relationship between this variable and 1970 rents.

16. To the extent that the real estate, housebuilding, and rental industries are effective in lobbying at the federal level, national tax and credit policies are subject to change, but this is unlikely to be a factor in local decisions about rent setting.

17. With few exceptions, very little empirical research has been conducted on the

processes by which rents are determined (for some exceptions, see Clark, Heskin, and Manuel, 1980; Krohn and Fleming, 1972; Manzer and Krohn, 1973; Stegman and Sumka, 1976; Susser, 1982; Vaughan, 1968). One of the authors of the present study conducted a series of interviews with landlords in Orange, New Jersey. In this section we summarize those results (for a full discussion, see Gilderbloom, 1982).

18. During the recent period of extremely high interest, "safe yield" investments in the form of government securities or liquid money market funds, a before-tax return of 18 percent on real estate investments would have been considered minimal by most investors.

# 9

# Rent Control and Abandonment in New York City: A Look at the Evidence

*David Bartelt*
*Ronald Lawson*

*One of the popularly held explanations of multifamily building abandonment is that it is caused by government rent regulation. This chapter challenges the link between rent control and abandonment. It finds that far more significant than rent regulation in producing abandonment are the residents' low incomes, creating a situation of insufficient effective housing demand.*

Opponents of rent control[1] have consistently charged that it is a significant, if not the principal, cause of housing abandonment and have cited New York City as the major example of this link (see Gilderbloom, 1981a, for a compendium of these charges). Our argument does not establish an alternative causal model of abandonment; we suggest instead that rent regulations have had only limited effect on housing abandonment and, further, that the data others have used to establish this supposed link demonstrate that factors other than rent regulations seem to be much more significant in generating abandonment. [*For further analysis of the causes of abandonment, see Chapter 10 by Ann Meyerson.*]

The roots of the argument that abandonment is the by-product of rent regulations are to be found in the political struggle over those regulations. As such, we see the link between rent regulation and housing abandonment, not as a necessary outcome of inhibitions on a "free market" of rental housing, but as a classic example of what Edelman (1980) has called "symbolic politics": Rent control became a politically manipulated symbol, central to the political objectives of the real estate lobby, a major constituency in the New York City political process. In this context, the symbol emerged as a kind of economic reality, with developers and bankers alike blaming rent control for their withholding of capital investment (although, in fact, this has been a long-term response to the availability of investments

An earlier version of this chapter first appeared as "Rent Control and Abandonment: A Second Look at the Evidence," in *Journal of Urban Affairs*, Fall 1982, 49–64.

that show a better return than housing, and had also occurred in many cities without rent regulations—see Sternlieb, 1970; U.S. Comptroller General, GAO, 1978a).

The argument linking abandonment to rent control can be summarized as follows: (1) Rent regulations constitute a subsidy to tenants of regulated apartments by their landlords; (2) this subsidy has a suppressive effect on landlord income, especially in lower-income housing (where the relatively poorer condition of the housing creates higher maintenance expenses); therefore, (3) rent regulations exacerbate the crisis of poor-quality housing by creating a no-win situation for the landlord. Caught in the income–cost squeeze, abandonment becomes an attractive option.

The question then becomes, To what extent does the available evidence confirm or contradict the link between rent control and abandonment? Roistacher (1972), analyzing the 1968 Housing and Vacancy Survey of New York City, has argued that rent regulations could hardly have been the root cause of housing abandonment. Her key finding was that in the housing inhabited by lower-income groups, which presumably was most vulnerable to abandonment, very few differences showed up between controlled and unregulated rent levels. Two factors were at work here: First, the income level of tenants placed a limit on the rent that could be demanded by the landlord, especially in areas where housing quality was on the decline, and second, because poorer tenants moved more frequently, the rents of their housing had increased more steeply than those of higher-income groups. As a result of turnover provisions, allowing substantial rent increase with each change of tenancy, poorer tenants tended to have abnormally high rents in controlled housing. While Roistacher, like Lowry and his associates (1971), found that, in general, landlords subsidized rent-controlled tenants, this subsidy was not present among renters of the class of housing where abandonment was in the offing. Roistacher provided substantial evidence that low income was the source of the gap between actual rents and economic rents (rents necessary for adequate maintenance and satisfactory profits) for the landlord, and her data suggested that, at that time, the removal of controls would have produced very limited rent increases among low-income tenants.

In a later study, Roistacher (1978) attempted to model the rent control–abandonment relationship. Using data from the period of vacancy decontrol between 1971 and 1974, when all regulated apartments became "free market" on vacancy, she estimated rents that would have accrued to landlords had all rent regulations been removed, and if the controlled stock had acted similarly to the decontrolled stock in the market. These rent estimates were generated irrespective of tenant income; that is, she predicted market rent for apartments then under some form of regulation. By comparing this theoretical rent level with the household characteristics of the occupants then in the housing, she obtained dramatic results. Specifically, she found that 77 percent of the aggregate theoretical increase in rents in the controlled stock and 82 percent of the increase in the stabilized stock[2] would be expected to come from households with incomes below $10,000 a year. Thus it is doubtful that these theoretical increases could in fact be realized.

Similar conclusions have been drawn by Stegman (1982a, 156–57): "Even with rent regulation, 57 percent of all renters in New York spend [in 1981] at least one-quarter of their incomes for housing. This suggests that for the foreseeable future, the more serious challenge to creating and maintaining a healthy rental market might be incomes, not the unresponsiveness of rent regulations to the costs of doing business."

An additional issue is raised by Roistacher who points out that the removal of rent regulations would not necessarily be translated into better-quality housing. That is, only if landlords' long-run prospects were affected by deregulation would there be much incentive either to upgrade properties or to reduce tax-delinquency levels. She argues that "where a neighborhood is in a disinvestment stage, the removal of controls is not likely to be an adequate incentive to overcome the disincentive to investment which results from neighborhood externalities" (1978, 29); and, in summary, "deregulation may not reduce tax delinquencies, may not promote building maintenance, but will result in higher rents which will dislocate households and/or place relatively heavy rent burdens on lower income groups" (1978, 31).

Thus, based on Roistacher's argument, deregulating the rental market would not guarantee that the abandonment process would cease, as there is no necessary connection between increased rents and maintenance expenditures.

Opponents of rent control have overlooked a serious problem facing New York City and its policy community—a problem of a housing stock that is too costly for its income base, whether or not rent regulations are in force. The recognition that what exists here is primarily an income problem, not a regulatory one, is a first step toward the development of strategies that could subsidize rents to the levels necessary for maintaining property. To the extent that the distribution of income is strongly fixed, then landlords' alternatives lie not so much in the abolition of rent regulations or the displacement of poor populations from one neighborhood or city to another, as with some increase in the amount of rent that tenants can pay.

The presumed relationship between rent regulations and abandonment is, in the main, a symbolic one, developed in the midst of landlord opposition to continued controls. The evidence is strikingly clear on one point: The removal of regulations is not likely to affect the levels of abandonment, and the institution of controls is unlikely to produce abandonment to any significant extent.

# Notes

1. Rent control in New York City dates back to 1920 (Spencer, forthcoming). Controls in effect during the late 1960s originated in 1943 amid the severe housing pressures of World War II, as part of the federal system of wartime price controls. When

the housing pressures continued during the postwar economic revival, New York State continued a strong system of rent control, but limited coverage to units built before 1947 in order not to inhibit the building of new housing. This system froze rent levels, except for a 15 percent increase at turnover, and could reduce rents for landlords who did not maintain their properties. Apart from the fact that the administration of the system was turned over to the city in 1962 (and then in 1984 was turned back to the state), and that across-the-board rent increases were allowed twice in 25 years, this system continued relatively unchanged until 1971. Key to the continuation of rent control during those years was the concept of a *housing emergency* operationally defined as a vacancy rate of less than 5 percent. Since the city's vacancy rate varied between 1.23 percent and 3.19 percent during these years, the emergency situation required for extension of the law was clearly demonstrated by mandated housing surveys (Marcuse, 1979b, 101).

2. "Rent stabilization," a form of industry self-regulation, was introduced in 1969; under this system, rent increases in buildings having six or more units built in the 1947–1969 period were limited by a formula tied to cost-of-living increases.

# 10

# Housing Abandonment: The Role of Institutional Mortgage Lenders

*Ann Meyerson*

*Building abandonment by landlords continues, despite the highly visible growth of gentrification in many older cities in the United States. As indicated in the previous chapter on the role of rent regulation in abandonment, there is considerable debate as to its causes, which has direct bearing on possible policy initiatives. This chapter reviews and critiques the prevailing theoretical literature on abandonment. The role of institutional mortgage lenders as mediators between broad economic and structural change, on the one hand, and neighborhood decay, on the other, is examined in detail.*

With all the talk of gentrification transforming the cores of many of our older industrial cities, one might view the problem of landlord abandonment of inner-city housing as *passé*. Has the phenomenon disappeared in reality as well as from public awareness? To anyone who has traveled recently in such cities, the answer is no. Abandonment continues, but its pace and geographic distribution have changed over the past 5 or 10 years. The cores of many cities that had previously experienced abandonment or decline (or government-initiated urban renewal spurred by decline) are, to a large extent, becoming gentrified. Abandonment is moving more and more to the middle rings—to the outer boroughs in New York City's case—squeezed between the gentrified core and the suburban periphery.[1]

This chapter, however, does not inquire into why abandonment continues to exist side by side with gentrification. Instead, it analyzes the phenomenon of housing abandonment itself, which first appeared as a distinct process in the late 1960s and dramatically increased in the early 1970s. The chapter attempts to conceptualize a new approach to abandonment starting from a review of the prevailing literature. Upon analysis, this literature fails to explain persuasively certain aspects of abandonment, such as its timing—the decisiveness, abruptness, and totalness with which it occurred in the early 1970s—and its occurrence in sound, relatively new structures that had not experienced a prior period of neglect. Relatedly, the literature does not seem to give proper weight to the role of financial institutions in shaping or initiating the abandonment process. Virtually all analysts agree that financial institutions play an important role in the functioning of inner-city housing markets, but many fail to integrate the role of these institutions into a theoretical understanding of the process. Recent events in the world of housing finance—the collapse of many institutional mortgage lenders and the restructuring of the industry as a result of problems stemming from an unprecedented period of rising interest rates, which originated around the same time as the first signs of abandonment [*see Chapter 4 by Ann Meyerson*]—make the past role of lenders in inner-city housing markets all the more worth reexamining.

The reconceptualized theory of abandonment put forth here suggests that lenders, far from following the market, as much of the prevailing literature postulates, have to a large extent played a leading role in the abandonment process. This leading role stems from their larger role as mediators of the macroeconomy. On the inner-city neighborhood level, they have been carrying out the effects both of complex transformations of the urbanization process and the deep structural "crisis of capitalism" that took place during the 1960s and 1970s. In David Harvey's words, "events of national import were being transmitted via the financial superstructure into the decision environments of local housing submarkets" (1975, 152).

The logic and coherence imposed on the urbanization process by the mediations of financial institutions go far toward explaining some of the questions raised above, such as the timing of abandonment. Because financial institutions have been pivotal in responding to crises in the capital accumulation process through their urban infrastructure investment behavior, and because they are very sensitive to conditions in capital markets, by necessity they played a key role in abandonment. More specifically, in mediating larger forces that were undergoing profound change, they were in a unique position to have an impact on inner-city housing markets rather abruptly. For example, by being drawn, in their capacity as mortgage lenders, to the suburban periphery and the Sunbelt because of changes taking place in the location of economic activity, and later being drawn to more liquid, nonmortgage assets as a result of rising interest rates, they affected mortgage availability in their historic, local, inner-city markets, which in turn influenced landlord abandonment.

Illustrative support for this view of the role of lenders in abandonment can be found by examining the investment behavior of New York City, in particular Bronx-based, savings institutions during the 1960s and early 1970s. Their apparent response to factors independent of conditions of neighborhood decline lends support to their mediating and initiating role in the abandonment process.

## Theories of Abandonment

First, it is necessary to define housing abandonment. Although it occurs with all kinds of properties, from single-family houses (when the resident owner walks away) to multifamily rental properties (when the landlord walks away), this discussion is primarily concerned with the latter. Abandonment of such properties occurs when an owner stops putting money into a building—stops paying maintenance and operating expenses, making mortgage payments, paying real estate taxes—and no longer expects to be able to collect rents or sell the property.

The literature on abandonment, so defined, can be divided among three kinds of theory: (1) dual theory; (2) orthodox economic theory; and (3) political–economic theory. The concern here is generally with the views of the causes of abandonment and, more specifically, the role of financial institutions.

## Dual Theory

Dual theory emphasizes social factors as primary in the decline or abandonment process. It postulates that there is essentially a behavioral foundation or cultural explanation for the economic decisions that result in decline. For example, it focuses on the personal relationships between landlords and tenants, the breakdown of which becomes the driving force behind neighborhood change (see Krohn and Fleming, 1972; Solomon and Vandell, 1982, 85; Vandell et al., 1974). Financial institutions enter the picture, if at all, after the landlord–tenant equilibrium has broken down and landlords have begun to undermaintain.

## Orthodox Economic Theory

The neoclassical residential land-use theory side of orthodox economic theory relies on the concept of filtering and consumer sovereignty to explain neighborhood change. It sees patterns in the growth and decline of neighborhoods as inevitable, "natural" events. Although institutional actors in the real estate system—landlords, financial institutions, noninstitutional lenders, realtors, government agencies, and so forth—are central, they are often portrayed more as reacting to market forces than shaping them.

According to this theory,[2] the household decision to leave the neighborhood triggers decline and abandonment.

> The real force behind neighborhood change is the impact of people moving in, moving out, deciding to stay or deciding to look elsewhere for housing. The dynamics of the neighborhood change process revolve around the household decision. Other people (bankers, brokers) make decisions and they are important and often critical, but it is the change in the resident population and the decisions behind that, that fuel the neighborhood change process. (U.S. HUD, 1975, 14)

And:

> The household decision is made on the basis of the household response to its own internal circumstances (and changes in them), to the feedback from its

present neighborhood and the people associated with it, and to the observation of conditions in the metropolitan area as a whole. (U.S. HUD, 1975, 16)

Owners–investors, for example, enter the picture in terms of reducing maintenance fairly late in the process, having been affected by households leaving and absentee ownership increasing. Bank redlining (a specific kind of intermediary action), moreover, enters in even farther along, *after* owners–investors have responded to the changing neighborhood.

According to this analysis, the process is inevitable once households leave and are not replaced by similar households. All the other actors passively "go with the flow."

Consumer sovereignty theory thus tends almost to exclude supply-side factors in its emphasis on the demand side. Although consumer preference clearly plays an important role in the neighborhood change process, this theory tends to take consumer preference at face value and not explore the structural or systemic conditions that influence those preferences.

Comparing this neoclassical orthodox theory with more mainstream orthodox theory on neighborhood decline or abandonment further helps reveal the problem of explicitly excluding supply-side factors. For example, Solomon and Vandell (1982, 84–85), in describing orthodox economic theory, and after discussing the demand-side factors covered above, include the supply side of the market as follows: "Supply side factors which may precipitate the decline process include relative increases in all capital and operating costs which affect a landlord's cash flows, hence the cost of supplying a unit of housing services."[3] Supply-side variables influence a landlord's costs, and demand-side variables influence a landlord's revenues. Either one can precipitate decline:

> Either declining demand or increasing costs of supplying housing services or both act to reduce an owner's net cash flow below that needed to offset the opportunity for more profitable investment elsewhere. . . . Landlords' expectations of the future are reduced, resulting in greater discounting of future returns. Maximization of profit strategies dictate that the landlord minimize his costs through disinvesting. This may take place in a short-term "end game" which quickly results in abandonment, or, in the case of greater commitment to the neighborhood, in a very long period of gradual decline. (Vandell et al., 1974, 24).

Thus, within orthodox economic theory one sees the theoretical focus shift from the household decision to move to the disinvestment activities of landlords. These phenomena are not mutually exclusive: Consumer preference and filtering clearly find a place within the interactive dynamic just described. The emphasis is shifted, however, with important implications for analyzing cause-and-effect relationships and developing intervention strategies. It is important to add that this more broadly construed orthodox theory also allows a major role for the actions of financial institutions as part of the supply-side factors.[4]

## Political–Economic Theory

Implicitly conflicting with both dual theory and orthodox economic theories of neighborhood change are political–economic theories. The fundamental critique they make of orthodox theory is that the latter separates market behavior from the institutional or class environment in which it operates. Within this framework, one can identify two prongs to the political–economic approach.

Some analysts have found that investment and disinvestment trends are by no means "natural," that institutional actors in fact shape rather than respond to market forces. As Bradford and Rubinowitz (1975, 79) state in their study of investment–disinvestment:

> While there is no Napoleon who sits in a position of control over the fate of the neighborhood, there is enough control by, and integration of, the investment and development actors of the real estate industry that their decisions go beyond the response and actually shape that market.

Similarly, Neil Smith states the following, in analyzing gentrification, a local housing market process not that dissimilar in principle from abandonment:

> Gentrification may be initiated in a given neighborhood by several different actors in the land and housing market. And here we come back to the relationship between production and consumption, for the empirical evidence suggests strongly that the process is initiated not by the exercise of those individual consumer preferences much beloved of neoclassical economists, but by some form of collective social action at the neighborhood level. . . . With private market gentrification, one or more financial institutions will reverse a long-standing redlining policy and actively target a neighborhood for construction loans and mortgages. All the consumer preference in the world will amount to nought unless this long absent source of funding reappears; mortgage capital is a prerequisite. Of course, this mortgage capital must be borrowed by willing consumers exercising some preference or another. But these preferences are not prerequisites since they can be socially created. . . . Along with financial institutions, professional developers have acted as the collective initiative behind gentrification. A developer will purchase a substantial proportion of the properties in a neighborhood, rehabilitate them, and sell them for a profit. (Smith, 1979, 545–46; see also Beauregard, 1986; Smith 1986) [*See also Chapter 6 by Barry Checkoway and Chapter 5 by Joe R. Feagin.*]

Furthermore, this political–economic literature emphasizes the central role of structural, macroeconomic trends stemming from the capital accumulation process. In other words, the needs of production—specifically, the need to earn profit—generate certain spatial–structural changes that profoundly determine consumer preference and landlord decision-making and thereby contribute to inner-city housing abandonment. Some of the broad trends affecting abandonment include suburbanization—involving population shifts; deindustrialization—involving labor market and income shifts; changes in public services and local government policies—involving disinvestment in selected neighborhoods ("planned shrinkage"); and differential land values alternatively discouraging and encouraging investment (Smith, 1979). These changes do not "naturally" emerge from the market but stem from the capital accumulation process, which is itself organized by institutional actors. The changes are in turn further utilized according to the necessities of the accumulation process.

To be sure, orthodox economic theorists also attribute a decline in demand to larger objective forces, such as

> the availability of residential alternatives on the suburban fringe; generally rising incomes; greater accessibility to distant locations through new transportation systems; the movement of jobs and industry out of the central city; the negative externalities of urban life . . . ; racial prejudice; the age and obsolescence of inner-city structures; the inferior quality of services and amenities in the inner city. . . . (Vandell et al., 1974, 21)

In the political–economic literature, however, these larger forces are primary in determining owner–investor, intermediary and household behavior, not secondary to personal circumstances or predilections. But, more important, it is not merely the fact of these structural conditions that is important in understanding the causes of abandonment but their emergence out of, and utilization by, the capital accumulation process. The consumer sovereignty view as well as broader orthodox economic theory do not emphasize or even locate the needs of production or private profit-oriented interests in the abandonment process. By leaving the profit drive (and its consequences) out of the whole host of *producers* active in the urban development process and focusing almost exclusively on *consumers*, they distort the true motive behind inner-city abandonment.

Several analysts have illuminated this political–economic, structural perspective on neighborhood change through various studies of urban development. The Fainsteins, in discussing the causes of urban disinvestment during the 1960s and 1970s, emphasize the principal role of the increasing domination of central-city space by blacks and Hispanics. But instead of seeing the presence of this population as producing individual racism and "white flight" (as well as alleged vandalism, etc.), as the orthodox theorists would postulate, the Fainsteins state the following:

> Because these populations were only a limited source of profitability for employers, merchants, and property owners, cities began to experience serious problems of both accumulation and realization. Labor elsewhere provided a higher return; tax revenues declined relatively and absolutely; retailing died; and the tenement landlord began to experience severe difficulty in meeting his costs. (Fainstein and Fainstein, 1982, 171)

Urban renewal was in part designed to remove these "drains on the economic base" (Fainstein and Fainstein 1982, 171). Thus, the analysis goes beyond stating the fact of the trend and describing behavioral reactions, to examine its material base and some of the underlying profit motives involved. Similarly, Piven and Cloward (1971) analyze the in-migration of low-income and unskilled blacks and Hispanics to northern cities as ultimately linked to the processes of agricultural mechanization in the South and rapid industrialization in developing regions such as Puerto Rico. The newcomers were largely made obsolete by these developments, which were motivated by profit maximization on the part of private firms.

Regarding the trend of suburbanization, often seen as the "filtering" mechanism producing unwanted, abandoned housing, Patrick Ashton (1978) provides an analysis that is quite different from that of the orthodox economic theorists. He sees the outmigration of middle-class whites as having its roots in earlier industrial decentralization. In so doing, it grew out of the needs of particular private profit-making interests. Ashton thus implicitly argues that mass suburbanization did not simply, if at all, stem from the preference on the part of middle-income, middle-class whites for space (single-family homeownership, trees, and a yard). [*See also Chapter 6 by Barry Checkoway.*] Whereas early upper-class suburban living was motivated by "a deteriorating quality of life, mounting taxes, and a loss of political control" (Ashton, 1978, 69), widespread development of suburbs in the early twentieth century essentially stemmed from the movement of industry out of the large cities (Ashton, 1978, 70). This movement, in turn, stemmed from (1) the growing costs (taxes and otherwise) employers shouldered of operating in the city's deteriorating physical environment, and (2) the "escalating hostility of urban class relations" (Ashton, 1978, 70; see also Gordon, 1976).

> The growing organization and militancy of urban workers challenged capitalist prerogatives and threatened capitalist profits. Capitalists perceived that by moving their industrial facilities to suburban communities they could reassert both economic and political control. (Ashton, 1978, 70–71)

Thus, to the extent that abandonment resulted from suburbanization and its "filtering" repercussions, it was not the result of simply constructing "residential alternatives on the suburban fringe" (see also Bradbury et al., 1982, 166). It is true that new suburban housing became available and that middle-income inner-city residents took advantage of it, but suburbanization did not simply spring from this market dynamic. The underlying roots of suburbanization, and therefore of abandonment, go back to decisions and constraints experienced by industrial corporations and by capital as a whole. These needs of production profoundly determined the resulting urban form and, in turn, consumer preference. Had their constraints or priorities, and therefore their locational decisions, been different, the spatial structure of our metropolitan areas would undoubtedly not appear as it does today.[5]

## Abandonment Reconceptualized

In summarizing this review of the literature on neighborhood change and abandonment, one finds dual theory too narrow in its applicability and insufficiently materially based; orthodox economic theories, which emphasize filtering and consumer sovereignty, one sided; and more mainstream orthodox theories making valid points but separating market behavior from the institutional and class environment in which it operates. The political–economic literature properly emphasizes the role of institutional actors together with structural economic conditions within the context of the capital accumulation process. Nevertheless, this analysis needs further refining. It needs to explain some important empirical observations that remain relatively unexplained by all the theories.

One striking observation about abandonment is the speed and abruptness with which it occurred in most cities, making it analytically distinct from the general problem of housing decay. According to Grigsby and Rosenburg (1975, 206),

> Decay is often not followed by abandonment, and, conversely, abandonment frequently takes place without a prior period of neglect. In fact concern over abandonment arises precisely because it appears in so many instances to precipitate, rather than follow, decay, striking solid structures in physically sound neighborhoods, not just those buildings in areas where deterioration has almost run its course.[6]

To a considerable extent, this empirical observation serves to refute the filtering theory of abandonment, but it also raises questions about the political–economic approach. The trends of suburbanization, deindustrialization, the in-migration of low-income minority populations, "planned shrinkage," and so forth are, for the most part, gradual developments that unfolded over a relatively long period of time—much longer than the time frame of abandonment. These trends convincingly contributed to abandonment. They do not, however, provide us with an explanation of how abandonment wiped out huge areas of sound housing so rapidly. To do that, one must not simply identify these simultaneously occurring trends but also determine the relationships among them and the particular mechanisms or actors bringing about abandonment, a complicated task, not easily amenable to empirical testing. The question becomes, How do all these structural processes interact to produce abandonment? How do we explain, for example, the timing of abandonment?

## The Role of Institutional Mortgage Lenders in Abandonment

An examination of the role of financial institutions in the urban development process can provide important insights on abandonment. Their mediations (between the structural conditions described by the political–economic theorists, on the one hand, and neighborhood housing markets, on the other) via their mortgage lending behavior play a key role in the abandonment process.

Financial institutions (particularly the savings and loans and mutual savings banks—the thrifts) "mediate" in the sense that they coordinate or mobilize the neighborhood-decline process, by perceiving and responding to long-term structural changes taking place around them, for example, changing relative wage rates, changing job opportunities, and migratory movements. "All of these forces are marshalled and given coherence in the urban context through the mediating power of the financial superstructure" (Harvey, 1975, 143). Lenders further facilitate these changes in their investment, as well as their disinvestment, policies. That is, they channel investment not only out of the inner city but to the suburban periphery and fast-growing Sunbelt areas. In this way, they function as stimulators of effective demand and facilitators of capital accumulation (Harvey, 1975, 141).[7] When they withhold funds from certain areas and invest them in other areas because of these larger forces, they also virtually create real estate speculation and new submarkets (see Harvey, 1975, 146).

There are further arguments to support the view that lenders often play a leading role in neighborhood change processes. First, on a more microlevel, the decision on the part of institutional lenders not to grant mortgages in an area or to force more stringent and higher-cost terms when loans come due causes owners to reevaluate their holdings radically. The withdrawal of bank credit increases the cost of financing and significantly reduces profit, particularly from refinancing or selling. Refinancing has been historically the source of most of the return on residential real estate (Sternlieb, 1971, 334). Without institutional lenders, owners who wish to sell must draw on noninstitutional lenders (who usually charge higher interest and require shorter repayment terms) or purchase money mortgages or both, which lowers the price (Devine, 1973, chap. 4, p. 19).

> Even if the owner chooses to sell, an acceptable sales price can only be secured if financing is available. Otherwise, the owner may have to reduce the price or make up the difference between the sales price and sufficient institutional mortgaging by offering the purchaser a purchase money mortgage. In this case, the former owner remains "locked in" to the parcel. He does not have the cash, which was the objective of the sale, except as the mortgage is repaid over a period of years; at the same time his collateral is subject to all the vagaries of the real estate market which may have occasioned the sale in the first place. (Sternlieb, 1971, 334)

Often, owners would rather not sell but hold on, gaining cash-flow profit and tax benefits while undermaintaining, and eventually abandon.

> The availability of institutional financing is one of the major determinants of the health and vitality of the real estate market. If the banks, savings and loan companies, insurance companies, and the like are willing to lend in an area, then owners can have confidence that their investments in properties are redeemable through ultimate resale or remortgaging. Without this assurance, landlords become locked-in; they know that capital improvements and investments will add little to the ultimate value of their properties; they may very well view even positive cash flows and operating profits from their properties as nothing more than the liquidation of capital values. The latter without financing are simply not redeemable. (Sternlieb and Burchell, 1973, 237)

Second, financial institutions have a very strategic impact on local housing markets in an environment of potential or real changing housing demand; they are also relatively conservative institutions. This means that lenders tend to *cause* decline by disinvesting as opposed to first perceiving indications of decline (e.g., population losses, owner undermaintenance) and then disinvesting. Lenders, far more than landlords, are in a position to take a longer view and affect housing markets on a wider geographic scale. For example, if the institution that historically services a local housing market embarks on a disinvestment strategy, all mortgagors in that area are potentially affected almost at once. In contrast is the more gradual and haphazard impact that demographic changes have on individual owners.

Institutional lenders are also more immediately sensitive than are landlords or homeowners to indications of possible risk to the collateral backing their loans. According to Leven et al. (1976, 196), householders are sensitive to "changes in the wind" that may "alter the neighborhood characteristics of [their] housing bundle," but lenders are more so:

> To lenders whose business is the financing of housing purchases, expectation is the very substance of daily operation; their calculations of probability have immediate and overt effect on the market. . . . Lenders' perceptions of probability are from the outset areal in nature: they too give heavy weight to the future neighborhood characteristics of the housing bundle. If they see a high probability that a neighborhood's income level will fall or that its racial composition will increasingly shift to black occupancy, their projection of property values will fall.

This would lead to more restrictive mortgage terms in order to avoid substantial loss in the event of foreclosure. And the perceived probability of continually falling values would lead to the withdrawal of financing.

Thus lenders may be "causing" decline in that they respond preemptively to indicators of future decline. Although they may have had little concrete experience of losses, their policies are formulated very conservatively. Their actions clearly alter the process of neighborhood decline, insure it, and perhaps cause it, in the sense that, had they not disinvested, decline might not have taken place at all (or perhaps not till much later), might not have taken place as abruptly and as comprehensively, and perhaps might not have taken place in relatively new, sound structures. Owners might very well have "hung in there," were it not for the actions of lenders.

A third source of support for the view that lenders play a leading role in decline or abandonment comes from empirical studies. For example, a national survey of abandonment conducted for the National Urban League concluded:

> Disinvestment, whether caused by owners who pocket the money that ought to go into property maintenance and improvement or by the "redlining" of neighborhoods by financial institutions, is a critical step along the abandonment road. If at this juncture in the life of a building or a neighborhood, kited values

can be deflated and investment capital found, abandonment probably need not follow. In those neighborhoods where abandonment has occurred, capital flight has always preceded actual abandonment by three to ten years. (Center for Community Change, 1971, 15)

The survey also found that of the seven cities studied, the two without widespread abandonment were also the only ones in which private capital was still available (Center for Community Change, 1971, 11–12).

In their study of housing in Newark (based on 567 properties surveyed in 1964 and revisited in 1972), Sternlieb and Burchell (1973) found that the withdrawal of institutional financing had significantly increased abandonment. Other forceful cases supporting the leading role of lenders were made by Wallace Smith who, in analyzing the redlining of nonwhite areas of Oakland, California, saw it as a key determinant of decline and a self-fulfilling prophecy (cited in Vandell et al., 1974, 80). Case et al. (1971) and Stegman (1972), argued that lenders have been overcautious in the inner city—they *can* profit from lending there—and thus they have been disinvesting on the basis of flimsy or nonexistent risk criteria, again initiating self-perpetuating cycles. MeGee (1973), Sternlieb (1966), and Von Furstenberg and Green (1970) all questioned the relationship between racial transition and mortgage risk and therefore criticized blanket redlining.

In fact, much of the literature on bank redlining, finding bias or prejudgment in lending behavior, implicitly supports the leading role of lenders in decline. Although many studies deal with the question of whether such redlining takes place and not so much with whether abandonment follows, the finding of credit withdrawal based almost exclusively on location (or racial considerations, which is almost always the same thing) strongly helps establish lenders as an independent causative factor in the neighborhood decline process (see Doyle, 1978; Marcuse, 1979a; Naparstek, 1977).

Thus, there is considerable evidence to support the view that lenders play a leading role in decline, often entering early in the process and either responding preemptively to real indicators of future decline or responding to false indicators of future decline out of prejudice or poorly conceived risk criteria. In both cases, they insure decline.

### Rising Interest Rates as a Cause of Decline

Lenders not only contribute to abandonment by interacting with neighborhood-related factors; their mortgage lending decisions are also heavily influenced by capital market and interest-rate factors. For example, the period of steeply rising interest rates after 1966, stemming from what many call the deep "crisis of capitalism" (Bowles et al., 1983; Crisis Reader Editorial Collective, 1978; *see also Chapter 3 by Michael E. Stone*), had a profound impact on the financial viability of savings institutions, and hence on the overall investment behavior of these lenders. They were increasingly unable to keep and attract deposits and thereby simply stay in business. In fact, one can see these financial difficulties as a key factor precipitating changes in lender behavior. But in this case, rather than respond solely to false or real indicators of future neighborhood decline, they responded to real indicators of their own financial vulnerability. This may then have caused them to disinvest prematurely from the point of view of neighborhood conditions or neighborhood mortgage risk and thereby precipitate abandonment. The fact that their problems, stemming from rising interest rates, began in the mid-1960s and that they often initiated immediate investment changes (to be described below) lends support to the view that lenders disinvested relatively early and may also help explain the abruptness of abandonment and its occurrence in relatively new, sound structures. This is not to discount the importance of the longer-term macroeconomic changes described above, but perhaps to see the latter as the underlying conditions under which the interest-rate problem unfolded. In other words, the preemptive and conservative mortgage disinvestment described above could have occurred at the same time as the interest-rate problem was unfolding. In fact, such disinvestment could have been reinforced by interest-rate problems. In other cases, the interest-rate problem could have defined the situation totally. In any event, high interest rates seem to have caused savings institutions to act decisively and immediately.

Specifically, when interest rates began to rise in the mid-1960s, beginning their "longest climb in the nation's history" (Clark, 1983, 23), they caused thrift institutions (1) to lose deposits to other depository institutions and the open market as rate-conscious depositors withdrew their savings to gain higher returns elsewhere; and (2) to experience an earnings squeeze between the low yields of long-term, fixed-rate outstanding mortgage loans and the increasingly higher rates they were forced to pay out to depositors in an effort to retain deposits.[8] Both deposit losses and the earnings squeeze forced them to borrow, to dip into surplus funds, to sell nonliquid assets at a loss, and, in some cases, to merge with healthier institutions [*see Chapter 4 by Ann Meyerson*].

The pressures that were building during the 1960s and 1970s culminated in a fullblown thrift crisis in 1981 as hundreds of savings and loan associations and mutual savings banks collapsed or were absorbed through mergers. The thrifts were finally bailed out by Congress in September 1982, but, at the same time, the entire financial system became deregulated and restructured. As a result of these financial difficulties, both in the 1960s and more recently, not only were the "riskiest" loans cut back, but long-term mortgage lending in general was reduced relative to other, more liquid investments. Liquidity became of paramount importance.

Research on the investment behavior of savings banks headquartered in New York City, particularly four key Bronx-based banks (a borough heavily impacted by abandonment), reveals that after each period of "tight money" (1966, 1969, 1973, and 1974), the sample banks' capital protection (net worth reserves) and earnings fell (see Meyerson, 1979, 217–26). They also suffered large nonrecurring losses during those periods. The banks then reduced mortgage lending and took advantage of new investment authorization to shift funds to high-yield and highly liquid investments (Meyerson, 1979, 269–70). Corporate stocks and bonds, liquid fast-maturing securities (such as federal funds and commercial paper), and obligations of states were the order of the day; together they constituted approximately 10 percent of the assets of the sample banks in 1965, 18 percent in 1970, and 25 percent in 1976. The profound shift away from mortgage investment is indicated by the fact that mortgage loans as a percentage of all assets peaked in 1965 at 80 percent and declined to 64 percent by 1976 (for all New York City–headquartered savings banks as well as for the Bronx banks). It is important to recognize the historic nature of this shift: The *raison d'être* of these savings institutions had always been mortgage lending.

These banks shifted their mortgage portfolios away from their traditional market of conventional mortgages on local multifamily properties. The most significant shift consisted of an increase in out-of-state mortgages. The percentage of multifamily conventional debt of all New York City savings banks invested in "distant states" (those not adjoining New York State) went from 2 percent in 1967 to 28 percent in 1976. For two of the Bronx banks, the percentage increased to more than one-third by 1979.[9] When considering all mortgage debt—government insured as well as conventional—the movement out of state was even more pronounced (almost all FHA–VA loans are on out-of-state properties): By 1976, over half of the four Bronx banks' aggregated debt was on property located outside of New York State.[10] The banks were also increasingly emphasizing nonresidential property, both in state and out of state; a shift, again, from their traditional residential market.[11]

These geographic and nonresidential mortgage portfolio shifts, in addition to creating a vacuum in their local areas with severe implications for neighborhood decline, represent an example of the mediating role of lenders in the decline process. They have indeed been playing a "marshalling" or "cohering" role of channeling urban infrastructure capital to the fast-growth areas, thereby stimulating effective demand and facilitating capital accumulation.

In addition to shifting to nonmortgage assets and out-of-state and non-residential mortgage loans, they also reduced mortgage lending in so-called healthy Bronx neighborhoods in the mid-1960s. In one such neighborhood, Bedford Park, the magnitude of lending on 100 sample residential properties was examined during five consecutive three-year periods between 1963 and 1977 (see Meyerson, 1979, 138–59; Schaffer, 1978). Before 1965, institutional lenders advanced a substantial amount of their 15-year cumulative refinanced mortgage debt on multifamily properties—over one-third of all lenders' refinanced debt (and almost 60 percent of that of the four Bronx banks), as opposed to 8 percent (and zero for the four banks) during the 1975–1977 period. Although refinanced mortgage debt increased during 1972–1974, a period in which one can assume many of the mortgages originating in the 1963–1965 period would be maturing for another round of refinancing, it was only one-third the amount of the 1963–1965 refinanced debt in the case of the four banks. Then, as sales activity continued and increased through 1975–1977, noninstitutional lenders (and purchase money mortgages) became active to accommodate these sales; institutions, which earlier in the 15-year period had dominated the financing of sales, withdrew from such activity during these last 3 years.

Similarly, a recent study of the disposition of "distressed properties" by Bronx savings institutions (Sarokin, 1982) found that these savings banks in the mid-1960s began to tighten up on loan terms (raising rates and shortening maturity periods) when balloon mortgages came due, again even in so-called healthy neighborhoods.

More recently, two studies have revealed related developments in the mortgage investment behavior of savings institutions. Between 1980 and 1983, an Arthur D. Little, Jr., study (1983) showed that savings institutions in New York City stepped up their squeeze on the refinancing of balloon mortgages, with devastating impacts on New York City's rental housing stock. In fact, substantial concern has been raised about the fate of soon-to-be-maturing loans if interest rates remain high. For example, a study prepared for the Federal Home Loan Bank of New York (1982) predicted that 22 percent of New York State federally chartered members of the Federal Home Loan Bank of New York would have a problem with multifamily balloon mortgage loans maturing in 1982, 1983, and 1984. These loans were maturing with average rates of 9.88 percent and had to be refinanced at rates of approximately 17 percent. According to the Arthur D. Little study (1983), some owners were required to make a significant paydown of their principal before refinancing; in some cases, no assured term was given on renewal; in other cases, mortgages were issued only on a variable-rate basis. Some owners were required to pay points or other fees prior to renewal; the terms of most renewals did not exceed 5 years, and many were for 1 to 3 years (as opposed to 10 to 15 years for refinanced mortgages in the past). "In a few transactions, the mortgage was renewed on the condition that the owner convert the building to a cooperative." Requirements of this type put extreme pressure on owners; many will try to get out by selling, converting to cooperatives, or abandoning. Coop conversion, for example, has become widespread in New York City as a result of the general climate of mortgage lending described above, as well as from such explicit stipulations as the one just quoted.[12]

Of course, all these changes in mortgage investment behavior on the local level could reflect some or all of the factors discussed so far: from macroeconomic forces such as suburbanization, to racial prejudice, to interest-rate problems. The cutting back on mortgage lending in the mid-1960s in "healthy" neighborhoods, however, particularly lends support to the leading role of financial institutions in decline and to the interest-rate-problem explanation. It does not, of course, definitively prove these conclusions.[13]

One conclusion that can be drawn from the data on New York City savings institutions is that factors other than neighborhood-related ones seem to play a role in lender investment. In other words, the choice is not between lenders disinvesting "out of the blue" and doing so because of neighborhood-related conditions (see Vandell et al., 1974, 83). There is some evidence that they disinvested when their financial viability problems made long-term, fixed-rate mortgage loans per se a poor investment.

It certainly can be argued that if the financial problems of these savings institutions had not been acute, the disinvestment process would likely have not been as abrupt, as dramatic, and as early. The banks would simply have shifted their mortgage portfolios to properties located outside the Bronx (as they had been doing since World War II) and not have reduced their total mortgage portfolios in favor of other than real estate assets, especially since they had gained authorization to invest in conventional mortgages outside the state. They did shift mortgage portfolios geographically after 1967 (as did all savings banks). However, they did not invest new asset growth in mortgage loans. The onset of higher interest rates created extreme pressure to maximize profits and, more important, to become liquidity conscious. This led banks to diversify their total portfolios and perhaps become more conscious of risk in their mortgage portfolios. The resulting disinvestment in Bronx mortgages, then, was due as much to the fact that mortgages are highly illiquid investments as to the fact that Bronx mortgages may have been considered "risky." Moreover, if neighborhood mortgage risk had been the chief motivating factor, the investment behavior of the sample banks might perhaps have diverged greatly from that of all savings banks. As conditions in the Bronx were deteriorating at a much faster pace relative to other areas, one might have expected the Bronx banks to have diversified away from mortgages more aggressively, and to have shifted their mortgage portfolios into out-of-state and nonresidential properties to a greater extent. Instead, their behavior did not diverge substantially from that of all New York City–headquartered savings banks suffering from the problem of high interest rates.

## Conclusions

The role of financial institutions goes far toward explaining abandonment. This is not to say that all abandonment occurs in conjunction with lender difficulties; some abandonment occurs in the absence of lending problems, and some neighborhoods remain stable (and some in fact undergo an upscale conversion) at the same time that lenders experience financial difficulties. But there seems to be, both logically and in some empirical situations, a strong relationship between abandonment and lender mortgage disinvestment, the latter particularly caused by problems stemming from rising interest rates.

This reconceptualized view of abandonment thus comes back to the earlier conclusion that lenders have played their role in neighborhood decline as mediators of the macroeconomy. But instead of mediating simply the macroeconomic factors discussed earlier (e.g., suburbanization, labor market shifts), they mediated capital market macroeconomic factors as well. The investment behavior of key Bronx-based and New York City–headquartered savings banks during the 1960s and 1970s reveals a definite reaction to an unprecedented rise in interest rates, leading to a reduction in their traditional mortgage lending role. Both aspects of the macroeconomy, operating on a national level, thus found their local, neighborhood expression via the coordinating or mediating role of financial institutions and ultimately contributed considerably to landlord abandonment.

It is likely that this abandonment trend will continue, particularly given the recent deregulation and restructuring of the financial system designed in part to deal with the interest-rate problem [*see Chapter 4 by Ann Meyerson*]. Now savings institutions will be both freer to invest in a variety of assets—including nonmortgage assets—and spurred to do so by intensified competition from other intermediaries as deposit rates become deregulated.[14] This undoubtedly means a further reduction in local mortgage lending, which, especially in the case of the thrifts headquartered in the older cities of the Northeast, threatens a loss of rental housing through abandonment and also through increased conversion to cooperatives and condominiums.

## Acknowledgments

The author wishes to thank Rachel G. Bratt, Jill Hamberg, Chester Hartman, and Emanuel Tobier for their helpful comments on an earlier draft of this chapter.

## Notes

1. Fainstein and Fainstein (1982) draw some interesting parallels between the development of American and European cities. Whereas, historically, until the middle 1970s, European urban centers differed greatly in their social geography from those of the United States—the former were preserved, served expensive consumption, and contained high-rise commercial and residential development, and the latter were desolate, partially abandoned, and dominated by low-income populations threatening the central business district—now we can discern a convergence between the two patterns brought about by the conversion of the cores of many U.S. cities to gentrification. But although the Fainsteins go on to analyze this conversion trend, they are quick to add that the dominant mode of inner-city disinvestment and poverty, on the one hand, and productive expansion in the suburban periphery and Southwest, on the other (a "self-reinforcing process of flight by business and the population," Fainstein and Fainstein, 1982, 172), continues in the United States. They conclude that core conversion merely "takes the problems of race and poverty out of public view" (Fainstein and Fainstein, 1982, 185) but does not eliminate them. Likewise, Smith (1986), in discussing gentrification, says: "The process has not yet become significant enough to reverse or even seriously counter the established trends toward residential suburbanization."

2. A HUD document titled "The Dynamics of Neighborhood Change," written in

May 1975, illustrates this neoclassical theory of neighborhood change. Five stages in the life cycle of a neighborhood are described, from "healthy" to "abandoned" (Healthy, Incipient Decline, Clearly Declining, Accelerating Decline, Abandoned). Abandonment is the final stage, when landlords "decide not to keep them [the buildings] up at all; they will accept *any* tenant they can get. As their income from the building decreases, they stop putting money into it; then they decide to stop paying taxes" (U.S. HUD, 1975, 13; emphasis in original).

3. Included are maintenance and repair costs—caused by aging, vandalism, rapid turnover, thefts; fuel costs—which are higher in older, more poorly insulated buildings; fire and theft insurance—which is higher because of higher risks; property taxes—which are higher because inner-city properties often are overassessed; and financing—which often is unavailable or more costly because of higher perceived risks.

4. For example, according to Sternlieb (1971), the problems of mortgage availability and cost rather than the operating aspects of the building per se are often the major ones forcing owners into desperate straits in declining neighborhoods.

5. Whereas Ashton does not address the inner-city housing implications of suburbanization, Smith's "rent-gap" theory can be seen as picking up where Ashton leaves off and linking suburbanization more specifically to inner-city abandonment. As Smith states: "The physical deterioration and economic depreciation of inner city neighborhoods is a strictly logical, 'rational' outcome of the operation of the land and housing market." The movement of capital to the suburbs made inner-city capital depreciation inevitable—ultimately producing a "rent gap," which later gave rise to revalorization or gentrification of the inner city. An important contribution Smith makes to the suburban investment–inner-city disinvestment analysis is the notion of the built environment as a key investment outlet or vehicle for capital accumulation at particular periods, dictated by the country's economic development (for example, see Smith, 1979, 541).

There are also political–economic, structural theories of declining effective demand in cities. Declining effective demand, like suburbanization, contributed to abandonment. Whereas suburbanization spurred outmigration of middle-income households, deindustrialization and the shifting economic base of older industrial cities caused inner-city rent-income ratios to reach their limit. Given wage levels, it became increasingly difficult to pass on the higher costs of operating buildings. For further discussion of deindustrialization, see Bluestone and Harrison, 1982; also, on declining effective demand, see Downs, 1983; Fainstein and Fainstein, 1982; Sternlieb and Hughes, 1975.

6. See also Sternlieb and Burchell, 1973, 329; Women's City Club of New York and 1978 New York City Housing and Vacancy Survey quoted in Marcuse, 1981a, 32–33.

7. In fact, David Harvey (1975, 139), along the same lines as Ashton, sees financial institutions as having played a key role in transforming the American city into a place "for the artificial stimulation of consumption," from one fashioned as "the workshop of industrial society." The mediations of the financial superstructure have been very important in facilitating an urbanization process (and urban policy) designed, since the 1930s, to deal with underconsumption. The very existence of financial institutions, for example, favors owner occupancy, and owner occupancy stimulates consumption (Harvey, 1975, 131, 136). Thus, "the financial superstructure mediates the relationship between the main dynamic of sustained capital accumulation on the one hand and the urbanization process on the other" (Harvey, 1975, 160).

8. The average cost of deposits soared, even with deposit ceilings. Several types of accounts earning more than 5½ percent time deposit accounts proliferated, with many banks paying more than 16 percent for some deposits. Fifty percent of liabilities at savings and loan associations and mutual savings banks were subject to market determined ceilings as of December, 1981; 22.5 percent and 8.5 percent of liabilities at savings and loan associations and mutual savings banks, respectively, were not subject to rate ceilings at all (President's Commission on Housing, 1982, 124–25).

9. "This rapid increase in distant state conventional mortgage investment indicates

that the banks were avidly taking advantage of liberalized statutory limitations on out-of-state investment instituted in 1966. During that year, the New York State legislature passed a law which allowed 20 percent of assets to be invested in conventional mortgages in distant states. Up until that time, banks were only allowed to originate FHA/VA mortgages outside of New York State and adjoining states" (Meyerson, 1979, 90).

10. The shifting of mortgage debt out of state reflected in large part the presence of numerous intermediaries in locations like the Northeast, which had already peaked in terms of construction and real estate investment. This competition pushed mutual savings banks to invest in mortgages out of state, usually the Sunbelt states, as out-of-state mortgages earned higher yields because the demand for mortgage money was greater there. The increasingly widespread use of private mortgage insurance also made these mortgages relatively riskless.

11. Also, during this period the banks began to invest heavily in Government National Mortgage Association certificates, which are government-insured pass-through securities backed by pools of mortgages. These investments enabled them to shift from direct mortgage investment to indirect, guaranteed mortgage investment, but usually for a different property market (i.e., largely properties using FHA–VA government-insured mortgages).

12. Whereas mortgage disinvestment on the part of institutional lenders can cause owners in the low end of the multifamily rental market ultimately to abandon their properties, it can also cause owners in the middle to upper end of the market to convert their properties to tenant cooperatives. With refinancing and/or selling as a rental property severely limited due to the actions of lenders, sale to tenants via coop or condominium conversion provides owners with a lucrative alternative. Financial institutions other than thrifts (e.g., commercial banks) usually come in to finance individual coop sales, as these loans resemble personal loans more than mortgages.

13. The more recent squeeze on owners of multifamily rental property also lends support to the importance of the role of financial institutions in decline and to the interest-rate problem as key factors behind their mortgage lending behavior. But whether the result will be housing or neighborhood decline as opposed to cooperative conversion, for example, remains to be seen.

14. New York State savings banks will be particularly affected as a result of recent legislation (July 1984), which gave them even broader powers than the federal deregulation legislation, the Garn–St Germain Act of September 1982. New York State banks will now be able to invest an unlimited percentage (as opposed to the prior 20 percent) of their assets in conventional mortgages out of state; likewise, an unlimited percentage (not 10 percent, as in the federal legislation) in commercial loans; unrestrictedly in stocks and bonds; directly in real estate development and ownership as well as leasing activities; and, regarding all assets, beyond a 75-mile radius of their headquarters [*see Chapter 4 by Ann Meyerson*].

# 11

# Residual Work and Residual Shelter: Housing Puerto Rican Labor in New York City from World War II to 1983

*José Ramón Sánchez*

*An important aspect of how the private housing market operates relates to how specific subpopulations fare in obtaining shelter. This chapter and Chapters 12 and 13 deal with the subpopulations of Puerto Ricans, blacks, and women.*

*Puerto Ricans in New York City are one of the most oppressed groups in terms of housing conditions and housing affordability. This situation does not stem simply from discrimination by housing providers or the high levels of poverty experienced by Puerto Ricans. The critical analysis presented here attributes the housing situation of Puerto Ricans primarily to their class position as an increasingly idle part of the reserve army of labor. This status affects their ability to secure decent housing, but their housing status also, in turn, affects their position as workers in the labor market, by limiting and constraining their economic and political behavior.*

Puerto Ricans living in New York City have had dismal experiences in attempting to acquire decent and affordable housing. The reasons for this are usually attributed to high levels of poverty and racial–ethnic discrimination on the part of housing providers, but a more important reason can be found in the economic and political liabilities that working-class existence imposes on Puerto Ricans in New York. Since the 1940s, Puerto Ricans have become an increasingly idle part of the reserve labor force, and this condition has helped to erode their capacity to demand and acquire satisfactory housing.[1]

By approaching the housing issue as a problem Puerto Ricans face as individuals and as a function of individual purchasing power, other studies have ignored the impetus to and limits on individual behavior by the built-in and historical processes of capitalist society (Eagle, 1960; Rosenberg, 1974; Rosenberg and Lake, 1976). This chapter argues that the housing conditions of Puerto Ricans can be approached legitimately only through an analysis of the relations Puerto Ricans have as a group to the contemporary capitalist system of production and to the struggle between classes. Analysis of the postwar period shows in particular that preexisting and emergent political and economic weaknesses (from racist victimization to poverty) were tied closely to the Puerto Rican class role and that these relations forged the Puerto Rican place as a reserve labor force in capitalist society that is especially vulnerable to housing market forces. As a reserve fraction of labor, Puerto Ricans typically have suffered periodic and prolonged bouts of unemployment and exclusion from productive activity resulting from general capitalist processes such as the constant drive by capital for cheaper sources of labor and the existence of productive sectors with seasonal requirements for labor. Landlords took advantage of the fact that these capitalist processes made Puerto Ricans relatively unimportant over the years to local sources of economic growth and as actual and potential wielders of political power. The consequence for Puerto Ricans is a level of housing distress combined with relatively high cost generally unmatched by other ethnic or racial groups in New York City.

But the problem does not end there. Although surplus-labor status and idleness have taken their toll on the Puerto Rican housing situation, these housing conditions themselves have had an important reciprocal effect on the employment and class condition of Puerto Ricans. Housing constrains and channels economic and political behavior in ways that are far more significant than the job-access problems attributed by some analysts to central-city segregation. The ultimate impact of their housing distress has been to help make Puerto Rican workers more available to capital: It perpetuates the role of Puerto Ricans as a cheap labor reserve poised, at demand, for either idleness or work.

## The Empirical Picture

The idea that poor people live in poor housing because that is all they can afford figures in much of the social science literature on substandard housing conditions. A corollary, equally common argument reads that "private enterprise usually cannot construct modern dwellings to rent or sell profitably at the prices such low-income families can afford to pay" (Gist and Fava, 1964, 549). These arguments claim a simple relationship between income levels and housing quantity–quality that seems logical and obvious. The facts concerning the Puerto Rican experience in New York since World War II confirm this relationship, but only on the surface. As Puerto Rican income and employment levels have dropped over the years, so have housing conditions for Puerto Ricans; but they have done so unevenly and in accordance with a much broader process involving the organization of production and consumption between classes.

Both nationally and in New York City, Puerto Rican employment and income levels have declined dramatically relative to other groups in society. In 1979, for instance, the median family income of all Puerto Ricans in the United States ($9,855) was much lower than that for Mexican-Americans ($15,171), blacks, ($12,674), or whites ($21,904). The 1979 median income for all Puerto Ricans in the United States was only 47 percent of the median for whites, compared with a 71 percent ratio in 1959 (National Puerto Rican Forum, 1980, 8). The Puerto Rican unemployment rate nationally was also one of the highest during 1980: 13.7 percent, compared to 10.3 percent for Mexican-Americans, 8.4 for Cubans, 6.3 percent for whites, and 14.5 for blacks (U.S. Bureau of Labor Statistics, 1981b, 3). The proportion of Puerto Rican females in the civilian work force (either working or unemployed) has also dropped over the last 30 years. A low point was reached in 1970 when only 29.8 percent of Puerto Rican females sixteen years and older were in the labor force. Recent increases have improved Puerto Rican female participation to 36.4 percent in 1980, but it still falls far short of the 51.7 percent figure for all U.S. females in this age category. In contrast, almost 39 percent of Puerto Rican women sixteen years and older were active in the work force during 1950, a figure higher than the 28 percent reported for white women at that time (Cooney and Colon, 1980, 60).

Not surprisingly, similar but often more severe economic conditions can be noted for those Puerto Ricans who live in New York City. There, for example, the median income of Puerto Rican renter households in 1980 was only $6,460, 71 percent of the median income for black and 48 percent that of white renter households. The decline of Puerto Rican income relative to other groups in New York City, furthermore, has been striking. In 1969, the median income of Puerto Rican renter households ($4,949), was 87 percent of the median income level for blacks and 60 percent that of white renter households (Stegman, 1982b, 140). The proportion of New York City Puerto Rican females active in the civilian work force dropped from a high of 39 percent in 1950 to less than 29 percent in 1970 but rose to 33.8 percent in 1980 (Cooney and Colon, 1980, 62; Mann and Salvo, 1984, table 16). These changes in Puerto Rican female participation in the labor force paralleled a completely opposite process among white females in New York, whose activity in the civilian work force increased from 35 percent in 1950 to 43 percent in 1980 (Cooney and Colon, 1980, 62; Eagle, 1960, 147; New York State, Department of Labor, 1982b, 3).

The thesis that housing opportunities are related exclusively to personal income would suggest that these reported declines in Puerto Rican income and employment levels would produce similar declines in Puerto Rican housing conditions. But on some measures the housing situation of Puerto Ricans has improved, on others it has stayed the same, and on still others it has worsened.

One of the few housing features where Puerto Ricans have shown any improvement has been in the area of overcrowding. Although 16 percent of Puerto Rican households were overcrowded in 1980 (more than 1.01 persons per room), this was a substantial decrease from the 40 percent figure in 1956. Most of this improvement can be linked to specific developments in housing affecting Puerto Ricans during the late 1950s and early 1960s. The first is the outlawing of subdivided apartments and rooming houses, which had been a major place of residence for Puerto Ricans in the 1950s. The second is the displacement caused by urban renewal and the tight Manhattan housing market and subsequent migration into new neighborhoods and apartments in the Bronx and Brooklyn. As whites moved out to the suburbs and new housing developments, vacated bigger apartments became available to Puerto Ricans who moved from Manhattan to the Bronx and Brooklyn, where in 1978 over 90 percent of the rental units had three rooms or more (Marcuse, 1979b, 91).

Nevertheless, the quality of housing for Puerto Ricans is as poor today as it was 25 years ago. Although the proportion of Puerto Ricans living in dilapidated housing today has decreased slightly since 1975, it is only one percentage point lower than it was in 1960 (Kantrowitz, 1969, 43; Stegman, 1982b). Measured by the presence of one or more serious "deficiencies which when taken together, prevent the housing from providing habitable shelter" (Stegman, 1982b, 107), almost one-tenth of all Puerto Rican house-households in New York City in 1981 lived in such uninhabitable quarters, almost twice the rate for blacks and three times that of whites.

The one area of housing that has clearly worsened for Puerto Ricans is the ratio of rent paid to income. In 1980, the median rent-to-income ratio for Puerto Rican renter households in New York City was 36 percent, compared with a 28 percent ratio for all New York City renter households (Stegman, 1982b, 159). In 1960, however, the median rent-to-income ratio for Puerto Ricans was only 20 percent, while for all NYC households it was 18 percent. Over the years, Puerto Ricans have had to devote progressively greater shares of their income for rent as their relative economic situation has declined.

As stark a picture as these facts present about the developing situation in Puerto Rican employment and housing, they do not suggest an easy fit with the idea of a simple income–housing relationship. Housing cannot be reduced to simple economic transactions where individuals exchange value for equal value. In capitalist societies, the act of selling, buying, or renting out housing involves more than a market determination of what housing will be sold or leased at what price. The market context actually obscures social and political processes that determine the distribution within society of the social wealth represented in housing (cf. Kirby, 1979). The following sections argue that the nature of the underlying process that characterize housing in capitalist societies is centered on historical patterns of class conflict.

# A Critique of, and Theoretical Alternative to, Housing as a Market Commodity

The idea that income alone determines housing conditions can mean that housing merely reflects larger income or class inequalities in the society. The concept of social or class inequalities, however, is generally ignored or opposed by studies that claim a simple income–housing relationship. Instead, most studies attribute low incomes (and the imposition of high rents on the poor) to personal flaws of one sort or another; for example, inadequate education or job skills, personal preference or ignorance, illegal or antisocial behavior, large families, or individual discrimination (Gist and Fava, 1964; Kristof, 1970; Sowell, 1981). The underlying strand in these explanations is the view that as a result of these behavioral and personal flaws, "certain groups in society are unable to compete in the modern world" (Murie, 1983, 213). The assumption that individual and household decisions and behavior are not restricted or compelled by broader social and economic structures gives no alternative but to attach personal blame.

The traditional explanations for the dire housing experiences of Puerto Ricans and other minorities also point to poverty or segregation and racism as main causal factors (cf. Eagle, 1960; Rosenberg, 1974; Rosenberg and Lake, 1976). This focus on individual or family behavior and purchasing power underestimates the role of class in housing processes. But, more to the point, it ignores the dissonant, empirically troublesome features of the Puerto Rican experience in housing.

The argument that the poor live in bad housing because that is all they can afford in some senses shows very limited insight. The correlation between the ability to pay and the quantity–quality of the good purchased would require very little elaboration were there not such recurring evidence of counterpatterns. Studies have found, for instance, that the poor often pay more than the general public for comparable or inferior housing, food, health services, and other necessities (Caplovitz, 1967). There is evidence of this in the Puerto Rican rent history.

The extreme poverty of Puerto Ricans places obvious limitations on their purchasing power but not on the rents they are frequently forced to pay. A number of studies made note of the high rents charged to Puerto Ricans during the 1950s. One study showed that Puerto Rican rents varied by less than a dollar from white rents (Eagle, 1960, 159). Another documented the many examples of rent gouging among the large proportion of Puerto Ricans living in subdivided apartments. In many of these cases, landlords had four to six persons living in one room at rents that were usually higher than the average rents charged for an entire apartment (Dworkis, 1957, 12).

Puerto Ricans, therefore, have a history of paying relatively high rents for inadequate housing. But they are not alone in this. A number of studies have documented the fact that poor, but especially black, renters and owners often pay more for shelter (McEntire, 1960; Rapkin, 1966). Research into this issue has reached the point where the existence of a black–white differential in housing price is hardly disputed. Much of the discussion now is over what to make of this. On one side, a discrimination-based argument is still popular, which points to an aversion to blacks or collusive practices on the part of white landlords, private owners, real estate agents, mortgage lenders, and government that limit the availability of housing to blacks and raise its price (see McEntire, 1960; Muth, 1973b). The major alternative arguments rely heavily on rational-choice models of human behavior to deny that discrimination plays a major role in black–white price differentials in housing (Lapham, 1973). Instead, these theories attribute housing-price differences between blacks and whites to the possibility that blacks prefer to consume less housing than whites or have a higher preference for integration (Muth, 1973b; Straszheim, 1973). In general, these theories argue that all actors, black and white, in the housing process conduct themselves as income maximizers and that housing-price differences thus merely reflect "wholly voluntary market transactions" (Muth, 1973b, 109).

Whatever their particular individual merits, neither the discrimination nor the rational-choice model provides an adequate explanation for why blacks and Puerto Ricans often pay more for housing. The assumption by both sides is that housing market transactions are composed solely of individual buyers and sellers, acting discriminatorily and malevolently, according to one argument, and rationally according to the other. This implies that these micro-level relationships are identical with and correctly reflect macroprocesses. However, such macroprocesses as government zoning policies, antidiscrimination legislation, and bank lending practices, to name but a few, obviously have a large role in either making possible discriminatory, or denying economically rational, transactions between individuals. While these theories agree that the poor and minorities often pay more for housing, they are unable to explain fully why this comes about.

So, low incomes alone cannot explain the oppressive housing situation of Puerto Ricans. The Marxist approach addresses this problem in two ways: It requires that housing be placed within the fundamental class conflict characterizing capitalist society, and it demands that housing be analyzed in terms of the historical development of this conflict. These methodological demands provide a basis for understanding the broader social implications involved in the purchase, leasing, and use of housing, as well as the nature of housing as a social product whose distribution and quality are tied to the interests and actions of particular individuals and groups.

Housing is an important factor in the contradiction and exploitation of labor by capital. Capitalist growth and capitalism itself are dependent on the exploitation of labor, making labor produce more than it needs for subsistence (Ginsburg, 1979). This fact produces both conflict and dependence. In order to exploit workers, capitalists must have workers who are available to work. Labor must be "reproduced" or, as Marx said, each day "a definite quantity of human muscle, nerve, brain, etc.," expended in production must be replaced so that tomorrow workers will "again be able to repeat the same process in the same conditions as regards health and strength" (Marx, 1977, 275). This need for labor reproduction is realized in a contradictory way, however. Counteracting worker, state, or capitalist efforts on behalf of working-class reproductive needs, especially in housing, is the exploitative process itself, the economic needs and interests of noncapitalist classes such as landlords, and intraclass differences within capital that result in different capitalist requirements for labor (Ginsburg, 1979). For example, wages are the principal means of subsistence for labor, but capitalists constantly seek to lower wages to increase profits. Capitalist growth itself may increase the need and demand for labor and, in this way, contribute to a relative shortage of labor and push the cost of labor upward.

Labor's need for housing and the economic role of landlords in capitalist societies give these factors a special place in the reproduction and thus the cost of labor. Unlike other purchases, housing is a relatively durable commodity, takes a big chunk out of working-class wages, is necessary for subsistence, and cannot easily be consumed in smaller portions as income decreases. Housing thus introduces specific tensions into the issue of working-class reproduction and labor costs. Inadequate or overpriced working-class housing, for instance, can affect the generation and appropriation of value by capital. An inadequately sheltered work force may be physically or mentally unable to perform its productive function, while overpriced housing can force workers to fight for higher wages in order to meet this need. Neither the quality nor the cost of housing is easy to maintain at tolerable levels, however, because housing is itself a commodity produced and sold for profit by various classes and class sectors (construction and finance capital, and landlords). Torn between its usefulness as shelter for workers and its function as an object of exchange for its owners, housing has historically tended to be more rather than less costly and less rather than more available to workers. The intervention of the state in regulating and providing housing for labor theoretically seeks to counteract these tendencies, but in most capitalist countries meets with little success (cf. Duncan and Goodwin, 1982).

The tensions housing introduces into the issue of working-class reproduction are not felt uniformly by all sectors of capital or labor. To the extent that the contemporary American capitalist class can be divided into subgroups, distinct "competitive" and "monopoly" sectors have specific relationships to labor, partly defined by the nature and level of reproduction for labor in each sector (O'Connor, 1973). The monopoly sector, that fraction of capital engaged in large-scale production, with products sold to national and international markets, has a regularly employed, stable, and organized work force paid relatively high wages. In this sector, job stability and high wages make housing cost less of a problem for workers, and thus for capital. Furthermore, in the United States, the housing needs of this sector's workers have been accommodated in large part through suburban homeownership. This housing form has been heavily encouraged and subsidized by the state in the post–World War II era [*see Chapter 6 by Barry Checkoway*] in an attempt to soak up idle productive capacity and ideologically incorporate this sector of labor into the bourgeois private property system (Marcuse, 1980a).

The reproductive conditions of labor are different in the competitive sector. Production there is normally small scale, sold at local or regional markets, and dependent on a low-wage, weakly or not organized, and irregularly employed work force. Work in the competitive sector is not only poorly paid but hard to come by, reflecting both seasonal and sudden changes in production and the generally large pool of workers (buoyed by a large reserve of idle labor) that competitive capital has to choose from (Gappert and Rose, 1975). The housing of these workers, especially those normally in the reserve army, has generally been inadequate and of little concern to competitive capitalists, for whom these workers function as an expendable labor commodity. The state has gradually assumed some of the housing subsistence costs for workers in this sector, but these efforts have generally been below the average levels of housing consumption for workers as a whole.

Thus the housing and general reproductive needs of labor are not a simple question of worker income levels but a broader contradictory class issue over which workers, capitalists, and landlords confront each other with varying and unequal amounts of economic and political power. The weakest position has generally been that of workers in the competitive sector, especially reserve workers. Puerto Ricans are typically found in the competitive and reserve sectors of labor, and for that reason they have suffered more than most from housing hardship.

Contrary to the predictions of economists in the 1950s and 1960s, the competitive sector of capital as well as competitive sector and reserve workers have not disappeared from New York City. At one time, the emergence of New York and London and Tokyo as world centers of finance and advanced corporate services suggested continued evolution of this sector and its eventual overall dominance within these cities. It was assumed that the work forces of these cities would be similarly transformed into a homogeneous body of well-paid, white-collar corporate employees (Gilpatrick, 1966). Actual developments have proven most of these predictions wrong (Ross and Trachte, 1983). Though substantial amounts of competitive-sector manufacturing have clearly disappeared from these cities, a significant (sometimes increasing) portion of competitive manufacturing and service capitalist sector survives and thrives largely on the basis of the volume of low-wage, easily discharged pool of reserve labor still in these cities (Simon and White, 1981). One account estimates the current size of the reserve army in New York City as at least 400,000 people, or 13 percent of the total civilian work force (Ross and Trachte, 1983, 411).

The contemporary circuits of capital on the world scale actually seem to encourage the existence and growth of reserve labor in "global cities" like New York (Frobel, Heinrichs, and Kreye, 1980; Portes and Walton, 1981). The reason for this is twofold. Basically, the exit of some manufacturing capital and the growth of the corporate service economy in the postwar period created a vacuum filled by (1) capitalists who occupy a subsidiary position in the service economy and employ office and janitorial workers, clerks and computer operators, messengers, and restaurant workers; and (2) capitalists who are able to take advantage of manufacturing processes that require low barriers to entry (apparel "sweatshops," for example) and depend on a large, cheap pool of willing and generally idle labor. Over the last 10 years, twin capital flows of this kind have grown large and dependent on the uneven employment of women, blacks, Puerto Ricans, other Hispanics, Asians, and undocumented workers. These groups form the principal components of a labor sector forced to comply with surplus status by a broad array of capitalist processes not unlike those described more than a century ago by Marx in *Capital.*

Among the categories of surplus workers identified by Marx, the notion of a "stagnant" work force seems most appropriate to the Puerto Rican case. The "stagnant" work force consisting of Puerto Rican, black, and other minorities is made redundant by the decay of particular industries or the flow of manufacturing and other capital elsewhere. Although this sector remains active as labor, it does so by being reduced to extreme levels of irregular and partial employment. It offers capital, as Marx said, "an inexhaustible reservoir of disposable labor-power" as a direct consequence of the fact that, in housing and other forms of subsistence, "its conditions of life sink below the average normal level of the working class, and it is precisely this which makes it a broad foundation for special branches of capitalist exploitation" (Marx, 1977, 796). Decreasing (or below normal) Puerto Rican subsistence, particularly in housing, thus not only taxes the Puerto Rican condition in New York City but drops them, along with other minority and undocumented labor, into a labor reserve that today helps to attract sweatshop and other "underground" operations to the city (Ross and Trachte, 1983). (This point is discussed more fully later in this chapter.)

# A Historical Analysis of Puerto Rican Housing

Although the reserve labor function of Puerto Ricans in New York City has had a major role in defining the housing condition for this group, its specific impact has varied over the years. In accordance with changes in capitalist demand for their labor since World War II, Puerto Ricans have experienced differing responses from the local state to their needs and demands as well as varied access to private and public housing resources. In fact, since World War II, three distinct periods show how the changing relations of class and production in the city created a context and class pressures favoring specific distributions of housing.

## Initial Changes: World War II to the Mid-1950s

The cheap-labor role of Puerto Ricans in New York immediately following World War II had a strong influence on the number of Puerto Ricans living in subdivided housing at that time. Although the housing Puerto Ricans found for themselves was usually bad, crowded, and overpriced, it was convenient to downtown Manhattan, where most Puerto Ricans worked. Subdivided housing also conformed to the social infrastructure of close personal networks and of shared expenses and responsibilities among family members and friends devised by Puerto Ricans in order to survive the migration process and work experiences in New York City (Sanchez-Korral, 1981). Finally, Puerto Ricans were led to accept these terrible housing conditions as a temporary measure by the apparent responsiveness of a municipal government eager to help (or to appear to help) with the housing and other adjustment problems of this cheap labor reserve.

A number of observers during the early 1950s were quick to recognize the important economic role of Puerto Ricans in New York as a cheap reserve work force (cf. Abrams, 1955). Newspaper reports and comments by government officials during the 1950s gave glowing tribute to the resourcefulness of the new migrants and to the benefits they brought the city. Academics and city officials kept careful watch during the early 1950s on the flow of Puerto Rican labor into the city, to insure an adequate supply of workers to fill an increasing number of low-skilled jobs. Warnings were issued periodically, whenever the yearly flow of Puerto Rican labor dropped too far below the number of available jobs. When Puerto Rican labor far exceeded the number of low-wage jobs, pleas were made to curb Puerto Rican migration and ship those already here back to Puerto Rico (Kihss, 1953, 1954). Some writers even argued that New York needed more cheap labor than Puerto Rico could provide. In an expansive 1954 report, Columbia University professor A. J. Jaffe predicted that if only "two-thirds of [Puerto Ricans] continue to enter operative and service occupations, then it would seem as though the Puerto Rican migration would be doing no more than filling the vacancies by death and retirement in these two major occupations" and thus not meeting the labor needs required for the continued expansion of these industries (Jaffe, 1975).

In 1949, New York City Mayor William O'Dwyer created the Mayor's Committee on Puerto Rican Affairs (MCPRA), while the government of Puerto Rico established offices in New York for the Migration Division of the Puerto Rican Department of Labor. As stated in an official publication, the general objective of these separate government bodies was "the integration of U.S. citizens from Puerto Rico into the life of the city" (Mayor's Committee, 1953, 4). Part of the function of these programs was to assist Puerto Rican workers with their housing problems: The MCPRA set up a housing task force that included the commissioners and other top officials from all city housing agencies, as well as Puerto Rican community leaders; the Migration Division distributed information about New York housing conditions and legal rights to the Puerto Rican community and set up housing clinics to deal with housing problems. Apart from a significant increase in the number of Puerto Ricans in the city's public housing projects (a 150 percent increase between 1953 and 1956), these programs did little for the general housing welfare of Puerto Ricans (Dworkis, 1957). This failure should not distract from the fact that, by their existence, these programs reflected a government realization that it was not enough simply to attract and bring cheap Puerto Rican labor to New York. Puerto Rican workers also needed a certain level of housing in order to function effectively as cheap labor. How to do that without jeopardizing the reasons for encouraging Puerto Rican labor to migrate to New York was to permit exploitation by capital and perhaps cheating by landlords. Achieving this delicate balance proved difficult for local government. While Puerto Ricans had few political resources to marshall on their own behalf, other groups had no such problem. The contradictory pressures on government were, in fact, underscored in comments made by New York City Welfare Commissioner Henry McCarthy, who was also a member of the MCPRA. In response to public demands to trim the welfare rolls, McCarthy argued:

> We cannot, on the one hand, attract Puerto Ricans to fill the need for workers in the garment industry, the hotel industry, or as domestic help without extending aid to them when illness or other misfortune strikes. Unskilled work cannot command sufficiently high salaries to build up resources to tide such workers over periods of unemployment or sickness, or the distress caused by desertion, or to care for children born out of wedlock. We cannot enjoy the benefits of Puerto Rican labor without assuming some additional welfare costs. On balance, the taxable values created by their labor must far exceed the additional welfare tax burden. (Kihss, 1957)

If McCarthy and city government did not live up to these remarks, it was because (as discussed later in this chapter) by the mid- to late 1950s changes in the New York City economy had begun to lower demand for Puerto Rican labor, making any concern for their welfare or for their reproduction as labor-power increasingly unnecessary.

Since the early 1950s, no local government body similar to the MCPRA has devoted an equal amount of attention to the housing needs of Puerto Rican workers. There may be several reasons for this, but the conclusion seems unmistakable that government neglect of the deepening crisis of Puerto Ricans is related to the decreased demand for their labor. As a consequence of this neglect, landlords were given free rein and were able to take advantage of Puerto Ricans in a variety of ingenious ways.

A very substantial portion of the Puerto Rican population in New York City lived in apartments and brownstones converted into single-room and roominghouse units during the 1950s. These conversions were a direct consequence of city laws passed at the end of World War II to permit more families to occupy the same amount of physical space. Between 1941 and 1950, fully 23 percent of the 147,000 unit net addition to the housing stock was of this converted type (New York City, Department of City Planning, 1978, 35). Conversion, in fact, produced more housing units than did public housing construction.

Eagle (1960) reported that in the early 1950s a minimum of one-third of all Puerto Ricans lived in converted units. Calculations based on this estimate indicate that Puerto Ricans actually represented the majority (53 percent) of all households living in converted units at the time. The impact of housing conversion on the Puerto Rican population thus was highly disproportionate, given the fact that Puerto Ricans were then only 2 percent of all New

York City households (Kristof, 1970, 324). As a group, Puerto Ricans thus had become an important source for the economic solvency of marginal landlords in New York. Public officials allowed this illegal practice to persist because it solved two knotty problems: housing a rapidly growing work force at minimum public cost and allowing a marginal landlord sector a means for short-term survival.

## The Transition: Mid-1950s to Mid-1960s

By the end of the 1950s, Puerto Ricans began to experience severe drops in employment. Puerto Rican females, in particular, were rapidly being squeezed out of the civilian work force. This restructuring of the economic role of Puerto Ricans, and of New York City's economy as a whole, had dramatic and unusual results on Puerto Rican housing conditions. A brief time of relative improvement in Puerto Rican housing in the early 1960s was followed by severe declines that have continued into the present. The forces rapidly shifting the New York economy toward corporate and personal services caused economic and population dislocations that proved only of temporary value to the ability of Puerto Ricans to meet their housing needs. The impact of these forces was particularly evident in the late 1950s.

By the mid-1950s, the employment of Puerto Rican males and females in the garment trades, small manufacturing, restaurants, and hotels had largely satisfied the cheap-labor needs of the New York City economy (Laurentz, 1980; Vernon, 1959). But the contraction of manufacturing, which accelerated during the late 1950s within New York City, decreased in an abrupt way the need for Puerto Rican, and especially female, labor. Since then, Puerto Rican employment and wages have been in a steady decline (cf. Glazer and Moynihan, 1963, 299). The public perception of a Puerto Rican labor force being made rapidly redundant soon shifted. Puerto Ricans were no longer seen as valuable but as expendable to local economic needs.

In a less clear way, a similar shift occurred in the way landlords and developers treated Puerto Ricans. What is interesting about the 1950s is the extent to which the housing experience of Puerto Ricans seemed to parallel increasing degrees of idleness. As Puerto Rican labor fell into greater disuse by capital, Puerto Rican claims to (any) housing and residential location became increasingly harder to uphold. The examples that follow illustrate the decisive yet subtle change that occurred.

Landlords, especially those with large holdings in downtown Manhattan, began to see Puerto Ricans as an obstacle to property speculation and development rather than as easy prey on which to unload dilapidated, overpriced apartments. The reaction from property owners to the decreasing importance of Puerto Rican labor in the local economy was summarized in a large, well-documented, and perceptive report by the prominent real estate firm of Brown, Harris, and Stevens (BHS). This report was one of the earliest published sources in the 1950s to identify a growing trend in the New York economy that emphasized corporate and personal services rather than manufacturing. The main concern of the BHS report was that property owners were being prevented from taking full advantage of this new trend by factors that obstructed office and residential construction in Manhattan and that forced middle- and upper-income "white-collar employees . . . to settle in private city peripheral or suburban dwellings" (White and Hebard, 1960, 41). Not surprisingly, the BHS report pointed to the large numbers of Puerto Ricans and blacks, who at the time accounted for over 40 percent of Manhattan's total population, as one such obstacle to real estate development. The BHS report argued that "most of these wage earners are in low-paying service and laboring jobs which do not permit them to pay economic rent for new building" (White and Hebard, 1960, 41). Just a few years earlier, however, the low wages of Puerto Ricans had not stopped landlords from overcharging Puerto Ricans for subdivided housing. What scared landlords about the economic situation of Puerto Ricans was not so much their low incomes but the prospect of manufacturing decline leaving them without income of any sort. On top of this, many Puerto Ricans occupied housing situated on sites that were rapidly becoming valuable for the construction of new office buildings and upper-income housing. The BHS report, for example, was especially critical of plans to build some low-income housing in the Upper West Side Renewal Area. "The problems of Manhattan housing cannot all be solved by pouring low rent housing into [the urban renewal area's] twenty blocks," they argued, for "not only will tax revenues fall, but more importantly the balance of the area will prove less attractive to those tenants who can afford to pay economic rent" (White and Hebard, 1960, 103).

The BHS report is an indication that, for at least some segment of their class, landlords in the late 1950s were no longer content to take economic advantage of Puerto Rican tenants because better, more secure profits were in the offing. By ridding themselves of tenants who were no longer useful to capital, landlords could prepare themselves to profit from the growth of the corporate economy and the need for office buildings and middle-income housing for its white-collar and professional employees. This shift in attitude was evident in other significant housing experiences of Puerto Ricans during the late 1950s.

The urban renewal program uprooted thousands of Puerto Ricans during the late 1950s and early 1960s from valuable land in what is now the Upper West Side and the Lincoln Center complex (J. C. Davies, 1966). The Puerto Rican housing situation became so uncertain that many Puerto Ricans found themselves used as interim, temporary tenants by landlords seeking to maintain rental income even after their buildings had been condemned and the original tenants had been evicted for urban renewal purposes. For example, Puerto Ricans renting apartments in 1959 at the site of the present New York University Medical Center found themselves evicted the following year and dumped elsewhere when developers were ready to tear down the buildings (Cook and Gleason, 1959, 189). Although the process was longer and more complex, the local government perception of Puerto

Ricans also changed, from a recognition of Puerto Ricans as a low-wage group with legitimate (and possibly unmeetable) housing needs to a view of Puerto Ricans as a minority beset with social problems whose presence in the city or in public housing had to be minimized.

In the late 1950s, the rising demand for public housing by economically ailing Puerto Rican and black workers was thwarted by a new government policy aimed at "desegregation," which favored the admission of white over Puerto Rican and black applicants (*New York Times*, July 4, Aug. 28, and Aug. 29, 1960). The suspension of this policy after strong protests from the Puerto Rican and black communities cannot change the fact that these admissions limits emerged precisely when decreased demand for cheap Puerto Rican (and black) labor in the local economy began to surface (cf. Price, 1979). Together, these developments in private and public housing suggest that Puerto Rican housing needs were affected by class processes that were more complex and general than those consisting of income-imposed limits on individual purchasing power.

Puerto Rican housing conditions did improve in the early 1960s, but this can be attributed to the legal banning of subdivided housing units, increased public housing construction and admissions, and improvements in the enforcement of local housing codes. More than a million whites left New York City between 1950 and 1960 (Tobier, 1970, 36). In this same period, over 77,000 public housing units were constructed. As this housing became available to Puerto Ricans and blacks, low-density local zoning ordinances enacted during the 1950s and early 1960s and code-enforcement improvements built into the Neighborhood Conservation Program of 1959 lowered the percentage of crowded, unsafe, and unsound housing. The impact of these processes on Puerto Rican housing conditions can be noted in the following changes: Dilapidated housing decreased from 22 percent in 1950 to 10 percent in 1960, roominghouse occupancy dropped from 15 percent of all Puerto Rican families in 1960 to 4 percent in 1968, overcrowding among Puerto Ricans dropped from 43 percent in 1950 to 39 percent in 1960, and rents increased 17 percent from $53 a month in 1956 to $62 a month in 1960 (Kristof, 1970, 372).

## Consolidation: The Mid-1960s to the Present

The forces affecting the transformation of the New York City economy, the housing market, and Puerto Rican labor seem to have matured since the mid-1960s. The new seems finally to have replaced the old. The corporate-based economy grew larger, healthier and dominant, making New York wealthy, at least on the surface. Many New York City residents, Puerto Ricans and blacks especially, found themselves again toiling for low pay and at irregular rates for low-skilled service and manufacturing jobs, however. Real estate formed the backbone for this period of economic growth. Property owners, developers, and speculators, particularly in lower Manhattan, were richly rewarded by the boom in the late 1960s in office building and luxury residential construction. Puerto Rican and other reserve workers suffered, as did many of their landlords before opting for arson or abandonment. Periods of idleness became more frequent and prolonged for Puerto Ricans. Some Puerto Ricans returned to Puerto Rico or migrated to other U.S. cities (Maldonado-Denis, 1976). Many of those who stayed in New York were not only forced to turn to "sweatshop" and other "underground" industries for employment but grew more dependent on government sources for their subsistence (Lopez, 1973).

The heaviest outpouring of Puerto Rican community activism and radicalization since Vito Marcantonio and East Harlem Puerto Ricans rocked the political establishment during the 1940s occurred in this period (Lopez, 1973; Maldonado-Denis, 1976).[2] Movements for school decentralization and militant organizations like the Young Lords exemplified the level and scope of politicization among Puerto Ricans. By the mid-1970s, when the New York City fiscal crisis helped establish as public dogma the idea that cities like New York simply spent too much (on minority workers' needs), the issue whether to rescue ailing Puerto Rican and black communities was rapidly being settled. The public relations gimmick that had Jimmy Carter standing in an empty, rubble-strewn South Bronx lot pledging a federal commitment to rebuild the area only delayed the public realization that government was fast retreating from these communities (Tabb, 1982). Support and maintenance of roads, sewers, fire, police, and other services in communities that could least do without them were being reduced, by newly cost-conscious political leaders (Marcuse, 1980b).

The city's role in housing during this period is revealing. Beginning in the early 1960s, there was a shift in housing subsidy programs away from working-class housing and toward middle-income housing. Between 1961 and 1970, public low-income units accounted for 14 percent of all housing construction in New York City, whereas during the preceding decade such units accounted for about 30 percent of all residential building. But while low-income public housing construction dropped sharply during the 1960s, publicly subsidized, middle-income housing rose dramatically. An estimated 29 percent of the city's total units built between 1961 and 1970 were publicly aided, middle-income projects (New York City, Department of City Planning, 1974). Government had clearly not shrunk from subsidizing housing, only from housing intended for low-income families.

The withdrawal of private and public funding for low-income housing coincided with the withdrawal of mortgage financing from inner-city, minority areas like Harlem and the South Bronx. [See Chapter 10 by Ann Meyerson.] Redlining, or the decision by banks and other lending institutions not to grant or extend mortgages in specific urban areas, had a severe impact on the New York housing economy. Some analysts, in fact, blame redlining for much of the housing deterioration and abandonment that has occurred over the last 20 years (Homefront, 1977; Tabb, 1982).

Trends in the private housing market have been devastating to Puerto Ricans because they are more likely to reside in private as opposed to public housing. As late as 1983, only 26 percent of all public housing tenants in the city were Puerto Rican; over 56 percent were black. Some of these differences can be attributed to the different sizes of the Puerto Rican and black populations (13 and 24 percent) in the city. But the greater incidence of poverty among Puerto Ricans suggests a greater need and eligibility for public housing. Despite population size differences, Puerto Ricans and blacks formed about equal proportions of the city's total 1980 population that lived below poverty (36 and 37 percent), as well as of those (37 and 40 percent) receiving Aid to Families with Dependent Children (Stegman, 1982b, 87).

Another facet of this policy shift lies in the general government withdrawal of program and fiscal support for the infrastructural and public service needs of Puerto Rican and black communities (Davidson, 1979). It can be argued that at least since the early 1970s, the allocation of city resources has developed into a policy whereby those areas considered not viable for capitalist investment and/or housing-related profit were deemed to be in decline and not worthy of additional public expenditures. The result of this "triage" policy, the withdrawal of housing and community rehabilitation funds, public transport, sewer and sanitation services, schools, and police and fire services, has been to accelerate the destructive process of population and housing loss, which served as the initial reason for withdrawing city resources in the first place (Marcuse, 1980b). A recent independent study found that, in fact, much of the arson or fire-related housing loss since 1970 occurred precisely because of reductions in adequate fire services for particular areas of the city (Wallace, 1981). This impact on housing was not an entirely unintentional consequence of policy decisions, according to this source, since the city had accurately anticipated it in detailed projections made by the Fire Department in 1970, before the cutbacks were made (Wallace, 1981).

Another form of public housing in New York City are the so-called *in rem* units, those taken by the city as a result of abandonment, tax delinquency, and foreclosure. Of these units, 112,000 were in the city's reluctant hands as of 1981, and more than 78 percent of the residents in the occupied units were black or Puerto Rican (Stegman 1982b, 211). City policy has been to resist taking responsibility for these units, and where it has had no choice but to take them over, it has attempted to auction them off, sometimes to gentrifiers, sometimes to private landlords who will re-milk them and eventually reabandon them (Bellamy 1979; Conway 1982). A small portion of these units has been given over to low-income tenants as cooperatives and sweat-equity ventures, with some city aid [*see Chapter 26 by Robert Kolodny*]. While many of the tenants in *in rem* housing pay little or no rent (Stegman [1982b, 208] reports that more than 25 percent of tenants in city-owned buildings were in rent arrears in 1981), the city has chosen not to take advantage of this new "public housing program" as a valuable resource for housing Puerto Ricans and blacks and other low-income households decently and permanently.

By the late 1970s an ironic and unexpected thing happened in the New York City economy: The devalued labor of Puerto Rican and other reserve workers again became attractive to capital in the form of legal and illegal manufacturing firms and subsidiary corporate services. The cheap and docile work force that capital had earlier searched for in southern U.S. and Third World locations has evidently been re-created in New York City (cf. Kempton, 1982). "Sweatshop" factories and other underground operations are one of the fastest-growing sectors of the New York economy, producing as many jobs, in some cases, as were lost on the legal side of their respective economic fields.

Most of the official reports and studies of the New York City economy continue to describe the manufacturing sector as in decline. One recent study, conducted for City Hall, stated that "during the period 1972–81, New York City lost over 50,000 jobs, or 34 percent, in durable goods industries . . . [and] 140,000 jobs, or 27 percent, in nondurable industries" (Bienstock, 1983, 28). While there has been substantial movement of manufacturing out of New York, such reports have underestimated both the extent to which such losses represent a shifting of manufacturing operations to illegal forms like "sweatshops," and the continuing role played by cheap and devalued labor in attracting capital for legal and illegal operations in New York City. A recent New York State Department of Labor report (1982a) indicated that there were 15 times as many apparel "sweatshop" firms operating today as in 1970, and, by the department's conservative estimate, these firms accounted for about 50,000 jobs, or almost all of the recorded job loss in the legalized apparel industry from 1970 to 1980. The results of a three-year survey of manufacturing in New York City found it in a healthy state in the city's outer boroughs (Interface, 1983). The report specifically mentioned the vitality of plastics, fabricated metals, and electric and electronic equipment manufacturing in outer-borough neighborhoods like Long Island City, Woodside, Jamaica, Staten Island, East Williamsburg, Greenpoint, and Sunset Park. The Federal Reserve Bank of New York (1983) also reported signs of an economic "turnaround" in New York, based in part on the growth of the manufacturing sector.

The retention and growth of manufacturing in its legal and illegal forms occur because labor in New York City has become relatively plentiful, cheap, and productive. This is demonstrated by government reports that indicate that the productivity (in this case, the ratio of total value added in production to total wages paid) of workers in New York State's apparel industry is 22 cents higher than it is in the rest of the country and is at its highest level in over 30 years (Kamer and Young, 1981; NY State Department of Labor, 1982a; *New York Times*, Dec. 26, 1984).

The unmentioned yet critical element in this rejuvenation, whatever its actual size, is the long decline in working-class living standards, especially as related to housing. The desperation bred by these housing conditions made workers more willing to accept whatever work capital had for them. Depressed conditions of working-class subsistence and the large size of the labor reserve, meanwhile, allowed capitalists to pay workers extremely low wages.

These recent developments in the Puerto Rican employment and housing situation suggest that the reserve role of Puerto Rican workers in the local capitalist economy remains intact. The reentry of Puerto Ricans into competitive sector and underground economic operations has a lot in common with the private and *in rem* housing in which most Puerto Ricans live—both are unstable, intolerable structures, each incorporating its own, ever-present threat to workers, collapse and ruin for the buildings, and migration for capital.

## Conclusion

Writing about working-class housing in nineteenth-century Victorian London, Anthony Wahl (1977, 5) claimed that it was the role of slums in the social system rather than the slums themselves that was constant and eternal. Wahl wrote that, under capitalism especially, slums serve "as part of the infrastructure needed to sustain a market for menial and more or less casual labor." Although generations and a continent removed from Victorian labor and its tenement experiences, this statement aptly describes the condition of Puerto Rican workers and their housing in New York City. There are differences, of course, between nineteenth-century London and New York in the 1980s, but these generally can be traced to changes in capitalism that nevertheless leave intact the need for both casual labor and city slums. The creation of public and private institutions, such as labor laws and unions, to manage disputes (and, ultimately, the contradiction between capital and labor), the growth of the state and public services, and the monopolistic and hegemonic growth of capital have produced a deeply fragmented working class in which some segments of labor are reduced to an existence of casual, irregular work, while others enjoy relatively high pay and some amount of job security (Edwards, 1979). Although capital still seeks to generalize idleness and casual employment (or the threat of it) to all of labor, such conditions of work have today become a specialized ethnic, racial, and sexual preserve within which housing provides a specific "infrastructural" or supportive role, as has been described here for Puerto Ricans.

The concept that housing has an infrastructural role in capitalism merely describes in systemic terms the idea that housing consists fundamentally of social relations between classes. Those approaches that attempt to understand housing as a function of individual income levels, discrimination, segregation, or competition ultimately prove incapable of grasping the full range of activities and consequences in which housing plays a major part.

In particular, the Puerto Rican experience in housing shows that variations in housing conditions are a function, not of simple individual purchasing power, but of the fractionated and unequal economic and political power held by the various classes. Puerto Rican housing conditions, in this sense, are best understood in terms of the imposition of productive idleness on Puerto Rican workers, rather than by any associated calibrations with individual income levels.

An actual historical analysis of the post–World War II class condition of Puerto Ricans in New York City during three distinct time periods revealed that identifiable differences in employment, housing, and government responsiveness were intimately associated. More often than not, employment processes suggested ongoing class changes for Puerto Ricans that corresponded to similar changes in the way Puerto Ricans were housed and treated by local government. The imposition of productive idleness and redundancy on Puerto Ricans, starting in the mid-1950s, weakened their claims both to good housing and to government assistance. This reserve-class status proved costly for subsequent Puerto Rican experiences in housing.

Ultimately, these housing conditions help to make for a below-normal level of subsistence for Puerto Rican workers that reinforces reserve-labor status. This is supported by recent evidence that Puerto Ricans continue to supply labor for competitive capitalist sectors, as well as for the current crop of sweatshop and other underground economic operations in New York City.

What the discussion of these various issues makes clear is that housing is a decidedly social and class process. Housing inequality is not a product of pure housing market processes nor of individual choice or purchasing power. Its roots lie deeply within economic and social processes in which classes, class fragments, and other social agents attempt to determine in economic and political terms who gets what in a housing stock of widely divergent value.

# Notes

1. Puerto Ricans can be considered part of the reserve labor sector because they experience long bouts of idleness and low-wage employment; more important, their political and economic history has been that of an auxiliary work force that is frequently manipulated and pulled into employment in accordance with capital's need for cheap labor.

2. Vito Marcantonio, a U.S. congressman of Italian descent, served the East Harlem district of New York from 1934 to 1950. Marcantonio was a radical with a machine-politics style. He was a strong voice for the independence of Puerto Rico from the United States, as well as an effective agent in helping his constituents deal with the bureaucratic obstructions of everyday government. He had a strong, loyal, and sometimes mobilized following among the Puerto Rican residents of East Harlem and other New York communities.

# 12  Minorities and Suburbanization

*Gary Orfield*

*Racial minorities are severely disadvantaged in the housing market because of lower incomes, their place in the occupational structure, and institutionalized discrimination in all segments of the housing system. Beginning with World War II, large streams of southern blacks headed to northern, midwestern, and western cities; later, Hispanic immigrants from Puerto Rico, Mexico, and other Central and South American countries joined them. Central cities became heavily, and in many areas predominantly, minority as whites left them for the suburbs, where housing and community facilities were newer and access to jobs was better. Substantial suburbanization of minority households has begun in the past decade, but for them "the suburbs" no longer are what they were for middle-class and aspiring-middle-class whites in earlier decades. The realities of suburbanization for minorities must be understood, and government policies must be fashioned, to prevent a repetition of the central-city ghetto formation process of the 1940s, 1950s, and 1960s.*

*It should be emphasized that suburbanization for minorities and low- to moderate-income people (historically, both denied entrance to the suburbs) is still an important and often positive development. It affords these groups greater freedom of housing choice and more options in terms of employment, education, and so on. The landmark Mount Laurel, New Jersey, Supreme Court decisions—excerpted and discussed at the end of this chapter—represent the first real attempt to bring about economic integration of the suburbs through zoning and builder incentives; whether this also will involve racial integration is an open question. The suburbs affected in New Jersey, unlike many of those discussed by Orfield, are stable, affluent and "exclusive." Whether these suburbs can be stably integrated racially and not deteriorate in the ways Orfield describes also is an open question.*

One of the biggest news stories to come out of the 1980 census was the fact that after decades of talk about breaking the barriers that kept blacks out of

An earlier version of this chapter was included in "Blacks, Demographic Change and Public Policy," proceedings of a conference at the Joint Center for Political Studies, Washington, D.C., September 1982, under contract to HUD, and was called "Black Population Redistribution and Housing Policy." Milton Morris, director of research at the Joint Center, has given permission for publication in this volume.

the suburbs, blacks were suddenly becoming suburbanites at an even more rapid rate than whites. Although blacks still represented only 6 percent of the nation's total suburban population, one black household in five was suburban, and the numbers were becoming very large indeed in some metropolitan areas. The statistics were widely reported as a sign of solid social accomplishment, an indication that open housing was a reality and that at least one of our most persistent social problems was well on its way to a solution [*see Chapter 18 by Citizens Commission on Civil Rights*].

Newspapers could and did point to some stunning changes, particularly for affluent blacks, whose residential choices had expanded greatly. For a black family in the elite suburbs of Washington, D.C., or Detroit or Los Angeles, living as accepted members of one of the nation's most affluent communities, housing segregation and the ghetto system might seem little more than a remnant of an unfortunate past, like the World War II relocation camps for the nation's amazingly successful Japanese-American community. Certainly the stories of blacks in such settings help to explain the white belief that housing segregation is no longer a serious problem. A national survey in 1981 reported, for example, that only 16 percent of whites thought that blacks faced discrimination in the housing market (*Washington Post*, Mar. 24, 1981, A2).

Yet other and radically different reports came from black suburbia and from emerging Hispanic suburbs. A controversial national study by the Rand Corporation, for example, pinpointed 14 "disaster" suburbs that had become thoroughgoing urban slums. The two worst areas, according to the study, were East St. Louis, Missouri, and Camden, New Jersey (96 percent black and 53 percent black in 1980). Both were "suburbs" only in the statistical sense that they were in the metropolitan area or Standard Metropolitan Statistical Area (SMSA) of a much larger central city—St. Louis and Philadelphia. They were really decaying industrial satellite cities. Such communities accounted for a substantial number of black "suburbanites." Although the Rand report pointed to a number of eastern and midwestern suburbs that were declining for purely economic reasons, it noted that all of the "troubled" suburbs in the more prosperous West were communities experiencing racial change or already largely minority. This controversial study was denounced as racist by the mayor of one Chicago suburb designated as troubled (*Chicago Tribune*, Aug. 26, 1982). All five suburbs cited in Los Angeles were predominantly minority. Compton, for example, was 75 percent black, 96 percent black and Hispanic, and extremely poor. Three of the troubled suburbs had large Hispanic majorities (*San Francisco Examiner*, Aug. 10, 1982).

Obviously we are talking about two completely different trends and two totally different impacts on the people involved. Yet both appear in the general statistics on suburbanization, the data that support the thesis of fundamental progress.

In the 1940s and 1950s, there was less differentiation among suburbs, and racial exclusion was so extreme that it made some sense to lump suburban areas together and argue that simply crossing the city–suburban boundary line was a fundamental racial breakthrough. Cities continue to change, however, and so do suburbs. Using a measure that had some rough justification a generation ago to assess progress in a very different social and economic setting can lead to extremely misleading results. The past 20 years have produced a series of developments that make analysis of what is happening far more complex. They include the following:

- Serious aging and physical and economic decay in portions of suburbia
- A strong outward white migration beyond suburbia, as it has traditionally been defined, to exurbia and small-towns
- Major regional shifts of wealth and economic opportunity producing metropolitanwide decline in some areas very important to minority families
- Emergence of Hispanics as a major demographic force in many metropolitan areas, making simple black–white analysis highly misleading in many instances (many Hispanics are counted as whites in the U.S. census)
- Growth of contiguous urban ghettos up to and across the city–suburban boundary lines in many cities

When we think about suburbanization, it is important to remember what were seen as key aspects of the suburban experience a generation ago and to look at where the same things are happening now. For example, we think about where families with means, with young children, with hope for good careers, and with personal mobility choose to locate. We look at areas with burgeoning economic growth and relatively affordable housing, with expanding school districts seen as desirable by young families.

The 1980 census showed a substantial net migration from metropolitan areas to nonmetropolitan communities and a substantial migration of white families from inner to outer suburbs. Public opinion studies show a broad desire to escape metropolitan areas altogether. Business magazines are full of stories about firms leaving metropolitan areas for friendly, controllable small towns with antiunion attitudes and low wages. In economic and social terms, there are good reasons to describe a number of the older suburbs, which are receiving black and Hispanic migration, as the equivalent of part of the central city of a generation ago, while the distant suburbs and even the growing small towns are taking on many of the aspects that were once seen as typically suburban. Celebrating the crossing of the suburban line today may be the equivalent of the celebrations in the black press of the black exodus from the rural South to the center of economic opportunity—the inner city—early in the century. It is celebrating what would have been a clear triumph a generation ago—at a time when its meaning has become highly ambiguous.

The other clearly outdated element of much of the analysis of suburban racial change is that the issue of simultaneous entrance of two major segregated minority groups—blacks and Hispanics—into suburban areas is being ignored. Because in the past blacks were clearly the dominant or only significant minority in the community, the suburban segregation problem was conceived of as a black–white issue, and progress was reported as blacks entered nonblack areas. Many of the poorest and most-depressed central cities, however, now contain large numbers of both blacks and Hispanics [*see Chapter 11 by José Ramón Sánchez*], and new census and school district figures show the same pattern emerging in some aging suburban areas. If an area's population is made up of 50 percent blacks and 40 percent Hispanics, then 90 percent of its people are members of groups that suffer great disadvantages in most metropolitan areas. While not a ghetto in the traditional sense, it is an area dominated by members of two groups with weak connections to the opportunity structure of the society and, often, considerable intergroup problems. Moving to such a community has a radically different meaning from moving to a stable, well-integrated suburb or an outlying white suburb. Ignoring this trend, particularly in areas with very large and rapidly growing Hispanic populations, throws the entire analysis into question.

The 1980 census data show that most of the increase in black suburban settlement during the 1970s took place in a relative handful of urban areas. Most of the dramatic growth came in metropolitan areas that had begun substantial black suburbanization before other cities.

In 1980, 25 SMSAs contained about three-fifths of all black suburbanites, and one-eighth of the entire national increase took place in the Washington, D.C., area. Almost 9 percent of the total *national* growth of black suburban residents took place in a single Washington suburb, Prince Georges County, Maryland (O'Hare, Chatterjee, and Shukur, 1982, 83–84). Inner Prince Georges County is now a large, integral, contiguous part of the Washington ghetto.

This brief review of national data and statistics from some of the metropolitan areas with the largest black suburban movements should indicate important differences between the meaning of suburbanization for whites and blacks. Blacks have arrived much later in significant numbers and often after the communities they are entering have ceased to be "suburban" in some of the characteristics most closely identified with the suburban ideal. These communities were not new and were not on the periphery of growth, but they were often older communities with a declining housing stock, shrinking school systems, and weakening fiscal situations. Black suburbanites were about one-third less likely than their white counterparts to be homeowners there. Though on the average, black suburbanites were more affluent than city blacks, they were a far more diverse group than white suburbanites, with about three times the white proportion of poor people and a far higher proportion of people living in suburban poverty pockets (Clark, 1979, 69–73, 90–91, 102). Blacks, of course, were vastly more likely than whites to be in, and stay in, suburbs that were in the midst of the ghettoization process.

These differences have great importance both for the possible gains of blacks from suburbanization and for the kinds of policies that could impede or facilitate access to equal opportunity in the suburbs. Obviously, many blacks are entering suburbs that have fewer resources, fewer connections to cities, less buoyant economies, more fiscal overburden, less affluent public schools, and much more isolation from the mainstream of upwardly mobile Americans than those that white suburbanites entered earlier. Blacks have gained less financially. Very few became property owners in the suburbs when the investments were smallest and the gains most spectacular. Most are still not property owners, and now they face much higher barriers to ownership. The rental market, rental construction, and rental subsidies are far more important to black than to white suburbanites. Black suburbanites, whose hold on suburban life is more precarious and whose gains have been smaller, also face the real possibility that a number of their communities will go through the entire ghettoization cycle, ending with segregated slums, falling population, and effective nullification of everything the early immigrants believed they had won. It has already happened in some areas.

Black suburbanization has occurred in a general policy vacuum and may well be pushed in still more unfavorable directions as a by-product of some of the policies now being pursued for very different reasons, without any analysis of their potential impact on these issues. Programs that inadvertently pump subsidized housing into precariously integrated suburbs, for example, can help turn black suburban migration into ghettoization. Suburbanization is one of the most important factors affecting middle-class black families in many metropolitan areas and an extremely important option for all minority families, whose opportunities are shrinking as basic central-city services are curtailed in such vital areas as education. It is very important that everything possible be done to avoid a repetition of all the mistakes of the central-city ghetto-formation process.

---

*Excerpts from unanimous 1983 New Jersey Supreme Court Mount Laurel II Decision (Southern Burlington County NAACP v. Township of Mt. Laurel [92 N.J. 158, 456 A.2d 390]), dated January 20, 1983, written by Chief Justice Robert N. Wilentz.*

We set forth in that [Mount Laurel I] case, for the first time, the doctrine requiring that municipalities' land-use regulations provide a realistic opportunity for low- and moderate-income housing. The doctrine has become famous. The Mount Laurel case itself threatens to become infamous.

After all this time, 10 years after the trial court's initial order invalidating its zoning ordinance, Mount Laurel remains afflicted with a blatantly exclusionary ordinance. Papered over with studies, rationalized by hired experts, the ordinance at its core is true to nothing but Mount Laurel's determination to exclude the poor.

Mount Laurel is not alone; we believe that there is widespread noncompliance with the constitutional mandate of our original opinion in this case.

To the best of our ability, we shall not

allow it to continue. This court is more firmly committed to the original Mount Laurel doctrine than ever, and we are determined, within appropriate judicial bounds, to make it work. The obligation is to provide a realistic opportunity for housing, not litigation.

We have learned from experience, however, that unless a strong judicial hand is used, Mount Laurel will not result in housing, but in paper, process, witnesses, trials and appeals. . . .

The constitutional basis for the Mount Laurel doctrine remains the same. The constitutional power to zone, delegated to the municipalities subject to legislation, is but one portion of the police power and, as such, must be exercised for the general welfare.

When the exercise of that power by a municipality affects something as fundamental as housing, the general welfare includes more than the welfare of that municipality and its citizens: it also includes the general welfare—in this case the housing needs—of those residing outside of the municipality but within the region that contributes to the housing demand within the municipality.

The state controls the use of land, *all* of the land. In exercising that control, it cannot favor the rich over the poor. It cannot legislatively set aside dilapidated housing in urban ghettos for the poor and decent housing elsewhere for everyone else. The government that controls this land represents everyone. While the state may not have the ability to eliminate poverty, it cannot use that condition as the basis for imposing further disadvantages.

The clarity of the constitutional obligation is seen most simply by imagining what this state could be like were this claim never to be recognized and enforced: poor people forever zoned out of substantial areas of the state, not because housing could not be built for them but because they are not wanted; poor people forced to live in urban slums forever not because suburbia, developing rural areas, fully developed residential sections, seashore resorts, and other attractive locations could not accommodate them, but simply because they are not wanted.

It is a vision not only at variance with the requirement that the zoning power be used for the general welfare but with all concepts of fundamental fairness and decency that underpin many constitutional obligations. . . .

We reassure all concerned that Mount Laurel is not designed to sweep away all land-use restrictions or leave our open spaces and natural resources prey to speculators. Municipalities consisting largely of conservation, agricultural or environmentally sensitive areas will not be required to grow because of Mount Laurel. No forests or small towns need to be paved over and covered with highrise apartments as a result of today's decision. . . .

As we said at the outset, while we have always preferred legislative to judicial action in this field, we shall continue—until the Legislature acts—to do our best to uphold the constitutional obligation that underlies the Mount Laurel doctrine. That is our duty. We may not build houses, but we do enforce the Constitution.

# SOME JERSEY TOWNS, GIVING IN TO COURTS, LET IN MODEST HOMES
*By Robert Hanley*

BEDMINSTER, N.J., Feb. 27—By late summer, the prosperous people living in newly built $210,000 town houses on a gentle slope here will have new neighbors moving into unadorned condominiums selling for $35,000 to $80,000.

The mix of elegant and more modest housing in the same development will be the first visible result of a year-old ruling by the New Jersey Supreme Court that municipalities across the state must zone for low- and moderate-income housing.

Judges, municipal planners, zoning experts and lawyers say scores of towns over the next decade will either agree voluntarily or be forced by judicial decree to accept such housing and a consequent recasting of their social and political fabric. . . .

The State Supreme Court first ordered suburban and rural communities to zone for low- and moderate-income housing in a 1975 decision.

The ruling overturned as exclusionary the zoning of Mount Laurel, a growing community in Burlington County on the outer ring of Philadelphia's suburbs.

The ruling produced mounds of lawsuits and many long and costly trials, but no housing for the poor.

Angry over the inaction, the high court reaffirmed the order in a unanimous Mount Laurel II ruling in January 1983.

It asserted that the municipal zoning powers granted by the State Constitution must be exercised fairly for everyone, and not favor the rich over the poor. . . .

In contrast with the earlier Mount Laurel ruling, the new one gives builders a financial incentive to construct low- and middle-income housing, legal experts said. . . .

In Bedminster, the struggle to keep out such housing is over after decades of resistance.

This Somerset County town, where zoning for many years required five acres for each single-family home, is acquiescing to 260 units of low- and moderate-income housing this year. By 1990, 684 more are to be built in the town in the north-central part of the state.

Construction is to start once the ground thaws. And within six months, newcomers of modest means will start coming to a world of wealth where 2,500 people now live in 27 square miles of countryside, and the steeplechase, the fox hunt and the horse farm reign.

Other towns are also feeling the impact of the year-old decision.

Mahwah, in Bergen County near the New York State border, recently enacted a new zoning law in response to a court order to provide 699 low- and moderate-income units.

Pequannock, in Morris County, is trying to settle a suit brought by the state's Department of the Public Advocate by agreeing to accept 500 units.

Officials of Warren Township, a prosperous community near Bedminster, have expressed a willingness to zone for 900 units despite mounting resistance from residents.

Under one aspect of the court decision, towns that rezone voluntarily to a judge's satisfaction are immune from zoning suits for six years.

East Windsor, near Princeton in Mercer County, is also rezoning voluntarily.

Branchburg, another Somerset County town, wants to comply by allowing construction of nearly 1,300 mobile homes for low- and moderate-income residents.

In Middlesex County, seven communities have been sued by developers. A court-appointed expert has recommended that the towns accept 10,242 low- and moderate-income units. A trial on the issue is scheduled in March.

And Mount Laurel, whose exclusionary zoning touched off the entire case, is negotiating to accept 92 low- and moderate-income mobile homes in a 456-unit complex as a first step toward meeting its obligation.

These seven cases are among 61 before three State Superior Court judges assigned to hear all Mount Laurel II litigation. The decision provided for all Mount Laurel cases to be heard by the three judges to speed up suits and avoid inconsistent rulings. Of these 61 suits, 57 have been filed by builders.

"As these cases get tried in the next year, we'll see a real flood of low- and moderate-income housing being constructed," said Kenneth J. Meiser, deputy director of the state's Division of Public Interest Advocacy, a watchdog agency.

Of the four suits not filed by builders, two came from Mr. Meiser's office and two from civil rights organizations. Years back, the legal effort was dominated by open-housing advocates and civil rights groups.

Builders are in the forefront now. The Mount Laurel II decision uses the builder as a wedge to insure open housing.

Under the decision, a builder is granted what is called a "builder's remedy" if a judge rules that a town's zoning does not provide for its "fair share" of low- and moderate-income housing.

Once granted a builder's remedy, a developer is allowed increased housing densities and agrees to construct 20 units of low- and moderate-income housing for every 80 units of high-priced housing. Profits from the sale of the expensive homes are meant to offset losses that builders incur by selling the modest housing below prevailing market prices.

The court viewed this profit-subsidy concept as the key to the carrying out of its order. "If builders' remedies cannot be profitable," the court said, "the incentive for builders to enforce 'Mount Laurel' is lost."

In addition to the builder's remedy, the decision provided another spur for construction.

Once a town persuades a judge that it has voluntarily rezoned to accommodate its "fair share" of low- and moderate-income housing, it receives a six-year grace period against builders' suits over such housing.

"Every single town has to get off the dime, or a builder can come in and it'll be like sitting ducks," said John Kerwin, president of the Hills Development Company, which is building the complex in Bedminister. "The longer it takes a town to figure this out, the greater the chances of builders telling them where the housing will go."

For decades, Bedminster's zoning required a minimum five-acre lot for a single-family home. Much of the land remains zoned for three- and five-acre lots.

But because of the Mount Laurel II decision, the Route 202-206 corridor near the busy woodland juncture of Interstates 287 and 78 has been rezoned to permit 6, 8, and 10 housing units an acre.

The 280 "Mount Laurel" homes will be part of a 200-acre complex of 1,287 condominium town houses.

Mr. Kerwin says his company can sell them for $35,000 to $60,000 because they will be small—567 to 997 square feet—and will not have basements, fireplaces, garages, custom cabinets or luxury features. The exteriors, however, will match the complex's $150,000 to $210,000 town houses farther up the hillside.

Under the court decision, eligibility to buy the "Mount Laurel" homes is pegged to income. Those earning up to half of the Bedminster region's median income of about $33,000 qualify to buy the low-income homes. Those earning 50 percent to 80 percent of the area's median income qualify for the moderate-income homes.

Mr. Kerwin says he believes the buyers of the new homes will be young married couples, single parents, teachers, police officers and the clerks and secretaries working in the new corporate headquarters that have sprouted up near Bedminster in recent years.

He does not foresee an influx of poor people from urban areas. "We do not have an affirmative action requirement under the decision," he said. "It's not a social or ethnic or racial obligation. It's a purely economic issue."

The [1980 State Development Guide] plan plays a key role in the Mount Laurel II decision by designating target areas for the bulk of such housing. The Supreme Court has asked that the plan be updated by Jan. 1, 1985, to provide more precise guidelines.

The plan written under the Byrne administration divides the state into four areas—growth, limited growth, conservation and agricultural areas.

The court decision requires that all municipalities in a growth area provide a "fair share" of low- and moderate-income housing within the surrounding region. Growth areas make up about a third of the state's land area.

Towns in limited growth, conservation and agricultural areas, which account for another third of the state's land, do not face the same "fair share" obligation.

They are required to provide only "realistic opportunities for housing for low- and moderate-income people who live within their borders.

Although towns in all four areas are encouraged to rezone voluntarily, their land-use ordinances will not come under judicial scrutiny unless a suit is filed.

As a practical matter, heavily urban areas, such as Newark and Paterson, will not be required to take additional low- and moderate-income housing.

Communities expected to be targets of lawsuits, housing experts said, are those in growth areas with sizable amounts of vacant, developable land and with restrictive zoning laws, such [as] those that require large lot sizes and prohibit mobile homes.

From the *New York Times*, February 29, 1984. Copyright © 1984 by The New York Times Company. Reprinted by permission.

| 13 | What Would a Non-Sexist City Be Like? Speculations on Housing, Urban Design, and Human Work |
|---|---|
| | *Dolores Hayden* |

*America's cities and housing have not kept pace with the changing needs of house-holds. Women have been entering the paid labor force in larger and larger numbers. Yet housing, neighborhoods, and cities continue to be designed for homebound women. This situation constrains women physically, socially, and economically, and reinforces their dependence. Some models of alternative housing and neighborhood designs that better meet women's needs are proposed in this chapter.*

"A woman's place is in the home" has been one of the most important principles of architectural design and urban planning in the United States for the last century. An implicit rather than explicit principle for the conservative and male-dominated design professions, it will not be found stated in large type in textbooks on land use. It has generated much less debate than the other organizing principles of the contemporary American city in an era of monopoly capitalism, which include the ravaging pressure of private land development, the fetishistic dependence on millions of private automobiles, and the wasteful use of energy.[1] However, women have rejected this dogma and entered the paid labor force in larger and larger numbers. Dwellings, neighborhoods, and cities designed for homebound women constrain women physically, socially, and economically. Acute frustration occurs when women defy these constraints to spend all or part of the workday in the paid labor force. I contend that the only remedy for this situation is to develop a new paradigm of the home, the neighborhood, and the city; to begin to describe the physical, social, and economic design of a human

This chapter was originally part of the text of a talk for the conference "Planning and Designing a Non-Sexist Society," University of California, Los Angeles, April 21, 1979. It also appeared under the title "What Would a Non-Sexist City Be Like? Speculations on Housing, Urban Design and Human Work," in *SIGNS* 5, no. 3 supplement (Spring 1980): 167–84. It is reprinted from *Women and the American City*, ed. Catharine R. Stimpson et al. Chicago: University of Chicago Press, 1981. © 1980, 1981 by The University of Chicago.

settlement that would support, rather than restrict, the activities of employed women and their families. It is essential to recognize such needs in order to begin both the rehabilitation of the existing housing stock and the construction of new housing to meet the needs of a new and growing majority of Americans—working women and their families.

When speaking of the American city in the last quarter of the twentieth century, a false distinction between "city" and "suburb" must be avoided. The urban region, organized to separate homes and workplaces, must be seen as a whole. In such urban regions, more than half of the population resides in the sprawling suburban areas, or "bedroom communities." The greatest part of the built environment in the United States consists of "suburban sprawl": single-family homes grouped in class-segregated areas, crisscrossed by freeways and served by shopping malls and commercial strip developments. Over 50 million small homes are on the ground. About two-thirds of American families "own" their homes on long mortgages; this includes over 77 percent of all AFL–CIO members (*Survey of AFL–CIO Members' Housing*, 1975, 16).[2] White, male skilled workers are far more likely to be homeowners than members of minority groups and women, long denied equal credit or equal access to housing. Workers commute to jobs either in the center or elsewhere in the suburban ring. In metropolitan areas studied in 1975 and 1976, the journey to work, by public transit or private car, averaged about nine miles each way. Over 100 million privately owned cars filled two- and three-car garages (which would be considered magnificent housing by themselves in many developing countries). . . .

The roots of this American settlement form lie in the environmental and economic policies of the past. In the late nineteenth century, millions of immigrant families lived in the crowded, filthy slums of American industrial cities and despaired of achieving reasonable living conditions. However, many militant strikes and demonstrations between the 1890s and 1920s made some employers reconsider plant locations and housing issues in their search for industrial order.[3] "Good homes make contented workers" was the slogan of the Industrial Housing Associates in 1919. These consultants and many others helped major corporations plan better housing for white, male skilled workers and their families in order to eliminate industrial conflict. "Happy workers invariably mean bigger profits, while unhappy workers are never a good investment," they chirruped.[4] Men were to receive "family wages" and become home "owners" responsible for regular mortgage payments, while their wives became home "managers" taking care of spouse and children. The male worker would return from his day in the factory or office to a private domestic environment, secluded from the tense world of work in an industrial city characterized by environmental pollution, social degradation, and personal alienation. He would enter a serene dwelling whose physical and emotional maintenance would be the duty of his wife. Thus the private suburban house was the stage set for the effective sexual division of labor. It was the commodity par excellence, a spur for male paid labor and a container for female unpaid labor. It made gender appear a more important self-definition than class, and consumption more involving than production. In a brilliant discussion of the "patriarch as wage slave," Stuart Ewen has shown how capitalism and antifeminism fused in campaigns for homeownership and mass consumption: The patriarch whose home was his "castle" was to work year in and year out to provide the wages to support this private environment (Ewen, 1976).

Although this strategy was first boosted by corporations interested in a docile labor force, it soon appealed to corporations that wished to move from World War I defense industries into peacetime production of domestic appliances for millions of families. The development of the advertising industry, documented by Ewen, supported this ideal of mass consumption and promoted the private suburban dwelling, which maximized appliance purchases (Walker, 1977). The occupants of the isolated household were suggestible. They bought the house itself, a car, stove, refrigerator, vacuum cleaner, washer, carpets. Christine Frederick, explaining it in 1929 as *Selling Mrs. Consumer*, promoted homeownership and easier consumer credit and advised marketing managers on how to manipulate American women (Frederick, 1929). By 1931 the Hoover Commission on Home Ownership and Home Building established the private, single-family home as a national goal, but a decade and a half of depression and war postponed its achievement. Architects designed houses for Mr. and Mrs. Bliss in a competition sponsored by General Electric in 1935; winners accommodated dozens of electrical appliances in their designs with no critique of the energy costs involved.[5] In the late 1940s the single-family home was boosted by FHA and VA mortgages, and the construction of isolated, overprivatized, energy-consuming dwellings became commonplace [*see Chapter 6 by Barry Checkoway*]. "I'll Buy That Dream" made the postwar hit parade (Filene, 1974, 189).

Mrs. Consumer moved the economy to new heights in the 1950s. Women who stayed at home experienced what Betty Friedan called the "feminine mystique" and Peter Filene renamed the "domestic mystique."[6] While the family occupied its private physical space, the mass media and social science experts invaded its psychological space more effectively than ever before.[7] With the increase in spatial privacy came pressure for conformity in consumption. Consumption was expensive. More and more married women joined the paid labor force, as the suggestible housewife needed to be both a frantic consumer and a paid worker to keep up with the family's bills. Just as the mass of white male workers had achieved the "dream houses" in suburbia where fantasies of patriarchal authority and consumption could be acted out, their spouses entered the world of paid employment. By 1975, the two-worker family accounted for 39 percent of American households. Another 13 percent were single-parent families, usually headed by women. Seven out of 10 employed women were in the work force because of financial need. Over 50 percent of all children between the ages of one and seventeen had employed mothers (Baxandall, Gordon, and Reverby, 1976).[8]

How does a conventional home serve the employed woman and her family? Badly. Whether it is in a suburban, exurban, or inner-city neighborhood, whether it is a split-level ranch house, a modern masterpiece of concrete and glass, or an old brick tenement, the house or apartment is almost invariably organized around the same set of spaces: kitchen, dining room, living room, bedrooms, garage or parking area. These spaces require someone to undertake private cooking, cleaning, child care, and usually private transportation if adults and children are to exist within it. Because of residential zoning practices, the typical dwelling will usually be physically removed from any shared community space—no commercial or communal day-care facilities, or laundry facilities, for example, are likely to be part of the dwelling's spatial domain. In many cases these facilities would be illegal if placed across property lines. They could also be illegal if located on residentially zoned sites. In some cases sharing such a private dwelling with other individuals (either relatives or those unrelated by blood) is also against the law.[9]

Within the private spaces of the dwelling, material culture works against the needs of the employed woman as much as zoning does, because the home is a box to be filled with commodities. Appliances are usually single-purpose, and often inefficient, energy-consuming machines, lined up in a room where the domestic work is done in isolation from the rest of the family. Rugs and carpets that need vacuuming, curtains that need laundering, and miscellaneous goods that need maintenance fill up the domestic spaces, often decorated in "colonial," "Mediterranean," "French Provincial," or other eclectic styles purveyed by discount and department stores to cheer up that bare box of an isolated house. Employed mothers usually are expected to, and almost invariably do, spend more time in private housework and child care than employed men; often they are expected to, and usually do, spend more time on commuting per mile traveled than men, because of their reliance on public transportation. One study found that 70 percent of adults without access to cars are female.[10] Their residential neighborhoods are not likely to provide much support for their work activities. A "good" neighborhood is usually defined in terms of conventional shopping, schools, and perhaps public transit, rather than additional social services for the working parent, such as day care or evening clinics.

While two-worker families with both parents energetically cooperating can overcome some of the problems of existing housing patterns, households in crisis, such as subjects of wife and child battering, for example, are particularly vulnerable to housing's inadequacies. According to Colleen McGrath, every 30 seconds a woman is being battered somewhere in the United States. Most of these batterings occur in kitchens and bedrooms. The relationship between household isolation and battering, or between unpaid domestic labor and battering, can only be guessed, at this time, but there is no doubt that America's houses and households are literally shaking with domestic violence (McGrath, 1979, 12, 23). In addition, millions of angry and upset women are treated with tranquilizers in the private home—one drug company advertises to doctors: "You can't change her environment but you can change her mood."[11]

The woman who does leave the isolated, single-family house or apartment finds very few real housing alternatives available to her.[12] The typical divorced or battered woman currently seeks housing, employment, and child care simultaneously. She finds that matching her complex family requirements with the various available offerings by landlords, employers, and social services is impossible. One environment that unites housing, services, and jobs could resolve many difficulties, but the existing system of government services, intended to stabilize households and neighborhoods by insuring the minimum conditions for a decent home life to all Americans, almost always assumes that the traditional household with a male worker and an unpaid homemaker is the goal to be achieved or simulated. In the face of massive demographic changes, programs such as public housing, AFDC, and food stamps still attempt to support an ideal family living in an isolated house or apartment, with a full-time homemaker cooking meals and minding children many hours of the day.

By recognizing the need for a different kind of environment, far more efficient use can be made of funds now used for subsidies to individual households. Even for women with greater financial resources, the need for better housing and services is obvious. Currently, more affluent women's problems as workers have been considered "private" problems—the lack of good day care, their lack of time. The aids to overcome an environment without child care, public transportation, or food service have been "private," commercially profitable solutions: maids and babysitters by the hour; franchise day care or extended television viewing; fast-food service; easier credit for purchasing an automobile, a washer, or a microwave oven. Not only do these commercial solutions obscure the failure of American housing policies; they also generate bad conditions for other working women. Commercial day-care and fast-food franchises are the source of low-paying nonunion jobs without security. In this respect they resemble the use of private household workers by bourgeois women, who may never ask how their private maid or child-care worker arranges care for her own children. They also resemble the insidious effects of the use of television in the home as a substitute for developmental child care in the neighborhood. The logistical problems that all employed women face are not private problems, and they do not succumb to market solutions.

The problem is paradoxical: Women cannot improve their status in the home unless their overall economic position in society is altered; women cannot improve their status in the paid labor force unless their domestic responsibilities are altered. Therefore, a program to achieve economic and environmental justice for women requires, by definition, a solution that overcomes the traditional divisions between the household and the market economy, the private dwelling and the workplace. One must transform the economic situation of the traditional homemaker, whose skilled labor has been unpaid but economically and socially necessary to society; one must also transform the domestic situation of the employed woman. If architects and urban designers were to recognize all employed women and their families as a constituency for new approaches to planning and design and were to reject all previous assumptions about "woman's place" in the home, what could we do? Is it possible to build non-sexist neighborhoods and design non-sexist cities? What would they be like?

Some countries have begun to develop new approaches to the needs of employed women. The Cuban Family Code of 1974 requires men to share housework and child care within the private home. The degree of its enforcement is uncertain, but in principle it aims at men's sharing what was formerly "women's work," which is essential to equality. The Family Code, however, does not remove work from the house, and relies upon private negotiation between husband and wife for its day-to-day enforcement. Men feign incompetence, especially in the area of cooking, with tactics familiar to any reader of Patricia Mainardi's essay "The Politics of Housework," and the sexual stereotyping of paid jobs for women outside the home, in day-care centers for example, has not been successfully challenged (Mainardi, 1970).[13] [*For a discussion of Cuban housing policy, see Chapter 33 by Jill Hamberg.*]

Another experimental approach involves the development of special housing facilities for employed women and their families. The builder Otto Fick first introduced such a program in Copenhagen in 1903. In later years it was encouraged in Sweden by Alva Myrdal and by the architects Sven Ivar Lind and Sven Markelius. Called "service houses" or "collective houses," such projects (Figs. 13.1 and 13.2) provide child care and cooked food along with housing for employed women and their families (Muhlestein, 1975). Like a few similar projects in the USSR in the 1920s, they aim at offering services, either on a commercial basis or subsidized by the state, to replace formerly private "women's work" performed in the household. The Scan-

FIGURE 13.1 Sven Ivar Lind, *Marieberg* collective house, Stockholm, Sweden, 1944, plan of entrance (*entré*), restaurant (*restaurang*), and day nursery (*daghem*): (1) entrance hall, (2) doorman's office, (3) restaurant delivery room, (4) real estate office, (5) connecting walkway to *Swedberg House*, (6) restaurant anteroom, (7) main dining room, (8) small dining room, (9) restaurant kitchen, (10) to day nursery's baby carriage room, (11) day nursery's baby carriage room, (12) office for day nursery's directress, (13) to *Wennerberg House*'s cycle garage.

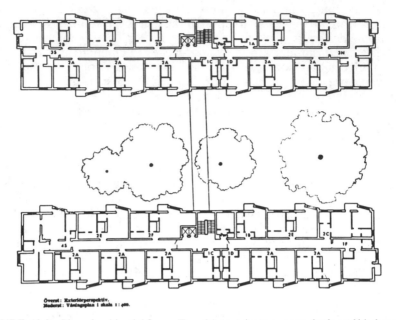

FIGURE 13.2   Plan of residential floors. Type 2A contains two rooms, bath, and kitchenette. Types 1C and 4D are efficiency units with bath and kitchenette. Type 4S includes four rooms with bath and full kitchen.

dinavian solution does not sufficiently challenge male exclusion from domestic work, nor does it deal with households' changing needs over the life cycle, but it recognizes that it is important for environmental design to change.

Some additional projects in Europe extend the scope of the service house to include the provision of services for the larger community or society. In the Steilshoop Project, in Hamburg, Germany, in the early 1970s, a group of parents and single people designed public housing with supporting services (Fig. 13.3).[14] The project included a number of former mental patients as residents and therefore served as a halfway house for them, in addition to providing support services for the public housing tenants who organized it. It suggests the extent to which current American residential stereotypes can be broken down—the sick, the aged, and the unmarried can be integrated into new types of households and housing complexes, rather than segregated in separate projects.

Another recent project was created in London by Nina West Homes, a development group established in 1972, which has built or renovated over 63 units of housing on six sites for single parents. Children's play areas or day-care centers are integrated with the dwellings; in their Fiona House project the housing is designed to facilitate shared babysitting, and the

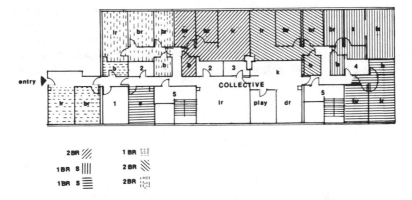

FIGURE 13.3 *Urbanes Wohnen* (urban living) *Steilshoop*, north of Hamburg, Germany, public housing for 206 tenants, designed by the tenant association in collaboration with Rolf Spille, 1970–1973. Instead of 72 conventional units, they built 20 multifamily units and 2 studios. Twenty-six mental patients were included in the project, of whom 24 recovered. Partial floor plan. Units include private bedrooms (br), living rooms (lr), and some studios (s). They share a collective living room, kitchen, dining room, and playroom. Each private apartment can be closed off from the collective space, and each is different. Key: (1) storage room, (2) closets, (3) wine cellar, (4) *buanderie*, (5) fire stairs.

day-care center is open to the neighborhood residents for a fee (Fig. 13.4). Thus the single parents can find jobs as day-care workers and help the neighborhood's working parents as well (*Architects' Journal*, Sept. 27, 1972, 680–84).[15] What is most exciting here is the hint that home and work can be reunited on one site for some of the residents, and home and child-care services are reunited on one site for all of them.

In the United States, we have an even longer history of agitation for housing to reflect women's needs. In the late nineteenth century and early twentieth century there were dozens of projects by feminists, domestic scientists, and architects attempting to develop community services for private homes. By the late 1920s, few such experiments were still functioning.[16] In general, feminists of that era failed to recognize the problem of exploiting other women workers when providing services for those who could afford them. They also often failed to see men as responsible parents and workers in their attempts to socialize "women's" work. But feminist leaders had a very strong sense of the possibilities of neighborly cooperation among families and of the economic importance of "women's" work.

In addition, the United States has a long tradition of experimental utopian socialist communities building model towns, as well as the example of many communes and collectives established in the 1960s and 1970s, which attempted to broaden conventional definitions of household and family.[17] While some communal groups, especially religious ones, have often demanded acceptance of a traditional sexual division of labor, others have attempted to make nurturing activities a responsibility of both women and men. It is important to draw on the examples of successful projects of all kinds in seeking an image of a nonsexist settlement. Most employed women are not interested in taking themselves and their families to live in communal families, nor are they interested in having state bureaucracies run family life. They desire, not an end to private life altogether, but community

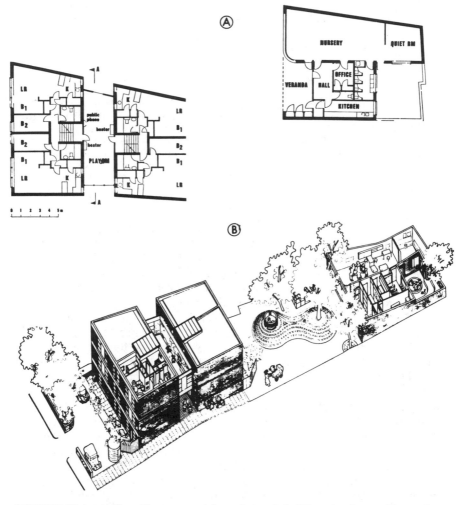

FIGURE 13.4   A, *Fiona House*, second-floor plan, main building, showing corridor used as a playroom, with kitchen windows opening into it; first-floor plan, rear building, showing nursery school. *B*, Axonometric drawing, *Fiona House*, Nina West Homes, London 1972, designed by Sylvester Bone. Twelve two-bedroom units for divorced or separated mothers with additional outdoor play space and neighborhood nursery school facility. Flats can be linked by intercom system to provide an audio substitute for babysitting.

services to support the private household. They also desire solutions that reinforce their economic independence and maximize their personal choices about child rearing and sociability.

What, then, would be the outline of a program for change in the United States? The task of reorganizing both home and work can be accomplished only by organizations of homemakers, women and men dedicated to making changes in the ways that Americans deal with private life and public responsibilities. They must be small, participatory organizations with members who can work together effectively. I propose calling such groups HOMES (Homemakers Organization for a More Egalitarian Society). Existing feminist groups, especially those providing shelters for battered wives and children, may wish to form HOMES to take over existing housing projects and develop services for residents as an extension of those offered by feminist counselors in the shelter. Existing organizations supporting cooperative ownership of housing may wish to form HOMES to extend their housing efforts in a feminist direction. A program broad enough to transform housework, housing, and residential neighborhoods must (1) involve both men and women in the unpaid labor associated with housekeeping and child care on an equal basis; (2) involve both men and women in the paid labor force on an equal basis; (3) eliminate residential segregation by class, race, and age; (4) eliminate all federal, state, and local programs and laws that offer implicit or explicit reinforcement of the unpaid role of the female homemaker; (5) minimize unpaid domestic labor and wasteful energy consumption; (6) maximize real choices for households concerning recreation and sociability. While many partial reforms can support these goals, an incremental strategy cannot achieve them. I believe that the establishment of experimental residential centers, which in their architectural design and economic organization transcend traditional definitions of home, neighborhood, city, and workplace, will be necessary to make changes on this scale. These centers could be created through renovation of existing neighborhoods or through new construction.

Suppose 40 households in a U.S. metropolitan area formed a HOMES group and that those households, in their composition, represented the social structure of the American population as a whole. Those 40 households would include 7 single parents and their 14 children (15 percent); 16 two-worker couples and their 24 children (40 percent); 13 one-worker couples and their 26 children (35 percent); and 4 single residents, some of them "displaced homemakers" (10 percent). The residents would include 69 adults and 64 children. There would need to be 40 private dwelling units, ranging in size from efficiency to three bedrooms, all with private, fenced outdoor space. In addition to the private housing, the group would provide the following collective spaces and activities: (1) a day-care center with landscaped outdoor space, providing day care for 40 children and after-school activities for 64 children; (2) a laundromat providing laundry service; (3) a kitchen providing lunches for the day-care center, take-out evening meals, and "meals-on-wheels" for elderly people in the neighborhood; (4) a grocery depot, connected to a local food cooperative; (5) a garage with two vans providing dial-a-ride service and meals-on-wheels; (6) a garden (or allotments) where some food can be grown; (7) a home-help office providing helpers for the elderly, the sick, and employed parents whose children are sick. The use of all these collective services should be voluntary; they would exist in addition to private dwelling units and private gardens.

To provide all of the above services, 37 workers would be necessary: 20 day-care workers; 3 food-service workers; 1 grocery-depot worker; 5 home helpers; 2 drivers of service vehicles; 2 laundry workers; 1 maintenance worker; 1 gardener; 2 administrative staff. Some of these may be part-time workers, some full-time. Day care, food services, and elderly services could be organized as producers' cooperatives, and other workers could be employed by the housing cooperative as discussed below.

Because HOMES is not intended as an experiment in isolated community buildings but as an experiment in meeting employed women's needs in an urban area, its services should be available to the neighborhood in which the experiment is located. This will increase demand for the services and insure that the jobs are real ones. In addition, although residents of HOMES should have priority for the jobs, there will be many who choose outside work. So some local residents may take jobs within the experiment.

In creating and filling these jobs it will be important to avoid traditional sex stereotyping that would result from hiring only men as drivers, for example, or only women as food-service workers. Every effort should be made to break down separate categories of paid work for women and men, just as efforts should be made to recruit men who accept an equal share of domestic responsibilities as residents. A version of the Cuban Family Code should become part of the organization's platform.

Similarly, HOMES must not create a two-class society with residents outside the project making more money than residents in HOMES jobs that utilize some of their existing domestic skills. The HOMES jobs should be paid according to egalitarian rather than sex-stereotyped attitudes about skills and hours. These jobs must be all classified as skilled work rather than as unskilled or semiskilled at present, and offer full social security and health benefits, including adequate maternity leave, whether workers are part-time or full-time. . . .

A limited-equity housing cooperative offers the best basis for economic organization and control of both physical design and social policy by the residents. Many knowledgeable nonprofit developers could aid community groups wishing to organize such projects, as could architects experienced in the design of housing cooperatives. What has not been attempted is the reintegration of work activities and collective services into housing cooperatives on a large enough scale to make a real difference to employed women. Feminists in trade unions where a majority of members are women may wish to consider building cooperative housing with services for their members. Other trade unions may wish to consider investing in such projects. Feminists in the coop movement must make strong, clear demands to get such services from existing housing cooperatives, rather than simply go along with plans for conventional housing organized on a cooperative economic basis. Feminists outside the cooperative movement will find that cooperative organizational forms offer many possibilities for supporting their housing activities and other services to women. In addition, the National Cooperative Bank has funds to support projects of all kinds that can be tied to cooperative housing.

In many areas, the rehabilitation of existing housing may be more desirable than new construction. The suburban housing stock in the United States must be dealt with effectively. A little bit of it is of architectural quality sufficient to deserve preservation; most of it can be aesthetically improved by the physical evidence of more intense social activity. To replace empty front lawns without sidewalks, neighbors can create blocks where single units are converted to multiple units; interior land is pooled to create a parklike setting at the center of the block; front and side lawns are fenced to make private outdoor spaces; pedestrian paths and sidewalks are created to link all units with the central open space; and some private porches, garages, tool sheds, utility rooms, and family rooms are converted to community facilities such as children's play areas, dial-a-ride garages, and laundries.

Figure 13.5A shows a typical suburban block of 13 houses, constructed by speculators at different times, where about four acres are divided into plots of one-fourth to one-half acre each. The 13 driveways are used by 26 cars; 10 garden sheds, 10 swings, 13 lawn mowers, and 13 outdoor dining tables begin to suggest the wasteful duplication of existing amenities. Yet despite the available land there are no transitions between public streets and these private homes. Space is either strictly private or strictly public. Figure 13.6A shows a typical one-family house of 1,400 square feet on this block. With three bedrooms and den, two-and-a-half baths, laundry room, two porches, and a two-car garage, it was constructed in the 1950s at the height of the "feminine mystique."

To convert this whole block and the housing on it to more efficient and sociable uses, one has to define a zone of greater activity at the heart of the block, taking a total of one and a half to two acres for collective use (Fig. 13.5B). Essentially, this means turning the block inside out. The Radburn plan, developed by Henry Wright and Clarence Stein in the late 1920s, delineated this principle very clearly as correct land use in "the motor age," with cars segregated from residents' green spaces, especially spaces for children. In Radburn, New Jersey, and in the Baldwin Hills district of Los Angeles, California, Wright and Stein achieved remarkably luxurious results (at a density of about seven units to the acre) by this method, since their multiple-unit housing always bordered a lush parkland without any automobile traffic. The Baldwin Hills project demonstrates this success most dramatically, but a revitalized suburban block with lots as small as one-fourth acre can be reorganized to yield something of this same effect.[18] In this case, social amenities are added to aesthetic ones, as the interior park is designed to accommodate community day care, a garden for growing vegetables, some picnic tables, a playground where swings and slides are grouped, a grocery depot connected to a larger neighborhood food cooperative, and a dial-a-ride garage.

Large single-family houses can be remodeled quite easily to become duplexes and triplexes, despite the "open plans" of the 1950s and 1960s popularized by many developers. The house in Figure 13.6A becomes, in Figure 13.6B, a triplex, with a two-bedroom unit (linked to a community garage); a one-bedroom unit; and an efficiency unit (for a single person or elderly person). All three units are shown with private enclosed gardens. The three units share a front porch and entry hall. There is still enough land to give about two-fifths of the original lot to the community. Particularly striking is the way in which existing spaces such as back porches or garages lend themselves to conversion to social areas or community services. Three former private garages out of 13 might be given over to collective uses—one

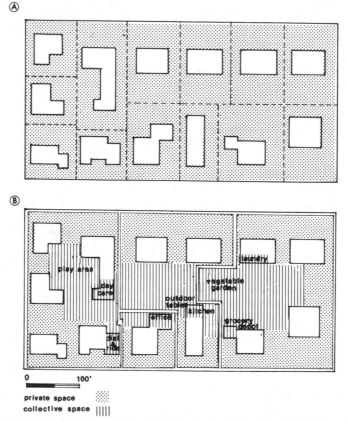

FIGURE 13.5   *A*, Suburban neighborhood, block plan. *B*, Proposed HOMES revitalization; same suburban block with new common space and facilities.

as a central office for the whole block, one as a grocery depot, and one as a dial-a-ride garage. Is it possible to have only 20 cars (in 10 garages) and 2 vans for 26 units in a rehabilitated block? Assuming that some residents switch from outside employment to working within the block, and that for all residents, neighborhood shopping trips are cut in half by the presence of day care, groceries, laundry, and cooked food on the block, as well as aided by the presence of some new collective transportation, this might be done.

What about neighbors who are not interested in such a scheme? Depending on the configuration of lots, it is possible to begin such a plan with as few as three or four houses. In Berkeley, California, where neighbors on Derby Street joined their backyards and created a cooperative day-care center, one absentee landlord refused to join—his entire property is fenced in and the community space flows around it without difficulty. Of course, present

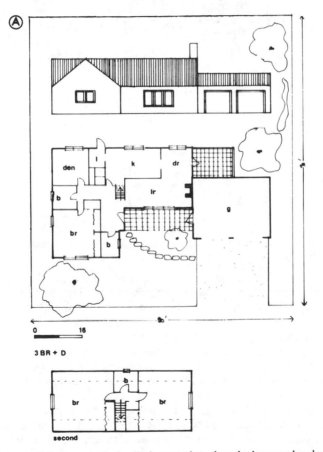

FIGURE 13.6  *A*, Suburban single-family house, plan, three bedrooms plus den.

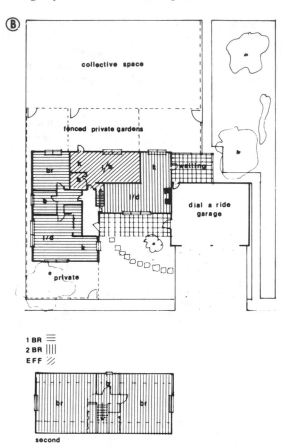

FIGURE 13.6   *B*, Proposed HOMES revitalization, same house converted to three units (two bedroom, one bedroom, and efficiency), plus dial-a-ride garage and collective outdoor space.

zoning laws must be changed, or variances obtained, for the conversion of single-family houses into duplexes and triplexes and the introduction of any sort of commercial activities into a residential block. However, a community group that is able to organize or acquire at least five units could become a HUD housing cooperative, with a nonprofit corporation owning all land and with producers' cooperatives running the small community services. With a coherent plan for an entire block, variances could be obtained much more easily than on a lot-by-lot basis. One can also imagine organizations that run halfway houses—for ex-mental patients or runaway teenagers or battered women—integrating their activities into such a block plan, with an entire building for their activities. Such groups often find it difficult to achieve the supportive neighborhood context such a block organization would offer.

I believe that attacking the conventional division between public and private space should become a socialist and feminist priority in the 1980s. Women must transform the sexual division of domestic labor, the privatized economic basis of domestic work, and the spatial separation of homes and workplaces in the built environment if they are to be equal members of society. The experiments I propose are an attempt to unite the best features of past and present reforms in our own society and others, with some of the existing social services available in the United States today. I would like to see several demonstration HOMES begun, some involving new construction following the program I have laid out, others involving the rehabilitation of suburban blocks. If the first few experimental projects are successful, homemakers across the United States will want to obtain day-care, food, and laundry services at a reasonable price, as well as better wages, more flexible working conditions, and more suitable housing. When all homemakers recognize that they are struggling against both gender stereotypes and wage discrimination, when they see that social, economic, and environmental changes are necessary to overcome these conditions, they will no longer tolerate housing and cities, designed around the principles of another era, that proclaim that "a woman's place is in the home."

## Acknowledgments

I would like to thank Catharine Stimpson, Peter Marris, S. M. Miller, Kevin Lynch, Jeremy Brecher, and David Thompson for extensive written comments on drafts of this paper.

## Notes

1. There is an extensive Marxist literature on the importance of spatial design to the economic development of the capitalist city, including Castells, 1977; Lefebre, 1974; Gordon, 1978; Harvey, 1973. None of this work deals adequately with the situation of women as workers and homemakers, nor with the unique spatial inequalities they experience. Nevertheless, it is important to combine the economic and historical analyis of these scholars with the empirical research of non-Marxist feminist urban critics and sociologists who have examined women's experience of conventional housing, such as Wekerle, 1978; and Keller, 1978. Only then can one begin to provide a socialist–feminist critique of the spatial design of the American city. It is also essential to develop research on housing similar to Kamerman, 1979, 632–50, which reviews patterns of women's employment, maternity provisions, and child care policies in Hungary, East Germany, West Germany, France, Sweden, and the United States. A comparable study of housing and related services for employed women could be the basis for more elaborate proposals for change. Many attempts to refine socialist and feminist economic theory concerning housework are discussed in an excellent article by Malos, 1978. A most significant theoretical piece is Movimento di Lotta Femminile, 1972.

2. I am indebted to Allan Heskin for this reference.

3. Gordon, 1978, 48–50, discusses suburban relocation of plants and housing.

4. Industrial Housing Associates, 1919. Also see Ehrenreich and English, 1975, 16.

They quote an unidentified corporate official (ca. 1920): "Get them to invest their savings in homes and own them. Then they won't leave and they won't strike. It ties them down so they have a stake in our prosperity."

5. Barkin (1979, 120–24) gives the details of this competition; Ruth Schwartz Cowan, in an unpublished lecture at MIT in 1977, explained GE's choice of an energy-consuming design for its refrigerator in the 1920s, because this would increase demand for its generating equipment by municipalities.

6. Friedan (1974, 307) somewhat hysterically calls the home a "comfortable concentration camp"; Filene (1974, 194) suggests that men are victimized by ideal homes too, thus "domestic" mystique.

7. Zaretsky (1976) develops Friedan's earlier argument in a more systematic way. This phenomenon is misunderstood by Lasch (1977), who seems to favor a return to the sanctity of the patriarchal home.

8. For more detail, see Howe, 1977.

9. Recent zoning fights on the commune issue have occurred in Santa Monica, Calif.; Wendy Schuman, "The Return of Togetherness," *New York Times*, Mar. 20, 1977, reports frequent illegal downzoning by two-family groups in one-family residences in the New York area.

10. Study by D. Foley, cited in Wekerle, 1978.

11. Research by Malcolm MacEwen, cited in *Associate Collegiate Schools of Architecture Newsletter*, March 1973, 6.

12. See, for example, Brown, 1978; Anderson-Khleif (1979, 3–4), research report for HUD on single-parent families and their housing.

13. My discussion of the Cuban Family Code is based on a visit to Cuba in 1978; a general review is Bengelsdorf and Hageman, 1979. Also see Fox, 1973.

14. This project relies on the "support structures" concept of John Habraken to provide flexible interior partitions and fixed mechanical core and structure.

15. Personal interview with Nina West, 1978.

16. See Hayden, 1977, 1978, 1979, 1979–80, 1981.

17. Hayden (1976) discusses historical examples and includes a discussion of communes of the 1960s and 1970s.

18. See also the successful experience of Zurich, described in Hans Wirz, 1979.

# Part II | The Role of the State

# 14

# Housing Policy and the Myth of the Benevolent State

*Peter Marcuse*

Afterword: The Myth of the Meddling State

*As the workings of the private housing market clearly produce a host of problems, particularly for low-income and minority people, we now turn explicitly to the role that government has played in interacting with private interests and shaping housing policy. On face value, one might assume that housing policy would be unambiguously aimed at alleviating housing problems. In the chapter that follows, this naive view is closely examined and found to be incorrect, hence the "myth of the benevolent state." The real reasons for federal intervention have had more to do with addressing crucial political and economic needs than with providing decent housing. In a recently written afterword, the author identifies a new myth that has gained increasing popularity in the conservative 1980s, the "myth of the meddling state." According to this myth, the state's past attempts to "solve the housing problem" have been consistently disappointing, often exacerbating problems. Again, this myth is found to be just that, and its implication that the private market can function well without state intervention is refuted.*

Much intellectual analysis of government policies is premised on the myth of the benevolent state. In brief the myth is that government acts out of a primary concern for the welfare of all its citizens, that its policies represent an effort to find solutions to recognized social problems, and that government efforts fall short of complete success only because of lack of knowledge, countervailing selfish interests, incompetence, or lack of courage.

In the field of housing the view that government policies are addressed to meeting real housing needs or solving housing problems has pervaded the mainstream of the professional literature for the past 30 years. On this basis efforts are made to determine the nature and scope of housing needs, their origins, the mechanisms by which they may be met, the context in which they must be dealt with. Evaluations gauge the results of housing programs

This chapter, without the afterword, originally appeared in *Social Policy*, January/February 1978. It is reprinted by permission of Social Policy Corporation, New York, N.Y. 10036. Copyright 1978 by Social Policy Corporation.

against the goal of providing adequate housing for all, and recommendations proposed to better achieve that goal are thought to contribute to improved housing policy.

The analyses informed by this view are not necessarily useless, and some, like Henry Aaron's (1972), are perceptive enough in their criticisms of policy outcomes. But the weakness of most such analyses arises from the assumption that decision-makers' mere exposure to the irrationalities in housing policy will be a major factor leading to their improvement. Even those politically sophisticated analyses that attend to interest-group pressures, popular prejudices, economic laws, regional conflicts, and the rigidities of bureaucracies still are premised on the belief that, underneath it all, there is a movement toward social amelioration. It is the contention of this chapter that this view of the benevolent state in general, and particularly in regard to housing, is radically and demonstrably false.

The very phrase "housing policy" is witness to this underlying myth. What is housing policy? It is the set of government actions (and inactions, in the sophisticated view) intended to deal with housing problems. Housing policy may indeed be criticized as illogical, incoherent, ineffective; a set of policies, rather than a single policy; a set of policies that is internally contradictory and even self-defeating in particulars; a policy lacking in focus, philosophy, clarity of goals, certainty as to priorities. Yet the underlying existence of a governmental thrust toward the solution of the social problems of housing—of a benevolent state—is implicit in the use of the phrase. The task of analysis is to make clear the goals of housing policy and the means of their achievement so that the benevolent state may act more rationally to solve housing problems.

Yet a historical analysis of government actions and inactions affecting housing reveals no such housing policy or any common thrust toward one. Housing policy is an ideological artifact—in Manuel Castells's phrase, not a real category. Hypotheses may be formulated as to what state actions one would expect to find if there were, in fact, a housing policy evolving from the efforts of a benevolent state to solve existing problems. These hypotheses may be tested and verified or invalidated. A good starting point may be the benevolent-state account of housing policy as moving from a restrictive approach, that is, the enactment and enforcement of housing regulations required by mid-nineteenth-century health problems, to the more positive contemporary approach of goverment provision of improved housing facilities.

According to this account substantial government action in the field of housing began in the United States in 1867 with New York's pioneering Tenement House Act. To stem the burgeoning problems of ill housing from which the poor suffered greatly, the Tenement House Act prescribed minimum standards for fire safety, ventilation, sanitation, and weather-tightness of roofs for accommodations rented to two or more families. This marked the beginning of a continuing effort to deal with the problems of ill housing by regulation. Such efforts are thought to be characterized by growing sophistication in definition, scope of coverage, level of standards, and methods of enforcement, culminating in contemporary housing codes and new building standards. State involvement in the actual provision of housing, rather than mere regulation, is seen as a different approach directed at the solution of essentially the same problems.

## Housing Regulation

Government actions impacted housing in the United States long before 1867, however. While detailed and extensive planning and public construction took place in colonial times in Williamsburg, Savannah, and Philadelphia, these early plans may be considered products of a declining feudal period rather than the responses to a new capitalist urban pattern. But the building regulation adopted by New York in 1766, creating a fire zone in which houses had to be made of stone or brick and roofed with tile or slate, begins a new lineage. It was made in anticipation of growth, in realization of an increasingly complex web of interrelationships within cities, in understanding that mores and social customs could no longer be relied upon to keep individuals from acting in their own private interests in such a way as to impose unnecessary risks on others. The Commissioner's Plan for New York of 1811, laying out a gridiron pattern to facilitate speculation in land, represented a further major involvement of government in the housing field. The admixture of government action with private enterprise was a continuing and escalating process well before the mid-nineteenth century.

The historic strands that went into the Tenement House Act of 1867, largely unenforceable and wholly unenforced, and the Tenement House Act of 1901, which finally created both meaningful standards and an adequate enforcement mechanism, are not hard to disentangle. First there were health problems, reported officially in New York City as early as 1834, and called attention to beginning in 1843 by the New York Association for Improving the Condition of the Poor, led and financed by wealthy merchants and businessmen (Lubove, 1962, 4). Smallpox, dysentery, tuberculosis, and other diseases were spawned in the slums, but it took the scare of the cholera epidemics in Europe in 1865 to generate real concern. Only by "sanitary reformation . . . can the inevitable epidemic be mitigated," one observer wrote in 1866, and *Harper's Weekly* prophesied that without health laws "the City of New York will be left to its own destruction." Lubove summarized (1962, 23): "Terror had succeeded where reason, enlightened self-interest and the pleas of humanitarians had failed." But, he noted further,

> it was not simply the danger of epidemic stalking out from the downtown ghettoes that panicked the middle class. True, the "stinks of Centre Street [lifted] up their voices," but important also after 1863 was the memory of the terrible July days when the poor streamed out from their gloomy haunts to burn, murder, and pillage. The draft riots, a turbulent protest of the immigrant

poor against what they believed was discriminatory conscription, helped prove to New Yorkers that they could not permanently ignore the social and moral condition of the immigrant. (Lubove, 1962, 12)

And as the Act of 1867 can be traced in part to the riots of 1863, so can the Act of 1901 be traced in part to the serious social and economic crises of the 1890s (Lubove, 1962, 83).

The political and social integration of the large immigrant population was also seen as directly related to housing standards:

> The housing reformer believed that if he could improve the housing of the poor, this would reduce the class and ethnic conflict splitting the urban community into enemy camps. Better housing was needed not only to protect the health of the entire community, but to Americanize the immigrant working-class populations, to impose upon it the middle-class code of manners and morals. (Lubove, 1962, 43, 21)

Both individual antisocial behavior and general economic productivity of labor were linked to the housing codes:

> Unless conditions improved [the New York Association for Improving the Condition of the Poor] warned [in 1865], the poor would "overrun the city as thieves and beggars—endanger public peace and the security of property and life—tax the community for their support, and entail upon it an inheritance of vice and pauperism." (Lubove, 1962, 7)

Lawrence Veiller, the father of the Tenement Act of 1901, sounded the theme of a "stake in society" and homeownership as an incentive "to work industriously, to be economical and thrifty," as part of the case for housing reform (Lubove, 1962, 132).

It is not necessary to impugn the motives of the leaders of the reform movement, of men like Lawrence Veiller or Jacob Riis, to argue that their actions served the self-interest of the rich. Certainly, liberals, idealists, philanthropists, and other persons of strong charitable inspiration contributed to obtaining passage of laws aimed at preventing the worst of housing conditions in the growing American slums. The point here is rather that the tenement house regulations in the United States, viewed historically, do not mark the beginning of enlightened governmental attitudes toward the slums. Instead, they form an integral part of state actions protecting the existing order from the dangers created by industrialization and urbanization. Regulations governing the use of fireproof construction materials, the provision of streets and highways and public utilities, the granting of franchises for transportation routes and services, and the banning of nuisances were all part of a process beginning well before 1867. Sam Bass Warner (1968, 109), referring to Philadelphia, articulated that process as follows: "The popular goal of the private city was a goal to make Philadelphia a moderately safe place for ordinary men and women to go about conducting their own business; the goal was never to help raise the level of living of the poor."

Historically, housing codes were not the beginnings of a benevolent concern for the housing of the poor; they were a continuation of the use of state power to prevent any disturbance—physical, social, or political—of the private conduct of economic affairs. That they also benefited the poor, and that persons of philanthropic motivations supported them, was neither a necessary nor a sufficient cause of their enactment.

In a historical account using real categories, then, the origins of tenement house reform and housing codes would be found in five different chapters: on the economic role and social assimilation of immigrants; on the growth and arrangement of the physical infrastructure of cities, including provisions for handling the external consequences of that infrastructure (this, under the broader category of processes of production); on evolving techniques for the control of deviant individual behavior (following Lubove's emphasis of environmental determinism); and on the devices for insuring domestic tranquility and social–political control of restive groups. Any treatment of the impact on state policy of the benevolent concerns of individuals would be a short one indeed.

## Public Provision of Housing

If housing codes were not the beginnings of benevolent policies addressed to remedying housing problems, neither was the public provision of housing for the poor a further manifestation of such concerns. New York City pioneered both in housing regulation and later in housing provision. But the development of the two was discontinuous, contrary to the hypothesis suggested by the myth of the benevolent state.

The New York Tenement House Act of 1901 was the largest single step forward in housing regulation; it created the widespread inner-court layout of apartment buildings in New York and was largely followed in the wave of legislation passed by other states in the two subsequent decades. It was also the basis for the Model Tenement House Act drafted by Lawrence Veiller in 1910 for use by other states.

But Veiller opposed public housing vociferously. He considered governmental assistance to the construction of housing to be socialistic and undesirable class legislation; it would be unfair competition to private capital and would promote the growth of cumbrous and mechanical government systems (Lubove, 1962, 179–80). Nor was he alone: Almost all of the early U.S. reformers agreed that "it was 'bad principle and worse policy' for municipalities 'to spend public money competing with private enterprise in housing the masses'" (Lubove, 1962, 104; see also Jackson, 1976, 121). Some outstanding housing reformers (e.g., Edith Elmer Wood) did indeed see housing regulation and public housing as directly interconnected, but it is only with the a priori assumption of a government continuously searching for the best solution to a problem of ongoing and benevolent concern that the linkage between housing codes and public provision of housing becomes direct or substantial. [*See also Chapter 20 by Rachel G. Bratt.*]

Nor did private philanthropic sponsorship of housing and the construction of model tenements on a charitable or limited-profit basis provide the foundation for subsequent public involvement. In the heyday of the model tenement movement before the turn of the century, a total of 10,000 persons were housed by it; during the same period it is estimated that 750,000 persons were housed in newly built private tenements in New York City. (Jackson, 1976, 110). No impact of the movement on subsequent public housing legislation can be found.

There is nothing obscure about the motivations for the public provision of housing in the United States. Instead of arising out of a benevolent concern for the poor, housing efforts were more closely related to the manufacture of war supplies to support American efforts in World War I than with concern to appease the discontent of returning veterans of that war (on the same order, although on a much smaller scale, as the Homes for Heroes campaign in England and Scotland during the same period), and finally with the provision of employment for the vast army of the unemployed following the Great Depression. A few individuals and organizations did indeed stick with the good fight for public housing throughout all these events; the historic events that shaped decisions, however, were not shaped by those stalwarts. Indeed, the three major phases in the history of public provision of housing in the United States—the World War I programs, the veterans programs after World War I, and the public housing programs that followed the Great Depression—were themselves largely discontinuous events to be found in different chapters of U.S. history.

The U.S. Shipping Board Emergency Fleet Corporation was created under the Shipping Act of 1916 and in 1918 was given the authority to build or requisition housing for "employees and the families of employees of shipyards in which ships are being constructed for the United States." Later in 1918 the U.S. Housing Corporation was established to help "such industrial workers as are engaged in arsenals and navy yards of the United States and in industries connected with and essential to the national defense, and their families" (Friedman, 1968, 95). These actions stem from no earlier involvement of government in housing; they appear right after discussions of tenement house regulations in accounts of housing policy because such accounts are arranged chronologically by artificial theoretical category rather than by organic historical development. The ancestry of these wartime efforts lies rather in the housing built in the factory towns of the late nineteenth century by burgeoning industries: textiles in Lowell, Massachusetts, and Willimantic, Connecticut, railroad cars in Pullman, Illinois, rubber tires in Akron, Ohio, coal in the anthracite fields of West Virginia, oil in Bayonne, New Jersey, even piano manufacturing (Steinway) in New York City. The parallels abroad are of course well known; they run from flax mills to candle manufacturers in England (Gauldie, 1974) to the giant coal and iron enterprises of the Ruhr in Germany, which likewise found it necessary to build housing for their workers if they were to harness an adequate and reliable work force. World War I created the same needs in the U.S. cities where production was centered, particularly in the ports, and the state lent its resources to private industry to help meet its needs. If housing units were to be publicly owned when built, their sale to private owners as soon after the war as possible was mandated, and in fact took place. Pullman, not Veiller, was the forebear of the first direct public provision of housing in the United States.

The same historical discontinuity marks what is generally taken as the next stage of supposedly evolving governmental concern with the condition of the poorly housed: the veterans' housing programs adopted by several American states, including Massachusetts and California, in the period following the end of World War I. Apparently unlike England and Scotland, where the postwar housing activities were directed at the areas of most severe shortage, the American programs assisted returning veterans to purchase single-family homes, regardless of the quality or suitability of their existing housing. Their lineage is as direct to Augustus Caesar and the housing of the returning Roman legions as it is to Lawrence Veiller and the tenement house reformers of New York City.

The Great Depression created the division between the policies of the 1920s and the 1930s. In the case of public housing the division is between policies unrelated to each other in terms of dealing with housing needs. The public housing program finally adopted in 1937 stemmed from concerns about social unrest among unemployed city workers; it hoped to deal with that unrest, not so much through the provision of better housing, but through the provision of jobs. The expansion of the supply of housing was not its goal; indeed, the demolition of an equivalent number of units (of substandard housing) was mandated in the U.S. Housing Act of 1937. As to the relationship to earlier efforts at housing regulation through restrictive codes, Veiller was prepared to testify *against* the Wagner bill in 1936 (McDonnell, 1957, 180).

If benevolence was the guiding principle behind state policies affecting housing, one would expect successive major housing acts—after 1937, these would include 1949, 1954, administrative and funding changes in 1964–1966, 1968, and 1974—to show an evolution of sophistication and effectiveness in dealing with the problems of bad housing. History shows no such pattern.

The Housing Act of 1949 did two things: it reinstituted the New Deal public housing program, dormant since World War II, and it laid the groundwork for slum clearance in the United States. The Housing Act of 1937 had coupled the removal of substandard housing with the construction of new public housing, but, as with early English legislation, the slum-clearance effects were hardly visible. The regressive consequences of slum clearance and urban renewal as practiced in the United States after 1949 are by now well known. The program has been criticized, correctly, as destroying more housing than it produced, moving out the poor to make room for the rich, and using public funds to purchase and clear valuable land near central business districts for the private benefit of downtown merchants, property owners, and the business community. Most of such criticism in the United States referred to these events as the "failures of urban renewal"

(Bellush and Hausknecht, 1967; Wilson, 1966). The critics speak as if these were perversions of its original intent; as if insufficient foresight, or inadequate understanding of market dynamics, or unanticipated changes in patterns of urban development had led to these consequences. Even radical critiques of the program often saw it as being diverted from its original purpose by local business cliques and real estate interests.

While the preamble to the Housing Act of 1949 calls for "a decent home and a suitable living environment" as the formal goal of national housing policy, the interests supporting Title I, which established the urban redevelopment program, looked to the act as a means of strengthening downtown areas and eliminating blighting uses adjacent to them. Their concern was not with rehousing slum dwellers but with tearing down slums—at least those casting a blighting influence on major business areas. Nonresidential blight was as obnoxious to them as residential. The very groups who were the strongest opponents of public housing in the United States—the National Association of Real Estate Boards, the United States Savings and Loan League, and, to some extent, the Mortgage Bankers Association of America—supported the principle of urban redevelopment. The first explicitly saw it as a way to "enable private enterprise to do the job that public housing was supposed to do" (Wilson, 1966, 81), in part by forcing slum dwellers out of cheap housing and into the higher-priced (and thus theoretically higher-quality) market.

The Urban Land Institute, sponsored by land developers and performing research functions for them, and the American Institute of Planners, through its president, Alfred Bettman, one of the early and nationally known proponents of zoning, specifically opposed any statutory requirement that urban redevelopment either clear only residential blighted land or be reused after clearance only for residential purposes. They slowly succeeded: first 10 percent, then 20 percent of projects were exempted from the original requirement that land to be cleared be predominantly residential; the requirement, in any event, only said "predominantly," interpreted as meaning 50 percent or more—a formulation that the imaginative drawing of project boundaries could render ineffectual. As one law review commentator lamented, a major reason for these developments, which flew in the face of the benevolent preamble to the original act, was

> the position of business interests which normally tend to support restrictions on federal expenditures, but are increasingly in favor of reconstructing blighted businesses and industrial properties. Foremost among these are department store owners and mortgage and other lenders concerned about large outstanding investments in downtown retail properties, now suffering competition from suburban shopping centers. (Wilson, 1966, 113)

Ten years later, major commercial banking interests, legal and accounting firms, national and international headquarters operations officers, and other specialized interests finding major central-city locations convenient could easily have been added to the list.

The changes that did occur in the urban renewal program in the 1960s and the passage of the Uniform Relocation Act (1970) giving major assistance to those poor displaced by urban renewal activities came about because the organized resistance of those being displaced was so powerful it could no longer be ignored. Either the process would grind to a halt altogether, or the protestors would have to be accommodated. Successive increases in relocation benefits, improvements in administration, and even obligations to construct replacement housing for the displaced were introduced until pro-renewal interests felt confident they had made sufficient concessions to enable them to proceed. And the program did proceed. Although changes are interesting to trace, they resulted not from greater awareness of residential needs, but from changing uses of central-city land. The nature of the program was not changed; the political price to be paid for it had simply been underestimated originally. The provision of relocation assistance was not a result of reawakened benevolence but of effective protest.

If benevolence was a major factor in the evolution of housing policies, one would expect to find the quantitative levels of production of public housing to be increasing as housing needs increased, and declining as needs declined. Such figures as are available (Aaron, 1972; U.S. Bureau of the Census, 1975b; U.S. HUD 1976) indicate a steadily growing need from 1930 through about 1949, and a rather steady decline in absolute numbers needed since 1949. The figures for publicly subsidized units, however, show an altogether different and almost opposite pattern.

The explanation is not hard to find. The U.S. Housing Act of 1937 was adopted to provide jobs, not housing; its construction standards were such that twice as many units might have been provided for the same cost had the provision of housing been its purpose. The private sector saw to it that no such result ensued. After World War II, in a period of major absolute housing shortage, assistance went to private builders and mortgage lending institutions in the form of financing aids and guarantees [see Chapter 3 by Michael E. Stone], and vast expenditures were made on infrastructure, highways, and related facilities. The suburban boom thus massively encouraged did not aid the poor; it led inexorably to the further decline of central-city housing, neighborhood deterioration, and reductions in public services available to the poor residents left behind by the governmentally encouraged outward movement. [See also Chapter 6 by Barry Checkoway.] Public housing, on the other hand, the only housing program directly providing shelter for the poor, was starved for funds throughout the postwar period.

Accelerated state support of housing construction for families below the level of economically effective demand was not forthcoming until a way was finally found to make it serve private profit. The process is a perfect example of, in Castells's words (1973, 12), "the constant tendency . . . to make the sectors of public subsidization profitable in order to bring them into line with the criteria of private capital so as to be able to transfer them gradually over to it." The first step was the turnkey construction process, which permitted private builders to do all of the construction on their own land and then sell the completed development to the public authorities. The second step was the perfection of the limited-dividend tax-benefit approach, which permitted private interests not only to build privately on public land but also to continue to own and manage the resultant publicly subsidized housing. They thus enjoyed the tax benefits of depreciation, with special acceleration provisions, agreeing in return only to limit cash profits. The tax benefits vastly exceeded in value the immediate cash benefit.

The final step, the Section 8 program of the Housing Act of 1974, permitted private interests to build, own, and manage housing intended for the poor, with no limits on profit whatsoever besides those nominally imposed by a requirement that rents be based on an administratively determined competitive level. The state nevertheless supported the payment of rent to the private owner through a subsidy based on the occupant's income. Any claim to benevolent intervention in the housing situation to bring about more rationally organized and improved housing for the poor was abandoned altogether in favor of a restricted income support to throw into the private market those whose own resources would make their participation in it otherwise profitless. Formal housing policy thus turns parallel to what has always been the largest public program providing housing for the poor: direct welfare payments. The difference between outright welfare and the newer programs is simply its restriction to certain forms of housing and its organization in such a way as to provide more direct benefits to private providers of the housing. [*See Chapter 17 by Robert Schur and Tom Robbins.*]

If the history of state programs directly assisting the positive provision of housing for the poor was to be written according to real categories, it would again be distributed among a number of chapters. The inception of the public housing program would be found in the chapter dealing with the economic and political consequences of the Great Depression. The Housing Act of 1949 and successive legislation dealing with urban renewal would be in the chapter dealing with the evolving economic role of the central city and its consequently changing spatial patterns. A separate chapter on the housing industry would explain much of the postwar evolution of public housing administration and finance. Struggles around housing would be best treated in a chapter tracing political conflicts since the war, most of them in the section on local politics. Benevolence might serve as a footnote in one or two of such chapters.

Housing policy as a category is not only artificial, but also creates a bias from its very use. For housing is a category of a social problem. The policies to be examined are then housing policies, that is, policies addressed to the solution of the housing problem. Thus we find ourselves by the very formulation of the problem granting the basic premise that a thoroughgoing analysis should begin by questioning: that there is in fact a coherent body of policies addressed to the solution of the housing problem. For if there is, then a benevolent state must be the moving force behind it, and the examination is confined to the forces and patterns that may encourage or interfere with the underlying commitments of such a benevolent state. But it is the very existence of a benevolent state that needs to be questioned, especially at a time when an apparently liberal shift in federal government administration makes the myth of benevolence particularly seductive.

# Afterword
# The Myth of the Meddling State

Since the first part of this chapter was written, in 1978, much has changed. The events of the 1960s, the civil rights movement, the ghetto rebellions, the War on Poverty, the student revolt, the mass movement against the war in Vietnam, all seem in the distant and almost-forgotten past. The hopes for a shift to more progressive policies following the defeat of President Nixon have been disappointed by the even more conservative policies of President Ronald Reagan. The shift to the right, the retreat from the welfare state, has become a pervasive trend in Europe as well as in the United States [*see Chapter 30 by Steve Schifferes*]. With this retreat has come an attack from the right on one of the underlying assumptions of welfare state supporters: the old myth of the benevolent state. As the right's critique has gained momentum, they have begun to put forward a new (actually old) set of beliefs, founded on an even more insidious myth. New times demand new myths.

The attempt to substitute a new myth—let us call it the myth of the meddling state—for the old provides an object lesson in the political uses of historical myths. The old myth of the benevolent state is not dead. Much of the liberal position is still based on it, and much (probably most) academic research on government policies still unconsciously assumes its validity. But it has lost its unquestioned and pervasive character; in day-to-day debates, it is on the defensive. In the process, its directly political–ideological role and the similar role of its replacement have become more obvious than ever.

According to the myth of the meddling state, the dominant factor in determining housing conditions is the free private market. Housing is provided, priced, maintained, and occupied in accordance with the laws of supply and demand. The market interaction of providers with occupants of housing is a sensitive barometer both of the cost of supply and the intensity and quantity of demand; where the supply and demand curves intersect is the optimal level of production and use. If demand is ineffective (i.e., if people do not have enough money), the remedy is to make it effective (i.e., see that they have, or can get, money); if supply does not respond adequately, the problem lies with inhibitions on its free action, which are primarily governmental regulation. Thus, to achieve the optimal housing situation, the removal, not the improvement, of government regulation is required. Government regulation of housing (government "intervention" in the housing market, in general) is unneeded and counterproductive: meddling.

The implications for government policy are clear. On the demand side, if all else fails, transfer payments (housing allowances); on the supply side, freedom from government regulation. The latter, in fact, should take priority over the former: In a "supply side" view of the economy, demand will ultimately take care of itself. Those who really want to work can get jobs,[1] and if they do not want to work, they do not want to make the tradeoff (going to work) necessary to get decent housing, so they are not morally entitled to it from the government. The conclusion: Get the government out of housing.

The myth of the meddling state is embellished by a reading of history that is as fallacious as that of the myth of the benevolent state, and has not even the excuse of wishful thinking to justify it. The state is pictured as essentially incompetent in housing; what it tries to do (as in the benevolent state myth, the assumption is that the state has in fact been trying to "solve the housing problem"), it does badly.[2]

• Public housing failed because it built impersonal, high-rise ghettos that bred antisocial behavior and prevented normal social controls from working.[3]

• Construction subsidy programs are inefficient because they substitute governmental regulation for market discipline. The competition for profits will control costs better than bureaucratic oversight (see President's Commission on Housing, 1982).

• Welfare rental checks do not insure their recipients decent housing because welfare recipients pocket the money and wreck their apartments, leading inexorably to abandonment (see Salins, 1980).

• Neighborhood blight and abandonment are the result of natural and inevitable market forces produced by declining population and disappearing jobs (see Kasarda, 1982; Sternlieb and Hughes, 1981).

• Government money spent in such neighborhoods goes down a rathole, accomplishing nothing in the long run (see Starr, 1977; Thompson, 1977).

• Citizen participation in shaping housing policy (or in managing housing) leads to no better end results, and just increases delays and costs.[4]

• Planning restrictions do likewise (President's Commission on Housing, 1982).

• Urban renewal programs prove that even public policies supposed to help the poor inevitably are counterproductive and do more harm than good.[5]

• The private market does a more efficient job of eliminating slums and providing housing than government can; witness gentrification in inner cities today.

That these are myths requires no extended demonstration:[6]

• The problems of public housing stem largely from its underfinancing, from the deliberate policy of holding standards down to prevent invidious comparisons with privately supplied housing (see Freedman, 1969), and from policies supporting, if not in fact producing, racial discrimination.[7]

• Public housing has been expensive to build because industry (and union) pressures on standards have been designed to maximize profits and employment, not produce cost-effective housing. While there are inefficiencies, and thus costs, resulting from government bureaucracy, they pale in amount compared to the costs incurred by surrendering to the pressure for private profits. The elimination of profit should certainly reduce, not increase, costs; if costs are still higher than they could be, it is because the pressure to make private profit still operates in many aspects of subsidized housing (see Freedman, 1969; McDonnell, 1957). [*See also Chapter 20 by Rachel G. Bratt and Chapter 17 by Robert Schur and Tom Robbins.*]

• Welfare tenants sometimes do not pay their rent because rent withholding is the only way that they can protest inferior housing (which much of welfare housing is, and was before welfare tenants moved in; that is often why it was available to them). The link between abandoned housing and welfare status is very tenuous; a vast amount of nonwelfare housing is deteriorating or abandoned. And welfare payments often are not adequate even to cover maintainence of rental units, let alone improvements.[8]

• Population declines (actually, the locational decisions of businesses and their consequences) clearly cause problems for many communities; but decline is neither natural nor inevitable, and results from the quest of business for ever-higher profits, and its insulation from having to pay the social costs of that quest (see Bluestone, Harrison, and Baker, 1981). It is significantly encouraged by government (see Goodman, 1979; Marcuse, 1981c).

• Problems created by business movement and population loss are greatly aggravated by public policies of cutback and neglect: at the extreme, triage (see Marcuse, 1982b). Far from being powerless to remedy neighborhood decline, a reversal of public policies could in many places prevent it from taking place.

• Planning regulations may indeed increase some costs of housing (by no means as much as is often contended). Yet what the market has produced without public controls has created even heavier social costs. The old-law tenements of New York City, the slum housing of working-class areas throughout the country, the pollution of the waters and the air, the devastation of the countryside through strip mining of coal and clear cutting of timber, traffic congestion and smog, noise and filth, suburban sprawl and downtown tension—these are what the market has historically produced, left to itself or encouraged. The cost of subsequently repairing such damage far outweighs the cost of prior regulation.

• Urban renewal can hardly be criticized as the failure of a housing program designed to help the poor. It was never that; it was from the outset a real estate–oriented program to protect and increase inner-city investment values, and as such it succeeded admirably (see Hartman, 1975). Good housing for poorer people was an afterthought. But at least it was a thought, and to some extent implemented; the Uniform Relocation Act provided benefits that private renewal and gentrification do not. The private market has never built good housing for working people (and certainly not for poor people) because it was never profitable to do so (see Jackson, 1976).

The historical record thus lends no credence to the view of the state as an outside agent incompetently and ineffectively meddling in the housing market.

Yet the myth of the meddling state is subtly undergirded by the very words used in conventional economics to discuss the state's role in housing. The propriety of the state's "intervening" in the housing market is the way in which contemporary economists and sociologists—the overwhelming majority of them at least[9]—phrase the issue. The implication is that the market can function very well independently of the state. The state has only meddled, in an effort to help the poor, and in doing so has made matters worse for them.

In fact, housing was always dependent on, and integrally tied to, state action. Housing is social through and through, in the arrangements for its production, its ownership, its financing, its management, its location, and its use. The state has been integrally involved from the beginning in every aspect of housing:

• Planning and building streets for it
• Regulating the materials of which it is constructed
• Providing transportation to it
• Taking care of the infrastructure to supply (and often supplying) electricity, water, sewage disposal, and gas
• Preventing inconsistent uses
• Providing means to enforce contracts and defining legal relationships so that contracts could be freely entered into
• Punishing interference with its use and damage to its structure
• Taxing (or not taxing) profits to be made from it
• Recording and protecting title to it
• Affecting the geographic distribution of demand through national and regional policies and of supply through monetary and fiscal policies
• Influencing the extent to which capital is used for it or diverted from it

The idea that the state "intervenes" in "private" housing is a linguistic distortion. The idea that what the state has done, it has done in the interests of the poor is standing history on its head.

The shift from the myth of the benevolent state to the myth of the meddling state is a textbook example of theory as rationalization for political policy. It is a result of a shift in power, not an evolution of ideas. It takes the myth of the benevolent state one step further, adding the distortion of incompetent meddling to the distortion of benevolence. Its purpose is clear, and blatant: to justify the reduction of state expenditures for social and redistributive programs, to make it easier to kill programs limiting the freedom of the private sector to make a profit. For housing, that means the elimination of government subsidies and the reduction of public controls over development and use.[10] From a social science point of view, it is hard to take the new myth seriously. From a practical political view, however, it has proven very useful to its beneficiaries: the profit sector.

The shift in power relationships that underlies the shift in myths is a striking one, and is revealed in the difference in the use of the two myths. The myth of the benevolent state is the underpinning of the welfare state. By suggesting a free-floating but ongoing effort by the state to improve conditions for all its citizens (an effort that a search through history hardly finds), it covers over the real causes of difficulty for working and poor people, and focuses attention instead on the details of program design, administrative implementation, and "social processes." It thus diverts attention from the conflicts and struggles that would be required to change conditions.

The myth of the meddling state is no longer concerned with papering over conflict. It acknowledges that, in the normal course of events, there are winners and losers, rich people and poor. It considers the successes of the rich to be proper, and rejects the claim that the state should attempt to redress the balance between rich and poor. The argument that the state is incompetent in what it does is used to justify abandoning any effort aimed at improving state policy, to rationalize a total abdication of "public" concern for the losers in the current round of conflict. In that sense, the myth of the meddling state is no longer concerned to deny the power relationships that the myth of the benevolent state ignored. The shift from one myth to the other reflects the self-confidence, indeed the arrogance, of the forces that are in power in the United States today.

# Notes

1. President Reagan, at a press conference in January 1982, when asked about the increase in black unemployment, said: "I made it a point to count the pages of help-wanted ads [in the local paper last Sunday]: in this time of great unemployment there were 24 full pages of classified ads of employers for employees." For a trenchant comment, see *Dollars and Sense* (Jan. 1984, 12).

2. *The Report of the President's Commission on Housing* (1982) sets forth the position here being criticized as comprehensively as is thus far available; Milton Friedman's public policy pronouncements often provide more generalized formulations.

3. See Oscar Newman's writings as an example of where this approach leads, and Chapter 20 by Rachel G. Bratt for an alternate explanation.

4. See Robert Einsweiler's account, in *Planning* 46 (1980): 15, of conversations with "leading planners" concerned about the political future of planning.

5. See the early work of Martin Anderson (1964), later President Reagan's domestic policy adviser.

6. For the best general account of the origins and impact of housing policies in the United States, see Hartman, 1975.

7. See National Committee Against Discrimination in Housing, 1967, and the series of opinions in the *Gautreaux* case in Chicago (first judgment on the merits at 448 F2nd 731 [7 Cir., 1971]).

8. See the recent studies by the Community Service Society of New York, 105 West 22nd Street, New York, NY 10011 for the situation in that state.

9. There are, of course, significant dissenters; see, for instance, Saunders, 1981; and Ball, 1983.

10. Or their redirection to benefit suppliers and/or higher-income groups (e.g., landlords' subsidy and homeownership support programs), in what I have elsewhere called the "siphon effect."

# 15

# How the Income Tax System Subsidizes Housing for the Affluent

*Cushing Dolbeare*

*Although the most visible federal housing interventions are direct-subsidy programs, these actually represent only a fraction of the total federal expenditure for housing. The ability of homeowners to deduct mortgage interest and property tax payments from income in calculating their income tax payments produces an aggregate federal expenditure that is many times the amount of direct outlays for housing. This favorable tax treatment for homeowners has many negative and inequitable side effects.*

*An Editors' Note appended to this chapter discusses the possible impact on housing of tax-reform proposals the Reagan administration released just as this book was going into production (mid-1985).*

This chapter is concerned with the federal spending for housing provided through the tax code, as opposed to the other major type of federal spending for housing, direct-subsidy-payment programs. The technical term for the former is "tax expenditure."

Homeowner tax preferences create inequities in the tax system and are inefficient as a subsidy mechanism. William F. Hellmuth (1977), in a paper prepared for a Brookings Institution conference, has commented on the effects of homeowner tax preferences on the tax system and the economy, as follows:

> They create horizontal inequities in the income tax system in that they provide tax savings for homeowners over tenants with comparable incomes, and differential savings between different homeowners with comparable incomes.
>
> They cause vertical inequities in the tax system. Since homeownership rises with income, the values of homes purchased increase as a proportion of income as incomes rise (that is, are income elastic), and the value of homeowner preferences is directly related to the marginal tax rate of the homeowner; high-income recipients benefit more from these preferences than do low-income recipients.
>
> They interfere with the allocation of resources between residential construction and other uses of resources. The tax expenditures favoring homeowners

lower the cost of housing services and increase the after-tax rate of return on investment in homes, relative to other choices that consumers and individual investors have for the use of their funds. Tax incentives thus draw more resources into housing than would occur in the absence of such preferences.

They also distort the housing market choices in favor of residential construction suitable for homeowners, creating a demand for more single-family homes and apartments for purchase than for rental units.

Further, these homeowner tax preferences are relatively inefficient and expensive if they are considered as incentives to promote homeownership and the construction of more homes. The incentives are most valuable to those with higher marginal tax rates, the income class that would find it easiest to buy homes in the absence of tax incentives. And the incentives for homeownership are much weaker for families in the lower tax brackets whose income levels also make homeownership more difficult. Tax incentives are, of course, of no value to those whose income is so low that they pay no federal income tax. And to the extent that the tax preferences increase the demand for owner-occupied homes, the price of such dwelling units rises and puts them further beyond the reach of low- and modest-income persons. The greater value of these preferences for persons with high incomes and high marginal tax rates is likely to draw more resources into the construction of large and expensive homes; on the other hand, income-neutral incentives would be likely to result in more dwelling units to meet the housing needs of more people.

The Congressional Budget Act of 1974 began to address the issue of the cost of tax expenditures by requiring a listing of all tax expenditures in the federal budget. These listings have since been contained in a Special Analysis that is an integral part of the annual federal budget. The act defines "tax expenditures" as "revenue losses attributable to provisions of the Federal tax laws which allow a special exclusion, exemption, or deduction from gross income or which provide a special credit, a preferential rate of tax or a deferral of liability" (Public Law 93–344).

By far the largest federal housing subsidies, both in cost to the Treasury and in number of recipients, are those provided through the tax code. In fiscal 1984, the cost to the federal Treasury of housing-related tax expenditures was estimated by the Congressional Joint Committee on Taxation at $43,665,000,000, based on information provided by the Treasury Department and the Congressional Budget Office.[1] The 1984 housing-related tax expenditures are listed in Table 15.1.

In contrast to direct expenditures, the major housing-related tax expenditures, contained in the Internal Revenue code, are not subject to annual review. Because appropriations for direct federal housing assistance programs must be adopted annually, and legislation amending and extending them is customarily also considered each year, they are the focus of far more attention than are tax expenditures. Some tax expenditure features have been inserted in the code with termination dates, so they are extended from time to time, but none has been subjected to the kind of review and decision-making by either Congress or the executive branch that accompanies requests for direct housing outlays and budget authority. Moreover, the

TABLE 15.1
HOUSING-RELATED TAX EXPENDITURES, 1984
($ in millions)

|  |  |
|---|---:|
| *Investor deductions* | |
| Historic-structure preservation[a] | 320 |
| Tax-exempt rental housing bonds[b] | 1,275 |
| Mortgage revenue bonds[c] | 1,785 |
| Accelerated rental housing depreciation[d] | 815 |
| Five-year amortization of low-income housing rehab[e] | 60 |
| Subtotal | 4,255 |
| *Homeowner deductions* | |
| Mortgage interest | 23,480 |
| Property taxes | 8,775 |
| Capital-gain deferral[f] | 4,895 |
| Capital-gain exclusion[g] | 1,630 |
| Residential energy credits[h] | 630 |
| Subtotal | 39,410 |
| Total | 43,665 |

[a] Credit (15–25 percent, depending on age and certified status) for expenses of rehabilitating old and certified historic structures.
[b] Exemption of interest on state and local bonds issued to finance construction or rehabilitation of rental housing occupied wholly or partly by lower-income people.
[c] Exemption of interest on state and local bonds issued to reduce the interest rate on home purchases by qualified owner-occupants.
[d] Depreciation of rental housing over a 15-year assumed life.
[e] Write-off in five years of expenses of rehabilitating housing occupied by lower-income (under 80 percent of median) households.
[f] Deferral of capital gains on sale of homes by owner-occupants, provided funds are invested within 24 months in another owner-occupied unit.
[g] Exclusion from income of up to $125,000 of capital gains (which can include those deferred from prior sales) on home sales by persons age fifty-five or over.
[h] 15 percent credit for up to $2,000 of the cost of energy conservation measures, such as insulation, and 40 percent credit of costs (up to $10,000) of alternative, renewable energy sources for heat, hot water, cooling, or electricity.

tax expenditures that have been given attention over the past several years, as Congress has endeavored to raise revenues by closing "loopholes," have been primarily those tax incentives designed to stimulate investment in housing. The major housing expenditures, however, are the homeowner deductions, which dwarf all other housing expenditures, either direct or through the tax system.

In summary, in 1984, federal expenditures on housing assistance were as follows:

| *Type* | *Percentage* | *In $ millions* |
|---|:---:|:---:|
| Direct outlays | 16.4 | 8,585 |
| Tax Expenditures | 83.6 | 43,665 |
| Investor | 8.1 | 4,255 |
| Homeowner | 75.4 | 39,410 |
| Total | 100.0 | 52,250 |

The Congressional Budget Office (CBO) estimated the cost of housing-related tax expenditures for 1985 at $55.2 billion. Investor deductions will rise to $5.8 billion, according to Joint Tax Committee estimates.

It should be noted that CBO and the Treasury, from which these tax-expenditure figures are drawn, do not count the failure to tax imputed rent as a homeowner deduction or tax expenditure, although many economists do. Imputed rent is "what a homeowner would receive by renting it [the home] out, less the costs of ownership, taxes, depreciation, and mainte-nance" (U.S. Congress, Congressional Budget Office, 1981). If the owner was renting the unit to someone else, she or he would be taxed on this income. The CBO notes that net imputed rental income has never been taxable in this country (although it has been taxed elsewhere) for two reasons: the fact that the concept has not been widely accepted by nonecon-omists and the practical difficulties of estimating the amount. A Department of Housing and Urban Development study (Simonson, 1981) estimated the cost of this expenditure to the Treasury in 1979 at from $14 billion to $17 billion. It would be substantially higher now.

While assisted housing payments (subsidies for all occupied units subsi-dized through HUD programs) have been rising steadily, though slowly, as additional units are subsidized, the cost of the homeowner provisions of the tax code is increasing far more rapidly (see Fig. 15.1). This is not the result of any conscious policy decision on the part of either the administration or the Congress to increase the federal assistance going to homeowners. Rather, it is the result of the interaction of changes in the economy with the provisions of the tax code. High housing costs, high interest rates, and an increasing number of homes with mortgages account for much of the increase. To a certain extent, the homeowner deductions stimulate borrowing for other

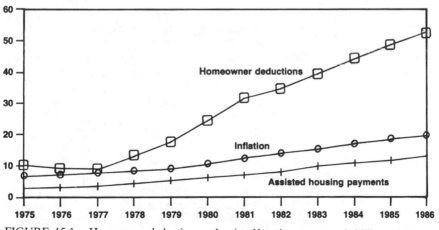

FIGURE 15.1.   Homeowner deductions and assisted housing payments, in billions of dollars.

purposes. During much of the past 10 years, for example, real interest rates have been negative after allowing for inflation and the tax deductibility of interest payments. Therefore, owners had a substantial economic incentive to refinance rather than pay off their mortgages.

It is worth noting that, with the exception of the capital-gain provisions, the homeowner provisions in the tax code were not inserted in order to provide assistance for homeownership. On the contrary, they are the result of a definition of income excluding interest and state and local tax payments, which was included in the tax code when it was first enacted in 1913. The definition had been carried over from an emergency income tax enacted during the Civil War. Until the broadening of the tax base and the rise in homeownership following World War II, it had had little impact.

Unfortunately, accurate figures on the numbers of homeowners benefiting from homeowner deductions are hard to come by because data on homeownership are kept by household and data on tax deductions are kept by taxpayer, and many households have more than one taxpayer. Nonetheless, it seems clear that fewer than one-half of all homeowners claim mortgage interest and property-tax deductions. In 1981, 26,425,000 taxpayers claimed these deductions; this is 48.6 percent of the total number of owner-occupied units in the inventory that year. (This figure overestimates the proportion of owners using the deductions, since some owner households had more than one taxpayer claiming these deductions).

While direct housing subsidies go almost exclusively to lower-income households, the homeowner deduction goes to upper-income households in a highly disproportionate manner; and since the dollars represented by the homeowner deduction vastly exceed the amount of direct housing subsidies, the overall pattern of benefits from government housing aids is extremely regressive. The following 1981 data illustrate this pattern:

• *For households earning less than $10,000 a year—25.4 percent of all households.* Only one out of eight households received federal housing assistance (of either type); only 6 percent received homeowner deductions; the average value of the homeowner deduction for those receiving it was $147; the average amount of federal housing assistance (of either type) per household in this income class was $125.

• *For households earning $15,000–20,000 a year—11.6 percent of all households.* Better than one out of four households received federal housing assistance (of either type); 25.9 percent received homeowner deductions; the average value of the homeowner deduction for those receiving it was $493; the average amount of federal housing assistance (of either type) per household in this income class was $167.

• *For households earning over $50,000 a year—7.2 percent of all households.* Six out of seven households received federal housing assistance (of either type); 85.1 percent received homeowner deductions; the average value of the homeowner deduction for those receiving it was $3,200; and the average amount of federal housing assistance (of either type) per household in this income class was $1,860.

There is a myth that low- and middle-income homeowners are the chief beneficiaries of homeowner deductions. The facts do not support this. Although about two-thirds of all households are homeowners, only 28 percent of the tax returns filed in 1981 claimed homeowner deductions. This was primarily because the majority of taxpayers do not itemize their deductions. Most low-income households own their houses free and clear, so they do not have mortgage-interest deductions to claim. For others, incomes and marginal tax rates are so low that it does not pay them to do so. Therefore, they do not benefit from the homeowner provisions. (That some households have more than one taxpayer also contributes to the low percentage, but this is a small part of the difference.)

The magnitude of the subsidy imbalance is such that a more equitable approach to federal housing assistance could provide a substantial portion of the funds needed to deal effectively with the critical housing needs of low income people. For example, Downs (1983) has estimated that a reduction of only 14 percent overall in homeowner deductions for mortgage interest and property taxes would produce enough revenue to fund a full-scale, entitlement housing allowance program.

It should be emphasized that it is neither necessary nor desirable to repeal homeowner deductions to redress the inequities of our present housing subsidy pattern. They could be capped or converted to tax credits, or some combination of the two. Converting the deduction to credit[2] would double the number of homeowners benefiting from the homeowner tax provisions, and would substantially improve equity. In 1981, less than 16 percent of the 11 million homeowners with incomes below $10,000 claimed deductions for mortgage interest and property taxes. Converting the deduction to a credit would enable an estimated 70 percent of these low-income homeowners to receive some tax subsidy. And if the credit were set at 15 percent (the lowest tax bracket under the Reagan tax reform proposals currently under consideration), the cost to the Treasury of the homeowner deductions would be reduced by $14 billion—which could substantially alleviate the housing problems of low income renters. Capping the amount of the credit that could be taken would increase both equity and tax revenues.

The important point is less the specific mechanism used than the urgency of addressing the basic inequity of a housing subsidy system that provides open-ended subsidies through the tax system to the affluent while denying them—primarily because of cost considerations—to low-income households that cannot otherwise obtain decent, affordable housing. It should be clear that a better distribution of our housing subsidies could, in fact, realize the goal of decent housing for all in this country.

## Notes

1. Estimates of the cost of tax expenditures are available from three major sources: federal budget documents, the Congressional Budget Office, and the Joint Committee on Taxation. Unless otherwise noted, the figures in this chapter are taken from relevant federal budget documents. In addition, the Department of Housing and Urban Development, in its annual Housing Production (formerly Housing Goal) Reports, publishes a breakdown of the homeowner tax expenditures by income groups. These figures have been used to estimate the cost of tax expenditures. It has been necessary to make some assumptions on the distribution of costs by income group in order to make estimates of the distribution of other direct and tax expenditures for housing assistance. To the extent that these assumptions bias the results, they overestimate expenditures for lower-income people and underestimate expenditures for upper-income people.

2. A *tax deduction* means that one's total taxable income is reduced by the permissible deduction; thus the value of that deduction is the amount of the deduction times the tax rate applicable to marginal income added at that income level. Since taxpayers with higher incomes generally are assessed at higher tax rates, the value of a tax deduction is greater to those with higher incomes. A *tax credit* allows the amount deducted—usually a fixed percentage of the expenditure—to be applied to the tax due. Since it is deducted from the tax due, at a given dollar level of deduction it is equally valuable to all taxpayers, regardless of their tax rate. Of course, the amount of homeowner expenditures for mortgage interest and property taxes will likely increase as income rises, and so the dollar amount of the tax credit will be greater for higher-income people.

## Editors' Note

As this book was going into production (mid-1985), the administration had just announced a sweeping proposal to simplify the income tax system. Exactly what revisions Congress will make in the plan, or whether in fact tax reform will be enacted, is of course not predictable. Some of the possible housing impacts of the administration's proposal are worth noting, in part for what they reveal of the profound impact tax policy has on housing consumption and investment, and in part because some version of these features likely will wind up in the tax code in the near future.

The principal elements of the administration proposal that affect housing are these:

• A lowering of tax rates (as part of a broader move to reduce the number of tax brackets and do away with most deductions), which consequently will reduce the dollar value of the homeowner deduction. This reduction in tax rates also will reduce the attractiveness of selling tax-sheltering limited partnerships in housing developments to upper-income investors, an arrangement that nonprofit housing groups have used to raise needed equity (albeit at the price of permitting the rich to lower their effective tax rates).

• Eliminating property tax payments as a deductible item.

• Creating a $5,000 limit on interest-payment deductions (beyond mortgage payments on one's principal residence), which in effect makes ownership of a second home far more expensive. ("Creative financing" proposals to circumvent this already are emerging; most notably, increasing the mortgage amount on one's principal residence, through refinancing, in order to generate enough cash to pay for a vacation home or other items that otherwise would be bought with credit without need of a mortgage or other loan.)

• Depreciation of investment property at a slower rate, thereby reducing the attractiveness of this form of investment as a tax shelter.

• Elimination of the tax exempt status of state and local housing agency bonds for constructing developments that provide housing for low-moderate income households.

• Elimination of the investment tax credit for renovating historic buildings.

What the overall impact of these or similar features might be is at the moment the subject of much speculation. Those in the real estate field are issuing jeremiads, predicting that such proposals will produce "a $300 billion destruction of value" (according to the chief executive officer of the National Association of Realtors—Hinds, 1984), as sellers are forced to lower their prices—10 to 25 percent, according to some economists, with the higher figures applying to the upper end of the market—in order to keep real monthly housing costs within the reach of housebuyers. Others in the real estate field predict a severe decline in rental housing construction and increased rents as landlords seek to cover their new, unsheltered costs with rent revenues. Still others claim that such proposals will kill the vacation-home industry.

What may be more important than the absolute value of the homeowner deduction and investment incentives is their value relative to other consumption and investment outlets also affected or unaffected by tax reform, in which case the reduced tax breaks on housing may be minimized or canceled out. But beyond overall consumption and investment impacts, the distribution of benefits and reforms by income class—a central theme of Cushing Dolbeare's chapter—must be a central focus of analysis.

# 16

# A Critique of Homeownership

*Jim Kemeny*

*Complementing the Chapter 15 critique of state subsidization of homeownership is this chapter, which sees homeownership, not as a "natural" preference but as the outcome of systematic discrimination against other forms of tenure. The result is a set of myths about the superiority of this form, particularly in English-speaking, capitalist societies. Such myths serve the interests of powerful groups that benefit from owner occupancy. Alternative forms of housing tenure and "tenure-neutral" housing policies can be developed, but only as part of a wider move toward collectivized social arrangements and wealth accumulation outside the housing sphere. These developments can increase overall social security and decrease pressure to use homeownership as insurance against hard times.*

The overwhelming emphasis on homeownership in English-speaking societies reflects an impressive consensus on the desirability of homeownership as a form of tenure and its inherent superiority over renting and other forms of tenure (such as co-ownership). The almost mystical reverence for homeownership is nicely reflected in the eulogy presented in an otherwise dry British Government White Paper on housing (United Kingdom, 1971, 4):

> Home ownership is the most rewarding form of house tenure. It satisfies a deep and natural desire on the part of the householder to have independent control of the home that shelters him and his family. It gives him the greatest possible security against the loss of his home; and particularly against price changes that may threaten his ability to keep it. If the householder buys his house on mortgage, he builds up by steady saving a capital asset for himself and his dependents.

This statement neatly sums up the principal myths about homeownership that pervade housing values in English-speaking countries—the psycholog-

Reprinted from Jim Kemeny, *The Myth of Home Ownership*, London: Routledge & Kegan Paul PLC, 1981, with the permission of the publisher.

ical and "natural" desire of owning, its inherent security of tenure (and by implication the inherent insecurity of other forms of tenure) and the capital asset which is produced. This commitment to homeownership has also been expressed in U.S. government publications, as well as by at least three U.S. presidents (Beyer, 1965, 249). . . .

Systematic discrimination in favor of homeownership has far-reaching consequences. It restricts real choice in housing tenure; it ossifies tenure patterns by discouraging two-way movement into and out of different forms of tenure; it stratifies housing tenure in terms of social class; and, by artificially stimulating the expansion of homeownership, it amplifies the limitations of homeownership as a form of tenure. In addition, policies to encourage homeownership are necessarily inequable . . .[*see Chapter 15 by Cushing Dolbeare*].

Perhaps the most telling argument against them is that they are morally unjustifiable even in terms of conservative ideology. Discrimination against comparable tenures reduces—or, rather, virtually eliminates—the ability of ordinary households to exercise real choice in housing tenure. More important from a conservative perspective, it prevents the emergence of a wide diversity of tenures and stultifies competition between tenures for households on the open market. Establishing a homeownership "monopoly" . . . by subsidies and other forms of political interference eliminates "free competition" and "the play of market forces" so beloved by conservative ideologues. Homeownership policies are therefore paternalistic and authoritarian, as well as being biased toward both the preferences of the rich and the interests of existing homeowners. If any semblance of equity and freedom of choice is to be introduced into housing policy, then the abandonment of current policies in English-speaking and other homeowning societies is an essential prerequisite. . . .

Homeownership will always be a major form of tenure in capitalist societies. The power of vested interests in owner occupation plus the social structural reasons why it is advantageous for households to have access to housing capital that can be privately spent to make up for deficiencies in the welfare state or to boost consumption are important reasons why many households become owner occupiers. Yet explanation in these terms is insufficient to explain the high or very high rates of owner occupation in some countries and among some socioeconomic groups. Much of the appeal of owner occupation lies in the fact that housing policies have been adopted that leave very little real choice for most households as to which form of tenure they can realistically choose. In turn, the widespread acceptance of tenure-discriminatory housing policies is based on a housing ideology that eulogizes homeownership and denigrates alternative forms of tenure. . . .

It would be naive to assume that this one-eyed view of housing tenure is an oversight by many politicians and academics and that all that is required is a more balanced perspective. It is clearly not coincidental that the ideological bias happens to support the vested interests of powerful groups that stand to benefit from owner occupation. At the same time, care must be taken not to take a conspiratorial view of housing-tenure ideologies. Rather, there is a symbiotic relationship between ideology and the power to determine policy. Once a system has been established that discriminates between tenures and in favor of privatization in society as a whole, there is a strong element of self-perpetuation involved. Discriminating in favor of homeownership will increase its attractiveness relative to other tenures, in terms of subsidies, sociolegal status, and eventually in sheer availability. This in turn will strengthen the likelihood that such a policy will be continued or even intensified. In addition, privatization in nonhousing areas of society will tend to increase the demand for privatized housing, which in turn will reinforce and stimulate further privatization in nonhousing areas.

This vicious circle is not at all peculiar to housing but operates in many areas where the state has been involved in providing communal facilities as an alternative to private ones. If public transport is neglected and services are poor, then most people will "naturally" prefer to be car owners. If, as in Britain, public telephones are limited in number and awkward to use, or if artificial limitations are placed on their use, such as preventing them from receiving incoming calls, then more people will "naturally" prefer to have their own telephone. If public radio is not allowed to compete with commercial stations but must be largely limited to catering for minority interests, as in Australia, then most people will "naturally" prefer to listen to commercial radio. If the standard of public education or public health is poor, then more people will "naturally" prefer to send their children to private schools or to take out private health insurance.

The major difference between all of these and housing is that, because of the long life of houses, it is not possible to make major alterations to existing arrangements over a period of much less than 20 years short of wholesale state takeover of owner-occupied housing. The need for sustained political effort over a long period, and the importance and highly personal nature of housing as a commodity, makes housing peculiarly vulnerable to the establishment and perpetuation of a vicious circle in which it can be argued convincingly that there is a powerful "natural" demand for homeownership. Indeed, the existence of a large homeownership sector is quite manifestly a major stumbling block to establishing tenure neutrality, even in a country such as Sweden, where the homeownership rate has been relatively low [*see Chapter 31 by Richard P. Appelbaum*].

The dominance of the homeownership ideology, particularly in English-speaking societies, has been fatal to the attempts by labor movements to develop alternatives, or even to articulate the possibility that there may be a competitive alternative. The widespread support for policies favoring homeownership ultimately derives from the ability of right-wing politicians to justify a tenure-discriminatory housing policy in terms of a coherent ideology. Before any real alternative policies concerning housing tenures can be developed an alternative perspective on housing tenures must be articulated. It is insufficient simply to oppose homeownership-oriented policies, and it is pointless to try to put forward alternatives without these being informed by a closely reasoned philosophy that makes sense in terms of policy to the ordinary household. The starting point, then, must be to counter the biased, one-sided view of housing tenures that develops in homeowning societies and to oppose it with an alternative that holds out the possibility of tenure choice, variety, and free competition within a broadly nonprofit framework. If this is done, as part of a wider move toward the development of collectivized social arrangements outside the housing sphere, then the basis will have been set for a radical change in direction.

This brings us back to the implications of the close relationship between patterns of tenure and the welfare state, on the one hand, and housing policies of political parties, on the other. The articulation of an alternative housing policy based on tenure neutrality can be carried out as part of a wider social policy of increasing (low-cost) socialized wealth. If this is done, then cost-renting[1] and other alternatives to homeownership will have considerably greater appeal, and there will be correspondingly less pressure on households to enter homeownership as an excessive form of insurance against mishap. If this is not done, but instead a tenure-neutral housing policy is introduced into a society where social security is minimal, then we can expect that the homeownership rate will be less affected, and owner occupation will almost certainly remain the majority tenure.

However, the problem of countering the myth of homeownership is formidable. The homeownership ideology is by now deeply entrenched in the housing folklore, as well as in the housing policies of most capitalist societies. Indeed, so much is this so that there is very little likelihood that tenure-neutral housing policies will ever replace the current homeownership policies in most countries, at least in the near future. The outlook is therefore grim, and for a long time we can expect that the general trend will be toward greater inequalities in housing, less real choice between comparable tenures for households, and greater discrimination against potential alternative forms of tenure to homeownership. This prognosis is borne out by the fact that even in Sweden, where some semblance of a tenure-neutral policy has been maintained for almost two generations, the pressures toward upsetting this balance appear to be mounting, and if present trends are maintained, Sweden is likely to move increasingly toward tenure patterns comparable to those in English-speaking countries [*see Chapter 31 by Richard P. Appelbaum*]. Much the same goes for Britain and Australia, where there is no constructive alternative to the pro-homeownership and anti–public housing policies of conservative parties. Indeed, housing policies in these countries appear to be becoming even more biased, particularly by way of attempts to reduce the attractiveness of public renting by introducing "market" or "fair" rents and by attempting to encourage more public tenants to buy homes they are renting [*see Chapter 30 by Steve Schifferes*].

Ultimately, the problem comes down to the way in which housing has been defined as a residual area divorced from the central policy-making area of social security. Once the far-reaching ramifications of housing for the whole of social structure are understood, it becomes possible to appreciate how crucial housing policy is to the viability of a welfare state. The residualization of housing is particularly noticeable in housing research. "Housing studies" have never been systematically integrated into the study of social structure as a whole. Much of the blame for conceptual confusion surrounding housing must therefore lie with those who have perpetuated the ghettoization of housing studies within sociology and social administration. The emergence of housing studies as a specialized field has been an unmitigated disaster for the understanding of housing tenure. The sooner housing studies become truly integrated into the study of the sociology of the family, the sociology of poverty, political economy, the sociology of ideology, urban sociology, and the study of the welfare state, to name but a few other specialisms, the sooner are we likely to enrich our understanding of housing tenures.

# Note

1. Kemeny uses the term "cost-renting" to refer to a system of averaging the construction costs of the entire housing stock and dividing them more or less equally among all households in order to give the advantages of historically lower housing costs to the entire population. The current homeownership system, whereby each household finances its housing on an individual basis, creates very different levels of housing costs for individual households, as a function of the length of time they have owned their homes (reflecting in turn historically lower construction costs and interest rates and retirement of individual mortgages). "Cost-renting" collectivizes the society's housing costs so that each household's housing costs can remain at a similar proportion of income throughout its lifetime. See the short book from which this chapter is excerpted for a fuller discussion of this concept and its implications.—EDS.

# 17

# Manhattan Plaza: Old Style Ripoffs Are Still Alive and Well

*Robert Schur*

## Manhattan Plaza Sequel

*Tom Robbins*

*Government assistance to limited-profit private developers of "moderate- to middle-income" multifamily housing has been highly vulnerable to criticism. Illustrating the housing policy theory articulated in Chapter 14 by Peter Marcuse is the case of the Manhattan Plaza project in New York City described here, which clearly shows how government programs—state-financed, limited-profit programs, the federal Section 8 program, and federal tax laws—primarily benefit private, wealthy interests and urban redevelopment schemes, and only incidentally produce housing needed by the majority of the people. The ways in which the government manipulates the affected interest groups and legitimates its actions are also revealed. Manhattan Plaza is by no means a unique example of how these programs facilitate (and were designed to facilitate) massive private profit making.*

## Part I

The curtain was dramatically rung down on the latest (but almost certainly not the last) act of the drama known as Manhattan Plaza in February 1977 when the Board of Estimate voted unanimously to approve $11.5 million per year (for each of the next 40 years) of housing assistance subsidies so that 1,698 apartments in the still-unfinished project can be rented to citizens who could not afford the rents required to sustain the project and repay the city its $90 million mortgage loan by means of which it has been built. The Board of Estimate's resolution provides that 70 percent of the apartments will go to members of the "performing arts" professions and the remaining 30 percent to lower-income residents of the Clinton neighborhood and the elderly.

The scene at City Hall . . . was indeed well mounted and produced. Of course, there was the usual array of city officials testifying that the plan was absolutely necessary and predicting dire consequences if it was not adopted.

This chapter, without the sequel, was originally published in two issues of *City Limits* 2, nos. 2 and 3 (February and March 1977). Reprinted with the permission of *City Limits*.

Predictably, the so-called community representatives from the Community Board and an anomalous organization known as the Clinton Planning Council gave their blessings. What added spice to the occasion, and assured front-page publicity, was the presence of that doyenne of legitimate stage and a senior citizen in her own right, Helen Hayes, and Oscar-winning movie actress, Estelle Parsons, who eloquently pleaded, in accents more familiar to Broadway than to City Hall, that the project be allowed "at long last . . . to open its doors to Clinton and the performing arts." As might be expected, they brought down the house.

Another piece of stage business that should not go unreported was the appearance that the Board of Estimate was effecting some sort of a "compromise"—one that was attentive to concerns of the Clinton community, the representatives of the performing artists that might soon move into the project, and even to the fiscal worries of the city comptroller.

From a play-reviewer's perspective, the production at the ornate, beautifully proportioned theater known as the Board of Estimate Chamber was a masterpiece. As a revelation of municipal housing and community development policy it was a disaster.

To understand fully the true motivations as well as the implications of what Manhattan Plaza is doing for and to the people of New York City, it is necessary to know the story of how, why, and by and for whom it got conceived, approved, and put together. Though the story of Manhattan Plaza may be known to some, its full implications have received little or no attention from the media. It actually goes something like this. . . .

Along about 1967, one Seymour Durst, a long-time wheeler-dealer in midtown Manhattan real estate, had assembled a lot of rundown property in the skid-row area of 42nd Street west of Times Square and on adjacent blocks in the Clinton neighborhood. Desirous of lightening the burden of these properties, he teamed up with a high-class developer by the name of Richard Ravitch and his HRH Corporation. Ravitch was a good deal younger in years than Seymour, but had already begun to make his mark as a builder of expensive "middle-income" housing projects.

Ravitch saw in Durst's deteriorating tenements and rotting storefronts a chance for a possible major killing (this is called "vision" in the planning industry), so he put together a proposal for a square-block, high-rise apartment complex running from 9th to 10th Avenues between 42nd and 43rd Streets. Calling it "Manhattan Plaza," Ravitch first tried to peddle the scheme to the State Division of Housing and Community Renewal. That agency turned down the scheme, basically because they concluded the apartments, projected to rent for $90–$100 per room per month, could not "sell" in that neighborhood.

Undaunted, Poor Richard turned his sights on the city, which, through the generosity of the state legislature, has the same right as the state to sell its bonds (and thereby hock its taxpayers for 40 years at a clip) to raise money to lend to developers of middle-income housing.

At this point, we should perhaps explain what "middle-income" means in the housing parlance of the Empire State. As a matter of actual fact, one doesn't find the words "middle income" anywhere in the New York State Private Housing Finance Law (more popularly called the "Mitchell-Lama Law" after its principal sponsors in the Albany legislature, Senator MacNeil Mitchell from Manhattan's West Side and Assemblyman Ferdinand Lama from Brooklyn—two astute lawyers who profited mightily representing developers who sought financing by using the law they, as legislators, had wrought). The law speaks only of "persons and families of low income." But the same law goes on to define low income in a most strange and peculiar way. It says that a family of one, two, or three members is "low income" as long as its annual income does not exceed six times the rent charged by the project; families of one or more persons are "low income" provided their incomes are not more than seven times the rent. There is, of course, no limit on the rent. So in a project where the rent is $100 per room per month, a four-person family occupying an apartment with three bedrooms and a terrace (which under the Mitchell-Lama regulations counts as 6.0 rooms and therefore rents at $600 per month) can earn up to $50,400 a year and still be classified, officially and legally and with a perfectly straight face, as "low income."

To return to our story—our intrepid developer, Mr. Ravitch, found the city fathers much more receptive to his plans and specifications. One can only speculate why. Perhaps because the mayor had the benefit of advice from a staff of "experts" known as the Department of City Planning; perhaps because the city was nearing (after decades of research and preparation) the publication of its long-awaited "Master Plan," which would confidently predict the rejuvenation and rebirth of West 42nd Street as a high-class strip of luxury hotels, shops, and apartment buildings; perhaps the brand-new administrator of the brand-new Housing and Development Administration (HDA) thirsted for a record number of new housing starts; perhaps . . .

Despite a few grumblings from local residents (who are always opposed to progress and enlightenment!) and others (who undoubtedly had special axes to grind), the plan sailed through HDA, the City Planning Commission, and the Board of Estimate, and Ravitch had his deal. The project was budgeted at a total development cost of $95 million. Under the Mitchell-Lama "low-income" housing law, the city would finance 95 percent or about $90 million; Ravitch and his corporation would have to put up "equity" of $5 million.

Ravitch's plan called for a project that would consist almost entirely of studio and one-bedroom apartments. Less than 10 percent of the units would have two bedrooms, and none would be larger than that. The intended tenants would thus be mostly single persons and married couples without children. At initially projected rents of about $100 per room per month (or $250 for a studio without a balcony and $350 for a nonbalconied one-bedroom unit) the project could only hope to acquire as tenants younger, upwardly mobile men and women who were making their way in businesses or professions located in midtown Manhattan and who would be intrigued by living quite close to work. . . .

And so the parties proceeded to a closing. Durst sold the land to Ravitch (probably at a tidy profit), and Ravitch signed with the city. Don't think for a moment that Poor Richard had to ante up $5 million in cash at the signing. That's not how Mitchell-Lama works. Richard had only to promise to come up with a total of $5 million as and when the city felt it was needed for expenses as the project progressed. At the initial closing, Ravitch, as a matter of fact, was only asked for $150,000 in cash—which he gladly put into the kitty. The city advanced, out of its mortgage proceeds, the rest of the money needed to get the construction underway.

Then, a strange thing happened. One day after the closing, Ravitch ceased to become the owner–sponsor–developer of the as yet wholly unbuilt Manhattan Plaza; he had sold his entire interest to a group of partners that included Estée Lauder, the perfume queen, Alexander Cohen, a millionaire Broadway show business luminary, and others—for the munificent sum of $12 million! For a cash outlay of $150,000, Ravitch became richer by $7 million in the space of 24 hours. Now you begin to see why Mr. Ravitch is considered by many to be the king of the local real estate developers and maybe also why Governor Carey appointed him head of the troubled New York State Urban Development Corporation.

But that ain't all! Ravtich and HRH still held a few cards in the game. His corporation had the building contract, worth some $60 million or more, including the built-in "builder's overhead and profit" and all sorts of professional fees, which the Mitchell-Lama regulations are so careful to specify. Through another corporation, Ravitch held the right to manage the project when it was completed—worth (courtesy of Mitchell-Lama regulations) around 4 percent of the then-anticipated gross rent roll of something in excess of $6 million a year, or an income of about a quarter of a million per annum.

Right from the start, Ravitch had already bailed himself out, at a 140 percent profit, and stood only to make more and more money. Why, one may ask, did Ms. Lauder and her partners so willingly enrich Ravitch and assume the risks of ownership of an as yet unbuilt housing development? The answer, in a word, is taxes. Much of the grease that enables the wheels of large-scale real estate deals to spin is furnished by the national government in the form of the Internal Revenue Code. On the one hand, the tax law requires rich people to pay huge percentages of their incomes to the government in taxes. . . . At the same time, the Internal Revenue Code offers all kinds of inducements to high-income taxpayers to reduce their incomes subject to tax. These inducements go by the apt name of "tax shelters." One of these shelters is called "depreciation," an interesting variety of which is known as the "double-declining balance" type and is very handy for owners of income-producing real estate. It works out about like this.

Suppose, as in the case of Estée Lauder and Company, you own a brand-new apartment house development that "cost" $102 million to put up (remember, Lauder and Co. paid Ravitch $12 million and the city was putting up $90 million for a total of $102 million). Assume that the land (which will always be there and therefore doesn't "depreciate") represented $7 million of the total project cost. The remainder, $95 million, can be depreciated. The period of time over which this depreciation can be taken is, for this kind of project, assumed by the tax collector to be forty years. That means that the property is assumed to decline in value (regardless of actual condition) at the rate of 2.5 percent of its cost, or by $2.375 million, per year.

However, if you use the legal double-declining balance method of depreciation, you take off twice $2.375 million, or $4.75 million the first year. What does this do to your tax bill? Let's see what might happen to the partners of Lauder and Co. Under the Mitchell-Lama law, the maximum profit the owners are allowed to make from operating the project is 6 percent per year on the cash equity—in this case, 6 percent of $5 million, or $300,000 per year. That would show up as taxable income to the partnership. But then, in year one, the partners subtract $4,750,000 of depreciation, leaving a net loss for tax purposes of $4,450,000. This loss the partners can use to offset other income on which, but for the loss, they would have to pay taxes.

Suppose the partners each contributed 10 percent, or $1.2 million apiece, to purchase from Ravitch the ownership of Manhattan Plaza. They would together own 20 percent of Lauder and Co., and they could therefore use 20 percent of the net loss from Manhattan Plaza, or $890,000, to subtract from otherwise taxable income. Suppose Lauder et al. have other net income (from salaries, interest on bonds and bank accounts, dividends on stocks, etc.) of $1.5 million. If they had no "losses" to subtract from this income they would have to pay [at the then-current U.S. income tax rates] a tax of $1,020,980. By using the net loss obtained from depreciation on Manhattan Plaza, they reduce their net taxable income to $610,000 and their actual tax to $397,980. They therefore save $623,000 in taxes, as a direct result of the depreciation loss on Manhattan Plaza. This saving represents a "return" of more than 25 percent on their $2.4 million investment—not a bad deal by any standards. And, of course, to this $623,000 should be added 20 percent of the net profit of $300,000 actually received from operating the project, or $60,000, making a total "gain" to the partners of $683,000, or 28.4 percent!

Of course, they don't "earn" quite as much in the succeeding years. In fact, under the double-declining balance method, their net savings in taxes become less each year. But after 10 years, by which time the annual net savings would become less than half of the sum saved in the first year, they will have "earned" an aggregate amount of almost twice their $2.4 million initial investment. At this point, the partners in effect would also own their 20 percent interest in Manhattan Plaza for nothing. They could then sell their interest to another millionaire in dire need of a tax shelter, save more tax money by the "long-term capital gains" provisions of the Internal Revenue Code, and go on to even bigger and better things.

The long and short of it is simply that the quick-turnover sale by Ravitch to Lauder and her friends was a very good deal for both sides—thanks to the U.S. Congress and the Legislature of the State of New York. [*See also Chapter 15 by Cushing Dolbeare.*]

Only—something went wrong between that initial closing and some time along about 1975, when the next scene opens.

The Master Plan's bright predictions for West 42nd Street weren't happening. Instead of shiny new buildings, the old dilapidated structures were still there. Only their former tenants, who operated pawnshops, one-arm luncheonettes, and second hand clothing stores, were being replaced by porno peep shows and massage parlors. Times Square, a few blocks to the east, was also sleazier and more unattractive than ever. New office buildings on Broadway—which were expected to be filled with bright, ambitious junior executives who would rush to live in Manhattan Plaza—remained empty and in foreclosure. Who, therefore, would want to live in the project? And it was no longer going to cost "only" $100 a room per month to live there. Along with the accelerating decline of Times Square and points west, the early years of the 1970s brought mounting inflation. The cost of money, reflected in the interest rate the city would have to charge if and when it ever got a permanent long-term mortgage placed on Manhattan Plaza, became double what it was when the project was first approved. Skyrocketing fuel, utility, insurance, and labor costs made it necessary to up the projected maintenance and operating expenses by very substantial amounts.

In short, by 1975, the developer and HDA were agreeing that the estimated rents would have to be increased from $100 to $150 per room per month (studios would begin at $375; one-bedrooms at $525 and the few two-bedrooms at $675—utilities, gas, and electricity included, of course). Even with the amenities of a swimming pool and health club, interior landscaping, and the like, the nagging question kept cropping up, Who will live there?

HDA made some kind of survey in 1975 or early 1976 and received a gloomy answer. At $150 per room per month, the project simply was not "marketable." There were not, it seems, anywhere near 1,698 individuals or families who would trade whatever housing they had, wherever it was located. for those high-priced apartments on 42nd Street and 9th or 10th Avenue. . . .

## Part II

By the middle of 1975, the parties in interest had realized, and began to acknowledge publicly, that the Manhattan Plaza project was getting into serious trouble. The "parties in interest," by this time, were principally the City of New York, which had by then paid out some $60 million or more of a $90 million mortgage for land acquisition . . . and construction, and Ms. Estée Lauder . . . and her co-investors, who had paid Richard Ravitch's development company $12 million to become the equity owners.

Ravitch himself was by this time a lesser party in interest. True, he was still the builder, but under the terms of the construction contract, he was being paid as he built, so he hardly stood to lose if the project was never completed or put into operation. . . .

Ravitch was probably more concerned about his reputation than his purse at this point. Summoned by Governor Hugh Carcy in 1975 to take over the reins of the state's ailing Urban Development Corporation (we might ask at this point just what Carey had insisted Ravitch do to avoid several patent conflicts of interest between his public and private posts), Ravitch launched some trial balloons about running for mayor either on the Democratic ticket or as an independent. His "image" in these situations was therefore of some importance.

Another party who began to make some noises was Seymour Durst . . . who had not only assembled the square-block site that he sold to Ravitch but who also held a lot of adjacent and nearby property, whose values stood to benefit substantially from a completed, occupied, and operating middle-income housing development. A collapse of the project would of course be very disappointing to Seymour's expectations for speculative increases in the prices of his neighboring holdings.

The "cause" of Manhattan Plaza's troubles was a combination of inflationary inceases in interest rates as well as in the projected costs of operating the project after it is finished—both of which factors inevitably have an effect on the rents that have to be charged to tenants. The "interest rate" issue is a matter over which the public has been gulled for years and may be worth a word of explanation.

The principal "subsidy" that the government (in this case the City of New York), through its Mitchell-Lama housing program, gives to encourage the construction of so-called middle-income housing is the fact that the financing for such projects is done by the city, rather than directly by private lending institutions. . . . There are actually two very attractive gimmicks embedded in this legislation.

First, "project cost" is an extremely all-embracing term. It includes not only the cost of acquiring the land on which the new housing is to be built, plus the cost of demolishing any old structures and relocating any tenants and other occupants of existing buildings, plus the cost of putting up the new housing, but a number of other items as well. One of the prettiest of these is a package of expenses that a developer must incur during the period of construction and which, if anything should happen that would prevent the project from being completed, would be totally lost forever. These items include interest on the money borrowed by the developer to acquire the land and erect the building until the building is completed and the tenants move in and start paying rent, the real estate taxes, water and sewer rents during the period of construction, the insurance premiums for fire, liability, and so on. Also tossed into the definition of "project costs" is a bundle of fees—such as the premium for title insurance, the rather stiff state tax on recording the mortgage (a million dollars or so for Manhattan Plaza), the city real estate transfer tax, and the fees charged by the Building Department for filing plans. Also, there are very healthy "allowances" for the inevitable lawyers' and architects' fees. These latter are figured in as percentages of the cost of construction. So if you are a big, established organization like Ravitch's HRH Construction Corporation and have a passel of lawyers and architects on your payroll, you may very well be able to acquire the necessary professional help for sums far less than what is "allowed." Nevertheless, the developer gets the full allowance — he simply pockets the difference between the "allowables" and the "actuals."

Then there is also the matter of "builder's and developer's fees." Part of this fee might be called a reward for being able to sell the project to the government. On a project where the "brick and mortar" construction costs amount to, say, $60 million (we guess that for Manhattan Plaza they are in that area and at that price of $33,000 per dwelling unit, the bare construction cost seems rather reasonable), these fees come to about $3 million.

The nicest thing about this item is that where the builder and the developer are the same entity, both fees are nevertheless paid in full. Thus Mr. Ravitch's company counted on a total of $3 million (aside from the $7 million profit made on the sale of the equity and aside from the excess allowances for legal and architectural costs) as its net profits on the project. Another pleasant accommodation that the city permits the developer is for the latter to "return" the developer's fee as a credit against the required 5 percent equity investment. Thus, the actual cash that a developer of a project the size and cost of Manhattan Plaza actually has to put up out of his or its own pocket can be as low as $2 million, rather than the $5 million that the developer is credited with having contributed.

The point is that all of these "extras" are paid for by the city, which adds them to the amount of money it lends to the project. This not only shifts the risk from the developer to the city, but it makes the mortgage that much larger—and hence means that the rents payable by the project's tenants will have to be that much higher in order for the loan to be repaid.

This loan given by the city to the developer is not made with funds in the general city treasury. Rather, the city goes out to the banks and borrows the money. It then re-lends the money to the developer. And here is precisely where the subsidy comes in. For, with another assist from the federal government, the banks (and others to whom the banks may resell their loans) do not have to pay any income taxes on the interest they receive on monies loaned to the city. This, too, can be a rather large gift consisting of money that the government doesn't get from taxpayers.

Actually, the idea in making interest paid by state and local governments taxfree is to make it cheaper for these units of government to borrow money. Wealthy investors will accept a lower rate of interest on loans to a city or state than they will on bank deposits (which are actually loans to banks) or to private businesses, since they are concerned about the net after-tax results rather than the gross interest rate as such. . . .

When the city first decided that it ought to help Dick Ravitch build Manhattan Plaza (back around 1967), the city was able to borrow money for housing projects at an interest cost of less than 4 percent per year. But even that low rate had experienced a sudden increase from a still lower level that prevailed during the early 1960s. The money "experts," both in and outside city government, were certain that this increase (of less than 1 percent from previous rates) was only temporary and that rates would soon go back to "normal."

The city was accordingly advised by these financial geniuses not to sell long-term bonds, but to borrow, for the moment, by issuing short-term notes, which could be replaced by long-term bonds when the market declined, as it was certain to do in the very near future. So, when it first started to lend money for Manhattan Plaza—under a 40-year mortgage—the city used money that it would have to repay in a year or at the longest two years. But when the time came to repay these short-term notes, the market had gone the other way—interest rates, instead of going back to their former lower levels, had gone still higher. Now the city was in a bind. Since it had been so sure that by the time it sold long-term bonds, the interest would be less, it had projected the interest it was going to receive from the Manhattan Plaza project at a lower rate than the interest rate for which it could sell bonds. If it readjusted the projections to reflect the actual interest rate, the rents would have to be refigured also, to provide the income required to pay the higher interest. Politically that would be undesirable. . . .

Unfortunately, the rate of interest payable on a long-term mortgage affects the cost of housing to a very significant degree, especially when virtually the entire cost of the project is included in the mortgage. Just as an example, for a project like Manhattan Plaza, a 40-year mortgage (that is, one where the $90 million principal sum is repaid in full over a period of 40 years), at 4 percent interest, would require payments of principal and interest in equal amounts per month over 480 months of about $350,000. Spread over the total of around 5,588 "rooms" (according to the city's way of counting them), a charge of $60–61 per room would have to be included in the rent. The same mortgage, at an interest rate of 7 percent per annum, requires monthly payments of almost $590,000 per month or $100 per room. Put another way, any variation of 1 percent in the interest rate would require a corresponding adjustment of just about $13 per room in the monthly rent. One now begins to see the potentially disastrous implications of any serious misjudgment of the interest rate for a project financed like Manhattan Plaza.

What the parties did, therefore, was to watch the interest rates climb ever higher as the 1970s succeeded the 1960s and the city's cost of borrowing finally reached such a ridiculous figure that the city was, in effect, precluded altogether from borrowing money in the private investment market.

Manhattan Plaza needed its financing placed under a long-term bond issue—almost always more costly than short-term financing. The 8 percent rate the city managed to get on its bonds meant costs of $110–115 per room/per month for debt service payments alone—somewhat more than the early projections for the entire rent.

Let's see who loses in this process. We don't have to look very far. Ravitch has already socked away his profits—he can't lose, except his reputation. Estée Lauder and Co. (the equity investors) could lose—possibly the whole $12 million they have sunk into the project, although in their tax brackets the capital losses could reduce the bite by at least 25 percent. So their maximum exposure, by the most generous standards, is not more than $9 million—still a tidy sum.

The big potential loser is the city—in for over $65 million already and for the full $90 million when and if the building is finished. What are its options?

One that presents itself would be for the city to continue to finance the project to completion and let the owners (the paper company that Ms. Lauder and her friends have formed to hold legal title to the property) rent the apartments for the best prices obtainable—most knowledgeable people guess this . . . would produce a shortfall of funds needed to make the mortgage payments to the city. The latter would therefore foreclose the mortgage, and the project would be put up for sale at public auction. According to at least one real estate specialist who has studied the Manhattan Plaza situation very carefully, the best bid that could be expected from any private investor-operator would not exceed $45–50 million—or about half of the city's investment. This would result in the equity owners being wiped out and the city sustaining a loss of $40–45 million. That loss would not only have to be paid (to the people who loaned the full $90 million to the city) over the period of any eventual long-term bonds, but until paid, the city would sustain a charge against its capacity to borrow money for other capital projects.

A second option would be for the city to buy into the property itself, crediting the purchase price against the mortgage. The city would, as landlord, rent the apartments for the best obtainable rents—say $110–115 per room per month. It would thereby sustain an annual loss, since the rents would be insufficient to make the payments due each year on the $90 million it will have borrowed. The guess heard around is that this loss would be on the order of about $4 million per year. That's a lot of money for New York City given its shaky fiscal position.

Still a third option would be to make a deal with the equity owners (Lauder & Co.). As we showed above, they are in the posture of possibly losing up to $9 million net after taxes plus a very lucrative tax shelter. A little tough bargaining by the city ought to produce an agreement whereby, in exchange for a promise by the city to forebear calling in its mortgage loan, Lauder & Co. puts up, over the next, say, five years, $1 million a year to help the city reduce the losses on the project. Since Lauder & Co. is allowed to earn 6 percent, or $360,000 a year, on the $5 million equity in the project, the partners would only have to cover $640,000 a year in new cash to meet such an obligation.

At the same time, a really hard-driving, fiscally frugal city might well ask Ravitch to make a small contribution out of the many millions he has already taken out of the project. Another million a year for five years from this source, added to the Lauder & Co. contributions, would cut the city's annual losses in half (and could be a big plus for Ravitch's political image). Two million dollars a year in the hole is, after all, a lot easier to take than $4 million.

Furthermore, within a few years continuing inflation and a real effort by the city, using a reasonable amount of federal community development funds and other aids from Washington, would upgrade West 42nd Street to make it a little more attractive to middle-income residents. City officials might have argued that the marketable rents for Manhattan Plaza would be high enough to cover the full debt service, plus maintenance and operations, plus some real estate taxes. It is quite probable, at any rate, that these costs would be substantially covered. Any remaining shortage would be more than compensated for by increased real estate taxes which the city would receive by raising the assessed values of the surrounding real estate (including those parcels owned by Seymour Durst)—a procedure that would be justified as a result of Manhattan Plaza's becoming a going concern tenanted by middle- to upper-middle-income occupants.

The city, of course, chose none of these options. Instead, it went the bureaucrat's favorite route of looking for an additional subsidy. Never mind that it may cost the taxpayers more in the short or long run; if it appears to make the city's books balance, that's really all that counts. The city found the "perfect" subsidy in the new federal Housing and Community Development Act's Section 8 housing assistance program—the most costly and expensive housing subsidy program yet invented by the fertile brains of the housing industry and the United States Congress.

Under Section 8, any family (plus single persons over sixty-two years of age) is eligible for housing assistance if its income is below a specified figure—initially this was 90 percent of the median income of the local metropolitan area. The assistance consists of the federal government paying directly to the landlord that portion of the "fair market rent" for the eligible family's housing that exceeds 25 percent of the family's income (for very large families, the subsidy begins above 15 percent of income). Section 8 rent subsidies are available, under different sets of guidelines, for newly constructed, substantially rehabilitated, and (provided it is in "standard" condition) existing housing.

While at least 1.5 million households are eligible for Section 8 assistance in New York City alone (especially after Roger Starr, while HDA Administrator, prevailed on the feds to increase the level of eligibility to the former Section 236 subsidy limits, or to about $16,000 a year for a family of four), there isn't quite enough money to take care of everybody. The most optimistic projections are that, at late 1970s levels of congressional appropriations, somewhat less than 1 percent of the "eligible" households will be able to receive assistance per year. Still in all, the program costs a lot of money— New York City's share being around $75 million a year (1977 figures).

What the city now proposed to do was to provide Section 8 subsidies for all 1,698 apartments in Manhattan Plaza. This would thereby enable the apartments to be rented to low- and moderate-income families for the full

$150–160 per room per month, with the tenants paying whatever rents equaled 25 percent of their incomes and the federal dollars being used to make up the rest. This is, of course, expensive. The city calculated that $11.5–12 million per year would be required in subsidies alone. This subsidy, under the Federal law, continues for 40 years (which is the same term as the Mitchell-Lama mortgage), so the total lifetime cost to the public of assisting 1,698 lower-income families to live in Manhattan Plaza has to be at least $460 million, or more than five times what it would cost to give away the mortgage entirely and let people pay only the $47 per room per month it would cost to run the project without worrying about any debt service (a rent that would enable individuals whose incomes exceed $6,025, couples with incomes over $7,900, and families with one, and in some cases, two small children earning $10,200 to live there). The point is, that with the $460 million built-in subsidy, the city is assured of getting its loan repaid, Estée Lauder and friends take their tax shelters (which will cost the federal government at least another $25 million of income taxes not charged or collected), and Richard Ravitch earns his full entitlement on the deal. The cost to the public fiscally? Only $485 million or a bit more over the next 40 years, or the paltry sum of $7,300 per year per apartment! That's an average of $608 per month in subsidies—or close to four times the amount that the average New York City renter household pays for its shelter.

Of course, the subsidy for this one project also uses up a good deal of the total amount of rent assistance available citywide—about 15 percent of the total and close to 40 percent of the subsidy allocated to the city (the state and federal governments each get a piece also to assist New York City landlords and developers of their own choosing). But then again, Manhattan Plaza is important, and how otherwise to avoid hurting some well-meaning and very well connected investors and realtors?

The city liked this idea so well that, without asking for anyone's further input, Roger Starr put in a quick telephone call to reserve the $11.5–12 million before it got misplaced anywhere else. As soon as the word got out, however, our old friend Seymour Durst sprang into action. This deal might be okay for the city, his sometime buddy Dick Ravitch, and for Estée Lauder and her playmates, but it didn't look like it would benefit Seymour. Putting these huge subsidies into all these apartments would instantly turn Manhattan Plaza into a low-income housing project. (Seymour must have noted a further Federal rule that, at least to the extent feasible, not less than 20 percent of the Section 8 allowances should go to "very low-income" tenants—households with incomes of less than half the median income for the region, or under $7,000 in the case of New York City). Low-income projects, as every realtor knows, do nothing for the surrounding neighborhood; if anything, their presence only depresses the values of nearby real estate. And Seymour Durst owns a lot of real estate right nearby to Manhattan Plaza. The Section 8 idea was not pleasing to Mr. Durst.

So Durst, with assists from the Broadway Association and the League of Theatre Owners, hired a couple of very smart lawyers, Albert A. Walsh (a former HDA Administrator and lobbyist for the local real estate industry) and Eugene J. Morris (who at one time or another has represented almost every large developer in this area). Walsh promptly filed suit against the city, seeking to block the Manhattan Plaza project on the ground that turning it from middle- to low-income housing constituted such a major change as to require City Planning Commission and Board of Estimate approval, to be voted on only after public hearings before those bodies.

As a stopgap measure it worked. The city was forced to agree, at a court hearing on Durst's motion for a preliminary injunction, that it would submit any plan to use Section 8 subsidies to the Planning Commission and the Board of Estimate. This concession meant also that the local Community Board would get a formal crack at the proposal, since even under the old city charter (this was during 1976) the City Planning Commission was obliged to refer proposals of this nature to the Community Board for an advisory opinion.

The resultant delay was used by the city to good advantage. Someone came up with a deceptively clever proposal. Since the concern is that Manhattan Plaza may become akin to just another public housing project, why not dress it up to appear like something else? Nearby Times Square is the heart of the entertainment industry. There are concentrated the city's theaters, the popular music industry, even the major radio and television networks' headquarters are just a stone's throw away on Sixth Avenue. Clinton and West 42nd Street is the closest moderately priced residential area. Many persons employed in "show business," especially those who work in the lower-paid ranks, already live in that neighborhood. Let's blunt the opposition to low income in general by making it low-income entertainment-industry. Let's, in short, turn Manhattan Plaza into a project to house people who work in the entertainment field but whose incomes are low enough for them to qualify for Section 8 allowances. Remember that Roger Starr got the Section 8 increased; the limits aren't that low, after all. Many part-time actors, actresses, and musicians and most full-time stagehands, grips, electricians, script boys and girls, and the like could make it under Section 8. And wouldn't anyone, even Seymour Durst, just love these types as neighbors?

Quickly handing out a "consultant contract" to benefit a long-time friend of the administration in housing, a survey was designed to "prove" that entertainment industry types would just love to live in Manhattan Plaza. As designed, the survey had to come up with the desired result. Letters were sent to the entire roster of union members belonging to Actor's Equity, Local 802 of the American Federation of Musicians, and other craft unions in the industry. The letters were, to say the least, a bit disingenuous. As an example, the form letter sent to thousands of musicians' union members living in and around New York starts out with the usual gushy real estate salesman's pitch for the project. In the heart of Manhattan's theater district—a new luxury housing development that you can afford—central air conditioning—24-hour security—roomy, modern, decorator-designed units. Rents will be "about" 25 percent of your income. Interested? Just put your name and address on the attached form and mail it direct to us (the "us" being Ravitch's management subsidiary), and we'll invite you to a special viewing (at no obligation) of the model apartments as soon as they are ready, which will be in a few short months. You will be able to see the models only by invitation. And remember: This offer is being made exclusively to entertainment industry union members. It's for you alone—the general public does not get in on the deal.

Note what the letter does not say. No mention that this is a government-assisted project. Not a word about maximum income limits. No hint that if your family is larger than three persons, this project can't be for you and that if there are even three persons in your household, only a handful of apartments will be available. Small wonder that an "encouraging" number of replies showing enough interest to request an invitation to see the model apartments were received.

The city administration was now ready to put the show on the road. First, a public hearing before the Chelsea–Clinton Community Board. The only opposition is from Durst and the Broadway Association. The League of Theatre Owners has been outflanked. How can they go against the unions, so many of whose members want to live in Manhattan Plaza? The Community Board is not completely sold. They like the idea. It gets the project completed, and it ought to help improve the sleazy, skid-row situation along West 42nd Street—a long-festering sore spot with local residents. But what about something for Clinton's own nontheatrical poor? Especially the senior citizens. The Board recommends that some units—say 20–30 percent—be set aside (with Section 8 subsidies) for Clinton residents; the rest are okay for the entertainment-industry people.

Next act is before the City Planning Commission. Again, a few opponents, but more speakers in favor and a good-sized crowd in the audience obviously pro the city's plan. A small question about the legality under state and federal civil rights and antidiscrimination laws of a plan that gives priorities on an occupation basis, but it's obviously so trivial that no one bothers to attempt an answer. The commission's calendar is cleverly put together. There are two proposals for consideration: one for 100 percent entertainment types; the other, an 80–85 percent entertainment-balance low-income Clinton residents mix. Everyone expects the latter to be voted. The commission closes the hearing and adjourns. As is its wont, it meets a few days later, in executive session, and records its vote. Surprise! 7–0 in favor of 100 percent entertainment-industry priority along with a lamely worded memorandum that worries about the rentability of the project to entertainment people (even with subsidies) if they know they will have to share the project with just plain poor people.

This last, of course, has its predictable, if not intended, effect. The Clinton community leaders and board members are righteously outraged. Our poor are just as good as "their" poor, they thunder. If they won't take some of our people, there won't *be* a Manhattan Plaza project.

So the lines are drawn for the final showdown. An early February afternoon at the Board of Estimate. The good folks from Clinton are mad enough to produce a big turnout. The chamber is packed. And here come the extra, added attractions. Miss Helen Hayes and Miss Estelle Parsons to plead the cause of housing for the performing arts. Shame on you, Seymour Durst! And the community gets its say for a fair deal for Clinton's poor and elderly. The voices of opposition to the $485 million rip-off are drowned in the swell of emotions.

Just a last note of caution to show us all that fiscal integrity has not totally been forgotten. The city comptroller, staunch guardian of the fisc and perennial candidate for higher office, interjects a note of caution. "After all," he says, "we're helping Mr. Ravitch and his friends by throwing all this federal money at their project. I think Ravitch ought to do a little something to show his gratitude. So I've asked him to come in to see me to discuss the matter and Mr. Ravitch has very considerately accepted my invitation and we're talking, right now, about Mr. Ravitch and maybe Ms. Lauder and her friends making a little contribution of, say, around $600,000 for some street furniture—trees—amenities—like that around the project. It's not quite settled yet, so I want any vote on this matter to be conditioned on my being satisfied that we have a fair deal here." Score one for the comptroller. The mayor and the HDA people are a bit upset; "For God's sake, don't blow the whole carefully arranged scenario," they are heard to mutter. But everyone assures them it is only a small thing, a little political sideshow that harms no one. And for those who know the larger stakes, of what importance can $600,000 be at this late stage? Ravitch may run for mayor too this year. If the $600,000 brings a few votes, what harm can it be?

The vote was foreordained and strictly anticlimactic. Unanimously in favor, with 15 percent or about 250 units for Clinton nontheatrical poor. Three hearty cheers, and away we go.

So, Manhattan Plaza will be finished, and Ravitch will earn his full builder's overhead and profit. And the city will peddle the $90 million mortgage for about 35 cents on the dollar and use the quick cash proceeds to help "balance" its 1977–78 expense budget and then we will settle down to paying the lenders with no city income from the rents and to helping our fellow citizens from all over foot the bill for 40 years of rent subsidies and tax shelters for Ms. Lauder, her co-partners, heirs, executors, and assigns. But that's still another story. . . .

## Manhattan Plaza Sequel
*Tom Robbins*

Seven years after the city's sign-off at the Board of Estimate, Manhattan Plaza's twin 46-story towers loom over a very different 42nd Street from the one Richard Ravitch surveyed in the early 1970s. Across the street, where a row of pornographic movie houses languished for over a decade, a new line of off-Broadway theaters—dubbed Theater Row and constructed with city aid—has taken their place. Also nourished in the Plaza's shadow is a ring of trendy restaurants and boutiques, which surround the project from Ninth to Tenth Avenues.

High up in the towers, tenants can look from their balconies directly down through an arched glass roof into an Olympic-size swimming pool where swimmers paddle through well-lit azure water. By the pool is a health club, and adjoining it are canvas-domed tennis and racquet-ball courts.

The buildings themselves boast many of the elegant trappings of upper-income housing: brick and glass-lined, carpeted corridors adorned with mirrors at jazzy angles, well-guarded and sparkling clean lobbies.

That chic-ness has rubbed off on the local community as well. In recent years, the Clinton neighborhood has been waging a fierce battle with gentrification and midtown office expansion as upper-income development steadily encroaches on an area once known as Hell's Kitchen for its steamy tenements and lawless streets. Newspaper ads now promote apartments renting for four-figure monthly charges "in the Manhattan Plaza area."

As anticipated, West Side real estate tycoon Seymour Durst has benefited from the massive increases in local property values. Rehabilitation is under way in a number of his buildings on 43rd Street facing the Plaza. [*For further discussion of real estate speculation, see Chapter 5 by Joe R. Feagin.*]

Also, after years of floundering, what looks like the final Times Square redevelopment proposal has been unveiled. Its high-rise office towers threaten to eliminate what is left of tawdry 42nd Street, creating new, legitimate theaters in its wake. Manhattan Plaza, the plan notes, will serve as the western anchor for this rebirth.

But aside from occasional complaining studies by the U.S. General Accounting Office or cynical references to the project at congressional hearings on the high cost of subsidized housing (a headline in a New York tabloid called Manhattan Plaza a "swank, federally subsidized luxury pad"), few in New York City seem currently troubled by the massive bailout arranged for builder Ravitch and his fellow investors.

Although he had some hesitation originally, Controller Harrison Goldin arranged long-term 8 percent government-backed financing for the project under the FHA Section 223(f) program. Mayor Ed Koch does not seem troubled either, even though, shortly after taking office in 1978, he angrily clamped a lid on high-rise construction for the poor. Nonetheless, he has continued to welcome middle- and upper-income towers wherever they arise. And Manhattan Plaza is clearly closer to that realm than "the projects."

None of the formulators of the Manhattan Plaza solution seems to have suffered either. Then housing commissioner Roger Starr, who cheerfully offered up virtually all of the city's Section 8 set-aside to make it work, went on to join the editorial board of the *New York Times.* From that perch he regularly advocates the "planned shrinkage" of poor communities and snipes away at attempts to get promised low-income housing built on the city's incomplete urban renewal areas.

Richard Ravitch, having been bailed out himself, won fame for reviving the state's Urban Development Corporation. Under that scheme the state has continued a yearly injection of funds into scandal-ridden and rapidly deteriorating projects, and the UDC has pulled out of the business of building affordable housing altogether. (The UDC's current projects are the massive West Side Convention Center, already $200 million over budget two years before completion, and new prison construction—low-income housing of a different kind.) Ravitch then went on to run the Metropolitan Transportation Authority, overseeing two hefty fare hikes before rejoining private business amid much hoopla in the press about ending his years of "service" and "self-sacrifice" to resume his former life.

Last but hardly least, the principals of Manhattan Plaza Associates continue to get their yearly operating costs underwritten by ongoing rent subsidies, as well as their (now quickly declining) tax depreciation.

On the surface, there is little to suggest that Manhattan Plaza is not the "Miracle on 42nd Street" city housing officials claim it is. As one Plaza tenant suggested, the project has worked so well because the developers "got the next best thing" to a market-rate development: "People who looked like luxury tenants—but weren't. We're sort of like paper dolls on display to help sell the rest of the neighborhood."

So if you close your eyes (as just about everyone has) to the fact that the subsidy allotted to Manhattan Plaza could have rehabilitated three times as many apartments for the poor (as the Pratt Center argued at the time of the hearing); that the city now has a homeless population estimated at close to 40,000, due in part to the elimination of low-income units; or that the town has now run totally dry of federal housing assistance—there is little to mar the Plaza's apparent success. An endangered housing project, built by a major developer and owned by important investors, was saved with timely federal low-income subsidies. The city (and Ravitch and Durst) still got their dream of a "market-rate" development that would transform the West Side.

## Slippage in the Subsidies

Yet Manhattan Plaza did not wind up exactly as predicted at that 1976 Board of Estimate hearing, and life amid the country's swankiest Section 8 project is not without its headaches. For one thing, not everyone gets a Section 8 subsidy. According to the city, in early 1984, 128 of the units had been rented at market rates. Another 28, begun under the Section 8 program, have since shifted up to market-rate levels because of upward fluctuations in tenants' income. These figures represent a threefold increase in the number of market-level tenants since 1980. Thus, a growing number of tenants are not lower-income, even by Manhattan Plaza's standards.

The erosion of subsidized units has helped to spur rumors that the complex will some day soon be sold as a coop, or gradually go entirely market level. In other words, having weathered the harsh housing market of the late 1970s with government aid, the owners may be tempted to cash in on the substantially revived situation of the mid-1980s. But there are still some 1,500 subsidized renters in Manhattan Plaza—70 percent of whom are drawn from the membership of the city's performing arts union, 30 percent from the Clinton community (of this group, half are elderly and the rest formerly lived in substandard housing).

But, while Manhattan Plaza's hefty subsidies sailed through both local and federal government reviews, in visible contrast was the treatment afforded the far smaller Taino Towers project in East Harlem. That development's large-family units (some as big as six bedrooms) required a Section 8 subsidy only slightly higher than those at Manhattan Plaza, which consists entirely of studio and one- and two-bedroom units. Constructed around the same time as Manhattan Plaza, the 656-unit Taino Towers complex traveled a far rockier political road. Built in response to decades of fierce organizing by East Harlem's Hispanic tenant and community groups to win decent, affordable housing for one of the city's poorest neighborhoods, Taino boasts some of the same amenities as Manhattan Plaza, such as balconies, a gym, an auditorium, and a greenhouse.

But Taino's apartments were held empty for several years while city and federal overseers made project sponsors jump every possible bureaucratic hurdle. Officials complained frequently that the housing was just too expensive to occupy—this while vandals daily invaded the vacant buildings, stripping away fixtures, the replacement of which made eventual rentals even higher.

It was the example of this project, along with the Booth Towers project in black Harlem, which aroused the mayor's ire and brought down his censure of "costly, high-rise towers for the poor." Manhattan Plaza, on the other hand, has remained politically unscathed. Although it was worth the high price in subsidies to conquer the "blighted" West Side, housing assistance for East Harlem should have been far less expensive, reckoned city officials.

Manhattan Plaza served a vital political and economic purpose for New

York City's power brokers and master planners. In one fell swoop, the developers' hefty profits were guaranteed, and the "Wild West" of Times Square and Clinton was readied for a plush and gentrified future. Sacrificing almost all of the city's low-income subsidies to do so—on a less-than-needy population—was still, they figured, a bargain. After all, it wasn't they who had to pay.

| 18 | The Federal Government and Equal Housing Opportunity: A Continuing Failure |
| --- | --- |
| | *Citizens Commission on Civil Rights* |

*Just as it is important to examine how the private housing market operates with respect to specific subpopulations (Chapters 11, 12, and 13), it is also necessary to look explicitly at how the state interacts with those submarkets. The two chapters that follow are concerned with government activity as it affects the housing of racial minorities and rural populations.*

*Although part of the discrepancy in the housing conditions of minorities and whites can be explained by the lower incomes of the former, income alone is not the full answer. Explicit policies of federal, state, and local governments, in concert with banks, developers, and real estate brokers, have created a dual housing market—one for whites and one for minorities (which is further broken down into blacks, Hispanics, Asians, etc.). This chapter focuses on the federal government's role in fostering housing discrimination against blacks and traces the outcomes of fair housing legislation.*

Residential housing—sales and rental—is a product of a chain of negotiations involving builders, real estate brokers, appraisers, lenders, and local governments. At any point, a decision made on the basis of the race, sex, color, religion, or national origin by any actor in the chain can deny a unit to an otherwise qualified individual.

For those who cannot afford to rent or purchase a decent home, the federal government has been the major provider, and it has played a major part in determining where that housing would be located and who would occupy it.

Reprinted from the Commission's *A Decent Home . . . a Report on the Continuing Failure of the Federal Government to Provide Equal Housing Opportunity*, Washington, D.C., 1983. This report was written for the Commission by Glenda G. Sloane, director for housing and community development at the Center for National Policy Review, Catholic University Law School.

# Federal Policy before 1962: Support for a Racially Dual Housing Market

Before 1962, there was no national policy favoring equal housing opportunity. For the most part, the disposition of property was dictated by local officials, elected and appointed, and influential members of the housing industry in accordance with accepted assumptions about race and property values, and race and credit-worthiness. As black people migrated to urban areas in the early part of the twentieth century, some jurisdictions adopted zoning laws prohibiting blacks and whites from purchasing, selling, or occupying property in a manner that would destroy the "racial purity" of a given block or neighborhood.[1] Where jurisdictions did not adopt such prohibitions, and as these ordinances were struck down as unconstitutional,[2] they were replaced by racially restrictive covenants between buyers and sellers, contracts that were enforceable in court until 1948,[3] and other operations of the private market that achieved the same results.

## Discrimination in the Private Market

The principal actors in the housing industry adopted practices that assured a racially dual market for blacks and whites. "Responsible" real estate brokers would not show houses or apartments to persons of a race not currently living in the neighborhood. If a seller accepted an offer under such circumstances, the sale could still be blocked by other key actors. Lenders would often refuse to make the loan, appraisers would substantially undervalue the property, or barriers could be posed by a restrictive covenant in the deed prohibiting the sale or occupancy of the property to a member of a racial or religious minority, or by neighborhood anger at the proposed sale, which was often made clear by overt action. Where violence occurred, law enforcement officers often failed to assist the victims of discrimination.

Racial redlining and racial steering maintained rigidly segregated neighborhoods, particularly outside the South, where the pattern was not as prevalent. The term "racial redlining" describes the practice of lenders who drew red lines to delineate areas of a city or town in which, because of the racial composition, they would not extend credit. Property insurers followed the same practice. Even where a neighborhood had not been redlined, an appraiser of the property who perceived it to be "unstable" or otherwise a poor risk because it was either all black, integrated, or in transition fixed a value that reflected this perception. The result was an appraisal well below the agreed-upon price. This, in turn, placed in jeopardy the value of all houses in that vicinity—further reinforcing the assumption that property values decline where neighborhoods become integrated.

Analogous to racial redlining, sellers of residential property did not show or give information to homeseekers in neighborhoods in which their race would be "incompatible" with the present residents. Homeseekers were "steered" into the appropriate parts of town.

An important factor in maintaining the dual market was the exclusion of minority real estate brokers from the white-only trade association, the National Association of Realtors (NAR)—until 1972 called the National Association of Real Estate Boards. From the local boards to the national board, blacks were effectively barred from operating in the market at large. The title "realtor" was made a registered trade name in 1950 so that only members of the NAR were entitled to use it. Local boards did not permit nonmembers access to multiple-listing services or educational and other services. Black brokers organized their own trade association (the National Association of Real Estate Brokers) in an effort to provide the services and status important to conducting a real estate business. . . .

Efforts by minority families to break out of the dual market in order to secure decent housing often were frustrated by other discriminatory practices. Real estate manipulators moved in to victimize both black and white homeowners and homeseekers. Brokers seized an opportunity to profit by promoting the initial sale in a white block to a black family and then representing to the neighborhood residents that black families were moving in and that it would be wise to sell immediately before the prices declined and the area became "undesirable." While minorities sometimes gained access to decent housing thereby, these techniques of "blockbusting" and inducing "panic selling" also assured perpetuation of segregated neighborhoods.

A black paid a high price for this housing. Because conventional financing was not available, particularly to the first families who bought in the white block, other arrangements were negotiated. A typical device was a land contract—a loan that carried high (sometimes usurious) interest rates, with balloon payments and no accumulation of equity.[4] When the families could not meet such onerous terms, they would lose the property and their investment, and brokers would again profit by the turnover.

## The Federal Government's Role in the 1930s

This pattern of racial exclusion and exploitation was the prevailing condition in the 1930s when the federal government entered the housing arena to prevent the housing industry from collapse and to protect the investments of homeowners. From the outset, federal policy adopted the assumptions of local governments and the housing industry about the desirability of a racially dual market and endorsed prevailing practices used to exclude and segregate minorities.

Only one program, public housing, explicitly recognized a right of participation by minorities and then only on a segregated basis. . . . Under the federal public housing program initially enacted in 1937, local housing agencies (LHAs) were required to provide units to low-income minorities according to a formula based on their proportion to all low-income families in the LHA's jurisdiction (U.S. Housing and Home Finance Agency, 1951). It was understood, however, that their housing accommodations would be separate. Other federal housing programs inaugurated in the 1930's—federal mortgage insurance (Federal Housing Administration [FHA]),[5] the Federal Home Loan Bank Board (FHLBB) System,[6] and the Federal National Mortgage Association (FNMA)[7], all designed to safeguard and facilitate homeownership—had no similar provision or even reference to the disadvantages blacks faced in securing decent housing.

The federal endorsement of local customs and practices of exclusion and separation was boldly expressed in a series of manuals issued by the FHA to guide underwriters in issuing federal insurance. The manuals warned about the dangers to property values of allowing minority entry into neighborhoods and provided a detailed blueprint for preventing such entry. The first manual, issued in 1935 to implement the 1934 law that established the federal mortgage insurance program, stated:

> Important among adverse influences . . . are the following: *Infiltration of inharmonious racial or nationality groups. . . .*
>
> All mortgages on properties in neighborhoods protected against the occurrence or development of unfavorable influences, to the extent that such protection is possible, will obtain a high rating of this feature. The absence of protective measures will result in a low rating or, possibly, in rejection of the case. (Quoted from *The Richmond School Decision: Complete Text of Bradley v. School Board of Richmond*, 1972, 172; *emphasis added*)

The 1936 FHA Underwriters' Manual specified techniques for avoiding such "infiltration":

> Deed restrictions are apt to prove more effective than a zoning ordinance in providing protection from adverse influences. Where the same deed restrictions apply over a broad area and where these restrictions relate to types of structures, use to which improvements may be put, and *racial occupancy*, a favorable condition is apt to exist. . . . (U.S. Federal Housing Administration, 1936, para. 228; *emphasis added*)

To guarantee these results further, the manual prescribed:

> Recorded deed restrictions should strengthen and supplement zoning ordinances and to be really effective should include the provisions listed below. The restrictions should be recorded with the deed and should run for a period of at least 20 years. Recommended restrictions include the following:
> . . .(G) Prohibition of the occupancy of properties except by the race for which they are intended.
> (H) Appropriate provisions for enforcement. (U.S. Federal Housing Administration, 1936, para. 266)

The 1938 manual advised the underwriter to examine the location to determine whether natural barriers might be effective in forestalling the incursion of adverse influences:

> Areas surrounding a location are investigated to determine whether incompati-

ble racial and social groups are present, for the purpose of making a prediction regarding the probability of the location being invaded by such groups. If a neighborhood is to retain stability, it is necessary the properties shall continue to be occupied by the same social and racial classes. *A change in social or racial occupancy generally contributes to instability and a decline in values.* (U.S. Federal Housing Administration, 1938, para. 937; *emphasis added*)

Thus, the framework established by the federal government in the 1930s for the preservation and expansion of the housing market (a framework that remains largely intact today) was governed by an explicit endorsement of racism. The theories articulated in FHA manuals and other policy statements led to the rigid separation of blacks and whites in public housing, to the exclusion of minorities from white neighborhoods assisted by federal funds, and to refusals to provide mortgage assistance in minority neighborhoods.

## Federal Policy in the 1940s

Federal policy did not change with the onset of World War II when the increased migration of blacks from the South to the cities of the Northeast, Midwest, and West expanded the black ghettos. . . .

Before the war ended, Congress acted to provide veterans "all that a grateful nation can furnish them in the way of compensation for the sacrifices and offerings which they have made" (*Congressional Record*, Mar. 22, 1944, 3284). Popularly known as the GI Bill of Rights,[8] its primary aim was to give returning veterans hospitalization and education benefits, but included as well a guaranty and loan program to enable veterans to purchase and rehabilitate homes and farms.[9]

After the war, the federal government became the prime mover in aiding the housing industry to meet the pent-up demand for new houses. The Housing Act of 1949 set a national housing objective for the first time: "the realization as soon as feasible of the goal of a decent home and a suitable living environment for every American family."[10] By insuring home mortgages for middle-income buyers and guaranteeing mortgages for veterans,[11] the federal government underwrote the development of large subdivisions of single-family homes in areas outside the central cities, areas that previously were sparsely populated and lacked water and sewer systems, roads, and schools (U.S. Commission on Civil Rights, 1974, 43; see also National Commission on Urban Problems, 1968, 99). Other federal assistance brought the roads and the infrastructure. But federal policy did not seek to assure that minorities would have a share in the new housing boom or its benefits, much less that housing subsidized by federal funds would be available without discrimination.[12] While overt endorsements of the use of discriminatory techniques such as racially restrictive covenants disappeared from FHA manuals after the Supreme Court's 1948 opinion ruling that such covenants were unenforceable, the federal government did not challenge racial practices in housing. Meanwhile, the segregative and exclusionary practices of the real estate industry remained unchanged and received the imprimatur of many state laws, such as a 1946 Michigan statute that wrote into law a code of ethics stating that realtors should not introduce into a neighborhood "members of any race or nationality . . . whose presence will clearly be detrimental to property values."[13]

As a result, when the Federal Housing Administration conducted a survey in the late 1950s, it found that less than 2 percent of the housing built after the war under the FHA mortgage insurance program was sold to minorities and that 1 percent was housing built in all-minority subdivisions (U.S. Federal Housing Administration, 1959).

## The Growth of the Suburbs in the 1950s

The growth of new residential communities with their new employment centers made possible by federal funds adversely affected the older central cities. The departure of the white middle class and jobs meant losses of revenues to the cities. The movement of employers to the suburbs placed the jobs beyond the reach of many inner-city residents (National Committee Against Discrimination in Housing, 1967; *New York Times*, Dec. 13, 1981). While the new communities needed funds to establish facilities and services to serve their growing populations, the older cities were in dire need of funds to maintain and upgrade an aging infrastructure for declining and less affluent populations. . . . With or without a conscious racial intent, the desire of local governments to maximize resources and minimize the need for services led to the creation of homogeneous communities, largely white and middle class—a suburban band around an increasingly poor and minority-populated center city.

The inequities between city and suburb were acknowledged by few. In the late 1950s, a few cities and states attempted to deal with persistent racial discrimination and the growing role of government in subsidizing it. The first state and local laws prohibiting discrimination in housing adopted in the 1950s applied only to public housing, that is, housing provided through direct federal funding.[14] The federal government remained silent, and continued to support the establishment of white enclaves in the suburbs through FHA and Veterans Administration (VA) programs, and segregated and increasingly minority-occupied public housing in the central cities.

In public housing, the federal government provided no incentives for the burgeoning suburban communities to establish their own local housing authorities, and state laws limited the territory in which existing LHAs were permitted to operate (National Committee Against Discrimination in Housing, 1974).[15] Even where an LHA had authority to operate outside the jurisdiction, it was easy enough for communities to exclude public housing entirely. The federal law required that a cooperation agreement be executed between the local governing body and the local housing authority to enable a project to go forward.[16] With few exceptions, communities decided not to be burdened with poor people and minorities and simply refrained from entering into agreements. Local veto power effectively kept low-rent public housing out of the suburbs and concentrated in the central cities where it was increasingly minority and isolated in areas of low-income and minority concentration.

## The Central Cities in the 1950s

Intended to aid central cities, the Urban Renewal Program, enacted in 1949 and amended in 1954 to assist in the elimination of slums and blight, helped to revitalize some areas but severely dislocated minority families who lived in the path of local development.[17] Directives to local agencies to assist these families in finding new housing were largely ignored.[18] For minorities whose choice was severely restricted to certain areas, equal access was crucial if they were to secure decent, affordable housing. Lacking fair housing requirements, the program operated to push displaced minorities into overcrowded, substandard, segregated neighborhoods, often creating more slums and blights. Urban renewal earned the title "Negro Removal."[19]

Federal policy in support of segregation in public housing and discrimination in FHA and VA programs persisted after the 1948 Supreme Court decision in *Shelley* v. *Kraemer*,[20] outlawing the enforcement of racially restrictive covenants, and the 1954 *Brown* decision, which made clear the unconstitutionality of "separate but equal" public facilities.[21] In the late 1950s, when some state and local fair housing laws were extended to cover housing with FHA mortgage insurance and VA guarantees, FHA and VA agreed to cooperate with state and local agencies by not doing business with any developer found to have violated that law. The measure of the federal commitment is found in the failure of the government to suspend or bar even one builder or developer from participating in the FHA or VA programs (U.S. Commission on Civil Rights, 1973a, 6).

Finally, after officially mandated segregated public housing was challenged successfully as a violation of the Fourteenth Amendment in suits brought following the *Brown* decision,[22] the Public Housing Administration repealed its policy of neutrality that permitted support of segregated projects but left the problem of implementing the judicial decision to the local agencies, maintaining that tenant selection was not a federal responsibility.[23]

At the same time that the suburbs were developing as white and middle class, the cities remained a patchwork of black and white neighborhoods. As white families moved from homes adjacent to black neighborhoods, the overcrowded ghetto would expand in that direction, a move often made possible by real estate brokers who engaged in "blockbusting." Often desperate for adequate housing, minority families agreed to pay prices above market value often on terms and conditions that were outrageous, if not illegal.[24] Because FHA and VA, consistent with accepted market practices, would not insure mortgages on houses in neighborhoods that were "socially inharmonious," minorities were denied the benefits of the low- or no-down-payment mortgage loans that lenders made when federal insurance was available.[25] The FHA and VA would routinely refuse to consider applications from integrated and minority neighborhoods—thereby redlining large areas of the city.[26]

Minorities were fair game for unscrupulous real estate speculators in large part because the homeownership assistance afforded by the federal government to hundreds of thousands of white families was unavailable to them.

To maintain these homes usually required an income beyond their capability; as a result, the residents could not keep their houses in repair, and neighborhoods began to decline. Others could not meet onerous debt service and lost their houses to foreclosure. In many cases minorities purchased homes under land contracts under which . . . failure to make a payment meant eviction and a total loss. With the tacit support of the federal government, discrimination and segregation in housing continued through the 1950s.

In 1959, the U.S. Commission on Civil Rights (1959) issued its first report to the President and the Congress. One-third of that report described in detail the history of federal complicity in perpetuating housing discrimination and segregation. The report recommended (p. 538):

> That the President issue an Executive Order stating the constitutional objective of equal opportunity in housing, directing all Federal agencies to shape their policies and practices to make the maximum contribution to the achievement of this goal, and requesting the Commission on Civil Rights. . . . to prepare and propose plans to bring about the end of discrimination in all federally assisted housing. . . .

## Federal Policy, 1962–1968: Beginnings of a Fair Housing Policy

In the presidential campaign of 1960, when federally subsidized discrimination in housing emerged as an issue, candidate John F. Kennedy stated that, if elected, he would issue an Executive Order to eliminate this injustice with "a stroke of the pen" (Wofford, 1980, 58).

### The Executive Order on Equal Opportunity in Housing

Two weeks after his inauguration, President Kennedy met with members of the Civil Rights Commission and assured them that he would issue an Executive Order on equal housing opportunity. But other considerations intruded, including an administrative effort to pass a housing subsidy bill that required support from southern congressmen and the need to obtain Senate confirmation of the appointment of Robert Weaver as the first black person to head the Housing and Home Finance Agency (Wofford, 1980, 140). (Weaver later became the first black cabinet member as secretary of the Department of Housing and Urban Development). Such political factors led the president to delay his stroke of the pen for almost two years from the date of his promise. On November 20, 1962, Executive Order 11063 on Equal Opportunity in Housing was signed by the president.[27] The first expression of a national policy on equal housing opportunity, the Executive Order was a limited document, narrowly constructed to cover only federally assisted housing contracted for *after* the date of the order. The federal financial regulatory agencies that supervise a substantial number of mortgage lenders were eliminated from coverage at the last moment.

The order prohibited discrimination in projects agreed to after November 20, 1962, and called for the abandonment of discrimination in federally assisted housing that originated before that date.[28] Severe sanctions were made available where violations were found.[29] Recipients could be cut off from funding; housing developers and realtors could be barred from future participation in federal housing programs should they violate the proscription against discrimination.[30] In addition to the programs administered by the Housing and Home Finance Agency (predecessor to the Department of Housing and Urban Development), the Veterans Administration and Farmers Home Administration programs were covered.

But the order was inherently defective and soon the inadequacy became apparent. The absence of sanctions against discrimination in federally assisted housing contracted for before the date of the order in combination with failure to include mortgage lenders supervised by the financial regulatory agencies resulted in a prohibition against discrimination that applied to less than 1 percent of the then-existing housing inventory and 15 percent of new construction (Sloane, 1976). Efforts to secure voluntary nondiscrimination policy commitments from members of the industry were unsuccessful. The perception of those who marketed housing—sales or rentals—was that adopting such a policy would place them at a competitive disadvantage. The only way to achieve the fair housing objective was to subject everyone to the same standard. Based on this experience, the President's Committee on Equal Opportunity in Housing (established by the order) asked President Johnson in its annual reports of 1964 and 1965 to extend the order to include lending institutions supervised by the federal financial agencies. No action was taken by the president.

Over the course of four years, only a few builders or developers were barred from participating in the FmHA or VA program, (U.S. Commission on Civil Rights, 1973b, 42), and the Urban Renewal Administration required a covenant running with the land to bar discrimination in all sales of property negotiated through a locality's urban renewal program.[31] But the patterns of segregation built up over the years remained largely unaltered.

The limited effectiveness of the order is not wholly attributable to its restricted terms. Implementation was in the hands of the agencies that administered the housing programs. They shared an identity of interest with regulatees. Thus, when, under the Executive Order, complaints of discrimination were submitted, they were viewed by many federal officials from the perspective of the housing industry. . . . Neither the President's Committee nor any other body had authority over the agencies. . . . Because the primary responsibility of the housing agencies was the achievement of the programs' objectives (e.g., to build public housing and insure or guarantee home mortgages) and not to enforce equal opportunity objectives, considerations of discrimination received little attention. Equal opportunity requirements were viewed as obstacles to the efficient and timely execution of the agencies' mission.

In addition, the ongoing relationship between the federal agency and the persons or organization with which it routinely did business did not include the homeseekers or the public housing tenant. Federal housing personnel dealt only with the mortgage lender, the builder, or the local housing and urban renewal agencies (i.e., the providers and not the consumers of the federal benefits). They were the people the area office staff knew, understood, and trusted. Some federal officials had received training in the housing industry, and some viewed the industry as a source of future job opportunity.

A third structural weakness was the separation of the small corps of equal opportunity staff from the operation of the program and the failure to give this staff any authority or significant role in program decisions that directly affected the elimination of discrimination from the operation of the program. The final decisions were made by the program officials, and as a result, discriminatory policies continued in effect despite advice and counsel from equal opportunity officers.

In retrospect, it is clear that the Executive Order did not result in concrete progress in opening up the market to minorities or eliminating segregation in public housing. Its importance lies principally in the fact that for the first time the guarantees of the Constitution against government discrimination in housing were buttressed by a policy statement by the executive branch. . . .

The Executive Order also serves as an example of the limitations of voluntary efforts unaccompanied by legal standards and requirements as the remedy for discrimination. The order covered and provided enforcement authority only for federally assisted housing. As noted above, it applied therefore to less than 15 percent of all new residential construction in the country. Existing housing that changed hands also was unaffected by the order unless repossessed by the FHA or VA through mortgage foreclosure. With 85 percent of the nation's housing under no federal constraints against discrimination, the President's Committee attempted to persuade the housing industry trade associations and individual lenders, builders, and brokers to adopt nondiscrimination policies. The committee was unsuccessful. . . .

## Title VI of the Civil Rights Act of 1964

In 1964 Congress added its voice with enactment of Title VI of the Civil Rights Act.[32] Not a fair housing law, it nonetheless did bar discrimination in federally funded activities including housing.[33] While assistance given by way of contracts of insurance or guarantee was expressly excepted from coverage, the Executive Order continued in force and covered FHA and VA programs.[34]

While the legislature joined the executive in barring discrimination in federal subsidized housing programs, the vast portion of the private market remained untouched, particularly as FHA's share of the market continued to decline to a point where it accounted for less than 15 percent of new construction (U.S. HUD, 1976b, 50). At the same time, new programs were introduced to increase the supply of housing for low- and moderate-income persons and the Executive Order and Title VI were major steps in assuring disadvantaged minorities access to these units.

The President's Committee continued to seek an extension of the order to include more of the private market. In 1965 President Johnson decided that housing discrimination was so invidious and pervasive that legislation was required to root it out of the marketplace.[35] The House of Representatives passed a far-reaching fair housing law the following year,[36] but a filibuster prevented it from coming to a vote in the Senate.[37]

Of course, the moves to eliminate housing discrimination were not carried on in a vacuum. In addition to school desegregation and voting rights initiatives, Title VII of the Civil Rights Act of 1964 prohibited discrimination in employment and Title II in public accommodations. While it was clear that where people lived had a direct impact on where their children attended school and where they could work, there was a reluctance to tackle housing discrimination. The reluctance was based in part on indecisiveness about the appropriate federal role in securing fair treatment for all people in the housing market. The Thirteenth and Fourteenth amendments to the Constitution, adopted after the Civil War, had established a federal responsibility to redress discrimination in governmental functions such as voting and public education, an obligation being assumed belatedly in the 1960s. In reaching discrimination in private employment, Congress was able to identify federal interests in removing impediments to national productivity and the defense capability of the country. In housing, however, legislators, backed by the influential lobbying of the housing industry, argued that a prohibition against discrimination would intrude on rights of private property and personal choice. This view was held tenaciously despite the federal government's long record of nonneutrality in racial discrimination and its growing role since the 1930s in shaping the racial demography of city and suburbs.

The enactment of Title VI and the promulgation of the Executive Order made only a small impact on the operation of federally assisted programs. The in-migration of blacks to cities and the out-migration of whites had meant that an increasing proportion of those eligible for public housing were minority families. Local political pressures continued to result in the confinement of public housing projects to neighborhoods that were already largely minority and low income. Under Title VI regulations that addressed the dual problems of tenant and site selection, the federal government continued to defer to LHAs methods for complying with the prohibition against discrimination. One approved or permitted method was a freedom of choice plan for tenants, and a site selection process that favored sites having "the greatest acceptability to eligible applicants regardless of race, color, religion or national origin" (U.S. Housing and Home Finance Agency, 1965, 7).[38] Finally, in 1967 the Public Housing Administration announced that this formulation was unacceptable and significantly modified the regulations.[39]

Most segments of the housing industry receiving assistance from the FHA and VA continued doing business as usual. And, of course, private, nonfederally assisted housing was not yet subject to any federal directive.

Title VI was not left solely to interpretation by the executive branch. In 1966, six black tenants or applicants for public housing in Chicago filed a lawsuit against the city, the Chicago Housing Authority (CHA), and HUD, alleging the establishment and maintenance of a racially discriminatory public housing system. The proceedings on the complaint against HUD were stayed until the disposition of the CHA case. After a finding of liability against the CHA in 1969,[40] the courts considered and found that HUD had violated the Fifth Amendment of the Constitution and Section 601 of Title VI "by knowingly sanctioning and assisting CHA's racially discriminatory public housing program."[41]

While the longevity of the case, 1966 to 1980, including consideration by the U.S. Supreme Court, may distinguish it, the finding of HUD liability under Title VI and the remedy applied to CHA and HUD were groundbreaking. HUD was not permitted to justify its acquiescence to CHA's illegal activity by claiming deference to local discretion. With respect to CHA, the Court's order was limited to activities within the CHA's jurisdiction. It directed the CHA to build its next 700 family units in predominantly white areas of Chicago and thereafter at least 75 percent in such areas or in Cook County. Was HUD's activity to be restricted as well to boundaries coterminous with the CHA's jurisdiction? The Supreme Court said no: "Here the wrong committed by HUD confined the respondents to segregated public housing. The relevant geographic area for purposes of the respondents' housing options is the Chicago housing market, not the Chicago city limits."[42] The Court did not require a metropolitan area order, but held that the district court has the authority to direct HUD to take remedial action by dealing with private developers outside the city limits. On remand, an agreement was entered into to enable public housing tenants and those on the waiting list to secure housing throughout the Chicago Metropolitan Area (U.S. HUD, 1979c, 28, 29).

# 1968–1980: The Emergence of a Federal Fair Housing Policy

Three major developments in 1968 changed the status quo dramatically.

In April, responding to the grief and anger engendered by the assassination of Martin Luther King, Jr., Congress swept aside its lingering doubts and enacted Title VIII of the Civil Rights Act of 1968, a broad prohibition against discrimination in private and public housing.[43] The act established an assistant secretary for equal opportunity, a position not found in any other department.

In June, the Supreme Court, in *Jones* v. *Mayer*,[44] reexamined the reach of the Reconstruction Civil Rights Act of 1866[45] and concluded that it was broad enough to provide black citizens with redress against private as well as government discrimination in housing transactions.[46]

In August, Congress passed a Housing and Urban Development Act authorizing new housing programs for low- and moderate-income families that promised volume and choice of location. . . .[47]

This confluence of actions had potential both for eliminating discrimination against minority families who could afford housing in the private market and for creating decent housing in a choice of locations for lower-income minority families.

## Title VIII of the Civil Rights Act of 1968

Title VIII established the national objective of fair housing and provided *some* of the mechanisms essential for achieving that goal. It created a right of private action for victims of discrimination as defined under the law[48] and gave the attorney general authority to institute litigation where there was a pattern or practice of discrimination.[49] A third road for seeking relief was provided through the Department of Housing and Urban Development.[50] The statute, however, merely authorized HUD to receive, investigate, and conciliate complaints of housing discrimination.[51] The failure to provide an administrative enforcement mechanism proved to be a serious flaw in the act, since the expense and delay involved in court litigation has deterred many victims of discrimination from taking that route.

With respect to federally assisted housing and urban-related programs, Title VIII directed the secretary and "all executive departments and agencies [to] administer their programs and activities . . . in a manner affirmatively to further the purposes of this title. . . ."[52] Thus the law expressly required government agencies to do more than prohibit discrimination in the operation of their programs. Title VI regulations in effect at the time Title VIII was enacted already required recipients to act affirmatively to undo the effects of past discrimination, but their application to so small a portion of the housing market could not have great impact.[53]

The entrenched patterns of segregation and discrimination in the housing market now seemed susceptible to reform, provided that decent housing at reasonable cost could be made available (through new construction and rehabilitation) to those families too poor to find units in the private market.

## Housing and Urban Development Act of 1968

This condition, which would make the new Title VIII useful to low-income minority families, was addressed in the Housing and Urban Development

Act of 1968. The act set targets for addressing the housing needs of the nation, including the needs of low- and moderate-income families. Until 1968, the public housing program was the major provider of housing for low-income families. From its inception in 1937 to the enactment of the new housing programs in 1968, little more than one million units had been built. (Private industry produced more than this number in a single year.) Recognizing the extent of the unmet need, Congress set a 10-year goal of 26 million units, 6 million of which were to be new and rehabilitated units produced with public assistance.[54] The mechanisms for meeting these needs included not only subsidized rents (§236),[55] but an innovative program to make homeownership a reality for lower-income families by subsidizing the interest payments on home mortgages (§235).[56] To remove obstacles to the dispersal of housing opportunities, the act permitted federal assistance to go directly to the private market without the veto power that local governments exercised under prior programs by refusing to give approval or enter into cooperation agreements.

# Implementation of the 1968 Laws

In the early years, the Housing and Urban Development Act fulfilled some of its promise. Although the pace for reaching the ambitious goals set was later slowed, the §235 and §236 programs did generate an annual rate of 600,000 new or rehabilitated units over a 4-year period. This was more than half the number produced by all subsidized programs over the preceding 30-year period.

Other goals of the program proved more intractable. Although local approval was no longer required, public officials devised other methods to exclude unwanted housing or unwanted people. Resistance to subsidized housing was vocal in middle-class city neighborhoods and suburban communities. Local governments applied zoning ordinances, building permit procedures, and other land and building controls to fend off would-be developers of §235 and §236 projects. Although discriminatory, often blatantly so, the actions went largely unchallenged by either the Justice Department or HUD.

## HUD Implementation of Title VIII

Government inaction on fair housing was evident in the time it took HUD to issue any regulations to implement Title VIII. While the complex regulations governing the new subsidized housing programs were published within two months of passage of the act, four years elapsed before a few, limited fair housing regulations were adopted in 1972.[57]

In other words, where subsidies to the housing industry were at stake, HUD was able to gear up and develop rules, handbooks, forms, applications, and manuals setting forth operating procedures for its own staff and applicants (including private developers and local public agencies) on such complex matters as housing costs, market rents, and tenant eligibility. But, in dealing with its regulatory responsibility to prevent discrimination, the agency could take no steps to interpret the provisions of Title VIII for its own staff, the industry, or the public.

## Affirmative Fair Housing Marketing Plans

The fair housing rules that were adopted applied only to housing projects provided with federal assistance, the same class covered by the Executive Order—although Title VIII covered most of the private market in 1972. HUD required developers to formulate an affirmative fair housing marketing plan to attract that segment of the population least likely to apply for their housing.[58]

The plan encouraged the use of advertising and community contacts to reach the targeted population, promoted the employment of minority salesmen and saleswomen, and required the applicants to set goals for occupancy by the targeted class. As units were sold or rented, the developer was required to submit reports on the race of the occupants.

Applicants for participation in all FHA mortgage insurance and assistance programs had to secure approval of their plans in order to qualify for federal benefits. Projects subject to affirmative marketing requirements included those serving low- and middle-income persons. It was evident from the outset that even well-intentioned developers did not have the necessary knowledge or understanding to either devise or implement such plans. In fact, most developers had operated for years on the assumption that the goal was a homogeneous development. Obviously guidance, if not reeducation on techniques for attracting a racially diverse clientele, was required. HUD provided little assistance and often approved plans that were uninformed and nonresponsive. . . . Racial occupancy reports were most often not submitted, and most HUD offices did not press the matter. Nor did HUD monitor the developers' implementation of their plans, for example, by checking newspapers to determine whether proposed advertising actually appeared. Little incentive was provided for developers to improve or implement their marketing plans should the goal appear elusive.

## Location of Federally Assisted Housing

The other facet of the rules dealt with the location of the projects. It gave priority to projects that demonstrated improved living environments for lower-income persons generally; and that were located near employment centers, public transportation, and schools.[59] Locations that promoted desegregated housing patterns were given high priority.[60] This last criterion became the subject of intense controversy. In response to the proposal, many expressed the belief that the rule would prevent the construction or rehabilitation of low-income housing in areas of racial concentration. When the rule was made final, HUD stated that it "is designed to assure that building in minority areas goes forward only after there truly exist housing opportunities for minorities elsewhere."[61] To assure that these were not mere token opportunities elsewhere, the rule specified that they be "sufficient" and "comparable."[62]

The rules on affirmative marketing and site selection were intended to be complementary. Site selection was to encourage the location of housing for low- and moderate-income families in predominantly white areas and affirmative marketing was to conduct outreach programs to inform minorities of these new opportunities. (Conversely, developers in locations in integrated or minority areas were to market to white low- and moderate-income families.) Middle-income subdivisions (which were not subject to the site-selection criteria) were to achieve open occupancy through affirmative marketing.

## The Results of HUD Practices and Policies

The results were not encouraging. In white suburban areas, assisted projects that were permitted to go forward were largely occupied by white residents—elderly people and working-class families. (Resistance to subsidized housing continued in many suburban communities.) Sales in subdivisions containing a significant number of single-family homes were largely unaffected by the new rules. Minorities who received subsidies were generally confined to housing opportunities in the inner city—many of them in existing housing units rather than new projects (U.S. Commission on Civil Rights, 1971). And it was in the sale of existing housing that corrupt and fraudulent practices most frequently occurred. Real estate speculators would make cosmetic improvements in dilapidated units and sell them to minority families unable to meet basic credit standards. When maintenance costs or other factors led to default, foreclosures occurred without any counseling or assistance to the family. FHA officials nodded at and sometimes participated in the fraud (U.S. HUD, 1974). Later, some would cite experience with the existing housing program as proof that homeownership for low-income people was unfeasible. . . .

To a large extent, the failure to expand housing opportunities was attributable to the failure of the federal government to regulate and to enforce the civil rights requirements applicable to both recipients of federal assistance and to the private market. As the implications of the 1968 laws were recognized and suburban resistance mounted, leadership at the highest levels of the federal government wavered. In a June 1971 statement on federal housing policy, President Nixon said:

> [w]hether rightly or wrongly, as they view the social conditions of urban slum life many residents of the outlying areas are fearful that moving large numbers of persons—of whatever race—from the slums to their communities would bring a contagion of crime, violence, drugs, and the other conditions from which so many of those who are trapped in the slums themselves want to escape.

While Mr. Nixon did not embrace these fears as his own, neither did he exercise leadership to counter them. Federal authority, he said, was "quite properly" limited "with respect to the essentially local choices involved in local community planning. . . ." It would be a "violation of the law," he said, to employ "Federal coercion or Federal money" to force integration (*New York Times*, Feb. 18, 1975).

In 1973 the momentum in production of §236 units came to an abrupt halt when President Nixon declared a moratorium on the programs, and the most promising resource for increasing the supply of decent housing for low- and moderate-income persons throughout metropolitan areas thus was terminated (U.S. HUD, 1974).

# The Housing and Community Development (HCD) Act of 1974

In 1974, Congress, in enacting the HCD Act, took a major step in revamping the categorical programs administered by HUD.[63] While loosening controls previously exerted by the federal government over the expenditure of funds for housing and community development purposes, the primary objective of the new law was to benefit low- and moderate-income persons. It also extended the reach of fair housing requirements. Communities were given far more discretion in determining how to meet their needs, but they were required to meet basic equal opportunity ground rules.

Prior to the 1974 act, applicant jurisdictions selected from an array of programs those they perceived best calculated to benefit their communities. But they were required to compete for these funds and to meet strict and detailed program requirements. Congress, however, did not require that the needs of the disadvantaged or minorities be met for jurisdictions to receive funds for parks, sewers, or recreation centers or other community needs. Federal funds were obtainable by affluent communities to benefit affluent residents. Most often, those communities effectively barred minorities from living there. Few had adopted laws or taken other steps to prohibit discrimination in the sale or rental of housing. Title VI had a "pinpoint" provision that permitted sanctions only with respect to the funded program in which discrimination was proved.[64] For example, if discrimination in a federally assisted housing project was established, funding for a sewer system serving that project would be approved in that the sewer system would serve all in the project regardless of race.

The 1974 Housing and Community Development Act eliminated the categorical programs in favor of a block-grant approach.[65] Communities applied for a sum, based on a legislated formula, for specific activities that they described in detail, including the type and location of the activity and the beneficiaries. Applicants had to demonstrate that the funds would be used principally to benefit lower-income persons. Included as part of the application was a Housing Assistance Plan (HAP) that set forth the housing conditions, needs, and goals of the community. Needs and goals were identified by family size and tenure.[66] In addition, the needs of special segments of the population (i.e., racial minorities and handicapped people) had to be identified with precision.[67]

## The Housing Assistance Plan

Of particular pertinence to equal housing opportunity was the statutory requirement that the HAP include an estimate of lower-income persons "expected-to-reside" in the community as a result of the growth of employment opportunities.[68] As noted, beginning in the 1950s, corporations and industries began moving out of central cities into suburbs and exurbs, leaving behind those employees unable to find housing they could afford nearby. Conditioning block grants on the applicant's willingness and capacity to provide housing to meet this need was viewed as an important step in bringing together job opportunities and those who needed them most, particularly minorities and women.

As early as the mid-1960s, federal civil rights agencies noted that the location and relocation by employers in suburban areas that did not prohibit discrimination in housing, did not have housing affordable by low- and moderate-income families, or were inaccessible for lack of public transportation obstructed compliance with the Equal Employment Opportunity Law (U.S. Commission on Civil Rights, 1970).[69]

The President's Committee on Equal Opportunity in Housing and the U.S. Commission on Civil Rights concentrated on the federal government as a major employer that was relocating to areas inaccessible to lower-income employees. The President's Committee worked with several agencies to assure job security to minority employees of agencies located or planning to relocate outside the district. One step was the designation of a housing officer to assist employees to find housing near their jobs. In 1970 the Civil Rights Commission documented these problems and the efforts to deal with them.

The problem persisted after the enactment of the Fair Housing law in 1968. The Equal Employment Opportunity Commission began to consider methods for dealing with the relocation of private companies in areas where there was inadequate or no affordable housing for low- and moderate-income employees. A 1971 memorandum prepared by the Office of General Counsel concluded that "a corporate relocation or proposed relocation to a suburban area where minority workers do not reside constitutes a violation of Title VII unless the corporation has taken steps to assure equal employment opportunity.[70] It then suggested what these steps might be, including the provision of "housing arrangements."[71]

While the HCD Act was not concerned directly with the problem as addressed by the EEOC counsel, it provided the link that would produce, if implemented, low-cost housing near employment opportunities.

Further, under the 1974 act, applicants were required to delineate the general locations that were suitable for low-income families and to develop a fair housing strategy to assure that these units and the entire housing market would be accessible to minorities without discrimination.[72] The site-selection standards continued to apply to specific project applications. Part of the strategy had to be designed as well to promote desegregation. It took several years to accumulate a body of experience on how best to implement these provisions. By 1980, however, communities were aware that housing activities would be subject to some degree of oversight and sanctions if necessary. (Section 109 of the HCD Act prohibits discrimination and §111 permits cutting off funds, reducing funds, or conditioning funds on correcting deficiencies.)[73] Applicants for community development funds that had not met their goals to house low-income families were warned by HUD that they must begin to correct the shortfall.[74]

The failure of jurisdictions surrounding cities with substantial minority populations to take steps to house low-income families was merely a continuation of past exclusionary practices and policies. Thus, HUD's insistence on meeting family housing goals was an essential factor in expanding opportunities for lower-income minorities to live outside central city ghettos. . . .

# Fair Housing Enforcement, 1968–1980

If the burden of eliminating discrimination from the housing market was not to fall on individual victims, federal action that would result in institutional changes in the way brokers, lenders, and developers operate was vital. In addition, such action had to take into account the role of local governments that, through the exercise of land-use authority, were major agents in controlling the production, cost, and location of housing in their communities. Clearly, many localities had used this power to keep minorities from moving in.

## HUD Enforcement

HUD's principal role under the law was to utilize its authority to investigate complaints, institute procedures to carry out the mandate to execute its programs in a "manner to affirmatively further" fair housing, conduct studies and surveys, assist local fair housing agencies, influence members of the housing industry, and refer significant cases of pattern or practices to the Justice Department. Basic to HUD's fulfilling its responsibility to administer Title VIII was an interpretation, through rulemaking, of the provisions of the law: What acts constitute a violation, who may sue, who may be sued, what is the standard of proof for establishing a violation? Interpretive regulations or guidelines were needed for the use of HUD staff, judges, injured persons, the housing industry, attorneys, and state and local fair housing agencies.

The issuance of such interpretive rules and guidelines in the 1960s by the Department of Health, Education, and Welfare (HEW), which in 1980 was split into a Department of Health and Human Services and a Department of Education, had proved a crucial factor in securing progress in school desegregation under the 1964 Civil Rights Act.[75] Similarly, guidelines issued by the Equal Employment Opportunity Commission, defining the elements of discrimination and addressing difficult issues such as the use of tests as qualifications for employment, had brought advances in job opportunities for minorities and women in the 1970s.[76] While courts remained the ultimate interpreters of the law, they relied heavily on the expertise of federal agencies to assist in such interpretations.[77] HUD, however, did not follow the lead provided by federal agencies in other areas and a critical opportunity for progress was lost.

Another weakness in HUD's enforcement in the private sector arose under the Title VIII provision that directs HUD to identify state and local laws that are substantially equivalent to the federal law.[78] Once recognized, HUD refers complaints from those jurisdictions to the agencies charged with administering the laws. For the most part, few state and local agencies were adequately funded or staffed to deal with those complaints in timely fashion. As a result, complaints languished in the agencies until in some cases HUD sent its own personnel to relieve the backlog. In fair housing cases, the impact of delay on the victim is particularly severe, since he may lose irretrievably the opportunity to obtain the house or apartment from which discrimination had barred him. Moreover, delay may curtail the possibility of legal redress. Under Title VIII, the 180-day statute of limitations has been deemed by some courts to apply from the date of the alleged discriminatory act, regardless of the timely filing of the complaint with HUD.[79] Thus, a complainant who waits for HUD or state agency action may be barred from seeking judicial relief.[80]

Another instrumentality HUD has used to carry out Title VIII is an office for voluntary compliance charged with seeking agreements from the industry to promote the fair housing objective. The best-known agreements were consummated with the National Association of Realtors and the National Association of Home Builders (U.S. Commission on Civil Rights, 1970). In turn, a number of local realtor and builder member organizations entered into separate agreements to follow through on those of their national organizations.

While the agreements ratified the change in basic policy of the housing industry, few commitments were made and fewer concrete actions were taken to actually open up housing opportunity. The agreements, for example, called for fair housing posters designed by HUD for display in realtors' offices, model homes and apartments, and so forth, and educational programs designed to explain the law. In return, realtors and builders who were subject to the Affirmative Fair Housing Marketing regulation and signed an agreement were relieved of their obligation to formulate and implement an Affirmative Fair Housing Marketing Plan (AFHMP)—the heart of HUD's Title VIII fair housing program. The tradeoff clearly advantaged the industry, which had opposed and continued to oppose this type of regulation. Those who filed AFHMPs found that neither the plans nor their implementation were subject to close HUD scrutiny. Thus, the development of white subdivisions and multifamily rental projects continued largely undisturbed.[81]

## The Justice Department

The Justice Department's early strategy under Title VIII was to bring as many cases in as many geographical areas as possible to convince those in the business of providing housing that the law was going to be vigorously enforced. Cases were filed attacking patterns and practices involving block-busting, steering, and discriminatory rental policies. Three hundred cases, an average of 32 cases a year, were filed between 1969 and 1978 (U.S. Congress, House, Subcommittee on Civil and Constitutional Rights, 1979). In three cases, the Justice Department challenged municipal government's use of its zoning and other authority to block housing that was to be open to minority as well as white families.[82] The Justice Department also succeeded in persuading the courts that the standard for judging violations of Title VIII was not whether an act was racially motivated but whether, without a compelling reason, it disadvantaged a racial group. These issues were the subject of private litigation as well, which resulted in a substantial number of favorable decisions.[83]

Unfortunately, success in court did not always result in the building of housing. Such opportunities were lost in a lengthy litigation process that resulted in higher construction costs and the loss of the federal subsidy commitment. Nonetheless, important precedents were established, including the obligation of defendants found in violation of Title VIII to take affirmative steps to undo the effects of their past discriminatory practice.[84] Outreach to the minority community through advertising media and local community groups, employment of minority rental agents, reporting progress or lack of it to the Justice Department, and cooperating with fair housing organizations to promote choice were among the steps ordered.

In the late 1970s the Justice Department decided to give greater priority to cases challenging restrictive land use practices that prevented minorities from residing in communities or certain parts of communities. The department recognized that most zoning laws were adopted initially to control the use of land and had no racial content. However, as the methods by which communities successfully excluded minorities were declared illegal or otherwise neutralized, zoning restrictions were utilized to effect the same end. Typically, a builder applied for a variance that would downgrade land from minimum one or more acreage requirements in order to permit the construction of multifamily low-cost housing. When it became known that the project was to be federally funded and subject to federal equal-access requirements, the request for a variance was rejected. The shift to a strategy of challenging such zoning actions under Title VIII was prompted by a belief these suits would have a greater impact, if successful, than suits against many small operators in the private market.[85] In addition, the Civil Rights Division sought to line up enforcement programs designed to end segregated housing with those designed to end segregated public schools.[86] Because the location and occupancy of subsidized housing as determined by local governments often has a segregative effect on schools, the Justice Department evolved an innovative schools–housing strategy that would establish liability on the part of the local government for housing segregation and lay the foundation for a remedy that would include provisions for housing action consonant with the school desegregation plan. Such a combined approach, the department reasoned, would ultimately decrease the need for school busing, as housing became more integrated.

Several recent studies demonstrate this interrelationship. It is commonly understood that housing segregation results in segregated neighborhood schools. What is not commonly understood is that where schools are racially identifiable as black or white, they tend to be used to steer prospective homeseekers to choose housing so that neighborhood and school segregation are perpetuated. Further, there is now growing evidence that large-scale school desegregation is followed by significant reductions in housing segregation.

This effect first shows up as reduced levels of white enrollment loss (Farley, Richards, and Wurdock, 1980). In a study that compared pairs of cities with and without metropolitan school desegregation, those cities that had desegregation had experienced roughly twice as much housing desegregation over the 1970s as their counterparts.[87]

## Private Litigation

In the many cases where the Justice Department does not bring a lawsuit, victims of discrimination are free to retain private lawyers to file a case. But private actions have not made major inroads on the marketplace or provided large numbers of individuals with relief for discriminatory housing practices. Although attorneys' fees are available where the litigant cannot "financially assume" those costs himself, the fact that the lengthy litigation process often prevents victims from gaining the house or apartment of their choice and that damage awards with some exceptions have been limited has deterred many from undertaking the ordeal of litigation.[88]

## Judicial Interpretation of Title VIII

In the cases that have been brought under Title VIII, the courts have given a liberal interpretation to the law. Beginning in 1972, the Supreme Court defined broadly the interests at stake in preventing housing discrimination, holding, for example, that white apartment residents who were not directly injured had standing to challenge a discriminatory rental policy because it denied them the benefits of interracial association.[89] Other examples of generous judicial treatment of Title VIII are the inclusion of discriminatory practices not expressly prohibited by the act but that make housing unavailable because of race.[90] Examples include racial redlining of neighborhoods[91] and land-use ordinances that prevent minorities from residing in communities.[92]

An important and divisive issue that arises under Title VIII is whether the plaintiff must show a discriminatory intent or purpose to prove a violation. While the Supreme Court has not decided this issue, a number of courts of appeals have applied some version of an "effects" test in determining the existence of a violation of Title VIII.[93] The use of an effects test permits successful challenges to housing practices that adversely affect minorities if they are not essential to meet a business need. Plaintiffs need not meet the difficult, sometimes insurmountable burden of proving that the harmful practices were prompted by racial animus.

The limited impact of these decisions is attributable to the defects of private litigation noted above and to the fact that the Justice Department can only bring pattern and practice cases and has limited resources to prosecute a large number of these necessarily complex cases.[94] In addition, HUD has no authority under Title VIII to order or otherwise secure remedies, and most injured persons do not even consider HUD a useful alternative.

After a decade of experience under the fair housing law, two conclusions seemed warranted: (1) Those responsible for administering the law had not fully utilized their authority to eliminate discrimination; and (2) the law itself had serious deficiencies that needed correction through legislative amendment.

## Amending Title VIII

In 1979, the Carter administration voiced support for amendments to the fair housing law, which would have added the needed administrative enforcement mechanism, extended coverage to the handicapped, and made other technical improvements in Title VIII (U.S. Congress, Senate, Subcommittee on the Constitution, 1979).

The major elements of the bill included the creation of an administrative forum designed to be more expeditious and less costly than litigation, with administrative-law judges deciding discrimination complaints when conciliation fails; authorization for a court proceeding to hold a house or apartment off the market while the discrimination claim is being decided; extension of the statute of limitations from 180 days to 2 years; extension of the availability of attorneys' fee awards to all victims of discrimination; and extension of the protection of Title VIII to people discriminated against because of a handicap.

The bill passed the House of Representatives,[95] but ultimately failed in the Senate in December 1980 when its proponents fell 5 votes short of the 60 needed to end a filibuster mounted by senators who opposed some of the reforms and wanted to change Title VIII to require proof of intent, rather than the current effects test.[96]

In December also, the Carter administration belatedly sent to Congress a comprehensive set of Title VIII regulations designed to improve enforcement of the law. But the days of the Carter administration were numbered, and the regulation did not become final.

While several important initiatives (e.g., litigative efforts to attack land use barriers, legislative efforts to strengthen the fair housing laws) were undertaken in the Carter administration, the last half of the 1970s, like the first half, was marked by an uncertain federal thrust and wavering political leadership.

As a candidate in 1976, Jimmy Carter had said: "I have nothing against a community . . . trying to maintain the ethnic purity of their neighborhood" (*New York Times*, Apr. 7, 1976). He spoke of "black intrusion" into white areas and the bad effects of housing "a diametrically opposite kind of family" in a settled community. Candidate Carter later apologized for his use of the "ethnic purity" phrase (which echoed the 1930s language of FHA manuals) and promised to enforce federal law, adding, however, that he would not "arbitrarily use Federal force to change neighborhood patterns" (*New York Times*, Apr. 9, 1976).

As president, Carter devoted little attention to the issue, and his 1978 urban policy statement "A New Partnership to Conserve America's Communities" made little reference to any need to secure access by urban minorities to jobs, housing, and public services in the suburbs (Taylor, 1978). Meanwhile, some advocates of low-income housing, frustrated by the delays caused by suburban resistance in securing integrated housing, called for more housing in the inner city, even at the cost of reinforcing segregation. Fears were also voiced privately that if housing opportunities for minorities and low-income families were dispersed, the political base of minority elected officials would be diluted and eroded. And the housing industry, led by the politically powerful National Association of Realtors, threw millions of dollars into the effort to prevent any significant strengthening of fair housing laws.

## Summing Up

In this political atmosphere, it is not surprising that the trumpet call of 1968—the Supreme Court's *Jones* v. *Mayer* decision and the two landmark housing laws (Title VIII and the 1968 Housing Act)—had faded by 1980. The major elements of contemporary federal policy, decent housing and equal housing opportunity for all, remained in place, but the steps taken to implement this policy did not come close to matching the work the federal government had previously done in constructing a segregated society.

With the adoption of national fair housing policies in 1968, however, many had hopes that the 1970s would tell a different story. But the first analyses of the 1980 census suggest a less sanguine prospect. Using the standard measure of segregation, the index of dissimilarity, which ranges from zero (no segregation) to 100 (maximum segregation), one recent study found that most of the cities of Michigan had changed little during the decade.[97] In the first nationwide in-depth study of racial patterns in housing, demographer Karl Taeuber of the University of Wisconsin confirms the Michigan findings for cities across the country. Taking the 28 cities with at least 100,000 blacks, he calculated the index of dissimilarity, on a block-to-block basis, for 1970 and 1980 (Taeuber, 1980). He found that the average declined from 87 in 1970 to 81 in 1980, or about six points. If that rate holds in the 1980s and beyond, it will take half a century to eliminate half the segregation in these cities. . . . [*See also Chapter 12 by Gary Orfield for a discussion on racial segregation in suburban areas.*]

Studies of earlier decades documented the stubborn persistence of segregated housing patterns in American cities. Discrimination, mostly subtle but effective, was documented in a HUD study of housing market practices conducted in 1977 (U.S. HUD, 1979c). This study, which sampled the behavior of housing agents in 40 American cities, found that the chance of a black person's encountering discrimination on one visit to a real estate agent was 15 percent and on one visit to a rental agent was 21 percent; if one visited a series of four agents, as many people do in the course of a housing search, the odds of being discriminated against increased to 50 percent and 75 percent, respectively. (And this is a conservative estimate, as it fails to take into account "steering" practices—showing black families homes only in neighborhoods where blacks predominate.) Similarly, a replication of the HUD study for Chicanos in the Southwest found that they faced discrimination on the basis both of ethnicity and skin color (U.S. HUD, 1979a). Later studies in several cities carried out by fair housing centers found that these practices have continued into the 1980s in places like Boston and Grand Rapids (Feins, Bratt, and Hollister, 1981). In some cases, discrimination that has traditionally been on the basis of race and ethnicity is being supplemented or supplanted in the rental market by discrimination against families with children.

Thus it is clear that the federal government must initiate and implement a more aggressive strategy to undo the persistent and pervasive patterns of segregation by race and income. Yet the initiatives and policies of the past few years by the executive branch and the Congress are not likely to increase choice for minorities, women, or lower-income families. The sharp reduction in housing assistance for those unable to secure housing without subsidies of some kind [*see Chapter 21 by Chester Hartman*]; the failure of the Department of Justice to pursue cases that would leave a significant impact on segregation and discrimination or even to bring a quantity of suits that would demonstrate a determination to eliminate violations; the abandonment of programs in support of metropolitan areawide strategies; the minimal efforts to investigate for, and assure compliance with, the fair housing laws; and the absence of a funded counseling program to assist those whom the laws are intended to benefit—all are adverse to the achievement of the national fair housing objective. Most discouraging at this time is the failure of the executive and legislative branches to agree on amendments to strengthen the Fair Housing Law and extend its protection to the disabled and to families with children.

While the progress of the past 25 years will not be undone, the challenge is to take action that will yield visible evidence that segregation and discrimination are on the wane.

# Notes

1. *Buchanan* v. *Warley*, 245 U.S. 60 (1971).
2. Ibid.
3. *See Shelley* v. *Kraemer*, 334 U.S. 1 (1948).
4. See, e.g., *Contract Buyers League* v. *F.&F. Investment Co.*, 300 F.Supp. 210 (N.D. Ill. 1969).
5. National Housing Act, Public Law 73–479, 48 Stat. 1246 (1934) (codified as amended in scattered sections of 12 U.S.C.).
6. Federal Home Loan Bank Act, Public Law 72–522, 47 Stat. 725 (1932), 12 U.S.C. §1421; 15 U.S.C. §57 (a) (1976 and Supp. I 1977, Supp. III 1979, Supp. IV 1980 and Supp. V 1981).
7. Title III of the National Housing Act, 12 U.S.C. §1723(a) (Charter Act).
8. The Serviceman's Readjustment Act of 1944 (38 U.S.C. §1801 *et seq.*, June 22, 1944).
9. Ibid, Title III.
10. Housing Act of 1949, Public Law 81–171, 63 Stat. 413 (1949) (codified as amended in scattered sections of 12 U.S.C., 31 U.S.C., 38 U.S.C. and 42 U.S.C.).
11. Mortgages for veterans were guaranteed by the Servicemen's Readjustment Act, Public Law 78–346, 58 Stat. 284 (1944), as amended.
12. The benefits conferred on homebuyers included tax deduction for mortgage interest payments and local property taxes, community-provided infrastructure, new school systems, and the incentives for corporations to locate in new industrial parks in order to provide a stable and substantial tax base to support the growing community.
13. *Bradley* v. *Milliken*, 317 F. Supp. 555 (1970).
14. See, for example, New York Laws 1950, chap. 287, p. 961; Montana Laws 1959, chap. 195, p. 422; Michigan Public Acts 1952, chap. 2958, p. 836; Massachusetts General Laws Ann., chap. 121, §26FF (1957), amended by Massachusetts General Laws Ann., chap. 151B, §§1-4 (West 1982); Pennsylvania Statute Ann., tit. 35, §1664 *as amended* (Purdon 1977); Minnesota Statute Ann., §462.481 as amended (West 1963).
15. In fact, the federal requirement that a cooperation agreement be executed between a local jurisdiction and the local housing authority (see note 13) had a discouraging effect. See *Mehaley* v. *Cuyahoga Metropolitan Housing Authority*, 355 F. Supp. 1245 (1973) (Three-judge court), 355 F.Supp. 1257 (1973) (One-judge court), *rev'd.*, 500 F.2d 1087 (1974).
16. See United States Housing Act of 1937, Public Law 75–896, 50 Stat. 888, 42 U.S.C. §1415 (7)(b)(i), as amended.
17. The Urban Renewal Program was introduced pursuant to the Housing Act of 1949. See note 10.
18. *Garrett* v. *City of Hamtramck*, 335 F.Supp. 16.
19. Ibid.
20. See note 3.

21. *Brown* v. *Board of Education*, 347 U.S. 483 (1954).

22. *Davis* v. *Housing Authority*, 1 Race Rel. L. Rep. 353 (1956) (E.D. Mo. 1955). See also *Heyward* v. *Public Housing Administration*, 238 F.2d 689 (5th cir. 1956), *dismissed on other grounds*, 154 F.Supp. 589 (S.D. Ga. 1957), *argued sub. nom.*; *Detroit Housing Commission* v. *Lewis*, 226 F.2d 180 (6th Cir. 1955); *Eleby* v. *Louisville Municipal Housing Commission*, 2 Race Rel. L. Rep. 815 (1957) W.D. Ky); *Askew* v. *Benton Harbor Housing Commission*, 2 Race Rel. L. Rep. 611 (1957) (W.D. Mich. 1956); *Kankakee County Housing Authority* v. *Spurlock*, 3 Ill. 2d 277, 120 N.E. 2d 561 (1954) (*Semble*).

23. Memorandum from Joseph Burstein, general counsel, Public Housing Administration to Walter A. Simon, director, Philadelphia Regional Office, Dec. 21, 1962; repealed, PHA Low Rent Housing Manual §205, 1, p. 7 (1965).

24. See case cited, note 4.

25. See notes 6–7.

26. Ibid.

27. Exec. Order No. 11063, 27 Fed. Reg. 11527 (1962), as amended by Exec. Order No. 12259, 46 Fed. Reg. 1253 (1980), reprinted in 42 U.S.C. §1982 app., 1217–1218 (1976). The U.S. Commission on Civil Rights had recommended again in its 1961 Report that an Executive Order be issued that would specifically cover "all Federal agencies concerned with housing and with home mortgage credit."

28. Ibid., para. 4002, §101.

29. Ibid., para. 4003, §102; see also para. 4008, §302; para. 4009, §303; para. 4010, §304.

30. Ibid., para. 4008, §302.

31. Letter from William L. Slayton, Urban Renewal Administration, to the Commission on Civil Rights, May 18, 1961.

32. Title VI of the Civil Rights Act of 1964, Public Law 88–352, 78 Stat. 252 (codified as amended at 42 U.S.C. §2000d [1976 and Supp. IV 1980]).

33. Section 601 of Title VI provides:
   No person in the United States shall, on the ground of race, color, or national origin, be excluded from participation in, be denied the benefits of, or be subjected to discrimination under any program or activity receiving Federal financial assistance. (42 U.S.C. § 2000d [1976])

34. Section 605 of Title VI provides:
   Nothing in this subchapter shall add to or detract from any existing authority under which Federal financial assistance is extended by way of a contract of insurance or guaranty. (42 U.S.C. §2000-4[1976])

35. In early 1966, President Johnson sent a message to Congress concerning legislation for combatting racial discrimination in which he said:
   I ask the Congress to enact the first effective Federal law against discrimination in the sale and rental of housing. . . The time has come for the Congress to declare resoundingly that discrimination in housing and all the evils it breeds are a denial of justice and a threat to the development of our growing urban areas . . . The time has come to combat unreasoning restrictions on any family's freedom to live in the home and the neighborhood of its choice. (Equal Opportunity in Housing 2312 [P-H][1971])

36. H.R. 14765, ibid., 2312–13.

37. S. 3296, ibid.

38. See also note 18.

39. The Department amended Title VI regulations by adding a provision under "discrimination prohibited." Approved by President Johnson on October 19, 1967, it required that local housing agencies assign eligible applicants to dwelling units based on (1) when the application is received; (2) the type of unit available; and (3) factors affecting

priority which are not incompatible with Title VI objectives. Equal Opportunity in Housing 2310 (P-H) (1971).

40. *Gautreaux* v. *Chicago Housing Authority*, 296 F.Supp. 907.

41. *Gautreaux* v. *Romney*, 448 F.2d 731, 739–740 (1971).

42. *Hills* v. *Gautreaux*, 425 U.S. 284, 299 (1976).

43. Title VIII of the Civil Rights Act of 1968, Public Law 90–284, 82 Stat. 81 (codified as amended at 42 U.S.C. §§3601–3619 [1976 and Supp. IV 1980]).

44. 392 U.S. 409 (1968).

45. 42 U.S.C. §§ 1981–1982 (1976 and Supp. IV 1980).

46. 392 U.S. at 422-37.

47. Housing and Urban Development Act of 1968, 12 U.S.C. §1715(1), §1715z-1 (1976).

48. 42 U.S.C. §3612 (1976).

49. 42 U.S.C. §3613 (1976).

50. 42 U.S.C. §3610 (1976).

51. Ibid.

52. 42 U.S.C. §3608(d) (1976 and Supp. II 1978).

53. 24 C.F.R. §570.601 (1982).

54. Section 1603 of the Housing and Urban Development Act of 1968.

55. Section 201(a) of the Housing and Urban Development Act of 1968, 12 U.S.C. §1715z–1 (1976).

56. Section 101(a) of the Housing and Urban Development Act of 1968, 12 U.S.C. §1715z(i) (1976).

57. 24 C.F.R. §§200.1–200.935 (1982).

58. 24 C.F.R. §200.625 (1982).

59. 24 C.F.R. §200.710 (1982).

60. Ibid.

61. 37 F.R. 204 (1/7/72).

62. Ibid.

63. Housing and Community Development Act of 1974, 42 U.S.C. §§5301–5320 (1976 and Supp. IV 1980).

64. §602 of Title VI of the Civil Rights Act of 1964, 42 U.S.C. §2000d–1 (1976).

65. 42 U.S.C. §§ 5301–5320 (1976 and Supp. IV 1980).

66. §104 of the Housing and Community Development Act of 1974, 42 U.S.C. §5304 (1976 and Supp. IV 1980).

67. Ibid.

68. 42 U.S.C. §5304(a) (4) (A) (1976 and Supp. IV 1980).

69. Civil Rights Act of 1964, Title VII 42 U.S.C. §2000e (1964).

70. Memorandum to William H. Brown, III, chairman, from Stanley P. Hebert, general counsel; John de J. Pemberton, Jr., deputy general counsel; Martin I. Slate, attorney, Employment Discrimination by Relocation of Plan and Corporate Headquarters, July 7, 1971, 2.

71. Ibid., 13.

72. 24 C.F.R. §570.601(b)(3)(1982).

73. 42 U.S.C. §5309(a)(1976); 42 U.S.C. §5311(a)(1976).

74. HUD Reports on Conditions for FHEO FY 1978, 1979, 1980; unpublished.

75. 34 C.F.R. §270 (1981).

76. Uniform Guidelines on Employee Selection Procedures, 29 C.F.R. §1607.1 (1982).

77. *Griggs* v. *Duke Power Co.*, 401 U.S. 424 (1971); *Green* v. *County School Board*, 391 U.S. 430 (1968); *U.S.* v. *Jefferson County Board of Education*, 372 F.2d 836 (5th Cir. 1966), *aff'd en banc*, 380 F.2d 385, *cert. denied*, 389 U.S. 840 (1967).

78. Section 810(c) of the Civil Rights Act of 1968, 42 U.S.C. §3610(c)(1976).

79. Section 812(a) of the Civil Rights Act of 1968, 42 U.S. C. §3612(a)(1976).

80. *Warren* v. *Norman Realty Co.*, 375 F.Supp. 478 (1974); *aff'd* 513 F.2d 730 (1975); *Warren* v. *Perrino*, 585 F.2d 171 (1978).

81. See note 53.

82. *City of Lackawanna*, 318 F.Supp. 669.

83. See, e.g., *Williams* v.*Matthews Co.*, 499 Fed 819 (8th Cir. 1974).

84. *Hills* v. *Gautreaux*, 425 U.S. 284 (1976); *U.S.* v. *City of Parma*, 494 F.Supp. 1049 (N.D. Ohio 1980), *aff'd in part* 661 F.2d 562 (6th Cir. 1981).

85. See note 72.

86. *U.S.* v. *Yonkers Board of Education*, 518 F.Supp. 191 (S.D. N.Y. 1981).

87. The power of this effect is illustrated by the experience of Riverside, California. After 15 years of busing students for desegregation, only 3 schools still require students to be brought in in order to achieve a racially mixed student body; the other 14 have sufficiently integrated neighborhoods that they have converted back to walk-in schools but are racially balanced.

88. Section 812(c) of the Civil Rights Act of 1968, 42 U.S.C. §3612(c)(1976).

89. *Trafficante* v. *Metropolitan Life Insurance Co.*, 409 U.S. 205 (1972).

90. Section 804(a) of the Civil Rights Act of 1968, 42 U.S.C. §3604(a)(1976).

91. *Dunn* v. *Midwestern Indemnity Co.*, 472 F.Supp. 1106 (1979); *Harrison* v. *Heinzeroth Mortgage Co.*, 430 F.Supp. 893 (1977); *Laufman* v.*Oakley Building and Loan Co.*, 408 F.Supp. 489 (1976).

92. *Metropolitan Housing Development Corp.* v. *Village of Arlington Heights*, 558 F.2d 1283 (7th Cir. 1977), *cert. denied* 434 U.S. 1025 (1978); *U.S.* v. *City of Black Jack*, 508 F.2d 1179 (8th Cir. 1974), *cert. denied* 422 U.S. 1042 (1975).

93. *Robinson* v. *Twelve Lofts Realty, Inc.*, 610 F.2d 1032, 1038 (2d Cir. 1979).

94. Section 813(a) of the Civil Rights Act of 1968, 42 U.S.C. §3613 (1976).

95. Fair Housing Amendments Act of 1980, H.R. 5200, 96th Congress, 2nd sess.

96. On December 9, 1980, by a vote of 54–43, proponents of the bill failed to secure cloture.

97. Letter from Reynolds Farley to Gary Orfield, reporting calculations made by David Goldberg and other colleagues at the University of Michigan Population Studies Center, September 15, 1981.

# 19

# Rural Housing Policy in America: Problems and Solutions

*Linda Kravitz*
*Art Collings*

*Relative to urban populations, the housing problems of rural Americans have been neglected. These problems are less visible, and the tools for solving them—credit, building industry capacity, political organization—have been lacking. The government's efforts in this area have been divided between the Department of Housing and Urban Development (HUD) and the Farmers Home Administration (FmHA). The latter, which has primary responsibility in rural areas, is part of the Department of Agriculture, and this has meant subordination of housing activities to farm and agricultural concerns, and to the concerns of large rather than small farmers.*

Rural areas,[1] with a fourth of the nation's population, have a third of its occupied substandard units and an even higher share (38 percent) of its substandard units occupied by poverty-level households[2]. While the proportion of rural housing stock lacking complete plumbing dropped dramatically—by three-fifths—over the last decade, plumbing is still a severe problem in the chronically poverty-stricken areas of the southern "black belt," Appalachia, the Ozarks, Indian trust land, and along the Mexican border. Although the decline in rural units lacking plumbing is heartening, it is offset by other considerations: a relatively constant level of rural units that are structurally deficient (U.S. Bureau of the Census, 1975a, 1981a, vol. E, table A-3), prevailing contamination of the rural water supply (Francis et al., 1982, 19), and the resettlement of former occupants of units lacking plumbing into mobile homes (Housing Assistance Council, 1983, 13), which have structural and durability problems of their own. Finally, the 1970s decline in rural poverty that accompanied the decline in units lacking plumbing has since been reversed, with discouraging implications for housing affordability (U.S. Bureau of the Census, 1982d, table 4).

Rural households in poverty differ from their urban counterparts in ways that should (but often do not) significantly influence rural housing policy. These include the lack of local lending (Mikesell and Davidson, 1982) and infrastructure resources, which are often prerequisites to major housing improvements; the greater proportion of rural poor homeowners ineligible for most existing direct housing subsidies; formidable obstacles to the provision of adequate temporary housing for the migratory farm labor force; for many rural residents, the inseparability of dwelling concerns from farm problems, credit needs, and encumbrances; land-title and land-ownership patterns impeding housing development in the most persistently poor regions; and the tenure problems peculiar to mobile-home occupants as owners of structures placed on leased sites.

Striking examples of infrastructure defects in rural areas are water and sewer systems. A 1982 representative survey of 22 million rural households, done by Cornell University under contract to the Environmental Protection Agency, found that almost two-thirds of all rural households had water judged unacceptable for at least one major contaminant, with coliform bacteria the most common pollutant. Households with low incomes (under $10,000) and low education (less than high school) were more likely to have bacterially contaminated water. About 370,000 rural households haul water on a regular basis from an off-premises supply (Francis et al., 1982).

The predominance of homeowners among the poor is another characteristically rural feature. The urban ratio of two poverty-level renters for every poverty-level owner is reversed in rural areas, where two-thirds of the 2.8 million poverty-level households are homeowners. There are more poverty-level owners of substandard dwellings in rural than in urban areas, and four times as many poverty-level owners of homes lacking plumbing. According to the *Annual Housing Survey*, rural homeowners are more likely than their urban counterparts to live with other housing deficiencies, including inadequate heating equipment and general dilapidation (U.S. Bureau of the Census, 1981a, vols. C and E, table 5 A-1 and A-4). Severe structural problems such as the lack of plumbing nullify the advantages usually attributed to homeowners, including the ability to use homes as investments or as collateral for credit. Even the advantages of equity in the land and some control over tenure disappear for the majority of rural mobile "homeowners," most of whom , as noted, rent their sites.

Confusion over land title cripples the attempts of many rural households to obtain credit for mortgages and home repair. The heir property problems of Southern blacks (i.e., property inherited for generations without wills or clarification of title), the status of Spanish and Mexican land grants in the Southwest, claims by whites and Indians for the same land, and the trust status of Indian reservations have presented obstacles to the improvement of living conditions for rural minorities (Treuer, 1982; U.S. Department of Agriculture, FmHA, 1980a, 1980b, 1980c, 1980d).

The deplorable state of housing for migrant farmworkers is a rural problem that has persisted despite recurring media exposure and congressional hearings. The most recent major survey of migrant housing, conducted in 1980, concluded that nearly 800,000 new or substantially rehabilitated seasonal units were needed to shelter adequately the migrant stream throughout the country (U.S. Department of Agriculture, FmHA, 1980c, 1). The census does not report the quality of units not occupied on a year-round basis, and its count of units that lack plumbing or are overcrowded thus omits a very large proportion of the migrant farmworker housing stock. However, a U.S. Department of Agriculture Economic Research Service study (1980) estimated that 75 percent of existing migrant farmworker units lack complete plumbing.

Finally, the rural poor differ demographically from their urban counterparts. The majority of rural poverty-level heads of family households are "working poor," and most families have both parents present. Nearly three-fifths of the household heads of rural poverty-level families were wage earners in 1979, compared to a little over two-fifths of urban poor families. Nearly a fifth of the rural poor, as compared with a tenth of the urban poor, was elderly (Getz and Hoppe, forthcoming).

Less than a fourth of the rural poor received public assistance, including Aid to Families with Dependent Children, Supplemental Security Income, or General Assistance; by contrast, more than 30 percent of the urban poverty population received such assistance. It is likely that the relatively low rural proportion is due to the combined effects of the number of families with a father present or with working household heads, and the exclusion from welfare assistance of both those groups in most of the states with high rural poverty rates. Twenty-seven percent of metropolitan but only 18 percent of nonmetropolitan poverty-level renters are in public housing or receive government assistance in renting privately owned units (U.S. Bureau of the Census, 1982d, table 20). Local resources for progress against poverty are scanty. Rural communities, with a lower median income (U.S. Bureau of the Census, 1981a, vol. E, table A-2) and higher unemployment[3] and poverty rates, have relatively weak tax bases compared with urbanized areas. Moreover, a number of studies have documented that the potential for local self-sufficiency that lies in the rich natural resources of many high-poverty areas, such as the mineral and timber resources of Appalachia and the Deep South, is undermined by absentee ownership and control (Gaventa, 1980).

## Past Federal Policy and Performance

The continuing high levels of substandard housing conditions in rural regions characterized by persistent poverty suggest that public resources have not been sufficiently targeted to the neediest and that a link exists between rural housing problems and poverty that has not been effectively addressed by government housing programs. In fact, over the 50 years of their existence, federal rural housing program resources have moved away from both a focus on the neediest and a treatment of their housing needs within the overall context of poverty.

The federal rural housing effort has evolved from the New Deal strategy of helping the rural poor through relief, restructuring the economy, and land redistribution, into a strategy to stabilize the "creditworthy" portion of the rural population through an infusion of credit resources (Baldwin, 1968, 85–157). Federal rural housing subsidies had their beginnings in the New Deal, with the Resettlement Administration (RA) programs for rural rehabilitation and resettlement of the poor to areas where they were expected to become self-sufficient. Its successor agency, the Farm Security Administration (FSA), continued these efforts and developed a third program, the tenant-purchase program authorized by the Bankhead-Jones Farm Tenant Act of 1937, under which tenant farmers were assisted in purchasing their farms. Both the RA and the FSA were committed to the eradication of rural poverty, a commitment that was greatly weakened in the current descendant, the Farmers Home Administration in the Department of Agriculture. However, the formidable tools they developed for delivery of resources, including a network of 1,945 county supervisors who solicit applications for loans, assist borrowers in developing farm and home budget plans, and supervise loans, were retained by FmHA.

With the termination of the Farm Security Administration in 1946, federal rural housing assistance became split along lines that still exist: FmHA got the tools for rural delivery of housing resources but was given very few resources to assist poverty-level households; the housing problems of the poor were to be dealt with through the programs of housing agencies that eventually evolved into the Department of Housing and Urban Development (HUD), all of which were urban oriented and had little capacity to deliver assistance to rural areas. HUD's current housing subsidies have also not been designed for, or equitably shared by, rural areas. HUD's rural delivery of low-income housing resources has been limited by its centralized administrative structure, with regional and area offices based in metropolitan areas; it has also been limited in program approach by an urban bias, termed "Metropollyana" by early leaders in the rural housing field (Margolis, 1973). For example, HUD's programs are not designed to produce small housing projects efficiently or treat scattered housing problems.

Under the 1949 Housing Act, FmHA was assigned responsibility for providing mortgage credit to qualified farmers—rather than the general rural low-income population—to enable them to obtain decent, safe, and sanitary living conditions. It was not until the 1961 Housing Act, which expanded FmHA's scope of services to nonfarm rural families, that funds were appropriated for construction of rental housing for rural low-income families; and it was not until 1974 that FmHA was authorized to provide rent supplements to low-income rural residents. HUD's urban-oriented programs had long before provided these forms of assistance to the urban poor.

On the whole, if the United States can be said to have had a federal rural housing policy, its most consistent themes over the last few decades have been that homeownership is the natural rural tenure pattern, that the basic rural housing problem has been a lack of mortgage credit for home improvement and purchases, and that the most helpful contribution the federal government could make is the provision of mortgage credit to rural areas. (Unlike HUD's major lending programs for homeownership and housing construction and rehabilitation, which provide mortgage insurance or interest subsidies for loans originated in the private sector, FmHA provides what in effect are direct government loans for its construction and rehabilitation programs; the difference reflects the shortage of adequate private lending resources in rural areas.) Thus, the vast majority of beneficiaries of FmHA program benefits have been households considerably above the poverty level, deemed to be "creditworthy," and unlikely to burden the government with loan defaults.

The long-term challenge for rural housing advocates has been to create a low-income subsidy resource that can exploit FmHA's well-established delivery capacity. The most realistic hopes for housing the rural poor decently rest on a strategy of building on FmHA's natural interest in rural development and its delivery network of state, regional, and county offices.

# FmHA, the Rural Housing Delivery System

FmHA's housing portfolio amounts to nearly 2 million loans and grants (mostly the former) totaling about $40 billion. The agency is credited with having made it possible for more than 1.3 million ill-housed rural families to move into adequate homes and provided some 15,000 communities with water and wastewater systems (U.S. Department of Agriculture, FmHA, 1983).

## Homeownership

FmHA's primary housing resource is the Section 502 homeownership loan program, introduced in the 1949 Housing Act. It is currently funded at about twice the level of FmHA's rental housing program, whose Section 515 (construction financing), Section 521 (interest subsidy), and Section 521 (rental assistance programs) were authorized in 1962, 1968, and 1974, respectively. FmHA makes long-term (currently 33-year) loans to low- and moderate-income borrowers, and subsidizes the difference between market rate and the rate the borrower can afford to pay with 20 percent of income, down to a 1 percent interest rate. With the typical $40,000 house financed by the program, the effective income floor is currently about $9,600; on the average, borrower family income is now about $11,800. Although the income range served is far lower than that reached by any other government homeownership program, it is clearly unable to assist poverty-level households (with incomes below $9,000) unless significant savings can be achieved in the cost of the house.

Some savings have been achieved in "self-help" projects. According to a 1978 survey by Rural America (1979, A-7), modest units constructed in large part with the owner–borrower's labor may cost up to a third less than contractor-built housing, making some houses affordable for poverty-level households. In spite of such documented advantages, and although authorized to provide Section 502 loans to self-help groups and to cover the costs of supervision, FmHA support for, and interest in, self-help projects has remained minimal. One reason is that the paperwork involved in small-scale self-help projects is generally greater on a per-unit basis than for other kinds of development; another is that unconventional kinds of development tend to be slighted by government bureaucrats.

Other attempts to bring the FmHA homeownership program within reach of poverty-level households have focused on lowering the cost of the homes through modified building design and standards. While FmHA formerly had more flexible standards, it grew more conservative in the late 1960s, as a consequence of experience with shoddily built houses that ultimately amounted to a loss for the borrower and the agency. (One vivid example of this was the proliferation of often badly installed manufactured homes such as those of the Jim Walter Corporation, described in Chapter 7 by Tom Schlesinger and Mark Erlich, which FmHA reluctantly financed under congressional pressure.) Since then, FmHA has developed an image of conservatism in its unbending adherence to the Minimum Property Standards (MPS) adopted by HUD in 1968 and later modified by FmHA to include more rigorous thermal efficiency standards. FmHA retained "marketability" and "livability" criteria after they were dropped by HUD in 1983, and its standards continue to leave little to the imagination of the builder.

However, FmHA's resistance to change is gradually being overcome by political pressure, including the Housing and Urban–Rural Recovery Act of 1983, which requires the agency to accept housing that meets HUD's family housing standards or one of several voluntary national building codes. Other provisions in the 1983 legislation, which require FmHA to make mobile homes eligible for subsidized interest loans, are cause for concern among many rural housing advocates worried about the questionable safety and energy standards of these houses. The new provisions have caused the agency to reconsider its previous resistance to "warm and dry" houses— small, heavily insulated dwellings that cost less than the traditional FmHA-financed house because they lack certain amenities normally required by FmHA. Their low purchase price would permit them to be initially cost-competitive with mobile homes, and their energy efficiency and durability would give them life-cycle cost advantages. These "warm and dry" houses could presumably meet the affordability objectives that ostensibly motivated the congressional demand that FmHA subsidize mobile-home purchases.

The FmHA housing program used by homeowners who cannot afford FmHA mortgage loans is the Section 504 Very Low-Income Home Repair Loan and Grant program. Section 504 provides grants not exceeding $5,000 to elderly and handicapped homeowners and loans not exceeding $7,500 at 1 percent to other low-income households, to make basic repairs that eliminate hazards to health and safety. Although in great demand, Section 504 loans have been underused because of the lack of time and interest on the part of FmHA county supervisors.

The Housing and Urban–Rural Recovery Act of 1983 provides for a new Rural Housing Preservation Grant Program, to serve low- and very-low-income households. Designed by the National Rural Housing Coalition, it provides grants to nonprofits and units of state or local government, on a competitive basis, for the rehabilitation of rental or owned housing.

## Rental Housing

The FmHA rental housing construction program (Section 515) provides 50-year mortgages for low- and moderate-income rental and cooperative housing, with a subsidy covering interest down to 1 percent, depending on the incomes and rent-payment ability of the tenants. Since 1978, FmHA has provided rental assistance (Section 521) to accompany units produced under this program. HUD's parallel Section 8 program has also been used with the Section 515 program. The average household income in the current stock of about 200,000 units is $7,500, and over three-fourths of the units are in what is termed the "lowest-income category," the average income for which is under $6,000.

With the general cutbacks by the Reagan administration in direct rental unit production programs, syndication of these Section 515 housing projects has become a major means of producing rural moderately low-income rental housing, although syndication may drive up costs: the more expensive a building, the greater the depreciation benefits.

FmHA rental resources also include loans (Section 514) and grants (Section 516) for the construction or rehabilitation of farmworker housing. Both have been underused largely because of local opposition: The farmworker program has produced only 23,000 units over its 22-year lifetime, mostly year-round units in home bases rather than for workers in the migrant stream. Moreover, due to the nature of the USDA and FmHA's general commitment to farmers, the interests of farmworkers (and workers' housing) has often become secondary to those of the growers.

Cooperative projects are also eligible for FmHA rental subsidy, yet only a handful of rural cooperatives have been funded. Many of the projects rejected by FmHA have been ill conceived, but the primary reason for inactivity has been FmHA resistance to the cooperative housing concept, reflecting its bias toward traditional notions of single-family home-ownership.

A major problem in many rural communities is the lack of land, or suitable land, zoned for rental housing. Additionally, local governments seem inclined to approve rental projects only for the elderly. This situation is compounded by the existence of "paper" housing authorities, which operate no units, and local housing authorities that, having built a certain number of units, do not wish to become further involved in low-income housing. FmHA is a reactive agency that responds only to applications. If the low-income housing needs of such badly served rural areas are to be met, FmHA needs a standby affirmative authority directly to purchase, develop, own, and operate rental housing.

## The FmHA's Failings

FmHA's most apparent limitations stem from its original conception, which grew out of a compromise with congressional conservatives irate over the Farm Security Administration's aggressive outreach programs and the latter's unwillingness to abandon the more daring "socialist" projects inherited from the Resettlement Administration. After lengthy congressional investigations of its "un-American" activities, FSA was terminated in 1946. FSA's successor, FmHA, was brought more in line with the thinking of its umbrella agency, the U.S. Department of Agriculture; was stripped at first of all but credit tools; and was restricted in its functions to simply stabilizing the family farmer.

As a subordinate agency, FmHA's greatest handicap is the Department of Agriculture's often conflicting priorities, interests, and bureaucratic procedures. The department has had a notable bias toward large farms, as reflected in its farm price-support programs, its research, its extension services, the kinds of people appointed to top departmental posts, and its relation to congressional committees. Current problems with the department had been anticipated by FmHA's predecessors. Sidney Baldwin's historical account of the 1930s and 1940s describes why many felt the new agency should be completely separate from the Department of Agriculture:

> There was consensus among all those concerned that the creation of such an agency, outside of the USDA, would probably free the proposed agency from the bureaucratic snares of an old-line executive department, where ossified administrative procedures, preoccupation with the commercial farmer and his problems of price and production, and entrenched conservatism would probably stifle the energy and imagination needed for launching bold new programs. (Baldwin, 1968, 91)

The Agriculture Department has its own set of priorities, and rural housing is not high on the list. Generally, the department bureaucracy is not sympathetic to social programs, particularly those that involve subsidies. The complex internal structure of the department, moreover, requires FmHA programs to go through a range of the department's budgetary, congressional liaison, and legal offices, any one of which has the power to stop or modify what the agency wants to do.

Moreover, department interference seems to have successfully undermined development of any sense of social mission within FmHA. This has helped create negative attitudes about disadvantaged people. The National Farmers Union cited employee attitude problems as contributing to farmer applicant difficulties (National Farmers Union, 1982), although the primary problems were interest rates. For example, after an initial period of forbearance, many FmHA loan officers feel an obligation to foreclose on delinquent borrowers, regardless of some later possibility for compromise or rescheduling. Once foreclosure has been instituted and the U.S. attorneys have moved in court, FmHA prefers not to compromise, even if the borrowers (defendants) develop a plan to save their homes. FmHA's reasoning is that the foreclosure process is cumbersome and costly and consumes time, during which the government's collateral may lose some of its value. Such negative feeling toward its clientele has transcended the policies of particular administrations, although the emphasis on reducing the delinquency rate through foreclosures and "voluntary conveyances" has been particularly marked under the Reagan administration.

Despite the conservatism of the FmHA staff, they are technically expert and experienced, and have a surviving core of commitment for addressing rural low-income needs that, given emancipation from the Department of Agriculture yoke, could find an effective outlet. In the meantime, its position within the department denies FmHA the opportunity to formulate its own specific policies and programs.

Reformation of the present approach to rural housing requires both improved programs and an improved administrative structure. In programmatic terms, what is needed are housing subsidies deep enough to serve poverty-level households, and comprehensive approaches that can relate housing to the agricultural and general development needs of nonurban areas.[4] If a reformulated rural housing delivery system is to carry out effectively and conscientiously these myriad functions, it must be removed from the Department of Agriculture. A new Rural Security Administration should be created, which would abosrb the existing delivery network of nearly 2,000 FmHA county offices. FmHA's mix of programs, often criticized because it has led to the subordination of housing to other agency priorities such as agriculture, could become an advantage if FmHA were liberated from the overwhelmingly large-farm interests at the Agriculture Department. Inadequate housing is but one manifestation of poverty, and a rational approach would be to treat it in concert with other manifestations (such as the lack of community facilities), as well as the causes of poverty itself.

# Notes

1. Except where noted, the term *rural* is used throughout this chapter to signify areas defined by the Census Bureau as rural: open country and communities of fewer than 2,500 residents. It is not equivalent to *nonmetropolitan* (generally referring to cities and places with fewer than 50,000 residents), but applies to communities within metropolitan as well as nonmetropolitan areas. It is also not equivalent to the Farmers Home Administration (FmHA) Service Areas, which include open country, communities with up to 10,000

residents that are rural in character, and communities with up to 20,000 residents that are rural in character and are outside Standard Metropolitan Statistical Areas (SMSAs). In general, FmHA Service Areas are what we term *nonurbanized*, as they fall outside the Census Bureau's *urbanized* areas.

2. Since the 1970 census, the Census Bureau has not counted dilapidated units in the housing inventory because their measurement was too difficult to conduct reliably. The measures of substandard quality used by federal housing programs in recent years have been lack of complete plumbing and overcrowding (more than one person per room), both of which are reported and cross-tabulated by the census. The *Annual Housing Survey*, carried out since 1973, does measure some structural deficiencies; according to HUD (U.S. HUD, 1982a), it indicates a fairly constant level of housing deficiencies since 1973 in the nation as a whole, in spite of the improvement in plumbing facilities.

Unless otherwise noted, data are from the Housing Assistance Council's October 1983 survey and its subsequent analyses of census data on rural poverty.

3. The unadjusted 1983 nonmetropolitan unemployment rate was 10.1 percent as opposed to 9.4 percent in metropolitan areas, according to the Bureau of Labor Statistics at the Department of Labor. Adjusted for part-time and discouraged job-seekers, the nonmetropolitan unemployment rate was 14.9 percent of the work force, compared with 13.1 percent in metropolitan areas.

4. A detailed, reformulated rural housing program is available from the authors at the Housing Assistance Council, 1025 Vermont Avenue NW, Suite 606, Washington, D.C. 20005.

# 20

# Public Housing: The Controversy and Contribution

*Rachel G. Bratt*

*Public housing represents the most direct federal government effort to produce housing for low-income people, and the only program that produces publicly owned housing. Although the program was designed to address a variety of pressing political and economic problems stemming from the Great Depression, and although it was opposed by private homebuilding and real estate interests, which consistently undermined it, public housing has actually performed better than is widely believed. To the extent that the program has not been successful, some of the major reasons for its problems are clarified here. The concept of public ownership of housing has not yet been given a fair trial, but, despite its current lack of funding, it remains one of the only real options for producing shelter for low-income people.*

There is a widespread belief in this country that the public sector is unable to build or manage decent housing. Rhetoric describing public housing developments as vertical ghettos, pictures of notorious projects such as Pruitt-Igoe in St. Louis being demolished, and news reports detailing the financial plight of many large housing authorities have reinforced this notion.[1]

The conventional wisdom about the failure of public housing has gone almost unquestioned. Although a handful of studies addressed this issue during the 1970s (Genung, 1971; *Journal of Housing*, April 1973; Meehan, 1975, 1979; Rabushka and Weissert, 1977), there is need for a current evaluation of the public housing program. The purpose of this chapter is to examine the record of public housing in providing decent, affordable housing to low-income people. In other words, Is the conventional wisdom of most policy analysts, journalists, and the general public accurate?

The issue is particularly significant because it is apparent that there is a need for more low-rent housing units. In most large cities the vacancy rate for low-rent units has fallen below 3 percent, and demand for subsidized units far exceeds supply. In New York City alone, over 165,000 households are on the Housing Authority's waiting list (*Mayor's Management Report*, 1983).[2]

Since most housing analysts agree that the private sector cannot build unsubsidized housing that is affordable to low-income people, the public sector has a critical role to play. Some analysts have suggested that this role should include more and better public as well as community- or tenant-owned housing (Achtenberg and Marcuse, 1983; Hartman and Stone, 1980). [*See Chapter 28 by Emily Paradise Achtenberg and Peter Marcuse and Chapter 29 by Chester Hartman and Michael E. Stone.*] Yet, in making these suggestions, proponents have had to face up to the legacy of public housing as this country's major publicly assisted housing program and the only one that involves government as opposed to private ownership. It is difficult to argue that public ownership and management is the answer as long as conventional images persist. A clear look at the record is needed. Does the record of public housing warrant a renewed commitment to this program? To what extent has it been successful in providing housing to low-income people? To the extent it has failed, what have been the contributing factors? Did the public housing program provide a fair test of the concept of public ownership? And what lessons can be learned for improving the program?

## Public Housing—A Historical Overview

The country's first major subsidized housing program was not enacted until the need for better housing could be coupled with another national objective—the need to reduce unemployment resulting from the Great Depression. [*For a discussion of earlier small-scale public housing initiatives, see Chapter 14 by Peter Marcuse.*] Section 1 of the United States Housing Act of 1937 made clear the dual objectives of the legislation: "to alleviate present and recurring unemployment and to remedy the unsafe and insanitary housing conditions and the acute shortage of decent, safe, and sanitary dwellings for families of low income. . . ."[3] Although the need to stimulate the economy was key to creation of the program, other forces determined its shape.

Probably the major factor that contributed to the form of the public housing program was the extent of the opposition to it. While the 1937 Housing Act held out the promise of jobs and apartments for the deserving poor, there were still many dissenters. President Roosevelt himself had to be coaxed: A large-scale public housing program had not been part of the first phase of the New Deal (Friedman, 1968). Organized opposition came from several interest groups, such as the Chamber of Commerce of the United States and the United States Savings and Loan League. Also in the forefront of the opposition was the National Association of Real Estate Boards, whose president summarized the views of the private homebuilding industry as follows:

> Housing should remain a matter of private enterprise and private ownership. It is contrary to the genius of the American people and the ideals they have

established that government become landlord to its citizens. . . . There is sound logic in the continuance of the practice under which those who have initiative and the will to save acquire better living facilities and yield their former quarters at modest rents to the group below. . . . (quoted in Keith, 1973, 33)

Within Congress, conservative members labeled public housing a socialist program and opposed it on the grounds that it would put the government in competition with private property (Friedman, 1968; Keith, 1973).

Largely as a concession to the private housing industry, the public housing legislation included an "equivalent elimination" provision requiring local housing authorities to eliminate a substandard or unsafe dwelling unit for each new unit of public housing built. Public housing could replace inadequate units, but it was not to increase the overall supply of housing, since that could drive down rents in the private housing market.

The argument that public housing should not interfere with the private market logically led to the view that public housing should be clearly differentiated. This had important implications, for example, for its physical design: Public housing, with its austere appearance, is usually easily distinguished from the overall housing stock.[4]

The early public housing program was shortlived. World War II interrupted all non-war-related programs, and public housing construction fell victim to defense needs. However, because thousands of units were in the "pipeline" prior to the war, it was not until 1944 that production virtually stopped (Table 20.1). Before the program was reactivated in the 1949 Housing Act, the real estate lobby launched an all-out attack on public housing. The familiar cry of socialism and the warning that public housing would destroy the private building industry were again heard. President Truman, a supporter of the program, responded with this pointed counter-attack:

> I have been shocked in recent days at the extraordinary propaganda campaign that has been unleashed against this bill [Housing Act of 1949] by the real estate lobby. I do not recall ever having witnessed a more deliberate campaign of misrepresentation and distortion against legislation of such crucial importance to the public welfare. The propaganda of the real estate lobby consistently misrepresents what will be the actual effect of the bill, and consistently distorts the facts of the housing situation in the country. (quoted in Keith, 1973, 96)

Ultimately, proponents of public housing prevailed, but the legislative intent was clear: Public housing was to serve only those people who could not compete for housing on the private market. Private interest groups were willing to tolerate public housing as long as it was explicitly serving a different consumer.

But not all low-income people were eligible for a public housing unit. From the program's inception, it was aimed at providing housing only for the deserving, temporarily poor—the "submerged middle class" (Friedman, 1968). The program therefore targeted those who could not find decent, affordable housing on the private market—but not the so-called unworthy poor and those with no means to pay rent.

The expectation that tenants should pay their own way expressed itself in the formula the federal government devised for financing public housing. Tenant rents were to cover all operating expenses, exclusive of debt service. Only the principal and interest on bonds, which were floated by the local authorities to construct the buildings, were paid by the federal government, through annual contributions contracts. Thus the federal government covered the long-term debt financing, while ownership and management were vested in local public agencies. This arrangement worked well during the early years of the program.

Following World War II, however, the country's demographic picture began to shift and so did the population served by public housing. As Federal Housing Administration (FHA) and Veterans Administration (VA) mortgage insurance and guarantee programs became available to vast numbers of new homebuyers, and as the interstate highway system took

TABLE 20.1
PUBLIC HOUSING COMPLETIONS, 1939–1983

| Year | Units | Year | Units |
|------|-------|------|-------|
| 1939 | 4,960 | 1962 | 28,682 |
| 1940 | 34,308 | 1963 | 27,327 |
| 1941 | 61,065 | 1964 | 24,488 |
| 1942 | 36,172 | 1965 | 30,769 |
| 1943 | 24,296 | 1966 | 31,483 |
| 1944 | 3,269 | 1967 | 38,756 |
| 1945 | 3,080 | 1968 | 72,638 |
| 1946 | 1,925 | 1969 | 78,003 |
| 1947 | 466 | 1970 | 73,723 |
| 1948 | 1,348 | 1971 | 91,539 |
| 1949 | 547 | 1972 | 58,590 |
| 1950 | 1,255 | 1973 | 52,791 |
| 1951 | 10,246 | 1974 | 43,928 |
| 1952 | 58,258 | 1975 | 24,514 |
| 1953 | 58,214 | 1976 | 6,862 |
| 1954 | 44,293 | 1977 | 6,229 |
| 1955 | 20,899 | 1978 | 10,295 |
| 1956 | 11,993 | 1979 | 44,019 |
| 1957 | 10,513 | 1980[a] | 15,109 |
| 1958 | 15,472 | 1981 | 18,000 |
| 1959 | 21,939 | 1982 | 28,529 |
| 1960 | 16,401 | 1983 | 23,000 |
| 1961 | 20,965 | | |

*Sources:* President's Committee on Urban Housing, 1968, 61; U.S. Department of Housing and Urban Development, 1980b, 204; and U.S. Department of Housing and Urban Development, proposed budgets, FY 1982–1985.
[a] Completions for 1980 to 1983 are for fiscal years, not calendar years.

form, most of the submerged middle-class residents of public housing surfaced, to assume full-fledged suburban middle-class status [*see Chapter 6 by Barry Checkoway*]. As a further concession to the private construction industry, the 1949 Housing Act limited public housing to very-low-income people by requiring that the highest rents be 20 percent lower than the lowest prevailing rents for decent housing in the private sector, and by authorizing the eviction of above-income families (Kolodny, 1979a; National Center for Housing Management, Inc., n.d.). Publicly provided housing thus was now to be available only to the very poor. Once public housing was reactivated, and could no longer claim to be a depression-stimulated support for the temporarily poor, it became clearly defined as permanent housing for people who were more or less separated from society's mainstream.

As a result of these postwar changes, vacated units were quickly occupied by a new group of tenants, many of whom had very low incomes and multiple problems. The large housing authorities of the Midwest and Northeast also began to accommodate black migrants from the South. In addition, displacees from the urban renewal and highway programs, the majority of whom were members of minorities, were given priority for public housing units. By 1978, over 60 percent of the residents of public housing were minority-group members (U.S. HUD, 1980b), whereas from 1944 to 1951 nonwhite families represented between 26 percent and 39 percent of all public housing tenants (Fisher, 1959).

By the 1960s, serious problems with the financing formula had surfaced. Inflation was having an increasing impact on operating costs, while rental income remained static. Starting in 1961, the Public Housing Administration (later merged into HUD) made the first in a series of attempts to alleviate this problem by authorizing additional subsidies up to $120 per year for each elderly household. Within a few years, these subsidies were also provided on behalf of handicapped, displaced, large, and very-low-income families (Kolodny, 1979a).

During the 1970s, the overall problems facing public housing worsened. Inflation continued to boost operating expenses, and many buildings that were, by then, 20 or more years old began to show signs of aging and the need for major repairs. At the same time, rental revenues were either declining or, at best, not keeping up with expenses.

In an effort to insulate tenants from having to make up operating cost shortfalls, Massachusetts Senator Edward Brooke sponsored legislation (known as the Brooke Amendments, 1969–1971) that capped rentals at 25 percent of income and provided additional operating subsidies.[5] Between 1969 and 1972, operating subsidies nationally rose from $12.6 million to $102.8 million (Sherwood and March, 1983). Between 1971 and 1982, operating subsidies jumped more than tenfold, to $1.3 billion (U.S. Congress, Congressional Budget Office, 1983a). However, these subsidies have begun to decline as Reagan administration housing cutbacks have taken effect.

Since 1975, operating subsidies have been provided through a mechanism known as the Performance Funding System (PFS). Funding levels under PFS have been set by examining the costs of a sample of housing authorities considered to be well managed and then using these costs to determine reasonable expenses for all authorities. One of the major criticisms of the PFS is that operating subsidies are based on past funding levels and do not take into account the actual cost of providing an adequate level of management services (Struyk, 1980; U.S. Congress, Congressional Budget Office, 1983a).

Thus, the original funding formula, by excluding funds for operating and maintenance costs, undermined the public housing program. Despite the assistance provided by the operating subsidies, many repair problems worsened to such an extent that very large sums of money were needed to remedy the most physically dilapidated projects. A modernization program, now called the Comprehensive Improvement Assistance Program, received $1.7 billion in fiscal years 1981 and 1982 and $2.5 billion in fiscal year 1983.

The highly polarized nature of the debate surrounding the 1937 Housing Act also helped shape the administrative structure of the public housing program. Administration was to be decentralized and participation by locales was to be voluntary. According to Lawrence Friedman, "For legal[6] and political reasons and to disarm conservative opposition, a decentralized program was desirable. Local initiative would govern as much as possible; states and communities would be allowed to opt out if they wished" (1968, 105).

This meant that decisions about public housing—whether to build it and where to locate it—would be made by local officials, who would be under significant pressure from their constituents. The decentralized structure also reduced the potential for the federal government to either enforce more progressive policies or to override local decisions.

The right of local communities not to participate in the public housing program guaranteed that within metropolitan areas public housing would be most prevalent in large cities. As a result, low-income people, already lacking housing options, were to be restricted still further: The choice to move to the suburbs usually was not available to them. Thus, local control over the program meant that little or no public housing was built in more affluent areas.[7]

As the program evolved, accommodating increasing numbers of blacks and other minorities, local control over public housing contributed to patterns of racial segregation, with white areas effectively keeping out blacks [*see Chapter 18 by Citizens Commission on Civil Rights*]. Large cities, with large minority populations, also served a high percentage of minorities in their public housing developments. As of 1976, 83 percent of public housing tenants in 20 large cities were members of minorities, compared to 61 percent for the overall public housing population (Kolodny, 1979a; Struyk, 1980).

Thus, opposition by the private homebuilding industry, maintenance and operating fund shortfalls, and class and racial segregation have continuously plagued the public housing program. As early as the 1950s, some of public housing's most ardent supporters began to lose heart. Catherine Bauer Wurster, one of the key proponents from the 1930s, bemoaned "The Dreary Deadlock of Public Housing" and commented: "After more than two decades, [public housing] still drags along in a kind of a limbo, continuously controversial, not dead but never more than half alive" (1957, 140).

The uncertainty and controversy that have always surrounded the public housing program are reflected in the sporadic rates of public housing production. Between 1939 and 1943, 160,801 public housing units were made available for occupancy, with 61,000 units completed in 1941 alone. In the postwar years, production reached over 58,000 units in both 1952 and 1953 (Table 20.1).[8] During the late 1960s, as concern about urban unrest mounted, there was a sharp increase in public housing production, compared to earlier in the decade. Following enactment of the Housing and Urban Development Act of 1968, in which Congress set a private and public production goal of 26 million new or substantially rehabilitated units over the following decade, including 6 million for low- and moderate-income households, public housing completions reached an all-time high: Over 91,000 units were completed in 1971. However, rather than signal a renewed commitment to public housing, the high levels of construction were short lived. In 1973, President Nixon called a halt to all federally subsidized housing programs. Since then, the program has limped along, with the full impact of the moratorium being felt from 1976 to 1978. With very few new authorizations for public housing development in the Housing and Urban-Rural Recovery Act of 1983, production will virtually come to a halt once projects currently in the pipeline are completed.

The history of public housing not only reveals how several key forces and decisions shaped the program but also reflects how the government has changed its thinking about its role in subsidizing housing for low-income people. Although the public housing program started out with management and ownership resting solely with the local public housing authority, as the program came under attack in the mid-1960s, the private sector was looked to as a way to rescue it.

The Section 23 program was authorized in 1965. Known as the leased housing program, which served as a prototype for the housing allowance idea [*see Chapter 21 by Chester Hartman*], it enabled low-income families to rent units in privately owned housing. The housing authority entered into long-term contracts with landlords and paid the difference between the unit's market rent and a proportion of the tenant's income. Over 100,000 units were financed through this program before it was superseded by the Section 8 Existing Housing program in 1974.

The "turnkey" form of public housing was also introduced in 1965. Under this program, a developer enters into a contract with a local housing authority to construct a project. The developer then sells the project (or "turns the key" over) to the housing authority at the stipulated price. Since 1965, about one-third of all new public housing projects have been built by the turnkey method, but it is unclear whether it has reduced either the time or costs of development or improved quality (Kolodny, 1979a; Meehan, 1979). From the developers' viewpoint, the turnkey program has been enormously popular. In 1968 the president of the National Association of Home Builders suggested that new public housing authorizations be directed primarily into that program. Calling it "the first attempt in the 30-year history of public housing to use, for the lowest income brackets, the tremendous resources and productive capacity of the private homebuilding industry," he cited the program for exemplifying "the proper role of Government in helping private industry to expand into areas not attainable without such help" (U.S. Congress, Senate, Committee on Banking and Currency, 1968, 293).

In addition to these changes in the public housing program, other subsidized housing programs were including a new role for the private sector. In 1959 private entrepreneurs were given their first opportunity to produce subsidized housing. The Section 202 program enacted in that year provided direct below-market interest-rate loans to private nonprofit sponsors of elderly housing. The Section 221(d)(3), Section 236, and Section 8 programs, enacted in 1961, 1968, and 1974, respectively, also invited sponsorship of multifamily subsidized housing by private for-profit groups.

Thus, while the early history of the public housing program was characterized by staunch opposition by the private sector, over the past two decades private interest groups have evolved into active supporters of most housing subsidy programs. Although they are still opposed to conventional public housing, they are certain to support government programs explicitly geared to stimulating the homebuilding industry and providing new investment opportunities.

## Public Housing Tenants and Projects

Public housing currently provides homes to about 3.5 million people, and its 1.2 million units represent less than 1.5 percent of the nation's housing stock. An evaluation of public housing requires a clear image of the projects and who lives in them. Public housing projects have often been characterized as large, dilapidated, old high-rises in central cities, inaccessible to public services and shopping, occupied mostly by minority, single-parent, welfare households with many children, who generally are dissatisfied with their accommodations. To what extent does the conventional image of public housing residents and the developments match reality?

### Tenants and Tenant Perceptions

Popular perceptions concerning the characteristics of public housing tenants turn out to be relatively accurate. Only 39 percent of the public housing tenantry is white, and among the white population, almost 70 percent of the households are elderly. In contrast, minority households tend to be much younger (only about 30 percent are elderly) and have several children. More than 50 percent of all black households and nearly 60 percent of all Hispanic households living in public housing have at least two children. Over three-quarters of all public housing households are headed by single adults, usually an elderly person living alone or a single parent with children. Finally, the incomes of over half of all public housing tenants are dependent on welfare (Kolodny, 1979a).

Interesting data on resident perceptions of public housing come from three studies of local housing authorities.[9] In the first study, Meehan (1975) analyzed why households moved away from St. Louis housing authority projects between 1954 and 1969. He found that while some discontent was clearly evident, with about 20 percent finding better alternatives, nearly half of the moves were precipitated by reasons that had nothing to do with dissatisfaction with the projects. Meehan concluded:

> The point that emerges most strongly from an examination of the tenants in the public housing program . . . is that conventional public housing, for all its inadequacies and faults, served a real and important human need that would not otherwise have been served. Had the alternative been significantly superior, the occupants would have voted with their feet and done so willingly and openly, recording their dissatisfaction for all to see. . . . (p. 135)

Despite the overall willingness of tenants to stay, Meehan was quick to point out that all was far from well with the projects.

> The conditions by the end of the 1960s were deplorable in most cases and unspeakable in some. . . . What is impressive is the extent to which the population was willing to live in such generally unappetizing facilities. . . . The need of the population should be kept separate and distinct from the failure or success of any particular attempt to cope with it. The fact of the need for cheap and decent housing is the evidence that justifies continued efforts to provide it. . . . (p. 136)

In a second study, researchers interviewed almost 2,000 Wilmington, Delaware, public housing residents to ascertain their views on the quality of life in the projects and solicit ideas for improving management. Other than expressing concerns for personal safety and a desire for more police protection, tenants, by and large, did not complain about other problems:

> . . . even as the image of public housing steadily deteriorates and its few remaining supporters speak in softer tones, tenants keep clamoring to get in.
> Is it not ironical that people should want to move into this housing of last resort? And that people in public housing don't want to leave? Even some tenants who can afford better alternatives in the private housing market don't want to go. Every year public housing authorities have to evict people who exceed the income limitations of the program but who would stay if permitted. We have, in short, a paradox: Nobody likes public housing except the people who live there and those who want to get in. (Rabushka and Weissert, 1977, xvi)

The study found that the overwhelming majority of tenants do not accept the tarnished image of public housing: Only 12 percent of the total sample reported that they were ashamed to be living in public housing. Elderly tenants were even more favorably disposed than family respondents; only 1 in 40 was ashamed to be living there. Concerning adequacy of their housing units and the quality of housing authority management, more than 60 percent of tenant family heads and over 90 percent of the elderly tenants reported no problems.

In a third study, 530 residents of Boston's public housing developments were interviewed. Despite the fact that the Boston Housing Authority has been seriously troubled and several projects have received much adverse publicity, more than two-thirds of the respondents reported they were either very satisfied (32 percent) or somewhat satisfied (35 percent) with the condition of their housing (Boston Housing Authority, 1983).[10]

Additional information about the general levels of satisfaction of public housing tenants comes from a survey of residents at 10 public housing developments in various parts of the country. According to Francescato et al. (1979), more than twice as many residents indicated they were satisfied (56 percent) as were dissatisfied (24 percent) with where they lived; 20 percent indicated that they were neither satisfied nor dissatisfied.

Thus, while conventional wisdom assumes low satisfaction levels among public housing tenants, the surveys cited above make clear that the majority of residents report positive feelings about their housing.

## Physical Characteristics, Condition, and Design

Despite its concentration in large cities, public housing is still far more dispersed than many believe. Almost two-thirds of all public units are administered by the 2,775 housing authorities that operate fewer than 6,500 units; the 22 largest public housing authorities administer the remaining one-third of the units (U.S. Congress, Congressional Budget Office, 1983a). In addition, most public housing developments (54 percent) are relatively small, having fewer than 200 units; most family public housing units (75 percent) are in low-rise buildings (four or fewer stories); only 7 percent of all family public housing projects are both high-rise and have more than 200 units; and public housing projects are an average of 17 years old (Perkins and Will, 1980).

Concerning the condition and design of public housing, the available evidence is mixed: Public housing, overall, is not in bad physical shape, but its design has been justifiably subject to criticism. Based on a sample of nearly 700 public housing projects, Jones et al. (1979) concluded that less than 4 percent of all projects were in bad or very bad condition. Projects in good or average condition were rated as "troubled" if they were reported to have five or more other significant problems. Altogether, Jones et al. found that only 7 percent of all public housing projects, accounting for 15 percent of all public housing units, were troubled. A second study found an even lower problem rate. Perkins and Will (1980) studied a national sample of 350 public housing projects and concluded:

> The vast majority of the housing stock is in good condition. While some of it is not attractive, these units appear to successfully comply with the MPS [minimum property standards] physical standards. Rehabilitation is required largely due to the aging of structures and systems, to the normal wear and tear of building components, minor vandalism and changes in state and local codes. A sound and adequately funded routine maintenance program as well as routine modernization is needed to improve upon and preserve the generally good condition of public housing. (p. 13)

Perkins and Will found that a small number of projects exhibited "chronic problems." A chronic-problem project was defined as one requiring in excess of $2,500 per unit to correct violations of basic health and safety standards and bring the building up to minimum property standards. According to the study, only 6 percent of all projects, containing 7 percent of all public housing units, exhibited chronic problems.[11] These projects would require about $621 million (1980 dollars) to bring them up to minimum property standards and to correct major violations. An additional $885 million would be needed to bring the remainder of the public housing stock, which is basically sound, up to these standards.[12]

Jones et al. further examined the extent to which projects with stereotypical characteristics—large, old, urban, and family (as opposed to elderly)—were likely to be troubled. They found that almost three out of every four projects with these attributes were untroubled, although projects with these characteristics were three times more likely to be troubled than were other public housing projects. Perkins and Will further found that most of the chronic-problem projects were not large, high-rise projects but small, low-rise, family projects: 62 percent of these chronic-problem projects were small, family, low-rise; only 9 percent were large, family, high-rise.[13]

Further evidence that high-rise public housing can provide decent shelter comes from New York City. The housing authority in that city administers over 174,000 units in predominantly high-rise buildings[14]—more than 10 percent of the nation's public housing stock—and has a reputation for having one of the best public housing programs in the country, boasting a very low vacancy rate and long waiting lists.

To summarize, the conventional wisdom of what constitutes a physically bad project is not borne out by the evidence: Most stereotypical projects do not exhibit severe problems. Although projects with stereotypical characteristics present problems more frequently than the rest of the public housing stock, they represent only a small percentage of all public housing developments.

To what extent has the overall poor design of public housing contributed to creating troubled projects? Jones et al. (1979) report that site and design factors are among the most significant variables. Sixty-three percent of troubled projects were reported to be adversely affected by project design and site deficiencies (e.g., project size and lack of defensible space—space under the control and surveillance of the residents), compared to only 4 percent of untroubled projects (Jones et al., 1979).

As discussed earlier, the design of public housing, in large part, has been shaped by the private sector's insistence that it not be competitive with private housing. Public housing administrators, furthermore, continually have tried to prove that public housing could make do with less. According to Albert Mayer, a noted architect:

> Housing officials, federal and local, have . . . been excessively on the defense. They have sought to escape attack by being undeniably virtuous, and penurious, and inoffensive, practicing stark economies, squeezing down space, minimizing community facilities, eliminating anything that could be thought of as "glamorizing." . . . As a matter of fact, there was a great competition to achieve virtue. It was a source of pride to the authority that discovered closet doors could be eliminated. Thus such housing officials sold the birthright of public housing, producing the dullest stuff imaginable . . . and getting exactly the same opposition and vituperation anyway. (Quoted in Kolodny, 1979a, 20)

By going along with the notion that public housing should provide only minimal accommodations, administrators may have given the opposition its greatest ammunition. Indeed, many public housing projects—overly modest and austere—did evolve into bad housing. The public sector's quest to provide no-frills housing, combined with the private sector's unrelenting demands that public housing be different from the rest of the housing stock, undermined the notion that public housing could also be attractive housing.

## Management

Management has a significant impact on the quality of public housing. Since the 1960s, inadequate management has been cited as a serious deficiency of many large housing authorities. Problems have revolved around two broad issues: financial mismanagement, and inadequate or insensitive handling of tenant-related matters.

HUD's inspector general recently found that of the 134 largest public housing authorities, 30 were financially troubled. (HUD considers a housing authority financially troubled if it fails to maintain adequate operating reserve funds.) Although these housing authorities represent only 1 percent of all housing authorities, together they administer 23 percent of the units in the entire conventional public housing program (U.S. HUD, 1983c). Another study by HUD's inspector general cited public housing authorities for intentionally underestimating income in order to get additional subsidies (U.S. HUD, 1984a). However, the Council of Large Public Housing Authorities refuted many of the findings from the inspector general's second report, charging that it did not seek explanations for observed problems and preferred "to create an impression of willful PHA [public housing authority] wrongdoing for political and media purposes" (Sherman and Sherwood, 1984, 5).

In addition to financial matters, housing authorities are in charge of a wide range of activities that place them in close contact with tenants, such as rent collection, evictions, and routine maintenance and repairs. For some housing authorities, fulfilling these basic tasks has been problematic. For example, before being placed in receivership, poor management by the Boston Housing Authority created grim conditions in many developments. Disruptive tenants were seldom evicted and repairs went undone, with employees often doing no work at all. And because of political patronage, the housing authority became a deeply entrenched and isolated haven for the politically faithful.

According to the former court-appointed receiver of the Boston Housing Authority, the housing authority neither protected the tenants nor maintained the buildings:

> Ultimately, the withdrawal of institutional supports destroys any sense of cooperative capacity among residents, destroys any sense of community. Each family becomes an isolated fearful unit. Poverty has already impressed on them a sense of powerlessness—now the violence that consumes the community and frightens and humiliates them daily gives final proof of their impotence. . . . and the most savage thing is—having walked away from the poor, then everybody says (the media most of all) look at how those scum live. Isn't it foul how poor people live? . . . It's as classic a case of blaming the victim as I know. (Spence, 1981, 44)

Short of such overt negligence on the part of some housing authorities, insensitivity to tenant needs on the part of housing authority officials also has been documented. A nationwide survey of public housing authority commissioners by Hartman and Carr (1969) found a prevalence of antagonistic and negative feelings toward public housing families. According to the researchers, this "can lead only to conflict between tenants and management and probably serves to reduce the effectiveness of public housing as a supportive experience for poor families" (p. 17). A key reason why commissioners were not sympathetic to their clients may have been due to the substantial differences in socioeconomic status between the two groups. In contrast to the public housing population, commissioners were often middle- or upper-income white males who were well-educated businessmen and professionals. Similarly, Hartman and Levi (1973) concluded:

> . . . it is likely that at least some of the tension in public housing today derives directly from wide disparities in race and class between the managers and the tenants. Managers are likely to feel more responsible and responsive to the housing authority, their professional colleagues, and to the middle-class public than to their present clientele. (p. 135)

Over the years, HUD has instituted a series of programs to encourage better management procedures. Overall, the results of these initiatives have been mixed. Some of the programs were not fully implemented or evaluated, while others were only one-shot efforts (Kolodny, 1979a; Struyk, 1980). One of the most significant efforts to upgrade management was the

National Tenant Management demonstration, a program modeled after tenant-initiated management corporations in St. Louis and several other cities [*see Chapter 26 by Robert Kolodny*]. Frustrated by inadequate local housing authority management, tenants formed their own management entities. Based on the experiences of these tenant management corporations, HUD, with the assistance of the Ford Foundation, launched a three-year demonstration project.

> The National Tenant Management demonstration has shown that management by tenants is a feasible alternative to conventional public housing management under certain conditions. In the majority of the demonstration sites, the tenant participants—all long-time residents of low-income public housing, most unemployed, and the majority black and female family heads—mastered in three years the skills necessary to assume management responsibility for the housing developments in which they lived. . . .
>
> The evaluation of tenant management on a series of measured standard performance indicators such as rent collection and the quality and timeliness of maintenance, shows that the residents were able to manage their developments as well as prior management had and, in so doing, to provide employment for some tenants and increase the overall satisfaction of the general resident population. (Manpower Demonstration Research Corporation, 1981, 239)

Although the record of tenant management has been encouraging, it has not grown into a standard part of the public housing program. This reflects primarily the resistance on the part of central HUD officials, as well as opposition on the part of housing authority commissioners and managers (for the possible sources of this opposition, see Hartman and Carr, 1969; Hartman and Levi, 1973).

## Accessibility

The image of public housing as inaccessible to public services and other facilities is frequently accurate. Because public housing in large cities was developed quite late in their stage of development, much of the best land was often already built up. In addition, public housing development costs had to fall within prescribed limits, which also put pressure on local housing authorities to acquire the cheapest land available, usually in less desirable locations. But the most important factor contributing to the location of public housing relates to a key administrative aspect of the program discussed earlier, the power of local governments to determine the location of developments. Opposition to proposed projects was usually vehement, and, as a result, projects tended to be located less in existing neighborhoods than in more out-of-the-way areas. Local city councillors and chief executives were reluctant to antagonize community residents. Therefore, the easiest and most expedient solution was to build public housing in areas where no one lived or wanted to live. Boston's notorious Columbia Point public housing project was located on the site of the former city dump.

# Impact on Racial Segregation

Public housing has not furthered the goal of racial integration. In addition to the program's decentralized administrative structure, which gave local housing authorities the freedom to discriminate at will, segregation in public housing was also the policy of the federal government during the early years of the program [*see Chapter 18 by the Citizens Commission on Civil Rights*]. The Neighborhood Composition Rule, formulated by Interior Secretary Harold Ickes, stated that housing projects should not alter the racial character of their surrounding neighborhoods (Meyerson and Banfield, 1955). Although housing authorities were permitted to offer units to whites and blacks on an "open occupancy" basis, most authorities chose to provide "separate but equal" housing (U.S. Commission on Civil Rights, 1975).

As a result of these policies, the earliest public housing projects were built for occupancy by either whites or blacks. Bowley (1978) has described how, in Chicago, two of the first public housing projects were in white areas and were rented exclusively to white tenants; another early project was built for blacks only. Similarly, the original plan for Pruitt-Igoe in St. Louis was for two segregated projects, Pruitt for blacks and Igoe, across the street, for whites (Rainwater, 1970). Segregation patterns in Boston's public housing were also finely drawn. In 1940, the first project to accept blacks was completely segregated. The second project open to blacks had specific buildings earmarked "the colored section" (Pynoos, 1974).

New York, in 1939, led the states in barring discrimination in public housing. Massachusetts was next, in 1948, followed by Connecticut and Wisconsin in 1949. By 1961, three years before Congress enacted Title VI of the Civil Rights Act of 1964, which prohibited discrimination in all federally assisted housing, 32 states operated public housing on an open-occupancy basis (U.S. Commission on Civil Rights, 1975). In these areas, some inroads were made to reduce segregation in public housing. In 1960, 55 percent of the 886 projects located in communities with open-occupancy laws had mixed occupancy patterns. However, many of these projects had only a few minority families living in predominantly white projects, or vice versa (U.S. Commission on Civil Rights, 1975). For example, despite the early enactment of a fair housing law in Massachusetts, Boston's public housing stock was still highly segregated in 1960.

> 13 of 25 projects were more than 96 percent white; of these, 7 were exclusively occupied by whites. Of the 1,733 Negro families in 15 federally aided projects, 98.6 percent were in 7 projects, two of which were entirely black. Discrimination was even more evident in the ten state aided projects—3.6 percent of 3,675 units were occupied by Negroes. Of these, 122 Negro families were concentrated in 4 projects, one of which was entirely Negro. That the pattern of segregation was neither accidental nor a matter of location is vividly evidenced by two projects across the street from each other—Mission Hill is 100 percent white while Mission Hill Extension is 80 percent Negro. (Hipshman, 1967, 29)

Discriminatory practices persisted in many cities. In a landmark court case, *Gautreaux* v. *Hills*, plaintiffs successfully argued that the Chicago Housing Authority and HUD had carried out tenant assignments and site-selection procedures along racial lines (Peroff et al., 1979). Following almost a decade of litigation in various courts, including the U.S. Supreme Court (which decided the case in 1976), tenants in, and applicants to, Chicago public housing were invited to participate in a demonstration program that enabled them to move to private housing, using Section 8 certificates, anywhere within the Chicago metropolitan area.

Notwithstanding this effort and other changes in HUD site-selection procedures, the years of discriminatory practices have had their effect. At present, public housing, particularly family public housing, is still often segregated. In many cities, such as Boston, predominantly white projects and predominantly black projects may still be only a few blocks from each other.

As mentioned earlier, the decentralized operation of the program and the option of locales not to participate meant that a wide spectrum of cities and towns within a given metropolitan area would not be under the jurisdiction of a single housing authority. This has substantially reduced the accessibility of suburban and nonmetropolitan public housing to inner-city applicants, most of whom are minority.

It is important to emphasize that in its racially segregating policies the public housing program was operating within the norms of society. Discrimination in the private market was standard procedure, and public housing did nothing to challenge the system. [*see Chapter 18 by the Citizens Commission on Civil Rights*].

# Costs to the Federal Government

The costs of public housing have been examined by housing analysts in two major ways. Comparisons have been made, on the one hand, with direct income supplements and the Section 8 Existing Housing program and, on the other, with other subsidized new construction programs. As will be discussed below, only the second comparison is legitimate. The first is really a comparison between "apples and oranges" (Hartman, 1983a)—programs that subsidize households' incomes or rents in existing houses versus a program that actually builds and creates new housing. But, despite the shortcomings of this comparison, it is important to include it here because it has been a major argument used against the public housing program.

## Public Housing, Income Supplements, and the Section 8 Existing Housing Program

The costs of building new public housing have been compared to the costs of providing income supplements, also known as cash vouchers. One of the most influential early studies was performed by Eugene Smolensky (1968) who concluded:

> Economic considerations alone suggest that the most efficient scheme is to give those families now eligible for public housing a cash subsidy, which the recipient can spend as he wishes so long as he lives in standard housing. (p. 99)

This finding helped to stimulate a whole generation of analyses of the benefits and costs of public housing in comparison to other subsidy mechanisms. Within a few years, many other economists had published studies that pointed to the greater benefits of a direct cash subsidy, or housing allowance program. For example, both Aaron (1972) and Muth (1973a) concluded that excessive costs of public housing, compounded by the inequity of relatively few low-income households receiving large benefits, warranted a shift in federal housing policy to an income-supplement strategy.

Solomon (1974) continued this critique of the conventional public housing program, comparing it with the leased housing program, which, it was argued, most resembled a housing allowance or income strategy. He concluded that the public housing program provided "disproportionately large benefits" to each subsidized household. According to Solomon:

> If the goal of national housing policy were simply to provide a maximum improvement in the housing conditions of a few poor households (the small percentage of those actually receiving government assistance) without regard to equity and cost factors, a reliance on new construction would indeed be a satisfactory policy. But, given both the scarcity of federal resources in relation to overall need and the large number of eligible families receiving no assistance, any definitive judgment regarding program alternatives must also consider their equitableness, cost effectiveness, and political acceptability. (pp. 69–70)

This type of analysis, combined with growing frustration with the alleged high costs and other problems associated with the subsidized construction programs, resulted in a series of experiments, starting in 1970, to test the housing allowance concept, as well as enactment of the Section 8 Existing Housing program in 1974. Both these initiatives generated further research, which continued to make the already well-established and not surprising point that in the short run new construction costs more than simply supplying subsidies for existing housing.

Mayo et al. (1980) compared the per unit cost of public housing, leased housing (Section 23), Section 236 (with and without rent supplements),[15] and housing allowances. They estimated that the total annual per-unit cost for new public housing or Section 236 was 82 percent higher than the per-unit cost for housing allowances. Similarly, the Section 23 program was much less costly than the new construction programs. This point was again made by Wallace et al. (1981) in a study of the Section 8 New Construction and Existing Housing programs. For equivalent subsidy dollars, roughly twice as many households were able to attain decent housing through the Existing Housing program as through the New Construction program.

Equity is also cited as a major reason for opposing public housing and the other subsidized production programs in favor of income supplements. For example, President Reagan's Commission on Housing pointed out that past housing programs were not equitable "because they provide a few fortunate tenants very high quality housing at a price less than their neighbors pay for lower-quality housing" (1982, 3). Yet, its own housing allowance proposal was open to similar criticism: The Commission did not recommend that it be an entitlement program. Thus, as long as budgetary priorities preclude all eligible households from receiving benefits, any housing program is certain to have inequities.

Those who wave the banner of equity when assessing the public housing program appear to have a misplaced sense of social justice: The benefits of the nation's largest housing subsidy are enjoyed by households far more affluent than public housing tenants. All homeowners, regardless of income, are entitled to deduct mortgage interest as well as property-tax payments from their income for federal tax purposes. The result is that $40 to $50 billion in tax revenues are currently being lost to the federal government each year, with most of these savings accruing to upper-income homeowners—those earning over $30,000 per year [*see Chapter 15 by Cushing Dolbeare*]. "Large" benefits to public housing tenants are not nearly as large as the savings enjoyed by upper-income homeowners as a group. Cushing Dolbeare, president of the National Low Income Housing Coalition, has made the following astounding calculation:

> Benefits from federal housing programs are so skewed that *the total of all the assisted housing payments ever made under all HUD programs, from the inception of public housing in 1937 through 1980, was less than the cost to the federal government of housing-related tax expenditures in 1980 alone.* (Dolbeare, 1983b, 69; emphasis in original)

The public housing program also has been compared to the Section 8 Existing Housing program by examining the cost of operating existing public housing developments with the cost of subsidizing low-income families in existing private units under the Section 8 program. According to the Report of the President's Commission on Housing (1982), the direct costs of operating public housing are no higher than providing a Section 8 subsidy to a family living in existing housing. The national average of the cost of operating existing public housing, as a percentage of Section 8 Existing Housing program costs, is 93–100 percent (President's Commission on Housing, 1982). Further, a 1981 report prepared for the President's Housing Commission by HUD's Office of Policy Development and Research indicated that "average public housing costs were about $1,600 per unit in 1979, as opposed to Abt's[16] estimate of $1,560 for Section 8 Existing Housing for the same period. Keeping in mind that Section 8 Existing Housing has smaller average household and bedroom sizes, the net outlay cost of public housing was lower than that of Section 8."[17]

Thus, it seems clear that, at worst, the cost of operating existing public housing developments is on a par with the costs of the Section 8 Existing Housing program. Meehan (1979) showed that two older public housing developments in St. Louis actually cost about 30 to 40 percent less to operate than Section 23 leased housing. Even the President's Commission on Housing (1982) concluded: "While Federal costs [of public housing] have risen, the average cost is not out of line with private rental housing" (p. 32).

## Public Housing and Other New Construction Programs

A more legitimate assessment of the costs of public housing can be made by comparing it to other subsidized new construction programs. However, there is a considerable amount of disagreement on the costs of the public housing, as compared with both the Section 8 New Construction and Section 236 programs. Mayo et al. (1980) found that public housing and Section 236 had almost identical construction costs. In contrast, the General Accounting Office (GAO) concluded: "For units of the same quality, public housing is the least costly alternative over a 20-year subsidy life and it results in housing projects which are likely to provide service for much longer than privately owned Section 8 units" (U.S. Comptroller General, GAO, 1980, 113; see also U.S. Congress, Congressional Research Service, 1976).

Additional contradictory findings emerged from a third study, completed in 1982 for HUD. Using actual program data rather than the hypothetical estimates used in the GAO study, Urban Systems Research and Engineering, Inc. (1982) found that the total per-unit development cost for conventional public housing was as much as $10,000 more than for other subsidized new construction programs. The Section 8 New Construction program demonstrated consistently lower subsidy costs than the public housing program, with savings ranging from about $300 to almost $2,000 per year.[18] Some of the higher costs of public housing resulted from the construction of larger units, higher land and site development costs, and more costly structures, such as high-rise elevator buildings or very-low-density projects. This discrepancy is, in itself, an important finding. It underscores the fact that the studies to date have not controlled for a host of variables and that, without such controls, a clear comparison of the subsidy mechanisms used in the public housing and other new construction programs is impossible.

The issue of public housing costs can be summarized as follows: First, although this chapter has argued that the comparison is not a fair one because, in the case of public housing, new units are built, and in the housing allowance programs they are not, it is less costly to subsidize a household through the Section 8 Existing Housing program than to subsidize the *construction* of a new unit of public housing. Second, the cost of subsidizing households in *existing* public housing units is no higher than the cost of subsidizing households in *existing* private units through the Section 8 program. Third, no conclusions can be drawn about the cost of building new public housing in comparison to other subsidized new construction programs.

## Public Housing: Future Directions for Policy

There is no question that public housing has made a considerable contribution to addressing the low-income housing problem in this country. Millions of low-income families are provided with decent, affordable units with which the great majority of tenants seem to be satisfied. The cost of subsidizing households in existing public housing units is no greater than the cost of subsidizing families in existing units on the private market. Finally, the majority of public housing developments are reported to be in good condition. But public housing also has been disappointing on several measures. It has not promoted racial integration, and, often, the designs of the buildings have been bleak, accessibility has been poor, and management has been problematic. Yet, as the preceding review has demonstrated, many of public housing's failings have been due to the persistent opposition by private-sector critics who, from the program's inception, attempted to kill the program. While public housing cannot and should not be "let off the hook," particularly regarding racial integration and management, these problems are correctible and do not reflect inherent flaws in the basic concept of the public housing program.

   In view of the real achievements of public housing, why do the completely negative stereotypes persist? First, some of the most problem-laden projects are clustered in large cities, readily observable to many people. The vast numbers of successful projects are more dispersed and often are in small cities and towns. The reality that a handful of projects are, indeed, in serious difficulty may have created the myth that all public housing has failed. Second, the notion that public housing has been a failure is certainly what many interest groups want to believe and propound. Public ownership of housing is still not a popular concept, and a successful program that bypasses the private homebuilding and real estate industry would be just as unwelcome in the private sector today as it was when the program was enacted. Third, the media have tended to cover the failures within the public housing stock to a far greater degree than they have depicted the successes.

   Beyond the preceding attempt to clarify the actual accomplishments of public housing, several broad questions need to be addressed. First, to what extent is the program a fair test of public ownership of housing? Second, what should be the future direction of public housing? And, third, what options exist, aside from public housing, for providing decent, affordable housing to low-income people?

## A Test of Public Ownership

The public housing program was never given an optimum chance at success. Opposition by the real estate lobby continually undermined the program, and the private sector's insistence that public housing not be competitive with market housing virtually assured that it would be different and less desirable. In addition, the funding formula provided inadequate operating reserves, which led to maintenance and repair deficiencies. Eugene Meehan (1983) has stated:

> The public housing program, effectively if not deliberately, was designed to fail. The design remained unchanged long past the time when minor modifications might have produced a genuine test of the principle of public ownership and operation of low-income housing. Public housing was not tested and found wanting; it was condemned without trial. Of course, a genuine test might also have revealed public housing's failure. The point is, the test was not made. (p. 75)

When signs of problems in the public housing program became evident, there was a major push toward privatization, instead of trying to improve the public ownership approach. The major "innovations" in public housing that occurred in the late 1960s all embraced an expanded role for the private sector. The leased housing program depended on private landlords, and the turnkey program depended on private developers. Meehan has questioned the thinking behind this shift toward a greater reliance on the private sector:

> Why a transfer of control over development or operations from a public employee to a private entrepreneur was expected to lead to significant improvements in performance is uncertain. Some proponents of privatization simply opposed public ownership on ideological grounds and took the "failure" of public housing as evidence favorable to their position. Others accepted the popular belief in the superiority of private enterprise (as opposed to the intrinsic evil of public ownership). In most cases, supporters of privatization apparently had only the vaguest notion of how and why it would improve the housing program. (1979, 136)

According to Meehan, privatization was a costly error and

> . . . the assumption that privatization was justified because public ownership had been tried and found wanting was grossly mistaken. . . . The poor quality and performance of some of the conventional developments were no more a simple function of public ownership than the poor performance and quality of some recent turnkey developments were a simple function of private development. (1979, 205–6)

As mentioned above, many of the difficulties experienced by the public housing program stemmed from the continued opposition it faced, given its highly controversial nature in a "free enterprise" system. But the issue remains that it is the only federal housing program involving government ownership. This concept, although admittedly difficult to investigate within an environment committed to ensuring failure (or, at least the appearance of failure), still awaits a fair evaluation.

## Future Directions for Public Housing

Although we know that most public housing developments have provided relatively decent, low-rent shelter in the past, policy makers are confronted with two questions: What should be done with the existing stock of public housing, and, should more new public housing be produced?

The answer to the first question is clear. The existing stock of public housing represents a scarce and invaluable resource that must be protected and supported. Efforts to privatize, demolish, or convert the existing stock should be opposed. For the vast majority of projects, resources and supports should be made available to insure that public housing remains a viable option.

The second question is somewhat more complex. A revised public housing program, which would correct the defects in the existing program, should be launched. In such a program, adequate operating subsidies and modernization funds must be available; management in many housing authorities needs improvement, and tenants should be provided with more opportunities to participate in running their projects. In addition, much more needs to be learned about what makes a problem project or even a problem housing authority. Research is needed on why some housing authorities have been successful, while others have not. Similarly, we know very little about why some projects in a given city are virtually troublefree, while others, often only a few blocks away, are public disgraces. Any new public housing program would also need to pay special attention to design, siting, neighborhood amenities, and social service programs.

Public housing presents a clear and compelling case: The demand for low-rent housing is acute in many areas, and the public housing program alleviates a pressing need. Public housing has not failed; if anything, it can claim an impressive success: Despite the opposition to the program and the unrelenting efforts to sabotage it, public housing has provided shelter to millions of this country's poorest and neediest households.

## Alternatives to Public Housing

If this country is committed to its national housing goal, first articulated by Congress in the 1949 Housing Act—"A decent home and a suitable living environment for every American family"—then we must develop policies and programs to achieve it. Do any other options exist for serving the population served by public housing? Logical answers might be the Section 8 Existing Housing program, housing allowances, or even the unaided private sector.

For decades, there has been controversy over whether or not the public sector should even be involved with subsidizing housing. Yet it is generally agreed that the private sector is not geared to building housing where profit margins are the smallest or nonexistent—in the low-income housing market. For example, Robert Taggart has concluded: "The reason for public ownership in the first place is that the private sector cannot provide for the lowest-income families and has been insensitive to their needs" (1970, 137). Similarly, Anthony Downs has stated that he does not believe that "a modern industrialized society can totally eliminate the need for publicly owned and operated housing for certain large-sized groups unable to obtain decent quality housing in private markets" (1973, 68). The U.S. General Accounting Office noted that 82 percent of the total U.S. production of low- and moderate-priced rental housing was federally subsidized during the early 1970s (U.S. Comptroller General, GAO, 1978b). Finally, the President's Commission on Housing admitted that "the private market has been unwilling or unable to house many of these [low-income, single-parent, minority and large] families . . ." (1982, 31).

Since there is currently no serious contention that the private sector can provide the needed housing, it is clear that we must look to some form of public assistance. None of the other federal subsidy programs meets the needs of the low-income population. Evaluations of both the Section 8 Existing Housing program and the housing allowance experiments have demonstrated that the population currently living in public housing is inadequately served by these newer programs. Summarizing the available data on the housing allowance experiments and the Section 8 Existing Housing program, the President's Commission on Housing reported:

> Persons starting out in housing that does not meet the quality standards of the program are less likely to participate in a Housing Payments Program than those who start out in units meeting the program standards. . . . Large families, single-parent households, and minority families are more likely than other groups to live in substandard housing. Therefore these households are less likely to become program participants (1982, 26–27). [*See also Chapter 21 by Chester Hartman.*]

The Section 8 New Construction program also has served only a portion of the public housing clientele. For example, Wallace et al. (1981) found that only 20 percent of Section 8 New Construction units were occupied by family (as opposed to elderly) households and that few minority households participated in the program. In contrast, more than half of public housing tenants are families and about three-fifths are minority (U.S. HUD, 1980b).

Similar findings came from the U.S. Comptroller General, General Accounting Office:

> Section 8 was designed to serve a wide range of eligibles in accordance with local housing need estimates. GAO found, however, that housing produced under Section 8 has primarily been serving elderly and small nonelderly families. Very

little of Section 8 housing being built will accommodate families with children or large households. (1980, vi)

Among the major housing subsidy programs, public housing emerges as the only alternative for millions of poor people, particularly large families, single-parent households, and minorities. The program should not only be measured against an absolute yardstick of what it has or has not accomplished; it must also be viewed in terms of what other options are available for the people it serves. Although there is obviously much room for improvement, public housing fills an important void in the private housing market and houses a clientele that is served only partially by other subsidy programs. Indeed, the tenants' own perceptions provide clear evidence of the crucial role played by the public housing program.

In addition to public housing, a companion program is needed, in the form of a support and financing system for community- and tenant-owned housing. Using an array of federal, state, and local programs, as well as private resources, dozens of community groups have demonstrated an ability to develop and manage their own housing for low-income people (Bratt, 1984; Cohen and Kohler, 1983; Marshall, 1981; Portnoy and Pickman, 1984). [*See also Chapter 25 by Seth Borgos, Chapter 26 by Robert Kolodny, and Chapter 27 by Tony Schuman.*] Limited equity cooperatives also present an exciting opportunity for tenants to enjoy long-term security while insuring that vacated units will be affordable to other low-income people.

Public ownership, tenant ownership, and community ownership are critical strategies for providing decent low-rent housing. The key to all of them is that they do not treat housing as a commodity—an item bought and sold for profit. By placing control and ownership squarely in the hands of public or other nonprofit entities, a new housing agenda would be formulated on the assumption that decent housing is a "right"—a matter of public concern, not private exploitation or political whim [*see Chapter 28 by Emily Paradise Achtenberg and Peter Marcuse*]. A government that pursued this approach seriously would be demonstrating a genuine commitment to the goal of decent housing for all.

# Acknowledgments

The author wishes to thank Phillip Clay, Judith Feins, Chester Hartman, Terry Lane, Peter Marcuse, Eugene Meehan, Ann Meyerson, Mary Nenno, and Florence Roisman for their helpful comments on earlier drafts of this chapter.

# Notes

1. The conventional public housing program, which is the subject of this paper, must be distinguished from other publicly assisted housing programs. Several other federal housing production programs have also provided reduced rentals and are often thought of as public housing. Specifically, the Section 202, 221 (d)(3), and 236 programs have produced lower-cost housing by providing interest-rate subsidies on the mortgage loan. Unlike public housing, which is owned by a local public authority, ownership in these other publicly assisted programs is by private for-profit or nonprofit groups. (In Section 202, only nonprofits are eligible sponsors.) The Section 8 New Construction program, enacted in 1974, superseded the Section 236 interest-rate subsidy program, which had been enacted in 1968. The Section 8 program subsidized rentals by making up the difference between a fixed percentage of a low-income household's income and the fair market rental of the unit. Although some new Section 8 housing was built by local housing authorities, that experience will not be discussed in this chapter. The Housing and Urban-Rural Recovery Act of 1983 repealed the new construction and substantial rehabilitation components of the Section 8 program. The Section 8 Existing Housing program, which provides a subsidy to tenants in existing privately owned units, is still in operation.

2. Despite these figures, in recent years there has been considerable debate on whether there is a shortage of low-rent housing. See U.S. Comptroller General, GAO, 1979, and U.S. HUD, 1981a.

3. United States Housing Act of 1937. Public Law 412, 75th Cong., 50 Stat. 888; 42 U.S.C. 1401.

4. Early public housing (pre–World War II), however, had less differentiated architecture and more amenities than subsequent developments. This has been attributed, in part, to the work of housing reformers such as Edith Elmer Wood and Catherine Bauer Wurster, women who stressed the importance of including community facilities such as meeting rooms and playgrounds in public housing developments (Birch, 1978;Wood, 1919).

5. Under present HUD regulations, rentals are based on 30 percent of income for new tenants. Rentals for existing tenants will rise 1 percent per year for five years until 30 percent of income is paid. This new income limit was set in the Omnibus Budget Reconciliation Act of 1981. In July 1983 the House passed a bill that would have reinstated the 25 percent of income formula for all public housing programs. The final legislation enacted by Congress, the Housing and Urban–Rural Recovery Act of 1983, did not reinstate the 25 percent of income formula; it did, however, modify deductions on which income is based, thereby reducing rents for many households.

A proposal to assess tenant rent contributions more equitably has been made by Michael E. Stone (1983). He has argued that "any attempt to reduce affordability of housing to a single percentage of income—no matter how low or high—simply does not correspond to the reality of fundamental and obvious differences among households." That is, "a small household with a given income can afford to spend more than a large household of the same income; while a household of a given size can afford a higher proportion of income for shelter as its income rises." Therefore, according to Stone, "an appropriate standard of affordability for housing is a sliding scale, with household size and income as the principal variables . . ." (pp. 102–3). [*See also Chapter 3 by Michael E. Stone.*]

6. The major legal reason for a decentralized program was that a court decision "cast grave doubt upon the right of the Federal government to condemn property for housing purposes. . . ." Abrams, 1946, 255–56.

7. Additions to the public housing stock within the past decade have broken away from the earlier central city emphasis. In 1976 only 22 percent of new public housing units

were located in central cities (Kolodny, 1979a). This trend is both the result of HUD regulations (enacted in 1967), which required dispersion of public housing outside of "racially-impacted areas" (Kolodny, 1979a), as well as legislative amendments, beginning in 1956, which made single older people eligible for public housing and authorized the construction of housing specifically designed for the elderly (Olson, 1982). While many communities have avoided building public housing for families, they have been willing to build such housing for the elderly. Nearly half the public housing units completed in fiscal year 1979 were designated for the elderly (U.S. HUD, 1980b); 46 percent of all public housing units are at present occupied by elderly households (President's Commission on Housing, 1982).

8. However, even this fell far short of Congress's authorizations. The 1949 Housing Act authorized funding for 810,000 units—135,000 units per year over a six-year period. Through the 1950s and 1960s, whether there was a Republican or Democratic administration, completions lagged well behind congressional authorizations.

9. Three surveys of specific housing projects, while less generalizable, are also worth mentioning. Rainwater (1970) found that even in the Pruitt-Igoe project in St. Louis, in which most tenants showed little attachment to the project community and indicated an interest in moving, the great majority felt that their apartments were better than their previous dwellings. A 1964 survey of Easter Hill Village in Richmond, California, found that 75 percent of the tenants liked their house either "a lot" or "quite a bit." Despite these high satisfaction levels with their particular unit, a considerably smaller percentage of tenants (40 percent) reported that they felt positive about living in public housing, while another 25 percent said they were indifferent (Cooper, 1975). And a 1980 survey of a public housing project in Decatur, Illinois, disclosed that 43 percent of the adult residents reported positive feelings toward their environment; 40 percent gave negative responses; 17 percent were neutral. (Weidemann et al., 1982). A fourth study of why people were leaving public housing projects in Puerto Rico found that only a small percentage (5 percent) of those moving away had cited dissatisfaction with living in public housing as their main reason for moving (Hartman, 1960).

10. However, Paul Warren (1982), citing Annual Housing Survey data, notes that tenant satisfaction is lower among Boston Housing Authority nonelderly residents than among nonelderly renters of private housing with incomes below 50 percent of the median. Levels of satisfaction for elderly renters were almost identical. These findings might be tempered, somewhat, if we knew the answer to the following question: If public housing residents had to find units in the private market, would they be able to rent dwellings comparable to those occupied by existing private-market residents?

11. Although their definitions varied, both the Jones et al. and Perkins and Will estimates of the number of troubled or chronic problem projects are reasonably close. However, it is surprising that the two studies found the number of units involved to be quite different. Since we know that the larger projects tend to have more problems than the overall public housing stock, Jones's estimate of 15 percent of public housing units being troubled seems more plausible than Perkins and Will's estimate of only 7 percent.

12. In view of the expenditures under the modernization program—the Comprehensive Improvement Assistance Program, discussed earlier—Perkins and Will's estimates of costs to bring the project up to standards are probably too low. However, Perkins and Will's estimates were probably based on a lower standard than the improvements made under CIAP. To gain a clearer picture of costs to modernize public housing, HUD has contracted with Abt Associates to update the Perkins and Will study.

13. According to the Perkins and Will study, however, large, high-rise projects accounted for more than half (54 percent) of the projected modernization cost for chronic-problem projects. Small, family, low-rise projects accounted for only 14 percent of these costs.

14. In addition to managing and owning federally supported public housing units,

the New York City Housing Authority administers about 24,000 city- and state-subsidized public housing units. Several other states besides New York (e.g., Massachusetts and Connecticut) also have their own public housing programs.

15. The rent supplement program, which was used between 1965 and 1973 to further reduce rentals for Section 236 and other assisted housing, subsidized the difference between 25 percent of the tenant's income and actual market rent.

16. Abt is a research and consulting firm that received a HUD contract to study the Section 8 program. See Wallace et al., 1981.

17. Cited in a letter to Rachel G. Bratt from Joseph Riley, HUD economist, April 8, 1983.

18. In its response to Urban Systems Research and Engineering's report, the National Association of Housing and Redevelopment Officials has argued that the findings were misinterpreted and methodologically imperfect (Maffin, 1983).

# 21 Housing Policies Under the Reagan Administration

*Chester Hartman*

*Since 1981, the Reagan administration has waged war on traditional government housing programs for the poor. The administration is averse to the very concept that government has an obligation to provide the poor with decent, affordable housing. Analyses of the administration's budgetary proposals, budgets, congressional activities, and administrative actions document the specific paths chosen: elimination of programs that directly add to the low-rent housing supply; reduction in the existing stock of government-provided housing; requiring the poor to pay a higher percentage of their incomes in order to receive subsidized housing; introduction of housing allowances (vouchers) that rely on a private housing market that has traditionally failed the poor and racial minorities; and inadequate enforcement of fair housing laws.*

The Reagan administration is well on its way to reversing the federal government's 50-year-old role in providing housing aid for the poor. While federal housing programs never have been anywhere near large enough or good enough to meet the nation's housing needs, a clear federal commitment was there. It now looks as if the administration is trying to remove the federal government altogether from direct responsibility for meeting the housing needs of households for whom the private market is not working. This has been accomplished in part through the budget process, in part through administrative actions and regulations of the Department of Housing and Urban Development (HUD), and in part through legislation (although Congress, particularly the House of Representatives, has forced the administration to back down on many of its legislative proposals and to accept programs and budgetary expenditures it opposed).

A presidential commission on housing, appointed shortly after the

This chapter is a revised and updated version of portions of "Housing," in *What Reagan Is Doing To Us*, ed. Alan Gartner, Colin Greer, and Frank Riessman, New York, Harper & Row, 1982, and used by permission of *Social Policy* Magazine; and of portions of "Housing Allowances: A Critical Look," reprinted with permission from the *Journal of Urban Affairs*, Winter 1983.

Reagan administration took office, laid out the road map unambiguously: Its mandate was to reshape federal housing policies and programs in conformity with the administration's overall economic philosophy—in the commission's words, "the genius of the market economy, freed of the distortions forced by government housing policies and regulations that swung erratically from loving to hostile, can provide for housing far better than Federal programs" (President's Commission on Housing, 1982c; see also Hartman, 1983c). Guiding its recommendations were its "Statement of Principles," enunciated in the commission's October 1981 Interim Report:

- Achieve fiscal responsibility and monetary stability in the economy.
- Encourage free and deregulated housing markets.
- Rely on the private sector.
- Promote an enlightened federalism with minimal government intervention.
- Recognize a continuing role of government in addressing the housing needs of the poor.
- Direct programs toward people, rather than toward structures.
- Allow maximum freedom of housing choice.

The composition of the 30-member commission—19 from the banking, real estate, and construction business world, 7 lawyers, with no one representing the construction trades or housing–consumer rights groups, and only 3 female and 2 minority members, but 29 Republicans—made its recommendations a foregone conclusion.

Backed by the work of the President's Commission on Housing, the attack on federal housing programs has been fierce. There are several distinguishable strands to the strategy:

1. Termination of existing new construction programs for lower-income households
2. Sloughing off existing lower-income housing developments through deterioration, demolition, conversion, or sale
3. Extracting ever larger portions of lower-income households' budgets as a price for getting federally subsidized housing
4. Introduction of a new housing allowance program as the primary federal housing tool

## Shutting Off the Housing Spigot

Perhaps the most dramatic change is the virtual cessation of direct production of housing for families that cannot afford market rents. Ever since the 1930s, the federal government has been in the business—at times with vigor, at times with torpor—of producing public housing, or its newer version, Section 8. Some 3.5 million people live in public housing, in 11,000 projects, located in 3,300 cities, towns, and counties across the country. In a move to "privatize" this function (which traditionally had involved local government development, ownership, and management of housing projects), Congress in 1974 introduced the Section 8 program, which for the most part provides federal subsidies on behalf of lower-income households to private developers and owners, for the construction, rehabilitation, and leasing of units to be occupied by families with incomes up to a slightly higher maximum than are eligible for public housing. The various subcomponents of the Section 8 program (new construction, substantial rehabilitation, moderate rehabilitation, and leasing of existing units) have produced an additional 1.4 million units, housing some 3.5 million people.

These programs have had problems, to be sure, in location, design, management, and concept (creating enclaves of subsidized households can intensify existing social problems). But the more dramatic manifestations of these difficulties (blowing up St. Louis's Pruitt-Igoe project a few years back, for example) tend to overshadow the fact that for millions of Americans they provide decent, affordable housing that otherwise would be impossible to obtain. And in any case many of the problems with the public housing program are attributable to successful efforts by opponents of the program to hamstring it through inadequate subsidies and arbitrary restrictions—which then permits them to use this deviation from the private-market model as an object lesson that public enterprise "doesn't work." [*For further discussion, see Chapter 20 by Rachel G. Bratt.*]

The Reagan administration seeks to shut off the housing spigot altogether. Housing starts for all HUD lower-income housing programs (public housing, Section 8 new construction and substantial rehabilitation, Section 202 housing for the elderly and handicapped, and the tiny Section 235 homeownership program) have dropped steadily in this decade: from 183,000 units in 1980, to 119,000 in 1983, to 42,000 in 1984, to an estimated 28,000 in 1985. ("Starts" reflect the rather long pipeline period for authorization and planning, and so it takes several years before turning off the spigot shows up at the other end.) The administration's proposed 1986 budget (released in early 1985) calls for a two-year moratorium on *all* HUD assistance for additional lower-income housing, and for wiping out completely the rural housing programs of the Farmers Home Administration (Low Income Housing Information Service, 1985).

Other significant Reagan administration cutbacks, attempted and implemented, are worth noting:

• Community Development Block Grant (CDBG) outlays, about 30 percent of which in the past have gone to rehabilitate substandard housing, not only have not been increased to keep up with inflation but have been steadily cut—from $3.7 billion in 1981, to an estimated $3.5 billion in 1985, to a proposed $3.1 billion for 1986. And programs that formerly were subsidized separately have been folded into the CDBG pot, increasing competition for these monies. Furthermore, the administration has attempted to weaken the congressional requirement that CDBG funds primarily benefit low- and moderate-income households.

• Neighborhood Self Help Development grants were terminated, the kind of help that increases communities' ability to resist displacement pressures, which now force 2.5 million Americans from their homes and neighborhoods each year.

• Comprehensive Employment and Training Act (CETA) public-service jobs have been cut; among other effects, this results in higher home-heating bills for low-income households, mainly the elderly, as the various home-weatherization programs largely depended on CETA labor.

• The Legal Services program is under severe attack, with attempts to limit its effectiveness, cut back on its scope and budget, and perhaps eliminate it altogether. In the areas of displacement, tenants' rights, and housing program benefits, the Legal Services program has been a key force, both in providing gains for individual clients and in reforming the law.

# Destroying the Existing Subsidized Housing Stock

Beyond barring additions to the subsidized housing stock, the administration also has been attempting to do violence to an already-vulnerable supply of existing public housing. Much of the nation's subsidized housing stock is not in good shape. As originally conceived, the federal government's financial contribution under the public housing program was to pay for all construction costs, giving to local housing authorities an annual contribution, over the life of the (usually 40-year) bonds these authorities issue to raise the construction capital needed, which contribution would cover annual principal and interest payments to the bondholders. Ongoing operating expenses were to be covered through rents from tenants.

Federal financing did not allow for capital expenses for remodeling and replacement of utility systems that inevitably would be needed as the projects grew older.[1] The formula also did not envision that there would be a severely growing gap between the costs of operating public housing and the rents housing authorities would be receiving from tenants, which in turn are based on a percentage-of-income formula.

And so, beginning in the 1960s, the federal government provided local housing authorities with operating subsidies as well, which are crucial to the financial solvency of these agencies and to the ongoing health of the projects they own and manage. While these subsidies never have been adequate, the Reagan administration has sought to slash them to the point where maintaining decent living conditions is in many cases impossible. In the early years of the Reagan administration, these subsidies were increased from $1.1 billion in 1981, to $1.5 billion in 1982, to $1.6 billion in 1984 (following a slight drop in 1983, to $1.4 billion). But the figure is down to an estimated

$1.2 billion in 1985, and the administration's 1986 budget proposal calls for dropping operating subsidies to $1.0 billion, lower than the 1981 figure, despite a growing need for these subsidies and inflation.

Funds for the public housing modernization program—capital infusions primarily for older, large projects to permit major repairs to electrical, plumbing, and heating systems, replacement of appliances, landscaping, and other renovation work—are to be slashed by even greater amounts. After increasing new budget authority for this all-important program from $1.7 billion in 1981, to $2.6 billion in 1983, program funds were cut in 1984 to $1.6 billion, are estimated to be $1.7 billion in 1985, and the 1986 administration budget proposal allocates a mere $175 million for modernization to meet emergency needs only (Low Income Housing Information Service, 1985). To the extent that older public housing developments are not modernized, housing standards for their occupants fall ever behind the country's norms, and these projects run a higher risk of being shut down altogether by local housing authorities.

Cutbacks in programs to upgrade and salvage deteriorating public housing developments, of course, fit in with the administration's desire to reduce the existing supply of public housing by demolishing units and selling off others. The issue of how and whether older public housing projects will be retained is coming sharply to the fore, in two ways. One is that the federal government's hold on projects ceases to exist when the local authority's bonds are paid off (unless there has been an extension of that hold either through the workings of the modernization program, or through a housing authority's decision to continue to receive operating subsidies after expiration of the bond-repayment contract, which receipt, under a 1979 Housing Act amendment, entails a 10-year commitment to keep the units as low-rent housing).

Some public housing units built before World War II have reached the point where the locality is free to do with these projects as it wishes, and thousands more will reach the end of their original 40-year commitment over the next decade. Often these older projects, built originally on unappealing, out-of-the-way sites, now are hot properties as a result of gentrification, new transit lines, and other factors. (Alexandria, Virginia, is a prime example, where as a result of the D.C. area's new Metro system and "in" places like Old Town, developers and the city are teaming up to replace old low-rent projects with pricey residences and commercial uses.)

Other ways in which localities can gentrify public housing projects are to convert them to cooperatives or condominiums, or to "upgrade" them from family to elderly use. (Even the modernization program can result in loss of units as projects are "thinned out," often for motives related to gentrification. In San Francisco, for example, the modernization program for the Hunters Point project resulted in demolition of 156 of the project's 993 units, a move clearly tied to the development of new moderate- and middle-income units on an adjacent site by the city's Redevelopment Agency, which felt that the presence of so large a low-rent housing project next door would keep away the new development's hoped-for middle-income clientele.) HUD's ability, even under the 1979 Housing Act amendments, to grant waivers for the conversion or demolition of projects on which it still has a hold provides a huge loophole through which many projects may be shoved. (The introduction of housing allowances—discussed in detail below—may also facilitate elimination and disposal of the existing subsidized housing stock, by encouraging upwardly mobile families to leave, with only the lowest-income households remaining, thereby increasing the financial and social problems in the projects and the likelihood of abandonment, sale, or conversion. Twenty-five hundred of the 3,500 housing vouchers proposed in the administration's 1986 budget are designated for tenants displaced by demolition of public housing.)

HUD's encouragement to local housing authorities to sell off their older units in order to cut operating expenses (and advance the goal of putting the government out of the housing business altogether) could be disastrous for the nation's poor. A frightening example of this from across the Atlantic is, of course, England, where the Thatcher government, spiritual, political, and economic sister to the Reagan administration, is selling off tens of thousands of public housing units each year [*see Chapter 30 by Steve Schif-feres*]. In 1985, HUD selected 18 local housing authorities to participate in a pilot program to sell public housing units to their tenants.

The other way in which we may see a dramatic reduction in the nation's public housing stock is through neglect (often intentional) and deterioration to the point where demolition becomes the "logical" path to take. This neglect can be rooted in the inadequate funds most local housing authorities have had for many years for maintaining projects; the incompetence of some authorities is a contributing factor as well. But, as a recent National Housing Law Project handbook (1981) observes, "Such practices may reflect . . . deliberate political decisions to close out a project by attrition in order to get rid of it and replace it with something which the power structure and the city consider more desirable."

As an example, it is hard to avoid interpreting the virtual abandonment of Boston's Columbia Point in this light. Built in 1954 on a large garbage dump–landfill site jutting into Boston Harbor, this 1,500-unit high-rise project was a disaster from the beginning, stuck in the middle of nowhere with few public services, no stores, and hopeless transit connections. But as times changed, Boston discovered that the remainder of the barren spit of land could hold a new University of Massachusetts campus and the John F. Kennedy Presidential Library. And public housing was not seen as a desirable neighbor for these prestigious institutions. Malignant neglect of the project set in, repairs went unmade, vacated units weren't refilled, and it wasn't long before the housing authority, with its waiting list of 7,000 households, had 1,200 vacant units at Columbia Point. Suddenly came a proposal for "renewal" of the Point, a brand-new development, this time with commercial and community facilities, and designed not as a low-income ghetto but to house people of all income groups—although only 300 low-rent units were being included. In the process, 1,200 low-rent units will be lost, and a big tract of land, given to poor people when it was regarded as having little value, is to be taken away from them now that it has become a "hot property."

HUD's disposal of publicly owned dwellings extends to moderate-income developments as well. Many such projects, built primarily under interest-subsidy programs (Section 236 and the earlier Section 221(d)(3) program), as well as single-family homes built under the infamous Section 235 program, have come into HUD's unwilling hands, as insurers of mortgages upon which owners defaulted. Despite federal housing amendments requiring that such units be disposed of in a manner that insures lower-income occupancy, HUD continues to keep many vacant, allows the demolition of others, and disposes of still others without the necessary controls and subsidies to keep them in the subsidized moderate- and low-income sector.

## Making the Poor Pay Even More

One fundamental feature of federally subsidized housing programs has by and large been that people pay according to ability—a pretty dramatic departure from the dominant economic philosophy in the United States, and half of you-know-who's formula. The percentage of income people pay has been creeping up over the years, from slightly under 20 percent to a 25 percent standard (with some minor exceptions) throughout the 1960s and 1970s. The Reagan administration has decided that the poor should pay 30 percent of their income to live in subsidized housing. This change was introduced in 1981, with existing tenants to pay 1 percent more each year over a five-year period until the 30 percent figure was reached, and new tenants to pay 30 percent right off the bat. The change directly extracts money from the pockets of the poor so the government will have to pay less, and in dollar terms its impact is staggering. The figures that accompanied this 1982 budget proposal showed that during the first year, the "savings" to the government (i.e., extraction from the poor) would amount to $232 million; in 1983 it would be $538 million; in 1984, $1.018 billion; in 1985, $1.747 billion; and in 1986, $2.445 billion—a total just short of $6 billion over the five-year period.

The 1983 housing bill passed by Congress provided some rent relief for public housing and Section 8 tenants by increasing the standard deduction allowed for minors and elderly households, thereby reducing the base income to which the 30 percent figure is applied. But the exaction was still enormous. The administration, by contrast, had proposed eliminating most current deductions and exclusions, such as day-care expenses for working mothers and extraordinary medical expenses. On several occasions it also has attempted, fortunately without success, to convince Congress to amend the food stamp law so that the cash value of food stamps can be counted as income for purposes of determining public housing and Section 8 rents—in effect taxing these desperately needed food benefits by 30 percent. About half of all households in public housing and Section 8 housing receive food stamps. Even the Republican-controlled Senate Agriculture Committee rejected this draconian move. Since poorer households get more food stamps, the move, of course, would have stuck the lowest-income households with the biggest rent increases, in absolute terms and relative to their rent-paying capacities.

(Michael E. Stone, in Chapter 3, presents a critique of the entire concept that low-income households can afford 20, 25, or 30 percent, or any arbitrary across-the-board percentage-of-income figure for housing.)

## Housing Allowances: A Bad Idea Whose Time May Have Come

To the extent that the Reagan administration intends to continue a federal role in adding to the supply of housing available to the poor, it is to be primarily through housing allowances: consumer-oriented (demand-side) payments that permit low-income households to compete more effectively for available vacancies in the private sector. It is a cheaper way of providing housing aid, although, as will be seen, it does not do the same thing as past housing programs. Housing allowances also reduce government's role and conform to the market model of sovereign consumers purchasing goods and services in a responsive market ruled by the mutually beneficent laws of supply and demand. In theory at least, there is a certain amount of common sense to this approach: To the extent that the nation's housing problem is increasingly an income problem (i.e., consumers' incomes are inadequate to afford existing available housing), rather than one of a substandard housing stock, what government ought to be doing is providing housing-targeted income supplements.

What the impact would be of substituting housing allowances for previous programs that directly added to the supply of low-rent housing (such as public housing and the Section 8 New Construction and Rehabilitation programs) is predictable. In the early 1980s the major findings were released from one of the country's largest and longest social science experiments ever: EHAP, HUD's Experimental Housing Allowance Program (Abrams, 1983; Bradbury and Downs, 1981; Hartman, 1983a, 1983b; Struyk and Bendick, 1981). EHAP was launched in 1970, under the Nixon administration, a massive laboratory involving 30,000 lower-income households at 12 sites across the country, who received housing allowances for 3 to 10 years, at a total cost of $160 million. Various subexperiments were constructed around three major issues: supply effects, demand effects, and how such a program might be administered.

The most salient findings from the EHAP research, in terms of immediate policy concerns, would seem to be the following:

• Where the program is made available to all who meet eligibility criteria—the Supply Experiment, mounted in the Green Bay (Wisconsin) and South Bend (Indiana) metropolitan areas—after four years only 42 percent of eligible renter households and 33 percent of eligible homeowner households participated (homeowners were included only in the Supply Experiment).

• In the Demand Experiment sites, Pittsburgh and Phoenix, where extraordinary outreach efforts were made to contact a limited number of eligible renter households—the Demand Experiment did not offer benefits to all eligible renters—the participation rate among eligible renters contacted was a lowly 27 percent.

• While *enrollment* rates were higher for minority households and those with lower incomes, rates of *participation* (eligible enrollees who actually received housing allowance payments)—which in most of the experimental variations, as noted below, required meeting minimum housing standards—were lower for minority, poorer, and large households and those living in poor-quality dwelling units.

• In most of the subexperiments, participation in the program was made dependent on meeting a housing-quality standard. If the household was not already living in standard housing, the standard could be met by moving or having the defects cured. Where no housing-quality standard had to be met (that is, where recipients could live in any housing of their choosing within the experiment area), participation rates were 100 to 160 percent higher than among households that had to meet a housing-quality standard. Poorer, minority, and large households, and those living in poorer-quality housing, were even less likely to participate when forced to meet a housing-quality standard. When housing allowance payments were not tied to a requirement that housing standards be met, approximately two-thirds of the recipients did not live in standard housing.

• The EHAP payments (averaging $43 and $59 per month for the two Demand Experiment sites and $72 and $78 per month for the two Supply Experiment sites) could be used to purchase additional housing services (more and better space, a better location, etc.), to relieve the extremely burdensome proportion of household income most recipients were devoting to housing (*averaging* 40 percent prior to participation), or the benefits could be split between these two purposes. To the extent the second goal was chosen, the housing allowance of course is virtually identical to an income supplement: The housing allowance in effect replaces income otherwise allocated to housing, and the family's disposable income is increased by that amount, which is allocated to nonshelter consumption items. Data from the EHAP Demand Experiment (the one designed to test consumer behavior most carefully) show that only one-fourth of the allowance payment was used to obtain better housing; the vast majority was spent on other goods and services.

• Participation in the EHAP program triggered little mobility: Very few households chose to incur the financial and psychosocial costs and uncertainties of moving, or saw moving as a realistic possibility, given the limited

duration of the allowances (3 years under the Demand Experiment, 2 years under the Administrative Agency Experiment, 10 years under the Supply Experiment).
• The program did not produce negative market effects, that is, inflation in rents. Nor did it produce any positive market effects—stimulation of new construction or rehabilitation (beyond the minor repairs—requiring a cash outlay of considerably less than $100 on the average—which the housing-quality requirement sometimes triggered).

Although some analysts concluded that EHAP proved housing allowances were noninflationary (Struyk and Bendick, 1981, 15; Harold Watts in Bradbury and Downs, 1981, 49), the relatively small size of the program and the fact that recipients spent so little of their allowance money on housing render such conclusions noncredible. In Green Bay and South Bend, where supply effects were tested, the program increased total countywide rent expenditures by a minuscule 1.2 percent, hardly something that could be expected to induce an inflationary effect. EHAP in no way answered the question whether a housing allowance program that aided substantially everyone who needed help and operated in such a way as to encourage additional tenant expenditures for housing would inspire landlords to raise their prices. Given what is known of the housing market and how suppliers operate under the profit system, it is hard to maintain that a substantial amount of this federal housing subsidy would not, absent government controls on the market, wind up lining landlords' pockets.

Economist John Kain noted, in response to criticism, that

> market conditions in Green Bay and South Bend were qualitatively different from those found in large, old, decaying urban centers such as Detroit, Cleveland, or Newark . . . , HUD contracted with the Urban Institute and the National Bureau of Economic Research to adapt their housing market simulation models to an analysis of the probable market impacts of a full-scale housing allowance. . . . Both the Urban Institute and National Bureau of Economic Research simulations indicated that a full-scale earmarked allowance program might cause significant rent increases for both recipients and nonrecipients, and the bureau simulations pointed out the possibility that such a program might trigger large price declines and extensive abandonment in the worst neighborhoods. (Bradbury and Downs, 1981, 358–59)

As one of the volumes on the EHAP project summarized it, "the ironic result [is] that the greater the need for physical improvements in a community's housing inventory, the less its residents are likely to participate in a housing allowance program that includes physical standards" (Bradbury and Downs, 1981, 379). EHAP shows that if you live in good housing to begin with, housing allowances are pretty much an income supplement; if you don't live in good housing, you are not likely to be able to take advantage of the program either by moving to a better unit or inducing your landlord to remove code violations (assuming the program has a housing standard, which the administration's proposed program will have).

The supply of decent, moderately priced vacant units available to people living in substandard quarters does not exist in most areas—the overall vacancy rate is too low, the vacant units that exist do not match the need (by size, rent level, tenure, location) of those who need them and the prevalence of discrimination (on the basis of race, household size or composition, and source of income) keeps units out of the reach of needy households.

Highly relevant are the findings of studies of HUD's Section 8 Existing Housing program (which subsidizes rents in existing sound units). A January 1982 report by Pratt Institute Center for Community and Environmental Development showed that 27 percent of New York City residents who were issued Section 8 Existing Housing certificates since 1976 were unable to put them to use, and that in the 1980–82 period, that proportion had grown to 36 percent, in line with the city's ever-shrinking vacancy rates. Minority households and families with children were least able to find a suitable unit to which they could apply their Section 8 rent certificate (DeGiovanni and Brooks, 1982). And a 1979 General Accounting Office inspection of a sample of Section 8 Existing Housing units in Massachusetts, Illinois, Georgia, Arizona, and California revealed that "42 percent contained one or more conditions which violated Federal housing quality standards and/or endangered the life, health, safety, or welfare of the occupants or the public" and that "conditions in 18 percent of the homes were so serious that they were not considered decent, safe, and sanitary" (U.S. Comptroller General, GAO, 1979, ii).

Also relevant are the few studies that exist of the housing conditions of families receiving public assistance (which in effect is a housing allowance program, with little or no systematic official attention paid to how recipients fare in the housing market); each state's public-assistance grant level has an imputed element that covers housing costs, or a portion thereof. A 1969 U.S. Department of Health, Education and Welfare study concluded that "on the basis of available data, it is estimated that at least one-half of all assistance recipients live in housing which is deteriorated or dilapidated, unsafe, insanitary, or overcrowded" (U.S. HEW, 1969). And a more recent and localized statistic, from a special 1981 Census Bureau survey of New York City's rental housing market, is that 47 percent of all renter families receiving public assistance are living in housing in need of rehabilitation (Stegman, 1981, 9).

Nor is moving any guarantee that one's lot will be improved through receipt of a housing allowance (and in any case many families do not want to incur the financial and psychosocial costs of moving). The EHAP results indicate that "over half of the households initially failing [housing quality] requirements, who moved over a two-year program period, moved to units which also failed to pass" (Struyk and Bendick, 1981, 111). And the size of the allowance, the fact that it will be available for only a limited duration, and the fact that not everyone in a given building will get one, all mean that landlords are not likely to respond to additional demand dollars by improving their substandard units.

Regarding the size of the housing allowance, obviously a key factor in how useful it will be, the Reagan administration's proposed 1986 budget calls for a one-year freeze on "fair market rents" (the figure which, according to local market studies, is needed to get decent housing) in both the Section 8 Existing Housing and voucher programs. Thus, in areas of rising rents (i.e., most if not all areas), within a year the allowance would prove insufficient, even if one were lucky enough originally to find something at a cost below prevailing rent levels.

In short, there is no reason to believe that housing allowances will work, if by "work" one implies doing what past government housing programs have done, however imperfectly: Provide people with decent housing at rents they can afford. If by "work," however, is meant getting the government out of the housing sector, then it may be a different story. In a revealing and highly disturbing interview, published in the November 6, 1981, *Washington Post*, right after release of the Interim Report of the President's Commission on Housing, recommending housing allowances, HUD Secretary Samuel Pierce let out the administration's game plan, although delayed by a couple of years: "We hope by 1984 or '85, that we will have interest rates down enough that it will stimulate housing so that we won't have to use the voucher system. We hope that maybe we'll even get out of that." More recently, and more directly, a HUD Deputy Assistant Secretary stated at a panel discussion during the Urban League's 1985 annual convention, in Washington, D.C.: "We're basically backing out of the business of housing, period." It's obviously easier to terminate the historical federal role in housing lower-income families by getting rid of programs that have long-term commitments, like public housing and Section 8, substituting very flexible short-term commitments and gradually phasing them out. In its statement to the President's Commission on Housing (dated December 3, 1981), opposing the commission's voucher proposal, the National Housing Law Project stated:

> Any voucher program which is adopted must be an entitlement program, must not be the sole federal housing program, cannot be a replacement for existing public housing and Section 8 projects, must be a supplement to, not a replacement for income maintenance programs, must include provisions guaranteeing tenants' rights [as a result of much litigation over the years, public housing tenants have a range of rights generally not available to private-market tenants under most states' landlord–tenant laws] and must be distributed fairly.

But there's about as much chance of the Reagan administration adopting a housing allowance program with these characteristics as there is of getting it to cancel the MX missile in favor of a larger food stamp and Medicaid program.

One can certainly get behind using the existing housing stock more efficiently to provide low-income subsidized housing, if there is an adequate supply of such vacancies in a local housing market. But it is important to recognize that lots of these vacancies are substandard and that those who own and control them have profit maximization and not social goals as their motivation. And so programs must be shaped that use the available stock in ways that insure substandard units will be brought up to code; that landlords will not rent-gouge; that tenants are able to pay the cost of such housing without depriving themselves of other of life's basics; that insofar as possible people will not have to move from their homes and neighborhoods to get decent housing conditions; and that low-income homeowners also get needed help.

Beyond that, there are groups and areas for which the existing housing stock can provide little help, such as large families, migrant workers, Native Americans living on reservations, the handicapped, and large parts of rural America. Direct construction programs still will be needed if we are ever going to reach the congressionally mandated National Housing Goal of "a decent home and a suitable living environment for every American family." As EHAP has shown, short-term housing vouchers will not motivate anyone to produce new or substantially rehabilitated units, which, for all their defects, the older programs such as public housing and Section 8 did, with their 15- to 40-year subsidy commitments and direct public construction.

# The Retreat from Fair Housing[2]

While not a central feature of the Reagan administration's assault on federal housing programs—in part because the issue has always been of secondary importance in federal housing policy—housing discrimination should be discussed in terms of what the administration is and is not doing. The more general moves on the federal low-income housing programs and their beneficiaries, described above, have special impact on minorities. Because of their very low incomes, minority households disproportionately need and make use of traditional low-rent housing programs; thus, subsidy cutbacks and moves to dispose of existing low-rent developments have the largest impact on black and Hispanic households. Having to pay a large proportion of their income in order to live in subsidized housing also has a greater negative effect on minorities than others, due to their very low incomes. And because of the discriminatory workings of the private housing market, reliance on housing allowances or vouchers means that nonwhites will have to deal directly with discrimination as they attempt to use their subsidies in that market.

Beyond the more general effects, the Reagan administration has directly harmed minorities by its attacks on fair housing programs—programs that are all the more necessary when vacancy rates are tight and rent levels and housing prices are soaring. The specifics are these:

• Weakening of the Voluntary Affirmative Marketing Agreements (VAMAs), which HUD and the National Association of Realtors developed in 1975 to foster positive efforts to market homes in a nondiscriminatory way, through creation of Community Housing Resource Boards. Although voluntary action can be a useful supplement to rigorous enforcement of fair housing laws, there must be some sense of forcefulness even in programs that rely on voluntary cooperation, and HUD's weakening of the VAMA approach in late 1981 undercut this modest effort substantially. Under these Reagan administration amendments, the names of participating realtors cannot be publicized; representatives of fair housing and civil rights groups are subject to restrictive conditions that effectively bar them from membership on Community Housing Resource Boards; and these boards are prohibited from sponsoring or funding "testing" programs whereby discriminatory actions can be revealed by having matched white and minority prospective renters and purchasers approach given sellers, agents, and landlords.

• Cutbacks in the collection of data on race and sex of program beneficiaries, which obviously is essential to enforcing federal civil rights mandates. To an extent, this was carried out persuant to more general requirements of the Paperwork Reduction Act (which antedates the Reagan administration), but the way this act has been used by administrative agencies (which usually are not directly responsible for civil rights monitoring and enforcement) has the effect, if not the intent, of undermining enforcement of antidiscrimination laws.

• The more general retreat of the Department of Justice from active civil rights enforcement, crucial to effective use of Title VIII (the fair housing provisions) of the 1968 Civil Rights Act, under which HUD has no enforcement powers of its own. Although the number of Title VIII cases filed by the Justice Department's Civil Rights Division never has been very large (20 to 32 annually up to 1981), the Reagan administration's Justice Department has virtually abandoned this tool in its first two years, filing just three Title VIII suits, none of which, in concept or settlement, has the broad impact or precedent-setting value of many earlier suits. The department has announced it will no longer institute actions challenging discriminatory land-use practices, such as exclusionary zoning, and has abandoned efforts of the previous administration to incorporate housing remedies into school desegregation cases. It has also enunciated a requirement that discriminatory intent rather than effect be the standard of proof in exclusionary land-use cases, despite a federal court's warning, in *Metropolitan Housing Development Corp.* v. *Village of Arlington Heights* (558 F.2d 1283) that "a strict focus on intent permits racial discrimination to go unpunished in the absence of evidence of overt bigotry. As overtly bigoted behavior becomes more unfashionable, evidence of intent has become harder to find. But this does not mean that racial discrimination has disappeared."

As summarized in the recent report of the Citizens Commission on Civil Rights (1983, 78): "The Reagan Administration's Justice Department has dramatically slowed the pace of fair housing litigation and made policy changes likely to render much of the litigation that is brought ineffective."

The advent of the Reagan administration in 1981 marked a fundamental shift in federal housing policy. The philosophical and practical retreat from an aggressive government role in alleviating the housing problems of those the market cannot serve has been dramatic, as evidenced by the programs the administration has abandoned and attempted to abandon, as well as those it has introduced and proposed. What the consequences of the second Reagan administration will be for the future of housing in America cannot be firmly predicted. Much depends on the actions of Congress and various interest groups. Apart from the refusal by Congress to go along with everything the administration has proposed, there has been disturbingly little organized activity to protect past accomplishments of government housing programs. Despite the key role of housing in people's lives, we have yet to see a level of public education and political organizing commensurate with the clear need to withstand this attack and mount positive programs to advance and improve on what has been done over the past 50 years.

## Acknowledgments

Cushing Dolbeare of the National Low Income Housing Coalition, Florence Roisman of the National Housing Law Project, and Glenda Sloane of the Center for National Policy Review provided useful commentary on an earlier draft of this chapter.

## Notes

1. Local housing authorities were actually allowed to build up reserve funds for renovation, but in the 1950s, as these funds began to grow, the feds decided in effect to appropriate them, by requiring revision of the annual contributions contracts to lower the federal contribution. But, as noted, the change in public housing tenant composition and income structure, combined with rising maintenance costs and growing obsolescence of projects, made such reserves a thing of the past by the late 1950s.

2. This section is drawn largely from Chapter 4 of the 1983 report of the Citizens Commission on Civil Rights, other portions of which are excerpted as Chapter 18 of this book. For more detail and the original sources, readers should refer to the report itself.

# Part III | Strategies for Change

# 22 The Tenants' Movement and American Politics

*John Atlas*
*Peter Dreier*

*Clearly, change in the U.S. housing system is necessary. Furthermore, if the govern-
ment has contributed to the problem by serving the interests of housing producers-
investors, then one would have to be skeptical about appeals to the government based
merely on reason or equity. Truly progressive, fundamental change in the housing
system, as elsewhere in the society, is not likely to come about solely through government-sponsored reforms. Such change must involve broad-based, grassroots mass
mobilization.*

*From this general "organizing" perspective come a range of questions: Who should
be organized and around what issues? What are the inherent difficulties in or obstacles
to organizing? What reforms are the most critical and the most progressive at this time?
How do short-term reforms fit into long-term strategies for fundamental change?*

*This chapter looks to organized tenants as the crucial actors in stimulating change.
According to this view, tenants, whose housing situation is substantially worse than
that of homeowners, are now ready to assume a key role in building a political
movement to alleviate the housing crisis. Although historically their organizations
have not played a powerful role in shaping new directions for housing, several
relatively recent conditions may make them a more viable potential change agent.*

Tenants, long a sleeping giant in American politics, are beginning to wake
up. A new generation of middle-class tenants, seeing the "American
Dream" of owning a house slipping away, is joining the urban poor in a
growing renters' rights revolt across the country. Whereas two-thirds of all
American households could afford to buy a single-family home in the 1950s
(using the one-quarter of one's income rule-of-thumb), less than 10 percent
can do so today (Donohue, 1982). According to *Mortgage Banking* (magazine of the Mortgage Bankers Association of America):

> Households that entered the housing market from 1950 to 1973 experienced
> little difficulty in making a home purchase. Those entering the market from

This chapter was originally published as "Mobilize or Compromise? The Tenants' Movement
and American Politics," in *America's Housing Crisis: What is to Be Done?* ed. Chester
Hartman, Boston: Routledge & Kegan Paul, 1983. Reprinted by permission of the Institute for
Policy Studies.

1973 to 1978, having virtually the same income after adjustment for inflation, were forced to sacrifice to a considerable degree in order to become homeowners. And many of those entering the market in recent years have effectively been told that there is no room for them in the housing market. (Donohue, 1982)

Even the middle-class households that resist renting and decide to buy a home despite the obstacles find that the American Dream is not what they were promised. Couples are working two, even three, jobs to keep making the payments on their homes. Even so, mortgages in arrears and foreclosures have both risen steadily. A growing number of people simply cannot make it as homeowners. They will find themselves renters once again (Brooks, 1982; Husock, 1981). [*See also Chapter 3 by Michael E. Stone.*]

With the nationwide rental vacancy rate at its lowest point in three decades, construction of new rental housing almost at a standstill, and rents skyrocketing, tenants are finding themselves with their backs to the wall. They have lost the option to move. With a greater stake in their apartments, America's tenants are proving more willing to fight rent increases, condominium conversions, arbitrary evictions, and unsafe, poorly maintained buildings. Their activism is changing the relative bargaining positions of landlords and tenants. It is adding a new ingredient to the urban political scene. And it is a symptom of the deepening crisis of a political and economic system that relies on the private sector to provide decent, affordable housing.

The situation facing tenants has never been rosy, but as long as it was confined to the poor and the near-poor, society did not have to address it as a serious problem—unless, of course, the poor started to riot, as they did in the 1960s. Growing numbers of middle-income households, shut out of the homebuying market, are now facing the powerlessness and frustration that comes with renting. They may not have the same problems as slum dwellers—such as rats, roaches, and lead paint—but they still face many of the same problems that come with being at the mercy of landlords in a tight housing market. They face escalating rents, the constant threat of eviction, and poorly maintained buildings. Americans who were brought up with the notion that households should spend roughly one-quarter of their incomes for housing are now finding that they must spend 50 percent or more of their incomes just to keep a roof over their heads.

Traditionally, tenants have had few rights that would allow them to improve these conditions. Tenant–landlord law remains exceedingly biased against tenants, still a remnant of its agrarian and feudal origins (Rose, 1973). Except in New Jersey (which has a statewide "just cause" eviction law), in public housing, and in cities with rent control laws, landlords can evict tenants for almost any reason at all, not only failure to pay rent, and they can use the power of the courts to back them up. Besides the right to evict during the term of the lease (for nonpayment), landlords can force tenants to move at the end of the lease period for almost any reason whatsoever. (One consequence of the tight rental housing market since the late 1970s has been the decline in the number of landlords who even offer leases. Increasing numbers of renters are tenants "at will.") Homeowners are more secure; mortgage lenders and city officials can take possession of a home (the equivalent of a tenant's eviction) only if the homeowner fails to make payments to the bank or to the tax collectors.

Since the 1970s, in response to tenant protest, a number of states have adopted laws giving tenants more rights and landlords more responsibilities. These include the "implied warranty of habitability" (which guarantees tenants the right to minimum standards of decent housing and that they will not have to pay for "essential services" that they do not receive), and protection against "retaliatory evictions" for complaining to the landlord or local authorities about building maintenance. Other legal reforms deal with security deposits, the right to withhold rents, utility shut-offs, lockouts and seizure of tenants' possessions, standard leases, and housing discrimination (Blumberg and Grow, 1978; Rose, 1973). But because tenant-landlord laws are enacted at the state and local levels, these reforms have not been adopted uniformly; they exist only in areas where tenant activism has been strongest. Many tenants, therefore, are not covered by such laws.

In large part, what is missing is a broad political movement willing to fight for decent housing policy. The present housing crisis is a result of the failure of progressive forces to mobilize a majority for reform. It is a political question, a question of which groups in society will steer the rudder of government policy. Once again, the banking and real estate industries have a stake in the present policy of providing government incentives to the private housing industry. And once again, the poor and the working class—but this time, with the addition of the disenchanted, inflation-pinched middle class—have a stake in more progressive policy. This coalition can no longer go the route of making compromises with builders, bankers, and land speculators, as the progressive coalition did in the 1940s, and as many well-intentioned liberals continue to do today. It is no longer enough to seek a few more rent subsidy funds, a few more mortgage write-downs, and a few more public housing units. That route has been tried and found wanting. So today progressives are confronted with the same choice: *to mobilize or compromise?* If we are not to repeat the mistakes of the past, a broad political constituency must be mobilized to influence and elect government officials around a national commitment to solving the housing crisis by directing public funds into construction of decent, affordable housing for all. Political mobilization is the only route to a real housing solution.

The growing mobilization of tenants during the past decade is a symptom of the housing crisis and a symbol of that new direction. It is showing an increasing number of the nation's 60 million tenants that things will only get better if they organize politically to *expand* their rights and *protect their housing conditions.* On its own, the tenants' movement cannot overhaul American housing policy toward a more comprehensive solution, but it can move part of the way in that direction. Ultimately, we believe, it can form a political coalition with the labor movement, the senior citizens and consumer movements, the women's and environmental movements, and even the peace and human rights movement, to redirect national policy and priorities toward meeting basic human needs instead of wasting them on welfare for the rich, the corporations, and the Pentagon.

## The Sleeping Giant Awakens

Conditions appear ripe for the building of a political movement of housing consumers, particularly renters. With the proper leadership, tactics, and strategies, tenants could be organized into a relatively powerful movement capable of contending for power and advancing programs that solve the housing crisis.

But there are skeptics. Tenants, they say, are a difficult group to organize politically for a variety of reasons [*see Chapter 23 by John Cowley*]. For one, tenants' organizations have historically been difficult to sustain because of the transient nature of tenancy or because tenants viewed themselves as being on a way-station toward homeownership (Dreier, 1982a; Heskin, 1981a; Lipsky, 1970). The difficulty is compounded because to most people housing is a private matter, a refuge for the individual and family from the ravages of the work world. The workplace is a source of drudgery or competition, a continual test of one's worth and self-esteem. Physically as well as psychologically, one returns home to relax, to retreat, to get away from the pressures of work. People resist coming home after work to fight their landlords or mortgage lenders or to attend a city council meeting. Finally, housing, unlike work, is rarely seen as a collective, or social, activity. The relations of consumption—food, clothing, shelter—are more fragmented than the relations of production. As Weinbaum and Bridges (1976) note, the consumer, unlike the worker, "has no singular and obvious antagonist, but many antagonists: the state, the supermarket, the landlord, etc." Even if one socializes with one's neighbors and fellow tenants, improvements in housing are considered individual matters. In housing, there is a strong "do-it-yourself" ideology. One either improves one's own housing or moves out to bigger, better accommodations.

But times have changed. A number of conditions make the emergence of "tenant consciousness" and tenant organizing more likely. Four factors in particular have made a significant difference in increasing the likelihood of tenant protests in the United States.

The first has been the explosion of grassroots protest during the past decade. The image of the 1970s as a quiet "me decade," a reaction against the noisy protests of the 1960s, is misleading. Not only did many of the civil rights, student, and antiwar activists remain political through the 1970s, but a much broader spectrum of Americans joined the struggle for more rights and freedoms. Throughout the decade, environmental, women's, consumer, senior citizens', human rights, and neighborhood movements emerged, mobilizing millions of Americans around a wide variety of concerns and creating a political climate of what sociologist Daniel Bell (1976) calls "rising entitlements." There was, once again, a climate of protest in the nation, not just among the poor, but among the working and middle classes as well. This momentum carried through into the 1980s, with protest movements against nuclear arms, nuclear power, the dumping of toxic chemicals, and the Reagan administration's cutbacks of social and welfare programs, consumer and environmental protection, occupational safety, and education. Many of the people who distrusted the radical protesters of the 1960s were among those joining the protests of the 1970s and 1980s.

This growing climate of protest emerged gradually out of changing values. For one thing, the period taught people that "leaders" and "experts" were not always to be trusted, and that they would have to rely on themselves to protect their rights, because the "best and the brightest" often showed little regard for the everyday routines and values of America's vast middle. For example, the urban renewal programs of the 1960s, allegedly set up to "clear" the slums, actually bulldozed stable, working-class neighborhoods (Fellman, 1973; Fried, 1973; Gans, 1962b). As Boyte (1980) observes, "The experiences through which people replenish and sustain themselves resemble more and more a kind of 'social factory' where they are dominated and exploited as taxpayers and consumers, like they are exploited in the workplace." Infringement on these everyday routines thus became the focal point of protest. Tenant organizations, which deal with a basic necessity within which so much of everyday life goes on, draw a potential strength from this reality—far greater, in some respects, than what can be drawn from the typical exploitation of most consumer–seller relationships. Not surprisingly, women are disproportionately found among the leadership of tenant protest groups (Lawson and Barton, 1980).

The second condition was the increase in long-term tenancies. As the costs of homeownership skyrocketed during the 1970s, many tenants became locked into renting. For an increasing number of families, particularly those of the postwar "baby boom" generation, the American Dream was beyond their reach (Donohue, 1982). An increasing number, including the growing number of single-person, single-parent, and elderly households, would find themselves spending a long time as tenants. Gradually, and unwillingly, they began to think of themselves as long-term, rather than temporary, renters. In addition, even as tenants, they were no longer as transient as tenants once were. When housing choices are abundant, and vacancy rates high, tenants who do not like their apartments vote with their feet: They move (Fredland, 1974; Goodman, 1978; Rossi, 1955). This transiency had always made it difficult to organize tenant groups and to develop stable memberships and leaders. It also led to lower levels of political involvement and less of a stake in community issues. For example, tenants have much lower rates of voter registration and voting than do homeowners (Alford and Scoble, 1968; U.S. Bureau of the Census, 1979). By the mid-1970s, however, tenants had fewer options. The low vacancy rates make it more difficult for tenants to find another apartment and more likely they will stay where they are, even when they are dissatisfied with their apartments. With both traditional options—moving to another apartment or to a single-family home—less available, tenants begin to have a greater stake in the conditions of their apartment and to develop "tenant consciousness."

The third condition was the growing number of tenants living in large buildings or apartment complexes owned by absentee companies. During the 1970s, the economics of apartment ownership and management began to change. Until then, the vast majority of apartment owners were relatively amateur landlords who owned one, or just a few, small apartment buildings. For many, it was not a full-time job, but a sideline to earn extra money. Many lived in their own apartment buildings, knew the tenants on a first-name basis, knew their problems, and might even peg rent levels to their tenants' ability to pay. Such personal, paternalistic relationships between tenants and landlords, although often strained, tended to inhibit tenant activism. It is difficult, in that situation, to see the landlord as an "enemy": He may not have much more money than the tenant. Also, it is hard to organize tenants when only a few of them share the same building or landlord (Gans, 1962b; Krohn and Tiller, 1969; Vaughan, 1968).

During the late 1960s and early 1970s there was a boom of suburban garden apartment complexes and of high-rise apartment buildings in cities (Neutze, 1968; Schafer, 1974). One big reason for the growth in large apartment buildings was the urban renewal and federally subsidized apartment programs. Apartments rented by middle-income tenants were part of large buildings and complexes increasingly owned by absentee owners and run by professional property managers. These changes altered the nature of tenant–landlord relations. They became more and more depersonalized. Rent checks were sent to faceless professional management firms rather than handed or mailed to an individual landlord. Absentee owners, who buy apartments for their short-term tax advantages, have less incentive than live-in landlords to make repairs and maintain their buildings. As Roger Starr (1979) has noted, "Locked into a long-term relationship with someone whom he [or she] usually never sees, the tenant cannot truly understand why he [or she] should be asked to pay again and again for something that the landlord already made." A large number of tenants under the same roof, or within the same complex, who have the same landlord, creates the potential for the emergence of a critical mass of tenants who share grievances, form committees, and organize a tenants' group. This depersonalization of tenant–landlord relations and the growing scale of apartment life enhanced the potential for the development of tenant consciousness and activism. From our observations, most tenant activism is found in the large buildings and complexes. This situation is similar to the emergence of industrial unionism, which only occurred when the large absentee-owned factory— with a large number of workers employed by the same company—replaced the small mill where the employees and owner worked side by side.

The fourth condition is the changing role and perception of government and its relationship to big business. Increasingly, Piven and Cloward argue, the state has become "the main arena of class conflict. Working people who once looked to the marketplace as the arena for action on their economic grievances and aspirations now look more often to the state" (Piven and Cloward, 1982, 125). Americans expect the government to protect them from the worst abuses of the private "free market" economy. For the three decades after World War II, the government subsidized the private housing industry with mortgage insurance, roadbuilding programs that opened up the suburbs to new housing development, and tax breaks for homeowners and for rental housing construction. The steady, indeed dramatic, increase in homeownership during this period—from roughly 44 percent of all households in 1940 to about 65 percent in the early 1970s—in effect "co-opted" the potential for a significant tenants' movement. For those left behind in the rush to the suburbs—the urban poor, the minorities, the elderly—the private housing industry had little to offer. Public housing provided only a minimal safety valve for the poor. After the urban riots of the 1960s, the government increased its rent subsidy and low-income homeownership programs, but these met only a tiny fraction of the overall need.

The new realities of the 1980s, however, make it impossible for the private housing industry and the government to respond in the same way. Affordable housing, like health care, will increasingly come to be seen as a basic right, an "entitlement," that government should make available to all. Obviously, housing consumers will have the most to gain from this, but some sectors of the business community will also be concerned with rising housing costs. Like health care and education, housing is part of the "social wage"— the cost of keeping the labor force able to produce and reproduce itself, so that employers can have a steady workforce. Large corporate employers do not want to pay higher wages simply to permit their workers to put a roof over their heads. Already, in some areas of the country, employers are alarmed because rising housing costs are driving away, or making it difficult to attract, skilled employees (particularly professional-level employees). Some companies are even offering long-term reduced mortgages, or down payments, to lure potential employees to move (*Business Week*, July 27, 1981; Lindsey, 1981). Most employers, however, do not want to directly subsidize these housing costs.

As the cost of housing continues to skyrocket, some sectors of the business community will call for "cost containment," as they have already done for the skyrocketing costs of health care. Of course, business leaders will resist direct government ownership and production of housing, as they have resisted excluding the private sector from participation in any national health care legislation. But the very call for government to "do something" about housing costs will push politicians into looking for new solutions. In this situation, the housing industry, particularly land speculators and landlords, is especially vulnerable.

Although the housing industry is not an isolated enclave within the overall economy, it is sufficiently distinct from the major manufacturing and service sectors. Indeed, it is this group whose interests have been subordinated when the larger needs of business production were at stake. During both world wars, national rent controls were adopted, promoted by the wartime planners from the corporate world over the objections of the private landlords (Lebowitz, 1981). Other capitalist countries have adopted much stricter controls on housing costs—particularly land, building materials, and financing. As pressure from tenants, homeowners, and segments of the business community mounts, politicians will find it in their political self-interest to jump on the bandwagon to control housing prices. The debate over national housing policy will open up discussion of more public control of housing. In the short term, though, policies like rent control will meet with more favor from large corporate employers concerned about rising housing costs for their employees. Much as the decades-long struggle for Medicare and Medicaid set the stage for the current round of debates over the structure of health care institutions and the "right" to decent, affordable health care, we can expect a protracted debate over housing, with private real estate interests increasingly on the defensive. These circumstances set the stage for major reforms.

## Tactics and Strategies

Tenant activism developed steadily during the 1970s and early 1980s. Tenant groups now exist in almost every city and many suburbs. These include building-level, citywide, and several statewide tenant groups. A National Tenants Union (NTU) was formed in 1980 to help coordinate the growing number of tenant activities. In 1975, tenant leaders founded the national magazine *Shelterforce* to report on and encourage tenant activism. The publication has helped to give the movement a sense of identity and coordination, and its editors (along with New Jersey and New York tenant leaders) took the first steps to form the NTU. In addition, many of the grassroots, Alinsky-style community organizations that mushroomed in the 1970s, in low-income and working-class neighborhoods, took on tenant organizing as part of their multi-issue agendas. These groups—such as the Association of Community Organizations for Reform Now (ACORN), Massachusetts Fair Share, and Hartford Areas Rally Together (HART)—had a concern with the problems of older urban neighborhoods; this necessitated some focus on tenant problems. Also, the growing number of activist senior citizen organizations (e.g., the Gray Panthers and National Council of Senior Citizens) around the country made tenant problems one of their priorities, a reflection of the worsening housing situation among older Americans (Cliffe, 1982).

Just as the early stages of the modern labor movement fought immediately for "bread and butter" issues (wages and hours, job security, working conditions), so too does the current tenants' movement focus on defending tenants against skyrocketing rents, arbitrary evictions, unsafe building conditions, and interference with the right to organize. Their tactics include rent strikes, picketing and demonstrations, legal challenges, and electoral politics. The battleground includes tenants' demands for rent control, restriction on condominium conversions, building safety and maintenance, enforcement of housing codes, protection against landlords' "arson-for-profit," greater tenant voice in building management, and greater freedom to organize. The improvements in tenant–landlord law cited earlier—such as the "warranty of habitability" and "retaliatory eviction" protections—now make tenant organizing less risky.

It is possible to offer selective examples that provide some sense of the dynamics and range of tenant activism and landlord-tenant politics.

The success of the New Jersey Tenants Organization (NJTO)—with 80,000 dues-paying members, and an impressive string of electoral victories, plus the toughest tenant-landlord laws in the nation—serves as a model for the tenant movement around the country. NJTO was formed in 1969, with tenants from the middle-income suburbs near New York City living in large apartment complexes, as well as tenants from the slums of Newark and Passaic (Baar, 1977). From the outset, NJTO developed a three-pronged strategy to build "tenant power" in New Jersey. It combined (1) direct action tactics (such as rent strikes, demonstrations, picketing, and rallies) associated with grassroots organizing, to keep tenants in motion, heighten solidarity and give them media exposure, thus attracting the attention of politicians; (2) electoral politics, endorsing pro-tenant candidates for local and state elections, who would enact favorable tenants' rights legislation; and (3) litigation to establish protection for tenants engaged in direct action and to strengthen tenant–landlord laws. The organization's leadership recognized that all three were necessary to mobilize tenants and win victories. A strategy that relied too heavily on direct confrontations to win concessions from landlords and political officials would ultimately fail. The problem was that the rent strike, by itself, failed to expand tenants' rights and build stable organizations and grassroots leaders. It did not, for example, lead to any lasting control over rent increases or enforcement of housing codes. Tenants remained subject to arbitrary evictions at the end of their lease or, if they had no lease, on merely a 30-day notice. Many tenant leaders were harassed and evicted for organizing or even complaining to the building department or other government officials. Thus, NJTO recognized early the importance of developing tenants as a voting bloc and engaging in electoral politics.

The political response to NJTO's early efforts to register tenant voters and engage in election campaigns surprised even NJTO leaders. During the 1970s, NJTO engaged in direct action organizing while also winning court and legislative victories. It won pro-tenant laws on the issues of security deposits, evictions for cause, receivership, public disclosure of apartment ownership, and state income tax credits for tenants. More than 100 communities passed rent control laws. Tenant leaders were elected or appointed to serve on local rent control boards, watching out for tenant interests and encouraging tenant groups to monitor rent board hearings, formulas for rent increases, condo conversions, and landlords' claims of cost increases. Today there is a powerful and effective group of pro-tenant elected officials in the state legislature. Politicians respect tenants' bloc voting power and return NJTO's endorsement with other favors. For example, in return for tenants' help in electing him, the Essex County Executive, the second most powerful office in the state, provided funds to establish a Tenant Resource Center, which provides counseling and organizing help, and an NJTO leader was named to head the Center.

NJTO views election campaigns as organizing tools. At election time, the media and voters pay attention. Campaign workers can knock on doors and talk to people, not only about candidates and personalities, but also about tenant issues. Campaign workers help distribute NJTO literature and thus help promote the organization. An independent poll of New Jersey voters found that NJTO's endorsement gave politicians substantial credibility.

In California, tenants have organized along similar lines. . . . The tenants' movement exploded in 1978, following passage of Proposition 13, the tax-cutting amendment (Dreier, 1979). Throughout the state, tenants expected Proposition 13 to hold down rents; landlords even made such promises. But the anticipated windfall of rent rollbacks did not materialize; in fact, many of California's 3.5 million tenant households received notices of rent *increases* shortly after Proposition 13 passed. This set the stage for a significant tenant backlash. Throughout the state, tenants who had been hit by increases organized meetings to demand that landlords share their property-tax savings with tenants. Newspapers were filled with stories of outraged tenants, embarrassed landlords, and politicians jumping on the bandwagon. As public clamor mounted, some landlords agreed to reduce rents in order to avoid mandatory rollbacks and freezes. But tenant pressure did not subside. And when heavy real estate industry lobbying defeated a statewide bill requiring landlords to pass on their tax savings to tenants, the battle shifted to the local level. Tenant groups began to mobilize in communities across the state, demanding rent control. Experienced tenant leaders began to travel around helping local groups. A statewide organization, the California Housing Action and Information Network (CHAIN), was formed to coordinate local and statewide efforts. By 1981, more than 25 California communities, including San Francisco and Los Angeles, had already passed rent control laws, and more were considering them.

The tenants' movement has been particularly successful in Santa Monica, a coastal city of 90,000 in Ronald Reagan's backyard. In 1980, the tenants' movement there had passed strong rent and condominium conversion controls, and elected several members to the City Council. A year later, it secured a majority on the Council (its slate included a minister, two union activists, and several tenant activists), and Ruth Yannatta Goldway, the leader of Santa Monicans for Renters Rights, was elected mayor. Once in office, they enacted a radical program that went beyond tenant problems. This included increased police foot patrols and improved municipal services; increased fees on Shell's underground pipeline; prounion policies, such as requiring the union label on all city stationery and negotiating a favorable contract with municipal unions; and resolutions opposing U.S. intervention in El Salvador and nuclear proliferation. The City Council named citizen task forces on crime, women's issues, and other problems, and appointed progressive activists to such critical positions as city attorney, city manager, and other high-level jobs. The council also dramatically changed the city's development priorities; for example, it required one developer to build a park, day-care center, and affordable housing units in order to obtain a permit to build a highly profitable hotel complex near the waterfront (*Business Week*, Oct. 26, 1981; Shearer, 1982).

Although the tenants' movement is most advanced in New Jersey and California, similar activities have taken place in cities and suburbs across the country.

New York City is the home of the oldest and one of the most effective citywide tenant groups in the nation, the Metropolitan Council on Housing, started in 1959. In 1976, 86 percent of the 15,372 tenants in Coop City, a moderate-income housing project in the Bronx, participated in a 13-month rent strike, withholding over $25 million in rents (Newfield and DuBrul, 1977). The New York City tenants' movement spilled over to suburban Westchester, Rockland, and Nassau counties, where several communities passed rent-control laws (Lawson, 1980b) and to upstate New York as well. Local tenant groups in New York State formed a statewide New York State Tenants Coalition (recently renamed the New York State Tenants and Neighborhood Coalition) to coordinate activities and work together in Albany.

In Massachusetts, where tenant groups had been active throughout the 1970s in the older industrial cities, a statewide Massachusetts Tenants Organization was formed in 1981, triggering tenant activism in the middle-income suburbs and small towns, primarily around rent increases and condominium conversions. Rising rents spurred tenant activism for rent control in many other communities across the country. Washington, D.C., Boston, and Baltimore, for example, passed rent-control laws during the 1970s. (Baltimore's rent-control initiative, passed by the voters in 1979, was later overturned by the courts, on the grounds that only the city council, and not the voters, can enact this type of legislation, under Maryland's constitution.) In 1979 and 1980 alone, momentum for rent control existed in cities in at least 26 states (National Multi-Housing Council, 1981b).

Another emerging problem, the conversion of rental apartments to expensive condominiums, led to tenant activism in the late 1970s. Some 366,000 units were converted in the United States between 1970 and 1979, 71 percent of which took place in the last three years of that decade. At first concentrated in a few urban areas, by 1980, condo conversions soon spread to most metropolitan areas. Conversions are highly profitable for landlords, developers, and the banks that finance the process, but also result in widespread displacement. Most tenants cannot afford the price of condominiums, but with vacancy rates so low, they have difficulty finding another suitable apartment. As a result, tenant opposition has emerged to delay evictions by requiring a year or more notice, to prohibit evictions altogether, or to require tenant approval before conversions can proceed. By early 1981, some form of tenant protection against condo conversion had been passed in 24 states and the District of Columbia (Dreier and Atlas, 1981; National Multi-Housing Council, 1981a; U.S. HUD, 1980a).

While the tenants' movement has primarily been concerned with protecting tenants from rent increases and evictions, and with improving conditions, other issues have emerged as well. In Boston, for example, the Symphony Tenants Organizing Project (STOP) came together to investigate fires that had been sweeping the neighborhood for several years. It began by trying to enforce the housing codes, but soon discovered that many fires were deliberately set by landlords in order to collect the insurance from buildings that had been abandoned or allowed to deteriorate. By generating considerable publicity and pressure around this "arson-for-profit" scheme, STOP got action by law enforcement officials and insurance companies, including the arrest of 33 landlords, lawyers, insurance adjusters, public officials, and a state police lieutenant who had been bribed. STOP has continued to organize tenants around rent increases, evictions, and "gentrification."

In many older cities, abandoned housing has triggered tenant activism, including a tactic known as "squatting," in which tenants take over abandoned buildings and simply refuse to move (similar to workers' "sit-down" strikes). This tactic is used primarily by low-income tenants. Owners of these buildings often have not paid property taxes, so many abandoned buildings are owned by the city. Tenants have demanded that the city government allow them to fix these buildings with "sweat equity" and live there permanently. In 1981, ACORN (the Association of Community Organizations for Reform Now) coordinated a campaign along these lines in Philadelphia, Detroit, Boston, and several other cities [*see Chapter 25 by Seth Borgos*]. In New York City, several programs are designed to turn abandoned properties over to tenant and nonprofit community groups (Schur, 1980). [*See also Chapter 26 by Robert Kolodny.*] In most localities, squatting still meets official resistance, eviction, and penalties.

Some tenant groups have organized as unions, seeking collective bargaining between tenants and landlords. Typically, this strategy is in response to rent increases and poor maintenance. Tenants engage in a rent strike, as well as demonstrations and picketing, to force the landlord to sit down and negotiate with the tenants' group. Tenants hope that the landlord's legal fees, the withheld rents, and public embarrassment (one Boston group spread "wanted" posters, with the landlord's photograph and name on them, throughout the city) will force landlords to bargain. Because tenants risk eviction for such actions, it is not a widely used tactic unless tenants already have achieved laws protecting them from eviction—or have faith in a sympathetic judge. In Chicago, Boston, and elsewhere, tenants have negotiated settlements with landlords, contracts that recognize the tenants' union and through which tenants gain a greater voice over rent increases, maintenance, and other conditions. Yet in no city or state are tenants' collective bargaining rights written into law (although from 1978 to 1981 Madison, Wisconsin, had a "Rental Relations Ordinance" that required landlords to bargain in good faith with any legally constituted union of their tenants). Unlike labor unions, which are protected by the National Labor Relations Act, tenants' unions have no automatic right to be recognized when more than half of the tenants (in a building or with the same landlord) vote for a union.

Tenant groups have also organized against involuntary displacement due to "gentrification," when private developers (often with the aid of public subsidies or tax breaks) build an office complex, luxury residential center, hotel or convention center, or other major project. These developments often displace low- and moderate-income tenants—either directly (by tearing down their housing), or indirectly (by "upgrading" the neighborhood, attracting higher-income residents and boosting rent levels, or inducing condo conversions). These antidisplacement efforts, however, involve great difficulties, since typically such developments are seen as "revitalizing" the city, broadening the tax base, improving blighted neighborhoods (LeGates and Hartman, 1981). Tenants have little leverage, other than costly, complex, and drawn-out court battles (usually to deny government subsidies to such projects) or direct action civil disobedience (which can delay projects, but rarely stop them). The principle of revitalizing neighborhoods without displacement requires a direct challenge to free-market principles (i.e., controls on land speculation, ownership of nonprofit housing). It is only where tenant groups and their allies have more direct influence on government policy—as in Santa Monica, where they control local government— that the pace and direction of local development can be altered to stop displacement due to gentrification.

The discussion so far has focused primarily on tenants in private housing, but tenants in public housing have also engaged in rent strikes, direct action, and legal and electoral activity to improve living conditions, often gaining concessions from local housing authorities. In the United States, however, public housing accounts for less than 2 percent of all housing. Public housing is funded primarily at the federal level, but controlled by local housing authorities [*see Chapter 20 by Rachel G. Bratt*]. Federal funding priorities thus directly impact public housing tenants, as the Reagan administration's policy of increasing rents and lowering operating subsidies indicates [*see Chapter 21 by Chester Hartman*], but tenants have little influence over national decisions. The National Tenants Organization, formed in 1969, sought to organize public housing tenants at the national level, but exercised only minimal and fleeting influence for a few years (Marcuse, 1971). Local public housing tenant groups have won concessions over project maintenance and tenant in-put in decision-making [*see Chapter 26 by Robert Kolodny*], but local housing authorities are ultimately dependent on federal funds, and public housing has not been a priority of federal policymakers, in part because of the prejudice against public housing's predominantly low-income and minority-group residents.

Tenants in public and subsidized housing share few similar targets with tenants in private housing, thus making joint action unlikely. Public and subsidized housing, for example, is exempt from local rent control laws, often eliminating these tenants as potential allies with private housing tenants. Although these tenants frequently live in large complexes and share the same landlord (the local housing authority or a private developer with government sponsorship), they rarely form enough of a critical mass in any one locality to constitute an effective political bloc. Two of the largest mobilizations among subsidized housing tenants—the Co-op City tenants group in the Bronx and the Tenants First Coalition in Massachusetts—made some short-term gains, but soon fell apart (Brodsky, 1975). Tenants in state-subsidized housing in Massachusetts recently formed a statewide tenants group, as part of the Massachusetts Tenants Organization, to fight for their rights.

To counter the growth of tenant activism, landlords have also developed greater cohesiveness and coordination. Homebuilders and real estate agents have been influential in local, state, and national politics for decades (Lawson, 1980a; Lilley, 1971; Wolman, 1971). [*See also Chapter 6 by Barry Checkoway.*] But until recently apartment owners have not. Increasingly, however, they have begun to develop their own networks and organizations. The large apartment owners and developers have taken the lead, but they have consciously sought to include both "mom and pop" landlords, and even homeowners, in their efforts to broaden their appeal as defending "property rights" from government and tenant interference. Landlords have considerable resources at their disposal. Real estate interests are usually the major campaign contributors in local elections (Dreier, 1982b). During initiative campaigns on rent control, for example, landlord groups consistently outspent tenant groups by large margins. By vastly outspending tenant groups, landlords have recently defeated rent control initiatives in Seattle, San Diego, and Oakland (November 1980), in Minneapolis and San Bernardino (November 1981), and again in Oakland (November 1982). Well-organized tenants have, however, been able to defy the landlords despite these odds. In 1980, for example, California's landlords tried to undermine local tenant victories by sponsoring a statewide initiative that would have effectively eliminated local rent control ordinances. With help from their counterparts around the nation, the landlords raised and outspent rent control advocates, $4.9 million to $45,000, with expensive television, radio, billboard, and direct-mail campaigns. CHAIN, the tenants' statewide network, coordinated an effective grassroots campaign to overcome these heavy odds and defeated the landlords' initiative, 65 to 35 percent.

In 1978, the nation's large apartment owners and developers formed the National Rental Housing Council to provide local landlord groups with advice on media campaigns, legal tactics, and research against rent control and other pro-tenant demands. In 1980 it changed its name to the National Multi-Housing Council (NMHC), reflecting the growing number of condominium developers and converters among the landlords' ranks.

Following the defeat of the anti-rent-control initiative in California in June 1980, the NMHC proposed federal legislation that would deny federal housing funds to any city with effective rent controls—a proposal designed to knock the wind out of the tenants' movement's sails. The NMHC proposal was recommended by President Reagan's transition team on urban affairs in 1980 and again by his President's Commission on Housing in 1982 (both panels were heavily dominated by bankers and real estate people; see Hartman, 1983c), and proposed in Congress by Republicans in 1980, 1981, and 1982. It was defeated each time by an unusual combination of activist tenants and conservative legislators who saw it as an unnecessary federal interference in local affairs.

The burgeoning self-consciousness and activism among both tenants and landlords at the local, state, and national levels has made tenant-landlord conflict a significant feature of America's political landscape since the 1970s. Despite the growing momentum of the tenants' movement, the conflict so far has resulted in, at best, a stalemate. Growing numbers of city councils and state legislatures have been forced to consider tenants' rights legislation, and the number of pro-tenant laws continues to increase. But the overall picture is still one dominated by landlords and real estate interests. Most tenants in most communities are still not protected by rent or eviction controls. Even though tenants are often able to defeat landlord-backed proposals, these efforts force tenant groups to devote a great deal of their meager resources to these defensive holding actions.

## Future Directions

The tenants' movement, still in its infancy, has made significant progress but has a long way to go. Even at this early stage, it is worth reflecting on just where it might go and how it might get there.

The tenants' movement has its own agenda. For the most part, this is a defensive agenda, seeking to improve tenants' status vis-à-vis landlords. This includes, as has been mentioned, such remedies as rent control, restrictions on evictions, improved maintenance, condo conversion regulation, tenant voice in management, fair housing laws against discrimination, limits on speculation and gentrification, more public subsidies for renters, and reducing the risk for tenants who organize. Effective organizing around this agenda is the first goal of all tenant organizing. The tenants' movement is still primarily a local phenomenon, and it is still a minor actor on the larger stage of American politics. The sum of its local activities does not add up to a significant political force at the national level, where major housing policy decisions get made. The tenants' movement can ignore national politics only at its own risk.

Yet even the tenants' own limited agenda raises questions of long-term strategy and program. If strong rent controls and other reforms put the squeeze on speculative profits, more landlords may abandon their properties, convert them to condominiums, or cut back on repairs. And certainly they will be less likely to invest in new rental housing. Real estate groups, of course, argue that the pro-tenant reforms are destroying the nation's housing. This is obviously misleading, since the nation's housing crisis is much bigger than the landlords' declining profits. It has to do with the very nature of housing as a speculative commodity and the inability of Americans to afford housing on their incomes. It raises questions about both the private financing and construction of housing and the overall distribution of wealth and income in our society [*issues discussed at length in Chapter 1 by Emily Paradise Achtenberg and Peter Marcuse*].

But how should the tenants' movement respond to this reality of housing disinvestment? Already, tenant organizations are beginning to take advantage of this situation by advocating housing programs that turn over ownership and/or control to the residents at prices they can afford. This process should be encouraged. For many tenants, nonprofit and cooperative associations, sweat equity, or homesteading programs are the only short-term options, even though they run the risk of leading to a greater financial burden [*see Chapter 26 by Robert Kolodny and Chapter 27 by Tony Schuman*]. These options, however, provide valuable political lessons. When cooperative housing is a result of a political struggle—a squatters' action, a rent strike that drives the landlord out of business—those involved begin to develop greater self-confidence in common political action. The process of cooperative ownership and self-management itself helps people to overcome their cynicism and powerlessness. Moreover, tenant ownership and management is an important short-term means of ameliorating the most authoritarian aspects of bureaucratic and private landlord control.

The biggest limitation of this approach is the danger of gaining ownership without control. Most major expense items for existing apartment buildings are not subject to much control by the owners. Mortgage payments may take 40 percent or more of the rents. Property taxes take about another 15 or 20 percent, utility bills 10 to 15 percent, management staff 5 percent, and insurance 2 to 3 percent of the rents. In other words, at least three-quarters of the rent goes for costs that are beyond the tenants' control. The remaining costs, which the tenant-owners do control, have to cover the maintenance and repairs. Many buildings have high repair and maintenance costs and are poorly weatherized, since landlords have milked the building without spending money for needed upkeep. Eventually the tenant-owners may reach the point where they must choose between raising rents to cover increased costs, letting the building go into default and possible foreclosure, or seeking a "bail-out" from an outside investor. In short, changing ownership patterns in housing will not put all decision-making power in the hands of tenants.

Thus, tenant groups need to go into such struggles with their eyes wide open. Rent control and other self-help housing reforms are important stepping stones, but they are not the ultimate goal of a desirable housing policy. Their importance is in the process of building a political movement that can move beyond the tenants' immediate agenda. As such, these reforms are a direct extension of a broader economic program of greater economic democracy and public control of major investment decisions. The tenants' movement *raises political consciousness.* Tenant issues, particularly rent control, are powerful weapons in changing people's attitudes about what's right and wrong, and what is possible and impossible regarding private property rights. The underlying assumption of rent control is that landlords do not have a right to make as much profit or charge as much as they want. "What the market will bear" is no longer a fair measure of what is right. This can lead people to work for more democratic control over ownership and investment in housing. The tenants' movement also *builds grassroots organizations and wins victories.* Organization is necessary to develop leaders, to give people an opportunity to develop political skills (chairing meetings, talking to the press, making speeches, lobbying elected officials), and to shift people from being passive spectators to being active, self-confident citizens. It allows them to think, "You *can* fight City Hall." Victories improve people's lives directly and immediately. Rent control, for example, keeps their housing costs down. Anti-eviction laws and controls on condo conversions give people security and stability. These are necessary before tenants can start thinking about long-term solutions to the deeper housing crisis. Like the labor movement before it, the tenants' movement cannot begin promoting wider social goals until it has a stronger political foundation.

The tenants' movement is thus a building block for a more comprehensive political movement, and in its own way, contributes to that process, without which no housing reform is possible. As Lawrence Goodwyn has written about the populist movement in America:

> In their institutions of self-help, populists developed and acted upon a crucial democratic insight. To be encouraged to surmount rigid cultural inheritances and to act with autonomy and self-confidence, individual people need the psychological support of other people. The people need to "see themselves" experimenting in new democratic forms. (Goodwyn, 1978)

Thus, while fighting for their own reforms that bring them together in collective action, the tenants' movement cannot isolate itself from the broader struggle for social change. To avoid the cul-de-sac of ownership without control of housing, the tenants' movement needs allies who can work for more public control over land, utilities, and finance capital—that is, for a program of greater social ownership and finance of housing [*see Chapter 28 by Emily Paradise Achtenberg and Peter Marcuse and Chapter 29 by Chester Hartman and Michael E. Stone*]. In turn, tenants need to join these allies on a broader progressive agenda of democratic reform, of which housing is only one part.

This requires a coalition strategy. While tenants need to form their own independent city, state, and national organizations, they will also have to enter into coalitions with other progressive groups to win many of their demands. Issues will have to be designed that will bring public housing tenants, federally subsidized tenants, moderate-income private tenants, and moderate-income homeowners together. The tenants' movement potential is limited by its numbers. Many cities, but no states, have renter majorities. In the nation as a whole, tenants comprise less than one-third of all Americans. A political movement that does not broaden its base to address the concerns of a broad majority cannot expect to win a contest for political power in America.

During the past decade, fortunately, the nation witnessed a dramatic upsurge of political activism of all kinds: neighborhood groups, consumer and environmental organizations, welfare rights campaigns, the senior citizens' and women's movements, and peace and disarmament activism. Even the American labor movement has begun to emerge from several decades of conservative leadership and political decline. The massive union-sponsored "Solidarity Day" march in 1981 to protest the Reagan administration's program would have been unthinkable just a decade earlier.

Although all of these movements have their own immediate goals and agendas, they do have at least one thing in common. They are all under attack by big business, the New Right, and the Reagan administration. Reagan's election, and subsequent policies of redistributing wealth to the rich, big corporations, and the Pentagon, reflects the relative weakness of each of these movements at the national level. The neoconservative call for belt tightening in housing is paralleled in most other areas as well. While each movement goes its separate way, big business and New Right groups band together to support candidates and policies that run roughshod over workers, consumers, the elderly, women, the poor, the environment, and tenants. Only a common strategy that brings these movements and organizations together can hope to overcome the power of big business, because together they represent the majority of Americans.

This strategy of coalition politics is nothing new. It formed the basis of Franklin D. Roosevelt's New Deal, bringing together workers, farmers, minorities, and ethnic groups, and forging a new political force during the Great Depression. It both shifted political loyalties to the Democratic party and enfranchised millions of Americans who had not participated in the political system. Since the peak of the New Deal's popularity, however, voting participation has gradually declined (Burnham, 1980). In the 1980 presidential election, only 53 percent of the potential voters went to the polls. None of the candidates projected a program or a vision that appealed to the alienated, angry population. In most local and congressional races, the turnout is even smaller. Ironically, the vast majority of nonvoters are the very people who have been mobilized by the grassroots movements of the past decade. It is obvious that to be effective these movements have to bring their members and supporters into the electoral system and to elect progressives to public office who can translate their issues into policies. As a coalition these groups have to work together, promoting candidates who support their common goals and issues. Only now the New Deal program does not go far enough. The nation needs to go as far beyond the New Deal as the New Deal went beyond Hoover. The progressive coalition can no longer afford to make compromises of the type it made following the Great Depression. It must articulate and work for a program of democratizing major investment decisions (Carnoy and Shearer, 1980). It must recognize, as Starr and Esping-Anderson (1979) note, that the failure of liberalism has not been "excessive government interference in the private sector," but "excessive private interference in government policy." Our current housing crisis is only one example of that truth.

Tenant groups have had some recent experiences in building coalitions around progressive policies. In San Francisco, for example, the citywide tenant group helpeḋ forge a coalition of renters and homeowners called San Franciscans for Affordable Housing. It was made up of 35 groups, including labor, seniors', civil rights, women's, gay, and church organizations. The coalition sponsored a comprehensive housing program on the November 1979 ballot that included a tenants' bill of rights, assistance for low- and moderate-income homeowners (to construct, purchase, and rehabilitate homes), control over speculation, restrictions on condominium conversions, and strict controls on rent increases. Although the initiative lost, that loss came about primarily because the city's governing Board of Supervisors took steps to undercut it by unanimously passing a weaker set of condominium conversion and rent controls (Hartman, 1979).

An even broader coalition was initiated by the New Jersey Tenants Organization. NJTO leaders realized that the tenants' movement there had almost exhausted its single-issue agenda and needed allies to move beyond rent control. In 1981, it brought together the state's major progressive unions, a women's group (NOW), senior citizens', civil rights, environmental, and peace organizations to discuss working together in forthcoming elections. Each group had a list of candidates—some to defeat, others to help elect—in the state legislature elections. The groups discovered that despite some differences, there was considerable overlap in their lists of friends and enemies. They joined forces and established the N.J. Public Interest Political Action Committee. It intends to pool resources, money, and volunteers to elect common friends and defeat common enemies. The initial assumption is that any candidates who can gain the support of *all* these groups have a coherent progressive political outlook. But explicit discussion of long-range program and policy is premature, something that will emerge as the coalition wins victories and the groups develop greater confidence in each other's contributions to the collective goals. This is part of the dynamics of movement building that Goodwyn observed among the populists.

Obviously, it is important to develop a comprehensive program, for housing in particular, and for the larger economy in general. It is important to recognize that housing is not an isolated enclave but part of the larger economy that allocates scarce resources according to political priorities. For the coalition-building strategy to work, tenant and other groups must recognize their mutual interest not only in providing affordable housing, but in dealing with related issues of employment, public health, social welfare, and income distribution. No program of redistributing and democratizing the nation's wealth can hope to work, for example, without a dramatic shift in priorities away from wasteful military spending, so that resources can be directed towards providing for basic social needs and jobs. Similarly, no progressive program will work unless government revenues are collected more progressively and loopholes closed for big business and the wealthy. Finally, a progressive program requires more direct public, consumer, and employee participation in decisions about how resources are to be used and spent. This means, first of all, electing grassroots activists to public office, so that "government" itself becomes a vehicle for popular enthusiasm. Putting limits on campaign contributions from big business and overall campaign spending would certainly help reduce the influence of big corporations on the political system. More directly, however, consumers and employees should be elected to membership on corporations' boards of directors, as Senator Howard Metzenbaum's Corporate Democracy Act proposes, and ultimately exercise greater ownership and control of corporate wealth. One model is Sweden's Meidner Plan, a proposal to establish "wage earner funds"—a system of mutual funds collectively owned by Swedish employees who would gradually come to own the vast majority of shares in Swedish business. Finally, local and national government should have direct ownership and control over basic industries. This includes energy corporations, utilities, and railroads; a national health service; and a public bank that would provide loans on the basis of social priorities.

All this may seem a long way from a local rent strike and other tenant-movement concerns, but it is actually a direct extension of the logic of the tenants' movement. The American tenants' movement has made significant gains, although in the context of the nation's housing crisis it has only made a small dent. But crisis creates opportunities, for the tenants' movement, and for other progressive movements as well. The importance of the tenants' movement is its potential for politicizing and mobilizing a great part of America's population around immediate problems, then pointing the way toward larger solutions as part of a broad coalition to democratize American society.

# The Limitations and Potential of Housing Organizing

*John Cowley*

*Counterpoints to Atlas' and Dreier's enthusiasm about tenant organizing are provided in this and the following chapter. Here, housing organizing is contrasted with work-place organizing, and the former is seen to have inherent difficulties in terms of developing a strong and long-lasting opposition movement. For example, the isolation inherent in residential patterns often precludes building an effective and sustained movement. The author (who is British and whose perspective therefore is influenced by the existence of a strong and organized working class) is sympathetic to housing organizing as a strategy for change and uses the comparison with workplace organiz-ing as a tool with which to understand and, he hopes, remedy the problems the housing movement has encountered.*

Why is it that in this vital area of working-class life organizations of similar permanence to the trade unions do not exist? Why do tenants' associations appear so weak and ephemeral in comparison? . . . The capital–wage-labor relation is fundamental to the organization of capitalist society and governs the social process of material production upon which life depends. This is the basis for speaking of the primacy of production and the economic character of the struggle between the capitalist and the working class. In production the conflict between the principal classes is immediate and ever present, and results in the combination of workers and the formation of trade unions wherever there is production organized on a capitalist basis. In comparison, housing, where workers live in relation to their work, is a secondary, although clearly necessary, part of social existence.

But it is not simply a matter of correctly weighting these different ele-ments constituting the material conditions of existence of the immediate producers. It is not simply that the social relations governing housing are subordinate to those governing the social process of production, but also that whereas the capital–wage-labor relation is direct and immediate in the

Reprinted from *Housing for People or for Profit?*, London, Stage 1, 1979, with the permission of the author.

factory, it is not so in housing. Finance capital, which dominates the housing stock, is mediated by the different agents of the various tenures: the local [housing] authorities, the small private landlord or property company, the building society or perhaps one's own employer (as with the banks and insurance companies). Together, the secondary position of housing and the indirect form of capital's rule weaken the necessity for combination in the defense of common interests. Consequently, tenants' associations remain but a shadow of their counterpart in production. Organizations on the basis of residence are both weaker and much more transient. They come and go and rarely achieve a level of combination, with everyone joining in whether actively or passively, as is achieved in many work situations. Even the most famous rent strikes of this century fall far short of achieving the solidarity characteristic of industrial disputes.

The spontaneous generation of [housing] groupings is forever taking place. As forms of organization they can be divided into two main types: those formed to fight a specific issue and those based on representing the general interests of a group of tenants. The first type may be a group of private tenants resisting a change in their tenancies, or an increase in rent or service charges, or perhaps a pending change in ownership and the threat of purchase by a company known for its speculation in property. . . . Squatters' organizations tend to be of the same type [*see Chapter 25 by Seth Borgos*]. The organization exists to fight a particular issue, and its strength and survival depend on its ability to draw people into the campaign. . . . Most struggles are defensive, fighting evictions or rent increases, and are attempts to preserve a given situation and level of rent. But occasionally there are actions that are offensive. This applies particularly to the periodic attacks made on empty dwellings in periods of widespread homelessness. . . . These types of association come and go. Whether the battle is won or lost, the organization rarely outlives the struggle. If it does survive, then it usually does so quite changed in its character and purpose.

The other type of tenants' association is the one formed to represent more generally the interests of a particular group of tenants. Initially these may be formed as the result of a particular problem, such as the need for major repairs or the installation of central heating. But as associations they survive on the basis of their ability to represent the more general and particular interests of tenants. This type of association is mostly to be found on local authority housing estates [projects], although there are examples of similar general associations among private tenants. These associations also come and go, but their basis is of this general kind and they do tend to survive for much longer periods of time than the essentially single-issue associations.

It is quite probable that as many estates have tried and failed to organize themselves as have succeeded and that even more have never actually tried. But those that do succeed tend to be quite stable in their membership and leadership. Well-known local tenants' leaders tend to be such for a long time.

Unlike workplace organizing where the general interdependency of modern production and the mass character of the labor process is a basic condition for labor solidarity and unity, in housing, organizing goes against the social grain. The immediately given forms of family and personal life impose an isolation and fragmentation on social life which must be overcome in order to sustain any organization. . . .

Although the ideal of individual homeownership is strongly held, even without it the idea of one's own home, whatever the tenure, encourages individual, private forms of personal life and satisfaction of basic needs. The actual success over the past 50 years in providing large sections of the working class with their own exclusive dwelling, whatever its particular physical shortcomings, has helped make private the various activities of child care, cooking, laundry, and entertainment [*see Chapter 13 by Dolores Hayden*]. By so doing it has helped foster the individualist beliefs of capitalist competition and possession among workers themselves: The sanctity of the home and the desire, come what may, of keeping up appearances of respectability with neighbors encourages stoicism in the face of difficulties. These attitudes and responses are materially underpinned by the widespread indebtedness, through purchase of consumer durable goods on credit, of the individual family as a consuming unit. The continuous effort to maintain [consumer debt] payments has become part and parcel of the struggle to maintain a self-contained family life. So, contrary to the workplace experience, in their home life people are cut off from their fellow workers, separated from the rest of their family and isolated even from their neighbors. This atomization and isolation of individuals in home life is in constant tension with the most immediate relations of cooperation at the heart of the capitalist production process and its ancillary activities, and with the elements of a more open and public social life still to be found in corner shops, betting shops, laundromats, and pubs.

The fragile and transient character of tenants' organizations and the sporadic nature of housing struggles is rooted in the social relations of residential life that spontaneously divide and isolate people. Organizing tenants is a matter of working against division among people. This explains both its weakness historically and its secondary importance in class politics. But these limitations, this weakness within the very basis of tenants' organizing is also its greatest strength in that it *does* necessitate going against the given order of things and overcoming the spontaneously imposed fragmentation and isolation of capitalist society. This is why the major housing struggles have nearly all involved an enormous release of energy and creativity on the part of those involved. It is not simply that people have created organization where none existed and given leadership in situations with few parallels to draw upon; the very complexity of the housing situation has demanded ingenuity and the elaboration of direct forms of action, sometimes of enormous inventiveness.

This overturning of the given social forms of compliance characteristic of capitalist society happens again and again in all the major housing struggles. It is expressed most clearly in the central role played by women in most housing struggles, be they large or small . . . .Anybody who has ever been involved in any tenants' organizing will know that it begins with the women. They know the condition of the dwelling: the damp that brings mold to clothes in the bedroom, the draining board that is a health hazard, the faulty light switch, the window that cannot be opened, and the door that can be shut only with shoulder and knee. Given the responsibilities for home life that capitalist social relations impose on women, it is not surprising. But it is here in the dwelling, with the problems of its physical condition and monetary cost and its precariousness as a home, that from isolation women often come to act collectively.

On the other hand, very often in the formal arrangements of tenants' associations, in officerships, and in formal representations to the local housing department or the landlord, men take their accustomed place. Here we confront that complex mass of threads that tie individuals to the established order of things and yet need severing if there is to be a development of class politics and a growth in consciousness of the need for fundamental change. Here we confront the fact that in all their weakness as a movement, tenants' organizations are collective forms vital to the growth in class experience and consciousness. They are not permanent and so central as the trade unions, but they do contain a shared class experience and are bearers of class consciousness. Historically, past and future, through these organizational forms and the struggles that erupt, women shape and share the consciousness of class.

Tenants' associations, like trade unions, are limited in what they can achieve. They are class organizations in a capitalist society. They give strength to the working class, and are part of the spontaneously created organizations that help make the class a social force, with a shared experience and separate identity. But they are not in themselves the vehicles, any more than the trade unions are, for overthrowing the rule of capital. At various times historically it has been widely believed by activists in the trade union movement that they could directly through the industrial struggle bring about the overthrow of capital, ignoring the existence of the capitalist state and its apparatus of violence. In a somewhat similar way, but with far less serious consequences for class politics, some activists involved in squatting on empty property in the 1970s saw what they were doing as the direct appropriation of private property and a direct challenge to the capitalist order. The real need is to recognize the part that any tenants' organizations can play in the sharing, consolidation, and transmission of class experience. This is as true for tenants' associations as it is for the trade unions, and will remain so even if there is little growth in the actual permanency of these organizations.

Although localized and disparate, such collective forms remain points of class experience vital for the survival of class identity in a capitalist society, which forever is imposing its own forms and values upon people. This is why housing, however secondary it may be in terms of the overall struggle between classes within capitalism, remains a vital area of political experience. Although there is not the same immediate and direct conflict with capital as there is in industry, nevertheless there is the reality of the forms of capitalist social relations that effectively divide and weaken the working class. First and foremost there is the domestic situation: the position of the women in the family and the home. This fundamental social relation between men and women is affected by housing struggles and organization—not necessarily dramatically and lastingly, but to the extent that women's experience can become part of the shared experience of the class. Clearly it represents an area that is badly undeveloped and yet of immense importance for the future making of working-class politics.

Similarly, on the question of race, the consequences of internal splits within the working class are apparent. The problems of discrimination, fear, and prejudice abound and especially where housing problems are at their worst. It is precisely here where the problems are most acute and are most divisive that the possibility for exposing the problems and working to overcome them is actually at its greatest. People do not have to like their neighbors in order to unite together, but a shared struggle helps more than anything else in overcoming individual fears, dislikes, and differences. Again, tenants' organization poses sharply the practical problems involved in working to overcome such divisions . . . .

If the politics of housing is ever to be posed in terms of a real and lasting solution to the housing question as an ever-present problem, then the politics of accommodation to the capitalist order must themselves be challenged [*see Chapter 24 by Kathy McAfee*]. If this challenge is to have any historical significance, it must eventually find expression in a development of a politics and party organization that goes beyond Social Democracy and poses fundamental solutions to the real problems of capitalist society. But this is a task that in itself lies outside as well as inside tenants' organizing and requires a separate, although related, development. All that basic class organizations such as tenants associations and trade unions can do is to play their part in reproducing and helping to strengthen the identity and capacity of the working class as a social force. This involves developing its autonomy from the capitalist politics of reform. On the one hand, it requires struggling for organizational forms that are capable of asserting the immediate interests of people in specific class terms, which means they should be as genuinely collective and open as possible. On the other hand, there needs to be some basic idea of the solution that is concretely possible, historically, to the housing problem and that can guide and inform such work. . . .

The Social Democratic solution to the housing problem is for the state to provide for those in need. This development of the local [housing] authority tenure [public housing] meets working-class housing needs in a way that neither of the other main tenures [private renting and homeownership] can. . . . [*For a fuller discussion of housing policy and housing tenure in Great Britain, see Chapter 16 by Jim Kemeny and Chapter 30 by Steve Schifferes.*] But state provision of housing takes place within the framework and dictates of capitalism. This means that [public housing authority] housing is indebted to the private interests of finance capital, is poorly built and maintained, and managed by a rigid and paternalistic local bureaucracy. Local authority housing meets working-class needs more effectively than the other tenures, but does so in subordination to the interests of capital. [Public housing authority] housing should be seen for what it is: the only viable solution to the housing problem available under capitalism [*see Chapter 20 by Rachel G. Bratt*]. This is not to imply that its quality and general standards cannot be improved—they can. But how far will depend ultimately on the balance of class forces and the ability to shift the balance of the division of the social product away from capital to the advantage of labor. The [public housing authority] tenure, then, does not represent a socialist solution to the housing problem in the sense of anticipating the sort of housing that will exist under the conditions of a developing socialist society. On the contrary, the social ownership of housing that will develop in a socialist society . . . will be completely and utterly different [*see also Chapter 28 by Emily Paradise Achtenberg and Peter Marcuse, Chapter 29 by Chester Hartman and Michael E. Stone, and Chapter 33 by Jill Hamberg*].

Social ownership means that people's relations to the products of their labor and natural resources, and to each other, are no longer determined by their class position, but depend upon the relations governing their mutual cooperation in work and social life: Property will no longer be private, belonging to a section of society, but social in character. The immediate producers will own and control, through the forms of their social cooperation, the social process of production. Similarly with housing, people, through the collective arrangements of their community and neighborhood life, will have a real say in the type and quality of housing constructed and control its repair and upkeep. It will no longer be shoddily built for profit but will be produced and allocated in order to fulfill individual and social needs.

It will not be just a matter of sound physical structures that is at stake, but also the kind of space the dwellings and community facilities provide for the various activities of domestic life: child care, housework, entertainment, and relaxation. Under socialism these activities will progressively lose their narrow character at present imposed by private family life. This does not mean the abolition of an exclusive personal and home life, but rather overcoming its isolation and so strengthening the basis for individual participation in social life. In the past decade women have posed once again the question of their liberation from the narrow confines of domestic labor and stressed the social aspects of such work. They have demonstrated the possibilities for mutual support for those who suffer from domestic confinement, and the immense benefits for all arising from sharing child care and other tasks to do with the home, such as the cooperative purchase of food. These experiments represent not so much the forms of the future as an expression of present needs unfulfilled by the existing order of social relations. In themselves these developments suggest that, far from being a precarious refuge from a hostile world, the home could become a point of entry into the immediate life of the community [*see Chapter 13 by Dolores Hayden*].

Clearly the social ownership of housing will involve an entirely different organization of society from that which exists today. It will be based on common ownership, cooperation, and the equality of freely developing individuals. . . .

The struggle for working-class organizations that are not immediately subordinated to capitalist politics, and the development, only sketched here, of the idea of the social ownership of housing are the basic issues at stake in the future growth of the tenants' movement. It is in this context that the demands for the nationalization of land, the building industry, and private financial institutions will need to be formulated. It is also the context for exposing present attempts to incorporate tenants' organizations into the activities of the state through mechanisms of tenants' participation in control, when effective ownership in a material sense still rests firmly in the hands of the capitalist state and the institutions of finance capital [*see Chapter 26 by Robert Kolodny and Chapter 27 by Tony Schuman*]. In raising these points one is forced to face the present backwardness of any and all existing socialist politics in the sphere of housing.

Individuals, in their separate, private houses or flats experience only too directly the importance of good housing for the quality of life. But, given that housing is such a vital and sensitive aspect of the social relations of capitalist society, it needs to become a much more important focus of our political activity.

# 24

# Socialism and the Housing Movement: Lessons from Boston

*Kathy McAfee*

*In further analyzing the current status and potential of the housing movement, the author, based on experiences in Boston, argues that rent control and other defensive grassroots campaigns have provided limited benefits. A fundamental problem with these strategies is that they accept the profit nature of housing which, it is maintained, cannot coexist with achievement of the right to decent, affordable housing. There is a need for a program of housing decommodification—a substitution of public for private investment and collective for capitalist control. With this as the long-term, not immediately winnable, goal, there is still a need to organize around other, more limited reforms that are steps toward getting profit out of housing and that build the working-class organization, consciousness, and power necessary to achieve more fundamental change. In contrast to the Atlas–Dreier approach, the author maintains that tenants of different social classes do not necessarily have truly common interests and calls for political organization of working-class housing consumers, owners and renters alike.*

During the past decade the failure of capitalism in the United States to provide adequate housing for its own working-class population has become increasingly obvious. One result has been a rising level of tenant and community activism. But many housing organizers, including those of us who consider ourselves socialists, have not understoood the root causes of the housing crisis or have chosen, for idcological or tactical reasons, not to act on the basis of that understanding. We have approached the housing crisis as if it were a series of vaguely connected "housing issues," rather than as a fundamental aspect of the system's failure.

Meanwhile, the crisis is deepening. Low-income people in the cities are forced to double-up or move away as a result of rent increases, abandonment, or arson. And not only low-income people are affected; in cities and suburbs alike, the price of keeping a roof over one's head for many includes burdensome rent or mortgage payments, insecurity, neighborhood instability, and lowered expectations.

City officials point to showcase "revitalized" neighborhoods in an effort to distract attention from the spreading acres of weed-filled lots and boarded-up buildings. Closer inspection reveals that these pockets of prosperity have been carved out at the expense of the former residents and through the input of amounts of money and labor far beyond the means of the majority of city dwellers.

These things are not temporary distortions but are the inevitable outcome of capitalist logic applied to the housing market and in the context of the broader crisis of capitalism. Because of declining real incomes—and thus decreased ability to pay for housing—among unemployed and working people, housing investors find that it does not pay to build housing for them or rent housing to them, especially when the profits to be made from speculation and condominium conversion, for example, are so much more attractive.

Particularly in older cities, an increasing proportion of real estate profits are made, not by building and maintaining housing, but by buying and reselling existing housing, extracting ever-higher rents and prices, and uprooting entire communities in the process. Or, profits are made by milking and then abandoning or burning buildings, or by collecting government rent subsidies and proceeds from the sale of shares as tax shelters and then moving on to repeat the process in other buildings. Every day, thousands of housing investors make "sound business decisions" that result in the elimination of affordable housing units and even in the intentional destruction of housing.

Thus the roots of the housing crisis go deeper than Reaganism or recession. It will not disappear as a result of a change in the federal administration or an "upturn" in the economy. But the trend toward less, worse, and more expensive housing cannot continue indefinitely without leading to a dangerous level of chaos, alienation, and anger. People will be demanding solutions, and sectors of the ruling class may be forced to accept changes in the system of providing housing that are more basic than any they have been willing to consider thus far.

We in City Life, a socialist organization with 12 years of experience in housing organizing in Boston, are convinced that no substantial improvement in working-class housing and neighborhoods in the city can be brought about through the profit system in housing, however refined, reformed, or regulated. We believe any significant reforms will have to be based on the decommodification—or socialization—of housing [*see Chapter 28 by Emily Paradise Achtenberg and Peter Marcuse*].

We are not sure whether any such reforms can be won on a large scale in the near future, and we debate among ourselves how far a program of decommodification could go without a revolutionary transformation of the entire economy and society. But all of us feel sure that the current struggle over who will control and who will live in city housing and neighborhoods—which is at heart a class struggle—is going to grow more intense. This struggle presents us as socialists with the opportunity and the responsibility to help point the way toward an alternative to the outmoded and destructive system of housing for profit: a socialist solution to the crisis that is concrete, credible, and worth fighting for [*see Chapter 29 by Chester Hartman and Michael E. Stone*].

Most housing activists in Boston and other U.S. cities have not begun to do this. Most housing organizing has been defensive in its tactics and self-conception. The demands and programs put forward by housing organizers have usually been limited to measures to tax or restrict private investment in housing and commercial development rather than to replace it.

The kinds of solutions most commonly proposed fall into two main categories. Tenants are urged to lobby and vote for rent and eviction controls, regulation of condominium conversions, and other "renters' rights" measures [*see Chapter 22 by John Atlas and Peter Dreier*]. The versions of rent and condo controls usually called for would regulate the housing market to some extent. But at the same time, they are designed to protect the profitability of rental housing and avoid provoking disinvestment. Consequently, they are so moderate and limited in scope that they would benefit only a minority of tenants, mainly those with middle and high incomes. This kind of rent control, if it could be won in cities like Boston, would leave most working-class tenants—the great majority of renters—still paying far more than they can afford for housing [*see Chapter 3 by Michael E. Stone*], and in the context of continuing disinvestment and abandonment.

The other kind of housing reform most often proposed involves various kinds of government subsidies, including expansion of Section 8-type rent subsidy programs and mortgage subsidies to promote home and condo ownership by low- and moderate-income people. What programs of this nature boil down to is a form of welfare for landlords, developers, and bankers [*see Chapter 17 by Robert Schur and Tom Robbins*]. They shore up the real estate industry, a sector of capital that plays an increasingly parasitical role in the economy, while they exacerbate inflation in the housing market. The occupants of subsidized units may benefit, but those benefits are paid for mainly by working-class taxpayers, and the net effect is the redistribution of income upward.

In short, while many people propose tinkering with the capitalist housing system, almost nobody talks about replacing it. The slogan "Housing for People, Not for Profit," seen on signs and banners at so many tenant rallies, remains undefined or even contradicted by the specific proposals supported by folks waving the banners.

There are several reasons for this. First, many housing activists are not aware, or do not agree, that the commodity nature of housing is at the root of the current crisis. Imbued with capitalist assumptions and values, they cannot or do not want to imagine a real alternative. Others, including many socialists, are committed to the goal of building a broad alliance of tenants of all classes, and believe it would be a strategic error to try to build mass support for an explicitly anticapitalist program.

There are also many activists who remain within capitalist boundaries in their analysis and program simply because they feel it is unrealistic to try to push beyond these limits in the present political climate. If we cannot even win rent control, they reason, how can we win anticapitalist housing reforms? They see the weakness of the tenants' movement, the fading of liberalism, and the assertiveness of the ideological right and conclude that only very mild reforms, directed at the worst "abuses" of the system but not challenging it, have a chance of being won.

In our view, this line of reasoning is self-defeating because it limits its sights to programmatic proposals so obviously inadequate that they scarcely seem worth fighting for. This approach is also short-sighted in that it fails to recognize the rate at which the current system is deteriorating, the growing sense of desperation among working-class city residents, and their increasing openness to more radical alternatives, including socialist ones.

A more promising approach, we believe, is to put forward a program that calls clearly for the socialization of housing, a plan that makes an alternative to housing for profit at least conceivable, if not immediately winnable. This kind of program could provide the inspiration and sense of direction that most of the movements around housing currently lack. And, as conditions worsen, it will sound increasingly like plain common sense.

We in City Life recognize that calling for socialized housing and achieving it are two very different things. The formulation of a strong socialist program will not eliminate the need to organize and fight our battles one by one. We will still need to win limited reforms at first, and in the process build the working-class organization, consciousness, and power that will be necessary to achieve more fundamental change [*see Chapter 23 by John Cowley*].

But there is a crucial difference between organizing for reforms—such as rent subsidies—that reinforce the profit system and those that are steps in the direction of getting profit out of housing: for example, public takeover and rehabilitation of tax-delinquent or substandard apartment buildings. Equally crucial is the difference between fighting for step-by-step victories as if these were ends in themselves and fighting for the same reforms as part of a broader socialist program. For instance, if rent control were presented as *part* of an overall plan to eliminate housing speculation and reverse the trend toward the destruction of urban neighborhoods, we could be much more effective in mobilizing support for rent control.

City Life's position has evolved gradually as we have tried to analyze the successes and failures of 12 years of hard-fought battles over rent control, arson, and displacement in Boston and the neighboring cities of Cambridge and Somerville. Since City Life as an organization has been involved in most of these struggles, we must accept as much responsibility as anyone else for the mistakes that have been made. But as we have tried to understand the history of the Boston area housing movements, it has become increasingly clear that many of the weaknesses of these movements derive from the failure to come to grips with the real nature of the housing crisis and from an attachment to a liberal–reformist strategy that yielded some results in the late 1960s and early 1970s, but which no longer has any chance of success.

We can best explain what we mean by drawing examples and lessons from the actual experiences of the housing-related movements in and around

Boston. Many of these examples will strike a familiar chord with housing activists in other cities, since housing struggles have taken shape along similar lines in many parts of the country. Since Boston is one of the older, Frostbelt cities hard hit by deindustrialization, there are some housing disasters here, such as acres of wastelands created by arson, that are not seen in, say, San Diego. But other aspects of Boston's housing scene, such as rapid inflation of rents and house prices, downtown gentrification, deterioration of public and subsidized housing, and escalating conflict between renters and real estate interests, are typical of most larger U.S. cities.

But before summing up the successes and failures of the movements here, we need to understand the context in which these struggles have unfolded: the physical and economic transformation of Boston, in the planning stages since World War II years and begun in earnest in the mid-1960s.

## The Context

Over the past 15 years, Boston's housing market has been transformed in the wake of major public and private investment in so-called revitalization: urban renewal, downtown redevelopment, and planned displacement and gentrification. The late 1960s saw the destruction of older factory and warehouse areas near the central city, and the demolition of entire working-class neighborhoods to make way for luxury high-rise housing, government and commercial office towers, the expansion of elite medical and educational institutions, and the development of fancy shopping and entertainment districts. This redevelopment was seen by the ruling class of the city as central to the economic modernization of the region, including the replacement of many of the manufacturing industries with high-technology research and development, service industries (medicine, education, finance, insurance, real estate, and tourism), and the government infrastructure to support all of the above.

This transformation was accompanied by a restructuring of the labor market. Blue-collar jobs at the middle and upper end of the working-class pay scale were lost. These were replaced by a nearly equivalent number of mostly poorly paid, nonunionized jobs in the service sector, plus a significant number of technical, professional, and managerial positions.

This change in the composition of the employed work force had an impact on the housing market: There were a lot more households in the city whose incomes were fixed or falling and who could not afford to pay increased housing costs. At the same time, there was a growing sector that could afford to pay more. The location of their jobs in the "new" downtown gave them added incentive to move to or remain in the central city. It was this widening gap between these two sectors of the population—not some sudden change in the psyches of suburbanites—that was the basis of the "back to the city" movement and the displacement of the urban poor in downtown neighborhoods by the "gentry." [*See also Chapter 5 by Joe R. Feagin.*]

Of course, this gentrification was not the result of market forces alone. The trend was actively promoted by city government policies: the channeling of federal grants and subsidies into "upscale" areas, tax breaks and giveaways of public land and buildings to commercial and condominium developers, blockage by the city of low- and moderate-income housing development by community-based groups, and the undermining of rent control.

In line with these priorities, City Hall has implemented a policy of "triage," through the selective cutback of services to low-income and especially minority neighborhoods. Schools have been closed and bus routes, health centers, and other services withdrawn from communities that have been wounded—presumably mortally—as a result of lower resident incomes, disinvestment by landlords, and redlining by mortgage lenders [*see Chapter 10 by Ann Meyerson*]. Sufficient funds do not exist, the city claims, to keep street lights and traffic signals working or to board up vacant buildings in these neighborhoods. Meanwhile, over in Gentryville, public funds are poured into plush amenities like gas lights and brick sidewalks.

For years, arson-for-profit has been tolerated by city officials and has taken place on a frightening scale in both kinds of neighborhoods. In disinvested areas, arson enables property owners to bail out by "selling to the insurance company." It also reduces the numbers of residents from population groups considered as political and financial liabilities by the city government, and it clears land for future, profitable redevelopment. In areas that are undergoing gentrification, arson enables property owners to clear their buildings of tenants, especially those still covered by rent control, whose very presence reduces the market value of their buildings. (Small fires are a quicker and more reliable method of eviction than court procedures.)

As a result of all this, the "New Boston," with its gleaming skyscrapers, brownstone condos, and food boutiques, has its dark counterpart in the new "urban prairies": extensive burned-out blocks dotted by a few rotting buildings. Between these two extremes are the ailing but still viable residential neighborhoods, mostly on the outer edges of the city, where working-class tenants and homeowners struggle to heat and maintain their houses while footing much of the bill for the city budget through their property taxes.

## The Resistance

Boston residents have not accepted all this passively; they have fought back and resisted displacement, deterioration, and rising housing costs in many ways. Probably the most important, and certainly the most publicized, aspect of this resistance has been the long battle in which rent control was won and then lost again.

During the period from 1970 to 1972, a coalition of eastern Massachusetts tenants groups won passage of statewide rent control enabling legislation and the adoption of rent control in Brookline, Cambridge, Lynn, Boston, and Somerville. In Boston, the program covered all existing apartments except those in owner-occupied buildings with three units or less. It allowed landlords a "fair" profit based on the net income generated by the building in a standard base year prior to rent control, and established a limited number of "just causes" for which tenants could legally be evicted.

This version of rent control was in effect through 1975. The extent to which it kept rents down in Boston is debatable. Many landlords never registered their property with the Rent Control Board, and many gave rent increases without going through the required hearing process. Landlords able to hire lawyers and accountants usually had little difficulty in getting the rent board to approve increases that brought their rents up to the level that the market would bear at the time. A gaping loophole in the regulations permitting decontrol of "rehabilitated" apartments allowed enterprising landlords to decontrol and empty entire buildings and even entire blocks.

There is little disagreement, however, that even this weak form of rent control was a valuable weapon wherever *organized* tenants waged rent strikes or struggles for better conditions. Rent-control protections and the rent board hearing process gave tenants a greater sense of their own legitimacy and security in fighting back, without which many tenant organizing efforts would not have gotten off the ground.

Many of these campaigns had significant results: Evictions and rent increases were stopped, and landlords were forced to make major repairs and even sign collective bargaining agreements with their tenants. But the landlords against whom these victories were won were mainly representative of the old breed, who held on to their property for many years and made their profits primarily from rents. By the 1970s, many of these landlords were being replaced by another type for whom rental property ownership was primarily a tax shelter and/or a short-term, speculative investment, to whom income from rents was a minor consideration, and who would rather switch—to condos—than fight.

By 1975, these modern landlords and their partners in banking and construction were able to dominate the political struggle over housing in the city and to pull the underpinnings out from rent and eviction controls. In 1975, Mayor Kevin White won his third term after a campaign in which he stressed his support for rent control. But almost immediately after his reelection, to the background of a symphony of anti–rent control propaganda by the real estate industry, White instituted a program of vacancy decontrol, which allows rent control to be permanently lifted from apartments after the tenants have moved. This was simply the most politically expedient means of dividing tenants and killing rent control.

By this time the tide of speculation was already on the rise, and the demise of rent control opened the floodgates. Between 1976 and 1982, about 80 percent of the covered apartments were decontrolled. In areas undergoing gentrification, such as Jamaica Plain, rent increases of 300 percent to 500 percent over a few years' time became common.

The Boston tenants' movement, in the form of a citywide coalition of neighborhood-based groups, fought the adoption of vacancy decontrol in 1975, and organized in subsequent years to resist the complete elimination of remaining rent control regulations. The tactics used have mainly been lobbying city councillors, petitions, press conferences, and testimony at public hearings. If it were not for these efforts, probably even the remaining controls would have been removed. Still, the numbers of people mobilized in the campaigns to save rent control have never been very large, and the movement's impact was not great enough to prevent the reelection of overwhelmingly anti–rent control city councils since 1979.

Rent control is not the only goal for which Boston residents have organized in their struggle against displacement. Tenant unions have been formed to fight bad conditions, condo conversions, and rent increases, with tactics ranging from legal suits and harassment of landlords through rent strikes, both legal and extralegal. Neighborhood groups and citywide coalitions have mounted campaigns and suits against the use of public resources (city funds, land, buildings, and federal grants) to promote luxury and commercial redevelopment. Community groups and individuals have attempted to save abandoned houses and apartment buildings through sweat-equity rehabilitation (using the residents' own labor). Community development corporations have sought state and federal funds for nonprofit housing rehabilitation and development.

Residents of subsidized apartment developments have fought to prevent the federal government from completely abandoning HUD-owned and HUD-regulated multifamily projects. Public housing tenants have organized to resist the scandalous neglect of housing projects by the city and the city's attempt to hand over to private developers projects on land now considered too valuable for poor people. Coalitions of working-class renters and homeowners and progressive professionals have resisted the expansion of universities and medical institutions into surrounding neighborhoods, and have attempted to reverse disinvestment trends through antiredlining legislation and the channeling of home mortgage interest subsidies into targeted neighborhoods.

## The Results

Where do working-class tenants and homeowners stand after the past 10 years of struggle in Boston? For starters, a number of the worst slumlords have had their wings clipped or even been put out of business with the aid of rent strikes. Tenant unions in the neighborhoods of Jamaica Plain, Roxbury, Dorchester, and Mattapan—many of them organized with the help of City Life—have scored some impressive successes in stopping rent increases and evictions and preventing abandonment. To do so they have had to overcome barriers of language and race, landlord violence, and the bias of the courts in favor of property rights.

The combativeness and perseverance of these organized tenants point to the potential for a larger and more militant grassroots movement, especially among low-income tenants. Some veterans of these tenant unions have become dedicated and battle-wise activists, joining City Life committees as organizers, for example, and making links between tenant unions in different neighborhoods. But for the most part, tenant union efforts have remained isolated from each other and focused on individual landlords.

Meanwhile, the community movements against institutional expansion have managed to hang on to a few footholds for working-class housing in neighborhoods like Chinatown and Mission Hill; nevertheless, more units have been lost than have been saved or replaced. Public housing tenants have extracted some concessions but have not been able to reverse the overall trend toward further deterioration. Rent and eviction controls helped temporarily to slow the pace of displacement in some neighborhoods, but the majority of apartments have now been decontrolled, and no significant restrictions on condo conversion have been won.

In neighborhoods where disinvestment is the dominant pattern, including most communities with a black or Latino majority, conditions have grown steadily worse. A few dozen arsonists, most of them convicted as a result of detective work done by community activists, have served time in prison, but the arson wave continues unabated in low-income areas. The response of City Hall has been, "Knock'em down before they burn down." City Life and neighborhood organizations have fought this policy—reminiscent of Vietnam, of destroying Boston in order to save it. We have succeeded in holding off the bulldozers in some neighborhoods, but the forces that generate abandonment and make arson almost inevitable are still at play.

So, while the struggles to save existing working-class housing have been impressive, we have still lost more than we have saved. Has more been accomplished by those who have focused on trying to increase the supply of affordable housing through antiredlining campaigns, home mortgage subsidy programs, support for squatters, and sweat-equity rehabilitation programs? Measured in terms of benefits to low-income tenants and neighborhoods, the results have been as meager as the gains made through defensive struggles.

In a few cases, nonprofit community development corporations (CDCs) have succeeded in building or rehabilitating quality housing projects with low and moderate rents. The largest and best known is Villa Victoria, a 500-unit development in Boston's South End. The great majority of the residents, board members, management, and employees are Hispanic, and the project serves as a center of community and cultural life. By its existence, Villa Victoria has helped prevent the complete physical and spiritual dispersal of the Latino community from the South End. But while the energies of many Hispanic activists have been absorbed by building and managing Villa Victoria and defending the project against charges of discrimination against non-Hispanics, the relentless pressure of rising rents and condo conversion is driving the majority of Latinos out of the surrounding neighborhood.

As a relatively successful CDC, Villa Victoria is the exception that proves the rule. Most other CDCs have failed to save or create any significant amount of affordable housing. A number of churches and nonprofit community groups developed low- and moderate-rent apartment complexes in the late 1960s and early 1970s under HUD 236 and 221(d)(3) programs. Most of these projects were caught in the squeeze between rising costs and inadequate subsidies; many nonprofit as well as for-profit owners defaulted on mortgage payments, with ownership of the projects reverting to HUD. In recent years HUD has been rushing to get these projects back on the private market, offering them to investors on a silver, tax-sheltered platter. New owners of projects in "upscale" neighborhoods are being given the green light to raise rents and evict those who cannot pay the increases. In projects where rents have been kept low by Section 8 rent subsidies from the pre-Reagan era, HUD allows landlords to minimize maintenance in order to keep profits up.

More recent attempts at nonprofit housing development have been defeated by the pro-market, pro-gentrification orientation of the city, state, and federal government. For example, residents of Mission Hill had a tentative commitment of federal funds to build a large, mixed-income project on vacant land where 90 triple-decker houses had been demolished. The mayor's Office of Housing refused approval for the project on the grounds that the neighborhood already had "too much" subsidized housing. A plan for conversion of a vacant school in Jamaica Plain to mixed-income rental housing was sabotaged by City Hall on similar grounds. In June of 1983, the city asked for federal urban development subsidies to back conversion of the same school into condominiums with an average sales price of $90,000! Other would-be development groups have found that current HUD subsidy guidelines would at best enable them to produce a token number of low-cost units in predominantly market-rate or "moderate-income" projects, with "moderate" defined in the $30,000 to $40,000 income range.

What of the efforts to increase the housing supply in inner-city areas by channeling private investment in the form of home mortgage loans into targeted neighborhoods? Some Boston community groups have tried to combine the carrot of government-guaranteed mortgage funds with the stick of antiredlining legislation. No one has seriously tried to force mortgage lenders to invest in the most badly rundown neighborhoods, but in borderline areas with gentrification potential, local banks have been only too happy to oblige by granting loans to young professionals. In a few cases families that would not otherwise have been able to afford a house have received loans, but the net effect of these programs seems to have been an increase in the pace of housing price increases and a stimulus to gentrification.

Other groups have seen sweat-equity rehabilitation as the key to getting inner-city housing into the hands of low- and moderate-income residents [*see Chapter 26 by Robert Kolodny and Chapter 27 by Tony Schuman*]. But here again, those able to take advantage of this approach have been those who have started out with considerable resources. People with carpentry skills, people able to afford to hire a lawyer, buy materials, and take time off from work have been able to acquire vacant townhouses and single-family homes and make them habitable. But most people who obtained these houses already had housing and were looking for something better to live in—or invest in. Most sweat-equity efforts by people truly in need of housing, whether in legal or extralegal (squatting) situations, have ended in failure; residents' incomes are simply too low to cover the costs of needed maintenance and repairs.

Although the material gains have been small, tenant union organizing, rent strikes, and rent control and anti-condo agitation have helped to make housing one of the most hotly contested issues in the city. As conversations in beauty parlors or barrooms quickly reveal, working-class Bostonians are upset and angry about the high cost and shortage of housing and particularly about the deterioration of neighborhoods. More than a few of them are willing to do something about it. Protests over rent increases, condo conversions, school closings, lack of garbage collection, threats to HUD-subsidized developments and to public housing projects, arson, and city auctions of property to profiteers continue to flare up like brushfires all over the city, especially in black and racially mixed working-class neighborhoods.

Sometimes these actions are spontaneous; more often they are associated with organizations like City Life, ACORN, or neighborhood associations. Sometimes the protests remain confined to "established channels"; often tactics rapidly turn more militant: rent strikes, demonstrations, and disruptions at government offices and public hearings.

In addition to this activism, there exists substantial passive support for rent control. In the fall of 1982, members of the Boston People's Organization held a petition drive to place questions favoring moderate rent and condo controls on ballots in five state representative districts within the city. The questions passed easily in all five districts, with an average margin of victory of 73 percent. All of this suggests that there is fertile ground in Boston for the growth of a stronger, more unified housing movement.

## The Weakness of the Tenants' Movement

In spite of this apparent potential for growth, the tenants' movement in Boston today is weak and organizationally fragmented. Most of the neighborhood-based tenant organizations that formed around the tenant union and rent control battles of the early 1970s have disbanded or are shells of their former selves. (City Life, which began as the Jamaica Plain Tenants Action Group in 1973 and is now a strong, multi-issue, citywide organization, is an exception.) Several attempts to unite these groups into citywide coalitions failed during 1978–1982, and the momentum of the earlier period was never recovered. While the level of dedication and accumulated experience among housing activists here is enormous, the tenants' movement as such seems incapable of building on its own past efforts.

The tenants' movement in Boston cannot be said to have failed because it has been unable to stop displacement and the gentrification of the central city. Cities in nearly all the advanced capitalist countries are being reshaped in similar ways, and the movements against displacement in Paris and London have not had much more success than we have. There are also factors particular to Boston that may make it especially hard to build a strong citywide movement here: the virtual ownership of city hall by real estate interests, the absence of strong labor and black organizations, and the depth of racism in the city.

But of all the barriers that stand in the way of success for the tenants' movement in Boston, the greatest is the changing economics of urban real estate and the growing gap between the profit levels required by housing investors and the ability of tenants to pay the rents necessary to provide those profits. It is the failure of the tenants' movement to come to grips with this reality that is at the root of its weakness.

Many housing activists are aware, of course, that it is harder to win material gains under today's conditions. For the most part, their response to this realization has been one of strategic retreat, a decision—perhaps not always a conscious decision—to narrow the focus of their efforts and limit their goals to moderate, short-range proposals in the hope of at least cutting the movement's losses.

Our view in City Life is that only a bolder, more radical approach can carry us forward. The economic changes that have brought about a total sellers' market in housing and accelerated the destruction of housing and neighborhoods have drastically reduced the room for gains that might be achieved through regulation of the private market. The basis for "tenant power" as it existed in the late 1960s and early 1970s has been eroded. But these same changes have created the conditions—and the necessity—for a movement to save working-class communities and housing by substituting public for private investment and collective for capitalist control.

## Toward a New Direction

To develop this alternative, much new ground must be broken on both a theoretical and a practical level. This is work that City Life has only just begun, but even at this early stage we can describe some major differences between a liberal–reformist approach to housing issues and organizing and a socialist one. By analyzing the arguments and tactics used by reformist tenant organizations in recent years, we can get a clearer picture of the implications of this approach and the assumptions on which it is based, and we can sketch the outlines of a more promising alternative.

1. *In arguing for rent and condominium controls, reformist tenant leaders have failed to challenge the assumption that solutions to the housing crisis can*

*and must be found within the boundaries of the housing-for-profit system. It is precisely this premise that needs to be refuted.*

During every round of the rent control battle in Boston and elsewhere in Massachusetts over the past 12 years, the PR men for the Rental Housing Association and other real estate interests have stepped into the ring of reporters and TV cameras to tell the same sad tale. [*See Chapter 9 by David Bartelt and Ronald Lawson.*]

"If rent and condo controls are adopted," they say, "we can't survive. Investment in Boston's housing will decline. Buildings will have to be abandoned."

In other words: "If you try to restrict our profits to the 8 percent to 10 percent level, we'll take our money and put it into something that will yield us 15 to 20 percent, like condominiums on Cape Cod, tax-exempt bonds, or a silicon chip factory in Singapore," which is the kind of thing any rational capitalist would do.

When the tenant organizations have gotten their turn in the ring, far too often their response has been to apologize for rent control.

"You've got it wrong," they say. "Rent control won't cause disinvestment, or at least the kind of rent control we're proposing won't. You can't *prove* rent control is the cause of abandonment. Anyway, we don't want to eliminate the 'fair' profits, only the 'exorbitant' ones. We've got nothing against the good, responsible landlords. It's those greedy, law-breaking types we want to get rid of."

In effect, the tenants have conceded the most important points in the landlords' argument. They have accepted the notion that those who own the shelter of others have a right to profit from it. They have agreed that those profits must be protected, to some degree at least, so that landlords and bankers will continue to invest in housing. They have reinforced the assumption that holds up these arguments: that private investment is the only way housing can be developed, owned, and maintained.

Once these premises have been established, the rest of the real estate industry's position flows logically from them. The landlords come across sounding hard-boiled but realistic, while the tenants' movement is left with little more than a moral plea against throwing old folks and children out on the street.

The irony is that the real estate industry argument could be demolished more easily if the tenants' movement were not afraid to challenge it head-on by refuting the claim that increased private investment is good for everyone. We need only look around us to see the result of rising investment and increased property values: Most of us can no longer afford to live in the areas where this has occurred. And in the few cases where private investment, leveraged by public funds, has resulted in low- and moderate-rent housing, this has been possible only because working-class taxpayers have subsidized real estate profits from these projects. Private investment is the heart of the problem, not the key to the solution.

The fact is, any form of rent control strong enough to keep the average rent in Boston down to a level affordable by the average Boston renter—

never mind the really poor—would have to cause a significant reduction in rental housing profits. Certainly this would lead many if not most landlords who own housing for investment purposes to look elsewhere for a better return. In short, any version of rent control strong enough to be worth fighting for *will* cause some amount of disinvestment.

What would happen if the tenants' movement, instead of denying this reality, proclaimed it, and presented it as an opportunity to take the first steps toward getting housing out of the hands of private capitalists? What if our attitude were as follows:

"The landlords say rent control will put them out of business? Well, if they can't provide decent housing at rents we can afford, why should we allow them to remain in business? Let's start working on a better way to run housing."

2. *The programmatic proposals of the tenants' movement have been almost entirely defensive ones. Instead, campaigns for defensive measures like rent control must be accompanied by positive proposals for saving and increasing the supply of affordable housing.*

If we are going to advocate the restriction of rental housing profits, which is what rent control must do to be effective, then we have to come up with a plan for how housing can be developed and maintained by something other than investment for profit. In themselves, rent and condo controls do not point toward such a plan.

Many city folks already understand, on a gut level at least, that effective rent control is incompatible with the continued profitability of real estate, but no one has yet presented them with any alternative to a devil's choice between higher rents and increased abandonment. The tenants' movement's inability to do this has made it hard for us to make a convincing argument that rent control can benefit all working-class residents of this city.

A working-class homeowner, or even a tenant who is not facing imminent loss of her or his apartment, can easily see that the only neighborhoods where streets are being repaired, schools kept open, and housing maintained are those where landlords and banks are investing and housing costs are going up. That same individual may realize that the price of this investment is the displacement of one class of residents by another. The tenant may feel terrible about the fact that less fortunate friends and neighbors are being forced to move away. Yet it is perfectly rational for the tenant to expect that the adoption of rent control will increase the likelihood that the apartment building across the street may be abandoned.

Until we can show such a tenant another choice between deterioration and gentrification, we will not be able to persuade that person to become an active supporter of rent control. As important as rent control is, it makes sense only as part of a broader program that addresses the issues of neighborhood decay and the housing shortage.

3. *Plans for saving or developing housing that leave that housing dependent on private ownership and capitalist financing are doomed to fail, since the housing involved will be subject to the same economic pressures that are*

*eliminating existing affordable housing. Only plans based on the decommod-*
*ification—or socialization—of housing can be the basis for real solutions.*

The general outline of how a plan for socialization might be applied on a national scale has been laid out by Chester Hartman and Michael E. Stone [*see Chapter 29*]. In City Life we are working on how to apply a similar approach to Boston. City Life's Housing Platform for Boston focuses on housing issues around which there is already a great deal of organizing, struggle, and public debate. It proposes steps that, in the case of each issue, would take the housing involved *in the direction* of decommodification. In itself it would not achieve full socialization, which of course is impossible in the context of a capitalist-controlled government, financial system, and labor market. But all the measures contained in it would be steps toward decreased control and ownership by private landlords and financial institutions, and increased collective, nonprofit ownership and/or control by tenants, community residents, and the public.

For example, along with strong rent and eviction controls, the platform calls for the right of tenants to form unions and sign collective bargaining agreements with landlords, and for determination by local residents of development plans for city-owned and tax-foreclosed buildings and land. These proposals are not included because tenant and community control are solutions in themselves. These demands are there because they provide specific, short-range goals that working-class people can fight for while building power to win more far-reaching measures. Organizing by tenant unions to prevent condo conversions and by community groups to block luxury development projects can help—and have helped—to hold the line against speculation in strategic neighborhoods while providing a focal point from which to expand organizing.

The platform calls for increased resources for existing public housing, for foreclosure and permanent public ownership of HUD-subsidized developments, and for support for nonprofit, community-based housing development, and low-equity cooperatives. We talk about the measures not as a way of filling the gaps left by the private market but as steps toward the socialization of all housing. We describe our goal as tenant-controlled, publicly owned and financed housing, but we see other forms of collective, nonprofit ownership (except where coop conversions drive out low-income tenants) as steps in the right direction.

A more radical measure in the platform, aimed at the same goal, is the proposal for a city-financed, democratically controlled agency (The Community Housing and Land Trust) with the power to take over a certain number of absentee-owned apartment buildings per year, primarily buildings in substandard condition or in tax arrears. With funds from taxes on speculation profits and other sources, the buildings would be rehabilitated and operated as public housing or low-equity coops. This proposal is an essential component of any plan for strong rent control, which is bound to be met with threatened or actual disinvestment by landlords. By offering an alternative to abandonment, such a plan would also increase the incentive for tenants to form unions and struggle for control of their buildings. (Under current conditions, successful organizing sometimes results in landlord abandonment and leaves tenants worse off than before.) This proposal, along with an accompanying demand to stop all transfers of public, HUD, and city-owned housing and land to the private market, presents the concept of socialization in a concrete form.

The platform contains no measure to increase individual homeownership. By proposing the extension of rent control to owner-occupied two- and three-family houses, it aims to make investment in homeownership ("let your tenants pay your mortgage") less profitable. At the same time it recognizes that many working-class homeowners are hard-pressed, and calls for grants and loans for weatherization and repairs by low- and moderate-income homeowners.

Also included is a proposal to give homeowners who are unable to afford mortgage and maintenance costs and are therefore facing the loss of their homes the option of turning over title to their houses to a public agency. They would forfeit the right to sell their house for profit but would retain the right to remain there. The intention here is to separate the negative aspects of homeownership (the burden of debt and the temptation to exploit one's tenants) from the socially positive aspects (security of tenure and the incentive to improve one's home). Rather than say everyone should have a chance to own a house—an impossible goal—we say, everyone, whether they live in a house or apartment, must have the right to secure tenure and decent conditions.

The platform does not contain any proposals that would aid bankers and housing investors, such as home mortgage subsidies, loans to profit-making developers for low-income housing construction, or Section 8 rent subsidies. These kinds of programs underwrite the power and profits of the real estate industry in the guise of aiding low- and moderate-income people. They create increased public debts that must be paid for by current and future generations of workers [*see Chapter 17 by Robert Schur and Tom Robbins*].

The essential difference between City Life's and a social democratic approach is not whether or not we fight for reforms—all the proposals in our platform are, of course, reforms. Rather, the differences lie in the kinds of reforms we support (only those that promote public or nonprofit ownership and control and none that subsidize private capital), in the way in which we believe those reforms can be won (in response to pressure from below, not through top-down legislative or administrative measures), and in whether the reforms are presented as ends in themselves or as steps toward socialism and working-class power.

In organizing around the platform, we try to play up, not tone down, its radical implications, using the proposals to illustrate the contrast between present profits-first housing policies and the kind of housing system that would satisfy our needs. It is essential to make clear to the people with whom we organize that powerful interests stand in the way of our ability to win and keep reforms like good public housing, effective rent control, and even enforcement of antidiscrimination laws.

If, by some sleight-of-hand, we were able—without the support of a mass movement—to suddenly win legislation embodying our program, we would accomplish very little. Real estate capitalists, like any others, will respond to a threat to their interests by mobilizing all the resources at their disposal. We could expect threats of large-scale housing abandonment, foreclosures, and bank failures, refusals to back municipal bonds, and red-baiting and prediction of doom by the mass media. Unless those who stand to gain by our program were prepared for this and ready to respond with increased struggle, the laws would not remain on the books for long.

In fact, this is a moot point, since our program will not be adopted *except* in response to a mass movement that erodes the power of real estate interests at the grassroots level and disrupts the procapitalist consensus. And the only way a program involving the partial socialization of housing could be maintained and made workable would be by following up the initial measures with increased public investment and further socialization, requiring more mass support. There are no legislative or administrative shortcuts to socialism; it can be brought about only through class struggle.

The proposals in City Life's Platform for Boston are only first steps toward socialization. It is the growth of the movement that will make it possible first to imagine and later to win more far-reaching changes. Meanwhile, it is important to present very concrete, although limited, goals and demands because they give people a way to struggle for their own interests *now*, and in the process to develop the consciousness and power that will make socialization possible.

City Life's Platform is a platform for Boston; almost all its goals could conceivably be won and implemented on a city level. We chose this focus not because we think we can win socialism in one city or in one sector; obviously changes in state and federal policies are essential, and housing cannot be separated from other economic issues. Nevertheless, by focusing on one city and one main issue we can go a long way in dramatizing the conflict between working-class and capitalist interests and in identifying resources, which could be redirected right now to meet the needs of those whose labor produces them in the first place.

4. *In recent years, much of the organized tenants' movement has confined itself to strictly legal tactics, with a focus on lobbying the state legislature and city councils. We must move beyond this to build a movement with the power to alter the status quo by directly challenging the control over housing and land in the city by landlords, bankers, and judges.*

The early 1970s, when the tenants' movement fought to save rent control in Massachusetts, was a time of rent strikes, eviction blockings, and militant, disruptive demonstrations. It was the effect of this kind of direct action and the fear that the situation might get out of hand, more than the reasoned testimony of experts or the pleas of suffering constituents, that influenced state and city lawmakers to extend rent control.

This was even clearer in the case of the battle to win rent control in Cambridge in 1969. There, a year of lobbying, mass petitioning, and even a successful rent control referendum failed to persuade the City Council to pass rent control: The proposal was voted down in June and again in August. But six weeks later, after a series of well-publicized eviction blockings in defiance of the police and the courts, the same City Council suddenly reversed its earlier vote, and rent control was adopted.

Cambridge activist Pat Hammond explained the council's reasoning:

> Each time the issue of rent control was before them they asked themselves: "Will it control tenants better than no rent control?" As tenants became more and more organized, moving from scattered to militant resistance, organized tenant unions and a movement capable of blocking evictions; as tenants began to think and act collectively, autonomous of landlords, courts, politicians and their ideas of right and wrong, it became obvious that the "free market" wasn't working any more to keep tenants in their place. It was time for the council to place their chips on rent control. (Hammond, 1982)

The militancy and momentum of these movements proved hard to sustain after the mid-1970s. But the lessons of this experience seem to have been forgotten by the leaders of the rent and condominium control movements in Massachusetts and Boston today. This is particularly true of the Massachusetts Tenants Organization (MTO), a group launched five years ago by members of the Democratic Socialists of America, which is trying to unite a loose coalition of tenant unions and neighborhood groups behind its campaign for legislative housing reforms.

While the MTO does encourage the formation of tenant unions, the crux of its strategy is bringing "tenant power" to bear on City Hall and the statehouse through lobbying and the selective endorsement of political candidates. The organization's focus is strictly on renters' rights, narrowly defined and separated from other urban and economic issues. By building broad support for moderate, lowest-common-denominator proposals, the MTO hopes to win real, if limited, gains for tenants.

For example, when Boston's weak rent control ordinance was due to expire at the end of 1982, the MTO decided not to push for strong rent control or even for reinstatement of the moderate, pre-1976 version. Instead, the MTO came up with a proposal for a Rent Grievance Board to which tenants could appeal rent increases. It was a measure that appeared to have a chance of passage precisely because it would not impinge significantly on the interests of most landlords and developers, and indeed, after an intensive lobbying campaign, a watered-down version of the grievance board was adopted.

This pathetically weak measure has done little to stem the tide of rent increases. Most MTO members would agree, but they say they lacked the power to squeeze anything better out of the council at the time. This may be true, but the real shame lies in the fact that all the effort put into lobbying, press releases, and backroom negotiations did nothing to shift the terms of public debate on housing to the left, or to educate and prepare tenants for the kinds of programs and struggles that will be necessary really to improve housing conditions. A continuation of this strategy will insure that the movement will be in the same weak position next time around.

The MTO-sponsored Boston Tenant Campaign Organization (BTCO) followed a similar strategy during the 1981 Boston City Council race when it did door-knocking and fund-raising on behalf of six of the candidates who were already in the running. The six were chosen solely on the basis of their answers to a BTCO questionnaire on rent and condo controls. Although only one member of the "tenants' slate" was elected, the campaign was hailed as a victory by the MTO because it "made tenants a force to be reckoned with in Boston politics." Even had the entire slate been elected, this claim would be far-fetched, since the BTCO would have had no way to make the candidates who received their blessing accountable once they were elected. Pro-tenant campaign rhetoric has seldom inhibited the other councillors from voting against rent control.

It may make sense—as one element of a broader strategy—for a strong housing movement to endorse or sponsor candidates and legislation. But it will not be possible to *build* a strong movement by focusing primarily on the electoral process and short-term gains while steering close to the ideological mainstream. On the contrary, this approach creates and reinforces illusions about what can be won at the ballot box. It is based on the idea that power in this society flows from political office, when in reality, the questions of who holds office and what policies they set are *reflections* of power relations in the society as a whole.

Most officeholders—regardless of their campaign promises or the wishes of their constituents—make decisions on housing policy that favor banking and real estate interests. This is because the bankers and landlords have the power to direct the flow of housing and commercial investment and—as Mayor Kucinich learned in Cleveland—to use financial blackmail to threaten to bankrupt city governments and destroy political careers. We will not be able to get a better performance out of elected officials, even if we get "our own" into office, until we are able to challenge this power at the top with the countervailing power of a movement that exerts pressure for change from below.

To build this power we need to reject capitalist notions of justice based on the priority of property rights. We must challenge the authority of landlords and judges to extort, displace, and evict, through our actions as well as our arguments. We have to organize to disrupt their system, refusing to pay unaffordable—although legal—rents, and refusing to accept unjust—although legal—evictions.

Workers in the 1880s and 1890s did not win the right to strike by lobbying their congressmen. The labor movement of the 1930s and 1940s won legal backing only after taking direct, extralegal action that threatened the bosses' power at its source, the site of production. If the civil rights movement of the 1950s and 1960s had confined itself to tactics like those of the MTO, Jim Crow would still reign in the South. Just as in the past, we will be able to change the laws that oppress us only by building a movement that makes the enforcement of unjust laws impossible.

5. *A corollary of the strictly legal, reformist approach is the concept of "tenant power" based on a cross-class alliance of renters as an interest group.*

*What is needed instead is a movement that has as its priority the needs of working-class tenants and homeowners.*

The cross-class alliance strategy is based on the assumption that in the area of housing, middle-income and high-income renters have the same basic interests as low-income renters. More than that, middle-class tenants are seen as the motive force, the engine that drives the coalition, because they can provide more votes, funds, connections, and skills.

The assumption that renters of all classes have similar interests is valid only to a very limited extent. High-income and moderate-income tenants stand to gain from moderate rent and eviction and condo restrictions that give them more bargaining power with landlords and keep rents low enough to allow them more to spend on their "lifestyle," or to save for a down payment on a house or condo. These tenants want to avoid extreme or sudden rent increases; nevertheless, they can afford to pay rents high enough to keep supplying the landlords with profits. These people have been the main beneficiaries of the kind of moderate-to-weak rent controls that were won in Boston in the early 1970s and more recently in a number of California and New Jersey cities.

It would be naive to expect middle-class renters to go out on a limb and risk their own immediate gains for the interests of the greater majority of tenants, who can benefit significantly only from much stronger versions of rent control and other anticapitalist reforms that must accompany strong rent control. This is especially true when those middle-class tenants have been appealed to by the movement in terms of their individual, immediate economic interests alone. Furthermore, the very skills and resources that make middle-class tenants so valuable to campaigns for moderate rent control also put them in a strong position to limit and control the campaigns.

At City Life we are attempting to base our program and organizing strategy on the needs of people whose housing problems cannot be solved by rent control alone. This is not only because they are the majority but also because their interests lie in collective, noncapitalist solutions.

6. *In order to establish the basis for a multiracial, working-class housing movement, connections must be made both in theory and in practice between the situation of public and private housing tenants, and between "renters' rights" and other housing issues, such as arson and abandonment.*

With few exceptions, tenant organizations in Boston have failed to explain the housing crisis as a whole, but instead have focused on one issue at a time. They have not put forward an analysis of that crisis that exposes its roots and reveals the intimate connection between its gentrification–investment and its abandonment–disinvestment aspects. Because of this, the tenants' movement has failed to create the ideological, programmatic, and organizational basis for a common action and mutual support between people threatened with the loss of their homes to condo conversion and soaring rents, and folks on the other side of the tracks who are losing their homes to fire, decay, and abandonment.

The result is a movement weakened by divisions that, to a great extent, have developed along racial lines. The organizations and coalitions that have led the struggles for rent control since 1975 have been predominantly white, and have seldom succeeded in getting groups from the black, Latino, and Chinese communities actively involved. The reason for this is not that people of color have nothing to gain from rent control and condo restrictions. But other issues—deterioration of public housing, the threat to HUD-sponsored, low-income developments, arson, and abandonment—have been seen by people of color as posing the greatest immediate threat to their homes and communities, and have provoked them into taking action.

For the most part, the predominantly white tenant groups have not given direct support to these struggles. They have not accompanied their calls for rent control with proposals that speak to the problems of disinvestment and they have tried to steer clear of supposedly "divisive" issues such as public housing. This is not only because of racism and the fact that tenants in many neighborhoods are out of touch with the housing problems that affect minority communities. It is also because these problems require more radical solutions than most tenant organizations have been willing to endorse or even to conceive of. This is a loss to the white tenant groups because there is a great deal they could gain by allying more closely with people of color, whose hard experience has led them to see more clearly the need for militancy and for more fundamental change.

7. *The liberal–reformist approach tries to "keep ideology out of organizing," but the two cannot be separated. A socialist analysis and program are needed to strengthen and give direction to the movement for better housing. At the same time, we need to strengthen the grassroots movement in order to develop and to win our program.*

Many academic experts agree with City Life that socialization of housing is necessary, but will not say so except to other members of the elite inner circle of experts and organizers. Ordinary folks, they assume, are incapable of understanding a socialist program and would not support it if they did understand it.

Our experience suggests something quite different. Whenever we have presented our ideas about socialization and the steps to get there from here, the response has been overwhelmingly positive. When the alternative is continued devastation and insecurity, socialization does not appear to be a utopian fantasy or a threat to the American way of life. Most city folks do not need to be convinced that radical changes are needed—only that they are winnable and workable. The kinds of questions and doubts about our proposals that people express are usually very pragmatic: How would this plan apply to the lot across the street? How can we wring these concessions out of landlords and the government? How will tenant and community control of publicly owned housing work? Where do we begin?

If we make it our conscious goal, we can help people engaged in organizing around rent control, in tenant unions, against arson and abandonment, and so forth, to understand their own situation in terms of the overall housing crisis and the broader crisis of capitalism. We can also show them that something better *is* possible and that their own efforts are helping to make it more possible. This knowledge in itself helps make people feel stronger and better able to keep fighting when victories seem distant or small. This is one way that having a socialist program helps to strengthen the movement. It also provides a framework for alliances among people struggling around different kinds of housing issues and a set of guidelines to help people formulate their specific goals and demands.

Not surprisingly, people whose own housing prospects under the current system are bleak are most enthusiastic about the idea of socialized housing: tenants who have been "condo-ed out" more than once, homeowners who are unemployed and fear foreclosure, organized tenants who discover their landlord would rather walk away than put money into repairs. As housing options narrow, more people will find themselves in a position where a plan for increased public investment and socialization offers the only alternative to worse housing than they had before, or to homelessness.

But experience also has shown us that not only people who stand to gain in a direct, economic way can be won to the idea of socialization. People do not live in housing alone; they are part of families, neighborhoods, and communities—or at least they would like to be. Goals like improving the quality of life in one's neighborhood or the city as a whole, and of helping other folks obtain decent housing also motivate people. For instance, some of the most active members of City Life's rent control committee have been people who, as residents of HUD low-income projects, were not directly affected by Boston rent control.

Often the most important motivation is the experience of the struggle itself: the challenge and satisfaction of working with others for a goal beyond one's personal, material gain and the sense of community and solidarity that comes from being part of the movement. In this sense many tenants and community folks are not different from those of us housing organizers who became active, not to save the roof over our own heads, but to work for a better society.

The time to build a movement for socialized housing is ripe, but this does not imply that we should stop organizing against slumlords and arson, and for better public housing and rent control, in order to mount a national campaign for the socialization of housing. It is only through the process of direct organizing that we will be able to build the power to win our larger goal. Every instance of people fighting to save a building or a parcel of land can help us to build this power, especially when we win. But even when we lose, our power can grow if, in the process of struggle, people get better organized, gain skills and confidence and a better understanding of the system and the need to change it. It is our job as socialists to see that the organization gets built, the skills developed, and the connections made.

So, while we do need citywide, statewide, and national organizations and programs, we can not skip over the local stage. It will only be after the power of bankers and landlords begins to weaken, as poor and working people gain more direct control over urban housing and land, that the concept of treating housing and land as a socially owned resource will be taken seriously by policymakers who scoff at the idea today.

There is another reason our movement needs to be built from the bottom up. Socialization of housing—like socialism in general—can only go so far without a transformation of social relationships. The elimination of control by those who own housing for profit is only the precondition for this transformation. For socialization to work well, residents of buildings and blocks need to develop a sense of mutual support and responsibility and learn to work collectively. It is through the process of common struggle that this sense of community is developed or rediscovered. It is a gradual and uneven process, but it really does occur. All of us in City Life would surely have lost heart if we did not see ourselves and the people in the buildings and neighborhoods where we organize going through changes of this kind as we work and struggle together.

# 25

# Low-Income Homeownership and the ACORN Squatters Campaign

*Seth Borgos*

*One organized consumer response to the housing crisis is squatting—taking over vacant houses and fixing them up. The squatting campaign organized by ACORN in over a dozen U.S. cities, modeled after an earlier grassroots action in Philadelphia, has assisted hundreds of low-income families in acquiring low-cost housing. The approach rests on the conviction that unoccupied housing (e.g., housing that landlords have abandoned or city government has taken over because of property-tax delinquency) should be returned to the community as quickly as possible, and that squatters can play a major role in fixing up these dwellings to keep costs down. The desire for home-ownership is seen as a key motivating force behind the strength of a squatters' movement. Furthermore, squatting, as a tactic, demonstrates the principle that the right to decent housing takes precedence over the rights of property; it has the potential of forcing government to assume increased responsibility for low-income housing.*

By official estimates, there are more than 20,000 abandoned houses in Philadelphia. The densest concentration of these houses is in the neighborhoods of North Philadelphia, flanking Broad Street for hundreds of blocks from City Hall to the city line.

The characteristic housing form of North Philadelphia is the single-family, brick row house, narrow, unadorned, and unpretentious. For decades following their construction in the nineteenth century, these houses and neighborhoods provided a stable and affordable environment to lower-middle-class and working-class families. In the years following World War II, this environment was violated. Houses were purchased by speculators and subsequently abandoned; houses were foreclosed on and left vacant; houses were demolished, leaving gaps like missing teeth in formerly solid blocks. Paradoxically, as the number of vacant houses mounted, so did the number of low- and moderate-income Philadelphians who lacked safe and affordable housing.

On a bright cold Saturday in March 1982, 200 people gathered on the street in front of Calvary Church at 29th Street and Lehigh Avenue in North Philadelphia. After a round of speeches decrying the abandonment and neglect of their neighborhoods, the demonstrators marched a few blocks down Lehigh, chanting "two-four-six-eight, we want houses, we can't wait!" and "We're fired up, can't take no more!" Then they swept down a narrow side street, with TV cameras, plainclothes police, and curious onlookers in their wake. Passing houses draped with makeshift banners proclaiming *Welcome, ACORN squatters*, the crowd halted in front of a boarded-up house in the center of the block. A young black woman mounted the steps and addressed the crowd:

> I decided to squat because . . . we are in Richard Allen project and you know what that's like—the rats and the crime and the stink and all. . . . I need a house for my children! This is our moment. We are going to fix up this house and make it a place to live.

The crowd applauded. Two men with crowbars climbed the steps and pried the sheet metal off the doorway. The young woman raised her arm in a gesture of victory, and the crowd cheered. She turned and entered the house, followed by the cameras and the curious.

The house was in good condition, considering the neglect it had suffered; the young woman was pleased. Some neighbors brought brooms and plastic trash bags to remove the debris. The police remained outside, observing the scene and relaying perfunctory reports on their walkie-talkies.

Through the afternoon, the march snaked its way across the neighborhood, stopping every few blocks to tear the boards off an abandoned house. The ritual was reenacted at each site. Later, there was an impromptu barbecue on a vacant lot. The crowd slowly diminished as cars departed for parallel actions in South and Southwest Philadelphia. By the end of the day, squatters had seized 30 more houses in the city.

## Some History

To squat is to occupy property without permission of its owner. It is the time-hallowed response of the landless to the contradiction between their own impoverishment and a surfeit of unutilized property.

In nineteenth-century America, with its vast expanses of wilderness, squatting was a common way of life. Though widely sanctioned on the frontier, its extension to settled and urbanizing areas was more problematic. When gold was discovered in Sacramento in 1849, the boom attracted land speculators who acquired lots cheaply and rented them for thousands of dollars a month. Prospectors could not or would not pay these prices, so they settled where they pleased and formed a Settlers Association to represent their interests. The landowners responded in 1850 by getting a law passed that allowed evictions without the customary legal protections. In August of that year, a squatter was evicted from his land and thrown in jail. Members of the Settlers Association immediately united to defend him, and a shoot-out ensued (Royce, 1885).

A similar mode of squatting flourishes today in cities of developing countries around the world, from San Juan, Puerto Rico, to Capetown, South Africa. In cities such as these, swollen by migration from rural areas, housing for the poor is crowded, unsafe, or simply unavailable. The poor solve the problem by squatting on vacant land at the margins of the city. In some instances, squatters have succeeded in creating full-fledged communities, with streets, utilities, schools, and permanent houses. In other cases their settlements have been bulldozed by the authorities (Ross, 1973; Stren, 1975; *Washington Post*, May 20, 1983).

Squatting inevitably conveys a political message, critical of the existing system, even when squatters are not conscious of it. The symbolic authority of the act has not gone unnoticed by political movements seeking an effective protest tactic.

An example from our own history is the Bonus Expeditionary Force of 1932. Three hundred unemployed World War I veterans began a journey to Washington, D.C., to demand an advance payment of veterans' bonuses promised by Congress. The idea caught on, and some 20,000 veterans descended on the capital, where they squatted in vacant buildings and on federal land. The squatters were an embarrassment to President Hoover, who asked Congress to pay the way home of any veteran who wanted to leave. Few took advantage of the offer. Finally, Hoover called in the army. Six tanks and 700 troops rousted the squatters with teargas and burned their shacks. However, the protest could not be considered a failure; Hoover lost the election that year, and Roosevelt's New Deal provided some relief to the unemployed (Warren, 1967).

Later in that decade, a group called the Southern Tenant Farmers Union organized a protest by 1,700 sharecropper families who had been evicted from their farms. These families camped out beside a major highway in southeast Missouri. After confrontations with the police, they eventually won cash relief and resettlement in Farm Security Administration housing (Grubbs, 1971; Mitchell, 1979).

In the past 15 years squatters' movements have bloomed in the major cities of Western Europe. The character of these movements is explicitly political. Although some of the predominantly young squatters are motivated by personal housing needs, and a few disclaim political intent, the fundamental thrust of the action is a collective protest against policies that have created severe housing shortages in these affluent cities, and against the development-at-any-cost values that undergird these policies. The new European squatters have not yet succeeded in stemming the tide of development. But they have fought the authorities to a standstill in their own enclaves, and have established de facto "squatters' rights" on many occasions (Greenfield, 1981; Kearns, 1980).

This capsule survey suggests that governments may respond to squatting with repression or concession. Another common response is to "tame" squatting by licensing it within a restricted context. In the United States this has gone under the name of "homesteading."

The first national homesteading legislation was approved by Congress in 1862. It provided free grants of federal land to applicants who would improve the land for agriculture and reside there for at least five years.

The Homestead Act was the product of a 20-year debate over the disposition of public land on the frontier. Supporters of homesteading contended that it would encourage owner occupancy of land and accelerate settlement; they also saw homesteading as an "escape valve for the urban poor and a way of avoiding downward pressure on wages."[1] Opponents of homesteading argued that

> . . . giving away land would lower property values of remaining land and create an injustice to those who had paid for the property. They also argued that it would entice the unprepared and unwary into a highly risky venture. Finally, they argued that homesteading was an indiscriminate form of charity that helped those perfectly able to support themselves instead of those who legitimately needed public aid.

The initial homesteading proposals reflected the radical views of their sponsors: Grants were to be limited to the poor, and the sale of government land was to be curtailed. But many legislators felt that the urban poor would be unable to meet the expenses of moving to the frontier and improving the land. As finally enacted, the Homestead Act of 1862 contained no eligibility restrictions on income or assets. And the federal government continued to sell prime land to speculators and award large tracts to railroad companies.

On its own terms, the Homestead Act was a success. Hundreds of thousands of individuals received land grants, and many succeeded as farmers. The main beneficiaries of the program were families of moderate means who could afford the cost of travel, supplies, and equipment. The program declined as the frontier moved west to agriculturally marginal land, and it was finally closed down in the twentieth century.

A generation later, the concept of an "urban frontier" came into vogue, and with it came a new field for homesteading. Urban homesteading was a response to two distinct problems. One was the flight of private investment from inner-city neighborhoods, which led to a rapid increase in housing abandonment. In the early 1970s, Wilmington, Baltimore, and Philadelphia established experimental programs that sold abandoned houses for a nominal fee to homesteaders who agreed to rehabilitate them. The other problem was a growing inventory of vacant federally owned houses, generated mainly by foreclosures of FHA-insured mortgages (Boyer, 1973). In 1970, the FHA owned 21,000 single-family properties; by 1974 it owned 78,000.[2] Congress responded by authorizing a federal homesteading program in Section 810 of the Housing and Community Development Act of 1974.

During the congressional floor debate on this measure, proponents argued that homesteading of vacant federally owned properties would reduce the blighting influence of these structures and alleviate the shortage of housing for low- and moderate-income families. Opponents questioned whether lower-income families could afford the costs of rehabilitation and suggested that more affluent families would be the ultimate beneficiaries. "Middle-income and upper-income people are coming into Baltimore and paying $1 for these houses, and making mansions out of them," noted Representative William Barrett of Pennsylvania. Concerns were also expressed about the indeterminate costs of the program, and its unproven methods (U.S. HUD, 1977b). Interestingly, the debate did not break along conventional party or ideological lines. The leading proponents of the legislation were two representatives from Maryland: Marjorie Holt, a conservative suburban Republican, and Parren Mitchell, a black Baltimore Democrat. Among the more vocal skeptics were Barrett, a Philadelphia Democrat, and Republican Gerry Brown of Michigan.

The act that emerged from Congress in 1974 was, like the Homestead Act of 1862, a compromise. On the critical matter of homesteader selection, the legislation required that "special consideration" be given to the applicants' need for housing and their capacity to make the required improvements. The inevitable tension between the "housing need" criterion, which favored lower-income applicants, and the "capacity to repair" criterion, which favored higher-income applicants, was left unresolved. Although the houses were to be provided by the federal government, management of the program was entrusted to localities, which were given wide discretion over homesteader selection and other aspects of program administration. The language of the act suggested that Section 810 was conceived as a "demonstration" of the viability of homesteading in carefully targeted neighborhoods.

As the program was implemented in the years following its enactment, the issue of homesteader selection was conclusively resolved in favor of middle-income applicants. HUD initially provided local homesteading agencies with a special allocation of Section 312 low-interest rehabilitation loans, designed to encourage low- and moderate-income participation, although not limited to that purpose. But appropriations for Section 312 were steadily reduced after 1978, and no alternative mechanism was created.[3] Instead, HUD advised localities to use their Community Development Block Grants as a source of rehabilitation assistance. Some did so, but competition for CDBG funds was so intense that relatively little support was generated in this fashion.

Local officials concluded that providing homesteads to a tiny cadre of young, upwardly mobile families was a more prudent course than an ambitious low-income effort, and HUD did nothing to discourage this view. The program remained small, turning over less than 1,000 houses annually nationwide, and middle-class families received the vast majority of the houses in most cities. In 1979, the latest year for which data are available, the mean household income for homesteaders was about $17,000, only slightly below the national average of $17,700.[4] The absence of more recent data may be indicative of HUD's reluctance to engage the issue of homesteader selection.

Needless to say, the federal homesteading program—whatever its experimental merits—was having little impact on the twin problems of abandonment and low-income housing need, both of which were reaching crisis proportions in distressed cities such as Philadelphia. In 1977 many of the more than 20,000 abandoned buildings in Philadelphia were HUD owned; North Philadelphia alone had 5,000 HUD homes. The situation impelled a bold and charismatic neighborhood leader named Milton Street to organize a grassroots Walk-In Urban Homesteading Program—less euphemistically, a squatters' movement.

Street's organization put 200 squatters into HUD-owned single-family houses. The action produced a heated response from public officials. HUD Secretary Patricia Harris described the squatters as "no better than shoplifters" and the president of the Philadelphia City Council warned of the "beginning of anarchy." But the public generally supported the squatters, and the press was sympathetic as well. A *Philadelphia Daily News* editorial (Aug. 8, 1977) proclaimed that Street "is putting people who need homes into houses that have stood vacant far too long. . . . Rather than doing battle with Street, the Rizzo Administration and HUD should get behind the man and help him."[5]

Though loathe to "get behind" a man who had thoroughly embarrassed them, federal and city officials quietly capitulated. Half of Street's squatters eventually received title to their houses at nominal cost, fifty purchased their homes with FHA or conventional mortgages, and many of the rest remained in place under rental agreements with HUD.

## The ACORN Squatters Movement

Milton Street's example inspired a succession of squatters' movements in Philadelphia. The Association of Community Organizations for Reform Now, or ACORN, an established grassroots community organization in 10 states, opened a Philadelphia office in 1977. Its membership ranged from welfare recipients to middle-class professionals, but the heart of its constituency in Philadelphia, as elsewhere, was the working poor. The typical ACORN member, tenant or homeowner, was firmly attached to a neighborhood and committed to its improvement. And the most visible and pervasive blight in ACORN's Philadelphia neighborhoods was housing abandonment.

By 1979, two years after Street's initial squatting wave, the character of Philadelphia's abandonment problem had altered significantly. Embarrassed by its status as the nation's largest slumlord, HUD had rapidly liquidated its inventory through demolition, sale, and transfer of properties to localities. During the same period, the city of Philadelphia was gaining title to thousands of vacant houses, mainly as a result of foreclosure for nonpayment of taxes. Neighborhood activists began to shift their attention to the city-owned housing stock and to the city's Gift Property program, the local homesteading effort.

On paper, Gift Property was a conventional urban homesteading program, providing houses for $13 to families who agreed to rehabilitate them. Deeper scrutiny revealed systematic mismanagement and corruption. Somewhat irregularly, the program was administered, not by the city's housing bureaucracy, but by the office of City Councilman Harry P. Jannotti, a Democratic machine stalwart. In four years Jannotti had conveyed a few hundred homes, many of them to real estate interests and political cronies. One speculator had obtained 30 Gift Property houses, which he was renting out, in violation of program rules. In the meantime, 5,000 applicants languished on the waiting list, and the stock of city-owned houses seemed to be mounting, although the records were so poor that no one could say with certainty how many houses the city owned.

On March 7, 1979, 75 members of ACORN and the allied Kensington Joint Action Committee (KJAC) descended on Jannotti's office carrying scraps of paper with the addresses of 300 vacant, city-owned properties. They demanded that Jannotti match these properties to applicants within two weeks and that he release the waiting list of applicants along with a listing of all the houses previously conveyed under the program.[6]

When the two-week deadline was up, the group returned to find Jannotti's office locked and under armed guard. After ACORN threatened to sue for the files, the city agreed to release them. A week later, the records mysteriously disappeared in a "burglary." The campaign then shifted its focus to the City Council, where independent Councilmember Lucien Blackwell introduced a bill to remove control of the program from Jannotti. With the machine faction in command of the council, Blackwell's bill was consigned to limbo.

By this point, ACORN's leadership had reached certain conclusions. It was agreed that reform of the Gift Property program should remain an organizational priority despite the level of resistance from the city; the issue was so critical, and the conduct of the program so indefensible, that some kind of victory seemed assured if ACORN and KJAC could maintain the pressure. Second, there was consensus that a new and more militant tactic was needed. Squatting was the obvious choice. Finally, it was clear that ACORN's active membership could supply relatively few prospective squatters. The most likely squatters were applicants on the Gift Property waiting list and families like them. Mobilizing this young, transient constituency and integrating it with the existing neighborhood base became the primary challenge of the ACORN homesteading campaign.

Since Jannotti refused to release the waiting list, this constituency had to be located in other ways. The most effective mechanism was a flyer that proclaimed: *Need a House? Call ACORN.* The flyer cautioned that ACORN did not have houses to give away, but that, by organizing, the Gift Property program could be made to work. It drew thousands of phone calls to the ACORN office and hundreds of people to meetings in North, South, and Southwest Philadelphia. Some of those who responded had been on the Gift

Property list for years, others had never heard of the program. They were united by a deep dissatisfaction with their existing housing situation. Typically, they were sharing a cramped residence with relatives or living in one of Philadelphia's notoriously decrepit and unsafe public housing projects.

Prospective squatters were informed that squatting was illegal, physically taxing, and risky. There was no guarantee that any squatter would obtain title to a house. At the same time, they were told that squatting was morally justifiable in this instance, that it might be the only way to force the city into action, and that ACORN would put its full organizational weight behind the squatting effort.

Scores of people decided to take the risk. Before squatting, they were asked to take certain functional steps designed to reinforce their understanding and commitment. First, squatters were asked to identify five vacant houses in which they were interested. They then proceeded to check the deeds and property-tax records for these houses.[7] Next, they were required to sign a "squatters' contract," which obligated them to participate in meetings, rallies, and other activities generated by the campaign to reform Gift Property; this was to be a collective struggle, not just a battle for one's own house. Finally, squatters were instructed to obtain the signatures of 75 percent of their prospective neighbors on a petition endorsing the squatting action, and to obtain concrete assistance from these neighbors wherever feasible.

The squatting action itself developed certain regular features. There was always a rally to demonstrate neighborhood support for the squatter. Ministers and sympathetic elected officials were invited to participate in order to lend legitimacy to the tactic; two ministers removed the boards from the first ACORN squatter's house. The press was generally invited as well. After the boards were removed, neighbors and supporters remained through the afternoon, helping to clean the house and serving as a guard against evictions.

The first ACORN squatters moved in on July 27, 1979, impelling the City Council to resurrect Lucien Blackwell's reform bill. A public hearing on the bill degenerated into a shouting match, and 100 ACORN and KJAC members walked out when the bill was tabled. But they had succeeded in making Gift Property a major political issue and a liability for the machine faction on the council. Adding to the machine's woes was a string of indictments stemming from the federal "Abscam" investigation; Jannotti was among those indicted. In the fall elections, the machine's grip on the council was loosened, and a new mayor, William Green, was elected with a clear mandate to reform the city's housing programs. Control of the Gift Property program was subsequently transferred from Jannotti to the Office of Housing and Community Development, whose director was a mayoral appointee. The squatters had won their first victory.

With Jannotti out of the picture, the squatters "upped the ante." They demanded the deeds to the houses they were occupying and immediate reforms in the Gift Property program, including an orderly application process, free access to information, tighter restrictions on eligibility, and a tenfold expansion in the number of houses being turned over.

Green and his appointees did not readily accede to these demands. The pattern was one of alternating confrontation and negotiation. In response to each wave of squatting, the city offered some programmatic reforms, a commitment to transfer some deeds, and de facto legal amnesty for all existing squatters, in exchange for an agreement from ACORN and KJAC that no new squatting actions would be organized. ACORN and KJAC accepted the deal, subject to revocation if the city's performance was unsatisfactory. For a short while, peace reigned, but the city inevitably failed to fulfill all its commitments, and the squatting cycle began anew.

## The Philadelphia Model

Each cycle moved the program forward, and out of this conflict-ridden process emerged a new conception of urban homesteading—the Philadelphia model. The essence of the Philadelphia model was to conceive of homesteading primarily as a housing program rather than as a property rehabilitation program, and as a large-scale effort rather than as a showcase demonstration. The program had several key components:

• *Restriction of eligibility to low- and moderate-income families.* Local homesteading programs have tended to favor middle-income applicants, partly for political reasons, and partly on the assumption that middle-income families have more cash and more skills to apply to home rehabilitation and improvement. But if homesteading is conceived of primarily as a housing program, an eligibility standard based on need seems appropriate. Furthermore, the assumption that lower-income families cannot perform rehabilitation without massive assistance is questionable. The Philadelphia squatters insisted that the city's rehabilitation cost estimates were inflated, and they cited examples of low-income squatters who were rehabilitating their houses on a "self-help" basis with the assistance of neighbors and relatives. Their position was bolstered by an Office of Housing and Community Development study that concluded that there was no significant relationship between the income of Gift Property applicants and their success rate as homesteaders.[8] Philadelphia ultimately restricted eligibility to households whose income was 80 percent or less of the median for the Philadelphia metropolitan area.

• *Sufficient time to bring homesteads up to code.* Self-help rehabilitation by homesteaders "generally took longer to complete but produced work that was equal in quality to that performed by professional contractors," according to a report by HUD's Office of Policy Development and Research (Sumka, 1982). Yet some local homesteading programs require participants to eliminate all code violations with six months to a year. By contrast, the

Philadelphia model calls for a more extended, two-step process: one year to eliminate "all major housing code defects posing a substantial danger to life and safety," after which the homesteader receives the deed to the property, and two additional years to complete the renovation.

• *Financial assistance for rehabilitation.* Despite the importance of the self-help component in low-income homeing, structural repairs and renovation of major systems (wiring, plumbing, and heating) must often be performed by contractors. Few lower-income families can afford these expenses without some form of financial assistance.

The most common form of government assistance is a low-interest loan.[9] Because homesteaders do not have to make mortgage or rental payments, they are able to carry sizable rehabilitation loans if the interest rates are sufficiently low. For example, a $10,000 loan at 3 percent, payable over 10 years, requires a monthly payment of $95.56, well within the budget of most low-income households.

Philadelphia eventually established a program, known as Action Loans, precisely along these lines, but it does not allocate sufficient funds to make low-interest loans available to all homesteaders who need them. The program's credit guidelines also exclude some low-income homesteaders. In short, the city assimilated the technical components of the model, without implementing the underlying entitlement principle.

• *Production quotas.* The model calls for a monthly quota appropriate to the city's size, administrative capacity, and level of abandonment. The value of a quota as an accountability mechanism is obvious. It also reinforces the conception of homesteading as a program designed to have a real impact on the problems of abandonment and housing distress, in contrast to the well-intentioned irrelevance of many homesteading demonstrations.

The Philadelphia squatters demanded that the city convey 200 houses a month. City officials resisted the quotas, but expanded the program from an average of 5 to 10 houses a month to over 50. The demand for additional houses raised the question of why many abandoned properties were not available for homesteading purposes.

• *Aggressive solicitation of houses.* In Philadelphia, as in many other cities around the country, the largest proportion of vacant properties are neither city owned nor federally owned but privately owned and tax delinquent. Many of these houses have been abandoned for years. Eventually they will be foreclosed on for nonpayment of property taxes, and will be auctioned off at an event known as "tax sale" or "sheriff's sale." Those that remain unsold at sheriff's sale fall into public ownership, where they are potentially available for homesteading. But the process takes so long—five years or more is not unusual—that the houses may have fallen apart in the meantime. Thus, proponents of large-scale homesteading efforts have an interest in accelerating the tax foreclosure process or developing alternatives to it.

Before the squatters entered the picture, Philadelphia had developed one alternative: a "donor–taker" provision that allowed delinquent taxpayers to donate their houses to the homesteading pool and deduct the assessed value from back taxes owed. (This was the "gift" provision to which the program's name referred.) Under pressure from the squatters, the city began to use Community Development Block Grant funds to purchase low-value houses from their owners and bid on houses at sheriff's sale to prevent them from being acquired by speculators. City officials implemented a technical change that accelerated the acquisition of full title to tax-foreclosed properties by six to nine months. They also experimented with the use of "spot condemnation" powers derived from urban renewal legislation to obtain properties designated by homesteaders.

All these measures helped to expand the pool of homestead properties, but their impact was relatively minor. A more radical solution was proposed by Councilman John Street, Milton's brother, and ultimately adopted by the council. Street's ordinance permits the city to declare an abandoned house a public nuisance and contract with a Gift Property applicant to occupy the house immediately and commence improvements. If the city subsequently obtains title to the house, the homesteader may claim it; if the original owner manages to redeem the property, he must reimburse the city for contracted improvements, and the city in turn reimburses the homesteader. By short-circuiting the cycle of abandonment and foreclosure, the Street ordinance aims not only to expand the homesteading pool but to reduce the unit cost of rehabilitation, since houses "caught" earlier in the cycle are likely to require less extensive renovation.[10]

## The Road to Tent City

By the end of 1981, the City Council and the Office of Housing and Community Development had implemented many elements of the Philadelphia model. City officials continued to denounce squatting, but none of the ACORN and KJAC squatters had been evicted, and some had received the deeds to their houses.

The news of the success of the Philadelphia actions spread to ACORN affiliates in other cities, which began to scrutinize their local homesteading programs. The situation in some cities bordered on the scandalous. Detroit, with the largest inventory of HUD-owned houses in the country, had a tiny program limited to two neighborhoods; 12 houses had been conveyed in a two-year period. Detroit's general policy was to demolish vacant houses and "landbank" the property. In St. Louis, another city with a massive abandonment problem, the homesteading agency was refusing to turn over 32 houses that had been claimed from the federal government for homesteading purposes. The St. Louis Land Reutilization Authority, an autonomous state-chartered agency, owned 1,000 vacant houses, many of which had been languishing in its inventory for years.

HUD frequently cited the homesteading programs of Dallas, Texas, and Columbus, Ohio, as models. Both cities had turned over more than 300 houses to homesteaders, with few subsequent failures. But ACORN groups in Dallas and Columbus discovered that this "success" had been achieved by conveying most of the houses to middle-class families. Neither city had established an adequate rehabilitation program. These cities had a low rate of failure because they took few risks.

Local ACORN organizations responded to these findings with conventional protest tactics and squatting. Squatters and leaders from Philadelphia visited other cities to explain how it was done. By April 1982, there were more than 200 ACORN squatters in 13 cities; the largest numbers were in distressed cities such as Detroit, Pittsburgh, and St. Louis, but there were also squatters in Houston, Dallas, Tulsa, and Phoenix.

City and federal authorities cracked down hard in some locations. Squatters were arrested in Pittsburgh and St. Louis; a HUD Area Office manager led a midnight raid on a squatter's house in Dallas; the St. Louis Land Reutilization Authority filed a $500,000 civil suit against ACORN and the leaders of its squatting group. With rare exceptions, mayors denounced the squatters and refused to negotiate with them. But the response was more positive in some quarters: the Detroit City Council passed a resolution asking for the establishment of a large-scale urban homesteading program and clemency for the squatters; favorable columns and editorials appeared in the metropolitan newspapers of Fort Worth, Atlanta, and St. Louis; the St. Louis tax collector agreed to accelerate the tax foreclosure process on abandoned houses suitable for homesteading; Mayor Andrew Young of Atlanta agreed to negotiate; homesteading ordinances based on the Philadelphia model were introduced in Pittsburgh, St. Louis, and Detroit.

As squatting erupted around the country, the goals of the campaign became more diverse. The Tulsa squatting effort was part of a long-standing protest against redevelopment and displacement on the city's North Side. An ACORN group fighting public housing vacancies in Jacksonville, Florida, squatted briefly in a housing project to dramatize the issue. In cities such as Houston and Phoenix, which have relatively few abandoned houses, the squatters' primary goal was not to create large-scale urban homesteading programs but to challenge the complacent assumption that the poor are adequately housed in these Sunbelt communities.

During the same period—winter and spring 1982—the campaign began to develop a national focus. In cities such as Detroit and Dallas, a large portion of the vacant housing stock was still federally owned, giving HUD a more direct involvement in the issue. Furthermore, ACORN's national leadership was beginning to appreciate the symbolic power of squatting and its potential for broader impact. The leadership began to conceive of the campaign, not only as a fight for local homesteading reforms, but as a protest against the failure of the nation to provide decent and affordable housing to low- and moderate-income families. Squatting was to be the tactical vehicle for this protest, homesteading its programmatic vehicle.

As ACORN members became more familiar with the federal role in homesteading policy, they realized that HUD's interpretation of Section

810 legislation was the source of many of the problems they were encountering at the local level. HUD officials insisted that localities were free to design their own programs, but although this was technically correct in many instances, it was obvious that the cities took their cues from Washington. For example, squatters were often infuriated when cities refused to expand homesteading programs beyond a few targeted neighborhoods. City officials inevitably attributed this policy to HUD. The truth was a bit more complicated: HUD's regulations did not prohibit a more expansive approach to homesteading, but they strongly encouraged neighborhood targeting, as did HUD program literature and the agency's field officials. The federal agency also seemed unconcerned about the middle-class character of the program, the shortage of funds for homestead rehabilitation, and the disparity between the enormous scope of the abandonment problem and the minuscule homesteading effort.[11]

On June 5, 1982, ACORN members in seven cities squatted in HUD-owned houses despite threats of eviction and arrest from HUD officials. Two days later, more than 300 persons sat in at HUD offices in 12 cities. Both actions were intended to underline the federal responsibility for effective homesteading programs and for addressing the housing problems of low- and moderate-income Americans. In doing so, they set the stage for the culminating event of the "national strategy"—a squatters' Tent City in Washington, D.C.

Tent City was established on the Ellipse, a few hundred yards from the back porch of the White House, and housed more than 200 squatters from 10 cities. The squatters used a press conference, a rally, a congressional hearing, and a march on the HUD building to press their case for reform of the federal homesteading program. At the hearing conducted by the House Subcommittee on Housing and Community Development, Representative Fernand St Germain of Rhode Island told the squatters, "I don't consider you criminals. . . . You are doing the community a favor" (U.S. Congress, House, Subcommittee on Housing and Community Development, 1982a). The squatters demanded that homesteading efforts be targeted to low- and moderate-income families, that more vacant houses be made available for homesteading, and that more funds be allocated for low-interest rehabilitation loans.

In March 1983, Congressman William Coyne of Pennsylvania introduced a bill to reshape the federal homesteading program along the lines advocated by ACORN.[12] Despite HUD's opposition, the Coyne bill received bipartisan support in the Housing and Community Development Subcommittee and was approved by the full House as part of a comprehensive housing bill. Although that bill did not advance further, elements of the homesteading provisions were incorporated in the 1983 Housing and Urban-Rural Recovery Act. The legislation does the following:

- Gives homesteaders up to three years to meet local housing code standards.

- Gives homesteaders priority access to Section 312 low-interest rehabilitation loans.
- Requires local homesteading programs to stress housing need in the selection criteria for homesteaders.
- Establishes a $1 million demonstration program providing federal assistance for the acquisition of privately owned vacant houses for homesteading purposes.

The squatters did not get everything they wanted, but they recognized a victory, and so did others. A HUD official told an ACORN representative, "Congress listened to you folks, and we're going to have to listen to you too."

The congressional hearing and other Tent City activities were reported in the squatters' hometown newspapers and received some national media coverage as well. *Squatting for Homeless Gains Support* was the headline in the *Tulsa Tribune. ACORN Finally Gets HUD's Ear*, proclaimed the *Columbus Citizen-Journal.* By publicizing and legitimizing the squatters' cause, the D.C. action helped to sustain the momentum of local homesteading campaigns, which have since borne fruit. Bridgeport, Connecticut, and Des Moines, Iowa, have established homesteading programs based on the Philadelphia model. New funds for homestead acquisition and rehabilitation assistance have been appropriated in Phoenix ($200,000), Columbus ($800,000) and Brooklyn ($1 million). Mayor Coleman Young of Detroit, once an implacable opponent of the squatters, has announced a program to give away 500 properties, and the Detroit City Council approved a bill—modeled on John Street's nuisance abatement ordinance—that would permit homesteading in privately owned, tax-delinquent houses.

## Radical Principles, Friendly Terrain

Five years ago, single-family urban homesteading programs were, at best, irrelevant to the needs of poor people and at worst a means for their displacement. The notion that these programs could serve a mass, low-income constituency had limited credibility and had never been seriously tested. Today, this notion has not only acquired a concrete, programmatic form—the Philadelphia model—but is influencing local and national policies. This achievement can be credited almost entirely to the action of the squatters.

It would be gratifying to conclude that the squatters had succeeded in their broader objective of forcing government to take increased responsibility for low-income housing. But although the squatters undoubtedly drew attention to housing issues and disturbed the complacency of public officials, they were swimming against a powerful current. The Reagan administration budgets have cut federal housing programs more deeply than any other major area [*see Chapter 21 by Chester Hartman*]. This reflects not only the administration's antipathy to these programs but the weakness of the political constituency for housing. With or without Reagan, the immediate prospects for a renewed national commitment to low-income housing appear dim.

For many observers, therefore, the most remarkable aspect of the squatters' campaign is that it succeeded at all. During a period characterized by political reaction and social quiescence, ACORN mobilized hundreds of militant squatters, backed by thousands of organized supporters, and won significant policy reforms in the face of deep resistance from public officials. What made this possible?

Viewed nakedly as a tactic, squatting was enormously effective. Its visual drama and clarity drew TV cameras and newspaper photographers. Its programmatic clarity—filling empty houses with families who need shelter—lent it both power and legitimacy. To many among the public, the press, the ministry, and even to some housing officials, the moral logic of the action outweighed its patent illegality.

The combination of intense militancy and public legitimacy reflects the manner in which the campaign's tactics and programmatic demands embodied radical principles in a politically compelling context. The squatters insisted that they had a right to decent housing, and that this right took precedence over the rights of property. In the abstract, such principles do not command the support of a majority of Americans; national housing policy is certainly not founded on them. Yet in the particular form posed by the squatters, these principles were almost unassailable.

At a time when Americans were increasingly hostile to anything perceived as a "giveaway" program, the squatters proclaimed that they were not looking for a handout but an opportunity. They cast their demands in terms of individual initiative, mutual assistance, and the superiority of homeownership, all culturally sanctioned values in the United States. Their position was bolstered by the visible failure of the for-profit "private sector" to maintain housing in their neighborhoods. And homesteading had fiscal appeal as well; even with the provision of generous rehabilitation loans, it appeared to be a relatively inexpensive means of producing low-income housing, and it promised to restore abandoned property to the tax rolls.

Just as important as the campaign's external legitimacy was its internal dynamic. In the classic mode of community organizing, the squatters' campaign appealed to a fundamental need in a direct and immediate way. *Need a house? Call ACORN*—the flyer was sometimes criticized for its audacity, but it was the audacity of the appeal that drew hundreds of previously unorganized individuals to ACORN offices, just as the simplicity of the campaign's central premise—"The houses are ours!"—propelled them to action. As we have seen, ACORN eventually developed a fairly sophisticated critique of urban homesteading policy and a detailed program for reform. But these emerged from the campaign, rather than vice versa. The squatters understood the policy issues and embraced the policy demands because the issues and demands took their ultimate shape from the collective experience of protest.

Another factor in the campaign's success was ACORN's capacity to forge links between the squatters and its traditional neighborhood-based constituency. The neighborhood base provided squatters with material and psychological support, as well as public legitimacy. (Many TV news accounts included interviews with squatters' neighbors, who inevitably said they preferred to have a squatter next door than an abandoned haven for rats and junkies.) And ACORN's experienced neighborhood leaders contributed political and organizational sophistication, which tempered the youthful militance of the squatters without smothering it.

One reason that the cause of low-income housing has suffered defeats in recent years is the absence of a grassroots constituency to generate, monitor, and defend programs. Some low-income housing programs are too complex or diffuse to attract grassroots support; others, like public housing, are unwelcome in many communities. Homesteading, on the other hand, is blessed with two large, enthusiastic constituencies: families that need houses, and residents of neighborhoods with many abandoned properties. If the identification and mobilization of such "natural" constituencies is not a precondition for policy reform, it is certainly a major asset.

But this analysis of the squatters' campaign raises as many questions as it answers. Even if all the abandoned houses in the United States suitable for homesteading were turned over to poor people, could it have a major impact on the nation's low-income housing problem? Aren't the economics of low-income homeownership so daunting that it represents a dubious basis for policy, and a cruel and dangerous myth for the poor? [*See Chapter 26 by Robert Kolodny and Chapter 27 by Tony Schuman.*] Doesn't the appeal to values such as self-reliance and fiscal efficiency play into the hands of those who wish to absolve the government of responsibility for housing? If the objective is fundamental reform of housing policies, why not develop proposals and campaigns which confront the central issues of equity, entitlement, and resources in a comprehensive fashion rather than nibbling at their edges? In short, could one characterize the squatters' campaign as tactically instructive but peripheral to the main lines of strategy for housing reform?

The most superficial response is that the campaign encompassed a much broader range of issues than the management and design of homesteading programs. In the course of their efforts to obtain houses, the squatters had an impact on federal property disposition policies, the tax foreclosure process, housing speculation, redevelopment plans, and code enforcement. They disseminated new approaches to home rehabilitation financing, which benefited existing homeowners as often as homesteaders. John Street's "nuisance abatement" ordinance, a product of the campaign, was a radical innovation in local housing policy.

And squatting embodied much more than the policy demands of the squatters; it was a blatant challenge to the assumptions and values on which

U.S. housing policy is founded. The desperation of the squatters mocked the assumption that Americans are well housed; their eagerness to tear down the boards asserted the primacy of housing needs over property rights; their uncompromising demand for the deeds lent substance to the nascent principle of entitlement. Of course, they cast this challenge on friendly terrain: the social terrain of their home neighborhoods, the ideological terrain of the American Dream. But that is precisely what is instructive about their experience.

At present, comprehensive policy reforms such as the establishment of a national housing entitlement are improbable under any scenario; the costs are too high, the political constituency for reform too weak, the bias against government action too well entrenched. The only way to advance fundamental reform is through the accretion of small but principled victories, which undermine the hegemony of dominant values and assumptions and enhance the credibility of alternatives [*see Chapter 24 by Kathy McAfee*]. When these victories involve ordinary people in the criticism and formulation of policy, they build an informed popular constituency for change. Hence, the key to the strategy is identifying friendly terrain—campaigns that can mobilize large numbers of people on their home grounds and win a broad base of public legitimacy.

Where is this terrain? Our own view is that it is most likely to be found in two areas. One is the effort to lend rental housing some of the characteristics of equity: security of tenure, predictability of costs, control over quality [*see Chapter 22 by John Atlas and Peter Dreier, Chapter 24 by Kathy McAfee, Chapter 26 by Robert Kolodny, and Chapter 29 by Chester Hartman and Michael E. Stone*]. The other is the effort to make homeownership affordable to the lowest-income groups, whether in the conventional form, homesteading, or new forms such as cooperatives and mutual housing associations.

Is the expansion of low-income homeownership a realistic policy goal? [*For a critical look at prohomeownership policies, in general, see Chapter 16 by Jim Kemeny.*] Here we would simply note that despite the historical legitimacy of the goal and the development, over the past decade, of promising new mechanisms to achieve it, policymakers have been reluctant to test these methods on a mass scale. Conservative opposition to new initiatives was expected, but the squatters also encountered ambivalence and resistance from politicians who had traditionally supported low-income housing efforts.

Indeed, one of the recurrent ironies of the campaign was the extent to which unexpected support from political conservatives and moderates was offset by resistance from liberal mayors, housing officials, and their legislative allies. The William Green administration in Philadelphia and the Andrew Young administration in Atlanta were lukewarm, at best, to homesteading reform, while Mayors Kevin White in Boston and Coleman Young in Detroit vehemently opposed any concessions to the squatters. Representative Stewart McKinney, a Republican moderate from Connecticut, was one of the strongest backers of homesteading reform in the House of Representatives, while the support of Michigan's liberal Senator Donald Riegle, ranking Democrat on the Senate housing subcommittee, was unenthusiastic and unreliable.

This pattern is in part attributable to crude political considerations; squatting was a rebuke to the folks in power at City Hall, regardless of their political complexion. But there was also a strain of principled opposition, which, if sincere, carries a scent of paternalism. Some officials insisted that poor people could not renovate their houses adequately without massive financial and technical assistance, and refused to support the expansion of homesteading opportunities unless such assistance was guaranteed. Since the necessary funds were not likely to be forthcoming from hard-pressed city treasuries or the federal government, this was in effect a stand against the squatters. Others argued that low-income homeownership was an expensive luxury, theoretically desirable but practically unattainable, and hence a diversion from the primary thrust of low-income housing policy. These officials tended to see the squatters' demands as an implicit criticism of existing publicly subsidized housing programs, to which they remained committed. Finally, there was a deep reluctance, engendered by the perceived failure of ambitious social programs in the past, to take programmatic risks of any kind. Better to stick with the tried-and-true, it was reasoned, even if per unit costs were high and relatively few persons were housed, than go out on a limb with low-income homesteading.

The squatters would have none of this. They insisted that they could make their houses livable; financial assistance would make the process faster and smoother, but they wanted the deeds regardless. Of course there were risks, but the risks were acceptable because even a problematic house was better than what they likely would find on the private rental market. The squatters felt that homeownership, far from being a luxury, was the only way to escape the domination of others. They drew strength from the same values that legitimated their militant actions to the wider public. As ACORN leader Grover Wright informed a congressional panel, the squatters "are here because they have an insatiable desire to become a part, an integral part of this great American life" (U.S. Congress, House, Subcommittee on Housing and Community Development, 1982a). Such "myths" are the engine of change.

## Notes

1. This quotation and the account of the 1862 Homestead Act are drawn from U.S. HUD, 1977b, 1–29.
2. Statistics on the HUD-owned houses are available from HUD's Office of Single-Family Housing, Preservation and Sales Division.
3. The Reagan administration attempted to close down Section 312, but succeeded

only in cutting off new appropriations. The program is currently funded entirely by loan repayments.

4. U.S. HUD, 1983a, is the best source of data on the federal homesteading program.

5. The account of Milton Street's campaign is drawn from Hartman, Keating, LeGates, 1982, 68–71.

6. The best account of the early stages (1979–1980) of Philadelphia ACORN's squatting campaign is Adamson, 1981.

7. Potential squatters were asked to check deeds and property-tax records because squatting was encouraged only in city-owned houses and in seriously tax-delinquent houses owned by persons outside the neighborhood—in short, houses where the squatter had a reasonable chance of obtaining the deed, and where squatting was unlikely to create conflict within the neighborhood.

8. The study, conducted by the Planning and Policy Research Department, was unfortunately never published.

9. A good sourcebook on assistance mechanisms is U.S. HUD, 1980d.

10. The ordinance was introduced as Bill 1202 on April 1, 1982. The program, known as "1202A, Emergency Nuisance Abatement," is administered by Philadelphia's Office of Housing and Community Development.

11. Regulations for the Section 810 program are in 24 CFR Part 590. The ambiguous language on neighborhood targeting is in 590.7(a).

12. The bill was introduced as H.R.2150 on March 16, 1983, and later incorporated in the Omnibus Housing Bill, H.R.1.

# 26

# The Emergence of Self-Help as a Housing Strategy for the Urban Poor

*Robert Kolodny*

*This chapter discusses another self-help strategy that has been used by tenants in multifamily buildings. Abandonment or severe undermaintenance of privately owned rental housing and poor management in public housing developments have stimulated tenants to try to improve their living conditions in a variety of innovative ways. Management, control, and/or cooperative ownership by tenants are seen as key to these strategies. The actual contribution of self-help, from aiding tenants in meeting immediate crises to generating resident mobilization and community redevelopment, is assessed.*

Self-help, which has become a staple among neighborhood housing remedies in the 1980s, either did not exist or went unnoticed before about 1970. In earlier years, when lower-income renters grew exasperated with their housing circumstances, their reflex was to assume the role of aggrieved consumers and disenchanted voters. They complained to rent regulators, code enforcers, and elected officials; formed tenant organizations; conducted rent strikes; and sometimes joined other groups to lobby for pro-tenant legislation. During the 1970s, however, conditions in several older cities prompted residents to try on some new and unaccustomed roles. A small but visible number of households that had always been consumers in the housing market became, instead, producers and suppliers of rehabilitated housing and management services. In New York, St. Louis, and then in a number of other American cities, groups of primarily lower-income minority residents were prompted by their rapidly deteriorating housing to assume a direct hand in housing provision—as managers and handymen/women, nonprofit developers, rehabilitation contractors, and even as construction workers.

These new roles emerged when the more established tactics did not seem

An earlier version of this chapter appeared as "Self-Help Can Be an Effective Tool in Housing the Urban Poor." Reprinted by permission from Vol. 38, No. 3, *Journal of Housing.*

to be getting results. This rediscovery of self-help in an urban setting has enlarged the range of strategies available to cope with housing deterioration and abandonment. These include resident management of public housing projects and tax-foreclosed multiple dwellings, conversion of rental buildings to tenant-owned cooperatives, sweat-equity urban homesteading, and a number of variations on user-initiated and -controlled housing development and management.

These efforts have been popularly dubbed "self-help"; the designation fits, for they have obvious kinship to the most familiar forms of mutual aid among squatters in developing countries. As it has in the Third World, a desperate need for housing prompted most of the American projects. And they rely in varying degrees on the substitution of labor for money by cash-poor families. Urban self-help in a developed economy, however, seems to involve a more fundamental redefinition of the housing consumer's role. It shakes up taken-for-granted and long-established arrangements in the provision of rental housing.

The significance of this modest flowering of self-help continues to be debated. Many observers were skeptical at the outset and remain so. Some view these developments as merely material for the "Sunday supplement," heart-warming instances that make good newspaper copy but are too isolated to matter. They constitute a small, rear-guard action that cannot cope with the social and market forces at work in low-income neighborhoods. Others have judged the principle of turning low-income consumers into the producers, owners, and operators of housing as a breakthrough and one key to a solution of housing problems. While such developments are familiar in a general way to many, they have been subject to little independent evaluation, and there is not much documentation.

# De Facto Cooperatives and Conversions to Tenant Ownership

The earliest urban housing efforts readily identifiable as self-help arose in New York City at the beginning of the 1970s. In buildings that had been abandoned by their landlords, occupants began collaborating with one another to make repairs, maintain essential services, and secure the premises. In some cases the arrangements were sanctioned by a court that had authorized the withholding of rent in order to remedy unacceptable conditions. More often, the tenants' assumption of management prerogatives was extralegal. They simply filled the vacuum created by the landlord's departure and assessed themselves enough rent to cover operating costs.

These de facto housing cooperatives were arising almost exclusively in the city's most troubled neighborhoods. They were primarily motivated by desperate living conditions and the residents' lack of housing alternatives. One extraordinary aspect was the largely spontaneous emergence of this activity, which developed independently in a number of separate locations.

In some cases, with the encouragement of Community Legal Services lawyers and a handful of advocates inside the city's housing agency, the tenants began to seek financing to acquire and rehabilitate their buildings and convert them to de jure cooperatives.

A study undertaken by the author in 1973 identified some 37 projects with nearly 2,100 units either completed or in the process of rehabilitation and cooperative conversion (Kolodny, 1973). An additional 35 projects with roughly 3,100 units had received at least preliminary approval from some public source of financing.[1] What was equally remarkable were the signs that, in an even larger number of landlord-abandoned buildings (the actual magnitude was unknown), residents had organized in a last-ditch effort at self-help. Since there was no established system of outside support for such groups, it was not surprising that many could not sustain what they had started. But the potential for a large-scale mutual-aid strategy represented by these efforts was impressive.

In many ways, the most dramatic self-help ventures were the sweat-equity projects. While they were part of the cooperative conversion movement, they were distinct in two important ways. The projects involved totally vacant and derelict buildings, and the would-be cooperators sought to undertake the rehabilitation work themselves. Thus the self-help aspects went beyond tenant ownership and cooperative management to direct participation in reconstruction.

Because sweat equity is undertaken by a "housing underground," the activity is not always easy to measure. Estimates made by the author show some 24 projects with 274 units already in occupancy at the beginning of 1981 (Kolodny, 1979b; updated by author). Thirteen additional projects were in construction as of that date and a minimum of a half-dozen more had received preliminary loan approval. The buildings were generally small by New York standards, and even if all pending projects had gone forward, the total number of units involved would amount to no more than 500.

As with the other homegrown rescue operations, these emerged as largely independent efforts in some of the city's most devastated districts. Initially, self-help was seen as an end in itself (promoting self-reliance) and as a device for securing inexpensive, rehabilitated housing and mutual ownership. The voluntary labor—"sweat"—was to reduce the cash costs of renovation at the same time it represented the down payment—"equity"—for each participant.

As they developed and attracted at least token support from public agencies, these projects added training and employment to their housing aims. The complexity of the physical structure and its mechanical systems and the complications of an urban setting were making insupportable demands on most volunteers—requiring a year or more of full-time, but unpaid, construction work. The solution was public manpower training funds that provided modest hourly wages to workers and helped pay for instruction, construction supervision, and organizational overhead.

While grafting an employment program onto what was already a highly ambitious experiment in reversing housing abandonment tended to dilute the self-help principles and complicate the administrative and organizational aspects of homesteading, it explicitly recognized the relationship between jobs and housing. The participants in sweat equity were primarily minority youths between sixteen and twenty-five years old, the bulk of them "hardcore unemployed." Construction work was both an appropriate and socially respected potential source of employment. Moreover, and this was only dimly perceived at the outset, regular wages for at least most of the would-be occupants were essential to the long-term financial viability of the rehabilitated housing developments.

## Tenant Management in Public Housing

In 1969, the residents of nine St. Louis housing projects launched what was virtually the first and probably the most notorious rent strike in any publicly assisted housing in the country (Baron, n.d.; Fleishman, 1979). The strike, which lasted eight months, was precipitated by dissatisfaction with the condition of the developments, but, above all, by the imposition of very substantial rent increases. The strike brought the local authority, which was already in disarray and near bankruptcy, to its knees. The terms of the eventual settlement spelled out a total reorganization of the authority and required it to explore with the residents the feasibility of tenant management. In 1973, following a lengthy period of negotiation and on-the-job training, the residents in two projects comprising a total of 1,256 units signed a contract with the authority. It gave them full management responsibility for the sites, subject to the federal rules and regulations governing all public housing projects. While the authority continued to have fiscal responsibility for public housing in St. Louis, it negotiated with the tenants to arrive at annual operating budgets for each site.

In 1976, two additional family developments signed management contracts, making a total of nearly 2,700 apartments under tenant operation. Overall policy is set by the Tenant Management Corporation (TMC) board, made up of unpaid elected representatives. Most staff positions, including the manager's, are held by residents, who are paid wages generally equivalent to those paid conventional housing authority employees. The TMCs have overseen substantial upgrading of the projects, which they inherited in an advanced state of underoccupancy and physical deterioration. [*For a further discussion of the problems of public housing, see Chapter 20 by Rachel G. Bratt.*]

Tenant management now has had 12 years of evolution in St. Louis. Early attention focused on doubts about the residents' discipline and their ability to perform the routine, "hard" management functions. An independent evaluation of the mature program has not been made, but there seems little question that the TMCs have mastered traditional real estate management.[2] What is most interesting is the extent to which this has logically led them in new directions. The problems of housing a population overwhelmingly made up of welfare-dependent, female-headed households confronted the TMCs with the need to rethink their roles as managers. To a far greater extent than most other public housing in the country, the St. Louis projects have developed programs in education, recreation, health, and other social services; special care for children and the elderly; job training; and direct tenant employment. What is most striking is the way in which the linkages among these programs have been exploited. The TMCs' extensive day-care centers, for example, provide employment for some residents and freedom to seek it for others. The need to feed the day-care children has in turn generated training and employment opportunities in food preparation, creating a new, local industry that now serves meals to the TMC's senior citizens as well.[3]

Tenant management also has taken hold in Newark, New Jersey. A set of circumstances remarkably similar to those in St. Louis led to an equivalent turn to tenant management in a 1,200-unit high-rise development. Again, the settlement of a bitter rent strike called on the parties to consider the possibility of tenant management in two large, family projects.[4] The tenants in one of the two projects eventually rejected the alternative. The judgment of independent professionals who were under contract to assist them was that they were not, in fact, ready to take over. In the second, the development that had played the central role in the rent strike, the resident corporation, has been managing the site since 1979. It has reported improvement in a series of objective indicators of hard management performance. As in St. Louis, the Newark tenants have sought to add employment and social service programs to the routine management functions. The entire venture, however, is now threatened by the severe financial problems of the Newark Housing Authority.

## Official Demonstrations in Self-Help

The efforts in New York, St. Louis, and Newark have authentic self-help and grassroots origins. There were no public programs directly encouraging such activity. Indeed, considerable ingenuity was required to bend existing statutes and regulations to fit these unorthodox approaches, and there is evidence of substantial skepticism and resistance on the part of public agencies. Subsequently, however, several of the formulas were adopted, and in that sense endorsed, by the federal government as part of national demonstration programs.

### *Multifamily Urban Homesteading Demonstration*

In 1978, the Department of Housing and Urban Development began a Multifamily Urban Homesteading Demonstration in New York City. It utilized the Section 312 rehabilitation loan program, coupled with job-training funds, to test the full potential of an expanded and regularized sweat-equity program. Four neighborhood development groups were to be involved, and rehabilitation of a total of nearly 250 units in 24 buildings was contemplated. Additional funds were made available to support the demonstration's overhead, give groups adequate technical assistance, and evaluate the results.[5] The first phase of the demonstration was carried out by two community-based sweat-equity groups. One organization in the South Bronx—the most devastated part of New York—was to have rehabilitated four buildings. It actually started three and completed only one. The organization's own internal problems foreclosed any real test of the concept. The second group, on Manhattan's Lower East Side, was to have done seven buildings; it started three, and completed only two. The shortfall appears to be largely a consequence of the organization's inability to handle the scale of operations originally planned and the intricacies of the financing arrangements themselves. The second phase, undertaken in two new neighborhoods in Brooklyn, was more successful. Eight of the nine buildings planned have been completed.

## Multifamily Homesteading Technical Assistance

Once the New York demonstration got under way, HUD contracted to have the self-help approach spread to other cities. The Multifamily Homesteading Technical Assistance Project operated in Boston, Chicago, Cleveland, Hartford, Cincinnati, Oakland, and Springfield, Massachusetts. A private firm, in partnership with the nonprofit champion of self-help projects in New York, Urban Homesteading Assistance Board (UHAB), provided technical assistance to local governments and neighborhood groups in developing sweat-equity projects of their own. No final evaluation of the efforts appears to have been done, although a guidebook with some case studies was issued (Dialogue Systems, Inc., 1983). A majority of the dozen projects contemplated were completed, but there is no ready way to judge their achievements in either financial or organizational terms.

## National Tenant Management Demonstration

In 1976, prompted by the apparent success of tenant-operated public housing in St. Louis and the active interest of the Ford Foundation, HUD agreed to a national demonstration in tenant management. Six local housing authorities were selected to participate. By the end of the three-year effort, four public housing projects at the four authorities most committed to the concept had converted to tenant management. As in St. Louis, all residents over the age of seventeen automatically became members of the nonprofit tenant management corporations. Each TMC elected a board of directors. Following their own training in property management, finance and accounting, social service programs, and community organization, they hired a management staff from among the residents.

Two evaluations of these efforts have been undertaken. The first, completed shortly after the TMCs took over full management responsibility, was conducted by the organization hired to oversee the demonstration for the foundation and HUD (Manpower Demonstration Research Corporation, 1981). It was lukewarm, acknowledging that TMCs in some instances did as well as or better than housing authorities but judging that, overall, the results did not justify the additional expense. Four of the participants nevertheless found the early results sufficiently promising to persuade HUD to continue funding them for another two years. These four projects—in Jersey City, Louisville, New Orleans, and Rochester, New York—continued under tenant management once the supplemental funding was exhausted, relying entirely on their share of the authority's operating budget, as did two of the original four St. Louis projects.

Meanwhile, the number of TMCs is expanding. An early tenant-management project in Boston continues to be run by residents. Jersey City has added a second TMC on its own and plans to sign a management contract with a third in 1986. Louisville has a second project being managed by residents in a joint venture with an outside consulting firm. Residents in a Washington, D.C., site are managing, and the idea is being actively explored in Cleveland, Chicago, New York, and several other cities.

A second evaluation of the four demonstration TMCs, undertaken by the author after there was more independent management experience to review, was more positive (Kolodny, 1983). It identified dimensions of the experiments beyond property management, noted that the TMCs had refined their operations so that they required no special subsidy, and pointed out that additional successful sites had been added with very modest start-up costs. The study concluded:

> Tenant management is not an unalloyed success, but in surviving and to some extent prospering at most of the sites where it has been introduced, it shows more potential and usefulness than it is generally given credit for. . . . [I]f the objectives in the administration of low rent housing are broad and multiple and include local empowerment, expanded employment opportunities for residents, leadership development, and some progress toward the revitalization of severely depressed residential districts, then tenant management would seem to have substantial if not fully realized possibilities. (Kolodny, 1983, 68)

## Alternate Management Programs

In New York City, continued landlord abandonment of privately owned rental housing [*see Chapter 10 by Ann Meyerson*] has brought large numbers of units—many of them still occupied—into municipal ownership through real estate tax foreclosure. Borrowing from the cooperative conversion and de facto tenant-control experience, the city, in the last half-dozen years, has developed a unique array of what it calls alternative management programs.[6] Instead of operating all properties itself, as was customary when the extent of tax delinquency was much smaller, the city now contracts out management responsibility for some, with the clear hope that this will lead to eventual sale of the property to residents or others.

Under the tenant interim lease program (TIL), an organized group of occupants can manage its own building and make modest repairs while considering whether it wishes to become the cooperative owner. In the community management program (CM), neighborhood organizations are given contracts to operate troubled properties, to oversee minor and major rehabilitation, and to train tenants for the possibility of ownership.

As of January 1, 1985, the city reported that a total of 130 buildings with 3,470 units had been sold to tenant cooperatives under the TIL program. Some 293 additional properties continue under resident management; the city hopes that most or all of them will be converted to coops and taken off its hands. Under the CM program, an additional 27 coops have been created, totaling 485 units. One hundred forty-nine properties remain in the program. How many might become coops is uncertain.

It is too soon to know the staying power of the new ownership arrangements, but almost all remain self-managed, and it is clear that the original small flowering of self-help in the city has become a modest garden.

## Institutionalizing Sweat Equity

Under pressure to support the sweat-equity activity, New York has launched both a Sweat Equity Loan Program and a Homesteading Loan Program, following an earlier homesteading demonstration. A total of 38 properties have been assisted with, or promised, loans under these relatively new commitments, which have been slow in moving from announcement to reality. So far, 9 buildings with 65 apartments have completed renovation and formally organized as cooperatives.

## Multifamily Homeownership Demonstration

In 1979, using New York as a laboratory, HUD launched a homeownership demonstration for rental buildings, which was then exported to other cities [*see related discussion of HUD's "homesteading" program in Chapter 25 by Seth Borgos*]. The program, known as the Section 510 Demonstration (after the section of the 1978 Housing Act used as its authorization) as well as "Coops for Neighborhoods," is complex, involving elaborate partnerships among community groups, private developers, and public agencies using sophisticated financing arrangements (Holin, 1982). A key element, however, is borrowed more or less directly from the cooperative conversion experience—transfer of ownership of rehabilitated tenements to their occupants.

Success is reported to have been spotty. Only one of the New York pilot efforts is judged to have lived up to expectations. Of the six sites in other parts of country, only half could be termed qualified successes, and in none of them were all the program objectives achieved (Sumka, 1984).

# The Emergence of User-Controlled Strategies

Growing disillusionment with the familiar means of providing rental housing services in lower-income districts was clearly one reason for the emergence of user-initiated strategies. The private real estate industry has long been under attack for the poor quality of ghetto housing. But the current impatience gained extra conviction from the widespread patterns of disinvestment and abandonment in older urban neighborhoods. This visible evidence was reinforced by a vague but venerable antiprofit, antilandlord sentiment among leaders and organizers of these ventures. Even the advocates of private-sector solutions are now inclined to agree that in portions of the standing private stock, there are no longer incentives sufficient to attract or retain investor owners or operators.

At the same time, a consensus was emerging among a number of neighborhood activists that the public sector could no longer be relied on to own and operate rental housing for lower-income families [*see Chapter 20 by Rachel G. Bratt for discussion of this "conventional wisdom"*], or to effectively regulate and police private owners. The view that government is ill equipped to be in the housing business has been long held by conservatives opposed to public intervention in the housing market. The difference was that many in the self-help movement rejected private-sector participation as well.

The current disillusionment with the public sector derives from the lengthy period of deep trouble encountered by public housing beginning in the mid-1960s, the enormous problems encountered under the two major interest subsidy programs (Sections 235 and 236 of the 1968 Housing Act), and the apparent inability of federal and municipal governments to mitigate the impact of private-sector withdrawal from the standing stock. This consumer disenchantment was played out against a backdrop of general impatience with government and widespread criticism of its reputed inefficiency.

The issues this new outlook posed were threefold: Who, then, was left who could assume reliable, day-to-day responsibility for this stock, both public and private? Who was to assume responsibility more generally for housing improvement and redevelopment in the inner cities? Finally, if declining market conditions in some neighborhoods reversed, how were residents to preserve their investment after holding out during the worst times and protect themselves from future displacement?

The fact that each of the important self-help developments occurred in the most troubled neighborhoods among groups with extremely limited housing options and high levels of dependency seems more than accidental. Charles Abrams (1971) called squatting a "trespass of desperation" [*see Chapter 25 by Seth Borgos for a discussion of homeowner squatting*]. Circumstances turned the residents of New York City tenements and St. Louis public

housing into squatters by default. Their assumption of control hardly qual-
ifies as trespass, but it certainly was fueled by the desperation of those with
few options. Apparently, conditions have to deteriorate badly before these
kinds of alternatives emerge. These efforts owed little to a *petit bourgeois*
interest in ownership for its own sake or alternatively to a radical ideology
that advocated expropriation of private property and community control.
The central issue was to gain sufficient control to remedy painful housing
conditions.

The emergence of urban self-help must also be understood against the
background of the poor people's and civil rights movements of the 1960s and
the consumer and neighborhood movements of the 1970s [*see Chapter 22 by
John Atlas and Peter Dreier*]. The agitation for local ownership, community
participation, and neighborhood control that emerged in minority communities certainly helped to give the principles of self-determination and
self-help currency and a certain legitimacy in the public mind. Tenant
management and mutual ownership required residents to put themselves in
the new and previously scorned role of landlord. Moreover, it required
considerable imagination to conceive of themselves as the owners of property where many had been long-term tenants, to say nothing of being the
owner or operator of something as substantial as an apartment house
(Kolodny, 1973). Without the assertions of consumer rights and the resur-
gence of neighborhood-based voluntary action, it is unlikely that such a
dramatic reversal of roles would have occurred.[7]

## Tinkering with Tenure Forms and Management Arrangements

Resident participation customarily has been seen as but a minor adjunct to
housing policy—therapeutic for low-income households; a safety valve for
landlord-tenant tensions; a way, perhaps, of humanizing the bureaucracy; a
training ground for skills in democracy. The self-help activity, however, has
potentially a much greater significance. It can be viewed as one test of what
can be achieved without additional subsidy in solving the problems of
housing low- and moderate-income households. Viewed in policy terms,
self-help emphasizes changes in the traditional incentive structures and
institutional arrangements we have employed to develop and run housing,
rather than increases in subsidies and changes in financing arrangements.
This is not to say that experimentation along these lines does not cost
money, which it certainly does. The central proposition being tested,
however, is whether a transfer of ownership or a reversal of managerial
arrangements in themselves might provide improved housing and housing
services for the same amounts already expended, or equivalent quality for
less (the savings accruing to the consumers, the public, or both).

Improving housing services while holding budgets constant is potentially
achievable, for example, through readjusting expenditure priorities and

operating standards to reflect tenant wishes, or through giving tenants a significant role in the monitoring of management performance, thereby increasing efficiency. Examples of mechanisms for cost cutting include offering residents the opportunity to substitute labor for cash by accepting a volunteer role in maintenance and management, and giving them incentives to employ "peer pressure" with neighbors to minimize rent delinquency and property abuse.

Beyond these basic propositions, there is the equally significant principle that employing residents in the delivery of residential and related services offers a way of multiplying the impact of expenditures on housing. It gives tenants a chance to earn wages and thus attacks the problem of the increasing gap between operating costs and rent revenues on the demand side.

Finally, there is in this activity an attempt to escape near total dependence on the "service economies" emerging in the older neighborhoods. These areas are producers of little that is valued in the larger society. Increasingly, they are dependent consumers of publicly provided goods and services, the market economy that once provided many of these services having withered. This is a local economy that not only lacks diversity, but also is heavily subject to the whim of a single centralized source of economic activity. Capturing ownership or control of facilities may offer limited but nevertheless psychologically real devices for limiting that dependency and giving residents a role in production as well as consumption.

## Self-Sufficiency and the Limits to Cut-Rate Remedies

These efforts do not necessarily ignore or deny the need for increased subsidization and income assistance. Their emphasis, however, is on exploring a new structure of relations among the actors in housing. The implicit objectives are to make the best of what we now have and to see what improvements can be extracted in the absence of massive new forms of housing subsidy and/or a significant redistribution of income through employment programs and tax policy. There is a clear link between the self-help activity and the assumption that the halcyon days of social programs are over, that subsidy levels will stabilize or decline, and that cutback planning is the only prudent and realistic kind. Particularly in New York and in the sweat-equity projects, the promise was put forth that self-help might so reduce costs that the poor would be insulated against the vagaries of housing programs, fickle state welfare policies, and the fortunes of the larger economy. The project also attracted interests that advocate energy self-sufficiency and appropriate technology. One of the earliest sweat-equity projects had both solar panels and a power-generating windmill installed on its roof. The general ethic of conservation and recycling was carried over from the building renovation into the redevelopment of vacant lots for open space and vegetable gardening and plans to use basements for aqua-farming and cottage industry.

There is nothing wrong with linking housing to other forms of self-help, and indeed it may have been inevitable that sweat equity would be adopted as a model for meeting other needs. But it points up the fact that self-help is a two-edged sword. On the one hand, it is a way to assert user interests and redirect resources more thoroughly to meet the needs of the intended beneficiaries. On the other hand, the dedication to going it alone and trying to make do without external assistance and support (what might be dubbed the "Little Red Hen Approach") can play directly into the hands of public agency and private-sector interests who would, if they could, relinquish all responsibility for social housing [*see Chapter 27 by Tony Schuman*]. Thus, control can be transferred without the resources required to make it work. This insulates against demands for more resources while simultaneously neutralizing criticism and protest, since consumers become their own land-lord or managing agent. Indeed the public agencies can be made to look good by comparison if the self-help venture, as is likely, founders. The point is that the flexing of consumer muscles and the simultaneous emergence of self-help coincide dangerously with a mood in the public sector to bail out of difficult or "impossible" situations and the political and financial liabilities that accompany them.

Indeed, some activists on the left charge that self-help strategies are playing right into the hands of government agencies that are trying to reduce social expenditures and evade the responsibility to provide everyone with decent housing (Homefront, 1977, chap. 3). They argue that, while self-help may appear superficially attractive, it is really just another form of privatization that will return to haunt participants as costs rise with no continuing claim on public subsidies to help meet them.

Surely it is romantic fancy to think that the poor and powerless can become so totally self-reliant that they will cease to depend on the redistributive powers of the public sector to improve their lot. Thus, the question that must be asked about these ventures is this: Are they only stopgaps, diverting poor households from real solutions, or do they point the way to a significant increase in these people's ability to reallocate resources in their favor over the long run?

The evidence is sketchy and unsystematic, but it would seem premature to attribute substantial cost savings to the self-help formula. In St. Louis and Newark, the deterioration of the public projects had proceeded so far, and management operations had been so curtailed prior to the tenants' taking over, that before-and-after comparisons are meaningless. The research that accompanied the more controlled national demonstration indicated that there are no dramatic economies in tenant management. Indeed, providing adequate housing for large low-income families in urban settings may simply cost more than most housing authorities have to spend. If tenants in these two cities are better off, part of the explanation may lie in the additional resources they have been able to attract for "soft" management activities.

As regards sweat equity, the author has assembled some rough cost comparisons with more conventional types of rehabilitation (Kolodny, 1979b). Costs to occupants are indeed reduced as a result of public subsidy. The donated labor and manpower stipends substantially reduce the mortgage amount required and thus the cooperator's debt service payments. Free technical assistance, waiver of fees, the nominal sales price set by the city for sweat-equity properties, and its real estate tax abatement and exemption provisions for rehabilitated housing all help to reduce monthly costs further. Savings in the actual costs of development, however, when the dollar value of all these contributions is added in, average probably no more than 15 percent as a result of the self-help approach. For individual projects, particularly those where there were no labor subsidies and work was voluntary, cost savings have been very substantial.

Part of the difficulty in analyzing such accounts is how to acknowledge the significance of the employment generated. In self-help homesteading, the housing expenditures are doing double duty, creating jobs for local residents as well as shelter. This, and training for employment, are among the clear benefits of the self-help approach, particularly in tenant management where the positions have proved to be relatively permanent.

Actual cost reductions are, of course, not the only measure of the possible virtues of self-help. If the same dollar is spent but better services are provided, this is an equally notable achievement. Again, there is no systematic evidence, but it is the clear consensus of informed observers that there is increased housing satisfaction among residents. This may be due to (1) objective improvement of services; (2) a reordering of priorities in what gets attended to and what gets neglected; (3) a sense of being in control of the immediate man-made environment, even if it is not objectively better; or (4) all three. It seems quite plausible that one thing self-help and user control does create is greater tolerance for existing conditions. This is because the relationship between rental income and the quality of services is more direct and visible. Where residents choose not to spend more money to remedy deficiencies, they at least recognize that they are deferring improvements in order to keep rents low, or because they simply cannot afford them.

What also can be said with considerable confidence is that, without self-help, much of this housing would have been lost permanently. Newark's tenant-management project was near the epicenter of the riots that occurred in that city in 1967. It was two-thirds vacant and boarded up at the end of the rent strike, and most sensible observers considered it a terminal case. The St. Louis projects were in only slightly better condition; meanwhile, the authority was in virtual receivership and clearly incapable of managing the projects at any acceptable level. (A companion project, the massive Pruitt-Igoe, was finally emptied because of intolerable living conditions and the structures were torn down.) The coop conversion and sweat-equity projects that succeeded in New York were saving buildings from almost certain total abandonment and then rapid devastation. As an antidote to abandonment, self-help certainly earns high marks, both in terms of restoring troubled publicly assisted housing and reclaiming orphaned, privately owned units. Indeed, it is impossible to compare it directly with alternative mechanisms for salvaging derelict housing since, in such settings, there is virtually no competition.

## Self-Help Housing and Community Development

The generally overlooked lesson of the St. Louis tenant management experience is that housing improvement may not, in itself, be the most significant result of expanded consumer roles in housing production, operation, and ownership. The ongoing contract with the housing authority has provided a permanent operating base from which the tenants can address their other needs. Thus, housing management, which in the beginning was the *problem*, over time has afforded the *opportunity* to work on community development at a much more ambitious scale.

By 1985, several of the St. Louis TMCs were well embarked on what can be considered a third phase of their evolution. One TMC participated in the construction of 100 turnkey townhouse units, which it conveyed to the housing authority and now manages. Two corporations are codevelopers of 675 units of new rental housing, now fully occupied on a neighboring site. The TMCs are also partners in the conversion of an empty local school building into Section 8 housing and in a plan to build a commercial shopping center to serve the housing projects. The TMCs' share of the proceeds from these projects is being plowed back into programs and services for the TMC residents. In addition to the revitalization of their districts and the enhanced services, the TMCs have secured a large number of the resulting construction jobs for tenants and other low-income persons.

It seems fair to say that without the legitimacy earned through competent real estate management and without the institutionalization of the tenants' common interests in the form of the TMCs, none of this could have occurred. Yet, despite the fact that what started as protest and grew into self-help has developed into a sophisticated corporate form, the TMCs have managed to maintain some autonomy from the larger system and their accountability to their own constituency. A long-time adviser to the resident corporations describes the evolutionary result of tenant management as a kind of "community socialism."

In New York, the strongest of the original sweat-equity groups are engaged in tenant organizing and advocacy, housing management, social service, and youth programs that go well beyond their housing rehabilitation activity. They have been important constituents of a citywide coalition that agitated and negotiated for a better shake for poorer neighborhoods in the allocation of public resources and for a more flexible and sympathetic administration of public programs.

By contrast, several of the national demonstrations that have adopted these formulas have encountered this paradox: Schemes that seem to have worked when developed by the parties most directly affected do not translate easily into programatic terms and have become "muscle bound." What is more, shifts in design that appeared to make sense in order to regularize an approach for wider application tampered with its essential elements. In HUD's sweat-equity homesteading demonstration in New York, for example, the construction workers were no longer prospective occupants, but only manpower trainees. Aspects of self-help remained in the efforts, but this central element was dropped. The St. Louis experience gives hope, however, that self-help can be institutionalized without a major loss of autonomy.

Involved in the pragmatic and urgent task of finding immediate remedies to severe housing problems in both the public and private stock are some larger issues relating to national housing strategies. A number of the most interesting efforts can be seen as rough tests of the limits of the contribution that improved management (taking this term in its broadest sense) can make to the solution of the nation's housing problems. If we are attentive, we may be able to learn the extent to which improvements in management skill and practice, experiments in recasting the relationship between the producers and consumers of housing services, and efforts at tenant organization and community development at the building or housing complex scale, can, and cannot, substitute for deeper subsidies, more equitable distribution of economic resources generally, and a larger public hand in the ownership and operation of housing for those the market does not serve.

In the midst of this experimentation and often desperate scrambling, the role of occupants, in terms of both responsibility and control, has been fundamentally redefined and residents are being identified as a management resource. This has already been the pattern in some of the most distressed public housing, as in St. Louis and Newark, and in the abandoned private housing stock of ghetto districts in cities like New York. These are resource-poor settings in which there is a premium on taking maximum advantage of remaining resources, where necessity sometimes helps mother invention, and where the loosening of established ways occasionally allows innovative remedies to be employed. Still, the total of these efforts is modest when measured against the scale of the problem. Moreover, these efforts are vulnerable to being lionized and puffed up out of all proportion by their supporters. They are subject to being alternately exploited and then cut off by public agencies vacillating between wanting control, on the one hand, and needing "receivers" for problems they cannot cope with, on the other. Nevertheless, the efforts demonstrate that mutual aid is possible in urban settings and that it is effective in meeting immediate crises. The boldest of these ventures may well be teaching us something new about how housing improvement strategies can be used as a basis for resident mobilization and large-scale community redevelopment.

# Notes

1. No comprehensive follow-up study of these particular projects has been undertaken, but it does not appear that a large number were completed. The city's fiscal crisis intervened, along with a federal moratorium on housing subsidy programs. Meanwhile, rehabilitation costs rose, and for a variety of reasons the municipal housing agency became less sympathetic to tenant ownership. For a recent review of the status of some of the early cooperatives that survived, see Lawson, 1984.

2. For an early evaluation of the tenant management experience, see Center for Urban Programs, 1974, 1975.

3. For a thoughtful reflection on the TMCs' experience by a participant and a discussion of their community development activities, see Baron, 1978.

4. Some sense of the turnaround achieved can be gleaned from Stella Wright Resident Management Corporation and Newark Redevelopment and Housing Authority, n.d. For impressions of a British houser who visited the project and another tenant management effort in Jersey City, see Power, 1979. For a general account of the St. Louis effort and six other experiments in tenant management, see Diaz, 1979.

5. For some preliminary findings of the evaluation, see Stegman, 1979a, 1979b.

6. For the most recent official report on these programs, see *The In Rem Housing Program*, 1983; for an evaluation of the programs, see also Sullivan, 1982.

7. For a description of the locally based housing organizations that emerged in New York during this period, see Schur and Sherry, 1977.

# 27

# The Agony and the Equity: A Critique of Self-Help Housing

*Tony Schuman*

*While the self-help ethic, be it in housing or other areas, has a virtuous aura, applying it on a mass scale as a program to solve the low-income housing problem raises some disturbing questions. Several important dilemmas emerging from the self-help movement are explored here, such as the limited cost reductions possible given the salience of financing and other nonlabor costs; the difficulties of translating skills learned on the job into permanent construction trade employment; and the reduction of pressure on government to assume primary responsibility for meeting the housing needs of those the market cannot serve. On the other hand, this strategy can provide valuable insights into how the housing and economic systems function, which in turn can lead to broader demands and the building of strong political coalitions.*

Criticism of self-help is a heretical undertaking in the context of Western moral and social thought. It flies in the face of biblical injunction, the Puritan work ethic, and the pioneer spirit. Indeed, who can offer anything but encouragement to those who, unable to compete for housing in the private market and neglected by inadequate public programs, provide shelter for themselves and their families through the sweat of their brows? But a problem arises when this individual solution to the housing question is elevated to programmatic dimensions suggesting wide applicability and success on a mass scale. The following remarks attempt to suggest directions that might strengthen self-help housing and lead to a more generalizable response to the housing question in the United States.

## The Growth of Self-Help

While the cooperative, self-help tradition in the United States may be traced to the barn raising and quilting bee in the era of westward expansion, its

This chapter is an updated and expanded version of a chapter that appeared in *The Scope of Social Architecture*, Volume 1 of *Columns: Architecture and Society*, edited by C. Richard Hatch. Copyright 1984, Van Nostrand Reinhold. Reprinted by permission.

application to multifamily urban housing is a recent development. Several factors explain this upsurge. The cycle of disinvestment (leading to housing abandonment) and reinvestment (by a new urban "gentry") has resulted in the displacement of hundreds of thousands of households.[1] At the same time, the rapid increase in tax foreclosures has put many buildings in city hands, potentially available to tenants at low cost.[2] This combination of pressure and opportunity has promoted self-help as a means of preserving both the housing stock and community profile of low-income neighborhoods.

The scope of resident-initiated housing activity is broad, ranging from rent strikes and tenant management to development and sponsorship of rehabilitation and new construction. Self-help housing, more particularly, involves two programmatic ideas: desire to reduce construction and operating costs by investing "free" labor, and cooperative ownership of buildings to guarantee security of tenure. These ideas are clearly combined in the sweat-equity approach pioneered by the Urban Homesteading Assistance Board (UHAB) in New York City, now codified in a municipal homesteading program.[3] Since this approach serves as a model for similar efforts in other cities, it is of more than local interest to examine the pitfalls and shortfalls of the sweat-equity process.

## Benefits of Self-Help

Four potential benefits are claimed for self-help housing:

1. *Reduced construction and operating costs.* Savings result from the donated labor of the participants in construction (and eventual maintenance) and the use of public subsidies to produce below-market mortgage interest rates.

2. *Employment and skills training.* Residents working under the supervision of experienced builders learn skills useful in building maintenance and are prepared for employment in the construction industry.

3. *Control of urban land.* With the housing shortage forcing rents upward and making working-class neighborhoods ripe for redevelopment, cooperative ownership offers the hope of retaining a part of the housing stock for low- and moderate-income families.

4. *Strengthening of community and individual identity.* The effort required to carry out a rehabilitation project in the face of adverse economic conditions, bureaucratic red tape, and inevitable construction snags are powerful molders of collective consciousness and self-esteem. The process serves to decommodify both labor power and housing, providing an opportunity for dignified work whose product is appropriated directly by the workers. Self-help housing also offers design flexibility capable of meeting the needs of nontraditional user groups who are ill served by conventional housing programs.[4]

# Pitfalls

All the potential benefits have been realized to some extent in every self-help project, and this is the great merit of the approach. At the same time, each has also revealed serious problems that suggest that self-help housing will need greatly increased assistance to become a viable option, and that much more radical programs must be developed if we are ever to realize the promise of a decent home for every American. The problematic aspects can be explored by reference to the benefits described above.

1. *Reduced costs.* Recent trends indicate that the gap between housing costs and income continues to grow. According to the 1980 census, median rents rose 125 percent nationally over the past decade, while median incomes went up only 98 percent (*New York Times*, Apr. 20, 1982). Inflation in construction materials, land costs, interest rates, and unpredictable fuel oil prices indicate the situation will only worsen in the near future. The net result is that those who need it most are increasingly unable to afford even self-help housing, despite the reduction in initial costs and the economies involved in cooperative management and maintenance.

There is no reason to believe that the gap between income and housing costs will narrow. On the contrary, the historical inability to correlate costs and incomes indicates that the discrepancy is a structural aspect of capitalism, viewed as a long-term secular trend [*see Chapter 3 by Michael E. Stone*]. Because housing costs are affected much more by mortgage rates than construction costs, sweat labor itself is unable to solve the dilemma posed by the rent-income gap.[5] As a result, self-help housing is heavily dependent on government subsidies. Neither the economic nor the political climate suggests that these subsidies will soon be available in sufficient quantity. One self-help advocate now acknowledges, "We are getting blown out of the water by costs."

2. *Employment.* The potential benefits here are restricted at the outset to the younger and more energetic of the poor. Excluded are the elderly, the disabled, women with child-care responsibilities, and employed people who could not support themselves and their families on the modest stipends that have been available to self-help labor through vehicles like the recently defunded CETA program. For participants in self-help, training in the building trades offers little beyond its eventual application in building maintenance. With the construction industry in difficult straits, and the minority groups most active in self-help housing largely excluded by racism, there is little likelihood that self-help training will lead to permanent employment. Once trainees have completed rehabilitating their own housing, during which time they were compensated through the CETA program (at least in the early New York experiments), they lose their only source of income, with few prospects for regular employment.

It has been argued that there are more than enough potential construction jobs available in rehabilitating the housing stock of our beleaguered cities to employ the self-helpers and ease the unemployment problem generally. The idea is appealing for both economic and social reasons. However, there are substantial obstacles to realizing such a program on more than a token scale. First, there would be competition from the construction unions wanting a piece of the action. Second, with the virtual elimination by the Reagan administration of direct federal housing subsidies, housing rehabilitation is largely restricted to gentrifying areas attractive to private capital. If the rehabilitated housing were to meet the social goal of sheltering low- and moderate-income households, it would require not only construction subsidies but also deep operating subsidies and a commitment to the right of people to remain in their communities regardless of their status in the economy.[6] This last concern goes right to the heart of the question of control of urban land.

3. *Control of urban land.* Despite the efforts of New York City's innovative Alternative Management Programs, several of which aim at the disposition of city-owned housing to tenant cooperatives or not-for-profit community organizations [*see Chapter 26 by Robert Kolodny*], the amount of housing thus retained for low- and moderate-income households is negligible compared with the wave of coop conversions and gentrified brownstones that is transforming the class and racial character of New York's older neighborhoods.[7] In more remote and derelict communities, such as the South Bronx and Central Brooklyn, where gentry fear to tread, a policy of "planned shrinkage" has been proposed to spur the out-migration of poor residents.[8] From an accounting standpoint, this would rid the city of dependent, service-consuming tenants and open up vast tracts of land for redevelopment.

What is at issue here is the very definition of a city. While community residents see the city as a place to live and work, raise children, and pursue their educational, cultural, and recreational needs, the private real estate sector sees the city as an opportunity for investment, a locus for the accumulation of capital. Commenting on proposals to rehabilitate low-rent housing in the West Side Urban Renewal Area in New York, the *New York Times* (Dec. 1, 1979) editorialized that it would be irresponsible to permit continued low-yield use of the land when private investors stood ready to renovate the area for high-income families: "The city's obligation is to demolish the obsolete buildings and sell the land for as much as possible."

Municipal policy in older industrial cities like New York and Newark is to recapture the housing stock as a tax-paying resource, even if this objective puts housing beyond the reach of low-income families. As these cities reorganize their economies in the face of massive industrial flight, the captive pool of unskilled labor is seen as a liability rather than a resource. Put crudely, unskilled workers are superfluous to an increasingly service-sector economy, and so is their housing. In this context, the ability of the urban poor to remain in the city at all depends on their willingness to subsidize their own existence. But self-help housing cannot compete with private interests. A few buildings may be salvaged, but urban land is controlled by capital.

4. *Community and individual identity*. Self-help housing is an intense, energizing, and creative undertaking. In the absence of public or private support, community residents have taken a stand in defense of their communities. People have been "reborn" in a socially conscious and collective manner.[9] Newly rehabilitated buildings stand as rays of hope amid piles of rubble.

The impact of the self-help experience on its participants is difficult to measure and varies widely from group to group. The most passionate advocate of self-help is the English architect John F. C. Turner, whose book *Freedom to Build* has been a Bible for the movement. His view stresses the values of self-sufficiency, autonomy, and decentralization, and suggests that self-help housing is an expression of individual liberty. Adherents of this viewpoint present optimistic assessments of the process, and support the concept with a fervor approaching "sweat ecstasy." There is an implicit assumption that small communities can be sustained internally and *independent of larger economic and political forces*. The model calls for an expanding number of local efforts, leading to the eventual incorporation of like communities in a new, self-governing network—society is transformed from the bottom up.

This view reflects both a populist orientation, distrustful of a government controlled by giant corporations, and a conservative anarchist perspective, wary of centralizing tendencies in large-scale organizations. But to the extent that self-help is seen as a starting point for transforming society, there are several instances in which it works at cross-purposes to this goal.

There is an inherent tendency in self-help to reduce the value of labor power, to have a depressant effect on wages, despite a general agreement that the maldistribution of income is a primary source of our housing problems to begin with. The willingness of self-help workers to labor for low wages, or even without compensation, competes with the demand for an adequate living wage.

By assuming the burden of providing shelter for themselves, self-help groups reduce pressure on government to maintain its legitimacy by alleviating the failures of the private market with social programs.[10] This implicit willingness to manage the contradictions of the capitalist housing market is sometimes acknowledged explicitly by the participants.[11]

The absorption of discontent through self-help housing activity also has a dampening effect on accumulated grievances, which might erupt into social conflict with broader implications. Major efforts at reform in the United States have generally followed open social strife, from the Draft Riots of the Civil War to the "Great Society" programs that followed the urban riots in the late 1960s. The point is not lost on advocates of the status quo.

The precarious financial picture of self-help housing has led more than one community group to enter joint venture agreements with private investors through the sale of equity shares.[12] The joint-venture limited-partnership approach, while outside the pure sweat model, demonstrates the pressures to conform to the private market for housing. Although no neighborhood group can be faulted for seeking critical financial assistance, there is at least an element of irony in the attempt to solve housing problems by reinforcing the tax-shelter and investment mechanisms that maintain a housing system based on profit rather than need.

Because the same economic forces that threaten the viability of self-help housing on a project basis prevent its applicability on a large scale, the question of consciousness is a critical one. The natural desire for control over one's housing does not alter the fact that self-help groups do not command sufficient economic resources to make it work. Likewise, recognition of the indifference and inefficiency of central government does not alter the fact that the government alone has the political power and economic resources to provide housing for those unable to compete in the private market. If the pitfalls of self-help housing are predominantly economic in nature, the shortfalls stem from its failure to challenge the structure of the economy. The root of the dilemma is the privatization of the housing question, the attempt to solve a collective social problem—the provision of decent, affordable housing—at the level of an individual building.

## Shortfalls

Because the housing question arises from the disparity between housing costs and income, there are three logical means of addressing the problem: raise wages, lower costs, or subsidize the difference.[13] As self-help groups complete the construction phase and take on the management and maintenance of their housing, the underlying economic problems come to the fore. It is especially instructive, therefore, to see how the groups approach the question of financial solvency.

Because self-help groups tend to view the housing problem as outside the labor market, the issues of wage levels and income distribution are generally not addressed [*for another view, see Chapter 11 by José Ramón Sánchez*]. Instead, a number of proposals have been put forth aimed at further lowering production costs. There have been a few attempts to lower the cost of materials through cooperative purchasing or the creation of small shops to fabricate items such as kitchen cabinets. But most efforts focus on easing the size and terms of the mortgage itself.

In this light, the most encouraging development in self-help housing circles is the call for permanent operating subsidies. While not actually closing the cost–income gap, this demand at least acknowledges its existence. It marries a practical response to the problem with a historical and theoretical understanding of our capitalist housing system. The underlying premise is that rents should be based on income—an obvious point of unity with all low- and moderate-income tenants. The idea itself is hardly radical. Both public housing and the recently curtailed Section 8 subsidy program are based on the principle that tenants should not have to pay more than 25 or 30 percent of their income in rent.[14]

The demand for permanent operating subsidies is attractive for several reasons. First, it is national in scope and addresses the housing problems of millions of needy families in addition to the relatively small number engaged in self-help. Further, the subsidy issue raises three fundamental questions that go to the heart of our socioeconomic structure: the structure of present housing subsidies, the ideology of homeownership, and the means of financing additional operating subsidies.

The prevalent notion is that existing housing subsidies are for the poor. This is not so. The present beneficiaries of federal housing subsidies are overwhelmingly middle- to upper-income investors, landlords, and homeowners rather than low-income housing consumers. The principal vehicle for subsidy is the Internal Revenue System, which offers highly regressive deductions to homeowners for local taxes and mortgage-interest payments and gives housing investors generous write-offs for depreciation [*see Chapter 15 by Cushing Dolbeare*].

But just as important as the issue of unequal benefits through tax policy is the way in which these homeowner subsidies have, ironically, reinforced the idea of homeownership as a symbol of the free-market system. In the words of Herbert Hoover, an enthusiastic booster of the "Own your home" campaigns in the 1920s, "To own one's own home is a physical expression of individualism, of enterprise, of independence, and of freedom of spirit."[15] [*See Chapter 16 by Jim Kemeny.*]

In this regard, it is not surprising that self-help housers are so taken with the idea of ownership. They are hostile not only to private for-profit ownership of housing but also to public ownership. But the obvious alternative to indifferent public agencies or rapacious landlords—control through cooperative nonprofit housing—turns out to be an illusion when residents cannot meet carrying costs. And while New York City has been generous in its tax abatements for builders of luxury housing, there has been no public discussion of tax relief for low-income housing cooperatives. Ownership may in fact mean control when we are talking about giant corporations that command enormous capital resources and government attention, but it does not mean control for the disenfranchised poor.

The recognition of the need for permanent operating subsidies can shift attention from the ideological issue of ownership to the practical question of control in terms of security of tenure. To provide this security, new public financing mechanisms will be necessary to provide the requisite level of subsidy. The National Low Income Housing Coalition proposed replacing the present tax-*deduction* mechanism with a tax *credit*, which would have provided more equitable assistance to moderate-income homeowners and would have increased federal tax revenues by an estimated $3.5 billion in

1982. Had these savings been applied to direct outlays for rental housing, it would have increased the present level of funding by approximately 40 percent (Dolbeare, 1981).

At the local level, *City Limits* magazine presented two approaches to revenue raising in New York in their December 1983 issue entitled "Where the Money Is." A joint project from Pratt Institute's Center for Community and Environmental Development and the late Paul Davidoff's Metropolitan Action Institute at Queens College called for a Housing Trust Fund to generate capital for low- and moderate-income housing from a variety of sources, including contributions for inclusionary zoning and office development and dedicated set-asides from existing taxes. The second proposal, by Peter Marcuse, called for a Luxury Housing Tax that would have the dual merit of raising additional subsidy money through a tax on high-rent apartments and luxury coop sales and of encouraging retention of lower-rent units by exempting them from the tax.

# A Strategic Role

Despite its shortcomings, self-help is a currently necessary activity and a useful training ground for local housing activists. The participants are brought into direct confrontation with market forces and financing schemes. In this sense, it is precisely because self-help does not "work" as a solution that it has potential. The self-respect and fighting spirit of the self-help housers, coupled with their manifest commitment to preserving their neighborhoods, inevitably leads them to defend their physical and emotional investment. As they come to grips with the high cost of housing operation, they are obliged to consider various cost-reducing strategies, including mortgage and tax default. They are also pushed to act in coalition with other self-help groups and to reach out to other low- and moderate-income tenants.

The demand for operating subsidies anticipates the pressures to default and can help the self-helpers concentrate on those issues that are, in fact, within their control—the day-to-day decisions regarding the management of their housing, from tenant selection and eviction policy to maintenance and repair priorities.

The demand for permanent operating subsidies socializes the housing question. It insists on housing as a matter of need and of right, that housing is a necessity and not a luxury, and that it must, therefore, be treated as a public good and not as a commodity [*see Chapters 1 and 28 by Emily Paradise Achtenberg and Peter Marcuse*]. By themselves, of course, subsidies cannot solve the housing question. The social context for housing includes issues of employment, education, health services, and discrimination by race and gender, among others. But the demand is a practical one, one that can be implemented incrementally, and one that can provide an ongoing experiment in public responsibility with local control.

Self-help groups, for example, are in an excellent position to demand targeting of existing housing subsidies for buildings in not-for-profit cooperative, community, or public ownership. The groups will also be in the forefront of the demand for greatly increased housing subsidies, having demonstrated that hard work cannot surmount the failure of the private market.

It has been argued by some that advocacy of self-help is a dangerous diversion, shunting attention from the structural aspects of the housing problem into a bottomless pit of small-scale self-exploitation. To the extent that self-help is seen as a solution to the housing question, these fears are well grounded. But in the absence of a mass movement for decent housing as a public responsibility, the self-help sector can be a valuable starting point.

# Notes

1. A recent study of displacement, defined as "people losing their home against their will," estimates that 2.5 million Americans are affected each year and that, beyond this total, "some 500,000 lower-rent units are lost each year, through conversion, abandonment, inflation, arson and demolition" (Hartman, Keating, and LeGates, 1982, 3).

2. The foreclosure process has produced its most dramatic results in New York City, where over 8,000 buildings were under municipal ownership as of October 1982. Of this total, 3,727 buildings were occupied, making the city the unhappy landlord for over 36,000 units housing over 100,000 people. See *The In Rem Housing Program*, 1982.

3. The Urban Homesteading Assistance Board (UHAB) is a nonprofit housing service established in 1973 to advocate and provide technical assistance for self-help housing groups. The initial UHAB approach was to use voluntary "sweat" labor to perform most of the construction work, under the supervision of paid, skilled (and licensed) professionals. UHAB helped the groups secure legal and architectural assistance and negotiated grants and low-interest loans for seed money and construction costs. For an account of UHAB's history, and a case study in self-help housing rehabilitation, see Laven, 1984.

With UHAB's assistance, New York City's Department of Housing Preservation and Development (HPD) launched an Urban Homesteading Program in 1981, with the city performing work requiring licensed professionals and the homesteaders doing demolition, roofing, carpentry, and interior work. The homesteading program provides a budget of up to $6,000 per unit for this work. See, *The In Rem Housing Program*, 1982.

4. This design flexibility could be in the form of unit size and mix or in the provision of special facilities such as day care, workrooms, greenhouses, or even a mosque. See Laven, 1984.

5. Even when cash outlays for rehabilitation work are kept to a minimum, residents are hard-pressed to carry the maintenance and operating costs of low-income cooperatives. An HPD official recently estimated that 20 percent of such tenants would require Section 8 subsidies to meet expenses (*New York Times*, Dec. 19, 1982). This is surely a light estimate of need for tenants in New York's *in rem* housing stock. According to Stegman (1982a), over half the tenants in city-owned housing pay over 35 percent of their income in rent. Median income for these tenants is $6,865 versus $11,001 for all renters; the median gross rent–income ratio is 35.7 percent for *in rem* tenants versus 28 percent for all renters.

6. Housing abandonment and neighborhood decay are, of course, by-products of

fluctuations of the free-market economy produced by the mobility of capital. The social impact of plant closings, capital flight, and other encumbrances of a capitalist economy are highlighted in Bluestone and Harrison (1982). A study by Homefront (1977) underlines the relationship between abandonment and shifts in the local labor market in terms of availability of mortgage financing and the profitability of rental housing in New York.

7. While the Division of Alternative Management (DAMP) at HPD may be justly proud of the 12,464 units in 523 buildings at present headed for continued low-income occupancy under private, not-for-profit, or cooperative ownership, this is still a drop in the bucket compared with the 7,766 buildings in the city-owned inventory, most of which are headed for demolition. In fiscal year 1982, only 112 buildings were sold under DAMP programs, while 1,001 were demolished (*The In Rem Housing Program*, 1982). And although the pace has slowed somewhat, the wave of conversions from rental to coop housing continues. In 1980 alone, there were 15,000 conversions. And beyond conversions is the rapid escalation in rents in gentrified neighborhoods. Median monthly gross rents in Manhattan increased 172.1 percent from 1970 to 1981 (in current dollars; 25.3 percent in constant 1967 dollars—see Stegman, 1982a). As George Sternlieb, director of the Center for Urban Policy Research at Rutgers, observed succinctly, "We lose housing from the bottom and replace it at the top" (*New York Times*, June 6, 1981).

8. The phrase "planned shrinkage" was coined by New York City Housing Administrator Roger Starr in 1976 in proposing a triage approach to urban redevelopment (*New York Times*, Feb. 3, 1976). Although the notion was roundly criticized by community advocates and never became official city policy, it has become a de facto reality due to abandonment, arson, and service cutbacks. The result is acres of land in areas like the South Bronx, which stand ready for redevelopment through mechanisms such as President Reagan's proposed enterprise zone legislation.

9. For an upbeat account of the impact of collective housing action on a group of Lower East Side tenants, see *El Corazón del Loisaida*, a half-hour film by Marci Reaven and Bienvenida Matias, available from Unifilm, Inc., 419 Park Avenue South, New York, NY 10016.

10. The premise of James O'Connor's argument is that "the capitalistic state must try to fulfill two basic and often mutually contradictory functions—*accumulation* and *legitimization*. This means that the state must try to maintain or create the conditions in which profitable capital accumulation is possible. However, the state also must try to maintain or create the conditions for social harmony" (O'Connor, 1973, 6; emphasis in original). The point here is that self-help housers, in some measure, absolve the state of its responsibility to maintain its legitimacy through social expenditures for housing.

11. See, for example, Hackney, 1984, for an account of a housing project in Macclesfield, England.

12. Early efforts using this mechanism are Inquilinos Boricuas en Acción (IBA) in Boston's South End, and Los Sures in Brooklyn's Williamsburg neighborhood.

13. These options were identified over a hundred years ago by Frederick Engels. "Capital does not *want* to abolish the housing shortage," Engels wrote, "even if it could; this has now been finally established. There remain, therefore, only two other expedients: self-help on the part of the workers, and state assistance" (Engels, 1970; emphasis in original).

14. The rent–income ratio of 25 percent was not scientifically derived but emerged as a "reasonable" cap until President Reagan upped the ante to 30 percent in 1982 [*see Chapter 21 by Chester Hartman*]. An alternative method of calculating income available for housing, by first subtracting all nonshelter necessities from household income, shows that for millions of families, even 25 percent of income for housing is far too high [*see Chapter 3 by Michael E. Stone*].

15. Quoted in "Signs of Life: Symbols in the American City," published in conjunction with exhibition organized and designed by Venturi and Rauch, Architects and Planners, for the Smithsonian Institution, 1976. See also Wright, 1981.

# 28

# Toward the Decommodification of Housing

*Emily Paradise Achtenberg*
*Peter Marcuse*

*Proceeding from their analysis of the housing problem* [Chapter 1] *and expanding on the ideas of Kathy McAfee* [Chapter 24], *the authors propose the "decommodification" of housing—removing the production, ownership, and financing of housing from the profit sector. Housing must be made available on the principle of socially determined need, not profitability. The strategic implications of these proposals, in terms of their potential for political organizing, are explored.*

A significant factor in the housing and neighborhood gains of the postwar period, to the extent that they have been achieved, has been the role of popular struggle. During the Great Depression, the threat of massive unrest around issues of housing and job security led to moratoria on mortgage foreclosures, the enactment of the public housing program, and a variety of federal supports for homeownership. In the 1960s, housing again became a direct political issue largely through black-led tenant protests linked to the civil rights and welfare rights movements.

## The Limits of Housing and Neighborhood Struggles

These efforts achieved some gains of considerable importance for the poor. For example, massive rent strikes in St. Louis, Newark, and elsewhere led to major reforms in the public housing program [*see Chapter 26 by Robert Kolodny*]. Local urban renewal struggles in white ethnic as well as minority communities forced significant concessions in the form of replacement housing, relocation benefits, and resident participation. These efforts also

Originally published as "Towards the Decommodification of Housing: A Political Analysis and a Progressive Program," in *America's Housing Crisis: What Is to Be Done?* edited by Chester Hartman, Boston: Routledge & Kegan Paul, 1983, 218–30. Reprinted by permission of the Institute for Policy Studies.

helped to launch the new subsidized housing production and neighborhood programs of the Great Society.

Despite their successes, the housing and neighborhood struggles of the 1960s remained fragmented along tenure and racial lines, and were limited in focus to particular issues or targets. They failed to broaden their concerns beyond local demands or generalized calls for "social justice" or "community control." Nor did they come to grips with the systemic nature of the housing crisis. As a result, when the worsening problems of the economy in the early 1970s made further concessions more difficult, the protest movement (in housing and other areas) all but collapsed. Thus the stage was set for President Nixon's 1973–74 freeze on subsidized housing, the defunding of "categorical grant" programs, the urban "fiscal crisis," and the beginning of the ideological attack on housing standards.

The 1970s saw the growth of a geographically widespread neighborhood movement, involving primarily homeowners and dealing with a range of economic issues. With a more diverse agenda than the 1960s protest movements, these groups won significant legislative and regulatory reforms, including nationally mandated disclosure requirements for mortgage lenders aimed at stemming the tide of neighborhood disinvestment. But the neighborhood movement has been unable to respond effectively to the problems of skyrocketing mortgage interest rates and scarce housing credit, which have made it impossible to improve housing and still keep it affordable.

At the same time, there has been a recent revival of tenant activism around the issues of high rents and condominium conversions in revitalizing areas [*see Chapter 22 by John Atlas and Peter Dreier*]. But while rent control has helped to mitigate the skyrocketing cost of housing to consumers, it has not addressed the problems of housing deterioration and abandonment. Very strict rent control (were it ever enacted) might even exacerbate these problems. Moreover, rent control in today's inflationary economy does not suffice to make housing affordable, especially for lower-income households.

Now that the political counterattack on housing is in full force and housing and economic conditions are worsening, there is an opportunity to develop a broad-based progressive housing movement that can unite low- and moderate-income tenants and homeowners around their common interest in decent, affordable housing and adequate neighborhoods. The growing elusiveness of homeownership for the vast majority of tenants and the decreasing ability of low- and moderate-income homeowners to benefit from their housing as an investment make tenure distinctions less important, while increasing neighborhood problems create a basis for common action. Moreover, the traditional housing solutions of subsidies and tax incentives for the rich, combined with federal credit manipulations, seem less and less workable even to those who view them as in general desirable. Needed is a program that can alter the terms of existing public debate on housing, that challenges the commodity nature of housing and its role in our economic and social system, and that demonstrates how people's legitimate housing needs can be met through an alternative approach.

# A Program for Housing Decommodification

## General Principles

As shown in Chapter 1, the housing problem is rooted in the commodity treatment of housing and in the general relationship between housing and private capital in our society. Racism and sexism, primarily linked to the needs of capital, significantly influence the nature of our housing problems. The dominance of capital in relation to housing is expressed in the organization of housing ownership, production, and finance; in the use and disposition of land; in neighborhood development and service patterns; in the particular housing problems of minorities and women; and in the allocation of resources both to and within the housing sector.

The following program for housing decommodification, broadly defined, has as its primary goal:

> To provide every person with housing that is affordable, adequate in size and of decent quality, secure in tenure, and located in a supportive neighborhood of choice, with recognition of the special housing problems confronting oppressed groups (especially minorities and women).

Just as the "commodity treatment of housing" is a possible shorthand for the root of the housing problem, "decommodification" is a possible term for a program to eliminate the housing problem. The terms are apt, to the extent that they focus on the relationship between housing provision and private profit, and call for a housing system in which decisions are made without regard to profit.

But speaking of the "commodification of housing," at least in the Marxist theory from which it stems, both says too much and too little to be an entirely adequate formulation of the problem. Too little, because the term "commodity," strictly speaking, focuses on the form of *production*, while issues of distribution are also critical to housing. Too little, also, because housing is neither produced nor distributed solely for the profit of producers and providers, but also to maintain the general stability of the system (in both an economic and a political sense). It is thus sometimes supplied even at the expense of direct housing producers, as during wartime or emergency price and rent controls. And in a profit-oriented economy, even where housing is partially or totally removed from the commodity market, it may be far from decent, affordable, or secure (squatter settlements, company housing, and public housing are a few examples).

Nor is it necessarily so that *all* aspects of the housing supply system need to be "decommodified" to solve the most serious current problems. As Jill Hamberg points out in Chapter 33, Cuban economists still speak of housing as a commodity as to aspects both of its production and distribution. Within that system, the ways in which housing is produced and distributed are indeed overwhelmingly subject to social control, yet limited scope is still given to conventional considerations of cost and "profitability." Likewise, in a society of plenty, if some should want more, and be willing to work harder or distribute their resources differently, there is no reason why they should not be allowed to buy more, nor why suppliers should not be allowed to sell them more, even if the commodity in question is housing and the purpose of the sale is profit. Thus decommodification says a little too much, also.

"Commodification" and its opposite should be understood here, not in the narrow sense discussed above, but as referring to the provision of housing for the purpose of producing or guaranteeing profit (including interest and land rent) for private interests, both within and outside the housing sector.

The program calls for decommodification in the very broadest sense, not only in the way that housing is directly produced, financed, owned, and disposed of, but also with regard to housing resource allocation, decision-making, and use patterns generally. The objective, broadly stated, is to limit the role of profit from decisions affecting housing, substituting instead the basic principle of socially determined need.

## Social Ownership

*Control the speculative private ownership of housing and expand the amount of housing under public, collective, community, or resident ownership that is operated solely for resident benefit and subject to resident control, with resale for profit prohibited.* An essential first step in the decommodification of housing is to eliminate the cost of speculative ownership and the arbitrary control that profit-oriented owners have. In the short run, this suggests the need for increasingly strict regulation of privately owned rental housing (e.g., as to rents, condition, occupancy terms, evictions, demolition, resale), and for measures to curb the speculative buying and selling of private homes. Housing already in the public sector should also be preserved, upgraded, and reoriented in the direction of social ownership, with increased control by residents in place of centralized, bureaucratic control.

In the long run, as much housing as possible should be converted away from ownership for profit. Social ownership can take a variety of forms, including direct ownership by government or nonprofit entities, collective ownership by resident-controlled corporations or neighborhood councils, nonequity or limited equity cooperatives, or nonspeculative resident ownership of single-family homes. What matters is not the precise legal ownership structure, but that the housing has the attributes described above and is permanently removed from the speculative market. Residents of socially owned housing would pay rent based on true ability to pay, resulting in rent-free housing for many (or equivalent income support). And residents would have the right to permanent occupancy as long as they comply with reasonable tenure obligations (including noninterference with the rights of others).

## Social Production

*Upgrade and expand the housing supply, and increase social control over the housing production process (including housing design, development, construction, and materials production).* To provide an adequate supply of housing, the existing housing stock (ownership and rental) should be upgraded as rapidly as possible to appropriate standards of safety, liveability, space, and energy efficiency. In addition, the rate of new housing construction should be increased to meet the needs of newly formed households, to replace lost or unrepairable units, to reduce overcrowding, and to facilitate adequate mobility and choice.

Certainly in the foreseeable future most aspects of housing production will continue to be performed by the private sector—but in order to meet these goals at reduced cost, the production process must be increasingly subject to public control. Government subsidies and financing assistance can be conditioned on the provision of social benefits (such as job creation for lower-income and minority residents, or the allocation of development profits for community use), with the housing thus produced ultimately transferred to the public or to resident groups for social ownership. The long-term goal is to move toward social ownership of the materials production industries, an increasingly strong public and community development sector, and perhaps a growing role for worker-controlled and public construction companies.

## Public Financing

*Reduce the dependence of housing production, ownership, and improvement on private mortgage credit, and increase public control of housing finance capital.* Our analysis (and the experience of Western European countries) shows that even with social ownership and production, as long as housing remains dependent on private mortgage credit, it will continue to be expensive to society and in short supply [*see Chapter 3 by Michael E. Stone and Chapter 4 by Ann Meyerson*]. To address this problem in the short run, regulatory measures should be devised to allocate more private credit to housing, and alternative public sources of housing credit should be developed (such as state housing banks and public pension funds). In the long run, housing production and rehabilitation should increasingly be financed through direct government spending—in much the way we build military facilities—with direct grants to public and community developers for the production of socially owned housing. This housing would be permanently debt free, with no mortgages or bonds to repay. At the same time, as a growing portion of the existing stock is converted to social ownership, the mortgage debt on these properties could be paid off (over time) and permanently eliminated. [*See Chapter 29 by Chester Hartman and Michael E. Stone for a detailed description of this plan.*]

## Social Control of Land

*Control speculative private use and disposition of land, and preserve and expand the supply of land under public control and ownership.* Land is a scarce public resource, given value by public action and having pervasive influence over community life. Its control is an indispensable element in planning for society's housing (and other) needs, and its rising cost is a significant deterrent to housing development. To reduce land costs and insure an adequate supply of developable land for housing, increased public control over the private use and disposition of land is needed, through a variety of regulatory, tax, and planning measures. The existing supply of socially owned land should be preserved and expanded through such measures as government and community land-banking, moving toward broad social ownership of land suitable for housing use and progressive land-use planning.

## Resident Control of Neighborhoods

*Limit the adverse impact of profit-oriented development and service patterns on lower-income and minority neighborhoods, and increase control by residents over neighborhood decisions, on a nonexclusionary basis.* Increased residential security and improved living conditions for lower-income and minority residents will require a reorientation of neighborhood development and service patterns to reflect social and community needs rather than profit considerations. At a minimum, this means that any private development activity (especially if publicly assisted) should be regulated to minimize its adverse impact on lower-income and minority neighborhoods (impacts such as direct or indirect housing or job loss). While private developers should be held accountable for these social costs, the public benefits of private development activity should also be maximized, for example, by providing jobs, housing, community facilities, or services for lower-income and minority residents in conjunction with such activity.

Similarly, public planning for the design and delivery of public services should be responsive to community (and especially to user) needs. In order to achieve this accountability, the residents of lower-income and minority neighborhoods should be increasingly involved in development and service decisions. Neighborhood control does not need to be increased for the rich, the powerful, and the entrenched, who already control not only their communities but most decisions in the society at large. It is, however, a progressive force in those communities whose residents do not have access to privileges and power, and whose ability to manage their own destinies is limited, rather than buttressed, by the power of capital. Resident control in any neighborhood should operate within a basic nonexclusionary framework, and should not be misused to exclude or deny access or opportunity.

## Affirmative Action and Housing Choice

*Eliminate the discriminatory, exclusionary, and oppressive uses of housing, especially in relation to racial minorities and women; and provide housing in forms and locations that address the special situation of oppressed groups, including the right to remain in place or to move to other neighborhoods of choice.* Special steps must be taken to address (and redress) the particular housing problems confronting oppressed groups in our society. These include increased, affirmative efforts to control and ultimately eliminate the pervasive forms of discrimination and exclusion that currently exist in the housing market [*see Chapter 18 by the Citizens Commission on Civil Rights*]. Housing resources must also be targeted for the revitalization of existing minority communities, in order to protect and affirm the right of minority residents to enhance their social and political cohesiveness by remaining in place if they choose to do so. At the same time, the right of mobility for minority residents must be expanded by providing increased housing options in other neighborhoods of choice, without diminishing the prior commitment to neighborhood revitalization [*see Chapter 12 by Gary Orfield*]. Affirmative efforts are also needed to develop housing of appropriate size, type, and design to free women from domestic oppression and exploitation.

## Equitable Resource Allocation

*Allocate available resources for housing and neighborhoods based on need; and provide adequate resources through the public sector, raising the necessary funds through progressive means.* Resources currently available for housing and neighborhoods (from the private as well as the public sector) should be increasingly targeted for purposes that benefit lower-income and minority households. In the long run, in order to provide decent, affordable housing and viable neighborhoods, the level of resources allocated to housing and the role of the public sector must be substantially increased. A major shift in public spending priorities (most notably away from military spending) as well as increased taxes on corporate and individual wealth and profits would be required in order to generate the needed revenues in a progressive way. At the same time, a progressive, nonspeculative approach to housing production, finance, and ownership would make it possible to use these increased resources with much greater cost effectiveness.

# Strategic Implications

What are the strategic implications of a program for housing decommodification in the United States today, given current political and economic conditions?

Certainly, the experience of other modern Western industrial societies suggests that many of these proposals can be quite compatible with a private market economy, at least under some historical circumstances. Strict rent controls, for instance, have appeared as a feature of the private housing market in virtually every Western European country since World War II, in some cases since World War I. England and West Germany both have more than 30 percent of their housing stock outside the private, profit-oriented sector, under government or nonprofit ownership. Significant construction has been done by the public sector in England [*see Chapter 30 by Steve Schifferes*]; controls over land use in France are virtually all-inclusive in key development areas. The share of the public budget allocated to housing is from two to five times higher in Western Europe than in the United States, and even residential investment as a percentage of GNP is considerably higher (6.4 percent in West Germany and 7 percent in France, as compared to 4.4 percent in the United States, between 1970 and 1978; UN Economic Commission for Europe, various years).

Yet in the U.S. context today, any major effort to reduce opportunities for private profit in housing development, ownership, and finance, and the tax reforms and income redistribution required to accomplish it, may well require far-reaching political and economic change. The pursuit of a progressive housing program is likely to challenge deep-seated ideological buttresses to the established system. In the context of the current capital accumulation crisis, the stakes (on both sides) are even higher. A program for housing decommodification can therefore become a critical element in the development of a broad-based movement for increased social control over investment and production in the society as a whole. For this reason, the program should not be viewed primarily as a legislative platform (although legislation may be based on it), but as a *political* program strategically linked to organizing efforts for progressive change [*see Chapter 23 by John Cowley and Chapter 24 by Kathy McAfee*].

Thus, progressive housing strategies should address immediate organizing (as well as housing) needs and should be relevant to ongoing organizing agendas. But they should also help to reveal the systemic nature of the housing crisis, and the possibility of an alternative approach. Finally, these strategies should help to unite diverse constituencies within the housing sector (such as lower-income tenants and homeowners) and should offer the potential for promoting coalitions between organized housing consumers and other progressive groups. Some examples are suggested below.

## Social Ownership

One possible application of the program would involve the broadening of local tenant organizing efforts into more affirmative struggles for social ownership [*see Chapter 22 by John Atlas and Peter Dreier and Chapter 24 by Kathy McAfee*]. Campaigns for increasingly strict control of rents, evictions, ownership conversion, speculation, and occupancy conditions in private rental housing could be coupled with the development of programs for public takeover of buildings in noncompliance with this regulatory scheme, as a first step toward social ownership. The burgeoning squatters' movement in cities that have already acquired a substantial inventory of abandoned, tax-title buildings [*see Chapter 25 by Seth Borgos*] could go beyond its current focus on individual "self-help" and homeownership to provide new models of nonspeculative public, community, and collective ownership (or ownership by individual residents with appropriate equity and resale controls). Block grant, Urban Development Action Grant (UDAG), rental assistance, or other funds could be targeted to these properties for rehabilitation and operating subsidies.

Relatedly, tenants in privately owned, federally subsidized housing that is in various stages of mortgage default, assignment, or foreclosure could demand a write-down (or long-term deferral) of the properties' outstanding mortgage debt and conversion of the housing to social ownership (Achtenberg, 1985). This is contrary to HUD's current policy of remortgaging and/or selling these properties to the highest bidder, often without subsidies. Rehabilitation could be financed debt free by tapping the FHA mortgage insurance funds (financed in turn by mortgagor contributions and off-budget Treasury appropriations), and available rental assistance subsidies could also be provided. In this way, a growing portion of the existing private rental stock could be converted to permanently debt-free social housing that is relatively affordable and in good condition.

At the same time, any effort to increase social ownership should involve major local and national campaigns to defend existing public housing, by organizing against rent increases, maintenance and service cutbacks, and plans for private resale or demolition (Roisman, 1983). These efforts should be coupled with affirmative programs for a rent policy based on true ability to pay, adequate and permanent operating subsidies, modernization funds, and increased resident control of management.

## Neighborhood Control

In the neighborhoods, antidisplacement activities involving both tenants and homeowners can be broadened to address the need for social control over private investment decisions. Thus, local groups can demand that developers of downtown office buildings, or institutions expanding into lower-income neighborhoods, provide a specified number of jobs and/or housing units for lower-income and minority residents, to compensate for the direct or indirect social cost of such ventures. This same "inclusionary development" concept (Davidoff, 1983) is applicable where the developer receives public benefits (such as zoning variances, property tax breaks, UDAG grants, or even building permits). A portion of the development profits, tax increments, UDAG loan paybacks, equity syndication proceeds, or other revenues generated by these ventures could also be allocated directly to public entities or community-based groups to finance neighborhood projects, housing, or services in the impact area.

Campaigns to restore public services and jobs for public employees can be linked with demands for higher or additional taxes on new hotels, offices, and shopping centers, or on the profits of condominium conversion or real estate speculation. Finally, neighborhood groups can demand compensation (reparations) from business to offset the adverse impact of plant closings or new development on their communities (e.g., in the form of emergency housing assistance funds or grants for the production of new, lower-income housing). These strategies offer the potential for alliances with progressive workplace organizations, or with groups opposing public service cutbacks.

## Resource Allocation

Finally, efforts to oppose federal budget cuts for housing can be tied to demands for a reallocation of government spending priorities, elimination of regressive housing tax expenditures, and large-scale progressive tax reform. And alternative programs for housing production, finance, and ownership can be devised to show how the increased funds might be used in a progressive way. For example, the elimination of 100 B-1 bombers from the military budget would generate $28 billion for the construction of over 500,000 new housing units through direct government spending for (debt-free) social ownership. The elimination of housing-related tax expenditures for high-income investors and homeowners with incomes over $50,000 could provide about $15 billion for rental assistance to tenants in socially owned housing, to reduce shelter costs to more affordable levels. An additional 10 percent tax on corporate after-tax profits could add another $12 billion for neighborhood improvements (more than three times existing outlays for the entire Community Development Block Grant program). These campaigns should, of course, be linked with the efforts of other progressive groups to restore social spending and oppose U.S. militarism, at home and abroad.

In these ways, one hopes, programs and strategies to challenge the commodity nature of housing and solve our housing problems can become part of the solution to the problems of our economy and society as a whole.

# Acknowledgments

We gratefully acknowledge the prior work of Chester Hartman and Michael E. Stone [*see their Chapter 29*], and of the Boston Urban Analysis Group (Louise Elving, Kathy Gannett, John Grady, Marie Kennedy, Kathy McAfee, and Michael E. Stone), in which co-author Emily Paradise Achtenberg participated, in conceptualizing many ideas developed in this program.

# 29

# A Socialist Housing Alternative for the United States

*Chester Hartman*
*Michael E. Stone*

*This chapter presents a concrete program for a socialized housing sector. The program derives from an analysis that sees as the central housing affordability problem dependence on mortgage financing and the ever-higher prices and credit needs that result from buying and selling housing for a profit [see Chapter 3 by Michael E. Stone]. Building on existing examples of noncommodified housing in the United States (public housing, military housing, nonprofit developments, limited equity cooperatives), the authors put forward a program to construct and rehabilitate a growing portion of housing units via direct capital grants from the government, the housing never to be sold and never to bear mortgage repayment charges; and to socialize the rental housing sector and some owner-occupied homes (the latter principally among homeowners facing foreclosure and others unable to afford current ownership costs). Housing costs to consumers—for ongoing maintenance, utilities, etc.—would be cut on average by about two-thirds, and housing allowances would be available for households too poor to afford even these reduced costs. The scheme shows that the government's costs for such a program are well within what the society can reasonably afford.*

The central elements underlying the nation's housing affordability crisis are the reliance on credit and the constant resale of housing by profit-maximizing private owners, as explained elsewhere in this volume [*see Chapter 1 by Emily Paradise Achtenberg and Peter Marcuse and Chapter 3 by Michael E. Stone*].

In any society, housing costs a lot to build. Large quantities of materials and many different kinds of labor skills are needed to put a house together. Each building must be located on a unique plot of land and must be connected to utilities. Various sizes and types of houses are needed to accommodate different family needs, climates, and terrains. Despite in-

This chapter is a reconceptualization, with current data, of an article the authors first wrote in 1977, which appeared in *The Federal Budget and Social Reconstruction*, ed. Marcus G. Raskin, Washington, D.C., Institute for Policy Studies, 1978, and was reprinted, in slightly revised form, in *Urban and Regional Planning in an Age of Austerity*, ed. Pierre Clavel, John Forester, and William W. Goldsmith, Elmsford, N.Y., Pergamon Press, 1980.

creasing mechanization, housing is far too complex ever to become a fully standardized, relatively cheap, assembly-line product like cars.[1] [*For a fuller discussion of this point, see Chapter 7 by Tom Schlesinger and Mark Erlich.*]

Under our economic system, housing is even more expensive because the materials and industry used to produce it are privately owned. So the cost of building a house or apartment building also includes the profits made by private developers, builders, and materials producers. In addition, the land underneath houses is privately owned, so housing production costs also include the profits made by landowners and speculators.

Because of the tremendous production cost, builders and developers generally borrow most of the money they need to put up new housing. About 75 percent of all the money used to finance new housing production in the United States is borrowed (Schulkin, 1970). And since the sources of money for housing are privately owned and/or controlled, the cost of borrowing money—interest on construction loans—is another part of the cost of producing housing.

In addition, since most housing is privately owned, once a new home is completed, it is generally sold to a private buyer. Even a new apartment building will eventually be sold by the developer to a new owner. But few buyers are willing or able to put up the large sum needed to purchase a house or apartment building. So they generally borrow most of the cash needed to buy the finished house—again, from a private lending source.

Finally, since houses and apartment buildings last for a long time, they are generally bought and sold over and over again. With each sales transaction, the new buyer must borrow the money from a private lender.

Thus the housing industry and the housing market in this country are very dependent on borrowed money—on credit.

The interest charged on credit (mortgage loans) and the supply of funds available to the housing sector are determined in the broader credit markets, involving the supply of, and the demand for, credit from all lenders and users. Over the last two decades, these credit markets have become less and less able to provide an adequate supply of housing funds at costs commensurate with consumers' ability to pay. [*See Chapter 4 by Ann Meyerson.*]

The money borrowed to build, purchase, and renovate housing (plus money drawn out of housing that has appreciated in value, through refinancing) is, for the most part, a permanent debt cost attached to the housing. That debt cost is renewed—usually for a larger amount and at higher interest costs—each time a house is sold to another owner; and since houses are almost always sold on terms that maximize the seller's profit, that debt impact is intensified. This cost is borne by renters as well as homeowners, although for the former it is paid indirectly as part of the rent, with the landlord in effect passing this portion of the rent payment on to the lender through periodic debt repayments. And so debt repayment consumes the overwhelming proportion of occupancy costs for most households. For owner-occupied single-family units with mortgages, mortgage payments constitute on average 65 percent of occupancy costs.[2]

Thus, if public policy were to aim at solving the housing affordability and supply crisis by substantially reducing housing costs to the consumer, it surely would make sense to concentrate on the principal cost elements, through changes in ownership structures and financing mechanisms. And examples exist of alternative systems for furnishing capital, for relating capital costs to ongoing housing costs, and for ownership and control of housing that provide useful models and directions for a radically different housing system.

One example is public housing. Economically, what distinguishes public housing is that the owner is a public body whose purpose is to provide the best possible housing at the lowest cost, not to maximize profits by operations and eventual sale. Public housing is not repeatedly resold and refinanced, with a succession of owners paying ever higher prices and doing so by borrowing larger sums, generally at higher interest rates. This nonspeculative ownership feature characterizes most housing owned by socially oriented nonprofit entities as well—community development corporations, churches, unions, and so forth. The initial development costs are paid off once; thereafter, the only expenses are for operations and periodic modernization. That is, public housing is not a commodity. [*See also related discussions of the commodity character of housing in Chapters 1 and 28 by Emily Paradise Achtenberg and Peter Marcuse and Chapter 33 by Jill Hamberg.*]

On the other hand, public housing still is dependent on the private credit market for construction funds. The money to build it in the first place is borrowed from private lending sources, as it is for private housing. This capital is raised by selling tax-exempt housing authority bonds to financial institutions and individual investors. The federal government[3] makes subsidy payments to the local housing authority (under what is known as an "annual contributions contract") to cover the cost of bond principal and interest payments. Thus the government pays for the development costs, but it does so with interest over a period of (usually) 40 years, a term that may be extended if the federal government later allocates capital funds for modernization. Once the bonds are paid off, though, there are no further debt costs.

Public housing has another fundamental economic feature that distinguishes it from the dominant commodity-type housing in the United States, a feature closely but not necessarily related to its financing system. What people pay is a function of their income—30 percent as of this writing—regardless of unit condition,[4] amenities, age, location, or size. These rents are allocated to operating costs for the unit, while capital costs are covered via the federal annual contributions contract.[5]

A second, perhaps more interesting, example for our purposes is the military housing program—a form of public housing almost never recognized as such. Where the local housing market is unable to meet the housing demand created by the presence, construction, or expansion of a military installation (which very often is the case, since so many military bases are built in rural areas), each service develops off-base or on-base housing for its personnel (built by private construction companies, as is true of low-rent public housing). Some 450,000 units of family housing have been constructed by the military, a public housing program about one-third the size of the far-better-known low-rent public housing program established by the 1937 Housing Act. Most of this housing is financed through the annual congressional appropriations process: capital grants are used to cover all construction and modernization costs, with no use of credit whatsoever. Since the occupants receive their housing free, as part of the benefits package the military offers its personnel, all operating costs come via the appropriations process as well.[6] Also, military housing is neither operated for purposes of profit nor bought and sold (save in those instances where closure of an installation or reduction in its size leads to disposition and sale).

Thus, there are some instructive models in the United States of alternative sources and mechanisms of housing finance, which are tied to a nonprofit ownership structure that drastically reduces the long-term cost of housing to its occupants and to the government. These can serve as the building blocks for a more generalized system to reduce reliance on credit and replace commodity relations, which in turn would lower housing costs to the consumer dramatically and permanently. Indeed, this is the only way the affordability crisis can be dealt with at its roots.

## Outlines of an Alternative System

We propose that the positive economic concepts of existing government housing programs in the United States be used as the basis for a new housing system designed steadily to transform a growing portion of the housing stock from a commodity into a social good. Under this system, people would have the right to use and occupy their housing pretty much as they wish for as long as they wish, but would not be able to buy or sell for a profit. We also propose that a growing proportion of new construction and housing rehabilitation be financed through direct public grants. Together, these proposals would lead automatically to greatly reduced dependence on credit for housing. By eliminating debt service as an element in ongoing housing costs, expenditures for most households would be cut, on average, by nearly two-thirds.

The basic elements of the program we are advancing are as follows:

1. A substantial and growing proportion of new and rehabilitated housing would be financed through direct construction grants to various local and regional public and private nonprofit developers. Publicly financed housing would then have no debt costs to be repaid by the residents or the government.

Private entrepreneurs and individuals could continue to develop conventionally mortgaged units for owner occupancy in the private market as long as there were people with the inclination and means to demand such housing, but such housing would not be eligible for any public assistance.

2. All publicly financed housing, new and existing, would be permanently held in some form of social ownership.[7] This form of tenure would over time replace traditional homeownership and tenancy forms and the private, free-market buying and selling of housing for profit.

3. Maximum shelter costs for residents of socially owned housing would be determined according to ability to pay, with subsidies provided for residents unable to afford full costs.

4. Existing homeowners facing foreclosure because of financial inability to keep up mortgage payments or with incomes too low to afford both non-shelter necessities and housing costs [*see Chapter 3 by Michael E. Stone for a discussion of "shelter poverty"*] could convert to social ownership and give up their right to resell, in return for which they would be relieved of mortgage payments, possibly compensated for their equity, and have the right to remain in the house.

5. The existing private rental housing stock would be converted to social ownership, with reasonable compensation, over time, for present owners.

In short, we are proposing that a large-scale commitment be made to a socialist alternative to the private housing market. We believe that this alternative not only would be of great benefit to lower-income people but also would offer economic and social benefits for middle-income people at least as great as present homeownership benefits.

# Direct Grants for Constructing and Rehabilitating Social Housing

Under our program, a growing proportion of new housing construction and rehabilitation of older housing would be financed through direct government grants, just as the federal government now pays, in whole or in part, for highways, dams, bridges, penitentiaries, pipelines, and military facilities (including military housing, as noted above). Housing development could be undertaken by local housing authorities, nonprofit housing development corporations, labor unions, community organizations, and other social entities; private developers could also build and rehabilitate such housing (under "turnkey" arrangements similar to those employed as part of the public housing program), as could individual families, who would receive grants to build their own homes, providing they conformed to cost and amenity standards applicable to the social housing sector generally. On completion of the housing, regardless of who developed it, title would be vested in the local or state housing agency or a nonprofit social housing entity. This housing would not be owned by the residents or be bought and sold on the private market. (Housing could still be built and rehabilitated for conventional forms of ownership, by merchant builders and individuals, on their own land. Financing and other arrangements would be purely private, involving no government subsidies.)

Grant funds would be allocated geographically according to housing and community development plans prepared by local communities, metropolitan areas, states, and regions, taking into account existing housing needs, the expected amount of private, conventionally financed development, and long-range growth and development plans. Regional, metropolitan, and local housing agencies would approve plans and costs, and would disburse funds as the work proceeded, much as state housing finance agencies now do. The major change would be that agencies would obtain funds as grants from the federal government rather than through the sale of notes and bonds in the capital markets. The money paid out for building and rehabilitating the housing would therefore not have to be repaid; there would be no construction financing costs; and no long-term mortgages or bonds would be needed to pay off construction loans.

How much would a system of direct grants cost, and is it economically feasible? Obviously, the answer to these questions depends on the production levels one posits, but under any reasonable set of production goals it is clear that the United States is wealthy enough to finance the construction and rehabilitation of a very large social housing sector through direct government spending rather than a debt system that mortgages the future.

We propose, for illustration purposes, a 10-year program of new construction and rehabilitation that starts with 100,000 new units of social housing built with direct grants and increases that total by 100,000 units each year, and that rehabilitates a constant 300,000 units each year. Thus, at the end of 10 years, the social housing sector would be producing at the rate of 1 million new units a year, and would have achieved a total of 5.5 million units over the 10-year period, an average of 550,000 new units a year; and a total of 3 million existing units would have been rehabilitated.

Using an average figure of $60,000 per unit for new construction and $20,000 per unit for rehabilitating substandard existing housing,[8] we derive a first-year cost of $12 billion. Each year the cost (in first-year dollars) will rise by $6 billion, reaching $66 billion by year 10. If population growth continues to slow, and if considerably more effort is put into maintaining existing housing than is done at present, the $66 billion figure would gradually decline, once the most serious shortages and substandard units were eliminated. The construction and materials industry could respond to this public sector construction activity without having to cut back on private construction, since a portion of the effective demand for new private housing would be absorbed by public sector activity. In 1972, the industry produced 2.4 million new units, its all-time high; and the 1968 Housing Act set a 10-year goal of 26 million units, an average of 2.6 million a year. With a predictable, steadily rising level of government construction and rehabilitation grants, the building industry would be able to plan and expand.

The first-year cost of this element of our program, by way of comparison with other magnitudes, is one-third of 1 percent of the 1984 Gross National Product and less than 5 percent of the nation's fiscal 1985 military budget; what percentages of these comparative magnitudes the direct-grant program would represent in subsequent years cannot be predicted. The capital grants are of course one-time capital expenditures; there is no continuing payout of construction and rehabilitation costs.

# An Alternative to Traditional Forms of Tenure

The attractions of the existing homeownership system cannot be ignored. Everyone wants security against the threat of eviction. Tenants in this society have a permanent and inescapable anxiety about being so dislocated, even if they have adequate incomes. Homeowners have security against arbitrary eviction. Ironically, however, the very mortgage system that has enabled them to "buy" their home prevents their security from being absolute, for there is the danger of foreclosure—with the loss of investment as well as shelter. There is also the danger of tax foreclosure for unpaid property taxes (as well as the possibility of condemnation). Under our proposal for the elimination of mortgage payments and traditional forms of private ownership, residents would be guaranteed a security of tenure far exceeding that enjoyed even by homeowners under the existing system.

We propose a new form of tenure that not only strengthens the freedom that homeowners have from control by others of their personal living space but applies it to everyone, most notably to renters, who now have few such protections and rights. All occupants of social housing would have the right of continued occupancy and control over their living space. As long as they wished to remain, they would not be required to move, except for those few situations where eminent domain takings are truly unavoidable and in the public interest, or for certain kinds of otherwise unresolvable conflicts with neighbors.

How to deal with some of the traditional grounds for eviction—nonpayment, destruction of property, "antisocial" behavior—is not a question that can be answered easily. (Given the subsidy system outlined below, nonpayment cases would always be willful, not the result of an inability to meet payments.) One approach to the problem might be as follows: Recognizing that people have to live someplace, no matter what their behavior, attempts to deal with antisocial behavior should be independent of eviction. Eviction merely relocates poor behavior and inflicts it on other neighbors and properties; it does not eliminate it. (An exception would be poor relationships between specific neighbors not based on any pattern of such difficulties.) With housing payments set according to ability to pay, if a household refuses to make its payments, then those managing the housing could take steps to recover these amounts through court action, possibly wage garnishment. If a tenant's behavior is injurious to property or truly offensive to neighbors, a step other than eviction—injunctive court action, damages, counseling, separating feuding neighbors, etc.—would be the attempted remedy. [*See Chapter 33 by Jill Hamberg for a discussion of how such problems are treated in another country and social system.*]

Another highly valued and positive aspect of the current homeownership system is the freedom of occupants to modify the property, make repairs and renovations, and use the house in ways that personalize it, give it meaning, and adapt it to their changing needs. Secure tenure for all doubtless would increase this kind of informal, voluntary property caretaking and improvement. At present, renters get little benefit from this kind of upkeep and space adaptation because they have no security of tenure and feel that their own improvements may, ironically, produce a demand for higher rents. They are also deterred by the injustice of investing time and money on property that someone else is holding and operating for current and future profit. Thus, the personal and social benefits from secure tenure would have a complementary value in terms of property maintenance.[9]

The new form of tenure proposed here also would eliminate some of the more conservative, negative impulses produced by the present ownership system. Concern about the protection of property values—existing equity and an assumed potential for future value increases—is responsible for much of the exclusionary behavior homeowners currently exhibit against racial minorities, people with low incomes, and "incompatible" building types and land uses. Absence of anxiety about protecting one's investment (anxiety that often is based on misperception or on agitation by realtors and others) may produce less resistance to neighborhood diversity and socially beneficial construction programs. Reduction of the locked-in feeling that homeownership now tends to produce—again, out of concern for protecting one's investment or reluctance to incur heavy turnover costs such as brokers' commissions, loan origination and mortgage assumption fees, title insurance, attorneys' fees, and other closing costs—may produce a greater freedom to move in order to take advantage of employment opportunities or otherwise improve one's life.

But the strongest attractions of the traditional homeownership system are economic—especially the possibility of accumulating some wealth through mortgage retirement and rising property values. Any viable alternative has to confront the strength of this appeal.

Under the existing housing system, homeownership appears to offer three economic advantages. First, for an identical house, a homeowner will have somewhat lower monthly costs than a renter because there is no payment for the landlord's cash-flow profit and overhead costs. For mortgaged homeowners, the two-thirds reduction in ongoing housing costs offered under our proposed alternative form of financing and tenure would, however, dwarf this economic advantage.

The second economic advantage of ownership is the income tax benefit of being able to deduct mortgage interest payments and property taxes[10] from taxable income, as well as the fact that our tax system exempts from taxation the imputed rental income from property one owns and occupies. On average, the elimination of mortgage payments would save residents far more than they gain from existing tax benefits. The supposed benefits are exaggerated anyway—at least for the majority of homeowners. Most taxpayers with incomes under $25,000 do not itemize their deductions, and those who do are in fairly low tax brackets where the deductions provide relatively little benefit (Dolbeare, 1985). [*See also Chapter 15 by Cushing Dolbeare.*]

The third and most significant economic advantage is the ability to build up equity through homeownership. The initial equity is established by a down payment and is then increased through mortgage principal payments and rising property values. This wealth is seen as a hedge against inflation, since residential property values have, on the average, risen faster than inflation. It may be used to acquire a bigger or more desirable house, to withdraw cash for other uses through home-equity refinancing, as a retirement nest egg when the house is sold, or to pass on to one's heirs.

As long as the choice is between renting in its present form and homeownership in its present form, there usually are real economic advantages to owning, although they are overstated. When homeowners sell their homes and realize a gain from rising property values, they generally have to plunge right back into the housing market and spend the money for another house, which also has gone up in price. If the money received from selling the old house is not spent on another house within two years, under current (1985) tax laws it is subject to a capital gains tax (except for people 55 or older, whose capital gains from home sales, under most conditions, are exempt from taxation on a one-time basis, up to $125,000). This tax provides a strong incentive (to the nonelderly) to buy another house of equal or greater value, rather than use the cash for other purposes. Also, the new house likely will be mortgaged, and generally at a considerably higher interest rate than the house just sold.

But under a system where a house could be obtained with no down payment and occupied with no mortgage payment (but not sold on the private market), the money saved would more than compensate for the inability to sell and make a profit from a home. And a more rational housing system would eliminate the unequal benefits the income tax system offers to homeowners as opposed to renters [*see Chapter 16 by Jim Kemeny*].

For example, suppose a family bought a $80,000 house in 1985 with a $20,000 down payment and a $60,000, 25-year mortgage at 12 percent interest. Monthly mortgage payments would be $632. Suppose the family decides to sell after 15 years. By this time, they would have paid out a total of nearly $134,000—the $20,000 down payment and almost $114,000 in mortgage payments—$134,000 that they would not have had to pay out under our proposal. They would still owe about $44,000 of their $60,000 mortgage. That is, of their $114,000 in mortgage payments, about $16,000 would have been applied to principal payments that build up their equity. The other $98,000 would have been paid for interest.

Let us suppose that property values continue to soar, so that by the time the family decides to sell, in the year 2000, the house bought for $80,000 in 1985 might be worth $160,000. They sell for $160,000, pay the $44,000 mortgage balance, plus brokerage costs (6 percent) and other closing costs, amounting to at least $11,000, and are left with about $105,000 in cash. With their total outlay of $134,000, they have not come close to breaking even.

By contrast, if this family had acquired the same house under our model—with no down payment and no mortgage payments—and had put the $20,000 in a long-term Treasury bond paying 8 percent annually, compounded, plus the same $632 each month into a money market account paying 7 percent annually, continuously compounded, by the end of 15 years they would find themselves with nearly $264,000. They would have recovered their $134,000 outlay and have $130,000 (pretax) in savings. (We have used conservative figures on investment return for the resident–saver, under the assumption that widespread adoption of the financing system we propose would considerably reduce the demand for mortgage money; hence money market funds, which invest heavily in mortgage portfolios and pass-through certificates, would experience reduced yields for their depositors.)

We have made a series of calculations assuming that property values will increase at an even faster rate—7 percent annually, compounded, thus nearly doubling in 10 years. We have also calculated the results with considerably lower mortgage interest rates—down to 10 percent—on the assumption that substantially lessened demand for mortgage credit would drive mortgage rates down and cool off the economy generally. And we have applied a 35 percent income tax rate to the resident–saver's investment yield, reducing it to an after-tax figure. The comparative financial benefits of traditional homeownership versus the system we propose are offered in Table 29.1. The degree to which the resident–saver comes out ahead, at each of the mortgage-interest-rate assumptions and for various holding periods, is striking.[11]

We propose introducing this option, giving priority to those with the greatest housing need and least ability to afford what they need. The existing homeownership market would still be available for those who can afford its costs and those who, for whatever reason—whether it be hopes of economic gain or personal ideological commitment to traditional forms of homeownership—prefer the existing system. (A windfall profits tax might nonetheless be introduced to tax away some of these speculative gains.) Those eligible for, and choosing to enter, the alternative social housing system could cut their housing costs by two-thirds and eliminate the need to invest their personal savings in a down payment. The system we are proposing makes available an option that would, on the average, yield far greater financial benefits than homeownership and with less risk and greater liquidity for household savings. We think our alternative would be increasingly attractive, but people would not be forced to take it.

## Universal Operating Subsidies

A key element of our proposal is federal subsidies to all residents of social housing who are unable to afford the operating expenses—maintenance and repairs, utilities, property taxes,[12] insurance, and management—for their dwellings. These subsidies would not cover mortgage payments, since such payments would be an ongoing part of occupancy costs only for private, owner-occupied units, and since, as described below, most owners unable to

TABLE 29.1
COMPARISON OF ECONOMIC BENEFITS: MORTGAGED HOMEOWNER
VERSUS RESIDENT–SAVER[a]

|  |  | After 5 Years | After 10 Years | After 15 Years |
|---|---|---|---|---|
| Sales price of $80,000 home, at 7% annual value increase,[b] compounded, net 7% brokerage/ closing costs |  | $104,300 | $146,400 | $205,300 |
|  |  |  | NET GAIN[c] |  |
| *Mortgage interest rate (monthly payment)* | *Tenure form* |  |  |  |
| 10% | Homeowner | −4,900 | 10,200 | 45,900 |
| ($545.23) | Resident–saver | 10,000 | 32,400 | 72,000 |
| 11% | Homeowner | −7,900 | 4,000 | 36,700 |
| ($588.07) | Resident–saver | 10,400 | 33,900 | 75,900 |
| 12% | Homeowner | −11,000 | −2,100 | 27,500 |
| ($631.94) | Resident–saver | 10,500 | 35,400 | 79,900 |
| 13% | Homeowner | −14,000 | −8,300 | 18,100 |
| ($676.71) | Resident–saver | 10,900 | 37,000 | 83,900 |

[a]Homeowner: $80,000 home, acquired with $20,000 down payment and $60,000 mortgage with 25-year term. Resident–saver: Initial deposit of $20,000 at 8%, compounded annually, plus monthly deposit equal to homeowner's mortgage payment into money market account paying 7%, compounded continuously.

[b]In recent years, residential property values have, on average, increased at a rate about 2 or 3% above the rate of inflation. Assuming that consumer income will be unable to support continuation of such house-price inflation, or that the overall inflation rate will average no more than about 4 to 5% over the next 5 to 15 years, a 7% per year value increase is a reasonable assumption. If higher rates of inflation return and values increase at a higher rate as well, the resident–saver's returns from the money market fund deposits would likely remain competitive.

[c]Homeowner: Net sales price, minus down payment, total monthly mortgage payments and remaining principal. Resident–saver: Down payment amount invested at 8%, compounded annually; monthly deposit of mortgage payment equivalent into money market account paying 7%, continuously compounded; after-tax investment return computed assuming 35% tax rate, (yielding 5.2% net, compounded annual return on down payment amount, and 65% of total return on monthly deposits when taxed at termination of given time period).

afford mortgage payments could convert to social ownership for relief from these payments. Operating subsidies would not pay for the cost of capital improvements and renovations either. For socially owned housing, such costs would be covered by the direct grant program.

The amount of operating subsidy (housing allowance) a household would be entitled to receive would be equal to the difference between the operating expenses for its unit and the amount it could afford. A standard for determining reasonable operating expenses would have to be developed, based on the size of the unit, the building's age and kind of construction, the type of heating system, and the region of the country. A great deal of information of this sort is already collected regularly for private multifamily housing by the Institute of Real Estate Management, the industry trade association, and for subsidized multifamily housing by state and federal regulatory agencies. The HUD–Census Bureau's *Annual* (recently turned biennial and renamed *American*) *Housing Survey* also now collects such data for single-family, owner-occupied housing. The affordability standard should not be what now is embodied in federal low-income housing subsidy programs (30 percent of income), but instead should reflect the amount of resources a household would have available after meeting its nonshelter needs at some minimum adequate level, as suggested by Michael E. Stone in Chapter 3.

Based on national figures for 1983, the most recent year for which operating cost and household income data are available,[13] we have estimated that a universal operating subsidy, if used by all eligible persons, would have cost about $42 billion in 1983—$23 billion for homeowners and $19 billion for tenants. About 24 million households would have been eligible for such subsidies in 1983: 13 million homeowner households and 11 million renter households. The cost in 1985 would be about 10 percent higher, based on a 2 percent increase in the number of eligible households and an 8 percent increase in operating costs due to inflation. That is, in 1985 dollars, the cost of such a program would be close to $46 billion. But, as noted in the following section, it is not likely that all low-income homeowners would want to convert their homes to social ownership and receive housing allowances, and so this figure considerably overstates the amount that would be required.

## The Existing Homeownership Sector

As noted in the Editors' Introduction to this volume, in the third quarter of 1984 more than 6 percent of all mortgages were at least 30 days overdue in payment, and in high unemployment areas close to 1 out of every 10 mortgages was in arrears to this degree. Homeowners facing foreclosure, as well as other owners unable to afford current housing costs, would have the option of converting their homes to social ownership and getting relief from further mortgage payments. The residents could remain, with full security of tenure, but they would no longer have the right to sell their homes. The government would assume the mortgage debt and make monthly payments to the lending institution until the debt was paid off. Some upper boundaries, by income-asset and/or housing-consumption level, would have to be built into the program, of course, to prevent persons with considerable assets and luxurious living styles from unfairly securing government bailout funds and to prevent such funds from subsidizing excessive levels of housing consumption. There might be need for protection from other possible abuses as well, such as withdrawal of equity just prior to assigning one's house to the social sector; it might be necessary to add recapture provisions or to prohibit people from coming into the program if they had refinanced within a given prior period. Persons needing or wishing to turn their homes over to social ownership in exchange for relief from mortgage payments would be eligible for the universal operating subsidy outlined above, if their incomes fell below the point where they could afford ongoing operating costs. And funds would be available through the capital grants program for removal of code violations and for modest levels of modernization; it is, of course, in the society's interest to maintain and upgrade the stock of social housing.

For homeowners, this bailout scheme is obviously far superior to the existing foreclosure situation where the owner is forced to move and generally loses most or all equity in the property. A more generous program would not only permit residents to stay in their homes while relieving them of mortgage payments, but might also, with certain restrictions, permit them compensation for their investment—their original down payment plus accumulated principal payments, inflated to current value through use of the Consumer Price Index, plus the depreciated value of improvements. This equity amount might be set up as an account from which funds would be drawn to cover the amounts needed to subsidize the family (the difference between what the household pays under the operant affordability standard and actual operating and mortgage repayment costs). In effect, this would be a conversion of that equity into cash that must be devoted to housing expenditures, an equity conversion *cum* tenure security in practice unavailable to people now facing or on the verge of foreclosure proceedings. Should there be money left in the "account" at the time of death or movement to another residence outside the social sector, the remainder would be given in a lump sum to the household or the decedent's estate. And should the family exhaust its account while still in that residence or other social sector housing, it would, of course, be permitted to remain in place, paying an amount set according to the affordability standard, with the universal operating subsidy picking up the payments previously provided by the equity account. The program might also build in an option allowing people to take back title to their residence within, say, one or two years, should there be a change of heart or economic circumstances.

Assuming such a program were available to, and used by, all low-income homeowners, how much would it cost? In 1984, total mortgage payments by owner occupants of single-family homes on 10 acres or less amounted to about $120 billion, while mortgage payments for other owner occupants (those in multi-unit buildings, attached single-family homes, single-family homes on 10 acres or more, and mobile homes) were at most $15 billion.[14] Only about 16 percent of mortgaged single-family homes belong to households with incomes of less than $15,000 (most low-income homeowners are long-term owners with no outstanding mortgages); no data are available on mortgage status of owner-occupants in multi-unit buildings and mobile homes, but about 40 percent of such owner-occupants have incomes below $15,000 (U.S. Bureau of the Census, 1984f). Since low-income owners tend to live in homes which are smaller and older than the average, and with less than average debt (both because they own less costly houses and because of their longer-term ownership), mortgaged low-income owner-occupants probably accounted for no more than 10 percent of the $120 billion in total annual mortgage payments on single-family homes, and no more than 25 percent of the $15 billion mortgage payments on other owner-occupied units. If the government had to assume this entire mortgage burden for low-income homeowners, the cost would be less than $16 billion in the first year and would decline year by year as the remaining mortgages were paid off. Some low-income homeowners would probably decide not to take advantage of this program, even if they faced financial hardship, because of very strong attachment to traditional concepts of ownership or desire to pass unrestricted ownership on to their heirs; the $16 billion is thus an upper bound for the first-year public costs of assuming mortgages for low-income homeowners, and the actual figure would probably be considerably less.

As part of a program to eliminate substandard housing conditions and increase the supply of social housing, repair and modernization grants might also be made available to homeowners who do not choose to assign their homes to the social sector. As a quid pro quo for receiving these grants, such homeowners would be required to accept two conditions: (1) a lien on the property to return the grant amount, with interest, upon sale of the property; (2) a requirement that, upon eventual sale, the property be offered first to a social housing entity for purchase at the market price.

## Eliminating Private Rental Housing

Private profit-motivated ownership of rental housing is incompatible with the goal of decent, affordable housing for everyone in the United States. The dynamics of the profit system, coupled with the related workings of the tax system, lead inexorably to rent increases that produce formal and informal displacement and excessive rent-to-income ratios; to conversion of rental units to condominiums, with attendant displacement of existing residents; to undermaintenance, abandonment, and arson when they are the most profitable route for owners to take; to insecurity of tenure for the 60 million Americans who live in property others own; to generally strained relations between those who own or control and those who use residential property; and to investment in rental housing largely for its capital gains benefits and for its value as a tax shelter for income generated elsewhere, and thus to ownership transfers and maintenance/modernization practices that are inconsonant with responsible stewardship of the nation's housing resources. The system works reasonably well for those with sufficient income to absorb periodic rent increases and demand adequate maintenance and services, and with the ability to exercise options in the housing market. For renters without adequate income, power, and choice—the majority of all tenants—the system is an anachronism and clearly in need of radical overhaul. Housing should be provided according to the principles of maximizing affordability, security of tenure, and user satisfaction. And this, we believe, means converting the rental housing stock to social ownership and allocating no further government aids or subsidies to private profit-motivated rental housing.

What we propose is a compulsory buyout of the nation's entire rental housing stock. Existing mortgages would be assigned to the social sector and amortized with government funds. Landlords would be compensated for the amount of their cash equity—represented by down payments, inflated to current value through use of the Consumer Price Index—plus cash expended on improvements (appropriately depreciated). Such payments would be spread over time in the form of bonds (which would, of course, be marketable, should ex-landlords wish to convert them to immediate, albeit discounted, cash payment). Management of the rental housing stock, as discussed below, would be either by existing managers on contract to social housing entities or by resident-controlled or public managers.

A key issue obviously is fair compensation to landlords. "Market value," the traditional eminent domain compensation standard, would become meaningless, as the program would in effect destroy the market value of rental housing by eliminating the sector from the market economy altogether. As for whether mortgage principal repayments should be treated as part of the landlord's equity, these have in effect been made by the tenants all along via their rents. Fair compensation to the landlord would consist of the current value of his actual cash investment (similar to having put it in some long-term savings certificate), with additional return having been taken out over the course of his ownership of the property via cash outflow (excess of rental income over expenses) and tax benefits, plus, in many cases, cash withdrawal through refinancing. It is neither socially just nor necessary to allocate public resources to pay landlords for the speculative value appreciation of their properties, particularly when for the most part the landlord's money was not used to pay for holding the property during the period of appreciation. (To do so would, in any case, be financially unfeasible. In 1984, the total value of all private rental real estate, including rental units in owner-occupied buildings with two or more units, was about $1,050 billion, of which the total market value of the owners' equity comprised about $600 billion.[15] This sum is about 63 percent of the fiscal 1985 federal budget and one-sixth of the GNP in 1984. Moreover, such compensation, even if financially feasible, would aid the rich enormously, for about 85 percent of investment real estate is owned by the wealthiest 20 percent of the population [Upton and Lyons, n.d.].)

Expropriating the speculative increase in value of landlords' property and assigning the property to a public purpose bears some similarity to the workings of the urban renewal program introduced in the 1949 Housing Act, whereby local redevelopment authorities took private property by eminent domain, compensated owners in a way that disregarded the property's potential value, and then conveyed the property to another owner for what was (liberally) construed as a public purpose. This fundamental mechanism of the urban renewal program was consistently upheld by the Supreme Court and lower courts. Since creating decent, affordable housing conditions for the one-third of the nation that rents is a far more clear-cut public purpose than taking low-income housing and using the sites for convention centers, office buildings, luxury apartments, and sports complexes, there is good reason to believe these takings and the compensation system proposed could withstand legal challenge. The Constitutional requirement is only "nor shall private property be taken without just compensation" (Article V)—the definition of "just compensation" is certainly not immune to judicial and political reformulation.

The program would have to be carefully crafted to avoid and counter what likely would be a plethora of ingenious devices by rental property owners and mortgage lenders, designed to increase their compensation. The most obvious ploy would be to inflate artificially the amount of "equity" that must be repaid, through sham sales and cash transfers: in essence, trading properties among themselves via paper "sales" that show vast amounts of cash down payments. Stringent proof requirements and penalties to deter such ruses would be needed. Landlords also might try to extract as much cash as possible from their buildings via refinancing; to deter lenders from making such loans, a cut-off date after which the lender would be given only partial repayment of such cash equity refinancing might be one form of protection required. And arson ("selling out to the insurance company") is yet another escape route that must be closed, perhaps through reform of fire insurance regulations, to require that the local government be designated as "additional loss payee" for fire insurance settlements in the event of suspicious or incendiary fires. This would guarantee that the insurance money be used to reconstruct the building rather than to pay off the owner and/or lender who might otherwise try to walk away with the cash. The games landlords and lenders play are imaginative, and the program must be prepared to know and win them. To avoid government bailout of overmortgaged properties, the program also would restrict mortgage amounts repaid to no more than the building's appraised value; where lenders' poor judgment has led to excessive loans, those losses would have to be borne by the lending institution, as is now the case when owners default on such properties.[16]

As with current homeowners converting to social sector housing, residents of the current rental housing stock who cannot afford the operating costs of their unit (which will not include either the mortgage payments or equity buyout) will receive operating subsidies (housing allowances). Space and amenity standard ceilings would ensure that government funds are not used to subsidize luxury levels of housing; costs of housing services in excess of these limits would have to be borne fully by the occupants. All residents will have full security of tenure, as described earlier in the chapter. Buildings and units in need of rehabilitation would receive capital grants for this purpose, as described above.

When all rental housing is converted to social ownership, all rental income will be received by the social owners. Of the nearly 30 million renter households, approximately half can afford their present rents, which are sufficient to cover operating expenses and repayment of outstanding mortgages. Based on ability-to-pay standards [*see Chapter 3 by Michael E. Stone*], a large proportion of current tenants would pay rents in excess of the amount needed for full operating costs, mortgage repayments, and return on equity; these "profits," which now go to private landlords, would accrue to the social housing sector. This cash-flow profit to the social sector, conservatively calculated at $4 billion a year (5 percent of $80 billion, the portion of the $120 billion total annual income stream from rent payments that is derived from tenants of this half of the rental stock[17]), can offset some of the public costs associated with the buyout of the rental stock.

Of the other 15 million renter households, who cannot presently afford the full rent on their units, about 4 million can afford the cost of operating expenses for their units but not the full cost of mortgage payments in addition;[18] the public would therefore need to cover the mortgage payment deficit on such units—a sum which, assuming roughly even distribution of these households along the income scale, would amount, on average, to about one-half the mortgage payment for each unit. For the remaining 11 million renter households—those eligible for the universal operating subsidy (see section above)—the public would have to pick up the entire mortgage repayment cost of their units as part of the buyout. (Operating subsidies for these units, an ongoing income transfer to people of low income, are computed as part of the relevant section above, rather than as part of the cost of converting the private rental stock to social ownership.)

The outstanding mortgage debt of the entire rental housing stock was about $450 billion in 1984, and the market value of the equity in such housing was about $600 billion (see note 15 for calculations). No national data exist on the amount landlords must pay to service this $450 billion debt, nor on the terms (interest rate and amortization period) of this debt, and so a precise calculation of the repayment amounts needed is not possible. By creating a typical rental building that would plausibly reproduce the above ratio of mortgage debt to total market value,[19] we estimate the total annual mortgage payments on the entire rental stock at $60 billion, or an average of about $2,000 per unit per year. Since the 11 million units occupied by low-income renters include public housing units with no mortgages, and since the privately owned units have considerably lower-than-average market value, we assume the average annual mortgage payments for each of these units to be just $1,000, yielding a total annual public cost of $11 billion. For the 4 million units requiring partial public mortgage payment, we assume the public will pay one-half of this $2,000 per unit average cost; the total annual public cost for the mortgages on these units thus would be $4 billion. The total public cost for mortgage retirement on the rental housing stock would therefore be about $15 billion, offset by some $4 billion in excess rental income, for a total of about $11 billion in the first year, an amount that would steadily decline as mortgages are paid off.

To compensate private landlords for their equity, a formula based upon original down payment increased by the Consumer Price Index would lead to landlords being paid about 20 percent of the market value of their equity—employing the same average purchase model used for the mortgage repayment calculation (see note 19), and a CPI increase of 5 percent per year, compounded. With the market value of the equity equal to about $600 billion, this would mean public compensation of about $120 billion. By providing this compensation in the form of fully amortized, 40-year government bonds, paying 8 percent interest, the public cost would be about $10 billion a year; at 9 percent interest, the public cost would be about $11 billion per year. Adding in the landlords' cash investment in improvements (appropriately depreciated) would increase this figure by a small amount.

# Management and Maintenance of the Social Housing Stock

Ongoing operation of the socially owned housing stock would be under the overall supervision of local, metropolitan, or regional housing authorities. Multifamily housing might be managed by neighborhood organizations, user associations, other nonprofits, or the authority itself. Private developers building and rehabilitating housing with government grants under "turnkey" arrangements described in an earlier section might remain as managers of the development on a contract basis. Judicious, creative use should be made of the talents and experience of private building managers, many of whom are extremely competent in a field where experience and know-how matter a great deal. Owner-occupants of multifamily buildings should be retained to carry out the management function whenever they are willing to do so and have demonstrated past ability. With respect to single-family homes, the same management arrangements are possible. Or the occupants might choose to be responsible for making repairs themselves (except for major items), in the tradition of homeowners and do-it-yourselfers, in exchange for a reduction in housing payments. Maintenance and routine repairs would be covered via allocation of a portion of housing payments. Disincentives to use such services unnecessarily could be built into the plan by imposing a small charge for each repair visit. Extraordinary repairs and improvements requiring capital expenditures would be made through capital grants from the housing authority.

Movement from one residence to another within the social sector would be handled in a number of ways. Vacancies would be listed with the various social housing entities (in centralized fashion), and occupants of social housing wishing or needing to move, either within a given housing area or from one part of the country to another, would have priority for vacancies. Movement from one home to another would be far easier and quicker without the need to sell one's home. As the social housing sector grows, so will the amount of choice with respect to location, housing type, amenities, and the like. Direct trades between occupants of social housing would be permitted, employing the standard forms of notices, listings, and advertisements now used. Among occupants of social housing mobility might be considerably lessened, given the elimination of economic hardship as a reason for having to move. Physically modifying the house to meet a household's changing needs, as an option to moving, also would be far easier with the grant program proposed. Since absence of mortgage payments and down payments frees up funds that can be put into savings, if a household deems it necessary or desirable upon moving to return to the private sector, this should not necessarily be beyond their means.

## Program Cost Summary

To summarize the cost of the various elements of our program:

- The direct construction and rehabilitation grants will have a first-year cost of $12 billion, rising by $6 billion a year, and leveling off once the existing substandard stock has been rehabilitated and other catch-up needs are met; new construction would then be required only to meet net new household formation and to replace obsolete units.
- The universal operating subsidies are estimated at $35 billion in the first year, under the assumption that half of the eligible lower-income homeowners will choose not to turn their homes over to the social sector. The maximum first-year subsidy required, if all eligible lower-income homeowners chose to come under the program, would be $46 billion. How much this figure would vary over time is largely a function of changes in household incomes.
- Taking over the mortgages of lower-income homeowners facing fore-closure or otherwise unable to afford their housing payments will come at most to $16 billion a year (probably less, due to the voluntary nonparticipation noted above), an amount that will steadily decrease as mortgages are retired. Lump-sum payments of remaining accrued equity upon death or transfer out of the social housing sector will be an additional cost, but the amounts required would probably be

considerably less than the offsetting figure from the $16 billion to account for nonparticipants.

- Buying out the rental housing sector will cost about $15 billion a year for mortgage retirement (an amount that will fall each year) and $11 billion a year to compensate landlords for their equity. This total will be offset by rental revenues from upper-income residents in excess of what is needed for operating, mortgage repayment, and equity buy-out costs, an overage conservatively estimated at $4 billion. This reduces the total needed to $22 billion.

The combined cost of these elements comes to roughly $85 billion in the first year. Total costs in subsequent years should not rise by much. These first-year costs would amount to 2.5 percent of the 1984 GNP, and one-third of the current military budget. They are only about twice the amount of the tax expenditures we now bestow on a highly inefficient, ineffective, and inequitable housing system. The long-term benefits, as we have stressed, are a permanent and drastic lowering of housing costs for most Americans, a decrease far greater than any increase in personal taxes that might be required to cover these considerably increased government housing outlays. A shift in priorities away from destructive military spending to needed social spending would of course make it possible to fund this program without an overall tax increase, as would a shift to a more equitable tax system, one that demands more from corporations, wealth holders, and those in the higher-income brackets so that all Americans can achieve a decent basic standard of living. There is no question but that the program we advocate is economically feasible; the issue is one of politics.

## Where to Begin

We can point to several opportunities for introducing and testing our system. One clear example is mortgage foreclosure among homeowners. A substantial portion of the nearly 2 million homeowners currently more than 30 days delinquent in their mortgage payments likely would find the alternative we propose attractive; just as farmer groups are effectively organizing to oppose farm foreclosures and distress sales, so might lower-income homeowners organize to demand that government take over their mortgage obligations and provide operating subsidies for those who need them so that they can remain living where they are and not join the growing ranks of the homeless.

Another opportunity for introducing our system is with single-family homes and multifamily projects built under various HUD programs, where the owner has defaulted on the mortgage and HUD has taken over, or can take over, title as mortgage insurer. A quarter-million units of housing in these programs have come into HUD's hands to date.[20] Instead of selling off these developments and homes to private owners, HUD ought to be forced to retain them in public or private nonprofit ownership, to write off the remaining mortgage against its insurance funds or through the use of special government subsidies, to establish a rent structure based on operating costs alone, and to make available operating subsidies for low-income residents who are unable to afford full operating costs.

At the local level, most cities and counties come into possession of a great many properties each year as a result of property tax foreclosure proceedings, and many more such properties that are way behind on their taxes could be taken over by local governments under more aggressive and accelerated proceedings. Another potential source of properties for local government takeover are so-called gift-house programs, whereby owners delinquent on their property taxes can donate the property to the city in return for both forgiveness on the property tax bill and a substantial federal and state income tax writeoff. [*See Chapter 25 by Seth Borgos for a description of such a program in Philadelphia.*] Local governments generally are reluctant to take over tax-delinquent properties because they do not want to assume responsibility for their occupants or to be in the low-rent housing business (beyond the federally subsidized public housing program). But organized neighborhood pressure can force a city to act in a way that protects the housing stock and assists the residents. [*See Chapter 26 by Robert Kolodny for a description of such pressures and responses in New York City.*]

Making use of these approaches, local governments could either retain ownership or transfer ownership to another social housing entity; work out some modified payment arrangment with the mortgage holder, if there is one; and establish a rent system based on operating costs alone, with operating subsidies available for those with incomes too low to afford housing costs even without mortgage payments included. Local political organizing—among residents of such buildings (which often are fully or partially occupied at the time of landlord abandonment), those on public housing waiting lists, and others in need of decent affordable housing— would be a key to implementing this approach.

Rental buildings with serious code violations might be another source of acquisition for the social housing stock. Under receivership provisions of housing and health codes, such buildings could be removed from private landlord control. A social owner (perhaps an organization created by the tenants) would be appointed as receiver, with legal authority to collect rents and make repairs; mortgage-holders' claims would be subservient to these obligations to create decent living conditions. Landlords would be given a deadline (say, one year) for negotiating a sale to the tenants as a limited equity cooperative or to another social owner. If negotiations were unsuccessful, condemnation proceedings would be used to obtain title from the landlord.

Various forms of "reverse annuity mortgages," designed for elderly homeowners occupying the valuable, illiquid asset that is their home, offer another opportunity. In exchange for a lifetime annuity generous enough to permit a decent standard of living, elderly homeowners might will their homes, which usually are mortgage-free, to a social housing entity. An experimental program of this kind already is operating in Buffalo (Edmonds, 1984).

Public funds now used to subsidize housing rehabilitation and construction ought to carry with them a corresponding set of conditions requiring eventual conversion to social housing status. Community Development Block Grant funds, housing capital raised through tax-exempt bonds floated by state and local government agencies, and new "housing trust funds" of the type recently created in Maine, New York, and California (using that state's surplus tideland oil revenues) should be made available only in conjunction with programs that foster the goals of nonspeculative ownership and the permanent elimination of mortgage debt. Relatedly, new "linkage programs," whereby local governments in San Francisco, Boston, and other cities require office developers to provide housing (or contributions to a housing trust fund) to compensate for the added housing demand these commercial structures generate, should have similar features. And like conditions could be made part of agreements community groups reach with lending institutions as a result of Community Reinvestment Act negotiations and "deals."

Finally, strong efforts should be made among various private nonprofit housing enterprises to revise their programs so as to institute the nonspeculative social ownership form outlined here, as a permanent element of the housing they produce. Such groups as James Rouse's Enterprise Foundation (and its affiliates in nearly two dozen cities), the Nehemiah Project in Brooklyn, the BRIDGE Housing Corporation in San Francisco, lending consortia of insurance companies and banks (the Chicago Housing Partnership, Boston Housing Partnership, New York City's Housing Partnership Mortgage Corporation and Community Preservation Corporation, etc.), Boston's Inquilinos Boricuas en Acción, and MUSCLE in Washington, D.C., all can be educated and lobbied to facilitate this shift in the structure of housing in the United States.

The above are only some examples of beginning moves toward the program we are proposing. In general, wherever there is a public "handle" in the form of aid or controls, or a socially oriented motivation on the part of the private sector, these can be used to move toward the decommodified, credit-free housing system we describe.

## The Political Dimension

In this chapter we have tried to show that it is economically feasible to develop a socialist housing program that would compete with, and steadily replace, the private housing and mortgage markets. It is important to recognize, though, that the political barriers to realizing this program would be more than just the obvious resistance from landlords, developers, real-tors, speculators, and lenders, whose interests would be immediately threatened.

Achievement of this program would further undermine the existing economic system. Substantial tax reform and massive housing subsidies that did not flow back to wealthy institutions and individuals would probably lead to lower profits, flight of capital, and reduced investment generally. Public spending for housing would not fully compensate for this tendency. The broader issues of public enterprise, economic planning, and control of the economy inevitably would have to be confronted.

Questions of land-use planning and control of land costs will inevitably come to the fore, leading to the need to develop an overall land-reform program that would go far beyond housing and would confront both the existing land-tenure system and the fragmented and parochial pattern of land-use controls.

A program that would provide people with secure tenure, no mortgage debt, and decent housing, at a cost based on their real ability to pay, would substantially reduce the anxiety caused by low wages and job insecurity in the labor market. That is, workers' bargaining power would be increased, and greater militancy might follow. The success of the housing program would thus tend to undermine the social control wielded through the labor market.

The achievement of such a program would require a broad-based and powerful political movement strong enough to force the state into the primary role of meeting the basic needs of all its people, rather than assisting in capital accumulation on behalf of the entrepreneurial sector and legitimating the present system through conflict management and maintenance of the existing social order [*see Chapter 14 by Peter Marcuse*]. A political movement of this type undoubtedly would not want to limit itself to housing when there are other fundamental and pressing issues, such as jobs, food, and health. Furthermore, even though the housing program would not necessarily require basic changes in these other areas, it would require substantial tax reform to generate the needed revenues in a progressive way; to the extent it was achieved, there would be many claims on the additional revenues.

Finally, there are dangers associated with the possibility of actually implementing aspects of the program. Some elements of the program we have suggested might be picked up and adapted to help rationalize the present system, ease some social pressures, prop up the construction industry, bail out mortgage lenders, and stave off financial collapse. But any demands for reform that do not occur as part of a total transformation of the society always have this contradictory quality. This does not mean that the demands should not be made; it does mean that such reforms should not be seen as an end in themselves but as part of a clear and conscious political strategy. That is, the kind of program we are suggesting should not merely be injected into high-level policy debates among a small number of people; it should be part of a political program, part of the process of broad-based organizing. Then, struggles to enact and control it will be successful even if the program is distorted or only partially achieved—in the sense that it will help build political organization and consciousness, without illusions about the possibilities of reform and how more fundamental change is brought about.

## Acknowledgments

The authors are grateful to Michael Tanzer for his helpful commentary and to Barbara Philips for her editorial suggestions on our earlier (1978) version of this chapter; and to Rachel G. Bratt, Peter Marcuse, and Ann Meyerson for their comments on the draft of this updated version. Dialogue with the authors' colleagues in the Institute for Policy Studies' Working Group on Housing over the past two years has been enormously helpful in clarifying ideas and programmatic details. Leslie Corn performed heroic typing feats at various points in our work.

## Notes

1. The material in this and the five subsequent paragraphs is drawn from Stone and Achtenberg, 1977.

2. Of the 54.7 million owner-occupied housing units in 1983, expenditure information was compiled only for the 43.5 million units in single-family structures on less than 10 acres and with no business on the property. Of these, 27.8 million—about two-thirds—had mortgages outstanding. Median monthly mortgage payment was $299; and median total cost for mortgage payment, real estate taxes, insurance, and utilities was $463 (i.e., median nonmortgage costs were $164). These figures yield the mortgage-payment-to-total-cost ratio of 65 percent given in the text, a figure that, according to *Annual Housing Survey* data, has been remarkably stable since 1974. It is worth noting, for comparison, that for owner-occupied units without mortgages, the median monthly cost was $166, which is virtually the same as the $164 median nonmortgage expense for mortgaged homeowners (U.S. Bureau of the Census, 1984f).

The ratio of median mortgage payment to median total cost does vary somewhat by income class, from a low of 54 percent to a high of 70 percent. For income classes below $15,000, the ratio is in the 54 to 59 percent range, whereas for income classes of $15,000 and more, the ratio ranges from 61 to 70 percent. This modest but significant difference between lower- and higher-income mortgaged homeowners is clearly due to the fact that most lower-income homeowners took out their mortgages prior to the past decade of rapidly rising prices and interest rates. Indeed, in 1981 homeowners below $15,000 in income constituted only 18 percent of all homeowners with mortgages but 52 percent of all homeowners with no mortgages.

Similar national data do not exist for renter-occupied units, but with landlords' often greater reliance on multiple layers of debt financing, the percentage of rent dollars allocated to mortgage repayments probably is of the same magnitude.

3. Several states and one city (New York) have smaller public housing programs that supplement and parallel the federal–local program, with the state or city government playing essentially the same subsidization role the federal government plays.

4. However, for units in such poor condition as to present a threat to the occupants' life, health, or safety, federal regulations, enacted following litigation brought by Legal

Services attorneys on behalf of tenant clients, allow for rent withholding until the defects are removed (National Housing Law Project, 1981).

Larger families, who occupy larger units, and the elderly actually pay slightly less than 30 percent, since there are deductions from the income base for minor dependents and elderly adults.

5. When, as has been true for years in most projects, tenants' rent-paying abilities are inadequate to insure rents that cover full operating costs, the federal government gives additional operating subsidies to the local housing authority. Such operating subsidies have generally been inadequate to meet the needs caused by the growing gap between tenants' incomes—an increasingly lower percentage of median U.S. household income—and the rising costs of operating public housing units, especially older ones with higher maintenance costs, costs that generally, unlike tenants' incomes, increase roughly at inflation rates. [*See also Chapter 20 by Rachel G. Bratt.*]

6. Co-author Hartman is currently completing a research project on military housing, which focuses on those elements that most markedly distinguish it from the low-rent public housing program, and which might serve as a useful precedent for a radically different approach to solving the nation's housing crisis. In addition to its financial system, the entitlement nature of the military's public housing program (a feature no other government housing program embodies) and the program's ability to achieve true racial integration in its residential complexes are the foci of the study, which is scheduled to be completed in early 1986.

7. Throughout this chapter, the terms "social ownership," "social housing," and "socially owned housing," which are widely employed in Great Britain and Europe, will refer to the full range of not-for-profit forms and entities for developing, owning, and managing housing—whether these are governmental, quasi-governmental, or private nonspeculative.

8. The figure on per-unit new construction cost is derived from 1984 data on the value of private residential construction put in place—a total of $135.1 billion, $102.8 billion of which was for new construction (public spending for housing *and* redevelopment in that year was only $1.6 billion, a minuscule fraction of the private spending figure). This spending produced 1.75 million new housing units. Average construction cost for new one-family units was $67,000 per unit, and for multifamily housing $46,000 per unit, or a weighted average of $58,600 per unit for one-family and multifamily housing combined (U.S. Bureau of Census, 1985a, 1985c). These figures do not include the cost of acquiring land, which represents about 12 percent of the cost of the average one-family home, but do include the cost of interest and fees on construction loans, which represents about 15 percent of total development costs, including land loan costs that would not exist under a system of direct grants (telephone interviews with Cheryl Garney and Dean Crist, Economics Division, National Association of Home Builders, July 19 and August 12, 1985; the cost breakdowns are based on a 1982 association survey of builders; similar data are not available for multifamily construction). Since the addition of land costs and the exclusion of construction financing costs just about offset each other, we have simply rounded off the per-unit construction cost at $60,000 for use in our calculations. The actual figure might be somewhat lower, since our program likely would produce a higher proportion of multifamily construction and a lower proportion of luxury housing than was true in 1984. Existing methods of construction, the fragmented character of much of the construction industry, and growing trends to centralization and vertical integration in the rest of the construction sector [*see Chapter 7 by Tom Schlesinger and Mark Erlich*] add considerably to unit costs as well. By providing a high and stable flow of units, our financing proposal would assure construction workers of much more secure employment, might lower hourly wage rates while increasing overall worker income, and would make production economies much more feasible. The $20,000 per-unit figure for rehabilitating substandard rental units is a rough estimate based on scattered data from local rehabilitation efforts.

9. In those few situations where tenants have real security of tenure, the personal benefits and the potential for improvements and upkeep of the housing stock are striking. In Boston's West End neighborhood—the "urban village" (Gans, 1982b) that urban renewal bulldozers tore down in the late 1950s—the small tenements were occupied by residents with long-established ethnic, friendship, and even familial ties to their land-lords, who often resided in the same building. Families lived in the same apartment for 20, 30, and 40 years, with low rents and (until the shock of urban renewal) the full expectation that they could remain living there as long as they wanted. The result was an enormous amount of investment of money and time in apartment improvements by tenants. Inter-viewers surveying the West Enders under a study sponsored by the National Institute of Mental Health of the impact of displacement and relocation were astounded at the fine interior condition of apartments in this urban "slum" (Hartman, 1963).

10. As this book was going into production, President Reagan's recently released tax-reform plan was under review by Congress. One key feature of the plan is the elimination of all state and local taxes as deductible items in calculating federal income taxes. Thus, property taxes would not be deductible if Congress approved this part of the tax reform. See "Text of President Reagan's Address on Taxes," *Washington Post*, May 29, 1985, and Editors' Note at the end of Chapter 15.

11. It is interesting to compare the results of these calculations with those we generated for the original version of this article, published in 1978. At that time, we used the then prevailing range of mortgage interest rates—7, 8, and 9 percent—and we posited a 5½ percent rate of return on the resident–saver's down payment and monthly deposits (for house value, the same compounded 7 percent annual increase was assumed); we also used 10-, 15-, 20-, and 25-year holding periods instead of 5, 10, and 15 years.

With a 7 percent mortgage interest rate, at the end of 10 years the resident–saver was only slightly better off than the homeowner, an advantage that widened with higher mortgage interest rate assumptions. But even at the 9 percent mortgage interest rate, the gap was only $9,100; by comparison, after 10 years, at the 13 percent mortgage interest rate, Table 29.1 shows a $45,000 gap. Under our earlier calculations, the homeowner was better off after 15 years, but only when mortgage interest rates were as low as 7 percent; after 20 years, the homeowner was better off under the 7 and 8 percent mortgage interest rates; and after 25 years, at the 7, 8, and 9 percent mortgage interest rates.

The effective deregulation of interest rates for depositors through expansion of the number of easily accessible and secure savings instruments and facilities, and the sharp rise of mortgage interest rates above the average expected annual property value increase create an entirely different picture with respect to our revised table. At all mortgage interest rates presented, and for all holding periods given, the resident–saver now comes out far better than the homeowner (advantages that would only widen for 20- and 25-year holding periods). It also is worth noting that even at a 12 percent mortgage interest rate, slightly below what currently (mid-1985) prevails, at the end of 10 years—longer than the average single-family home now is held by a given owner—the typical homeowner does not fully recover down payment plus accumulated monthly principal and interest pay-ments upon sale, even when property value doubles over that time. High interest rates and the nature of repayment schedules mean that the average homeowner is doing little more than paying enormous interest sums to the lender, in exchange for an elusive and illusory capital gain and some modest security of tenure. The old homeowner's jest, "The bank is my landlord," thus approximates reality.

12. Not essential to our program, but certainly desirable, would be replacement of the highly regressive and inefficient property tax with a more progressive and efficient means of supplying this basic financial support for local government. As of 1982, local governments obtained $79 billion in revenues from the property tax (25 percent of all local government revenue, and 40 percent of their revenue from their own sources—U.S. Bureau of the Census, 1984g, table 438). Local governments generally support forms of economic and land development that maximize property tax revenues, regardless of

overall planning considerations or negative effects, such as the displacement of residents or small businesses. A public financing reform shifting local government financial support to more progressively raised taxes (heavier taxes on corporations and progressive federal and state income and wealth taxes) would decrease these unhealthy pressures on local governments; would eliminate what in effect is a sales tax on the most basic consumption expenditure (and which therefore impacts most heavily on the poor, who devote a far higher proportion of their incomes to basics); and would correspondingly lower operating costs for housing and hence the level of operating subsidies required under our program.

13. Average operating costs per room per month were about $37.50 in 1983 (based on data supplied in a telephone interview, Kenneth Anderson, Institute of Real Estate Management, Chicago, September 6, 1985). The modal number of rooms occupied by households of various sizes and tenure in 1983, obtained from the U.S. Bureau of the Census (1984f), was then used to determine average monthly operating costs for households of various sizes and tenure. Affordability standards similar to those in Chapter 3, for various sizes and incomes, were then used to compute the average operating subsidy for households of various incomes, sizes, and tenure. The average subsidy for each type of household was then multiplied by the number of households of that type given in the U.S. Bureau of the Census (1984f).

14. The $120 billion figure for mortgage payments is based on two separate estimates that differ from each other by under 3 percent. The two estimates both start with published 1981 data on homeowners' mortgage payments, and then extrapolate, using other kinds of housing and mortgage data that are available through 1984.

First, for 1981, using median mortgage payment as an estimate for the mean mortgage payment (since mean is not available, median is used, although it is lower than mean and hence the result will be on low side) and the number of mortgaged one-family owner-occupied units (from U.S. Bureau of the Census, 1983a), total estimated mortgage payments for these owners for 1981 was $88 billion.

The first method of extrapolation utilizes the increase in home mortgage debt between 1981 and 1984. At the end of 1984, mortgage debt outstanding on one-to-four-family homes was $1,347.0 billion, at the end of 1981, it was $987.2 billion (Federal Reserve System, 1984, and telephone communication, March 18, 1985); the increase was thus $368.8 billion. Of all the one-to-four-family homes in the United States in 1981, about 64 percent were owner-occupied, one-family, detached units (U.S. Bureau of the Census, 1983a). Allocating the increase in mortgage debt proportionately would make the debt increase on one-family, owner-occupied units $236 billion between 1981 and 1985. While some of the debt outstanding in 1981 was refinanced by 1984, the most direct way of estimating the *increase* in mortgage payments from the 1981 level is simply to determine the annual debt service cost on the $236 billion increase. Based on an average interest rate over this period of about 13 percent and a term of 25 years, the increase in annual mortgage payments would be $32 billion. Added to the figure for 1981, we arrive at an estimate of $120 billion for 1984.

The second extrapolation method utilizes the component of GNP for personal consumption expenditures for owner-occupied housing, which was $206.3 billion in 1981 and $274.7 billion in 1984 (U.S. Bureau of the Census, 1983b, 746, table 1336; U.S. Bureau of Economic Analysis, telephone communication, February 22, 1985). This GNP component includes nonmortgage housing expenses as well as mortgage interest (principal payments are considered repayment of debt, not consumption) and includes all owners, not just owners of one-family houses. The ratio of mortgage payments by one-family owners to personal consumption expenditures for housing by all owner-occupants was 42.5 percent in 1981 and consistently very close to 42 percent for prior years, reflecting the relative stability in the three ratios: mortgage cost to total housing costs; mortaged one-family housing to total one-family housing; and one-family, owner-occupied housing to all owner-occupied housing. Applying the 42.5 percent ratio to the

1984 GNP component yields an estimate of $117 billion for mortgage payments by one-family-homeowners in 1984.

The two figures—$117 billion and $120 billion—differ by less than 3 percent. Because both figures are extrapolated from the 1981 estimate of $88 billion, which is on the low side, the higher of the two 1984 estimates has been used in the text.

Finally, it should be noted that mortgage payments for owner-occupants in multifamily structures, attached single-family houses, single-family homes on 10 acres or more, and mobile homes have not been included in the $120 billion estimate because neither the *Annual Housing Survey* nor other sources provide any expenditure data for such owners. In 1981 and 1983 these categories of owner-occupied housing together equaled about 20 percent of the number of owner-occupied, single-family detached units, and of these over one-third were mobile homes. Since most of these housing units tend to be smaller than single-family detached housing, often located in areas where values are not rising very rapidly, and are largely occupied by long-term owners with lower incomes than those of owners of single-family detached homes (median income in 1983 was $18,800 for such owners but $26,100 for owners of single-family houses—U.S. Bureau of the Census, 1983a, 1984f), their mortgage payments are, on average, considerably less. Thus, aggregate mortgage payments by such owner-occupants probably equal only 10 to 15 percent of those by owners of single-family detached homes, i.e., about $12 to $18 billion per year; the text uses the midpoint of this range.

15. The procedure for estimating the total market value of rental housing in 1984 involves extrapolation from earlier years plus allocation among building types and ownership forms.

The procedure is based on the published value through 1982 of the gross stock (replacement cost at current prices) and net stock (depreciated replacement cost at current prices) of residential real estate for private, nonfarm, one- to four-unit buildings and five-or-more-unit buildings (U.S. Bureau of the Census, 1983b, 747, table 1337).

The value of the total gross stock was then extrapolated from 1982 to 1984 by applying (a) an inflation factor, plus (b) construction spending. The inflation factor used was the compounded two-year percentage increase in the median sales price for new one-family homes (U.S. Bureau of the Census, 1985b, table 10; construction spending figures from U.S. Bureau of the Census, 1983b, 740, table 1321; U.S. Bureau of the Census, 1985a).

It should be noted that extrapolating on the basis of factors (a) plus (b) above understates gross-stock increases by leaving out increases resulting from additions and alterations and the value of land under new housing, but overstates the gross stock by leaving out losses to the inventory. To test the extent to which these effects cancel each other, the method was first used to extrapolate from 1980 to 1981 and from 1981 to 1982. The 1981 projection was 0.58 percent less than the actual figure for the total gross stock, whereas the 1982 projection was 0.26 percent more than the actual. These errors are so small as to give great confidence in the validity of the method.

The estimated total gross stock for 1984 was then allocated between one-to-four-unit structures and five-or-more-unit structures. From 1980 to 1982, the proportion of total value of residential real estate in one- to four-unit housing decreased slowly and linearly, while correspondingly the proportion in larger buildings increased (U.S. Bureau of the Census, 1984b, 747, table 1337). Consistent with this, from 1980 to 1981 and from 1981 to 1983, the proportion of all units that were in one- to four-unit structures decreased in each period, while the proportion in five-or-more-unit structures increased, although the rate of change from 1981 to 1983 was less than from 1980 to 1981 (U.S. Bureau of the Census, 1982c, 1983a, 1983d). Finally, consistent with both of the above, from 1980 through 1984, the proportion of housing starts in one-to-four-unit structures was less than the proportion of the total stock in one-to-four-unit structures, and conversely for five or more units (U.S. Bureau of the Census, 1983b, 744, table 1329; U.S. Bureau of the Census, 1985c, table 1). The shifting proportion from 1980 to 1982 thus was expected to continue at least through 1984; the allocation proportion used for 1984 was simply a linear extrapolation of the trend in the 1980–1982 proportion.

The gross-value estimates for 1984 were then translated into net-value estimates, since depreciated replacement cost at current prices is a much more realistic measure of market value than is historic construction cost at current prices. Again examining trends from 1980 through 1982, it was noticed that the ratio of net to gross value for both one-to-four-unit and five-or-more-unit buildings decreased year by year, due to the declining rate of new construction compared with the previous decade (i.e., aging of the stock). However, substantial increases in construction in 1983 and 1984 would have reversed this decline. So, in this part of the estimate, the ratios used were those for 1980 (rounded to two significant figures) rather than extrapolation of the 1980-1982 trends. The resulting estimates for the net stocks in 1984 were $2,550 billion for one-to-four-unit buildings and $500 billion for five-or-more-unit buildings.

The values by type of structure were then allocated by type of ownership, using the *Annual Housing Survey: 1983, part A, table A-1*. Since 92 percent of all units in buildings of five or more units are renter occupied, and since most of the owner-occupied units in such buildings are condominiums and hence have higher market value per unit than the average rental unit, it has been assumed that 90 percent of the $500 billion net stock in five-or-more-unit buildings—i.e., $450 billion—is for the rental units. Of all the units in the one-to-four-unit buildings, just 24 percent were renter occupied, but less than half of these rental units were in one-unit detached houses, while over 90 percent of the owner-occupied units were in one-unit detached houses. Assuming that the per-unit value of units in the one-to-four-unit stock other than one-unit, detached homes is equal to the per-unit value of units in the five-or-more-unit stock, yields a value of about $2,000 billion in one-family, detached units and $550 billion in one-to-four-unit buildings. With rental units constituting 14 percent of the one-family, detached stock, their net value was about $280 billion in 1984; of the units in two-to-four-unit structures, 58 percent were rental, representing a value of about $320 billion. Adding these two estimates and the $450 billion estimate for the five-or-more-unit rentals yields a total net value of rental housing of $1,050 billion in 1984.

Finally, mortgage debt by type of structure was allocated by type of ownership in the same manner. At the end of 1984, mortgage debt on one-to-four-family houses was $1,347.0 billion and on multifamily housing $161.6 billion (Federal Reserve System, 1985). Assuming that debt-to-value ratios are, on average, about the same for owner and rental properties of the same structural type (but not necessarily for different-size structures), about 22 percent of the debt on one-to-four-unit buildings and 90 percent of the debt on five-or-more-unit buildings would be attributable to rental units. Outstanding mortgage debt on rental housing would thus have been about $450 billion at the end of 1984.

16. The compensation mechanism proposed in the text might appear to treat landlords differently from mortgage holders, since landlords would have their cash investment in the property returned to them at a rate that would be somewhat less than the speculative increase generated by the market, while lenders would get their investment back amortized at whatever interest rate the loan bore. This apparent imbalance might provide an incentive for landlords to try to extract equity prior to buyout, through refinancing (with lender cooperation, since lenders would be assured of full repayment), or to increase their apparent down payment through sham sales.

There are several ways of overcoming this apparent imbalance. One would be to pay off lenders with long-term bonds at moderate interest rates—that is, lenders would recover the amount invested but would not be assured of the rate of amortization and the interest rate of the outstanding mortgage loans. This would create a disincentive for lenders to agree to refinance prior to public buyout.

Another approach would be to treat landlords' equity and mortgage indebtedness together under a single compensation mechanism. The government would pay an established price for each property, in the form of long-term bonds issued jointly in the names of landlord and lender. It then would be left to the two bond owners to negotiate their respective shares and rates of repayment. A reasonable compensation formula would establish the buyout price as equal to the original purchase price, adjusted for inflation using the CPI, plus depreciated value of expenditures for capital improvements—but in no case would the price be more than current market value.

While treating landlords and mortgage holders equally, thereby reducing the incentive for landlords to try to extract their equity through refinancing prior to the buyout, strict controls and retroactive limits on sales would still be needed to avoid having to buy out at inflated prices generated by sham sales.

Under this latter approach, public compensation might be higher, as the CPI inflation factor would be applied to the larger base of the original purchase price rather than the original down payment. In fact, the public cost would depend on whether the mortgage debt on the property had increased more or less than the CPI over the period of ownership. If there had been a lot of refinancing or additional mortgaging, then this approach would actually be less expensive than the one in the text, as it does not guarantee compensation for excessive financing subsequent to the original purchase. Calculations of the range of public costs for these alternative methods of compensation are not included here.

17. The $120 billion figure was derived by multiplying the median monthly rent for all renters, as reported in the U.S. Bureau of the Census, 1983d ($315), by the number of renter households (29,914,000), converting this total to an annual figure, and increasing it by 6 percent to account for inflation between 1983 and 1984. Since median rents are below average rents, the figure is conservative. Since the upper half of the rental stock, by income and rent levels, will generate a proportionately large amount of the total revenue, we have put this portion at two-thirds, rather than half.

18. Chapter 3, by Michael E. Stone, calculates the number of shelter-poor renters for 1981; extrapolating this figure to 1984, using compounded inflation rates, yields the 15 million total. Eleven million of these households, as noted in the text above, is our calculation of those eligible for the universal operating subsidy. The remaining 4 million are estimated to have high enough incomes not to need operating subsidies but insufficient to pay rents that cover full mortgage payments.

19. The typical rental building we posit was purchased 10 years ago, with a 10 percent down payment and a 20-year mortgage (or, as is more likely, multiple mortgages) averaging 12 percent interest, and has increased in value, on average, 5 percent a year, compounded.

20. This figure includes nearly 150,000 units of Sec. 221(d)(3), Sec. 236, and Rent Supplement housing—about one-third of all units built under these multifamily programs—that HUD either owns, has already sold off after taking title, or for which the agency currently is mortgage-holder (Achtenberg, 1985). Some 100,000 Sec. 235 single-family units have come into HUD's inventory since the program was introduced in 1968, most of which have been sold off or demolished (telephone interview, Zenora Addison, HUD Division of Housing Information and Statistics, November 8, 1985). Very large proportions of the rest of this HUD-insured stock are in serious financial trouble; a 1978 HUD study showed that fewer than one-third of all Sec. 221(d)(3) and Sec. 236 developments were financially sound (HUD, 1978), and given the increasing gap between operating costs and tenants' incomes, it is likely that even fewer would be so rated today.

These figures do not include HUD's inventory of units in its mortgage insurance programs that do not involve a subsidy, Sec. 203(b) and Sec. 221(d)(2) single-family homes, Secs. 207, 213, 220, 231, 608, and other multifamily projects. As of 1984, HUD had taken into its inventory more units from its unsubsidized multifamily programs (154,000) than from its subsidized multifamily programs (telephone interview with Emily Paradise Achtenberg, Boston, November 14, 1985). While occupants of units in unsubsidized programs generally are not low income, an equal potential exists for bringing these units as well into the social housing sector.

# 30 | The Dilemmas of British Housing Policy

*Steve Schifferes*

*In evaluating ways to move forward from the current housing situation in the United States, much can be learned from current and historical practice in other countries. The next four chapters deal with housing in countries that have had more progressive government housing policies than ours. These chapters can provide us with a vision of what is possible and in some cases can lead to an examination of the pitfalls that may lie ahead if certain strategies are chosen.*

*Although the political–economic system in Britain is fundamentally like our own, it is striking that Britain has a vastly larger publicly rented housing stock—the largest in Western Europe—6 million units, or almost one-third of total housing stock. Relatedly, housing policy is a major issue in national politics, in sharp contrast to the situation in the United States. This chapter traces the evolution of British housing policy, particularly analyzing the factors that facilitated the coexistence of a large public housing sector with an active private sector. Recently in Britain, as in the United States and elsewhere [see Chapter 20 by Rachel G. Bratt and Chapter 31 by Richard P. Appelbaum], the continued viability of publicly owned housing has been threatened. Thus, although Britain's experience shows us what can be accomplished toward decommodifying housing within a capitalist system and a predominantly private housing market, it also points out the vulnerability of these efforts. The political and programmatic lessons for those working on strategies toward decommodifying housing in the United States are enormous.*

In 1977 two contradictory events took place that symbolized the current dilemma of British housing policy. On the one hand, the Housing (Homeless Persons) Act came into effect, guaranteeing the right to housing for all family and elderly households that were homeless.[1] On the other hand, the Labour government took what proved to be decisive steps in limiting the growth of public sector housing by introducing controls on the number of units local governments could build. Thus ended over half a century of expansion, during which time the central government had guaranteed an open-ended subsidy for all housing built by local governments ("council housing"). Under the present Conservative government, the public sector has begun to shrink as hundreds of thousands of tenants have been allowed to buy their council houses at reduced prices.

The gap between a recognition of housing need and the provision of housing resources for the needy lies at the heart of Britain's housing dilemma. At its center lies the question of the future of the public housing sector. For decades it had been widely accepted that only an expansion of the supply of public sector housing could provide the resources for meeting housing need. Indeed, the strength of this belief and its broad-based political support are demonstrated by the fact that Britain has the largest stock of publicly owned rental housing in Western Europe, some 6 million units, or almost one-third of the total housing stock. The Homeless Persons Act was feasible only because of the size of Britain's public housing sector, which generated enough units to house the homeless.

But in recent years serious doubts have arisen from many parts of the political spectrum about public housing. And the political middle ground has shifted, with even the Labour party questioning its commitment to public sector housing. First, questions have been raised about the physical standards of public sector housing. There has been increasing evidence of major design faults and a need for improvement of large portions of the public housing stock. Second, concern has focused on the way in which public housing seems to reproduce inequalities in the wider society, with the poorest and most deprived families allocated the worst housing within the public sector. Third, among the vast majority of the population, including many who live in public housing, there is an apparent preference for owner occupation. The left and right differ on how they interpret these developments, the right arguing that the public sector has failed and should be replaced, as much as possible, by private housing, the left believing that it should be retained and expanded, but reformed and improved. This chapter traces the evolution of British housing policy in an attempt to analyze to what extent public housing, in a capitalist mixed economy, can be insulated from market forces.

## The Historical Legacy

It is important to understand the political and social preconditions in Britain that allowed the growth of so large a public housing sector. The growth of public housing in the United Kingdom can be explained only by the creation, over a major part of this century, of a political consensus as to its desirability. Such a consensus was not inevitable, as some liberal historians of the welfare state (for example, Bruce, 1961; Foster, 1973; Gilbert, 1971) have argued, and owed far more to a militant labor movement than has previously been acknowledged. But its maintenance over a long period—and among all welfare state services, housing requires a long time to have any effect, as housebuilding in any one year has a limited impact on the housing stock and housing market—required political agreement. As with the rest of the British welfare state, that consensus between the two political parties was forthcoming in the prosperous years after World War II. In the 1950s broad political agreement emerged in Britain on the right balance between state intervention and a free market economy—a balance endorsed by both Conservatives and Labour. This compromise was for the state to provide welfare services and income support, ranging from free health care to a guaranteed income for the poor, but for the economy to be run primarily by private enterprise. Thus Labour curbed its demands, made in 1945, for massive nationalization of private companies; and the Conservatives accepted the expansion of state-run services such as health, education, and housing. But the foundation of public sector housing policy had been laid earlier, in the years between the first and second world wars.

## Homes Fit for Heroes, 1915–1930

The long-lasting consensus in housing policy was forged in the midst of Britain's struggle to win the world's first total war. The first major state intervention in the private housing market in Britain came about, not via liberal policymakers, but as a result of protest by munitions workers about high rents. The total mobilization for World War I had led to a massive increase in the number of munitions workers in Britain's major industrial cities, such as Glasgow, Sheffield, and Birmingham, and therefore to overcrowding and high rents. The government wanted to boost production by changing work practices and introducing unskilled workers and women into factories hitherto dominated by skilled trade unionists. In 1915, the skilled workers, led by local Labour parties, began a campaign against high rents that culminated in a series of rent strikes. The government panicked. It introduced a national system of rent control and security of tenure for the duration of the war. Many industrialists supported the rent freeze, preferring to buy industrial peace at the expense of the private landlord (Englander, 1983; Melling, 1983).

Many of the countries involved in World War I found that they had to introduce temporary rent controls, but in Britain such controls were not lifted when the war came to an end. One government committee after another found that it would be unfair to lift rent controls until the postwar housing shortage, caused by the cessation of building during the war, was eliminated. And there was growing political agreement that only the public sector could provide enough houses to eliminate the shortage. The coalition government, headed by Lloyd George, elected at the end of the war in 1919 had pledged to provide the returning soldiers with "Homes Fit for Heroes." The production of private rental housing had dried up after the war as small private capitalists sought other, more lucrative investments. And owner occupation was still out of reach of the vast majority of the population (Swenerton, 1980).

The public sector building program had a rocky start, as the first attempts at public subsidy (in 1919) foundered on the greatly inflated housebuilding costs of the early postwar years. Housebuilding costs tripled in two years, leading to substantial program cutbacks. But by 1924, during the first Labour government (whose housing minister, John Wheatley, had been the architect of the Glasgow rent protests), council housing was put on a firm financial and administrative basis with a planned program of expansion over 15 years paralleled by an expansion of the building trades to meet the extra demand. Although Wheatley's target of 1.5 million homes over 15 years was not met, almost 1 million public sector dwellings were constructed in the interwar years, enough to eliminate the absolute shortage of the immediate postwar period.[2]

The pattern of public sector building set in this period has prevailed in Britain until today. Largely at the behest and to the benefit of the Labour party, local governments built and managed public housing, using central government subsidies. There was no limit on the number of centrally subsidized dwellings each council could build—an incentive to expansion initially resisted fiercely by the Treasury—and the central government commitment extended for 40 years, each dwelling financed by a revolving loan fund. As the Labour party gradually came to power in the major towns throughout Britain, its pledge to increase the housing program played an important part in its success, and the new council tenants were its most loyal supporters.

## The Campaign to Abolish the Slums, 1930–1945

Although this early public housing program was a success in its own terms, by the 1930s it had begun to run into problems. It was the intent of the early Labour housing policy entirely to replace the private rental sector, in which nearly all working-class people lived, with public rental housing of a better standard and lower rent. The problem was that with rent control keeping private sector rents down, public housing was too expensive, even with subsidy, for the poorer members of the working class who lived in the worst slum housing. The prospect of further subsidy became remote in the 1930s, with the coming to power of a Conservative-dominated government committed to cutting public spending in the wake of the 1931 run on the pound. At the same time, private and government surveys showed the extent of the slum problem, with the majority of the urban population living in appalling conditions (see Bowley, 1945). Finally, by the 1930s the private housing market for owner occupation had revived in a big way, with an owner-occupation boom fueled by cheap mortgages provided by the expanding building societies (savings and loan associations) operating nationally (Ball, 1983; Merritt, 1980).

The result was a major shift in housing policy, accepted by both political parties in the 1930s, toward slum clearance as the main objective of public housing policy. The desire to have the public sector tackle the bottom rather than the top end of housing market—and essentially substitute for the failure of the private sector to provide adequate housing for the poor—led to a consensus-based, rather than radical, housing policy; but it did involve major shifts in attitude, particularly by the Conservative party.

In the first place, in backing massive slum clearance in the 1930s, the Conservatives finally severed their ties to private landlords, whose lack of political support had been all too evident in the First World War.[3] Many large industrialists had also accepted public sector building in order to get a better-housed workforce. For the kind of slum clearance proposed involved declaring vast areas of inner cities unfit for human habitation and having the local governments take them over and demolish them, without paying compensation to the owners of such property.[4]

Other major changes followed the decision to concentrate on slum clearance. In order to insure that the poorer slum residents could afford the new public housing being built for them, a new system of rent pooling had to be introduced, combining the subsidy accounts of different kinds of dwellings (formerly, the rent for each house was set individually on the basis of its construction costs less subsidy). This allowed introduction, at local discretion, of a sliding scale of rents based on income, a "rent rebate" scheme. Over 200 housing authorities had adopted such a system by 1938 (Schifferes, 1974).

In addition, housing standards suffered (1) because cheaper construction costs and smaller houses were needed to insure lower rents; and (2) because rehousing all the people who had been crowded in the inner city meant higher density—and eventually high-rise buildings.

Finally, the social composition of public housing changed, from skilled workers to largely unskilled workers. This was the result both of rent policy, which dictated cheaper, less desirable houses, and allocation policy. Councils began to develop rules and systems (the "waiting list") to give first preference to families with children in housing need. "Housing need" was defined by most housing authorities as applying to people who had lived for a specified time in specified bad conditions (no inside toilet, damp flat, etc.). People were given points for each condition, and had to reach a total number of points to qualify for rehousing. The total varied among different housing authorities, and at different times within the same housing authority, depending on how many dwellings were available for rent.

This allocation system was reinforced by a policy of guaranteeing public sector dwellings to those whose slum homes were knocked down by clearance schemes, without their having to wait their turn on the waiting lists. These persons were also most likely to be unskilled workers (see Lambert, Paris, and Blackenby, 1978).

## The Postwar Consensus, 1945–1970

Although the main parameters of housing policy were established in the 1930s, it was not until after World War II that the means to implement them fully became available. The sacrifices of that war had created a mood for sweeping reform that led to the election by overwhelming majority of a

Labour government in 1945. The defeat of Winston Churchill, and his eventual replacement by Harold Macmillan in 1955, led to a Conservative party also pledged to constructive participation in the work of building up a welfare state. The war had also left a legacy of physical control by the state over the whole of the economy—all manpower, materials, and production in the wartime economy had been centrally directed. Labour continued many of these controls in the period of postwar reconstruction and economic crisis. In addition, it created a national town planning system that tightly controlled the use of land for development.

The result was that Labour found it had both public support and the means to implement a massive expansion of public sector housing to eliminate the wartime shortage and clear the slums. All private housebuilding, and the use of land for private housing development, was banned, and a massive program of public housing began. Ambitious development plans included the creation of new towns to "decant" the overcrowded central-city population, high-rise apartments with green space in place of terraced back streets, and by the 1950s major new innovations in the use of prefabrication and stressed concrete to speed up building.

In addition, rents were kept low by a far more generous level of central government subsidy, and indeed dropped below private sector controlled rents (which had been frozen again at 1939 levels when war broke out). Those with no income, under the new National Assistance scheme created as part of the post–World War II reform of the income maintenance system, were guaranteed their full rent from the state as well as a subsistence income to meet their other basic needs (since 1966 called Supplementary Benefit). Although the Conservative government elected in 1951 supported public housebuilding, albeit slightly less enthusiastically than Labour had done, the unleashed demand for public housing at very low rents and good conditions was such that local councils could not keep up with demand, and waiting lists continued to grow. During the 1950s and 1960s, builders came along with more and more technological fixes to produce public sector homes more quickly and cheaply than ever before—all of which eventually produced more unsatisfactory buildings than ever before. And councils struggled to produce more and more elaborate waiting-list systems to regulate demand for public housing (and within public housing, transfer to more desirable dwellings; Short, 1982). But while public sector housing was growing, so was owner occupation, fueled not only by new building but by a massive desertion of landlords from privately rented housing. Particularly in cities, larger homes were split up into flats and sold into owner occupation.[5] The growing affluence of the working class, many of whom purchased their privately rented homes as sitting tenants, contributed to the growth of owner occupation as well.

The result of these developments was a transformation in housing tenure and housing conditions in Britain. The rented housing sector was transformed from one based on private to one based on public housing, with the poorest households especially moving into public housing. But for the

TABLE 30.1
HOUSING TENURE IN ENGLAND AND WALES, 1914–1985
(in percentage of units)

|  | 1914 | 1950 | 1985 |
|---|---|---|---|
| Privately rented | 90 | 53 | 7 |
| Publicly rented | a | 18 | 30 |
| Owner-occupied | 10 | 29 | 63 |

*Source:* Department of Environment, *Housing Policy Review* (London: HMSO, 1985), Technical Vol. 1,
   chap. 1; Central Statistical Office, *Social Trends*, no. 15 (London: HMSO, 1985), table 8.1.
a Less than 1%.

majority of the population, including the skilled working class, owner
occupation became the tenure of choice. The physical conditions of the
housing stock improved dramatically, with newer public sector stock replacing older privately rented housing. The high rate of public sector building
contributed to the elimination of absolute shortage, overcrowding, and the
sharing of accommodation by families (see Tables 30.1 and 30.2). And many
more of the elderly and "problem" families, including many single parents,
now had the benefit of public housing (Lansley, 1977; U.K. Department of
the Environment, 1977).

# Recent Trends in Housing Policy:
# Cuts, Rights, and Privatization

The postwar consensus in housing policy, and indeed in other aspects of the
welfare state and the mixed economy, began to break down in Britain in the
1970s. The 1974–1979 Labour government was the victim. The problems of
economic decline, culminating in Britain's humiliating approach to the
International Monetary Fund for a loan in 1976, with the fund's insistence
on major public-spending cuts, destroyed the illusion that the public sector
could go on expanding. And the sharp rise in inflation, which in turn led to
major disparities in wage rates between different groups and strikes against
the Labour government's pay-restraint policy, cleared the way for the
radical monetarist views of Margaret Thatcher's Conservative government.
In this climate of cuts and crisis, housing held a uniquely bad place.

   Margaret Thatcher's Conservative government, which came to office in
1979, has shattered the welfare state consensus and is now engaged in testing
the limits of its right-wing reforms. Like Ronald Reagan, Thatcher is finding
those limits greater than she first thought. But nowhere has the British
welfare state been more vulnerable than in the area of public housing. First,
unlike other welfare services (e.g., health and education), the majority of

TABLE 30.2
HOUSING CONDITIONS IN ENGLAND AND WALES, 1931–1981
(in millions of units)

|  | 1931 | 1951 | 1971 | 1981 |
|---|---|---|---|---|
| Multiperson households sharing (including married couples or single parents living as part of another household) | 2.2 | 2.3 | 0.8 | 0.5 |
| Overcrowded households (living at over 1.5 persons per room) | 1.2 | 0.6 | 0.2 | 0.1 |
| Living in dwellings unfit or lacking basic amenities (inside toilet, bath, or running water) or requiring major repairs | N.A. | 7.5[a] | 4.0 | 2.1 |
| Total households | 10.2 | 13.3 | 16.8 | 19.1 |
| Percentage in unsatisfactory conditions (eliminating duplication) | N.A. | 69 | 24 | 11 |

*Source:* U.K. Census; Department of Environment, *House Condition Survey* (London: HMSO, 1971, 1981).
[a] Does not include disrepair.

the population does not use the service but relies on the private housing market. Second, housing, which is financed by public borrowing, has a more direct effect on government overspending than other services and has always been the prime target of the Treasury spending ax. Third, the legitimacy of public housing itself as a solution to the housing problems of the country has been widely questioned, and the political agreement on the nature of the nation's housing problem has evaporated.

## The Crisis of Public Sector Housing

Nothing was more damaging for the public housing program than the media-inspired campaign against public housing of the 1970s. On the one hand, it was widely believed that real housing need had been eliminated by the construction of so much new public housing and that many people in public housing were not needy, and many others did not pay their rent. On the other hand, new problems were identified as consequences of the public sector slum-clearance program, which made its continuance undesirable. Traditional working-class, inner-city communities had been broken up and dispersed in new, isolated developments; unsatisfactory forms of housing— notably tower blocks (high-rise housing)—had replaced the terraced working-class streets. Mothers could no longer supervise their children, nor could residents keep the area free of vandalism, graffiti, and crime; and people no longer wanted to live under the paternalistic management of large bureaucratic housing authorities that decided what color they could paint their flat and front door (Coleman, 1985; Wilmott and Young, 1957).

Such claims, undoubtedly exaggerated, became more and more the common currency of political debate in the 1970s; they interrelated with the growing social stigma of the public sector (as the skilled working class moved away into owner occupation) to weaken political support for its extension.

This atmosphere served to magnify greatly the very real problems of public sector housing that were emerging by the mid-1970s, and strengthened the Treasury's hand in pressing for cuts—a continuous pressure over the last decade, and a largely successful one. Housing has gone from being one of the largest government spending programs to one of the smallest, and *half* of all public-spending cuts achieved by both Labour and Conservative governments have fallen on the housing budget.

The first target of spending cuts was, ironically, the modernization program for public housing itself, which was subjected to a fixed spending limit in 1975. In the decade since then, the accumulated repair and modernization problems of many (though not the majority) public sector dwellings have continued to mount. Although relatively few public sector homes are "unfit for human habitation," many are less than desirable as modern residences. The most serious problems exist in the many hundreds of tower blocks built in the "crash programs" of the 1950s and 1960s slum-clearance campaigns. The prestressed lightweight concrete building methods used were seriously defective, and many blocks are now under consideration for demolition. In addition, many more modern council flats suffer from problems of dampness (mold growing inside), the result largely of their inappropriate (and very expensive) heating systems. Many more flats and houses lack modern central heating systems, or are small and cramped by modern design standards. Many of these are products of the 1930s slum-clearance drives. The cost of dealing with the backlog of accumulated repair and modernization problems in the public sector has been estimated by the local authorities to be at least £20 billion—that is, 10 times the current annual capital spending by government on *all* public housing, including newly built housing (Association of Metropolitan Authorities, 1984).

The crisis in public housing also was related to the disappearance of the slum homes that public housing was meant to replace. By the 1970s it had become clear that the days of area clearance were coming to an end, as vast tracts of bad housing in major cities no longer existed. Rather, bad housing was now more dispersed throughout the country, and its problem was increasingly disrepair rather than the lack of basic amenities such as an inside fixed bath and toilet. In general, bipartisan policy was shifting from clearance to improvement. The key question was who would do the improving.

The 1974 Labour government came into office with ambitious plans for "municipalization"—the acquisition by local government through compulsory purchase—of much of the private rental sector, which was where bad conditions were most concentrated. But local authorities were not well equipped to manage and improve the diverse stock of dwellings they acquired before the public-spending ax struck in 1976. In total, local authority renovation work—for both newly acquired and newly constructed purpose-built, public sector dwellings—fell by two-thirds, from an annual rate of

180,000 dwellings in 1973 to 60,000 dwellings in 1975 (U.K. Department of the Environment, 1977). Some renovation was also undertaken by private voluntary organizations known as housing associations, which received capital grants from the government to do the work. These associations generally managed fewer dwellings than did local authorities, and associations that focused on inner-city rehabilitation tried to concentrate their programs in a few small neighborhoods rather than acquire properties over a wide area, as had been the pattern with local public housing authorities.

Even the elimination of all these capital programs was not enough as the government approached the financial crisis of 1976. The growing capital expenditure of building new public housing units also came under scrutiny. In the summer of 1976, the government announced a freeze on all building projects outside the major conurbations.

To understand the significance of this freeze, which eventually led to an elaborate system of housing capital controls, it is necessary to understand the permissive nature of the financing of British public housing up to that time. Local authorities since the 1920s had been given almost complete freedom to build and manage as many public housing units as they wanted. Unlike the situation in the United States, the central government in the United Kingdom did not lay down any conditions in detail concerning rent levels, management practice, or design (except for broad controls on the total cost of each housing project). Instead, the central government pledged to pay a subsidy (at first a fixed sum for a given number of years, later a percentage of total capital costs) to help keep cost and rents down. It was up to each local authority to balance its own books, set its own rent levels, and, at its discretion, make additional contributions from local tax revenues to meet its costs.

Local authorities were allowed to pool their debt and rents, thus creating a cross-subsidy. That is, rents from older dwellings that had been largely paid for helped cover the costs of new borrowing to build more units. Compared with the U.S. practice, this was an important strength of the British system. The "profits" from the difference between the historic cost and the current costs of different dwellings could be retained within the public sector and redistributed [*for further discussion of these concepts, see Chapter 16 by Jim Kemeny*]. But it was the weakness of this system of debt financing in a period of rapidly rising inflation that fatally undermined the financial basis of council housing in the 1970s and opened the way for major cutbacks.

The total central government subsidy to local authority housing doubled in the first three years of the new Labour government, creating, in an atmosphere of cuts and crisis, irresistible pressure for spending restraint. The central government subsidy cost rose for three reasons. First, the cost of servicing the debt on existing public housing rose with interest rates (as most local authority housing debt was held in relatively short-term instruments). Second, local housing authorities attempted to expand their building programs to meet housing needs. And third, since housing and land costs were rising faster than general inflation, expansion of the housing program appeared extremely costly (e.g., for some larger urban housing authorities, a 5 percent increase in the dwelling stock resulted in a 50 percent increase in total debt)—although the combination of high inflation and high interest rates produced "front loading" of new debt charges that, while expensive to pay off initially, would later become less burdensome in real terms.

So, for the first time, the public sector building program was to be subject to a fixed upper limit on total cash, through an appropriations system, introduced by Labour, known as HIP—the Housing Investment Program. The government assigned each local housing authority a maximum number of permitted dwellings and limited other capital spending programs (such as modernization) as well; eventually, all capital spending was to be lumped into one block grant, and local authorities could decide whether cuts would fall on modernization or new construction. The overall size of the Housing Investment Program nationally was determined by the Treasury, and the Department of the Environment then divided up the total allocation, partly through negotiation with local authorities, and partly through a fixed formula based on various indices of housing need. This financial mechanism had a dramatic impact on public sector building programs, which up to then had been rising rapidly under Labour. Public sector housing starts rose from 113,000 in 1973 (one-third of total housing starts) to 174,000 in 1975 (60 percent of all housing starts) and then collapsed to 107,000 by 1978 (one-third of all starts) (Merritt, 1979; U.K. Department of the Environment, 1977).

Far worse was to come under the Tory government. By 1980 public sector starts were down again by half, to 56,000, and since then they have been at a level of 35,000 to 40,000 dwellings a year (one-quarter to one-fifth of all housing starts). This level of cutback has had less impact than might have been expected because so large a public sector generates a significant number of relets (vacancies that occur when tenants move or die). Total new occupancies in public housing were 475,000 in 1976; by 1981–1982 they had dropped only to 438,000, despite a drop in lettings of newly built units, from 131,000 to 56,000 (U.K. Central Statistical Office, 1985). That turnover is going up is largely the result of another strand of Conservative policy—a sharp rise in the rents of council housing, which leads more people to decide to leave the public sector.

For although the Labour government cut back massively on new construction of public housing, it did this partly to be able to maintain subsidies to existing council tenants. It allowed local authorities to keep rents low, far lower than the so-called economic rents based on the cost of construction. This, Labour hoped, would retain the political support of the 6 million council households. The Conservative government had no such compunction and felt that excessively low public rents encouraged overconsumption of public housing. They were determined to reduce them, and they did so with a vengeance.

From 1970–1971 to 1984–1985, central government spending on subsidies fell from £1.4 billion to £360 million, a drop that would be even greater if one were to take inflation into account, and as a result rents (excluding heating and property taxes) increased from an average of under £6 a week in 1978–1979 to almost £15 a week in 1984–1985, and substantially higher in the high-cost big cities. As a percentage of average male earnings, the percentage absorbed by rent increased from 6.6 percent to 8.8 percent (U.K. Treasury, 1985). By 1984–1985, however, relatively few public sector households were made up of a nuclear family with an employed father. Most were therefore shielded from these rent increases because, as we see in the next section, they received help with their rent from another system of income-related subsidies: Housing Benefit.

## The Growth of Housing Rights

Although public housing provision has been cut back in Britain in the last decade, paradoxically the period also has seen the growth of the concept that everyone has certain housing rights, which the state in the last resort should underwrite. The wide currency given to the term *housing rights* by all political parties has not meant total agreement on the meaning of the term. For example, the Conservatives attach great importance to *the right to buy* the public housing unit one lives in; Labour believes in the right of private tenants to *security from eviction* from their home. But there has been surprising agreement among all parties on the *principle* that everyone, regardless of income, should be entitled to a decent home at a price he or she can afford. Disagreements have been greater in relation to the means best suited to reach that end (and there is also some disagreement as to whether "everyone" includes families with children, all married couples, or single people under the age of twenty-six who might want a home of their own).

One important extension of the principle of housing rights by the Conservatives is in the area of income support for people of low incomes who must pay high rents. As mentioned earlier, since 1948, people in Britain with no income receive a state minimum benefit called Supplementary Benefit, and their rent normally is paid in full whether they live in the public or private sector. The Conservative government has always favored replacing general subsidies to all council tenants (based on construction costs) with more targeted subsidies based on income, on the grounds that the latter system reduces the incentive for local municipalities to build more public housing. In 1972 the Conservatives therefore introduced, as part of a package of public housing rent increases, a national scheme of relatively generous financial assistance for employed low-income households, to help them pay their rent. This entitlement program rebated to people in both public and private rental housing a portion of their rent, based on their income, upon application to the local housing authority. In 1982–1983, the current government amalgamated the two schemes—the housing element of Supplementary Benefit and the rent rebates—into one system, called Housing Benefit, under which all people in need of rent assistance, whether they live in public or private housing, are employed or unemployed, can receive aid.

This area has become the fastest-growing component of housing expenditure in the Thatcher government and thus is finally coming under scrutiny. Rent rebates had doubled, from £275 million to £550 million, in the three years before amalgamation into Housing Benefit (1979–1982). Following amalgamation, rebates tripled, from £1 billion in 1982–1983 to an estimated £2.9 billion in 1985–1986. Almost 4 million council tenants, or two-thirds of the total, receive income-related housing benefits today, as do 1 million private tenants, or more than one-third of that sector (U.K. Department of Health and Social Security, 1985; U.K. Treasury, 1985).

As part of its recently announced social security review, the government has declared its intention to reduce spending on the housing benefit by a massive £500 million. This is being done by reducing the number of low-income households that qualify for rent assistance. Thus the benefit is being redistributed from the poorer to the poorest households. However, the government has not abandoned the principle that those in severe financial need should be entitled to receive government help in paying their rent. (Lansley and Goss, 1983).

Another area in which housing rights is still strongly entrenched is within the concept of security of tenure, or "just cause" eviction. In the private rental sector, the Conservatives have again decided that the political cost of abandoning security of tenure would be too high to pay, despite the Conservative belief that to do so would stimulate more private rentals to come onto the market.

Nor are Conservatives proposing to abandon Labour's extension of security of tenure to private tenants living in furnished rooms, which was part of a law passed in 1974. Instead, they supported Labour's plan to extend security-of-tenure legislation to cover public sector tenants, who had previously been excluded, and the 1980 Housing Act accomplished this. Broadly, the act stipulates that for public and private tenants, landlords have to go to court and show that they have a valid reason for evicting a tenant. Aside from causing a nuisance and not paying rent, evictions can be made by private landlords for a number of other reasons—for example, if they need the property for their own use. In the public sector, municipal landlords have management grounds available—such as the need to vacate the premises for modernization—but in such cases they must guarantee to rehouse the evicted tenants.[6]

Public and private tenants were granted other ancillary rights in 1980, such as the right to carry out improvements to their homes, and, for public sector tenants, the right to sublet or rent out rooms. However, British law has not developed the concept of the warranty of habitability; there are relatively weak powers available to force landlords to take action if the property becomes uninhabitable, and the government is proposing weakening these still further (U.K. Department of the Environment, 1985). Security of tenure has been weakened by ingenious legal arrangements that landlords have devised to let property outside the rent acts, the most notable of which is the license agreement,[7] which is very common in London and other large cities. The courts have taken an ambiguous line toward the legality of such agreements, however, and the most recent case (*Street* v. *Mountford* [1985]) has, in an obiter dictum, suggested that they are largely illegal.

Undoubtedly the most important bipartisan measure extending the concept of housing rights was the Homeless Persons Act of 1977. This established the right of individuals in priority need [*see note 1 for definition*] to have accommodation "secured for their occupation" by the local municipal housing authority. Since the act came into force, about 500,000 households have been helped, with the bulk of that number eventually rehoused in public housing. At present, about 20 percent of local authority lettings are going to the homeless, who are presenting themselves at a rate of 90,000 households a year, double the rate when the act came into force. Most households are either newly formed or never had secure accommodation, although a growing number are unhoused as a result of mortgage arrears. The bulk of households rehoused (65 percent) are families with children; pregnant women and the elderly each make up around 10 percent (Donnison and Ungerson, 1982; U.K. Central Statistical Office, 1985).

Two main problems have emerged in implementing the Homeless Persons Act. The first is a geographical problem. Homelessness is concentrated in the large cities, above all London, where the housing authorities have the fewest number of suitable units; and within the large cities, homelessness is concentrated in certain areas of inner-city housing stress, especially inner London. The Homeless Persons Act places the obligation of providing housing on the housing authority to which the person initially applies; the act provides no real mechanism for sharing the different levels of demand for housing, for example as between inner and outer London boroughs, and in London there are 32 separate housing authorities. One of the problems of Britain's public housing system in general is that there is relatively limited mobility within it, and virtually none between local housing authorities. Thus, families often cannot be accommodated in public housing for months, or even years, and must wait in cheap hotels paid for by the local authority.

Second, the priority-need group excludes single people and couples without children, who make up most of the demand for new housing. This group is increasingly buying small flats when it can afford to, but poorer single people and young couples are excluded from the mainstream of the housing system. The bitterness of this group perhaps was the swing vote for the Conservatives' most politically attractive housing right: the right to buy.[8]

## The Privatization of Housing

Labour's appeal for council tenants' votes in 1979—by keeping rents low and offering them more rights in their homes—was less attractive to many of these tenants than the Conservative policy that gave them the opportunity to purchase their dwellings at 30 to 50 percent below market cost, aided by council mortgages. This right of sitting tenants to buy their council houses became the main housing program of the Conservative government elected in 1979. Its appeal was that it essentially transferred part of the historic cost advantage of most public sector dwellings to the individual tenant instead of sharing it among all tenants.

These would be advantages for some public sector tenants. But they accrued only to those lucky enough to live in a desirable public sector dwelling, and well-off enough to be able to afford to buy. For the majority who remained in public housing, chances of moving to a more desirable property were decreased. And the loss of the cross-subsidy from the rents of properties sold would eventually lead to higher rents for the rest (U.K. Parliament, 1980).

As we have seen, council housing rents more than doubled from 1979 to 1983, the Conservatives' first four years in office, because of cuts in subsidies. The result has been that, in some areas, public housing now makes a profit, which contributes to keeping property taxes down for everyone else. In other, inner-city areas, council rents have soared so high that some tenants pay half their earnings for rent. The steep rent hikes have had a hidden purpose: to encourage privatization. For many, the costs of buying are not very different from current rents.

The broad aim of the Conservative government is to roll back the size of the public housing sector, which, the government believes, places limits on the spread of owner occupation to an even larger section of the population. In addition to selling off existing housing (so far, about 10 percent of the stock has been sold), the Conservatives have gone further than previous governments to prevent any new public sector construction by local councils; local authority construction levels are down four-fifths from what they were under Labour. The Conservatives have also prohibited acquisitions from the private sector ("municipalization"), except by the private, nonprofit housing associations.

In addition, the Conservatives have introduced several measures to help the private sector. First, they are encouraging local authorities to sell back to private developers land they have banked for future public housing construction. Next, they are asking them to build for sale, and even offer houses to "partly rent, partly buy" (equity sharing) as a way of stimulating owner occupation. Finally, they have increased tax credits for larger mortgages. This last measure means that regressive "tax expenditures" on mortgage relief for owner occupation—at £3.5 billion—now exceed the cost of income-related help for poorer tenants (U.K. Treasury, 1985). [*See related discussion for the United States in Chapter 15 by Cushing Dolbeare.*]

These measures all suggest that the Conservatives may have realized that they have reached the limits of council house sales as a means of expanding owner occupation. Sales of publicly owned dwellings increased from 55,000 in 1979–1980 to 204,000 in 1982–1983, but have fallen to an annual rate of about 100,000. It seems that, factoring in new construction, the rapid fall in the absolute size of the public sector has stabilized.

The sale of council houses shows that there is a substantial number of highly desirable dwellings, built by the public sector, that people would like to own. In large part, these are the 75 percent of the public sector dwellings that are houses, rather than flats (few of which have been sold). Because flats are disproportionately concentrated in large cities, sales have been disproportionately in rural areas and medium-size towns, and under the Conservatives' rule, this has led to a further distortion of investment. Local municipalities have up to now been allowed to keep the bulk of their capital receipts from sales and reinvest them in new building or modernization (which the government saw as a further incentive to encourage local authorities to sell); these capital receipts now constitute half of all government capital spending on housing. But these receipts generally are accruing to the authorities with the least housing need, and there is no mechanism for redistributing them nationally (U.K. Central Statistical Office, 1985).

Sales of public dwelling units would have been higher if there were more employed heads of households living in public housing. But half of all public sector tenants are not economically active (i.e., they are retired, unemployed, and single parents with children), up from 25 percent in 1968. Among the elderly, only 3 percent considered buying their home, in contrast to 32 percent of council tenants who were part of families with children (U.K. Central Statistical Office, 1985).

The increase in the size of the owner-occupied sector under the Tories, from 57 percent to 63 percent, has not been without its problems. In the first place, unemployment has affected many people who took out mortgages. At present, the impact of unemployment is lessened by the fact that, for those without income, Supplementary Benefit normally meets mortgage interest payments in full. Nevertheless, the government's recently announced Social Security Review proposes to change this (U.K. Department of Health and Social Security, 1985).

Second, there is a growing problem of disrepair in the owner-occupied sector among older properties (built before World War I) that are now largely owned outright. The 1981 House Condition Survey showed that one in four homes in the private sector was in unsatisfactory condition, an increase in disrepair of 20 percent over five years. The government's response was to introduce a very generous system of outright grants of 90 percent of the cost of repair work for property built before 1919, available on a first-come first-served basis, regardless of income, as long as applicants met the qualifying criteria on age of house and need for repair. As a result, 250,000 owners, mainly among the better-off, had received assistance by 1983–1984, and spending on grants to private owners had risen from £90 million to £911 million in five years, making it the fastest-growing component of housing expenditure, and almost the size of net central government capital spending on housebuilding (U.K. Department of the Environment, 1985). Since the 1983 election, Treasury pressure on this area of spending has been intense, and the government has announced its intention of replacing the grant system with a loan system that targets assistance more toward those with low incomes.

Thus the Tories have been caught in the contradictions of their own policies. Encouraging owner occupation, after the one-time free ride of council house sales, has turned out to be an expensive business. And the social differentiation that they favor in the public sector (reserving council housing for the poor and the old) has limited their ability to reduce the public sector stock further. They now recognize that a substantial rented sector—about one-third of the housing stock—is likely to remain, and most of it will be in the public sector (U.K. Treasury, 1985).

## Some Conclusions and Lessons

Britain has gone further than most capitalist countries in intervening directly in the housing market. Virtually a century of struggle over housing as a political issue has firmly established the idea that the provision of decent housing is a right for which the state must take major responsibility. Even among Conservatives, there is acceptance of state responsibility for helping with housing costs for the poor, and indeed acceptance of state responsibility for the homeless.[9]

It is also clear from the British experience that the main help for the poor and badly housed came from direct state provision. Legal regulation of private rental housing in Britain was politically acceptable because it was part of a broader strategy of state provision. Security from eviction insulated tenants from the immediate consequences of private market pressures, but could not in itself provide better-quality dwellings.

What can also be seen from the British experience is that when the public housing sector reaches a certain size, it begins to mirror the class structure of the wider society. The methods used in allocating public housing seem to have led to a situation where the poorest and neediest households are occupying the least desirable units. This is clearly illustrated by the workings of the Homeless Persons Act. Homeless families have a desperate need for accommodation, and generally they will take any unit offered to them by the local housing authority. Units become vacant, however, because people want to transfer to other, more desirable dwellings. So vacancy rates in public housing are highest in the least desirable project, which then fills up with "homeless families," who often have many other social problems.

Moreover, the sale of public sector dwellings is reducing the degree of social differentiation in public housing by "creaming off" the best 10 to 20 percent of housing units, the more desirable ones that people want to transfer to, thus clogging the transfer system by which people in the public sector could improve their housing chances within the sector.

But if the social composition of public housing is increasingly dominated by the poor and non-wage earners, concern is also now focusing on how the public sector has excluded certain kinds of households. Public housing does not cater to the poor, nonfamily households that traditionally lived in private rental housing. With the decline of this sector, many young people now find themselves prematurely forced into owner occupation; among developed countries, Britain now has the highest rate of homeownership in the under-35 age group (*Building Society Association Bulletin*, April 1985).

Thus there are tensions in attempting to implement a public sector policy of decommodifying housing in a mixed economy with a predominantly private housing market. Those with housing needs are likely to want to enter public housing, and are likely to be at the desperate end of the scale, unable to insist on any better standards of public housing. Those wanting to leave their present housing stand to gain from being in the private sector. This suggests that (1) the definition of housing need must be as wide as possible in the public sector if its social composition is to remain mixed; and (2) the inequitable arrangements of indirect government subsidy that apply to the owner-occupied sector through the tax system need to be rethought. No postwar government, in either the United States or the United Kingdom, has dared to challenge mortgage tax relief for owner-occupiers, despite the fact that such tax relief is far more generous to the better-off. In the British context, as long as an increasing proportion of households, especially non-family households, feel they can get housed only by becoming owner-occupiers (because they are not eligible for public housing), the prospects for ending mortgage tax relief are remote.

The idea of expanding public housing provision to include the nonpoor and the not-so-needy may seem remote to those in the United States who are struggling to preserve the existing, far smaller public housing supply and subsidy levels. But the political collapse of support for the expansion of public housing in Britain is not unconnected with its increasingly narrow social base. For the same reason, it is apparent that making rent dependent on income (Housing Benefit) has had the same effect: It stigmatizes state housing as being just for the poor and narrows its social base even more. However, so comprehensive an entitlement program as Housing Benefit was feasible in Britain in the first place only because most of the poor were in public housing where the state directly controls rent levels, and hence total costs were at least manageable. In contrast, rent levels in some parts of the private sector are difficult to control despite legal curbs; hence the program could become an open-ended subsidy to landlords. The state can also control its costs in the long run more effectively if it does so directly, and thus direct public provision has the advantage of efficiency. (In Britain, for example, with the National Health Service, total health expenditure as a percentage of GNP is less than half what it is in the United States.) Particularly in regard to housing, where most costs are capital costs, in the long term the state, by owning directly, reaps the benefits of historic costs.

In the British experience, however, not enough attention was paid to the supply side of providing public housing, and this largely caused the financial difficulties of the 1970s. As happened in the 1920s, housing construction costs rose faster than the general rate of inflation. Neither the public nor the private building sector in Britain has been able to solve the problem of low productivity in the building industry, which has become even more acute in Britain given the need for contractors increasingly to concentrate on repair and improvement rather than new construction. And there is no doubt that the inability to tackle the problem of high and rising land costs also has reduced the possibilities of public sector expansion, especially in big cities.

The private rental sector is under pressure in the United States as well, although it has not declined as fast in numbers or quality as it has in Britain. The British experience suggests that, rather than try to stanch the flow of disinvestment in private renting, a more radical program of selective take-over is required. Smaller administrative units than municipalities may be more effective in managing and rehabilitating this kind of housing. Rent control in Britain can be seen as a way of managing the decline of the private rental sector so as to protect those in it from the failure of market forces to insure them a decent home. British housing policy has not prevented the owner-occupied private market from becoming dominant, with increasing problems of access for new arrivals and the accumulation of greater wealth for those who were already well-off. But it has enshrined in institutional terms the principle that provision of housing can be based on need as well as profit. The reality of a functioning public sector of the size that exists in Britain cannot be eliminated easily. In a time of retreat, that in itself is an important asset.

The central dilemma of British housing policy outlined at the beginning of this chapter has not been resolved. Some in the present government would like to roll back the language of housing rights and entitlements altogether, seeing it as part of the process of inflated claims on the state's resources that cannot possibly be met. But the degree of public support for the principle of state intervention for those in genuine need has limited the government's freedom of action in this as in other parts of the British welfare state. At the same time, the existence of a large public sector has provided a means of making available needed resources that have cushioned the impact of the cuts in programs. So the day of reckoning, when real choices between principles and resources must be faced, has been postponed. But the longer the postponement, with its concomitant reduction in publicly provided housing, the more expensive will be the ultimate cost of living up to the ideals that are enshrined in the British welfare state.

# Notes

1. Under the Homeless Persons Act, local housing authorities have an obligation to "secure that accommodation was available" only for households in priority need. These households are defined in the act as families with dependent children (under age 16 or under age 19 if in full-time education), those over retirement age, pregnant women, and those vulnerable because of serious physical or mental illness or disability.

2. No modern account of the interwar years exists, although the author is currently completing a history of Labour party housing policy under John Wheatley. The best account is still Bowley, 1945. For the growth of owner occupation, see Ball, 1983; Boddy, 1980; Merritt, 1980.

3. The decline of the private landlord in Britain as both an economic and a political force has been going on for a very long time and has its roots in the nineteenth century, although the consequences of the decline became clear only in the interwar years (1919–1939). Among the reasons for the decline of private landlords in comparison with their strength in the United States was that their political power at the local level counted for less because policy in the United Kingdom is much more made at the national level (there is no state level of government in the United Kingdom, and cities are creatures of Parliament); moreover, their economic position was undermined in the 1920s by the emergence of national capital markets—the building societies, operating throughout the United Kingdom (unlike savings and loans in the United States) that represented an attractive investment for middle-class property owners. So the vested interest in property as a tax shelter never developed in Britain, nor (under the British constitution) did landlords have resort to the courts to claim that their rights were being undermined by rent control. But in the longer view, two developments were clear by the early twentieth century: (1) Private landlordism was not very viable economically as a method of providing decent housing for the majority of the population, and was likely to become less so as demand for better standards of housing increased; and (2) the political economy was becoming more attuned to "corporate" solutions, where the state intervened on behalf of larger industrial and financial interests, and traditional small private traders (e.g., landlords) counted for less. For two illuminating studies of this (probably European-wide) phenomenon, see Maier, 1980; Offer, 1982.

4. The Conservative housing minister, Neville Chamberlain, argued that just as when the health inspector seizes meat declared unfit for human consumption, the butcher does not get compensation (because it has no salable value), so housing in such bad condition as to be unfit for human habitation (by the same public health inspector) has no salable value, only a site value. When the public health inspectors were empowered to declare whole areas unfit, rather than individual houses, slum clearance got under way on a large scale.

5. Studies made in the 1960s (notably Cullingworth, 1961; Nevitt, 1966) showed that a private landlord could make more by selling his property to an owner-occupier than by continuing to rent, and that this was likely to be true even if rent control was abolished, due to the favorable tax position of the owner-occupier vis-à-vis the private landlord (there is no accelerated depreciation in the United Kingdom). So the larger, more commercial landlords were tending to sell off their properties, and the landlords who remained in the sector tended to be "mom and pop" elderly owners of one or two properties who were not aware of the economic realities of their situation. The larger commercial landlords did retain a fair amount of flats until the 1970s because building societies would not give mortgages on such units until that time (unlike the situation in the United States, the majority of the private rented sector was single-family, rather than multifamily units); but flat "break-up" and conversion of larger properties into small flats for sale into owner occupation has accelerated in the last decade as more young households begin living separately in their first home as owner-occupiers.

6. For a comprehensive overview of the pre-1980 Housing Act situation, see Cutting, 1979.

7. Under English case law, a nonexclusive occupation agreement—where no one person has exclusive use of any part of the premises (e.g., when two people share a Pullman sleeper carriage)—can apply to residential premises and does not create a tenancy but merely a license to occupy. If it did create a tenancy, then the provisions of the rent acts (e.g., security of tenure) would apply. In the last 20 years, courts have found it

increasingly difficult to draw the line between genuine licenses and sham agreements designed to evade the rent acts, and a series of judgments in the mid-1970s seemed to allow landlords the freedom to issue license agreements for what otherwise would seem ordinary tenancies. But the most recent House of Lords judgment has reversed this.

8.  Voter surveys done in the 1979 election showed that the largest swing away from Labour and to the Conservatives was among the young and among council tenants who wanted to buy their homes. This was widely interpreted by both political parties as evidence of the failure of Labour's housing policy to appeal to these groups.

9.  To explain why U.K. Conservatives accept state responsibility more than U.S. conservatives do is an essay in itself. Perhaps one could point to the role of the state in the United Kingdom as always being more than that of the laissez-faire "night watchman," and the British Conservative party as always containing a large section ("one Nation" conservatives, such as Disraeli, who opposed the ravages of liberal laissez-faire capitalism) that believes in paternalistic help for the less fortunate (see Blake, 1985). One could also ask why the United States stands out as a country where the prevailing political ideology has always been against state intervention, perhaps because the state was formed at a time when political liberalism and economic individualism seemed most closely linked. This of course is also the subject of fierce debate; the starting point might be Hartz, 1956.

# 31

# Swedish Housing in the Postwar Period: Some Lessons for American Housing Policy

*Richard P. Appelbaum*

*Sweden, with a mixed socialist–capitalist economy, has probably gone further than any country in the world in insuring that all its residents are decently housed. It is virtually a slumless society; housing-quality standards are very high; an impressive array of planned, high-density new suburban communities has been developed; and housing costs are subsidized as needed so as to be in the range of all income groups. Sweden's approach has combined a range of nonmarket (nonprofit) alternatives with extensive regulation of investment, development, and management in the private housing market. Housing production goals and plans, land-use planning, extensive public financing, and reinvigoration of local housing authorities were the basic tools. A long tradition of democratically controlled cooperative housing has been a central element, employing national-level financing at attractive terms and technical assistance to local tenant-owner associations created by the national cooperative organization. Recently, however, as in England, the gains achieved over the past two decades appear to be threatened by a move toward greater privatization and homeownership, as opposed to public and cooperative tenure forms, as Swedes reach a certain level of affluence. Nonetheless, as the United States faces increasingly severe housing affordability problems and as the private sector remains unable to deliver satisfactory, moderately priced housing for lower-income Americans, the approaches and programs that Sweden has used so successfully may provide useful models here.*

In the mid-1960s both the United States and Sweden made public commitments to assure adequate housing. In 1965, amid much fanfare, Sweden embarked on its 10-year program. The United States began 3 years later, in the 1968 Housing Act, which set a 10-year production goal of 26 million units. The rates of new construction envisioned were unprecedented in Western countries. Annual construction rates of 10 to 13 units per 1,000 people were to increase the housing stock in each country by over one-third.

The United States, lacking any real means to implement its goals, fell short by 8.4 million units of the projected 26 million, or about one-third (U.S. Bureau of the Census, 1984f, table 1328). The majority of units finally constructed were destined for middle- and upper-income households. Low-income targets—2.6 million in total—were achieved in only one year, 1976.

Sweden, by way of contrast, surpassed its 10-year target, constructing more than 1 million units for its 8 million inhabitants during the period from 1965 to 1974. This represented an average annual increase of 20 percent to 25 percent over previous construction rates (Nesslein, 1982, 241). With housing defined as a public right, construction was directed toward the publicly owned and cooperative sectors. In 1970, for example, 43 percent of all construction was undertaken by nonprofit municipal housing companies, with an additional 16 percent done by cooperatives. Owner-occupied houses accounted for 28 percent of the total, with private rental housing amounting to only 13 percent. A complex system of subsidies and housing allowances assured that no person need spend more than 20 percent of his or her income on housing. By the mid-1970s it appeared that supply had been brought into balance with demand and that Sweden had achieved its goal of providing adequate and affordable shelter to its population.

The following pages examine the means by which the "Swedish miracle" was achieved. Sweden's approach is of particular interest to the United States in that national policy sought to develop nonmarket alternatives alongside traditional (albeit highly regulated) ones. Swedish policymakers expected that such alternatives would, over time, prove more attractive than owner-occupied houses and private rentals. These alternative housing forms were to be achieved by means of inducements or "steering mechanisms" that redirected private investment toward nonprofit forms of tenure. As we shall see, these mechanisms included interest subsidies, land-use planning, and controls on prices and rents—all within the context of a vastly expanded public commitment to the housing sector.

Yet the Swedish zeal for a "middle way" has not been without its problems. In attempting to socialize housing within a market economy Sweden was able to achieve a great many of its objectives; but difficulties have not been far beneath the surface. In particular, the economic and ideological appeals of homeownership have continued to remain strong as the Swedish population has become increasingly middle class. As a result, some of the gains achieved over the past two decades now appear to be threatened, although no one in Swedish public life seriously questions the overall approach that has proven so successful.

Despite its shortcomings, a compromise approach such as Sweden's has direct relevance to the political reality in the United States today. As larger numbers of Americans become marginalized by the marketplace, the promise of security and affordability through nonmarket alternatives should prove increasingly attractive. In the final section of this chapter I offer some suggestions for American housing policy that draw on the Swedish approach, learning from both its successes and its failures. This is not to suggest that Sweden's housing programs can simply be grafted on to American politics; only that we can benefit from the Swedish experience.

# The Third Stream: Nonmarket Alternatives

By the time that a nonsocialist governing coalition interrupted 44 years of unbroken rule by the Social Democrats in 1976, Sweden had achieved phenomenal success in its housing policy. The roots of the present-day programs originated immediately after World War II when the Social Democrats began to think of housing in terms of what came to be referred to as the "socialist market."[1] By the end of World War II, partly as a consequence of rapid urbanization, the people of Sweden were among the most poorly housed in Europe, particularly in the rapidly growing metropolitan areas of Gothenburg, Malmo, and Stockholm. Thirty-eight percent of the 2.1 million dwellings were owner occupied, with most of the rest involving various forms of tenancy—mainly private rentals (35 percent) or rentals based on employer–employee relationships (10 percent). Only 2 percent were rentals in public housing, and 5 percent were cooperatives (Lundqvist, 1981, 1).[2] It was in this context that the Social Democrats sought to encourage the provision of nonmarket housing, and at the same time to "re-educate" the public to the virtues of more communal tenure forms in contrast to the privatizing tendencies of the conventional suburban home.

In 1945 the Royal Commission on Housing and Redevelopment, which had been in existence since 1933, issued a report calling for a comprehensive national housing policy. Under the commission's program, all risks were to be socialized; speculation would be eliminated. The program became the guidepost for three decades of Swedish housing policy. Its objectives are summarized as follows:

1. To eliminate the housing shortage by means of a Fifteen-Year Programme (1946–1960). The output of new housing was to be stabilized at a level that would be sufficient to meet the increase in the number of households and also meet the need for improving housing standards and urban redevelopment.

2. To raise space standards by increasing the production of dwellings containing at least two or three rooms and a kitchen. The use of one-room flats as family housing was condemned.

3. To raise equipment standards in new housing and to improve older dwellings. Standards for rural housing were to be brought up to the same level as for urban housing.

4. To keep down rent levels, partly through government action, so that spacious, modern, family dwellings would be within reach of average wage earners. It was considered that an average industrial worker should pay no more than 20 percent of his wage for a fully modern flat consisting of two rooms and kitchen.

5. To encourage public financing of housebuilding.

6. To invigorate local authorities in their housing activities.

7. To discourage speculative building by offering favorable loan terms to individuals, housing associations and local authorities. (Headey, 1978, 74)[3]

Before examining in some detail exactly how these objectives were to be achieved, it may be useful to comment briefly on the political context of Swedish housing policy.[4] The "organizing of Swedish society" (Headey, 1978, 60) into politically active interest groups was largely completed during the decade following World War II. These groups, which can be classified as supporting either the Social Democrats or the bourgeois parties (as they are called in Sweden), play a central role in Swedish politics. On controversial issues they are represented on the Royal Commissions, which generate national policy as well as build consensus. Interest groups are thus consulted frequently and formally, and in exchange they play important roles in eventual policy implementation.

In the housing sphere, those groups generally supporting the Social Democrats' programs include the construction, trade, and white-collar unions; the League of Municipalities; the large cooperative associations; the National Association of Swedish Public Housing Enterprises (SABO); and the National Tenants' Union. The "pro-bourgeois" interest groups include the university graduate and higher civil servants unions; farmers' organizations; employers and industrialists federations; private builders; landlord and homeowner associations; and the banks. The very success of the Social Democrats' housing program has served to build the strength and membership of those groups that supported it. General public opinion, at least until very recently, has also strongly favored the Social Democrats' approach: before they became relatively affluent, most Swedes supported programs that promised cheaper public and cooperative housing, housing allowances, and other forms of subsidy (Headey, 1978, 64).

The stage was set for the present approach at the beginning of World War II when housing construction all but ceased. In the face of rapid urbanization, public demand soon outstripped supply in the larger cities. In response to the perceived failure of the private market, the Social Democratic government became heavily involved in housing production, subsidizing over 90 percent of wartime construction from 1942 to 1945. Building targets were met each year (Headey, 1978, 72). The increased state intervention clearly favored nonprofit builders and working-class consumers at the expense of developers, private investors, landlords, and potential homeowners. It was made possible partly because of the national consensus generated by the war, but also because of the Social Democrats' decisive electoral victory in 1941, when they obtained a clear majority for the first time since winning power in 1932. When the war ended, the Social Democrats could therefore point to past successes, relying on the administrative legacy of greatly enhanced wartime planning. It is against this backdrop that the vision of the 1945 Royal Commission must be assessed.

The Social Democrats by no means had free rein to promote a thoroughgoing socialist housing program. Although they were to hold office continuously from 1932 until 1976, during most of this 44-year period they were forced into coalition governments. (Legislative majorities were held only from 1941 to 1951 and from 1967 to 1973.) As Headey (1978, 59) summarizes the Social Democrats' position, "retention of power hinges on 5 percent of voters and seats, so that public opinion and the parties and interest groups which represent centrist opinion have to be carefully cultivated. Compromise is a political necessity not just a national characteristic." At the same time, the importance of almost half a century of Social Democratic governance should not be underestimated: The party became strong and disciplined, both nationally and locally (where it held power as well), while administrators and bureaucrats could be reasonably confident that the government's housing programs were relatively permanent.

## Cooperative Housing in Sweden

The cooperative movement was Sweden's first major alternative to private rental housing, with its origins preceding the Social Democratic government by about two decades. [5] The principal cooperative organization—the National Association of Tenants' Savings and Building Societies (HSB)—was founded in 1923–1924 on the initiative of the National Tenants' Union, at a time when wages were falling and rents rising.[6] HSB developed a two-tier structure—a regional savings society, which also provided technical assistance, and local tenant–owner associations, which the national organization aggressively sought to create. By offering depositors who eventually purchased coop units preferential interest rates, HSB was able to raise substantial amounts of capital to increase greatly the amount of cooperative construction under its sponsorship. The association was (and is) run democratically, with elected boards based in the local projects. HSB thus combined building and savings, cooperative ownership, and mutual assistance. It grew rapidly during the 1930s, becoming a nationwide movement. As its capital base grew, HSB was able to acquire suppliers' firms and manufacturing facilities, and to engage in bulk purchases. At the present time, HSB estimates its total membership at almost 350,000.[7]

A second cooperative association, Svenska Riksbyggen, was founded in the 1940s, at a time when 40 percent of the members of the building trades were out of work. Riksbyggen's membership base was in the trade unions, and it was originally intended to revitalize the home construction industry by building public housing units as well as cooperatives. Smaller than HSB, it currently manages some 180,000 dwelling units. Together HSB and Riksbyggen account for two-thirds of all cooperatives and approximately 1 of every 10 dwelling units in Sweden (Lundevall, 1976, 38).

The cooperative movement in Sweden was highly self-conscious about its goals, seeking no less than the transformation of housing tenure in the country. It sought to provide quality housing at prices that working people could afford, removing housing from the inflationary effects of the marketplace. The cooperative form of tenure itself—a hybrid between tenancy and private ownership—was appealing in that it promised security while presumably discouraging "privatization." Until 1969, resale controls prevented units from being resold at market prices, thereby guaranteeing price stability as well. It was anticipated that once cooperatives had acquired a significant segment of the market, private rents would be forced down in competition.

## Public Utility Housing

While cooperatives were therefore a part of the socialist vision of housing as a "social right, rather than a private good,"[8] the cooperative movement came to occupy the conservative position within the Social Democratic approach to housing. The more radical position, favored by the socialists, was to deny private ownership forms altogether, in the form of a greatly expanded "public utility housing" sector. Under this approach, private landlords would eventually be displaced by more public forms of ownership. This was to be achieved through the massive construction of flats by nonprofit municipal housing companies, financed by the central government and facilitated by significantly enhanced local empowerment. [*See Chapter 30 by Steve Schifferes for discussion of a parallel development in England.*]

The Housing Provision and Building Acts of 1947 allocated to the municipalities responsibility for solving the housing shortage, along with the right to decide how all land within the municipal boundaries was to be used (Svensson, 1976, 5–13). This "planning monopoly" made possible extensive land banking, long-range planning, and the construction of public housing units on municipally owned land. Municipalities were given the rights of expropriation and first refusal on land, and later (in 1973) were given the right to expropriate existing rental housing that failed to comply with building standards (Jussil, 1975, 176–77).[9] The national government viewed its role as providing enabling legislation and financing; the localities had the responsibility for planning and construction.

By 1980 there were some 250 municipal housing corporations throughout Sweden, and they had produced two-thirds of all rental construction during the previous decade. One-quarter of all dwelling units were owned by these companies—amounting to half of all rentals. Within the cities, close to three-quarters of all new housing construction occurred on municipally owned lands. Tenancy in public housing extended well into the middle class; indeed, an objective of the massive public housing construction that occurred from 1965 to 1974 was to "de-class" this form of tenure. As with the cooperative movement, the long-term strategy underlying public housing was to increase the market share to the point where public housing became price leading. Since such units were provided on a nonprofit basis, this in turn would make housing generally available at lower prices (Lundqvist, 1981, 1).

Thus, Swedish postwar housing policy, particularly from 1965 to 1974, sought through heavy governmental subsidy and strong local planning to "steer" new construction away from the private sector and toward the public rentals and quasi-private cooperative ownership preferred by the Social Democrats (Jussil, 1975). By 1980, 25 percent of all housing units were

owned by municipal housing companies, and 15 percent were in cooperatives. At the same time, the share of private rentals had declined to only 20
percent of the market, with owner-occupied homes making up the balance,
or about 40 percent (SI, 1980, 2–3).

Table 31.1 summarizes recent trends for the multifamily housing stock.[10]
One can see that almost two-thirds of all units built in 1945 were private
rentals, while approximately one-fourth were in cooperatives and 1 out of 11
in public enterprises. Cooperative housing construction peaked in 1960 at 38
percent and subsequently has fluctuated around postwar levels. Private
enterprise construction had declined to only 12 percent by 1979, while public
enterprise construction increased to 68 percent in 1975 and declined somewhat thereafter. As a consequence, the multifamily housing stock went from
80 percent private rentals in 1945 to 38 percent in 1975. Cooperatives at that
time accounted for almost a fourth of the multifamily housing stock.

## The "Swedish Miracle"

The accomplishments of the Social Democrats in achieving their housing
objectives from 1965 to 1974 were substantial by any standards. By allocating an annual average of 6.7 percent of GNP to housing,[11] a total of 1,005,600
units were constructed (Headey, 1978, 48). The 10-year program witnessed
the following:

1. *The large-scale construction of housing of a quality unimaginable two
decades earlier.* In 1945 only 21 percent of all dwelling units in Sweden had a
bath or shower, 36 percent had an inside toilet, and 46 percent had central
heating. These figures had improved only marginally by 1955. By 1974,
however, fully 93 percent of all households enjoyed central heating, shower
or bath, inside toilet, refrigerator, stove, and other modern amenities
(Headey, 1978, 50–51). Slum areas have been eliminated, although one
study estimates that "some 8,000 people have no decent home" (Wiktorin,
1982, 248).[12] While historically Swedish housing had been small and
crowded by American standards, this situation had also improved considerably by the 1970s, with a shift in construction to larger two- and three-
bedroom units.

Most significantly, working-class people enjoyed these amenities to the
same extent as those in the middle class. In 1974, for example, 97 percent of
salary earners lived in "modern" dwellings with a full range of amenities; the
figure for wage earners was 92 percent (Headey, 1978, 51–52). In fact, one of
the principal achievements of Swedish housing policy was to provide for all
Swedes the housing opportunities available in most countries only to the
middle class. Headey has summarized this accomplishment:

> In most countries—as in Sweden in the past—lower-income groups are con-
> strained to live as tenants of either private landlords or public authorities in

relatively poor, rundown neighborhoods. In modern Sweden, by contrast, working-class people, like middle-class people, have an effective choice of living in cooperative as well as tenant housing and also of being owner-occupiers. . . . The significance of this extension of opportunity should not be minimized. In most countries working-class people are not able to choose whether to live in town, close to work and entertainment, or to join the green wave living in simulated countryside. The Swedish worker is relatively fortu-nate in being able to house his family according to preference rather than according to the tyranny of what economists, accustomed to analyzing "free" rather than socialized markets, term "effective demand." (Headey, 1978, 50, 52–53)

There is some evidence that the lowest-income people are not as well housed as middle- and working-class Swedes. Immigrants, for example, are more likely to live in overcrowded conditions: One study in 1976 found that one-quarter of Finnish workers and almost one-half of immigrants from southern Europe were living two or more to a room (excluding kitchens and living rooms). The same study concludes, however, that "people with unsatisfactory housing conditions . . . [are] very marginal in proportion to the whole population," tending to be low income and low status, but otherwise heterogeneous in terms of ethnicity, household size, and social record (Wiktorin, 1982, 248–50).

2. *The creation of planned suburban communities.* For ideological as well as economic reasons, a great deal of housing construction consisted of large apartment complexes, particularly in the major metropolitan suburbs. In the Stockholm area, for example, close to four out of every five people lived in apartments by 1970 (Daun, 1979, 1); nationwide, the figure is currently almost half.

TABLE 31.1

MULTIFAMILY HOUSING IN SWEDEN: NEWLY COMPLETED UNITS
AND EXISTING STOCK, BY OWNERSHIP TYPE, 1945–1979
(percentages)

| | NEWLY COMPLETED UNITS | | | | | | EXISTING STOCK[a] | | | | |
|---|---|---|---|---|---|---|---|---|---|---|---|
| | 1945 | 1960 | 1965 | 1970 | 1975 | 1979 | 1945 | 1960 | 1965 | 1970 | 1975 |
| Private enterprises | 65 | 21 | 20 | 19 | 12 | 12 | 80 | 55 | 49 | 41 | 38 |
| Housing cooperatives | 26 | 38 | 27 | 22 | 20 | 27 | 11 | 22 | 24 | 24 | 24 |
| Municipal and public utility enterprises | 9 | 41 | 53 | 59 | 68 | 61 | 9 | 23 | 27 | 34 | 38 |
| Total | 100 | 100 | 100 | 100 | 100 | 100 | 100 | 100 | 100 | 100 | 100 |

*Source:* SR, 1980, 4, 6.
[a] 1979 percentages not available.

Suburban housing, particularly public housing projects built during the late 1950s and early 1960s, was often characterized by the alienating high-rise functionalist architecture often associated with Swedish public housing. Yet much recent construction has been in row houses and small flats in well-planned suburban communities built around service and commercial centers and integrated with highly efficient mass-transit systems. The visitor to the Swedish suburbs is struck by their "new towns" atmosphere—cluster development, large amounts of open space, children's play areas, centrally located shops, and a range of amenities seldom found in their U.S. counterparts.[13]

3. *The elimination of private landlords as a significant force in the determination of rents.* When the postwar system of rent control was lifted in Sweden in 1975[14] with the decontrolling of 350,000 private rental units in the larger urban areas (Nesslein, 1982, 237), the groundwork had already been laid for the operation of the "socialist market" in rent setting. A series of national laws, beginning with the Rent Act of 1968, established key safeguards for tenants, including mandatory collective bargaining between tenants' and landlords' organizations. Every year, representatives of the large nonprofit municipal housing companies negotiate rent levels with representatives of the National Tenants' Union. Under law, public sector rents then serve as guidelines for rents in the private sector. Rents are determined on the basis of "utilization value" only—equal rent for dwellings of equal quality.

Under rent control, rents reflected initial production expenses (with adjustments for rising costs); "utilization value" rent setting is designed to insure that newer, more costly units in a locality are not priced above older units of comparable quality (Nesslein, 1982, 237). Under this "fair rent structure," neither location nor capital costs are supposed to influence rents; only the size of a unit, its amenities, and its overall maintenance level are to be considered. This has resulted in a system that "leads to rent agreements that are independent of the property owner's actual costs" (Ronmark, 1981, 11). In practice this means that the large public and private rental companies must practice "rent pooling," whereby rents in their newer, high-cost units are subsidized by rents in older, lower-cost ones.[15]

Because of these "fair rent" provisions in Swedish housing laws, tenants are protected against large rent increases, a major source of involuntary displacement. Tenants enjoy other protections as well, particularly safeguards against arbitrary eviction. Swedish law also protects against eviction through "luxury renewal"—the upgrading of property so that it becomes too expensive for its present tenants. It is, in fact, very difficult for landlords to evict tenants who pay their rent on time. Disputes over lease conditions and violations, as well as rent levels, are handled by local rent tribunals, and, on appeal, by the National Housing Court. Landlords who fail to maintain their units adequately are subject to stringent controls. Under the 1973 Housing Renewal Act, local rent tribunals can force landlords to bring their units up to acceptable standards. The 1977 Housing Management Act

empowers the rent tribunals temporarily to suspend landlords from management duties until necessary repairs have been done; in extreme cases, the
right of landlords to mortgage their property can be suspended for up to five
years (Lundqvist, 1981, 26).

4. *The creation of a system of housing allowances, reaching almost 40
percent of all households* (Nesslein, 1982, 236), *that guarantees that no
household need pay an excessive percentage of its income on housing.* [*See
Chapter 21 by Chester Hartman for U.S. comparison.*] Allowances are based
on income, number of children, age, and housing expenditure. They extend
to households in all three forms of tenure, reaching 26 percent of homeowners, 33 percent of cooperative owner–tenants, and 42 percent of tenants in
public and private rental housing (Lundqvist, 1981, 20).[16] Support levels
were at one time pegged at one-fifth of household income, although the
inflation of recent years has made such a goal increasingly remote. Although
as recently as 1974 families with children spent an estimated 16 percent of
their income on rents, there is evidence that the figure for all households
may now be considerably higher, possibly approaching 25 percent.[17] For all
households receiving allowances, approximately one-third of housing expenditures are covered (Lundqvist, 1981, 20). For a typical working-class
family paying roughly one-quarter of its income for rent (approximately
$200 per month), allowances would cover 54 percent of rent payments (SI,
1980, 3). Unlike the American Section 8 program, housing supports thus
extend well into the middle class, so recipients are not stigmatized.

5. *Municipal land banking of almost all remaining developable land in the
major urban areas.* Public lands are then used for the construction of public
nonprofit housing units, leased to developers, or sold outright under stringent controls, with the consequence that three-quarters of all construction
done in the municipalities (excluding urban renewal) has been done on
municipal holdings (Heimburger, 1976, 31). Furthermore, under the so-
called land condition, state loan subsidies for the construction of rental units
are made only for projects built on land obtained from municipalities
(Svensson, 1976, 31–32). Since, as we shall see, such subsidies are in fact
sizable, this affords the localities further leverage over speculation and land
use generally.

Swedish municipalities, along with responsibility for assuring the provision of adequate housing, have been granted extremely strong land-use
planning powers in order to do so. National legislation empowers localities
to set construction, design, and equipment standards for all housing, regulating its type, location, and timing (Nesslein, 1982, 238). Under the
"planning monopoly," all development must reflect annual and rolling
five-year municipal plans. As noted, localities have rights of expropriation
and first refusal (Jussil, 1975, 176; Svensson, 1976, 14–32), with compensation laws designed to discourage speculation. They are also in a position to
get land-procurement loans and leasehold loans on highly favorable terms
(Jussil, 1975; SI, 1980, 3).

6. *The elimination of shelter poverty.* In Sweden, where the average

blue-collar worker earns $12,000 a year, an unsubsidized four-bedroom unit rents for about $245 a month (all utilities included). A comparable cooperative costs $40 less (estimated from Lundqvist, 1981, tables 5 and 6; SR, 1980, 8). According to Headey:

> There is now a housing surplus rather than a shortage and almost everybody lives in a good quality dwelling in a pleasant neighborhood. The government could reasonably claim that it had achieved its stated aim that "the whole population should be provided with sound, spacious, well planned and appropriately equipped dwellings of good quality at reasonable costs." (Headey, 1978, 86)

Nonetheless, new problems have emerged, and housing controversies are as fierce as ever in Sweden. Before examining some of these difficulties, let us look first at the mechanisms by which the Swedish government has "steered" housing investment in the direction dictated by the "socialist market."

## Steering Mechanisms

The Swedish government has used two principal means to achieve its housing objectives: legislation empowering localities to solve their own housing problems, and the financial mechanisms necessary to do so. I have mentioned some of the former: the "planning monopoly" and "land condition," rights of preemption and expropriation, and strong powers of code enforcement that at the same time prevent "luxury renewal." There are also provisions in the tax code to discourage speculation. Since 1968, the capital gains tax has been strengthened, with a rate of 75 percent for short-term gains, net of a small deductible (see Svensson, 1976, 28–29). The chief financial mechanisms have included housing allowances, loans to municipalities for land banking, and a system of interest subsidies designed to promote more public forms of ownership. Interest subsidies, in fact, constitute the main "steering mechanisms" by which the Swedish government is able to direct the marketplace toward socially desired objectives.

The financing of construction is based on large government subsidies to private borrowers (see Lundqvist, 1981, 17). Seventy percent of the total cost of land and development is financed through long-term (40-year) private "primary loans" at slightly below market rates.[18] A variable part of the remaining 30 percent is financed by "state housing loans"—the portion being larger for preferred forms of tenure. Thus, nonprofit municipal public housing corporations receive the entire 30 percent in state loans; cooperatives receive 29 percent; owner-occupied houses, 25 percent; and private rentals, 22 percent. This in effect means that no monies need be advanced for the construction of public housing, while cooperatives require only 1 percent of the total cost, detached homes 5 percent, and private rentals 8 percent.

This preferred investment hierarchy is reinforced by a parallel system of loan subsidies. New housing in Sweden has a "guaranteed mortgage interest rate" on the entire loan, set initially at extremely low levels, with government subsidies covering all interest payments in excess of the guaranteed rate. For cooperatives and rental units the guaranteed rate in 1981 was 3 percent for the first year of the loan, rising at 0.25 percent per year thereafter until reaching the market rate. For owner-occupied homes, the initial rate was 5.5 percent, rising considerably more steeply at 0.5 percent per year. Together, these financial mechanisms have worked well historically to discourage the production of single-family homes vis-à-vis other forms of tenure,[19] and to encourage the production of public rentals instead of private ones.

The "steering effects" of interest subsidies were originally to be secured by a tax system that neutralized any economic bias in favor of single-family housing. While homeowners in Sweden were allowed to deduct the unsubsidized portion of interest paid on mortgage loans from taxable income as if it were a business expense,[20] such an expense was to be set against the hypothetical income that would result from actually renting out the property— income which was then taxed at 2 percent (Headey, 1978, 86–87).[21] When nonsubsidized interest rates were also at 2 percent, taxes more or less offset the interest deductions (Headey, 1978, 87; Lundqvist, 1981, 21), and homeowners received no tax benefit by virtue of their tenure. [*See Chapter 15 by Cushing Dolbeare for U.S. comparison.*] As we see below, this is no longer the case.

## Some Recent Problems

By the mid 1970s, Sweden had pronounced its housing problems essentially solved. With the completion of the "one million" program, supply had in theory been brought into balance with demand. The minimum standard of two bedrooms for a four-person family was widely achieved. Speculation had largely disappeared because of a "balanced" market, the removal of most developable urban land from the marketplace, and the replacement of market rental pricing by a system of rent negotiations. The termination of the postwar system of rent controls as unnecessary in a "balanced market" was a direct result of these achievements.

The past five years, however, have revealed some fundamental problems.[22] Increasingly, affluent Swedes have begun to demand (and receive) detached suburban homes, despite more than 40 years of socialist "education" promoting the virtues of public housing and cooperatives. Whereas surveys in the 1950s indicated that only 30–40 percent of the population preferred to live in detached homes, the figure is now 80–90 percent (Daun, 1979, 2, 6). Today, 72 percent of all newly constructed units are single-family homes, a dramatic reversal from 10 years ago (see Table 31.2). Only one-fifth of all units are in public rentals. Vacancy rates in high-rises,

TABLE 31.2
NEW HOUSING PRODUCTION IN SWEDEN BY TYPE OF HOUSING, 1970–1979
(percentages)

| Housing Type | 1970 | 1975 | 1979 |
|---|---|---|---|
| Single-family (1–2 units) | 32 | 63 | 72 |
| Multifamily (3+ units) | 68 | 37 | 28 |
|  | (100) | (100) | (100) |

*Source:* SR, 1980, 5.

especially in suburban areas, rose in the early 1970s, although in some areas shortages are again being felt.[23] In some projects, middle-class Swedish tenants have been replaced by immigrant workers, who now number one-eighth of the total population. Segregation is regarded as a potentially serious problem.

## The Recommodification of Swedish Housing?

The highly successful cooperative sector has come increasingly to resemble ordinary homeownership. Coop members now have virtually total control over the use and resale of their units. This control was greatly reinforced with the removal of resale price controls on cooperative units in 1969. Before that time, Swedish law conferred control over equity appreciation on the directing boards of the major cooperative organizations, who generally limited price increases to the initial down payment, augmented for any improvements plus some compensation for the rate of inflation. In 1969, however, HSB dropped its resale price controls. A variety of reasons were given: the existence of a black market for coop units in the face of housing shortages, the difficulty of enforcement, and the unfair advantage conferred on owners of private homes.[24] The political climate in general was one of harsh criticism of the Social Democratic housing programs on the part of the nonsocialist media and parties, reinforced by housing shortages in the major urban areas (Headey, 1978, 83–86). The Social Democrats received their lowest popular vote since 1932 in the municipal election campaign of 1966 (42.2 percent). Decontrol of rents and coop unit prices were part of the general restructuring of the government's housing policies that followed.

Currently, coop members are free to sell their shares on the open market. There are pressures to make legal what already exists in fact—private ownership of cooperative units, or the condominium form of ownership.[25] As a result of these developments, there are strong pressures to convert rental units to cooperatives, especially in Stockholm, where a housing shortage is again being felt. While such conversions are at present a marginal problem in Sweden, where they do occur they are highly profitable, both because (as in this country) the combined value of coop units greatly exceeds the value of the building as a rental, and because under Swedish financing, cooperatives qualify for favorable terms on government rehabilitation loans.[26] Conversions, which tend to be favored by private landlords and tenants who benefit by acquiring their unit, are strongly opposed by the National Tenants' Union and the National Association of Swedish Public Housing Enterprises (SABO), which view conversion as a retreat from the "socialist market" and a threat to their political power base.[27] They fear that the most desirable rental housing will be sold off, lost to the inflationary market stream. Because of "rent-pooling," rents in all the remaining apartments could go up if the units converted were the older, less costly ones (Lundqvist, 1981, 28). The central cities, where much of the desirable rental housing is located, would then become gentrified, with resulting displacement and economic segregation. Tenants in the remaining rental housing would be left with the stigma that attaches to public housing in the United States.

The major cooperative associations have taken somewhat differing positions on the conversion issue. Although HSB stands to benefit from the management contracts it would gain, it has close historical ties with the National Tenants' Union and therefore has shown no interest in converting public housing to cooperatives. Riksbyggen, closely affiliated with organized labor, favors conversions, but under new cooperative forms that would end speculation. Under its spring 1981 "housing rights" program, for example, vacated units would be resold to the association, which would then sell it to another member. This would be equivalent to reestablishing equity controls on cooperative shares. Another Riksbyggen program (the "Stockholm Model") envisions the formation of cooperative tenant–management association boards in public housing, which would subcontract managerial responsibility from the companies (who would be represented on the boards). This would produce a "quasi-conversion," one that realizes the goal of cooperative management while leaving the unit legally in the public domain.

The nonsocialist governing coalition of 1976–1982 favored a return to market allocations in housing. A 1981 governmental committee, for example, charged with responsibility for developing legal options for condominium ownership, recommended "making possible a quite considerable change from tenancy to cooperatives," involving the conversion of as much as 40 percent of public rentals (cited in Lundqvist, 1981, 28). Needless to say, this would represent a dramatic reversal of close to four decades of Swedish housing policy. With the return of the socialists to power in September 1982, however, there are again pressures from the top for a return to the original ideals of the cooperative movement, in the form of resale restrictions such as those envisioned in Riksbyggen's "housing rights" program. It is highly unlikely that the Social Democrats will permit significant amounts of cooperative conversion as long as they remain in power.

The reasons for these recent trends away from the ideals of the "socialist market" are many and widely debated. They have partly to do with the very success of the Social Democrats in producing an affluent middle-class society that views homeownership with increasing favor. In the rental sector, the reasons also reflect dissatisfaction with bureaucracy and inflexibility in public housing management, where enormous municipal companies are seen as unresponsive to the needs of tenants. The once-radical tenants' movement is now a mass organization of some 600,000 tenants that functions primarily to negotiate rental agreements among tens of thousands of units.

## Some "Qualitative" Issues

These difficulties are widely acknowledged, and some tentative steps have been taken to confront what are referred to as the "qualitative" issues of Swedish housing (Headey, 1978, 93). Foremost among them are changes in the management of public rental units that would give tenants a considerably greater role to play (Lundqvist, 1981, 29–35). These changes range from slightly expanded managerial responsibility to codetermination, or joint tenant–management decision-making. Experiments with the latter have begun in public housing corporations outside of Stockholm (Nackahem) and Gothenburg (Alebyggen), where tenant committees help determine the budget for maintenance and are able to rebate savings to residents.

A somewhat more far-reaching approach, "selective tenancy," was launched by SABO in May 1981. Under this concept, the large, citywide corporations set up minicompanies in each housing complex, and tenants have access to the full budgeting process. Tenants are then able to choose how to spend the money allocated to their complex, setting, for example, higher or lower standards of service (with corresponding increases or decreases in rents). A major purpose of these programs is to promote the ideal of economic democracy among tenants, decentralizing at least one aspect— management—of tenant–landlord relations.[28] At present they are limited in scope, voluntary for the housing companies, and, according to Swedish tenant leaders, have not yet sparked the imagination of most tenants.

Other "qualitative" issues include equipping dwellings with services to benefit families in which both parents work and adapting dwellings to the special requirements of singles, divorcees, and old people living alone (Headey, 1978, 94).[29] Finally, a large part of recent Swedish research on housing has focused on the issue of energy efficiency. This is vital both because of Sweden's long and harsh winter climate, and because of the escalating costs of imported energy.[30]

## Preferences for Private Ownership

The principal problem, as viewed by the Social Democrats, remains the move toward more private forms of ownership. This is attributed to several factors. There is unquestionably an increased preference for owner-occupied housing, particularly in the suburbs. Although the demand for apartments remains strong in the larger cities, the high-rise public housing flats in the suburbs often combine the geographic and social isolation of suburban living with all the disadvantages of small apartments (Kemeny, 1978, 318). The costs of apartment living are also high relative to other forms of tenure. Because of the Swedish system of "rent pooling," rents on older units (with lower financing costs) are the same as rents on new units of comparable quality; as we have seen, the former subsidize the latter. Given the relative newness of the Swedish public housing stock, the high costs of recent construction have served to raise average costs, although the costs on newer units have been somewhat lowered. It will be some time before rent averaging brings overall costs down (Kemeny, 1978, 318).

These disadvantages of rental housing are reinforced by tax laws that increasingly work to the advantage of homeowners. Of the three forms of housing, owner occupancy is in theory the most expensive, once maintenance, heating, and utilities are taken into account. One study, for example, estimated that in 1978 an average homeowner spent $255 per month, compared with $245 for tenants and $205 for cooperatives (Lundqvist, 1981, 15). When the homeowner's tax deductions were taken into account, however, the cost of homeowning dropped to $195, the least expensive of the three forms. The study concluded that an "average homeowner could get almost one-fourth of his total housing expenditure covered by the increase in disposable income caused by the right to deduct his deficits on housing from his taxable income" (Lundqvist, 1981, 22). As Swedes have become increasingly affluent, even the middle class now confronts high marginal tax brackets. Homeowners' interest deductions are thus extremely attractive.

With the recent rise in housing costs and interest rates, homeowners' tax deductions have become the most rapidly growing form of government housing expenditure. In 1975, tax deductions for owner-occupants amounted to 33 percent of all governmental subsidies for the existing housing stock; by 1978 the figure had grown to 42 percent (Table 31.3). One

TABLE 31.3
GOVERNMENT SUBSIDIES TO EXISTING HOUSING STOCK IN SWEDEN, 1975–1978

| Form of Subsidy | MILLIONS OF DOLLARS[a] | | | | PERCENTAGES | | | |
|---|---|---|---|---|---|---|---|---|
|  | 1975 | 1976 | 1977 | 1978 | 1975 | 1976 | 1977 | 1978 |
| Housing allowances | 720 | 900 | 960 | 1,060 | 44.5 | 44.1 | 38.7 | 36.8 |
| Mortgage interest subsidies | 360 | 440 | 560 | 620 | 22.2 | 21.6 | 22.6 | 21.5 |
| Tax deductions for owner-occupants | 540 | 700 | 960 | 1,200 | 33.3 | 34.3 | 38.7 | 41.7 |
| Total | 1,620 | 2,040 | 2,480 | 2,880 | 100.0 | 100.0 | 100.0 | 100.0 |

*Source:* Lundqvist, 1981, table 7.
[a] Estimated at 5 Swedish kroner to the dollar.

recent estimate has found expenditures on tax deductions to be as high as 53 percent of the current housing total (IUT, 1982, 1–2). During the three-year period, tax expenditures relative to homeownership grew more than twice as fast as those on housing allowances and interest subsidies combined—122 percent versus 55 percent. This has placed a severe strain on Swedish fiscal resources.

While the nonsocialist government had encouraged these trends, the new socialist coalition remains committed to the old vision of "equal cost for equal quality," regardless of tenure. Sverker Gustavsson, director of the National Swedish Institute for Building Research, in June 1981 outlined to me a three-part approach he believed the Social Democrats would implement, were they to return to power.[31] First would be a systematic across-the-board attempt to eliminate what crowding remains, thereby addressing one of the chief objections to much of the public housing built during the 1960s. Second, there would be greater tenant participation in management, building on the tentative experiments at present under way. Finally, he foresaw a restructuring of the subsidy program, with the goal that no household should pay more than one-fifth of its income on housing. This could involve shifting subsidies away from housing allowances toward construction loan supports, so that housing would actually cost no more than one-fifth of income, without as great a need for (potentially stigmatizing) housing allowances.

How the Social Democrats will afford such a program is another matter. It is highly unlikely that the costly but popular tax breaks for homeownership will be abolished, for example. More likely will be the extension of comparable benefits to tenants, effectively reducing rents. While this would restore equity between the two tenures, it would also be extremely expensive. The Social Democrats' margin of victory in September 1982, while small, was decisive: The socialists received 45.6 percent of the popular vote and 166 seats (out of 349) in Parliament, compared with 45.1 percent and 163 seats for the three other parties combined.[32] The new government is confronted with an international economic recession, enormous public expenditures (two-thirds of GNP), and large budget deficits. The Swedish economy, like that of most other Western nations, has been stagnant, with declining investment and output. Rising import costs have led to sizable balance-of-payments deficits, with the resulting need to borrow abroad at high interest rates. Unemployment is close to 4 percent—high by Swedish standards. It is within this context that the Social Democrats confront the difficult task of resolving Sweden's present housing problems.

## Sweden and the United States: Some Lessons

The provision of housing in the United States represents a tremendous misallocation of this nation's finite resources. In 1981 sales of new and existing homes totaled $227.9 billion (National Association of Home Builders, 1982b; National Association of Realtors, 1982, 33). To pay this bill,

Americans went deeply into debt. The average housebuyer in 1981 required an income of $39,000 and spent over $800 per month (Christian and Parliment, 1982, 3). Yet, despite this vast expenditure, only 705,400 new homes were produced in 1981, a postwar low (National Association of Home Builders, 1982b). The largest part of sales expenditures—81 percent—went to trade existing homes at greatly inflated prices (National Association of Home Builders, 1982b).

If present demographic trends continue, the United States will need 2 million new housing units a year over the next decade just to keep pace with population changes. Only about half that many were built in 1983 (National Association of Home Builders, 1982b). With the average price of an existing single-family home surpassing $80,000 in 1983, compared with $23,400 in 1970 (National Association of Realtors, 1982), almost the only people who can afford to buy a house are those who already own one. A recent study by the U.S. League of Savings Associations notes that first-time housebuyers made up 36.0 percent of all purchasers in 1977, but only 13.5 percent in 1981 (Christian and Parliment, 1982, 4).

According to the 1980 Census of Housing, 37.2 percent of American households—26.6 percent of homeowners and 52.9 percent of renters—in 1980 paid more than one-quarter of their income for housing; 11.4 percent paid more than half. The poor, who are least able to cut corners on other items, suffer most. Among those who made less than $10,000 a year, 73.6 percent spent more than one-quarter of their income for shelter. Thirty-five percent of low-income Americans spent over half their income. These conditions have most certainly worsened from 1980 to 1984. They are a testament to the failure of liberal social policy.

For those most in need, the government has until now interceded with two main programs: public housing and Section 8 rent supplements. Fearing competition from public housing (which it claimed was the opening wedge of socialism), the real estate industry actively sabotaged the public housing program from the beginning, pressuring Congress to limit it to the very poor [*see Chapter 20 by Rachel G. Bratt*]. And by constructing buildings that are all too often aesthetically unappealing, the industry insured that "government housing" would carry the stigma of poverty, thus discouraging middle-class people from demanding such housing for themselves. Today, only 1.3 million American households (1.9 percent) live in public housing—one of the lowest percentages of any industrialized nation. Rent subsidies, which came in response to the 1960s ghetto riots, have never been sufficient to accommodate more than a small fraction of those who qualify. The current Section 8 program serves only an additional 1.8 million households (Dolbeare, 1983b, 7). Despite growing waiting lists for both programs, the Reagan administration has made cutbacks that will dramatically reduce their scope and effectiveness [*see Chapter 21 by Chester Hartman*]. The level of authorization requested by President Reagan for 1984 low-income housing programs was only 1.9 percent of the level provided in 1980 (Dolbeare, 1983b, 2). The United States spent only $8.5 billion on housing payments of all sorts in 1984, involving fewer than 4 million units, and reaching no more than one-fourth of all eligible households (Dolbeare, 1983b, 5, 7).

The report of the President's Commission on Housing, which calls for "free and deregulated markets" in place of government intervention, signals the abandonment of even this minimal public commitment to house the poor. The government's largest housing subsidy, homeowner deductions for mortgage interest payments, is in no danger of falling to the Reagan ax. This subsidy cost the government $34 billion in lost revenues in 1983 (Dolbeare, 1983b, 16), far more than all low-income housing programs combined, and more than the entire annual budget of the Department of Housing and Urban Development.[33] These benefits are extremely regressive; about 30 percent of them go to taxpayers with incomes over $50,000, who make up less than 5 percent of the population. The large majority of homeowners benefit only minimally from such deductions; 60 percent do not claim them at all (U.S. Congress, Congressional Budget Office, 1981).

The building industry in the United States already fears that as housing conditions worsen, pressures to regard housing as a public utility—as in Sweden—will prove attractive to politicians and planners. I believe they are correct. The marketplace has been unable to provide adequate shelter for all, and will prove increasingly incapable of doing so. The Swedish successes in housing began with the tenants' and cooperative movements in the 1920s and received a major boost with the commitments made by the government immediately after World War II. We are beginning to see the stirrings of such a movement here. I believe that the time is ripe for a comprehensive national housing program that would reflect the experiences of Sweden and other countries that have regarded housing as a human right. Such a program would commit the government to taking bold steps in order to guarantee that the needs of housing consumers are met. It would entail three broad components, complementing rather than replacing the private housing industry. Those who choose to rely on private housebuilders or landlords could continue to do so. But for the growing number of Americans who are ill served by the marketplace, there must be an alternative that attacks our wasteful housing system at its source: high interest rates, speculation, and inequitable tax policies.

The components may be summarized as follows:

• To end speculation and help assure long-term affordability, a third stream of nonprofit housing must be developed, alongside private homes and private rentals. This stream would consist of equity-controlled cooperatives and community-owned public housing. To reduce construction costs, financing should be made available to localities to permit the banking and holding of land for future development, insulating it from speculation. Both forms of housing should be administered democratically so as to provide residents with maximum opportunity to make decisions that affect their housing—decisions concerning maintenance, ongoing costs, and selection of other residents.

• The financing of housing production must be overhauled so as to reduce production costs and curb speculation. A principal objective of financing should be to direct investment toward third-stream forms of tenure. Such financing might take the form of deep interest subsidies, as in Sweden, or selective credit controls, where private lenders subsidize targeted housing by charging higher interest rates on other loans. In either case, subsidies must be linked to the production of housing that is removed from the speculation of the marketplace for the life of the housing.

• Finally, tax policy should be revised to steer investment productively. The use of such tax shelters as accelerated depreciation to encourage investment must be replaced with other inducements that do not at the same time result in speculation. Similarly, the regressive homeowner deduction should be replaced with a system of tax credits for both renters and homeowners, subject to a ceiling to insure against overconsumption and tax sheltering.

A thorough examination of Swedish (and other) housing programs suggests the strengths of these approaches and the pitfalls to be avoided. While an American housing policy cannot blindly adopt features of programs that have worked elsewhere, it does not have to begin with a blank slate either. We have seen how these ideas have fared in Sweden. Many have been tried in a limited way in the United States as well. It is time to begin a serious consideration of alternatives to the "free market" in our housing policy.

At a time when the federal government is busy dismantling the few progressive housing programs that exist in this country, how realistic is it to call for a greatly expanded public and nonprofit housing sector? We have seen how even in Sweden, with over four decades of experience with the "socialist market" in housing, there are still countervailing pressures to restore "free" market conditions, although the basic public commitment has never been seriously questioned. Sweden is a small, culturally homogeneous country with a tradition of cooperativism that can be traced back a millennium or more. In the United States, such conditions hardly prevail. Rather, one finds a deeply rooted populist antagonism against "big government" and "big business" that is being cynically exploited to benefit business at the expense of basic social welfare.

Yet despite current conditions—or perhaps because of them—I believe that the time is right to put forth a progressive housing program. These proposals simply assure what has long come to be regarded as a fundamental American right: a secure place to live. They envision a decentralization of housing delivery, with the federal government limited to setting standards and providing funds. They call for the creation of nonmarket alternatives for those who need them; the rest of the system is left intact, although I believe it will serve a decreasing number of households. Most important, these proposals are not radical; they are interim efforts based on tested American and Western European models. They may seem bold today, but that is precisely the reason to put them on the national agenda: Tomorrow they will be familiar.

# Notes

1. In Headey's (1978) terms, "'socialist' because it was intended to operate in accordance with governmentally imposed policy objectives and priorities, 'market' because competition among builders providing different types of housing (multifamily apartment blocks, single-family houses, etc.) for different types of owner and tenant was not wholly abolished" (p. 44).

2. Ten percent were characterized as "other," probably involving some form of tenancy (Lundqvist, 1981, 1).

3. Headey bases his summary on Greve, 1971, 63.

4. The following discussion is based on Headey, 1978, 57–97.

5. Another alternative—what is termed "self-help" construction in the United States (in Sweden it is called "small house building")—originated during the same period. It involves do-it-yourself construction on a cooperative and nonprofit basis, under the direction of a public agency (*Smahusavdelningen*) that arranges for everything except labor. Some 12,000 units were provided in the Stockholm area from 1927 to 1976, targeted at working-class households (Witt-Stromer, 1977). Another form is the "collective" house, dating to 1935 and the architectural school of Sven Markelius. Collective houses are large apartments with common kitchens and public space. This form, once seen as a major solution to the housing problem, has never amounted to more than a small number of units (Vestbro, 1979).

6. Lundevall (1976, 3–4) notes that wages fell 30 percent from 1920 to 1923, while rents rose 20 percent. HSB was not the first cooperative association in Sweden, but its influence in creating a national cooperative movement was decisive.

7. Members pay annual dues to the local organization and, in some cases, are required to deposit funds with the savings association as well. In exchange, they receive a place in the queue for units and the right to "codetermination" in the affairs of the local and national organizations, on the one-person-one-vote principle. Membership is open to anyone who chooses to join. See HSB, 1975, for a detailed discussion of HSB's history and operations, punctuated with numerous photographs and coop design renditions. For a more general collection of articles on the Swedish coop movement, see HPP, 1976.

8. Phrase of Sverker Gustavsson, director of the National Swedish Institute for Building Research, in personal interview, June 1981.

9. Compensation is at market value, although since 1972, in certain cases of rapid land inflation, it corresponds to market value 10 years before the taking, under the theory that the increased value reflects community-initiated improvements and amenities (Heimburger, 1976, 28–29).

10. Single-family housing tends overwhelmingly to be privately owned, although there has been a slight trend toward cooperative and public ownership in this sector as well. In 1976, for example, 94 percent of single-family homes were classified as privately owned, with 5 percent publicly owned and 1 percent in cooperatives. By 1979 the figures were 87 percent, 8 percent, and 5 percent, respectively (HPP, 1980, 13).

11. Investment levels reached a high of 7.4 percent of GNP in 1966–1970 and have averaged 6.8 percent since the early 1950s. The United States has invested approximately 4.6 percent (Headey, 1978, 179; Nesslein, 1982, 239).

12. This study goes on to note that slum "tendencies" remain: "In almost every municipality there exist at least a few badly maintained houses, more or less exclusively occupied by alcoholics, criminals and other social outcasts." Such houses are not geographically concentrated, however (Wiktorin, 1982, 248).

13. For a comparison of Swedish and American suburbs, see Popenoe, 1977.

14. Rent and price controls were enacted in 1942, with rent controls being gradually

phased out in smaller towns and urban areas throughout the postwar period. Rent control remained in effect in the major urban areas until 1975.

15. This is because the age of the unit is not supposed to be a factor in determining rents, apart from differences in quality that might be associated with age. Thus, a new unit with high capital expenses under law must charge the same rent as an old unit with low expenses, providing both are of equal quality. There is, of course, some divergence in practice from this ideal model of fair rent setting, although rents are far less variable in Sweden (when quality is controlled) than in most other countries. One study found that in a random sample of 83 public housing companies, two-thirds charged within 8 percent of the median rent for all units. Nevertheless, the same study found that the age of units continues to play a significant role in determining rents (see Turner, 1981).

16. For families with children, the percentage reached by allowances is quite high. Seventy-eight percent of renters with three or more children, for example, receive allowances (Lundqvist, 1981, 20).

17. Headey (1978, 57) estimated 15.6 percent in 1974, before the general price inflation of recent years. The International Union of Tenants reports that Swedish tenants now pay 27 percent of their income, on the average, although it is not clear whether this figure takes into account government housing allowances (IUT, 1982, 1–2). The cooperative society Riksbyggen provides a similar estimate, noting that poorer families pay higher percentages than wealthier ones; these estimates, however, are based on assumptions about "typical" expenditures rather than actual surveys. The role of housing allowances is unclear in this case as well (SR, 1980, 9).

18. First mortgages are provided by the Urban Mortgage Bank (established 1909); second mortgages by the Sweden Housing Loan Bank (established 1929). These are specially chartered commercial banks with funds guaranteed by the state; their loans are thus risk free (Headey, 1978, 66).

19. Lundqvist (1981, 18) demonstrates that recent (1980–1981) changes in the subsidy system have increased the bias in favor of tenancy and cooperatives.

20. Headey summarizes the origin of this tax expenditure as follows: "Tax relief on mortgage payments dates from the 19th century when Sweden was a rural society in which farmers had both the political weight and a genuine financial need to obtain relief from their debts" (1978, 66).

21. The imputed rent is a percentage of the house's assessed value, determined on a five-year assessment cycle. This system should be contrasted with that in the United States, under which interest and property taxes can also be deducted from income, while there is no requirement to offset imputed rental value against such expenses.

22. For a recent study that attributes all Swedish housing successes to postwar affluence and all the problems to "serious resource misallocation" and "housing market disequilibrium" resulting from excessive governmental intervention, see Nesslein, 1982. This study suffers, however, from a highly selective interpretation of secondary materials.

23. There were 26,628 vacant units in January 1974, of which almost four-fifths were in public housing (Headey, 1978, 90). In September 1974 the vacancy rate throughout metropolitan Stockholm was 7.2 percent; metropolitan Gothenburg, 10.0 percent; and metropolitan Malmo, 7.8 percent (Nesslein, 1982, 241). Since that time, the surpluses have declined, and vacancy rates are considerably lower (e.g., Stockholm was estimated to have a vacancy rate of only 1.6 percent in 1978; see Nesslein, 1982, 242).

24. Interviews in June 1981 with Rolf Trodin, director of Planning, HSB, and Olle Lindstrom, deputy managing director, Riksbyggen. According to Lindstrom, his studies found that 95 percent of all Riksbyggen sales in the early 1970s followed prices recommended by the coop board. He thus viewed the relaxation of controls as having little effect on prices in most cases, at least where the market was relatively "balanced" between supply and demand.

25. At present one cannot legally own a flat in an apartment building in Sweden.

26. Partly because of this latter reason, and partly for administrative reasons, coop conversions in Sweden attempt to sell a majority of units to existing tenants.

27. The National Tenants' Union has recently criticized conversions as part of the "wild speculation in housing" (Kjellberg and Burns, 1981).

28. The key aspect, of course, remains rent setting, which is achieved through a highly bureaucratized system of tenant–management negotiations that closely resembles organized labor wage negotiations. While the average tenant has a voice in this process, it is a very small one.

29. Facilities for the handicapped have long been a part of Swedish housing policy (see Beckman, 1976).

30. Paradoxically, many Swedish houses are now so energy efficient that the government currently sponsors research to determine the toxicity of different building materials in virtually airtight environments.

31. Personal interview, June 1981.

32. This means that the Social Democrats can govern without the necessity of forming a coalition government with the Swedish Communist Party, which kept 20 seats (with 5.6 percent of the vote). The remaining 3.7 percent of the popular vote went to a small "Christian" party and the new Green Party, neither of which received the 4 percent necessary to gain a seat in Parliament. See Leijonhufvud, 1982.

33. According to Dolbeare (1983b, 14), "The total cost of housing related tax subsidies in 1984 is estimated at over $40 billion." This includes mortgage interest and property-tax deductions, capital gains deferrals and exclusions, and tax-exempt bonds.

# 32

# A Useful Installment of Socialist Work: Housing in Red Vienna in the 1920s

*Peter Marcuse*

*For a brief period after World War I, the socialist-controlled municipal government of Vienna launched an all-out attack on inadequate and unaffordable housing. The approach included many of the components advocated by progressives today: rent control, city-supported cooperatives and self-help initiatives, land banking, and new construction programs. But beyond the quantifiable achievements of Red Vienna's policies was a fundamental concern for fairness and equity in the allocation of housing services. Progressives in the United States today may take inspiration from the fact that Red Vienna's housing program was implemented and "worked" for a brief period in a basically capitalist society.*

> Capitalism cannot be abolished from the Town Hall. Yet it is within the power of great cities to perform useful installments of Socialist work in the midst of a capitalist society. A Socialist majority in a municipality can show what creative force resides in Socialism. (Danneberg, 1931, 3:89)

These are the words of a participant in that effort, in "Red" Vienna after World War I. Robert Danneberg, president of the Vienna City Council, later died in the Nazi concentration camp where he was interned as a Jew and a socialist when Germany occupied Austria in 1938. At the time he wrote these words he pointed out proudly: "Vienna is the only city on earth counting millions of inhabitants that is governed by a socialist majority. . . ."

The widely accepted evaluation of the results of that government is typified by A. J. P. Taylor's summary:

> . . . in the . . . years [after 1922], an ambitious program of working-class housing, health schemes and adult education was carried out, giving "Red Vienna" a unique reputation in Europe. These schemes were financed principally by heavy taxes on property in Vienna, which virtually eliminated private income from house rents. House owners and middle-class tenants thus provided the means by which *the slums of Vienna were abolished.* (*Encyclopaedia Britannica*, 1959, 2:747; emphasis added)

Were the slums of Vienna indeed "abolished" by "useful installments of Socialist work" in this period? What "useful installments" led in this direction? Have they any meaning for us today, in very different times? This chapter addresses these questions.

The story of Viennese housing policy between 1918 and 1934, in the period of Social Democratic control of the city, is discussed here along the lines of the major programs, presented in the historic order in which they developed:

1. Control over the private housing market, including
   a. Rent and eviction controls
   b. Public requisitioning and allocation of private housing
2. Self-help and cooperative activities, including
   a. The squatters' movement and the "wild settlements"
   b. The internal organization of the self-help movement
   c. The cooperative movement and guild socialism
   d. The city's role in assisting these initiatives
3. The municipal construction program, including
   a. Tax and financing policies
   b. New construction of social housing
   c. Public land banking and direct construction

The chapter then attempts an evaluation of the nature of the Viennese accomplishment (and its limitations) and concludes with a section suggesting the factors that determined the nature of the Viennese program in the 1920s and its relevance for the United States today.

# Housing and Politics after World War I

In 1914 Vienna was the prosperous capital of an empire of 55 million people, the seat of the longest-reigning family in all Europe. By 1918 it was the capital of a defeated and impoverished state of 7 million, a rump state that many doubted could survive for long as a separate nation. Not only housing but society as a whole were in crisis in Austria in 1918.

The war had aggravated, but not caused, the housing crisis. A housing shortage had existed long before the beginning of the war and was as much the result of the emergence of capitalism and industrialization as of the war. Accounts of Vienna's housing in 1894 read much like Engels's of Manchester in 1845 or Booth's of London in 1889 or Riis's of New York in 1890 (Philippovich, 1894). Rents were high, quality low, and overcrowding chronic.

The war accentuated the housing crisis and changed its political context entirely. There was, of course, virtually no new housing built in Vienna during the war: 342 units were built in 1917 compared to an average of 13,051 a year in the years before the war (Hardy, 1934, 42). While the population of Vienna shrank slightly during the war, with residents, predominantly men, leaving for army and government service outside the city, the number of households did not diminish appreciably, and other workers came to the capital because of the expanded needs of the war. The absolute number of housing units in fact declined, in significant part because of the conversion of residential units to office use for war- and business-related purposes. By 1918 the vacancy rate was practically zero—the best estimate is that at the beginning of that year only 254 units were empty and available for occupancy in the whole city (only 105 by September 1919), and even these were not fit for occupancy (Hardy, 1934, 46). The resulting overcrowding is hard to imagine: Single-room apartments housed parents, children, grandparents, often married children with their families; frequently, space was let, not only to subtenants, but also to day lodgers.

The end of the war led to an even worse housing shortage. Returning soldiers swelled the ranks of those seeking shelter in the capital, as did refugees from the former provinces of the Austro-Hungarian Empire. Family formation, inhibited during the war, shot up. At the same time, the resources necessary for a significant construction program were depleted. The housing crisis deepened.

The political situation was equally critical. The monarchy ended in October 1918, shortly thereafter to be replaced by the First Republic. The Social Democrats, long a major party (they had 46.2 percent of the vote in Vienna in 1911, although much smaller representation on the primarily advisory representative assembly for the city), were the largest single party after the war. Yet the moderate Social Democrats, detested as they were by most of the old aristocracy, appeared to the Austrian establishment as very much the lesser evil: In Russia, in Hungary, and temporarily in other countries, Communist parties had come to power, threatening the very existence of capitalism, rejecting liberal parliamentary democracy in favor of the dictatorship of the proletariat. In comparison to these revolutionary parties, the reformist Austrian Social Democrats seemed trustworthy allies to the established powers. As Otto Bauer, the undisputed leader of the party through most of the 1920s, wrote, after the event: "Only Social Democrats could pacify the unemployed, direct the *Volkswehr* [the private army made up largely of returned veterans], and restrain the workers from the temptation to embark upon revolutionary enterprises which would have been fatal to the revolution" (Bauer, 1925, 95; cf. Rabinbach, 1983, 20).

That the Social Democrats, despite their commitment in theory to major social change, saw their role in Austria as stabilizing the new (and still clearly nonsocialist) status quo was clear. The local programs of the Social Democrats in Vienna can be understood only in this context.

> . . . The tasks of the new Socialist administrators of Vienna were to aid the national coalition government (which their party colleagues dominated) in avoiding a Communist revolution, to reorganize a practically bankrupt city, and

then to rebuild that city in the literal and the figurative meanings. (Gulick, 1948, 356)

"Rebuilding that city" meant, for the Social Democrats, first and foremost dealing with its housing problems. For the conservatives, by the same token, "the substitution of social policy for social revolution seemed a small price to pay for maintaining the economic and social status quo" (Rabinbach, 1983, 24).

# Rent Control and Requisitioning

## The Setting

The political factors that impelled the Austrian Social Democratic Party to make housing a central concern, even though its ideology had never antici-pated the fact (Marcuse, 1985b) included the pressing self-interest of its own members and natural constituency, the electoral situation, and the direct pressures of the ill housed, expressed through demonstrations and marches. On the economic side, the most decisive immediate factor was the inflation that was rampant throughout Central Europe.

The inflation had two asymmetrical effects on housing. For landlords and property owners, mortgages and other debts were effectively erased; with an inflation rate totaling around 10,000 percent over the four years im-mediately following the war, debts could be paid off with paper having a real value only a minuscule fraction of their prewar amount. Since the mortgages that were thus practically wiped out covered an estimated two-thirds of the value of Vienna housing, property owners in effect found the value of their property tripled by the inflation. For tenants, their real rents, to the extent that they could be held to the levels of 1914, were likewise reduced virtually to zero by the inflation. Inflation thus benefited both landlords and tenants. It buffered the otherwise even sharper level of conflict that the early housing policies of the Vienna City Council produced.

The Social Democrats won control of the Vienna City Council on May 4, 1919. Their first acts dealing with housing were simple and immediate: controlling rents and requisitioning underutilized apartments. They built on measures already implemented under the monarchy in the last year of the war, which had restricted evictions and prohibited "key money" payments, nonresidential conversions, and the holding empty of residential apart-ments.

## Rent Control

The formula by which rents were set broke rent down into four components[1] *[for a discussion of rent control in the United States, see Chapter 22 by John Atlas and Peter Dreier]*:

1. "Basic rent," theoretically the return to the landlord. It was set at 50 percent of the prewar gross rent, not increased for inflation.

2. "Maintenance rent," set at 150 times prewar rent, with conciliation offices in each municipality to permit increases where warranted, auditing or checking rights for tenants, and the power by tenants to compel landlords to carry out necessary maintenance work. In addition, statewide commissions were given power to increase maintenance rents overall based on increases in the cost of building materials and wages in the building trades. The law permitted rent increases on a showing that rents could not cover maintenance for a particular unit; after August 1, 1929, grants were available to tenants whose rents were thus increased beyond the level of affordability.

3. The tenant's proportional share of regular operating costs, such as water and sewage charges, chimney sweeping, garbage fees, and wages of the caretaker.

4. The tenant's proportional share of taxes. (The landlord, however, was paid a "commission" of 10 percent for collecting the Housing Construction Tax from the tenant—see below.)[2]

New construction was not covered by rent control. Nevertheless, very little new private building took place in Vienna through the 1920s. Normal market forces, rather than rent control, probably produced this result; levels of income were simply not high enough to afford the rents required to cover the costs of new construction (Danneberg, 1931, 59).

The system succeeded in keeping rents low. Where rents before the war had taken on the average more than 25 percent of a worker's real income, the comparable figure in 1922 was only 4 percent. In addition, tenants later had to pay the Housing Construction Tax. But their total payment still was less than one-quarter of its prewar level.

The effect the system had on landlords is less clear. On the one hand, the system itself was hardly calculated to return a substantial profit to landlords. The "basic rent," according to Gulick's calculation, ended up at only .0056 percent of the real prewar rent, and this, in the strict terms of the legislation, was to be the sole profit. On the other hand, that rent was net of all expenses. Some income also flowed to landlords via the maintenance component of the rent formula. There is no indication of net cash outflow, nor any record of landlord abandonment. The private market for housing remained active, if depressed; Danneberg (1931) suggests that half of all houses in Vienna changed hands in the decade after the war, sometimes at only one-tenth of their prewar value.

The results of rent control required the Social Democrats to consider further measures. Rent control had certain consequences that had to be dealt with:

• It did not insure adequate maintenance, since no higher profit could be derived from good maintenance than from bad. This may not in fact have been undesirable for tenants. Many may well have preferred to pay a lower rent (employment problems being what they were) for lower-quality accommodations than a higher rent for a better-maintained or improved unit. In any event, there was no assurance that ending controls would result in improved maintenance. Problems of maintenance probably came about as much because of low income levels and unemployment as because of rent control.[3] [*See related point made in Chapter 9 by David Bartelt and Ronald Lawson.*]

• It did not deal with the absolute shortage of housing, the homelessness and overcrowding that was prevalent throughout the city.

• It did not provide any mechanism for the allocation of units among tenants seeking them—the normal processes of the market, allocating among competing bidders according to ability to pay, being in effect suspended by rent control.

The extension of the housing requisitioning system and, later, new construction programs were direct responses to these problems.

## Housing Requisitioning and Allocation

The requisitioning system had two components, one dealing with the supply of units and the other with their allocation to tenants.

On the supply side, the conversion of units from residential to nonresidential use, as well as the merger of units, had been forbidden under the monarchy, and landlords were required to notify housing departments of vacant units. One of the first acts of the federal state council under the republic (proclaimed November 12, 1918; the specific order on requisitioning was adopted November 13) was to extend this legislation: Authorities were empowered to requisition vacant units as well as all surplus space in underutilized units. If a person owned more than one unit, he or she was to notify the authorities of that fact; excess units were subject to requisition. A waiver could be obtained if the owner paid a fine in an amount sufficient to cover the cost of the city's construction of a new apartment.

These powers were used actively, and various loopholes were plugged over the next few years. Requisitioning was extended, by decree of March 31, 1921, to all apartments with three or more rooms where the number of rooms exceeded the number of occupants by more than one. Administration was effective. Out of a total stock of something over 500,000 units, 44,838 dwellings were requisitioned from 1919 through 1925. At the high point of the requisitioning program, 9,385 units in one year were assigned through this process. This is more housing than was built in any single year under the subsequent municipal construction program.

On the demand side, tenants were assigned to units based on need (as was later done in assignment of new publicly built units). The system was elaborate, taking into account household size, tenant health, condition of

existing accommodations, existing crowding, length of residence, number of
children, and other factors. Points were allocated as follows:

| | |
|---|---|
| Austrian citizenship | 1 |
| Domicile in Vienna | 1 |
| Marital status: | |
|     Married less than 1 year | 1 |
|     Married or living together over 1 year | 2 |
| Each child under 14 | 1 |
| Each child over 14 | 2 |
| Residence in Vienna | |
|     Since birth | 4 |
|     Since August 1, 1914 | 3 |
|     For 1 year | 1 |
| Binding eviction notice without fault of tenant | 5 |
| Present unit unfit for occupancy | 5 |
| Disability: 60 percent–99 percent | 1 |
|     100 percent | 5 |
| Pregnancy, over 6 months | 1 |
| Illness made worse by present unit | 1 |
| Subtenancy, other than with parents | 2 |
| Each family member sleeping away from home without a room of his/her own | 2 |
| Overcrowding (2 adults or 1 adult and 2 children under ten in one room) | 1 |
| No kitchen | 1 |
| Applicant main tenant of adequate unit, not overcrowded | − 10 |
| Applicant subtenant of adequate unit, not overcrowded | − 5 |

Over 10 points total was first priority, 5–9 points second priority.

The city also ran a housing-exchange system to encourage housing exchanges among households seeking units of different size in different locations by publishing a newspaper with the relevant advertisements and providing listings and guidance through its local housing offices.

The requisition–allocation system was important not only to achieve substantive equity among those directly affected by it. It also served to inhibit the development of a "black market" in housing. Generally, a system of "key payments," bribes, and kickbacks accompanies a strict rent control system in an environment of housing scarcity. With the requisition–allocation system, a tenant had an alternate way of obtaining housing if a landlord asked for more than he was entitled to; the bargaining power between the parties was thus more nearly equal. The misallocation of units that rent control sometimes causes, with occupants staying in units too big for them because there is no economic incentive for them to move out, was also minimized.

For tenants, therefore, requisitioning corrected some egregious misallocation problems in the housing sector and contributed a surprising amount, but within obvious limits, to the supply of housing available to those in need. For landlords, on the other hand, the return on property was not changed by the requisitioning; both before and after assignment of a tenant, the maximum rent was set in the same manner.

## The Wild Settlements, Self-Help, and the Cooperative Movement

### The Wild Settlements

Requisitioning could add only a limited number of actual units to the available housing supply. The flood of those seeking housing in Vienna after the war—returning soldiers, emigrants from the old provinces, families newly formed, and so forth—far exceeded the number of underutilized units. It was out of the desperation created by the severe absolute shortage of physical shelter that the "wild settlements" were born.

The wild settlements are a fascinating aspect of Viennese housing history. They were part of a spontaneous self-help movement, probably the most widespread example of physical self-help[4] in housing in the twentieth century in an industrialized nation. They began as part of a movement that took over not only empty land but also railroad cars, boats, caves, and virtually any other available empty structure for housing. The "settlers"[5] occupied empty land, generally on the outskirts of the city, on which they built, with their own labor and with what materials were at hand, crude shelter from the elements and, ultimately, houses.

It was actually the need for food, not shelter, that started the train of events that led to the wild settlements. Vienna's green belt, including the Wienerwald, is of course world famous. Here, at the outskirts of town, on empty and overwhelmingly city-owned land, hungry men and women in 1916 simply began growing their own vegetables, without regard to the legal niceties of land ownership. It was only a short step to raising animals (goats and pigs, primarily), and building small stalls for them, as well as shacks for the storage of garden tools. The next step, born of desperation after the end of the war, was perhaps inevitable: Those most acutely in need of housing began using such shacks and expanding them for more permanent use. The combination of squatting on public land and self-help in construction had nothing ideological about it; it was the simple and logical product of dire necessity. [*See comparative material on squatting in the United States in Chapter 25 by Seth Borgos.*] To give an order of magnitude to the movement, in 1919 it was estimated that 14,000 households were occupying land on the outskirts of Vienna, and by 1921 the number was 30,000.

The material resources the squatters needed could not come from pure spontaneity nor individual or friendship-circle self-help, and there was no extant organized movement on which to rely. Further strands were essential to the evolution of the movement:

1. The internal informal organization of the housing settlements themselves, which both developed organically and drew on the experience of the preexisting and at first unrelated cooperative movement.

2. The formal organization of the settlers, in which their naturally evolved informal organizations were linked to, and sometimes merged into, the organization of the cooperative movement proper (making the latter one of the largest and most powerful organizations of residents in the city) connected in many ways to the guild socialist movement, the discussion of which is unfortunately outside the scope of this paper.

3. The involvement of the city of Vienna, in providing the resources, material and technical, to permit the movement to increase the amount and quality of the housing it was capable of producing and managing.

## The Internal Organization of the Cooperatives

Arrangements for the handling of self-help in general reflected the combination of ideological commitment to cooperative efforts and pragmatic recognition of the need to economize on costs. From every household, a minimum of direct labor equivalent to 15 percent of the total estimated cost of construction was demanded [*see Chapter 25 by Seth Borgos, Chapter 26 by Robert Kolodny, and Chapter 27 by Tony Schuman*]. The typical number of hours put in was 1,600, or 30 percent of construction "costs." What work was done depended on the individual's skills. Those who had skills in the construction trades used them both in building their own units and in working for others. Heavy work and light work were divided by physical strength—although the correlation was by no means automatically by sex, since women participated in every phase of construction, and some of the proudest photographs of the period portrayed women mixing cement and building forms for the pouring of concrete. Artists who joined the movement contributed as their share the painting of murals, and the decoration of house facades. But members of the bulk of households had no particular construction skills, and thus most self-help work went into the unskilled portions of site preparation, quarrying stone, acting as helpers to the more skilled. For the unemployed, the contribution of labor was no problem; for the employed, adoption of an eight-hour day in 1919 permitted a schedule of four hours a day at the construction site to be maintained, with eight hours a day on weekends. Settlers' labor was also put into the construction of collective facilities. These facilities were necessary because the developments were located at the outskirts of town, where adequate infrastructure was lacking. But building collective facilities was also ideological, to undergird and support the mutual assistance characteristic of the process. Thus meeting halls, "children's houses," and the like were generally provided.

The relationship between skilled workers and their unions evolved from one with many tensions to a close and cooperative one. At first, the unions saw the self-help movement as a threat. Criticisms were five-fold:

1. The homesteaders were violating the hard-fought-for eight-hour day.
2. The homesteaders were competing with union members and depriving them of work.
3. Property ownership led to political conservatism.
4. The quality of work was poor.
5. So much work on construction left no time for political activity.

It quickly became apparent that the self-help movement was in fact likely to increase, not decrease, the number of jobs available to members of construction unions. Skilled workers formed their own enterprises, and the cooperatives contracted with them for work they could not do themselves. At their high point, such worker enterprises employed 2,200 workers. Union opposition to the movement did not persist.

The ideological content of the movement increased steadily. It was reflected not only in the collective ownership of the housing built (*see below*) but also in the form of organization of the coops. Administration was centralized in elected (but almost always unpaid) directors and managers. The coops collected rents, purchased materials (including those for individual use, purchased centrally for economy), were responsible for most repairs, and set up reserve funds for longer-term maintenance and emergencies. But the coops saw their role as going well beyond providing shelter. They centralized the purchase of insurance, provided educational and health services, set up a museum, began a bank, and provided technical advice on farming and the raising of animals. They tried to inject the cooperative spirit even into such activities as purchasing furniture at wholesale and promoting the rationalization of household functions through the use of built-ins, thus hoping to permit more time for collective activities, particularly for women.

Some of their insistence on a particular vision of the proper life went quite far. Their regulations, for instance, were extensive. They prohibited lodgers (presumably in the interest of controlling density and use) and retained the right to approve subtenants. They regulated the kinds of fences used and the facades of individual houses. And they deliberately built uniformly so as to minimize competitiveness and ostentation, hoping that members would put equivalent pride into collective facilities. Perhaps the most striking regulation (to us today) was the one permitting only "temperance restaurants" in certain settlements.

## Forms of Ownership and Physical Construction

Both the legal and physical forms of housing produced by the self-help and cooperative efforts were much debated at the time.

The relationship between housing ownership and the cooperative form is complicated. In the history of the cooperative movement in Europe, cooperatives were frequently seen as a means of providing houses to be turned into individually owned homes after their completion. The Social Democrats in Vienna reacted very consciously in a different fashion: They wanted cooperative ownership as a matter of principle. [*See Chapter 31 by Richard P. Appelbaum for a discussion of the long-standing Swedish coop movement.*] The basic philosophic outlook of the cooperative movement, of the guild socialism with which the cooperative movement was identified, and of the Social Democratic Party reinforced the lessons that those engaged in self-help drew from their immediate personal experiences.

A few groups did permit individual home construction and individual ownership. Novy (1981) suggests two sensible criteria to distinguish the progressive cooperatives from earlier or alternate forms: no threshold in resources or skills to join, and no private appropriation of the benefits of cooperative activity. There was within the movement as a whole general agreement that individuals should not have title to the units they occupied,[6] to prevent the development of a new private market in housing that the whole movement, with its evolving guild socialist orientation, was dedicated to avoiding. It was a matter of discussion at first whether title should formally remain in the city (most of the units were built on city-owned land) or be transferred to cooperative associations—and if the latter, to a single comprehensive one or to more neighborhood-sized organizations. The last was the solution preferred by the large majority and was put into effect.

The physical forms of housing developed by the settlers were also a matter of much concern. The individual households who were the first squatters built single-family, free standing houses for themselves, generally on fairly sizable plots (400 square meters, or about 4,300 square feet), since food production was a central activity. For reasons of economy (both in building and land use), attached two-storey units soon became the norm, and lot size was reduced by half (there being less need for individual food production). Lots remained separate, however, in virtually all settlements; each household had its own front and back yard. From the point of view of physical form, the settlements could easily have been assemblies of individually owned houses.

The single-family house (whether detached or attached) was, however, the form most closely allied with individual private ownership, both in the popular mind and in the thinking of theorists. Single-family houses were identified with the *petite bourgeoisie* and conservative small peasants, in the working class and in the Marxist tradition. The typical socialist ideal housing, harking back to the early Utopians, consisted of large buildings occupied by many households together, often with common living, eating, and/or working quarters (Fourier's Phalanstere, for instance, or Owen's New Harmony, or Godin's Familistere). Thus there was a clear, and frequently expressed, hostility to single-family housing in the leadership of the Social Democratic Party, and to some extent within the guild socialist movement as well. This led also to criticism of the settlements and the settlers' movement. They were condemned by some as nostalgic attempts to recapture the benefits of an earlier, preindustrial era, understandable, perhaps, as a reaction against the evils of an alienated capitalist society, but an inherently conservative and politically reactionary manifestation in contemporary Vienna (cf. Novy, 1981, 28).

Women were vitally affected by these decisions as to physical form. Max Winter, an ardent advocate of the small settlements, contended that they were the ideal housing form for women, who would be freed of the necessity of going to work in a factory and could, in the freedom of open vistas and their own house and garden, invest their energies in growing vegetables and raising animals. Otto Bauer, on the other hand, emphasized the dangers of a *petit bourgeois* attachment to small landed property and pointed out the restrictions on the opportunities available to women living in isolated single-family houses. Feminists pointed out that apartments were clearly much easier to maintain and much less labor intensive for women (see discussion and citations in Pirhofer and Sieder, 1982, 360, and fns.63, 64, and 65). [*See also Chapter 13 by Dolores Hayden.*]

The movement away from the housing form of the settlements was fortified by the advent of the city's major municipal building program in 1924, in which the giant *Wohnhöfe* (housing blocks with inner courts) were the predominant form.

## The Assistance of the City Government

The organizing activities aimed at bringing together all those involved in the settlements, the cooperatives, and the guild socialist movement were highly successful. By 1922, various constituent groups claimed 100,000 construction workers, 45,000 settlers, and in the aggregate 1 million individuals as members. Given that the total population of Austria was 7 million, this was a force to be reckoned with. And reckon with it the city administration (and the leadership of the Social Democratic Party) did, as the evolution of the relationship between the settlers' movement and the city shows.

It was not ideological sympathy that first prompted the Social Democrats to provide the assistance of the City of Vienna to the squatters and the self-help movement. On the contrary, both the party leadership and the city administration reacted negatively to the illegal nature of the occupation of public land by the squatters and had to be pressured into assistance. But as the participants in the wild-settlement movement banded together, and as their small and informal organizations grew in strength, sophistication, and militancy, they demanded from the city not only legalization of their settlements—indeed, the city could do little else—but also building materials, supplies, roads, infrastructure and land for expansion. Huge demonstrations in downtown Vienna on September 26, 1920, and April 3, 1921, added strength and support to the movement. The alliance forged between the settlers and the cooperative and guild socialist movements added support to the settlers' program. The Social Democratic Party early saw its interests as best served by associating itself with the settlers, and Social Democratic organization among the settlers was much stronger than that of the Christian Social, the majority party at the national level.

At first, the city helped the independent organs of the settlers' movement; then it acted jointly with them, founding GESIBA, for instance, as a half-cooperative, half city-owned, nonprofit building enterprise in which the cooperatives and the unions participated. In the first year or so, the city bought and provided bricks, lumber, plumbing supplies, windows, and doors to the settlers and their cooperative associations. By 1920 it had taken over or founded firms to produce these items itself—partly forced to do so to bypass the consequence of the virtual producers' strike that was part of the campaign against its rent control policies.

By 1921 the assistance of the city to the self-help efforts of the cooperatives was very substantial. To begin with, the city-owned land on which self-help developments were generally built was provided without cost. Since the city was not retaining title to the projects, it was originally thought appropriate to provide construction financing in the form of loans, rather than grants, and an 85 percent loan–15 percent resident's investment formula was devised to cover the full estimated costs of construction, the loan to be secured by a mortgage. Initially, the remaining 15 percent was expected to be paid in cash. But that requirement was soon dropped (or rephrased so as to label labor contributed as equivalent to money), so there would be no financial barrier for participation. And the loans were soon written off as "irredeemable," the entire building cost thus being provided as a grant.

In the end, settlements that were physically similar to the early cooperatives were built solely by the city and conveyed to cooperative associations on completion, with a "rent" continuing to be charged by the city. This evolution seems to have been largely administrative and not the subject of extensive policy discussion. The approach helped make self-help developments more analogous to other municipally owned housing, where the costs of construction were also written off in their entirety.

# The Municipal Housing Construction Program

The golden age of Viennese social housing was the period from 1924 to 1927. But it did not come easily. Rent control and requisitioning were not enough to deal with the tremendous housing shortage, nor was self-help; new mass construction was required. The private market could not do what was necessary. New construction within the economic reach of ordinary workers, and certainly of the unemployed, was simply not profitable enough for a profit-driven housing industry, and the overall situation was not one in which the filtering process could be counted on to contribute much to low-income housing needs.[7] There was no alternative for an administration with a working-class constituency but to build housing itself. But first, it had to raise the necessary money.

## Tax and Financing Policies

The principles that formed the basis of Social Democratic tax policy might be summarized as follows:

1. Taxation of luxury goods rather than necessities. Thus, high taxes were levied on ownership of race horses, use of domestic servants, automobiles— then clearly a luxury good!—and taxis, brandy, various forms of entertainment,[8] sales at auction, luxury foods, etc.

2. Low or no charges for municipal services that constituted necessities for the majority. "Municipal monopolies" over the provision of gas, water, and transportation had been a mainstay of revenue generation for the imperial government; that explains why such services had been "socialized" during the empire. Charging high fees for such essentials seemed undesirable to the Social Democrats, and they reduced all these fees to virtually nothing. Thus, for many years Vienna had one of the cheapest transportation systems in Europe.

3. A steep progressivity in rates as well as in selection of sources of income to be taxed. Savings account interest, annuities, rental income over 2,000 crowns per year, capital gains, and income from investments were taxed, since the result was inherently likely to be progressive. Within most general taxes, likewise, the rate structure itself was progressive; figures for the housing construction tax are set forth below.

4. Earmarking, so that those paying a tax would know exactly why the tax was being collected, and a stable and predictable source of revenue would be available for the activity being supported.

Given this orientation, the city's approach to raising money for housing was logical. On January 20, 1923, effective the following May 1, it adopted the famous Housing Construction Tax (*Wohnbausteuer*), which was to be the chief means of financing its ambitious construction program over the next 10 years. It was a progressive tax on rents, going from 2 percent on the lowest rent to 37 percent on the highest. The tax was politically easy to implement because inflation coupled with rent control were holding tenants' rents far below their prewar levels. Thus, even including the rent tax, the total amount paid by most tenants was substantially less than what they paid before the war. Landlords' opposition tended to focus much more on the issue of rent control, and the tax was not a substantial source of controversy at the time of its passage.

The Housing Construction Tax was indeed steeply progressive. A few figures make the point:

- The top one-half of 1 percent of the units taxed accounted for 41.6 percent of the revenues generated
- The lowest 86 percent of the units taxed paid only 23.6 percent of the revenues
- The 90 most expensive houses paid as much tax as the 350,000 least expensive.

It was essential to the city's housing program that all capital costs be paid out of current revenues, not by borrowing [*for a similar proposal for the U.S., see Chapter 29 by Chester Hartman and Michael E. Stone*]. The logic behind this approach was simple: Housing construction would be a continuing necessity for the foreseeable future. Financing from borrowing, if continued over a period of years, would lead to an escalating cash outflow even with a constant level of construction and constant prices, simply because the costs each year would reflect debt service on an ever-larger level of debt. Thus taxes would have to be raised each year or the volume of construction would have to be reduced; neither was acceptable. Further, the conventional justification for funding housing construction out of future revenues (borrowing) is that future users would in fact pay for housing as they used it, that is, over a period of years and not all at once. But the Social Democrats in Vienna did not want to have the users pay the costs of construction, now or in the future. Rather, they saw housing as a public facility, to be provided by the community without charge, much like schools or highways. Only current operating costs were to be paid out of rents.[9] The astute political leadership realized that having bonds for past construction outstanding, with an ever-increasing debt service to be met, would create substantial pressures to increase rents to pay off these debts. They did not want to be subject to such pressures, fiscally or politically. Thus the decision to fund municipal activities out of current revenues and the quest for substantial and reliable sources for such revenues.

It speaks of the political acumen and visible logic of the taxing system adopted, and in particular of the Housing Construction Tax, that it became a prominent positive symbol of Vienna's achievement. Political leaders are not often proud of their taxes, and rarely is the name of a tax displayed in bold letters on the outside of the homes it was used to construct; yet the legend *Built with the Proceeds of the Housing Construction Tax of the City of Vienna* appears over the entrances to some of the best-known Viennese landmarks.

The earmarked Housing Construction Tax raised, on the average, about one-quarter of all revenues produced by city taxes. But the city had to add to the housing construction program from general revenues. In most years the earmarked tax in fact was more than matched by contributions from the city's general revenues. The 1930s depression forced the Vienna administration to curtail these additional contributions. It tried to make up the deficit by reforming the Housing Construction Tax to bring in even higher revenues. By 1933, however, new investment in housing was only about 24 percent of what it had been in 1930.

## The Long-Range Program

The long-range program to use the proceeds of the Housing Construction Tax was adopted in September 1923. It called for the construction of 25,000 housing units by the city over the next five years—given the circumstances, a very ambitious program, although only 40 percent of the annual rate of private building before the war. The goal was attained one year ahead of time; in 1927 the Council decided to construct 5,000 additional units that year, and in 1928 it enacted a new four-year program calling for 6,000 units a year. It again exceeded its goal in 1930 and 1931. During the First Republic, the City of Vienna built 80 percent of all new housing built in the city; by 1933, it owned 66,270—11 percent—of the city's 613,436 dwelling units.

But the type of construction, as much as its quantity, singled out the Viennese building program for international attention. Most of the funds went into the construction of large apartment blocks around spacious inner courtyards, the famous *Höfe*.[10] At first, one-third of the units were built in settlements near the outskirts of the city, but the proportion diminished steadily and was only 5 percent by 1932.

*Karl Marx Hof*, the best known of the large developments, was not atypical. It had 1,382 units, was built in an elongated shape (dictated by its site) at the edge of the built-up area of the City of Vienna, and was adjacent to a rail terminal. It was built around two large inner courtyards, which were the heart of the complex. Twenty-five shops were placed around its perimeter (commercial on the outside, community facilities on the inside). Only 18 percent of its lot was covered with structures, so each unit received ample light and air. With few exceptions, the units were sunny, all windows opened on the street or a large courtyard, many apartments had substantial balconies, floors were of hardwood except in kitchen and toilet areas, and storage space within the building was assigned to each unit.[11]

While each individual unit in *Karl Marx Hof* was small, effort was made to make up in community facilities what was missing in individual space—for reasons both of efficiency and social philosophy. Within the courtyard were two kindergartens, a youth center, a library, a dental clinic, a health insurance office with medical facilities, a pharmacy, a post office, two bathhouses, and two laundries with the finest and most modern equipment then available. Within the private units, also, effort was made to conserve space and permit housework to be done efficiently—built-in furniture and functionally laid out kitchens, for instance, were widely recommended as contributing to freeing the housewife of some of her more time-consuming labors.

The architecture was intentionally symbolic of the strength and dignity of the working class for whom it was built and by whom it was occupied. It was intended to be the socialist counterpart to the Baroque palaces of the late Hapsburg era on the Ringstrasse: glorifying the proletariat rather than the aristocracy, building *Volkswohnungspaläste* (people's housing palaces) rather than royal palaces, museums, and monuments.[12]

Planning for housing was long range. In 1923, well before the Soviet Union's first five-year plan, Vienna laid out its expected resources and goals for a five-year period, kept to its plan, and fulfilled it one year early. The predictability of revenues from the earmarked Housing Construction Tax, land banking, and a firm set of priorities contributed to making this possible.

Rents in the new developments were extremely low, set to be roughly equal to rents in private housing as limited by the rent control laws. They amounted to 3.4 percent of income for the average skilled or semi-skilled worker. Special provisions were made for rent reductions in cases of unemployment or illness; security of tenure was virtually complete.

As to management, contemporary accounts are (by current standards) curiously silent. There is no evidence of direct resident participation in management decisions; although there was a high level of resident organization, not only through social clubs but also politically, the management of the developments was apparently left entirely to the city administration. It is quite possible that some of the advantages that might have been provided by progressive physical planning were lost through old-fashioned hierarchical—indeed, patriarchal—management. Pirhofer and Sieder, for instance, recount in some detail the arrangements for use of the central laundry facilities, which indeed lightened the physical burden of washing. But it did not change the distribution of the labor that remained; indeed, the *Herr Waschmeister*—the overseer of the laundry, a man—forbade men or children to enter the laundry, and thus the help a woman might have had under other arrangements was lost to her by administrative action (Pirhofer and Sieder, 1982, 354). The basic sexual division of labor, Pirhofer concludes from his interviews, was not changed in the new municipal housing.

Other features of the planning and construction have drawn criticism, then and now. The architecture was out of step with the modernism of the Bauhaus; the architectural philosophy it expressed was different from that of many politically as well as aesthetically progressive architects in Germany, Sweden, and the Netherlands. Interior space standards were low, certainly in comparison to the United States, but also by some contemporary European standards. Transportation linkages were not always adequate. The new materials then much in vogue—glass, concrete, and steel—were used little, and the level of technology did not rise (in the words of a current commentator) "to the level of an experiment" (Ungers, 1969, p. 2, cited in Mang, 1978), in contrast to much German building of the same period.

A response to aesthetic criticism must be partly a matter of taste, partly a matter of social philosophy; the commitment to collective rather than private amenities clearly has physical and architectural consequences that underlie some of the disagreement on aesthetics. As to planning, the administrators of Vienna's housing programs acknowledged some of the shortcomings but believed that they had done very well in terms of the resources and alternatives at hand. The administrators deliberately eschewed high technology in the huge municipal developments because it was capital intensive and labor saving; Austria had a labor surplus, not a labor shortage, and the Social Democratic Party kept its eyes on the labor effects of its policies at all times. The housing construction program, in fact, did contribute to a reduction of unemployment in Vienna.

## Land and the Building Process

Public land banking was not new in Europe. Even before World War I, Viennese city officials had been slowly purchasing vacant land. Under the Social Democrats, the pace of acquisition quickened considerably. Land was bought quietly, often through fronts. The existence of a comprehensive range of housing programs helped effectuate each component part. Rent control kept prices down, thus avoiding the rampant price escalation that plagued so many other countries. Tax policies helped also: Unbuilt land ripe for development was taxed more heavily than other land, and capital gains on land sales were taxed separately and heavily. The city further had the right, when property was being sold, to step in, in place of the purchaser, and buy at the value stated for tax purposes, in order to prevent tax avoidance through understatement of the purchase price. Planning powers were also occasionally used to influence prices (e.g., downzoning just before beginning negotiations). As a result, the proportion of land owned by the city rose from 19 percent in 1918 to 30 percent by 1929.

In its efforts to hold down the costs of housing construction, the Viennese administration also entered the building materials and construction business in a big way. Largely through the mechanism of GESIBA, the city established its own brickyard; produced its own flooring, doors, and windows; operated a lime kiln, stone quarries, and a sawmill. In the mature phase of the program, the city prepared the building plans, provided all building supplies, and let construction out to private firms strictly on competitive bids. The net result was that the City of Vienna was able to build at substantially lower costs than private construction would have allowed. Perhaps even more important, it was able to prevent the emergence of a powerful private real estate and construction industry with the distorting influence that such interests have had in many other countries. [*See Chapter 5 by Joe R. Feagin, Chapter 6 by Barry Checkoway, and Chapter 7 by Tom Schlesinger and Mark Erlich.*]

## The Political Transformation of the Programs

The Social Democratic government of Vienna fell before the military onslaught of reaction in February 1934; the proud housing developments of the 1920s served briefly, but ineffectively, as fortresses of defense. Their sponsors, and many of their residents, were jailed, some summarily executed, some driven into exile, many surviving only to be persecuted and sent to their end later in the concentration camps of German fascism. The thrust of the city's Social Democratic housing programs could not avoid a similar end.

Two aspects of the conservative handling of socialist housing policies deserve special mention. One is self-help. Self-help was revived as an important feature of national policy but was used in a manner directly opposite to that of the days of the wild settlements. Conservatives in Austria, very like the Nazis in Germany, saw governmental encouragement of self-help as promoting certain conservative objectives: reducing the outlay of governmental funds for workers' housing; encouraging homeownership, with its baggage of rootedness, conservatisim, attachment to the soil; facilitating food production on individual backyard parcels, thus reducing pressure for governmental action; and harnessing energies otherwise not in productive use because of widespread unemployment [*see Chapter 26 by Robert Kolodny and Chapter 27 by Tony Schuman for parallel discussion of the negative aspects of self-help in the United States*]. In addition, self-help made some contribution to relieving the housing shortage, but this was secondary to the political purposes underlying its support. No collective effort or social organization, no common facilities, and no spirit of cooperation or vision of a better way of living were associated with the conservative version of self-help.

Rent control remained a component of conservative, and later fascist, housing policy, but for reasons very different from those of the earlier Social Democratic administration. After an initial and significant round of rent increases, tenant protection was not repealed. The logic was similar to that used in Nazi Germany, where rent control was introduced at the national level by Hitler in 1936. Austria's economic reconstruction, in the service now of entirely different interests, demanded some restraints on landlords. Too-sharp rent increases would cause corresponding pressure for better wages with which to pay the higher rents. But contrary to earlier programs, the right of landlords to a profit was fully acknowledged by the conservatives. And the programs of public housing construction, an integral piece of the comprehensive housing policy of which socialist rent control was a part, were no element of the conservative policy. The content of Red Vienna's housing programs came to an abrupt end in 1934, even if some of their forms survived to serve other purposes.

# Perspective and Evaluation

## Accomplishments

The accomplishments of the Viennese housing programs of the 1920s seem very impressive indeed:

- The city built over 60,000 units of housing in less than 10 years.
- All housing construction was fully paid for out of current revenues.
- Revenues for this purpose were derived primarily from a steeply progressive, productive, and stable tax, levied within the housing system and earmarked solely for housing use.
- Rents both in municipally owned and private housing were kept very low, amounting to less than 5 percent of income for most workers.

• Security of occupancy was given in all accommodations, public and private.
• Social services and community facilities, the infrastructure of neighborhood life, were built into the planning and construction process from the outset and were of a very high quality.
• Special attention was given to the situation of women within the typical working person's family, with efforts made to rationalize housework and provide collective facilities to relieve individual work. [*See Chapter 13 by Dolores Hayden.*]
• Architectural design and planning arrangements were thoughtful and innovative.
• Cooperative, collective, and self-help involvement of residents was pioneering and attracted international interest.

The evaluation of these accomplishments by contemporaries resulted in very high grades for the policies that produced them. Both the Viennese workers and the international housing community—architects, planners, housing theorists, political leaders, sociologists—saw Red Vienna as one of the most promising social phenomena of the time, a harbinger of a better world, with accomplishments in housing a tangible fulfillment of that promise. Building for a new humanity was seen as the essence of what was happening. "With us, a new age arrives" (*Mit uns zieht die neue Zeit*) was the slogan, and the housing developments of Red Vienna were its symbol. Delegations came from all over the world to see what the housers of Vienna had achieved, and world congresses addressed themselves to analyses of how it was done. No one doubted that its housing program would remain one of Viennese social democracy's most enduring memorials.

## Limitations

But there is a puzzle here. Although each of the accomplishments listed above is remarkable, none is unique, none is without its critics, none could not, individually, find its peer or even its superior in other countries. For example, the volume of housing construction was substantial, but it was not more substantial, proportionately, than that of the City of Frankfurt in an even shorter time, and it was substantially less than that of the United States in the same time period. In terms of the percentage of the housing stock built in the years shown, Vienna does not shine:

| Years | United States | Frankfurt | Vienna |
|---|---|---|---|
| 1926–1930 | 18 | 11 | 5 |
| 1924–1933 | 28 | | 11 |
| 1931–1940 | 11 | | |

To interpret these figures, other factors must be taken into account: Austria's lower per capita national income (even today only two-thirds that of the United States); the lower price paid for housing in Austria; the economic difficulties faced by Austria in the 1920s (much more akin to the 1930s than to the 1920s in the United States); the more rapid population growth in the United States, so that improvement in units per household there might show less of a difference than the proportional numbers built. Still, Frankfurt's situation was close to that of Vienna, and its accomplishment looks more impressive. Yet no one at the time, and certainly not the residents of the new developments, doubted that Vienna's achievement was a giant step forward.

Another example of the gap between the general perception and the objective fact: Some critics charged that the municipal developments had units with entirely inadequate interior space, were badly located in terms of transportation, were of inferior design and unimaginative architecture, and were technologically backward in architecture and construction. Responses to these criticisms cited limited resources, differences in taste, and differences in social philosophy (e.g., the preference to provide amenities communally rather than privately). But that the units were small, almost tiny, even by contemporary standards, is hard to deny. In the first municipal building program, adopted in 1923, units of two sizes only were provided: one of 38 square meters (about 414 square feet), the other with 48 square meters (about 520 square feet). With the new building program adopted in 1926, a larger unit, of 57 square meters (about 630 square feet), was also provided, but this was the largest unit available even for the largest families. In the earlier units, the kitchen served also as living room; after 1926, kitchens were made smaller to save steps, as part of the effort to lighten the housework burden. Private bathtubs were not provided; minimum kitchen facilities were only a water faucet and a gas cooking stove (or plate).

This then is the puzzle: Neither the absolute quantity nor the physical quality of housing in Vienna came anywhere close to justifying the near euphoria pervading the citizenry's feelings about its housing accomplishments. That euphoria is all the more remarkable when it is recalled that even in Vienna itself the level of housing construction in the years immediately preceding the war was more than twice as high as the average for the best years of the Social Democratic administration—so even the explanation of comparative improvement does not hold in absolute numbers. Certainly A. J. P. Taylor's comment that "the slums of Vienna were abolished" is an overstatement.

## Evaluation: The Permanent Contribution

The explanation for the puzzle perhaps lies in the fact that we misjudge (and the participants also misjudged) the real nature of the contribution Vienna's housing programs made to the lives of the majority of its residents.

The real contribution of Red Vienna's housing policies lies, I believe, in an aspect of housing policy to which it is difficult to give a name—in part because we are so little used to considering it a "real" aspect of housing. "Fairness" or "equity" are perhaps the closest to general terms for what is referred to here. "Symbolic" might be also be appropriate, except that it suggests appearance rather than reality, and this aspect of housing was a very real part of a real social rearrangement to the benefit of working people in Vienna. "Democratic' might be the best word, if it is clear that substantive democracy, not merely a set of formal procedures, is meant. It was what the city's housing policy *said* to the people of Vienna about their lives, their roles in society, the respect to which they were entitled and the importance of their welfare, their ultimate control over their conditions of life, that made the difference—even if they could not at that particular time provide for themselves the ultimate level of housing they wanted and believed they would eventually obtain.

Several examples illustrate the point. The first is *price*. For the average Viennese worker, the figures given above suggest that rent constituted less than 5 percent of income in 1928. The roughly comparable U.S. figure in 1929 was 26.1 percent.[13] If the quantity and quality of housing available to the average Viennese were substantially lower than that available to his or her U.S. counterpart, the amount paid was far less. The reason seems clear: There was a general shortage, not someone making an undue profit or holding back on supply until a profit could be made. One person's hardship was not another person's gain.

A second example involves the *allocation* of housing. In Vienna, virtually all housing built in the period in question was built publicly, and both this new housing and much of the older housing coming vacant were allocated on a publicly established point system based on conception of need. Low income, to the extent that it was relevant, might well give priority in assignment, since it would generally correspond with housing need. Further, rent control guaranteed that there would be no regressive reshuffling of occupancy in existing housing by income. In the United States in the same period, by contrast, there was no publicly built housing whatsoever. Both in existing and in newly built housing, the ability to pay—income and wealth—determined occupancy patterns; the best-off received the best housing, the worst-off got the worst. It might be expected that the social democratic system of Vienna in the 1920s would strike those affected by it as vastly fairer than the U.S. system at the corresponding time, even if statistically the U.S. system provided physically superior housing.

The *collective* features of Viennese housing policy provide another example of its equitable–democratic character. Community facilities—including libraries, schools, health centers, meeting halls, recreation spaces—were provided as part of a comprehensive and long-range housing program whose stated goal was to help achieve a good and fruitful life for all people. Such facilities could be taken as an indicator of the overall goals of society, of government, an indicator of the value attached to each individual regardless of birth or wealth—and perhaps particularly of the value attached to working people.

Nor were these aspects of housing granted by the state as the result of top–down action. Vienna's housing policies were fought for from the bottom, in election campaigns, in street demonstrations, in organizations, and in every aspect of daily life—sometimes even against the city government's immediate wishes. The workers who lived in Vienna's proud new projects felt, with reason, that these projects belonged to them. They were built by them, fought for by them, and defended by them with the limited means at their command when the attack came in 1934. Vienna's housing policies were part of a political and social program that constituted a whole, not a product of technical sophistication or benevolent government.

The improvement of housing as part of the total social and political—in the broadest sense of the word—life of the individual is thus perhaps the real achievement of social democratic housing policy in Vienna in the 1920s. It was not only the physical improvement of the private dwelling but also (even more?) the political control over its shape and its use, and the consequent improvement in the quality of residential life in terms of the price paid for it, the distribution of its benefits, the control of its direction, the provision of the neighborhood facilities and services necessary for its enjoyment, the collective and community-building nature of that enjoyment. These factors were what made Viennese housing policy the great achievement its participants saw it as being.

There were still limitations, even when seen in these terms. The policies of rent control, construction of large developments, and the allocation of private rented housing on the basis of need had nothing to offer home-owners—whether rich, middle-class, or poor—and there were many poor homeowners in the countryside around Vienna. This limitation had serious political consequences; if the Social Democratic Party could be labeled the "tenants' party of Vienna," this was both a strength and a weakness. Homeowners were fertile targets for recruitment by the forces opposed to democracy in Austria. To what extent a different housing policy might have retarded this development is an open question; it was not tried.

The impact on women of Vienna's housing policies is as yet too little explored, but some indications are that it was quite different from the impact on the average man. The very recent discussion by Pirhofer and Sieder on this issue is provocative. Relying largely on interviews of women who lived in the municipal developments in the 1920s, they conclude that the *petit bourgeois* family was reinforced through the city's housing policies: The father's patriarchal role was continued, women were less often employed outside the house (because child care by the extended family was seldom possible), the day-to-day management (e.g., of the collective laundries) remained in the hands of men, with conventional sexist results. It may well be that the contribution of municipal housing was in direct proportion to the nonhousing-based social, economic, and political position of the individual, with politically active men being at one end of the spectrum and isolated women with small children at the other end.

To complete the list of the results of Viennese housing policies, we would have to add the following as shortcomings:

- Substantial limitations in physical quantity and quality existed in the municipal construction program.
- Homeowners obtained no direct benefits from housing policies.
- Women were less positively affected than men; major changes in the structure of family life were not accomplished.

We would also have to add, as further accomplishments:

- Equity and fairness in the housing system as a whole—in allocation, rent levels, security of tenure, and taxation—were accepted by virtually the entire population.
- Housing contributed to a sense of dignity and the democratic nature of the society as a whole for workers and poor people, reversing the previous pattern of housing as a badge of inferior political, social, and economic status.

## Lessons from Vienna

Two major lessons may be drawn from the Viennese housing experience of the 1920s. The first has to do with the substance of housing policy, and is the conclusion of the evaluation just presented.

The successes of the Social Democratic housing policies in Vienna in the 1920s lay as much in their social as in their physical character, as much in the totality of the approach they represented as in the individual components. Tax policy, planning, architecture, construction, administration, control of the private market, collective and cooperative facilities and organization, housing-based political and social organization—all played important roles. Housing was not seen as purely shelter but as part of an overall reconstruction of life around goals of human dignity and public responsibility. Red Vienna's accomplishments in improving the physical quality of the city's housing achieved its proud status because it was seen, not as an end in itself, but as a part of an effort to build a better, fairer, more democratic life.

The second lesson to be drawn from the Viennese experience is a political one, and it requires a closer look at an aspect of the political–economic situation in Austria in the 1920s only briefly mentioned before.[14] National economic forces (indeed, international ones), not dissimilar to forces at work today, contributed significantly to creating a favorable position for certain aspects of Social Democratic housing policy in Austria in the 1920s.

In order to end Austria's rampant inflation and achieve integration with the economic system of the Allied powers (predominantly the United States), Austria's conservative national leadership agreed in 1923 to a wide-ranging set of monetary reforms and received substantial loans from the United States under terms of repayment considered onerous at the time. Partly as a result, Austrian industry was forced to become heavily export oriented. Its ability to be competitive on the international market, in turn, depended significantly on the level of wages paid workers inside Austria. In the political context of the time, pressure on militant labor activity such as the political and social repression witnessed in the United States with the Red Scare and the Palmer Raids of the early 1920s was not necessary—certainly given the alternative of cooperation with the Social Democrats in achieving the same results.

One way of achieving those results—keeping cash wages low—was housing policy. The figures for the impact of rent control have already been given; they show that rent control lowered the percentage of the average worker's pay going to housing from over 20 percent before the war to under 5 percent in the 1920s. The direct relationship between housing policy and wage levels, and the competitiveness of the Austrian economy, is commented on by Gulick, who comes to his conclusion without any preconceptions drawn from housing theory:

> The real wages of Austrian workers were extremely low. . . . This enabled Austrian industry to maintain a certain position as exporter on the world market. . . . Austrian industry could successfully compete on the world market . . . only because of the export premium industry received in the form of tenants' protection. Abolition of tenants' protection would have made increases in wages unavoidable . . . furthermore, a rise in wages would involve, for some time at least, an appreciable increase in a large part of the social burdens such as social insurance contributions. . . . (Gulick, 1948, 483–84)

In a footnote, Gulick explores the availability of direct evidence to prove this contention, and does not find much. Some manufacturers, indeed, opposed rent control vigorously. This Gulick explains in part by the availability of company-owned (and thus price-controlled) housing outside Vienna, in part by the political–ideological conservatism of some manufacturers. Neither the conceptualization nor the evidence is conclusive at this point. Before the war, in any event, the Chamber of Commerce of Vienna clearly was directly concerned to insure that there was adequate, reasonably priced housing for workers. Kainrath (1978) also supports the hypothesis about the influence of rents on wages, arguing that the monarchy in 1917 and the bourgeoisie in 1922 both understood the relevance of low housing costs to low wages, and the City of Vienna vociferously made the same point in defense of its policies in 1929.

Friedrich Hayek, in attacking rent control from an ultraconservative viewpoint in 1930 in Vienna, seems to take a different point of view, but in fact lends support to the hypothesis. He contends that rent control may force wages *up* because they reduce living costs during a strike and thus encourage militancy. Whatever the merits of that argument, he concedes that lifting rent control would increase the pressure on wages, and directs his argument against "the generally accepted view that rent controls help to keep production costs down" (Hayek et al., 1975, 76). He thus supports the point being made here, that there was a "generally accepted view" that rent control kept wages down, with the reasonable corollary that the desire to hold wages down was a major factor permitting rent control in Austria. Danneberg (1931) corroborates the point indirectly: He suggests there was only limited new construction because, in Vienna, "ordinary incomes are determined by such factors as the lowness of rents." As pointed out earlier, the Nazis in Germany adopted rent controls for a similar purpose.

Given the critical economic situation of business as a whole, the more parochial interests of the housing industry had to play a more subordinate role, at least temporarily. In a crisis, real estate interests are expendable (certainly the limitation of their interests is negotiable); it was Lord Keynes, after all, not Karl Marx, who spoke of the "euthanasia of the rentier."[15] Social Democracy in Austria was able to seize on this vulnerability of the real estate industry in the particular historical circumstances to forge a housing program at the progressive edge of anything that was seen up to that time, or perhaps even today.

It would be the rankest economic determinism to suggest that the logic just outlined was the sole factor leading to the housing policies of Red Vienna. Certainly the political situation, intimately tied to the economic situation but with a logic and evolution of its own, played an at least equally critical role. The volatile situation in 1918–1919 has already been alluded to; the Social Democratic Party's role in "maintaining order" gave it a fairly wide leeway for action on behalf of its constituency, and as long as the threat of worse alternatives hung over the head of the establishment, the Social Democrats' latitude for action remained broad. This was the situation throughout most of the 1920s.

Can a lesson be drawn from this history that is relevant to the United States today? The analogy on the political level seems slight, at the moment; on the economic level, it may be closer than at first appears. Politically, the level of conflict between the rulers and the ruled in the United States has not today reached even the level of the mid-1960s in the United States, let alone that of Vienna in the 1920s. But tensions clearly are mounting, and in many major cities the normal processes of economic and political adjustment do not seem to be functioning effectively to keep conflicts under control. Whether such conflicts will heighten or not remains to be seen; the indications are that they will. If they do, housing policies may again become, as they were in Vienna in the early 1920s and in the United States in the mid 1960s, a prize in a broader combat.

Economically, the recession of the late 1970s had a significant effect in eroding the level of business profits in the United States. International competition plays an increasing role, and the concern of U.S. business to control wages at home is of mounting significance. The control of housing costs can be a useful ingredient in meeting this concern. The business community as a whole may see some housing profits as an inexpensive chip to give up, and labor may see the control of housing costs as a chip winnable where the direct workplace concessions are not [*see the related discussion in Chapter 23 by John Cowley*]. The attempts to control health costs may provide an example, or at least lessons, for housing strategy. There is a difference of interests within the business community, in which the separate interests of the housing industry (builders, landlords, lenders, landowners) may be sacrificed to the interests of business as a whole. If such a split develops, the scope in the United States for programs looking like those of Vienna in the 1920s may be greater than might at first appear. This is the second, and perhaps the more important, of the lessons Vienna in the 1920s may have for us today.

# Notes

1. The most fully developed version of rent control was incorporated in the Tenant Protection Act of 1922, on which the description in the text is based.

2. To give some order of magnitude, for a typical worker's small apartment, Gulick (1948, 443, n.95) suggests the distribution in 1922 might have been: basic ("landlord's") rent, .18 schillings; maintenance rent, 5.40 schillings; operating costs and taxes, 15.00 schillings.

3. See the extensive, and often polemical, discussion in Hayek et al., 1975, 67ff. For a review of the evidence in the context of the current U.S. debate, see Marcuse, 1981a.

4. For a discussion of the different types of activity lumped together under the phrase "self-help," and an attempt to define categories more rigorously, see Marcuse, 1983. [*See also Chapter 25 by Seth Borgos, Chapter 26 by Robert Kolodny, and Chapter 27 by Tony Schuman.*]

5. "Settler" is the literal translation for *Siedler*. "Homesteader" conveys a bit more of the feel of the term at the time. The areas the settlers in Vienna occupied and built up were known as the *wilde Siedlungen*, literally "the wild settlements." But *Siedlung* in the German usage is much closer to "development" or even "small suburb"; "wild development" conveys the sense of the German better. For consistency, however, we use the term "settler" and "settlement" here.

6. The prevalent legal arrangement apparently provided that a household, on moving out, could recapture its initial cash investment, with interest at 5 percent, but since most investment was in the form of labor, the arrangement does not seem to have led to any view of housing as a profitable investment, and perhaps was not utilized much in practice. See Novy, 1981, 29.

7. There was substantial argument that rent control was responsible for the lack of construction (e.g., see Hayek et al., 1975). But new construction for the majority was not profitable, for incomes were too low to afford the necessary rents; and the number of wealthy who would have wanted new units, absent rent control, but did not because they had "bargains" under it, was trifling compared to the need.

8. It can be a source of delight to speculate on the debates surrounding the adoption of the following schedule of taxes: on slide shows to illustrate lectures, 3 percent; plays and operas, 4 percent; light opera and reviews, 6 percent; concerts, 7 percent; dancing lessons, circuses, and variety shows, 23 percent; sports, 26 percent; movies and balls, 28.5 percent; races, wrestling, and boxing matches, 33 1/3 percent!

9. This is a theoretically inconsistent position: Either housing should be provided regardless of ability to pay or it shouldn't. Practically, the compromise it represented made good intuitive and political sense. The result was also close to that achieved in private housing, where operating costs were the major component of rent under the rent control formula (see the earlier section on "Rent Control").

10. With a pleasant eclecticism in names, running from *George Washington Hof* and *Jean Jaurès Hof* to *Höfe* named after Friedrich Engels, August Bebel, Sigmund Freud, August Strindberg, Franz Joseph Hayden, Käthe Königstetten, Goethe, and Karl Marx.

11. The judgment of an article in the *Journal of the Royal Institute of British Architects* is representative of much opinion of the time: "The housing record of the city of Vienna is greatly to its credit, and that it should include a building of the quality and magnitude of the Karl Marx Hof is an index of the fact that Vienna possesses a lively sense of its duty to humanity, and the artistic and technical ability to express this duty in a manner equal to that of any of the great cities of the world" (1909, 677).

12. The architectural history refuted pat concepts about the relationship between ideology and architecture. The original plan was developed for the city by an independent architect. After review by the council, it was rejected, and an architect on the city staff, Karl Ehn, revised the plans and developed the final version. Ehn (1884–1957) had been on the city payroll as an architect under the monarchy, joined the Social Democratic Party in the 1920s, and later joined the Fatherland Front, applying for membership in the National Socialist Party. He remained in his position with the city through 1950. In his later work he is said to have shown the influence of the time of Schuschnigg and the Blood and Soil style of the Nazis (Mang, 1978).

13. Calculated from U.S. Bureau of the Census, 1975b, ser. G-846, p. 327.

14. The argument that follows is based on a theoretical analysis of the general historical determinants of housing policy spelled out in Marcuse, 1980a, 1982b.

15. Although Marx would also agree: "Landed property is different from other types of property in that, at a given level of development, it appears as superfluous and harmful even from the standpoint of the capitalist mode of production" (*Das Kapital*, 1909, 3:635).

# 33

# The Dynamics of Cuban Housing Policy

*Jill Hamberg*

## Urban Housing Policy in Nicaragua: A Comparative View

*Tony Schuman*

*This final chapter presents the book's most progressive model of a housing system, one that contrasts most sharply with that in the United States. The Cuban socialist revolution made housing an important aspect of its early reform agenda. Of particular significance was the 1960 Urban Reform Law, which outlawed private investment in housing for profit and put forth the goal of housing as a free public service rather than a commodity. Early measures included halting evictions, reducing rents, ending land speculation, and initiating self-help and government construction of housing. As Cuba's housing and overall development policy evolved over the next two decades, new measures were instituted to respond to changing realities. This process culminated in the comprehensive 1984 Housing Law, which promotes homeownership and greater resident participation in building and maintaining housing. Cuba presents a provocative case study of how housing can be provided in a country where profit has been eliminated as the driving force in the economy and the housing sector. The direct lessons for the United States are perhaps limited by the fact that Cuba is an underdeveloped country, but its experience does provide a vision of what a truly alternative system can accomplish.*

*In a short addendum, the urban housing policies of the 1979 Nicaraguan revolution are discussed. Nicaragua has permitted the continued presence of a private rental sector and has made extensive use of expropriation to control urban land development. These features are ascribable to the different political situation in Nicaragua from that in Cuba, with respect both to political–economic system and the considerable resources devoted to defending against an ongoing counterrevolutionary war.*

If postrevolutionary Cuba is as striking an example as one can find of the dictum that people make history, it is also an enduring reminder of the corollary: They do not make it under circumstances of their own choosing. The boundary conditions within which revolutionary ideals are unleashed and the emerging unanticipated consequences of the new programs implemented become central determinants of the evolution of actual policy. Housing policy is particularly instructive in this respect. The tensions between orienting vision and objective reality, between immediate priorities and long-term goals, and between centralized planning and the imperatives of popular participation—these, in effect, have defined the dynamic of development in this arena of public policy. This chapter explores the unfolding of Cuban housing policy, from the 1959 revolution through 1984, in an attempt to understand how and why policies developed as they did.

Aside from providing a basic description of what happened, tracing the evolution of Cuban housing policy can be useful in a number of other ways. First, it makes explicit the interaction between housing policies and broader development strategies in the process of building socialism. Second, it highlights the importance of viewing specific housing measures in the overall context of socialist development, rather than as isolated policies that may or may not appear "socialist" in themselves. Finally, it raises important issues of concern to housing activists in developing and developed capitalist countries about strategies for fundamental change. Should housing be seen as a public service, a commodity, or a little of both? What is the most appropriate tenure form: homeownership, renting, cooperative, or condominium? To what extent should equity and equality be the main goals in housing policy, and what is the best way to achieve them? How do these objectives relate to the allocation of other goods and services? What role should land rent and interest play in socialist housing policy? How should housing be used to promote balanced regional development and contribute to labor productivity and stability, and at the same time address the shelter problems of those most in need? How should decision-making and implementation be decentralized while directing limited resources to high-priority localities and population groups?

After a brief description of the housing situation before the revolution, this chapter describes the most important changes in housing policy in each stage of postrevolutionary Cuban development.

## Housing in Prerevolutionary Cuba

Cuba's housing situation before the revolution reflected the country's general level of development and its history of dependence on foreign powers, first as a Spanish colony and, after 1898, as a neocolony of the United States. The country's enormous sugar earnings and its role as the center of Spain's declining empire meant that Cuba urbanized earlier[1] and accumulated relatively greater wealth than most other Latin American nations. Much of this wealth was channeled into public and private building in urban areas, initially as an expression of Spanish colonial power, and then in the twentieth century as a major investment arena, with rampant real estate speculation after World War II.

The vast differences between city and countryside were also evidenced in housing. In 1953, more than four-fifths of the rural dwellings consisted of thatched-roof huts with dirt floors, known as *bohíos*, and less than 10 percent of rural houses had electricity or plumbing (IUA, 1963; J. M. Fernández Núñez, 1976). In contrast, the vast majority of urban dwellings had electricity (95 percent in Havana). But less than half the urban units had complete sanitary facilities, and only half were considered of acceptable quality. Six percent of Havana's population lived in squatter settlements. At the time of the revolution, between 650,000 and 750,000 units were considered substandard, that is, about half of the total stock of 1.4 million units.

In the two decades before the revolution, tenants acquired a series of protections and rights even more advanced than in most jurisdictions of the United States today. Cuba instituted rent control in 1939 and continued it in one form or another through the revolution (Cuban Economic Research Project, 1963; MINJUS, 1974). Rent control consisted of a combination of rent freezes or reductions for most units and some moderate increases, usually for newer properties. Numerous ways were found, however, to circumvent rent restrictions. The most frequent were unregulated subletting, furniture fees, and "key money" (Acosta and Hardoy, 1971; Vega Vega, 1962). Since each successive rent law brought previously unregulated new rental construction under some form of control, investors—aided by a 1952 law—responded by developing condominiums rather than rental units. These new apartments were sold on the installment plan, with mortgage holders charging usurious rates.

The shift to condominium construction was also in response to rent laws establishing a "right to occupancy"—that is, eviction only with just cause (Cuban Economic Research Project, 1963; MINJUS, 1974). Despite this right, an average of 70,000 evictions a year were ordered in the mid-1950s—out of a total urban rental stock of 460,000 units (J. M. Fernández Núñez, 1976).

The very existence of such tenant protections reflected in part the relative strength of the labor movement during much of this period and the substantial political weight of renters in cities and towns. In 1953 tenants represented nearly three-fifths of households in urban areas and three-quarters of those in Havana (IUA, 1963). But despite rent control, tenants paid on average nearly a quarter of their incomes for rent, high compared to other countries at that time (Cuban Economic Research Project, 1963; MINREX, 1965).

Postrevolutionary policies would be influenced by these factors: drastic differences of living conditions between city and countryside and among social classes within urban areas, long-standing rent control coexisting with high rents, and an established "right to occupancy" along with widespread evictions.

## 1959 to 1963: Postrevolutionary Housing Reform

The new revolutionary government's early housing policy was two-pronged: sweeping housing legislation affecting virtually everyone living in urban areas; and innovative construction programs reaching a small but significant fraction of those most in need. These measures were part of an array of policies—including the agrarian reform laws and the nationalization of the educational system, banks, and many industries—pursued to fulfill the promises of revolutionary leaders, undermine economic power of the very rich, and consolidate the revolution's political base.

## Urban Reform

The first housing law, halting all evictions, was decreed barely weeks after the January 1, 1959, revolutionary victory.[2] Several months later, most rents were reduced by 30 to 50 percent based on a sliding scale, with greatest reductions for the lowest rents. The law protected small landlords[3] and offered 10-year tax exemptions for owner-occupied houses built in the following 2 years. The intent was to discourage rental construction and channel investment into homeownership.

Existing and potential homeowners were aided as well by a series of "vacant lot laws" designed to stimulate construction and eliminate land speculation. These measures required most landowners either to start building within six months or sell their vacant or sparsely developed land to someone willing to do so.[4] Prices for land sales were set at a maximum of 4 pesos—then equivalent to $4 U.S.—per square meter.

Landowners still making installment payments on their lots had the total original price reduced, first by 30 percent and after October 1960 to the maximums permitted under the vacant lot laws. Owners of lots in subdivision developments where the infrastructure (e.g., roads, electricity, and water) was incomplete could withhold installment payments, but if the developer still failed to provide such services after a year, the government could step in and do so, placing a lien for the cost on the developer's assets.[5] [*See addendum to this chapter by Tony Schuman for a discussion of how Nicaragua has dealt with these and other issues in the early years of its revolution.*]

The Urban Reform Law, promulgated in October 1960, established the concept of housing as a public service, with the stated goal of eventually making it available at no cost to residents. The law prohibited private rental housing. Landlords were permitted to retain their own homes and a vacation house, but were forced to sell investment property, with current tenants having first priority to buy. Tenants would then amortize the price of their dwellings by continuing to pay their regular rent (in many cases already reduced in 1959) for a specified length of time, set at between 5 and 20 years, depending on the age of the building. The state acted as intermediary by collecting amortization payments from former tenants and in turn paying their former landlords in installments of up to 600 pesos a month, a generous sum, given that in 1962 average monthly wage and salary income in Cuba reached only an estimated 105 pesos (Brundenius, 1981).

No compensation was paid to owners of the infamous *cuarterías*, typical inner-city slum housing with families living in one or two small rooms and sharing sanitary facilities. The *cuarterías* became government property, with tenants' payments credited toward purchase of replacement housing.[6]

All mortgage agreements, both for former landlords and homeowners, were canceled. Individual lenders and private mortgage companies received no compensation, but commercial banks received bonds equivalent to the value of their mortgage holdings.[7] Homeowners and former landlords were still required to finish amortizing the principal to the government, but at no interest. Even the remaining principal was reduced if it exceeded two-thirds of the property's price.

Speculators, large landlords, and private mortgage lenders were clearly hurt by the Urban Reform Law.[8] But most small owners, many of whom held income-generating property for financial security in their old age, benefited. After receiving compensation for their properties, former landlords were assured a lifetime income of up to 250 pesos a month.[9] Small mortgage holders were also assured a lifetime pension, but no direct compensation. Small former landlords benefited not only because they received full compensation for their properties and an additional pension equivalent to their previous incomes but also because these payments were guaranteed; previously they had to contend with widespread rent delinquency.

The Urban Reform Law specified a second stage to begin soon thereafter (actually it began May 1961), in which the government would build housing and lease it with lifetime occupancy rights to new inhabitants who would pay no more than 10 percent of family income for rent. At a future time, later scheduled for 1970, a third stage was to begin, in which the government would lease housing free of charge. This goal of making housing a free public service reflected Cuban revolutionaries' early optimism—which they later criticized as overly idealistic—about possibilities for rapid economic development and accelerated transition to socialism (Castro, 1976).

The Urban Reform Law and related measures set the overall legal framework for housing for the next two decades. The consequences were enormous. They gave security of tenure and virtual protection against eviction for both homeowners and leaseholders. They ended private ownership of housing for profit and drastically reduced speculation in buildings and land. They also were among the principal measures to redistribute income in the early years of the revolution.[10]

Almost as significant were certain measures the Cubans chose not to adopt. There was little redistribution of housing. Small families living in large mansions remained in place, as did large families living in one-room slums. The only exceptions were unoccupied units speculatively held off the market or vacated by families who emigrated. These homes were used either for public purposes such as schools and clinics or distributed by trade unions and government agencies to families most in need. In these early years, eliminating the use of housing for profit was the main goal. Greater equality was to be achieved by improving conditions for those in the worst housing, not by lowering anyone's living standards. Forms of social and racial segregation were gradually eliminated by assigning vacant housing in the best areas to former slum dwellers, and later by workplace allocation of new government-sponsored housing, rather than by forced redistribution of occupied housing.

Urban land was not nationalized. Setting its maximum price at a low uniform rate may have severely restricted speculation, but it could not eliminate the underlying differential land rent deriving from variations in topography, location, and improvements. This was to have an important impact on density issues in later years.

## The New Housing System

The Urban Reform Law established two basic urban tenure forms. The overwhelming majority of tenants became homeowners as a result of the law, joining the one-third of urban families owning their homes before 1959 (IUA, 1963). Individuals were permitted to own no more than one permanent and one vacation home. Long-term leaseholding—under the legal concept of "usufruct"[11]—was gradually introduced as families were assigned new or existing government-owned dwellings. The security of tenure assured by usufruct leases was a logical extension of the prerevolutionary "right of occupancy." Other forms of renting were totally prohibited, except for short stays in hotels and vacation houses and apartments.

These two tenure forms differed with respect to housing payments and ownership rights. Generally, the amount of homeowners' amortization payments reflected three things: the size and quality of construction (basically the human labor involved in creating the dwelling); location and other characteristics of the site; and depreciation.[12] Homeowners were required to pay only until the official price was amortized. In contrast, long-term leaseholders' rents were based on ability to pay (no more than 10 percent of household income), without regard to unit size, quality, or location. Unlike homeowners, however, leaseholders were obliged to continue these payments indefinitely, without accruing equity. Regardless of tenure status, all residents were responsible for arranging and paying for normal maintenance and repairs within their own houses and apartments. Local government agencies were assigned the task of maintenance and major repairs of structural elements and common areas of multifamily buildings of 4 or more units. Only scant material and human resources were devoted to maintenance and repair through the mid-1970s, however, leading to severe deterioration of the housing stock.

The Urban Reform Law authorized individuals to buy and sell dwellings and land for housing, but only at government-set prices, calculated on the same basis as the forced sale to tenants and the maximums in the vacant lot laws. Moreover, the state was given first option to buy the property. For these and other reasons, relatively little legal private buying and selling of land and dwellings occurred for the next two decades, although "informal" sales were not uncommon.

Homeowners' heirs were entitled to receive their share of the official price of the deceased's dwelling. However, the right to remain in and acquire the property—by amortizing the share due the other heirs—was restricted to people living with the deceased for at least one year at the time of death. If a homeowner died and no one else was still living in the unit, the dwelling reverted to the state, which in turn divided the legal value among the surviving heirs. A homeowner, however, could convey the dwelling as a gift to any other household member (MINJUS, 1974). In the case of leaseholders, only close relatives who had lived with the deceased a certain minimum period of time could inherit the lease (i.e., the right to occupy the dwelling).

Security of tenure was thus virtually assured to both homeowners and leaseholders. Nonpayment was dealt with by deducting rent or amortization arrears, plus a small penalty, from salaries or other sources of income or assets (with total deductions not to exceed 15 percent of monthly income). Homeowners more than three months in arrears lost the right to buy their units but could continue in the same dwellings as leaseholders.[13]

Bothersome neighbors were usually handled by social pressure from neighbors and the block-level Committees for the Defense of the Revolution (CDRs), by social workers where appropriate, and through the criminal justice system when a law was broken. Squatters who illegally occupied vacant units about to be assigned to families in need were relocated to space in a *cuartería* (Hernández, 1962).

Exchange of houses was the most common way to move because vacant dwellings and new government-built units were assigned by the government and trade unions, and there was relatively little buying and selling. As the number of leaseholders grew, what happened to the tenure status of the respective "swappers" became an issue. In 1966 it was decided that each household would retain the tenure form it had in its prior residence (MINJUS, 1974).

Until the late 1970s, the only official way to find trading partners was through local Housing Exchange Offices, which maintained lists of potential swaps. Informally, people put up signs on their houses, at bus stops, in grocery stores, and so on. As one might expect, a number of individuals undertook a broker function, often organizing exchange "chains," a sequence of interrelated transfers among three or more households. The government agency authorizing the trade established a price for each dwelling based on the criteria stipulated in the Urban Reform Law. Homeowners trading for a unit with a higher price than their previous one paid the difference to the government in monthly installments. Owners "trading down" for a lower-priced unit were not compensated for the difference. Leaseholders, of course, continued to pay whatever they were paying before.

## Improving Housing Conditions

Government policy regarding distribution of housing, new construction, and improvements to existing dwellings followed seven main thrusts: (1) creating credit mechanisms to finance private building, (2) providing technical assistance for private self-built construction, (3) clearing the largest and worst squatter settlements and relocating their residents, (4) establishing and fostering a large government housing sector, (5) launching substantial construction activity in the countryside, (6) distributing vacant houses, and (7) upgrading urban and rural infrastructure.

Within weeks after the revolutionary victory, a novel way to tap a fresh source of credit and stimulate construction was implemented. The National Institute for Savings and Housing (INAV), created in January 1959, tapped proceeds from the national lottery to finance housing with no-interest or low-interest (up to 5 percent) loans. INAV financed over 8,500 units, built primarily by private contractors, in its first two years of existence (*Moncada's Program Achievements*, 1966).

The government, in addition, provided technical assistance to families wishing to build their own homes. The program was aided by low land values and government provision of free building permits and model architectural plans (J. M. Fernández Núñez, 1976).

To eradicate urban shantytowns, the revolutionary government briefly experimented with its first formal "self-help" initiative: the Self-Help and Mutual Aid program. [*See Chapter 25 by Seth Borgos, Chapter 26 by Robert Kolodny, and Chapter 27 by Tony Schuman for comparison with U.S. self-help housing.*] Each household contributed at least 24 hours of work a week, and small stipends were paid to the unemployed. Between 1960 and 1961, 3,400 homes were constructed by former residents of squatter settlements in developments of 100 to 150 units each, usually with local community facilities such as schools and clinics (J. M. Fernández Núñez, 1976).

The self-help approach was soon abandoned. Unskilled labor, high absenteeism, and labor force instability caused by participants obtaining jobs elsewhere contributed to low productivity and poor-quality construction. Moreover, officials concluded that it was a mistake to maintain socially marginal former shantytown dwellers living together, and isolated from the larger society, instead of integrating them into more stable working-class communities (Agüero, 1980). Despite these reservations, the program was effective in eradicating about 40 squatter settlements.

Some *cuartería* residents also received vacant or newly built housing, but in general older urban neighborhoods received little attention. Buildings deteriorated even further as their populations soared during the 1960s, fueled by the combined forces of a massive baby boom and increased migration to cities. Moreover, few resources were devoted to maintenance and repair. This early "benign neglect" of most urban areas, especially Havana, reflected the priority assigned to improving living standards in the countryside. Conditions in cities, although deficient, were far superior to those in small towns and rural areas, and therefore urban centers continued to attract migrants from the countryside.

Massive direct government building represented a major new commitment, considering that public construction had totaled only 1,400 units between 1945 and 1958 (J. M. Fernández Núñez, 1976). Most new units in urban areas were in single-family detached residences or four-storey walk-up apartment buildings. An early exception to this approach was *Habana del Este*, an ambitious 2,300-unit development built on mostly vacant land assembled by speculators before the revolution. Organized around the neighborhood unit and the superblock, this well-designed project combined high-rise and walk-up residential buildings with community facilities and commercial areas. Its spacious apartments were built to high standards using conventional construction technology (Segre, 1980). The neighborhood unit concept and the superblock henceforth became the mainstays of new urban developments (and many rural new towns as well), but the generous apartment sizes were later reduced, and prefabricated and semiprefabricated technologies were introduced.

State-sponsored housing programs also supported massive changes in rural areas. The agrarian reform laws distributed land to peasants and converted large plantations and ranches into state farms. Small farmers were assured their property would not be expropriated but were encouraged to sell their land voluntarily to state farms. One important incentive to do so was the provision of government-built, rent-free fully furnished dwellings located in rural new towns. This policy of "urbanizing" the countryside reflected Cuba's commitment to overcoming differences between rural and urban areas. To bring modern services and facilities to rural areas, it was necessary to concentrate residents in settlements large enough to make such services feasible. A related goal was to stem out-migration from rural areas and stabilize the work force.

Most of the 26,000 units built in rural areas during the first five years were grouped in 150 settlements, ranging in size from 20 to 25 houses to the several-thousand-unit *Ciudad Sandino* (Segre, 1980). Salaried workers, who then made up 70 percent of the agricultural labor force, were guaranteed stable, decently paid work (Estévez, 1982). They benefited from the extension of infrastructure and community facilities to remote rural areas but only received a portion of new government-built housing in the 1960s.

During the first five years, the government directly built or sponsored 55,000 new units. Nearly half of them were in rural areas, in contrast to the prerevolutionary period when almost all new standard housing was built in urban areas, especially Havana (J. M. Fernández Núñez, 1976). Construction in the private sector continued as well, with another 30,000 standard units produced with some degree of government supervision, financing, or technical assistance. Together this represented an average of 17,000 standard units a year, comparing favorably with the prerevolutionary average of 10,200 from 1945 to 1958 (J.M. Fernández Núñez, 1976). In addition, tens of thousands of units were built with no assistance; most were substandard, but many were of significantly better quality than that found in prerevolutionary shantytowns.

The distribution of vacant housing was nearly as important in magnitude as was new construction. For instance, from May 1961 to September 1962, nearly 20,000 vacant units were distributed. Sixty percent of these dwellings were assigned to the central labor federation for allocation through local unions to families with the greatest need, primarily those living in *cuarterías*. The remainder was allotted to families displaced by fires or vacate orders, veterans of the revolutionary war, and other high-priority sectors (Hernández, 1962).

Finally, latrines and cement floors were provided to more than 100,000 peasant dwellings, and electricity and other urban infrastructure were extended to thousands of houses in low-income urban neighborhoods (MIN-REX, 1965).

All these programs were facilitated by readily available materials and excess capacity in the construction industry immediately after the revolution, since building by large companies fell off sharply. Unemployed construction workers and other jobless people could be absorbed swiftly into new projects. But the combined effect of shortages created by the 1961 U.S.-sponsored trade embargo and the increasing demand for construction resources in other sectors of the economy soon forced a reappraisal of housing policies, including the volume and type of government-built housing and the role of private building. Overall priorities in construction shifted primarily toward industry, farms, and infrastructure and, in terms of services, toward schools and health facilities.

## 1964 to 1970: Mobilization and Disruption

In late 1964 Cuba held its first housing conference to evaluate past experiences and chart directions for future policy (Seminario Nacional de Vivienda, 1965). The conference's recommendations emphasized preventive maintenance, repairs, and rehabilitation to preserve the existing housing stock; government-aided self-help housing in rural areas, with the possibility of establishing savings and loan building cooperatives; and multifamily housing by the state construction sector. Participants stressed industrialized construction as the only possible way to expand housing production rapidly, but cautioned against hasty investments in imported systems without adequate evaluation of those used to date, and encouraged experimentation with new systems.

Only some of these strategies were actively pursued in the next half-decade. Housing production in general was subordinated to other needs of the national economy. During the early 1960s, Cuba's overall economic development strategy had emphasized basic industry and central control of economic planning and administration. By 1963 the limitations of this strategy became apparent, and development focus shifted to agriculture and related industries. Cuba did not yet possess enough skilled labor or infrastructure, nor did it have sufficient foreign exchange earnings to finance importing factories, machinery, and raw materials in large quantities. Sugar was Cuba's only export capable of earning substantial amounts of foreign exchange. In the short run, emphasis was put on expanding infrastructure and diversifying, modernizing, and mechanizing agriculture. A paramount goal was a 10-million-ton sugar harvest in 1970. Vast material and human resources were diverted to that harvest, thereby disrupting production in almost all other sectors of the economy. The harvest was the largest in Cuba's history—8.5 million tons—but still fell short of the target.

With most resources devoted to infrastructural and productive investments, the central government allocated meager resources to housing, building only 44,000 units from 1964 to 1970. In fact, from 1968 to 1971, state production plummeted to an average of only 5,000 units a year (J. M. Fernández Núñez, 1976), most of which was concentrated in small rural new towns near state farms and high-priority industrial settlements in the interior. Larger urban areas, especially Havana, were virtually ignored.[14]

Industrialized construction was pursued because of severe shortages of materials and labor, especially skilled labor, as more workers were attracted to higher-paying sectors of the economy. A lightweight prefabricated building system, originally developed in Cuba before the revolution, was used extensively for one- and two-storey construction, especially in small towns and rural areas. Experimentation also began with heavy prefabrication systems, employing technology from Western and Eastern Europe.[15]

In the first years after the revolution, private construction companies were still involved in producing housing, but from the mid-1960s on, just about all "private" construction was "self-built," in the sense that the household obtained its own materials, provided some or all of the labor (including the labor of relatives, neighbors, and friends) and hired self-employed building tradespeople as needed. At the time, a small proportion of these self-built units received materials and other assistance from local public agencies and workplaces. Land was obtained from a variety of sources: formal purchase from private owners, purchase or exchange of publicly owned land, and construction on land owned by the state or private individuals without a formal sale occurring.

The national government ignored private, self-built construction in the second half of the 1960s, except for sponsoring an architectural competition for models of self-help housing (MICONS, 1964). This neglect of self-built housing reflected the Construction Ministry's early overoptimism about the potential of industrialized construction and its distaste for traditional building methods. Nevertheless, self-built construction continued to be the main way new housing was created. These units did not appear in annual official construction statistics because understaffed local government agencies found it almost impossible to regulate, let alone count, new and subdivided units. Not until figures for the 1970 and 1981 censuses appeared did the magnitude of nongovernment construction become clear. Between 1959 and 1970, 416,000 houses and apartments were created, averaging 34,700 annually (see Tables 33.1 and 33.2). Only 100,000 were built directly by the

TABLE 33.1
TOTAL PUBLIC AND PRIVATE CONSTRUCTION OF HOUSES AND APARTMENTS, 1959–1984

| Period | TOTAL PUBLIC AND PRIVATE | | GOVERNMENT HOUSING | | ESTIMATED PRIVATE HOUSING | |
|---|---|---|---|---|---|---|
| | Number of Units | % | Number of Units | % | Number of Units | % |
| 1959–1970 | 416,400[a] | 100 | 99,600[b] | 24 | 316,800[d] | 76 |
| 1971–1975 | 212,000[a] | 100 | 81,000[c] | 38 | 131,000[d] | 62 |
| 1976–1980 | 246,000[a] | 100 | 82,000[c] | 33 | 164,000[d] | 67 |
| 1981–1984 | 331,200[e] | 100 | 120,000[f] | 36 | 211,200[g] | 64 |
| Total | 1,205,600 | 100 | 382,600 | 32 | 823,000 | 68 |

*Sources:* [a]CEE, 1984. Based on houses and apartments occupied in 1981 by year of construction.
[b]J. M. Fernández Núñez, 1976.
[c]CEE, 1980.
[d]Total minus government construction.
[e]Sum of public and private construction.
[f]H. Pérez, 1981, 1982, 1983, 1984.
[g]This figure is extrapolated from the 145,300 self-built houses and apartments completed from January 1981 to September 1983 (Estévez, 1984a).
*Note: Bohíos,* units in *cuarterías* (i.e., rooms without exclusive use of sanitary services) and improvised housing are not included.

government, and another 30,000 had some public involvement (CEE, 1984; J. M. Fernández Núñez, 1976). Note that the figures in the tables do not include *bohíos*, units in *cuarterías* (i.e., rooms without exclusive use of sanitary facilities), or improvised housing, nor do they reflect all units created by subdivisions of, or additions to, existing units.

The low priority given to new housing construction and housing maintenance and the economic disruptions of the late 1960s resulted in a growing national housing shortage, estimated to have reached at least a million units by 1970 (DCE-DD, 1976). But by then the housing system had been fundamentally restructured. The overwhelming majority of new and redistributed units went to those most in need, and geographic priorities had been shifted. Only 25 percent of new urban houses and apartments were built in Havana Province between 1959 and 1970, compared with 55 percent in the period from 1946 to 1958.

# 1971 to 1975: Institutionalization and Recovery

The failure to achieve 10 million tons in the 1970 sugar harvest had the positive effect of provoking a profound reassessment of almost all aspects of

Cuban life, including housing. The new direction emerging from this process is known in Cuba as the "institutionalization" of the revolution. In the political arena this included early experiments with elected municipal government and decentralized administration. In economic planning and administration, emphasis was placed on raising productivity, which had fallen sharply in the 1960s, and on utilizing scarce human and material resources more efficiently. Material incentives (both individual and collective) were strengthened to improve productivity, but moral incentives were continued as well.

The cash income of the Cuban population in 1970 was twice the supply of goods and services available, a problem that would influence housing policy. Most daily necessities were provided free of charge or at heavily subsidized prices, but relatively few nonessential consumer goods were available. This situation provided fuel for a black market and undercut attempts to use higher pay as a material incentive, thus contributing in part to the sharp drop in productivity and a rise in worker absenteeism. To correct this imbalance, the supply of some products was increased, and prices on many nonessential goods raised.

After relatively slow rates of growth in the 1960s, Cuba experienced a remarkable recovery in the first half of the 1970s. Growth in overall production averaged over 10 percent a year, with construction taking the lead,

TABLE 33.2

ESTIMATED AVERAGE ANNUAL PUBLIC AND PRIVATE CONSTRUCTION
OF HOUSES AND APARTMENTS, 1959–1984

| Period | TOTAL PUBLIC AND PRIVATE | | GOVERNMENT HOUSING | | ESTIMATED PRIVATE HOUSING | |
|---|---|---|---|---|---|---|
| | Total | Per 1,000 Pop. | Total | Per 1,000 Pop. | Total | Per 1,000 Pop. |
| 1959–1970 | 34,700[a] | 4.5 | 8,300[b] | 1.1 | 26,400[c] | 3.4 |
| 1971–1975 | 42,400[a] | 4.7 | 16,200[c] | 1.8 | 26,200[c] | 2.9 |
| 1976–1980 | 49,200[a] | 5.1 | 16,400[c] | 1.7 | 32,800[c] | 3.4 |
| 1981–1984 | 82,800[f] | 8.3 | 30,000[d] | 3.0 | 52,800[g] | 5.3 |

*Sources:* [a]CEE, 1984. Based on houses and apartments occupied in 1981 by year of construction.
[b]J. M. Fernández Núñez, 1976.
[c]CEE, 1980. Note that only 6,000 units were built in 1971, but annual construction averaged 19,000 from 1972 to 1975.
[d]H. Pérez, 1981, 1982, 1983, 1984.
[e]Total minus government construction.
[f]Sum of public and private construction.
[g]This figure is derived from the 145,300 self-built houses and apartments completed from January 1981 to September 1983 (Estévez, 1984a).
*Note: Bohíos*, units in *cuarterías* (i.e., rooms without exclusive use of sanitary services) and improvised housing are not included. Population figures are at midpoint of period (CEE, 1982).

expanding at an even faster pace (CEE, 1975). Increased productivity, better planning, and unusually high world market prices for sugar contributed heavily to the economic spurt.

## The Birth of The Microbrigades

By 1970, after more than half a decade of dismal rates of new housing construction, there was considerable pressure to step up building, especially in Havana and other large cities. Construction materials were still in short supply, but investment in production of cement and other products in the previous decade had improved the situation markedly. The biggest obstacle to expanding housing production was what appeared to be an acute labor shortage—a shortage that in fact was due more to the sharp drop in productivity and increased worker absenteeism in the 1960s. At the same time, citizens had demonstrated their willingness to participate actively in solving their housing problems in a variety of ways. One was the large number of self-built housing units created in the previous decade (see Table 33.1; Segre, 1980). Another was voluntary work on agricultural and construction projects, including housing, organized through the CDRs. Circumstances thus were ripe for the emergence of the "microbrigade" system in late 1970.

Microbrigades are teams of 25 to 35 employees from a given workplace, who work under the supervision of skilled workers and technicians from the Ministry of Construction to build housing for the workplace labor force, usually in the form of four- or five-storey buildings with 20 to 30 apartments in each. The Construction Ministry provides materials, land, equipment, supervision, and some skilled labor. Workers from the same workplace then decide which of their fellow employees should receive the completed units. Priority is given to those with the greatest need and outstanding job performance, but brigade members need not be selected. Brigade members are released from their normal jobs and those remaining at the workplace agree at least to maintain production levels. Many of those who stay on the job also spend a few hours on the construction project in the evenings or weekends. New residents of these apartments pay only 6 percent of family income, rather than the regular 10 percent, in acknowledgment of the "surplus work" contributed either as microbrigade members or by working more on their regular jobs.[16]

One of the microbrigades' explicit purposes was to tap a new source of labor by recruiting former construction workers and training new ones. Another, less explicit, goal was to foster greater workplace productivity, an important factor in the early 1970s before new economic planning and management mechanisms were introduced. Productivity was increased directly by fewer workers maintaining the same production levels. The microbrigade system also indirectly helped increase productivity and reduce turnover, since most government-built urban housing in the 1970s was distributed through workplaces, at least in part based on production performance. Another benefit of organizing microbrigades through workplaces, rather than through block-level CDRs, was that new housing could be located relatively close to workers' jobs.[17]

After a slow start in 1971, government housing construction increased dramatically, averaging nearly 19,000 units a year from 1972 to 1975 (CEE, 1980). Over half of these units were built by the microbrigades (Roca, 1980) and the rest by regular government construction workers. Havana and other large cities received a disproportionately large share of this construction, to compensate for their neglect during the previous period, but housing construction increased as well in rural new towns and areas of industrial growth.

Of the 212,000 houses and apartments created between 1971 and 1975, only two-fifths were government-built (see Table 33.1). Just as in the 1960s, the majority of new units continued to be self-built with little or no government aid, although there were exceptions at a local level.

## Urban Development

The microbrigade-fostered building boom of the early 1970s brought with it a new crop of large-scale housing projects on the outskirts of most Cuban cities, characterized by endless rows of four- and five-storey walk-ups in enormous superblocks. Occasional high-rise prefabricated buildings sprang up in a number of provincial capitals and with greater frequency in both central and outlying areas of Havana. These trends in site planning and design have continued to the present but have come under increasing scrutiny and criticism, as will be noted below.

Meanwhile, attention turned again in the early 1970s to urban slum areas. The already dilapidated inner city had deteriorated even further in the 1960s. This led to Cuba's first major urban redevelopment project in Cayo Hueso, a neighborhood bordering on Havana's downtown commercial area composed of old, rundown buildings, though not of such ancient vintage or historic value as colonial Old Havana. Families had to be relocated before demolition could begin. This process was slowed because few relocation units were available; most new housing in Havana was distributed by workplaces with microbrigades, and fewer vacant units came into state hands when emigration from Cuba dropped to a trickle after 1972.

The first buildings were five-storey walk-ups. In the second half of the decade there was further demolition, and on those sites several 12- to 18-storey towers were erected. High-rise construction was held to be necessary to maintain the area's high density while assuring larger units for each family and providing additional open space and needed community facilities. This was yet another position later called into question.

## Changes in Housing Legislation

The third stage of the Urban Reform Law—the period when leaseholders would no longer have to pay rent—was scheduled to go into effect in 1970. It was postponed indefinitely, however, because of the surplus cash in the economy; the government was not anxious to inject any more purchasing power. Nevertheless, certain sectors were granted exemptions from making housing payments. Rent-free leases had already been given to residents of rural new towns since the early 1960s and by 1967, to all *cuartería* dwellers. Exemption from paying rent was extended in the early 1970s to very-low-income families. The practical consequences of the decision not to distribute housing free to all households were minor, since by the early 1970s only a small minority made any rent or amortization payments. In 1972, 75 percent of all households owned their homes free and clear, and 10 percent were still making amortization payments; 8 percent were paying rent, and another 6 percent were living rent free in government-owned dwellings (Banco Nacional de Cuba, 1975).

Absolute security of tenure became increasingly difficult to maintain for a variety of reasons. For one thing, visiting friends and relatives who outstayed their welcome and divorced couples forced to remain together because of the housing shortage constituted growing sources of tension, irritation, and at times family violence. The divorce rate climbed sharply in the late 1960s, tripling between 1965 and 1971 (CEE–DD, 1979),[18] with the rate in Havana nearly twice the national rate and the housing situation there much tighter.

In 1971 the government responded by issuing regulations defining the "principal legal occupant(s)" (usually one or both spouses), other "legal occupants" (basically children and parents of the principal occupant[s]), and other "guest" occupants, who could stay as long as the principal occupants allowed. The new regulations were designed to deal with "guests" who were no longer welcome, including former spouses who were not on the original title or lease. The government prohibited individuals from expelling such unwelcome household members but established a procedure for the government to do so once the "legal residence" of unwelcome members (i.e., where they have a right to live because of family ties) could be ascertained. The police were reluctant to carry out such court-ordered evictions, however, and moving people back to their "legal" residences was in practice not always easy. Moreover, the courts soon became clogged with endless appeals, making such evictions even more difficult.

Residents of housing owned by or "linked" to workplaces faced a different kind of eviction threat. Dwellings constructed in rapidly developing industrial zones were frequently assigned to present employees or newly arrived workers and technicians, on the condition that the unit be returned to the workplace when employment there ceased.[19] In most cases, employees who retired or transferred to other workplaces in the same area had nowhere else to live. This presented a difficult dilemma. Regional economic development policymakers and local officials favored attracting skilled workers and technicians to developing areas in the interior—and keeping them there. Therefore they were reluctant to enforce the evictions, in the interest of maintaining a stable labor force in the region. But the individual workplace was faced with the problem of providing housing for new employees recruited from other areas.

Severe housing deterioration led to other forms of displacement. The most common was emergency removal of families from hazardous buildings. As the decade wore on, the number of families living in shelters for such reasons reached crisis proportions.[20] The Cayo Hueso urban renewal project also displaced households, but they were relocated in permanent, usually new, housing.

### Changing Trends in New Town Planning

General economic instability during the 1960s and the need to create new towns in haste meant that many were not well planned. The majority were small. Of the 246 new rural settlements constructed between 1959 and 1971, nearly half had fewer than 40 families. Most dwellings were single-family detached residences, which were soon considered too costly. Low density increased infrastructure costs, and traditional construction methods with low productivity added to the expense.

New towns constructed in the 1970s tended to be larger, composed of several hundred families. In contrast to the one- and two-family houses of the 1960s, most structures have been four- and five-storey walk-ups, often built with prefabricated technology. This was intended to achieve a number of goals: maintain high densities to reduce infrastructure costs and loss of agricultural land; promote equality between urban and rural areas through similarity of housing types; and provide greater opportunities for social interaction to help overcome traditional peasant isolation and individualism.

# 1976 to 1980: Consolidation and Development

Most of the changes initiated in the early 1970s came to fruition in the second half of the decade. A new constitution was adopted in 1976, which established elected governmental units on the municipal, provincial, and national levels—a system known as People's Power.[21] At the same time, the country's geographic and administrative structures were reorganized to increase the number of provinces, reduce the number of municipalities, and eliminate the intermediate level of "region." Numerous administrative and economic responsibilities previously concentrated in Havana were decentralized to the municipalities and provinces.

The country's first five-year economic plan began in 1976. After a decade of emphasis on agricultural investments, the plan reflected the shift back to industry. A new Economic Management and Planning System was approved in 1975 and gradually implemented starting several years later. The new economic system recognized that there are "objective economic laws" during the current stage of transition to socialism. These include the presence of the law of value, commodities, "profit," money, interest, etc., which function differently from those under capitalism because they are within the overall context of a planned economy.[22] The introduction of the new economic planning system would soon have an impact on housing policy.

The rate of economic growth did not keep pace with that of the previous five-year period because soaring energy costs, recession and inflation in capitalist countries, and a sharp decline in the world price of sugar made imports more expensive and curtailed foreign exchange earnings. Nevertheless, the economy developed at a steady pace. Industrial investment more than doubled, import substitution increased, and exports became more diversified.

## New Construction: Reassessment and Diversification

Housing policy developed in a number of directions. Planners were overly optimistic, expecting to reach annual construction of 100,000 units by 1980, mostly through an expansion of prefabrication. But centrally budgeted government production in fact declined slightly in the second half of the decade, compared with the years from 1972 to 1975. Prefabrication capacity grew more slowly than expected, and machinery and material bottlenecks decreased productivity, causing delays in planned production levels.

Between 1976 and 1980, 246,000 houses and apartments were created, an average of 49,200 a year (see Tables 33.1 and 33.2). Of these, an average of 16,400 were constructed directly by the government (including microbrigade housing); the rest, two-thirds of the total, were built privately. Government-built housing was disproportionately concentrated in areas where priority was given to attracting and retaining population, such as the Isle of Youth and the central provinces. A sizable share of state construction also went to large cities such as Havana where land scarcity discouraged extensive private building, and the government assumed major responsibility for providing housing to promote high densities.

On a national level, emphasis was still placed on developing prefabricated construction, particularly the most industrialized systems, as the main way to deal with the housing shortage. At least three other trends emerged as well: New assistance was given to self-built housing on a local level; resources were allocated to maintenance and repair of housing and other structures; and the role of the microbrigades was called into question.

Renewed interest in self-built housing came from several quarters. By 1975, housing analysts noted that the majority of new units continued to be built privately (Estévez, 1975). Rather than see this as cause for concern, it was pointed out that other socialist countries at similar stages of development also had a majority of their new housing built privately, especially in small towns and rural areas. Recommendations were made on how local and national government agencies could assist and channel private construction.

Perhaps the most important factor making public involvement in this process possible was the establishment of local units of People's Power. These units were assigned the task of distributing construction materials allocated by the central government and were encouraged to produce materials locally. Before long, experiments were under way in various parts of the country to provide materials and technical assistance and to regulate private construction more closely through building permits, licensing self-employed contractors, and so on.

The budget for maintenance and repair of housing and community facilities increased dramatically as a result of complaints expressed in meetings held periodically between local People's Power delegates and their constituents, and of government studies spearheaded by the construction committee of the National Assembly, Cuba's parliament (ANPP, 1978). Between 1977 and 1983, local agencies increased their maintenance and repair budgets fivefold (*Granma*, July 12, 1984). During the same period, the value of materials sold directly to consumers for maintenance, repairs, and to some extent new construction increased tenfold (although this figure in part reflects increases in prices of construction materials).

The microbrigades grew rapidly until 1975, after which their numbers leveled off, largely because resources were insufficient to establish a microbrigade for every workplace seeking to create one. In 1978 government officials proposed transforming or phasing out the program, a move based on a number of considerations (Castro, 1978; CTVU, 1983). First, microbrigade housing was generally of lower quality and higher cost than equivalent buildings erected by regular state brigades. Most microbrigade workers, who came from a variety of job classifications, continued to receive their regular wages from their own workplaces. Therefore, they earned higher wages on average than unskilled construction workers. On the other hand, microbrigade members who acquired craft skills began to receive higher wages directly from the Ministry of Construction. Moreover, most microbrigade members were assigned to work on labor-intensive traditional and semiprefabricated construction, since they still lacked sufficient skills for the more complex industrialized systems, which have a lower per unit cost than equivalent microbrigade housing.[23] Productivity also decreased because materials were insufficient to supply all the brigades adequately, thereby slowing the pace of work.

Second, the fact that most government-sponsored new housing in urban areas was distributed only through workplaces with microbrigades meant that many households with similar or greater need were left out. These included families housed in emergency shelters and people in severely overcrowded or deteriorated dwellings.

Third, proposals were under consideration to modify rent setting in housing distributed by the government. Existing leaseholders would continue to pay a percent of income, but future residents would pay according to the size and other attributes of their dwellings. Moreover, their payments would be set so that, over a number of years, full construction costs would be repaid, no matter who erected the buildings, microbrigades or state brigades.

Fourth, by the late 1970s the general labor situation had changed significantly. Overall productivity in the economy was increasing at a healthy rate, making it more difficult to remove workers without affecting production. In addition, growth in the construction sector meant that more state brigades of skilled workers were able to build with new prefabricated construction systems.

Finally, renewed attention to different forms of self-built housing, organized individually and collectively, offered other outlets for voluntary labor, often with more flexibility than the microbrigade system.

To deal with this situation, a number of alternatives were considered and debated at the 1978 convention of Cuba's Central Trade Union Federation. One was to convert most or all of the microbrigades into state construction brigades. Another was simply to phase out the microbrigades by not creating new ones. The labor federation opposed workplaces losing their role in distributing housing but agreed that there should be a uniform system of housing payment (CTC, 1978). The unions also sought to protect wage levels of microbrigade workers, no matter what alternative was selected. Everyone agreed that the microbrigades had represented not only a crucial response in a period of acute labor shortage but also continued to be a highly motivated, cohesive labor force, whose spirit should not be lost. The convention recommended that workplaces continue to distribute a certain portion of all new housing, but left open the possibility of some microbrigades being converted into state brigades, with no loss of workers' salary levels and seniority.

By 1983, microbrigades had completed 100,000 units, nearly half of all government-built housing in the 1970s and early 1980s (Veiga, 1984), and they were still going strong, a sign of their continued popularity and effectiveness. Their number has remained constant through the mid-1980s, although microbrigade housing represents a steadily declining portion of total new construction, as state brigades multiply and materials for self-built units become more available. Microbrigade members receive wages commensurate with their tasks as construction workers and are given preference when completed housing is assigned.

## Rural Housing and Agricultural Cooperatives

Rural housing policy was also modified in the late 1970s in response to the growth of agricultural cooperatives, labor shortages in agriculture, and wider availability of construction materials. In 1977 a new program was adopted that encouraged the remaining small private farmers, who still produced nearly half the nation's nonsugar crops, to form production cooperatives voluntarily. The land remains privately owned—by the cooperative rather than the individual farmer—but the government provides incentives by offering special credit and opportunities to purchase farm machinery. Among the most important inducements have been loans to purchase construction materials for housing.

The growth of cooperatives was slow at first, but by late 1984 they represented 60 percent of privately owned agricultural land (Martínez, 1984). The importance of this new strategy can be appreciated from figures on the progress of new town construction. By 1978, 347 new rural communities had been built, containing 32,679 housing units and 154,968 inhabitants. Despite the magnitude of this achievement, it represented only 5.1 percent of the rural population (CEE, 1984; Martín, 1979). If the traditional model of building fully equipped new towns had been continued as the only strategy, it would have taken an estimated 30 years to transfer most of the privately owned land and group peasants in settlements large enough to provide at least some basic services and infrastructure (Castro, 1977).

When a cooperative is formed, individual farmers' landholdings are consolidated, and the government often swaps land or permanently leases it to the cooperative to insure an unbroken expanse for cultivation. Dwellings and other buildings are also demolished or relocated to more appropriate areas. Small communities are created, usually composed of relocated *bohíos* and makeshift houses, which then are gradually replaced by permanent dwellings. Electric lines are extended to the cooperative; when that is not feasible, small power plants are installed. These new communities start relatively small, but since the trend is for cooperatives to get larger, it is likely that the new communities will grow as well. Homes are usually single-family detached residences built with traditional methods or lightweight prefabricated systems. Labor is generally provided by cooperative members organized in small, informal brigades. Moderately high densities are achieved by concentrating single-family dwellings or by including one- and two-storey semidetached and row houses (Díaz de Villalvilla, 1984).

In the first years of the cooperatives, houses were allocated after they were built. Beginning in 1983, each house was assigned before construction so that individual farmers and their families could choose a preferred design (Marsán, 1983). Households also committed themselves to pay any extra charges for homes costing more than the standard credit assigned the cooperative. Based in part on the results of a 1980 architectural competition, the Ministry of Construction issued a series of model plans, offering 96 different design solutions for houses of varying sizes, layouts, and materials. This new system has the advantage of combining collective labor and individual preferences. The cooperative as a whole also takes on the responsibility of building housing for elderly or disabled members and paying off their loans if necessary. Neighboring cooperatives have combined forces to produce cement blocks, establish carpentry workshops, and provide other forms of mutual aid (Ramírez Cruz, 1984).

The government is still building new rural communities and has started expanding existing ones. Starting in the late 1970s, however, most of the units have been assigned to salaried workers as part of a strategy to prevent agricultural labor shortages (Gomila et al., 1984). Material incentives to outstanding workers in key sectors, like the sugar industry, include "kits" of plans and materials for single-family low-cost housing. So far the strategy seems to be effective in keeping and attracting people, especially in the underpopulated central provinces. In any event, the rural population has been concentrating in larger country villages (CEE, 1984), largely the result of spontaneous migration and self-built housing, rather than deliberate government programs.

There will be a declining demand for labor in rural areas, as increased mechanization displaces workers from agriculture. In 1953, 41.5 percent of the labor force was employed in agriculture. By 1970, this had dropped to 30 percent and by 1981 to 22 percent, although the actual number of agricultural workers dropped only slightly during this last decade (Estévez, 1982; 1984a). Housing must be provided now for workers in certain locations to retain the labor force, but as urbanization of the countryside—both spontaneous and planned—progresses, housing needs will shift. Hence, two different housing models were requested in the architectural competition for rural housing in cooperatives: one that would last up to 15 years and one to last 30 or more years (CTVU, 1980).

# 1981 to 1984: New Focus on Housing

Despite the fact that housing received low priority for most of the revolution's first two decades, the 1981 census revealed that nearly half the country's stock of houses and apartments had been built since 1959 (CEE, 1984). Moreover, substantial improvement was evident in the availability of electricity, water and sanitary facilities, and basic domestic appliances. Nevertheless, serious housing problems remained. Public and private construction of houses and apartments averaged 45,800 units a year from 1971 to 1980 (see Table 33.2), barely exceeding the 45,000 units required annually to provide for population growth and replace lost units,[24] not to mention replace or rehabilitate the hundreds of thousands of deteriorated structures and diminish overcrowding and doubling up. Housing loss was particularly acute in the older parts of Havana where vacate orders, building collapses, and demolitions became increasingly common. By 1980, 8,180 displaced Havana families were lodged in shelters (*Granma*, June 6, 1980).

The baby-boom generation of the early 1960s reached adulthood in the 1980s, producing a sudden spurt in housing demand. Recently married young couples often doubled up with parents or continued living apart. In 1979, two-fifths of all households—and nearly one-half in larger cities—consisted of extended families (CEE–DD, 1981). Doubling up may have contributed partially to the late 1970s drop in the birth rate (CEE, 1982; Díaz-Briquets and Pérez, 1982) and to Cuba's high divorce rate (Estévez, 1984a).[25] Divorce, in turn, breaks up households, thus increasing the demand for housing.

Cuba's urban reform laws protected existing households against increased housing costs and provided relative security of tenure, but new households found it difficult to enter the system. The government-built stock, although increasing steadily, was primarily distributed through workplaces; alternatives—such as self-built construction, purchase of an existing unit, or illegal subletting—presented a variety of problems.

Self-built construction expanded rapidly in the early 1980s, with more than 182,000 such units built between January 1981 and September 1983 and another 88,000 under construction (Estévez, 1984a). While helping somewhat to ease the housing shortage, the surge in self-built housing brought with it other difficulties. Nearly half the units built from 1981 to 1983 were of poor quality and one-sixth were *bohíos*. Although less than one-third of Cuba's population is rural, half of the self-built homes were located in the countryside or small rural villages, reflecting greater availability of land and traditional building materials and almost no building regulation. Such rural construction helps stabilize the agricultural labor force but conflicts with the policy of promoting urbanization of the countryside.

In urban areas virtually all self-built units have been single-family detached dwellings, thereby perpetuating low-density sprawl. Indeed, since 1959, the populations of Cuba's largest cities have doubled, but their land areas have tripled (Estévez, 1984a). Building and zoning regulations have been either non-existent or inadequately enforced. Nationally no more than 6,000 building permits were issued in any year between 1981 and 1983, while urban self-built construction averaged more than 30,000 units annually (Estévez, 1984a). Provision of urban infrastructure has seriously lagged behind, and been hindered by, such uncontrolled growth (CTVU, 1984). No legal or financing formulas existed on a national level to enable households to join together to build multifamily structures, although local arrangements were not uncommon (Lezcano Pérez, 1984). Officials urged limiting the maximum size of new dwellings to spread scarce materials as widely as possible (Maciques, 1984; Tesoro, 1982).

Except for housing loans for agricultural cooperatives, few self-built units were officially financed through formal credit channels. Starting in 1979 the government extended credit for purchasing materials for housing repair,[26] but it is believed that most of these materials were used instead to create new units (Maciques, 1984). With few loans available, many new homeowners paid somewhat more than 10 percent of income for housing, at least initially. Small shantytowns reappeared in a few of the most rapidly growing areas in the interior where demand far outstripped the supply of housing and materials (CTVU, 1983).[27]

At the same time, some of Cuba's key housing policies came under scrutiny in terms of their effectiveness, efficiency, equity, and enforceability. First, small households living in large dwellings could not legally rent out rooms, while doubled-up young couples and divorced people still living with former spouses were desperate to find other accommodations.

Second, several policies—the ban on private rentals, limiting possession to only one permanent dwelling, and security of tenure—clashed with regional and economic development policies. By the early 1980s, government-built units "linked" to workplaces were increasingly occupied by people employed elsewhere. For instance, one-fifth of the units controlled by the Ministry of Heavy Industry were occupied by people employed in other workplaces; in some areas this figure reached more than one-third (*Granma*, Dec. 28, 1984). In numerous rural new towns, few residents still worked on the local state farms. On the other hand, many who did work at these farms and factories lived in substandard housing or commuted long distances to work (or both). Workers and technicians attracted to newly developing areas lived for extended periods in workers' hostels or tourist hotels waiting to be assigned housing.[28] Such precarious accommodations made it difficult to bring along their families, thus deterring transfers to labor-scarce areas. Indeed, officials consider housing nearly as important as wage incentives in guaranteeing a labor force in developing areas (*Granma*, Dec. 28, 1984).

Labor mobility and stability were further complicated by the fact that people temporarily working or studying elsewhere in Cuba or abroad could not legally sublet their dwellings. If they invited friends or relatives to occupy their permanent residences in the meantime, it might later be difficult to persuade or force these guests to leave, since they would have trouble finding housing.

Third, the major tenure types became mixed, sometimes in incongruous ways. Most "government-owned" buildings in fact housed both lease-holders and homeowners, since in housing exchanges tenure status was attached to the household, not the unit. After 1971, residents who built on public land or private land owned by others were required to pay 10 percent of income as rent. This was in addition to their own expense of constructing the unit; hence, many considered this policy unfair (Tesoro, 1982). Indeed, the ownership status of a number of housing situations remained murky, including self-built dwellings on land owned by others and new dwellings built as additions to or on the roofs of owner- or leaseholder-occupied units. As a stopgap measure, a series of new regulations was issued in 1982 eliminating some of the more obvious inequities and legalizing certain ambiguous situations.[29]

Fourth, a number of economic reforms in the early 1980s provoked a revival of illegal and extralegal markets (López, 1984) in housing as well as other sectors. The 1980 wage reform raised salaries for almost all workers. This, coupled with productivity bonuses, increased retirement and disability pensions, and higher prices paid to farmers once again put more money in people's pockets than there were goods available (Benjamin, Collins, and Scott, 1984). Modest price hikes in 1981—the first since 1962—on selected goods and services absorbed part of the demand and reduced state subsidies on many items, but excess spending power still sought other outlets. Hence, under-the-table payments in otherwise legal exchanges or sales of housing and land became more commonplace.[30] Isolated instances of illegal private subletting at free-market prices also emerged.

Fifth, courts were clogged with drawn-out appeals of evictions of unwelcome ex-spouses and other household members, and of workers living in "linked" housing who were employed elsewhere. Houses often remained vacant while disputes about occupancy rights or inheritance were resolved juridically (*Granma*, Dec. 24, 1984).

Finally, the tenure and rent-setting system was increasingly perceived as unfair. Only homeowners acquired equity and could sell and bequeath their property. Whether households became owners or leaseholders was often a quirk of fate: for instance, whether one's workplace had a microbrigade or whether sufficient materials were available locally for self-building. Furthermore, income-based rents, at first glance apparently equitable, began to be perceived as unjust. Many families paid relatively high rents for small or poorly located housing, while others spent little for large, centrally located units. In addition to appearing inequitable, this situation discouraged efficient use of space.

## The New Housing Law

In response to these and other problems, Cuba's National Assembly enacted a sweeping new housing law in December 1984, after widespread public discussion of draft legislation released in early November (Ley General de la Vivienda, 1984; Proyecto de Ley General de la Vivienda, 1984). Proposed amendments were the object of spirited debate in the National Assembly's year-end session, broadcast live to the entire country.

The new law converts leaseholders in government-owned housing into homeowners; permits limited short-term private rentals; fosters self-built housing construction by individuals and cooperatives; and updates existing legislation regulating housing management, maintenance and repair, evictions, and the buying and selling of land and housing. The law applies to all housing, not just that in urban areas. To coordinate housing activities and assure the implementation of comprehensive policies, the law established a National Housing Institute, which will regulate the following policies:

1. *Conversion to homeownership.* Cuba's 460,000 rent-paying families, representing one-fifth of all households (*Granma,* Nov. 7, 1984), will become homeowners by amortizing the price of their dwellings with their regular monthly rents. The total purchase price is calculated by taking a household's rent as of October 1984 and multiplying it over a 20-year period. Payments from past years are credited toward the total, but a minimum number of years must still be paid, ranging from 5 years for dwellings built before 1940 to 13 years for those erected after 1971. A family can choose to pay more rapidly; or, if household income falls so that amortization payments exceed 10 percent of income, the term can be extended. As an alternative, households can opt to have the total price based on the type of construction, usable floor area, location, extra yard space, and depreciation, an alternative benefiting higher-income households living in small, deteriorated, or poorly located dwellings.[31] The price based on this method is called the "legal price," to distinguish it from prices on the unregulated "free market" or those derived from income-based rents.[32]

Before the new law, another 740,000 households, almost one-third of the total, were considered neither homeowners nor rent-paying leaseholders. Many of them, including most residents of self-built housing and rural new towns, will acquire title to their homes without paying any amortization.[33] Certain leaseholders, however, will not become homeowners. These residents, who will retain their rent-free leases, include those living in single rooms with shared services, in structures beyond repair, or in units built with scavenged materials. This policy represents a continuation of the 1960 Urban Reform Law, which likewise did not grant homeownership to slum dwellers. The small number of nonowner households temporarily receiving public assistance payments will also remain rent-free leaseholders until their economic situation improves, when they will acquire their dwellings by paying the "legal price."

Thus, almost all households will acquire the same tenure status—homeownership—and will therefore have the same rights and responsibilities. Additionally, hundreds of thousands of households in ambiguous situations will have their tenure status clarified.

2. *Housing distributed by the government.* New government-built housing will be sold to high-priority families,[34] who will pay off the "legal price" of their dwellings with low-interest loans over a period of 20 years in high-rise structures and 15 years in all others. Prices for government-assigned existing housing also will reflect depreciation. Few families will pay the full price because they will receive credit for payments on their prior residence or its "legal price." If a household cannot afford the regular installments, however, the new law provides for lower payments over a longer term.[35]

Most state-built new housing will be distributed by local public agencies rather than by workplaces. Exceptions include dwellings "linked" to or owned by workplaces, those financed out of "social and cultural funds" created out of workplace profits, and those built by microbrigades.

3. *Sales, exchanges, and inheritance.* The new law permits free-market sales of land and housing and of the right to build on the roofs of single and multifamily housing. The state still reserves the right to exercise its option to purchase the property at the "legal price."[36] When households exchange dwellings, they will normally take their mortgage debt with them, but the new law permits the parties to exchange their debts or one party to assume the debt on both dwellings. The law allows inheritance of a home left vacant after its owner's death, even if the heir did not previously reside there. The law also updates regulations on the fate of dwellings owned by people who emigrate.

4. *Self-built housing.* The new law provides for active public involvement in fostering a variety of forms of self-built construction, including building by individuals and by cooperatives established on a temporary basis for the purpose of building multifamily housing. Once completed, apartments are owned as condominiums. Trade unions and other organizations are encouraged to promote such cooperatives among their members. Land or the right

to build on roofs can be purchased from private parties, as can permanent surface rights on state-owned land.[37] First priority for state land will go to cooperatives formed by trade unions planning to build near workplaces, then to other cooperatives, and finally to individual builders who fulfill certain criteria.

Low-interest loans are available to cover a wide range of building costs: materials for construction or repairs, land, architectural and other technical assistance, rental of tools and equipment, and contracted labor from self-employed licensed tradespeople or specialized government enterprises.

5. *Short-term rental.* Owners are permitted to rent rooms, with or without separate sanitary facilities, to no more than two households at any one time. Leases can be for a minimum of one week and a maximum of six months, and are renewable. There are no restrictions on the amount of rent charged. If the homeowner chooses not to renew the lease or there has otherwise been a breach of contract, and the renter refuses to leave, the owner can request the government to attach 50 percent of the renter's income, which in turn is paid to the owner. If after three months the renter household still refuses to leave, its members can be evicted.

6. *Management, maintenance, and repairs.* Occupants will continue to be responsible for normal maintenance and repairs of their units, but the government will contribute to costly major repairs of structural elements and common areas of deteriorated multifamily buildings. The National Assembly debated proposals for greater state involvement in such repairs, but these were rejected as unrealistic.[38] Low-rise multifamily housing will be "self-managed" by councils composed of all residents (in practice not unlike cooperative boards in the United States). Occupants will assume responsibility for paying a maintenance fee. High-rise structures will still be managed by local government agencies, but only a portion of the maintenance costs will be subsidized.

7. *Nonpayment, unwelcome household members, and illegal occupants.* All amortization payments, whether for existing, new state-built, or self-built dwellings, will be withheld from salaries or other regular income in the same way that installment payments on consumer loans have been for years (Alcalde, 1985). Only self-employed workers will pay directly, and if they fall more than three months in arrears, they can be declared "illegal occupants," risking eventual eviction. As long as he or she is not related linearly (i.e., parents, grandparents, and children), any member of a household can be asked to leave by the owner(s). Special provisions are made in case of divorce. The owner can request the local housing department to issue a 90-day eviction notice, and only limited appeals are permitted.[39]

Occupants held to be "illegal" under the new law—including squatters occupying state or private housing or land without permission—must return to their legal residences; if that is not feasible, the government will assign them a room or housing unit. If the illegal occupant still refuses to move, 30 percent of his or her salary will be attached for three months, and 50 percent for the following three months. As a last resort, the police may remove the recalcitrant party.

8. *Housing "linked" to and owned by workplaces.* To assure a stable work force, a limited number of housing developments will be designated as either "linked" to or owned by specific work places, military installations, or other political or social organizations. The National Assembly debated what to do with the tens of thousands of families without members employed in the workplaces to which their housing is "linked." Unable to reach consensus, the legislature tabled the whole issue of "linked" housing pending further study by the National Housing Institute, and left only broad provisions on this matter in the new law.[40]

## Revival of Capitalism or Transition to Socialism?

How far will the new law go toward resolving Cuba's housing problems? Does it represent a revival of capitalism? Will it lead to a significant redistribution of income and greater social segregation?

The new law will likely resolve many of Cuba's most pressing housing problems. It creates a standard tenure type (homeownership), regulates self-built housing, streamlines administrative and legal procedures, fosters greater resident responsibility for maintenance and repairs, and provides more flexibility by creating a short-term rental market.

Security of tenure remains one of the thorniest issues. The National Assembly debate on the new law illustrates the dilemma facing Cuban policymakers (*Granma*, Dec. 28, 1984). At issue was a proposal to guarantee that residents of "linked" housing who later shift jobs be relocated to similar units acceptable to them. Some deputies argued that such stringent conditions would make it virtually impossible to relocate anyone, while others contended that residents must be protected against abuses by workplaces anxious to reclaim "their" housing stock.

President Fidel Castro injected a note of realism into the deliberations. He observed that although workplaces have the right to relocate people, in practice they have nowhere to move anyone. Indeed, in Havana, households lodged in shelters and hazardous dwellings have first priority for any vacancies. He further pointed out that the threat of eviction is somewhat unreal: "The police just about won't put anyone out" (as quoted in *Granma*, Dec. 28, 1984). In fact, he said, the socialist government has never resorted to forced displacement through direct expropriation, even for major public works. Instead, persuasion has been used to relocate families to other, usually better, dwellings. He explained that the introduction of economic sanctions—withholding up to 50 percent of income—against illegal residents, unwelcome household members, and renters is designed to put more teeth into the law, since formal eviction is, in effect, a nearly empty threat. Unlike capitalism, where the drive for profits is the main threat to tenure security, in Cuba competing social goals are at the heart of the matter.

Aside from legal issues, the new law cannot of course resolve the problem of shortages of construction materials, tools, and equipment, though it will help channel available resources in a more effective manner.

Does the shift toward homeownership, "legal pricing" of government-built housing, and free-market resales and renting represent a move toward capitalism? Homeownership is one of several possible tenure forms acceptable under socialism; others include cooperatives and government ownership. Only private ownership by nonresident investors for the purpose of making profit runs counter to socialism. In Cuba housing is considered a form of "personal" property, not a means of production, and no one can own more than one permanent residence.[41] [*See Chapter 30 by Steve Schifferes and Chapter 31 by Richard P. Appelbaum for discussions of parallel shifts to homeownership in England and Sweden.*]

Cuba has no private real estate industry as such. Nor does it have private banks, developers, or construction companies. The only private source of labor is self-employed skilled construction workers, hardly a form of capitalism, since no one is making a profit off other people's work. Housing, like other goods in Cuba, is produced to meet the needs of the population. This social objective is quite different from the goal of profit, which guides most housing production in capitalist countries. However, housing does function in Cuba as a commodity—in the context of a *socialist* economy—in that construction materials, land, and government-built housing are produced for sale to individual households.[42] In addition, most housing and land can be resold, exchanged, and inherited. Thus, housing is unlike education and health care, which are public services universally available at no cost, but it is similar to food and clothing, which also function as commodities. Through rationing and low prices, a basic level of such necessities is assured to everyone. Consumers can then decide where to spend their discretionary income (e.g., eating better, wearing nicer clothes, taking more vacation trips, or occupying a bigger house), subject to the various distribution mechanisms of the goods and services in question.

Indeed, most new housing will still be allocated by social criteria, such as need or maintaining a stable labor force, rather than sold to the highest bidder. This includes government-built units, which will account for about half the new housing in the next 5 to 10 years, as well as publicly owned land sold to cooperatives and individuals for self-built housing. Since payments can be stretched out, paying the "legal price" will not discriminate against families with below-average incomes.

Differential land prices and interest, also frequently viewed as capitalist forms, are consistent with Cuba's current stage of transition to socialism. In Marxist theory, neither is a form of "value," but both have "prices." Under socialism, interest (i.e., the price of money) and land prices are used to promote efficient use of resources under conditions of scarcity (J. Fernández Núñez, 1981). Interest is set at varying rates for different personal savings account balances and types of loans in order to foster accumulation and ration credit.[43] Indeed, the interest rate on loans to purchase a new government-built unit will be a low 3 percent (*Granma*, Aug. 17, 1985). Official prices on urban land, proposed in the early 1980s to encourage higher densities on government-owned land (see below), reflect differential land rent based on such things as distance from downtown, accessibility, and infrastructure (González, 1982).

The two aspects of the new law that most resemble capitalism—free-market resales and short-term renting—do involve private unearned income. These transitional "free-market" measures mirror similar policies adopted in the early 1980s in other sectors of the economy where demand exceeded supply, thus creating a potential for speculation and black marketeering (Alcalde, 1985; López, 1984). After years of attempting to police millions of discrete private transactions, Cuban policymakers decided, as a short-run measure, to coopt the black market by directly competing with it, or by controlling it through legalization (see Benjamin, Collins, and Scott, 1984). Examples include farmers' markets selling produce at freely set prices, and state-run "parallel" markets offering selected nonessential or supplemental consumer goods at near-black-market prices.

Because owning more than one permanent dwelling remains illegal, it is highly unlikely that anyone could make an ongoing business out of buying and selling houses (Estévez, 1985a). The only way to make a "profit" is to trade down, either by moving in with someone else or to a unit of lesser value. This may happen once or twice in a lifetime, and unlike under capitalism, the "profits" cannot be turned into income-producing assets through the purchase of stocks, bonds, a factory, etc. (Estévez, 1985a). High free-market prices cannot result in displacement through increased real estate taxes, since no such taxes exist. Moreover, little or no social "resegregation" is likely to result. Wage differentials are moderate, and total family income depends as much on the number of wage earners as on their salary levels. Furthermore, Cuba does not have the kind of exclusionary zoning regulations that create and perpetuate racial and class segregation in the United States. Most neighborhoods have very mixed housing stock—old and new, large and small, in good condition and bad—and differences in land prices are not substantial (Coyula, 1985b).

Short-term renting, in contrast, does represent an ongoing source of private unearned income. It is seen as a transitional measure to provide more dwelling options for recently divorced people, married couples living apart for lack of housing, people doubling up with relatives, and employees temporarily transferred to other parts of the country (*Granma*, Nov. 21, 1984). The number of rooms potentially available is not insignificant. The 1981 census indicated that 140,000 dwellings had at least one extra room. However, these units represent only 6 percent of the total housing stock. Setting maximum rents was considered in the course of drafting the new law, but rejected as an administrative nightmare to enforce. President Castro noted in the National Assembly that he expects complaints about exorbitant rent levels and some redistribution of income toward "landlords," but that in the long run the only way to overcome this situation is to build more housing (Castro, 1985; *Granma*, Dec. 28, 1984). Presumably, the fact that renters will share the same dwellings with their landlords will temper some of the worst potential abuses.

Thus, little or no social segregation can be expected, and only limited redistribution of income to private owner-occupant landlords.

The impact of the new law will not be fully evident for several years. The first period will be devoted primarily to establishing new administrative bodies; transferring titles to new homeowners; resolving numerous disputes about occupancy and ownership rights; and designating self-managed, state-managed, and workplace-linked housing. At the same time, criteria for distributing housing, land, and materials must be set and building code and zoning regulations strengthened. Undoubtedly, in this transitional period new problems will emerge, but they can be expected to receive more prompt, comprehensive, and decisive action than in the past because of the existence of a high-level National Housing Institute devoted exclusively to monitoring, coordinating, and implementing housing policy.

## Housing Development and Redevelopment

The major changes in housing legislation and the spurt in government and private construction also sparked lively debate about future policy directions in a number of areas: site planning, building scale and design, urban renewal, rehabilitation, conservation, and resident participation.

Government housing output nearly doubled in the first half of the 1980s, and overall production reached over 8 units per 1,000 population (see Table 33.2), which compares favorably with levels in Western Europe in recent decades (Donnison and Ungerson, 1982). Two main developments made such dramatic increases possible: starting in 1980, housing received highest priority among "nonproductive" investments, with proportionately fewer resources invested in educational and health facilities (CEE, 1982); and the overall level of construction increased with the greater availability of materials. In fact, Cuba was able to export a portion of its cement output.

In response to the rapid decay and near collapse of sectors of older urban areas, officials moved to protect historic districts and develop plans to deal with other deteriorating neighborhoods. In the late 1970s Old Havana was declared a national landmark, thereby halting indiscriminate demolition; a comprehensive plan was completed; and greater resources were allocated for rehabilitating the main squares and their connecting streets (Arjona, 1981; Capablanca, 1982). Furthermore, UNESCO granted Old Havana "world cultural heritage" status in late 1982. Architects have thus been challenged to find ways to preserve not only Old Havana's hundreds of landmark buildings but also thousands of other structures in the historic district. They have also become interested in preserving other older areas, whether of historic value or not (Coyula, 1984; 1985a).

Nurturing a concern for conservation and renovation has not been easy. Construction agencies prefer clearance to provide the necessary work space for building high-rise structures. They also argue that new construction is less expensive than rehabilitation. Some members of the general public have also expressed doubts about the feasibility and wisdom of saving old, dilapidated buildings (*Granma*, June 25, 1982).

Attitudes and policies have begun to change, however (Coyula, 1982). As more rehabilitation was completed, the public could see tangible results. As more resources became available and rehabilitation workers became more skilled, the quality and quantity of renovation work improved. After some costly experiences with substantial rehabilitation, architects shifted to promoting moderate rehabilitation with ample resident participation, thereby keeping per unit costs below those of new construction. Moreover, historic preservation will occur with minimum displacement and without gentrification. Staged rehabilitation will make it possible for the majority of current residents to remain in the neighborhood (Segre, 1985).

Successful measures to reduce the shelter population and limit further displacement have also furthered rehabilitation and conservation efforts (Coyula, 1985a; 1985b). These measures include stepped-up state and private repair of severely dilapidated buildings, limiting vacate orders to more extreme situations, and assigning condemned buildings to shelter residents—in groups or individually—for rehabilitation (not unlike U.S. urban homesteading programs). [*See Chapter 25 by Seth Borgos.*]

The relation between density, site planning, and building design has come under scrutiny as well. Planners agree on the need to foster higher densities,[44] but debate the best ways to achieve this goal. Officials have noted with irony the apparent contradiction of policies that stress building 4- and 5-storey structures in rural new towns (to preserve agricultural land), while unplanned and uncontrolled growth in cities has perpetuated urban sprawl (Coyula, 1985a; Estévez, 1984a). Studies for the new Havana Master Plan indicate that even buildings in the capital average only 1.5 storeys (DPF, 1984; Rioseco López-Trigo, 1983). Seeking to foster higher densities, the plan emphasizes high-rise buildings in central areas. But the use of 12- to 18-storey structures has come under fire because of their higher per unit cost (extra reinforcement for high winds and earthquakes), greater use of imported materials (elevators, structural elements), increased energy drain, and greater difficulties in maintenance (Coyula, 1982; Gomila, 1982).[45] Even more important, high overall neighborhood densities have rarely been achieved with high-rise housing because low-rise community facilities and little-used open space occupy so much land. Recent policy shifts regarding high-rise housing in several other socialist countries have also influenced Cuban thinking on this matter (Coyula, 1985b).

Low-rise, high-density buildings have been urged as an alternative. Higher densities can be achieved in existing neighborhoods by encouraging "in-fill" building on small vacant lots and on the roofs of single-family and multifamily structures; both policies are facilitated by the new housing law. For older urban areas proposals have been made to build low-rise, high-density structures, combining the use of lightweight prefabricated technologies, designs more compatible with the surrounding area, and resident participation in the finishing work; some of these even incorporate existing facades (Coyula, 1985a; Gomila et al., 1984; Segre, 1985). Indeed, a number of architects and planners hope that the lessons learned from historic preservation and urban renewal projects, as well as positive design features of prerevolutionary housing, can be applied to construction in newly developing areas: buildings with mixed uses, maintenance of the street as the focal point (unlike the superblock), and use of interior courtyards and covered sidewalk arcades. Such designs seek not only to overcome the monotony in current housing design but also respond to findings of studies indicating that undifferentiated open space tends not to be well used or well maintained. Generous space standards between buildings, borrowed from cold, European climates, are not well adapted to tropical conditions, where shade is of the utmost importance.[46] Furthermore, many Cubans appear to prefer more central locations and traditional architectural styles, as demonstrated by a tendency to trade units in new suburban developments for inner-city housing, often in much worse condition.

Traditional superblock site planning in suburban areas and high-rise structures in many downtown areas will still be the dominant trend in government-built housing in the immediate future, but if these new experimental designs, once implemented, prove cost effective and attractive, the general direction of development is likely to change.

Other measures, not directly related to building design, have been adopted to foster higher overall densities. Several years before location was incorporated into the new housing law as part of housing cost, Havana urban planners proposed that differential prices be assigned to government-owned vacant land to be used for industrial, commercial, and community facilities (González, 1982). The pricing system would attempt to reflect real costs and benefits derived from such factors as travel time from the city's center, existing urban infrastructure and facilities, and soil and other site characteristics. Unlike the situation under capitalism, both landowner and "investor" in these cases are public agencies; hence the purchase price of land represents a transfer payment within the state sector. The intent is to force investors realistically to assess their land needs and the tradeoffs between land and construction costs in designing their facilities.

Although housing is receiving higher priority than in the past, and policies reflect greater realism, diversity, and flexibility, further increases in housing output were and are still limited by serious problems. In the early 1980s the Cuban economy enjoyed the highest growth rate of any country in Latin America (*Granma*, Jan. 4, 1985), but the world price of sugar remained well below its cost of production for most of this period, thus severely restricting hard-currency foreign exchange earnings. These earnings are necessary to import certain construction materials that Cuba cannot produce, or can produce currently only in limited quantities, including metal fittings, electric wiring and fixtures, bathroom fixtures, plumbing supplies, and elevators (López Blanco, 1982). Import substitution has progressed considerably, but this has limits, since Cuba simply lacks certain raw materials.

Heightened international tensions, particularly in the Caribbean and Central America, mean the diversion of substantial building materials to defense needs, which takes its toll on housing. Furthermore, government-sponsored housing is still plagued by problems of quality and bottlenecks in the construction process. Hence, the productivity benefits of industrialized housing are often more than neutralized by difficulties in coordinating the arrival of materials and the use of scarce machinery, which, in addition, is prone to frequent breakdowns (*Granma*, Dec. 12, 17, and 23, 1983).

Cuban planners estimate it would be necessary to build 130,000 units a year (or 12 per 1,000 population) during the last two decades of the century to replace lost housing, upgrade living conditions, eliminate overcrowding and doubling up, accommodate internal migration, and provide for demographic growth (Estévez, 1984a). Smaller families and a greater variety of household composition due to an aging population and low birth and high divorce rates will increase overall demand as well as influence such design features as number of rooms per unit, floor area per person, and building scale (Estévez, 1984b).

Cuba's need to expand exports and restrict imports will require a 4 percent reduction in construction in 1985 (H. Pérez, 1984). Therefore, government-built housing will expand less rapidly than originally projected. It will be concentrated in locations where a labor force to produce basic goods, especially exports, must be guaranteed (Castro, 1984).

## Conclusions

Cuba is justly proud of its housing accomplishments over the last quarter-century. Despite housing's low priority for so long, Cuba's record stands in sharp contrast to the rest of Latin America, where one-third to one-half of the urban population subsists in miserable slums and shantytowns and the rural population is even more poorly housed. Cuban families enjoy security of tenure and low shelter costs, protections that would be the envy of many U.S. and Western European households. These and other accomplishments, such as socially and racially integrated neighborhoods, resident participation in maintenance, management, and construction, and housing's role in promoting balanced regional growth, are all made possible by the fact that housing is produced to meet social needs, not for profit. Clearly, this basic socialist orientation is not a panacea, but it does provide a positive framework to guide how problems are approached. Within that framework, Cuba has demonstrated remarkable flexibility in correcting mistakes and revising policies in response to changing conditions.

Several simple but nevertheless useful observations can be extracted from the Cuban experience. Though perhaps obvious, they bear restatement because they are sometimes overlooked by housing advocates in developed capitalist countries seeking policies for radical change.

First, Cuba shows that many housing problems and issues found in capitalist countries do not disappear under socialism; they are simply handled differently.

Second, justice, equity, and fairness in housing—not to mention equality—are complicated issues, both theoretically and in practice, and are exceedingly difficult to implement adequately under conditions of scarcity.

Third, the commodity nature of housing and other apparently "capitalist" forms, such as homeownership, interest, and differential land pricing, may be present in socialism, but the overall context in which they function is different. Profit is not the driving force in the economy nor in the housing sector. This may lead us to reexamine whether the issue in capitalist societies is the commodity nature of housing or whether it is the presence of profit as the prime mover in the economy and the housing market [*see, for instance, Chapter 28 by Emily Paradise Achtenberg and Peter Marcuse*].

Finally, the transition to socialism does not occur in a neat, linear fashion, especially in a developing nation under economic, political, and sometimes military attack. The interplay of housing policies with broader economic development strategies means that housing shares with the rest of the economy both insufficient resources to meet social needs and the experience of uneven development—of resources, of institutions, of consciousness. The degree to which Cuba has addressed its housing problems with such limited resources is not only an inspiration to other developing nations but a challenge to capitalist industrialized countries to make better and more equitable use of the substantial resources at their disposal.

## Acknowledgments

I would like to thank the editors of this book and the following people for their insightful comments on earlier drafts of this paper: Frank Caro, Penny Ciancanelli, Robert Cohen, Ximena de la Barra, Chip Downs, Matt and Kim Edel, Jane Franklin, Mauricio Gastón, Richard Hatch, Kim Hopper, Peter Marcuse, Edwin Melendez, Ivelisse Mercado, Fred Rosen, Andy Scherer, Tony Schuman, Luis Sierra, and Karen Smith. I am especially grateful to Cuban-based architects Mario Coyula, Reynaldo Estévez, and Roberto Segre for their comments and generous assistance.

## Notes

1. In 1899, 28.5 percent of the Cuban population lived in cities of more than 20,000, a higher proportion than even the United States at that time, which had reached only 23.8 percent (Acosta and Hardoy, 1971).
2. Texts of the laws discussed in this section can be found in the following sources: For the Anti-eviction Law (Ley No. 26), Rent Reduction Law (Ley No. 135), and Vacant Lot Laws (Leyes No. 619 and 892), see Vega Vega, 1962. For Vacant Lot Law No. 218, see discussion in Estévez, 1959. For the Urban Reform Law, see Vega Vega, 1962, *Seis leyes de la Revolución*, 1973, and, in English, *Urban Reform Law*, 1966. See also discussion of these laws in Acosta and Hardoy, 1971, and J. M. Fernández Núñez, 1976.
3. Rents in units built before 1940, owned primarily by small landlords, were exempt from reductions if at legally controlled levels. No reductions were made for landlords collecting less than 150 pesos a month (then equivalent to $150 U.S.), or where the reduction would leave them with less than that amount.
4. Forced sale of lots could be sought for nonrental buildings for industrial, commer-

cial, or office use, as well as for owner-occupied homes. Such lots could not be resold for five years. Owners of small lots were exempted from paying real estate taxes.

5. As it turned out, the largest developers—who had held land off the market after the revolution, speculating on a change in government—soon fled the country, thus leaving the state with much of their property and full responsibility for installing infrastructure (Acosta and Hardoy, 1971).

6. Continued residence in slum *cuarterías* and squatter settlements was at first optimistically viewed as a transitory phenomenon. Therefore, little attention was paid initially to resolving the tenure situation of households living in such circumstances. By 1967, all *cuartería* residents had been granted lifetime rent-free leases on their dwellings.

7. Noninstitutional mortgage lenders received no compensation, since they were among the main promoters and beneficiaries of real estate speculation, especially in the 1950s. In practice they functioned almost as landlords, charging usurious interest rates as a way to circumvent the rent control laws. Bank mortgages, in contrast, were often insured and offered on more conventional terms.

8. Before the revolution, 5,000 big landlords (4 percent of the total) collected more than 100 million pesos in rent annually, with some even receiving from 3 to 5 million pesos a year (IUA, 1963).

9. In 1963, 117,000 former landlords were receiving 70 million pesos a year (IUA, 1963). By 1966, 39,000 former owners were still receiving amortization payments and another 40,000 were already collecting lifetime pensions (*Moncada's Program Achievements*, 1966).

10. An estimated 80 million pesos were transferred to tenants by the rent reduction law. The only other redistributive measures of greater impact were wage increases (150 million pesos) and the elimination of most forms of gambling (100 million) (MINREX, 1965).

11. Usufruct is a legal concept found in civil, or Roman, law jurisdictions (most of Europe, Latin America, and, to some extent, Louisiana). In common law systems (England and its former colonies), the closest equivalent is "life estate." These concepts are not directly comparable, however, since real property rights differ under civil and common law. Long-term leases on urban land and structures in common law countries resemble usufruct in practice, if not in legal theory. For a comparative discussion of usufruct and life estate, see Merryman, 1974, and McClean, 1963.

12. The sole exception was for owners of homes built on sites acquired through the vacant lot laws, who paid little for land, irrespective of location or other attributes.

13. A later regulation prohibited taking away the status of "buyer" if more than 75 percent of the home had been amortized at the time payments became seriously overdue (MINJUS, 1974).

14. Low rates of new construction in Havana and other cities were partially offset by the continued availability of housing vacated by people leaving Cuba. Nevertheless, the housing situation grew exceedingly tight. Despite large-scale emigration, from 1953 to 1970 Havana's population grew faster than the number of units, whereas the opposite was the case in Cuba's other provinces (DCE, 1970; Tribunal Superior Electoral, 1953). Average household size in urban areas increased slightly between 1953 and 1970. In response to this situation, residents in existing housing subdivided their units and converted commercial premises to residential use.

15. The José Martí district in Santiago was the first large-scale housing development to incorporate such a system. It used large panels from a factory donated by the Soviet Union in 1963 after Hurricane Flora devastated the eastern end of the island. Cuban architects eventually adapted the Soviet system, designed for Russian winters, to a more tropical climate (Segre, 1980).

16. For a discussion of how the ideological and practical aspects of Cuba's microbrigade system compare to self-help efforts in developing and developed capitalist countries,

see Segre, 1980, 1984. Cole, 1979, discusses the relevance of microbrigades and Cuba's housing policies in general for solving housing problems in the black community in the United States.

17. In the long run, this aspect did not prove completely effective. In larger cities, people change jobs with some frequency, and other employed family members may in turn have to travel long distances to reach their workplaces.

18. A 1970 university survey of divorced people revealed some reasons for the soaring divorce rate. In addition to the housing shortage, these included expanding rights and opportunities for women, increased protection and security for children, and greater independence for young people (see discussion of study in L. Perez, 1980).

19. An analogous situation in the United States would be company towns, family housing on military bases, and units owned by universities and hospitals for use by students and staff. A small portion of microbrigade units was assigned on a similar conditional basis.

20. Most Havana shelters are located in older hotels or large subdivided houses. Families are assigned rooms and share cooking and sanitary facilities (Marín, 1983).

21. Among other things, the constitution guarantees a series of economic rights, such as the right to a job, education, and health care, all of which exist in practice, not just on paper. Recognizing the impossibility of immediately providing decent housing to all, the constitution assures that the state will work toward that goal (*Constitution of the Republic of Cuba*, 1976).

22. For a discussion of how these concepts function in Cuba, see Acosta Santana, 1982; Navarro Alaluf, 1983; Oleinik, 1977; and Silverman, 1971 (the last reference for early debates). Kozlov, 1977, presents a Soviet view. See also Nove, 1983, and Wilczynski, 1977, for analyses of socialist economies by noncommunist writers.

23. In the early 1970s this was not much of an issue, since there were relatively few factories for prefabricated systems, but by the end of the decade that was no longer the case.

24. Demographic growth accounted for about 25,000 units a year (assuming an average of 4.23 people per unit, which was the national mean in 1981) and lost units for 20,000 (assuming 1 percent of the stock was lost each year; see CEE, 1984).

25. The 1970 divorce survey (see note 18), indicated that 64 percent of divorced people had lived in households that included, in addition to the nuclear family, other related or unrelated individuals (L. Pérez, 1980).

26. The People's Savings Bank, Cuba's main retail banking institution, granted an average of 10,500 loans annually for housing repair materials from 1981 to 1983 (Lazo, 1984).

27. The number of "improvised" housing units grew by 56 percent, from 2,370 in 1970 to 3,690 in 1981 (CEE-DCE, 1977; CEE, 1984). Nevertheless, this still represented less than 0.2 percent of the total 1981 stock. Three-fifths of these units were in the five eastern provinces.

28. For instance, Moa, the center of Cuba's nickel industry, had 36,000 permanent residents in 1984; another 22,000, mostly construction workers, lived in hostels (Pozo, 1984).

29. These regulations abolished the 10 percent rental fee for land, facilitated obtaining title to many self-built dwellings, and legalized prior and future sales of land and housing, with the government having only limited first option to buy (*Tribuna de La Habana*, Jan. 31, 1982). Such an option could be exercised when the house or vacant lot was in areas designated for resorts or public facilities or when residential use would conflict with the Master Plan for the area. In these cases, the owner of the property could choose to receive either compensation or equivalent property elsewhere. In addition, new regulations on housing exchanges ended the payment of difference in value when house swaps occurred between owners and clarified the tenure status of households in more complicated trades.

30. Since 1979, classified ads for housing exchanges have appeared in the monthly magazine *Opina* and in local dailies, thereby obviating the need for housing exchange offices. These ads sometimes explicitly state that the interested party is willing to accept or offer a "good deal."

31. Prices for usable floor area range from 48 pesos per square meter for the worst housing to 213 pesos for the best. Depreciation varies from 3 percent a year for the worst units to 1.5 percent for the best. The usable floor area of the unit, not the lot area, also serves as the basis for calculating the surcharge for location. The country has been divided into six location groups: Havana, Santiago, the other provincial capitals, other cities over 20,000 inhabitants, the remaining urban areas, and rural settlements. Within each location group there are a series of zones. Prices range from 0 to 27 pesos per square meter, although the spread within most settlements is much smaller (*Granma*, July 3, 1985).

32. This measure mirrors similar policies in Eastern Europe, where most countries use these factors in rent setting. With the exception of the Soviet Union, most Eastern European countries have increased housing payments and fostered homeownership, and in some cases sold state-built units to tenants. Private construction with varying degrees of state aid is also still common in rural areas, small towns, and even some cities (Morton, 1979).

33. Households living free in units owned by someone residing elsewhere in Cuba or in dwellings built as additions to homes owned by others will also become homeowners at no cost. Another small group of nonowners—principally many of those living in dwellings owned by people who died or emigrated—will become homeowners by paying off the "legal price" of their units.

34. In the past, priorities for distribution were set locally. For instance, Havana dwellings left vacant by the 1980 wave of emigration were allocated, with local CDR approval, to people living in shelters (*Granma*, June 6, 1980). In contrast, in rural Las Tunas province, preference was given to managers, technicians, and medical personnel working in local factories and hospitals but living in hotels and hostels; to families of people killed during Cuba's revolutionary struggle or while stationed with the Cuban military abroad; and to each municipality for distribution to high-priority families (*Bohemia*, May 29, 1981). The National Housing Institute is responsible for establishing general guidelines on priorities for local agencies to follow and monitoring compliance with these criteria.

35. Provisions for stretching out payments for future owners do not define "affordability," unlike those for current residents, where 10 percent is specified. It appears that permission from the central office of the National Housing Institute will be required in each individual case, and will only be granted when monthly payments are "considerably greater than 10 percent of the household's income" (*Trabajadores*, Sept. 14, 1985). Average monthly family income in 1983 was 307 pesos (*Granma Weekly Review*, Dec. 18, 1983). Households paying the entire price (i.e., not receiving credit for a previous residence) of a 7,000-peso unit over 15 years at low interest would have monthly payments of around 44 pesos, or 14.5 percent of average income. State-aided single-family dwellings costing 3,000 to 5,000 pesos would require some 21 to 35 pesos, or between 6.8 and 11.4 percent of average income.

36. The new law does not specify under what conditions the state would exercise its option to buy in private transactions. Most likely it will be used primarily in limited situations (see note 29).

37. If construction does not start within six months, the right to build is forfeited, and the land can be resold only to the state.

38. The draft law proposed that public agencies contribute to costly repairs for both single-family and multifamily units (whether common areas or not). The National Assembly rejected this measure on the grounds that the government should not promise what it cannot realistically as yet provide (*Granma*, Dec. 28, 1984). In addition, deputies from the oldest and most deteriorated parts of Havana proposed that residents of severely

dilapidated housing not be required to repair their units until the government makes at least basic repairs on the buildings. The majority rejected this amendment, arguing that local agencies could not be expected to repair all such buildings in the near future, and postponement of repairs on individual units would lead to further deterioration.

39. The draft law was amended to postpone enforcement of this provision for a year, to give people time to find other lodgings, now more feasible through the new short-term rental market. After January 1, 1986, unwelcome household members will have 30 percent of their income withheld for six months before an eviction order is issued, the withheld money becoming part of general government revenue.

40. The draft law specified that dwellings "linked" to and owned by workplaces would receive special treatment. For instance, their residents would be permitted to own another permanent dwelling. "Linked" housing would be sold at 50 percent of its normal "legal price" and would have to be resold to the workplace when the owner leaves his or her job. These dwellings could not otherwise be sold, exchanged, rented, or bequeathed. Units directly owned by workplaces would be rented on a short-term basis to high-level technicians, management personnel, and special visitors for little or no charge.

41. See also Roistacher, 1985, for a discussion of the conversion of publicly owned units to homeownership in Britain and the United States.

42. See note 22 for references that discuss the special nature of commodities under socialism. See Martín, 1979, for a discussion of housing as a commodity in Cuba.

43. Interest rates on savings accounts are set as follows (Alcalde, 1985): up to 200 pesos, no interest is paid, as an incentive to save more; from 200 to 2,000 pesos, 2 percent; 2,000 to 5,000 pesos, 1 percent; and over 5,000 pesos, 1/2 percent. The interest structure is designed to pay the maximum interest to average working people. The interest rate on loans for purchase of dwellings and materials to repair housing is 3 percent. In contrast, loans for consumer durables such as television sets and refrigerators are offered at 4 percent; auto loans, 9 percent.

44. Unlike the United States, where most suburban zoning regulations emphasize *minimum* lot sizes to promote lower densities, Cuba is considering establishing *maximum* lot sizes for self-built housing (Estévez, 1985a).

45. Social issues have sometimes been mentioned as a concern in high-rise buildings, but most Cuban policymakers believe that buildingwide resident councils and the CDRs can largely overcome the potentially isolating effects of such buildings.

46. An experimental prefabricated housing development on the outskirts of Havana will be using simple technologies to save energy (through cross-ventilation, reflective paints, landscaping, shade, and solar energy) and varied design features respecting the topography of the site. Cuban architects have received technical assistance from U.S. experts experienced in environmentally oriented design (see Groundwork Institute, 1984).

# Urban Housing Policy in Nicaragua: A Comparative View

*Tony Schuman*

The Nicaraguan revolution has drawn inspiration from the Cuban experience in a number of ways, from the conduct of guerrilla war that overthrew the Somoza dictatorship to the formulation of urban and agrarian reform programs after the Sandinista victory. Both countries have undertaken a radical restructuring of their societies aimed at redistributing income and developing social programs to improve living conditions for the rural peasants and urban workers. In terms of urban housing policy, the two countries share the overriding objective of transforming urban land from a speculative commodity to a social resource.

Despite these common goals, it is a mistake to assume that the Nicaraguan revolution is developing in ideological fealty to the Cuban model. There are important differences in historical conditions and political outlook. With over half its urban population living in marginal settlements lacking basic services and infrastructure at the time of the revolution in 1979, Nicaragua resembles more the less developed countries of Central and South America than the relatively more advanced Latin nations like Argentina, Uruguay, Chile, and Cuba. The extreme level of underdevelopment has prompted Nicaragua's revolutionary leadership to pursue a moderate course aimed at retaining the loyalty and managerial skills of the private sector and at maintaining normal economic relations with historic trading partners. The Sandinistas' commitment to political pluralism and a mixed economy reflects these practical considerations as well as the recognition of the broad spectrum of Nicaraguan society that supported the fight against the Somoza dictatorship.

Although confiscation of property belonging to Somoza and his associates transferred considerable holdings to state ownership, the private sector still (in late 1984) controlled roughly 60 percent of both national production and agricultural land. The Sandinista party, the FSLN, remains the preeminent political force, but opposition parties hold a third of the seats in the recently elected National Constituent Assembly. In addition, the influential Catholic Church, though split into traditional and "liberation theology" factions, is dominated by a conservative hierarchy hostile to the Sandinista government. Thus, the Nicaraguan revolution is under considerable pressure to preserve and expand the degree of political and economic freedom that evolved in the first five years after the fall of Somoza. This brief essay attempts to delineate how Nicaragua's urban housing policy has emerged in response to its own urban history and political orientation.

*Urbanization*

Although Cuba and Nicaragua share a history of Spanish colonial rule, with an economy based on export-oriented agro-exploitation and a legacy of uneven regional development, the two countries urbanized at different rates and different historical moments. Nowhere is this more apparent than in a comparison of the capital cities of Havana and Managua. Both capitals contained 20–25 percent of their national populations at the time of their respective revolutions in 1959 and 1979, but the timing and pace of urbanization had produced radically different configurations.

Havana, first as the center of the Spanish colonial empire in the Caribbean and later as the headquarters for a national bourgeoisie engaged in the sugar trade, developed early as part of a society that by the end of the nineteenth century was one of the most urbanized in Latin America. By 1959, although class differences were evident in housing conditions, Havana, as well as other large Cuban cities, had a relatively high level of urban infrastructure among Latin nations.

Managua, on the other hand, did not emerge as an important city until the late nineteenth century when it was a compromise choice for the national capital following the civil war waged between the conservative aristocracy based in Granada and the "liberal" coffee plantation bourgeoisie centered in León. Urbanization in Nicaragua came late and fast as a result of industrialization following the switch from coffee to cotton and sugar cultivation in the Pacific Coast regions after World War II. The nation's urban population jumped from 35 percent in 1950 to 58.6 percent in 1980. In Managua, much of this increase was absorbed in marginal areas around Lake Managua and, especially, on the periphery of the city, whose urban area grew by 70 percent from 1960 to 1977. Much of this peripheral growth took the form of "illegal" speculative tract developments after the 1972 earthquake destroyed 75 percent of the housing stock in the center city (Black, 1983, 147; MINVAH, 1982). At the moment of the Sandinista victory in July 1979, fully 65 percent of the population of Managua lacked one or more of the basic infrastructural elements: paved roads, fresh water, electricity, sanitary drainage, and storm sewers (MINVAH, 1982). In addition, a substantial number of people lived in overcrowded *cuarterías*, where entire families occupied one or two rooms with shared and inadequate sanitary services.[1]

# Urban Reform

The most sweeping housing measure, aimed at controlling speculation in the private rental housing market and thereby increasing the real income of the work force, was the Tenants' Law of January 1980. This law reduced all rents, most (88 percent) by half, and on future leases set a maximum annual rent of 5 percent of the property's assessed value.[2] The law also enabled the state, through the Ministry of Housing and Human Settlements (MIN-VAH), to take the *cuarterías* into receivership in order to make necessary improvements. Compared to Cuba's urban reform laws, the Nicaraguan legislation is perhaps most notable for what it does *not* do: It does not eliminate private rental housing. Cuba's law transformed the monthly rent into payments toward purchase, effecting a forced sale of privately owned rental housing and placing a blanket proscription on evictions.[3] Nicaragua's Tenants' Law may be seen as national rent control, discouraging speculation in rental housing and guaranteeing tenants' rights, but respecting certain rights of private ownership, including eviction for cause.[4] While legislation to eliminate private rental housing was discussed in Nicaragua, the issue has not been pursued because, apart from units owned by the Somoza family and their associates, which were confiscated, much of the rental housing stock was owned by working- and lower-middle-class people who supported the Sandinista struggle (López Román, 1982).

With respect to physical improvements in urban housing, Nicaragua has opted for a "site and services" approach based on limited government investment in infrastructure, coupled with self-built housing constructed by the occupants using scavenged materials or purchased goods, including prefabricated wood wall sections available with low-interest loans through the state-run Materials Bank.[5] Despite enormous housing need, estimated at 280,000 units nationally (MINVAH, 1984) and particularly acute in Managua, in the context of a wartime austerity budget Nicaragua simply cannot afford, in time or money, the level of state-assisted new construction initiated by Cuba in the early years of the revolution.[6]

The most urgent application of the site-and-services approach was to upgrade the 230 "illegal" settlements on the outskirts of Managua, mostly built after the earthquake, which housed over 50 percent of the city's population (MINVAH, 1982).[7] Ownership of these lands was considered illegal by the Sandinista government because of the failure of the tract developers (*lotificadores*) to furnish necessary infrastructure and services and/or provide sales certificates for the lots they sold. Under the Law of Illegal Settlements of September 1979, just two months after the Sandinista victory, the state was empowered to intervene in these settlements, with MINVAH acting as receiver of the monthly amortization payments pending transfer of title from the *lotificador* to the lot holder.[8] This revenue was used to pay for infrastructural development and to purchase 15 percent of the land area for communal services, as well as for topographical and planning studies as needed. If the amortization payments were insufficient to cover these costs, MINVAH was given the right to place liens on other assets and attach the bank accounts of the *lotificadores*. Security of tenure was guaranteed by the Title Law of January 1982, which conveyed title to lot holders who lived on their lots.[9] Previous mortgages for these residents were considered paid in full, although lot holders are obliged to continue payments to MINVAH to help finance the infrastructure work. The title transfers confirmed the intention of the earlier legislation to expropriate land in the illegal settlements, on the basis of past payments by the lot holders to the *lotificador.*

The same pressures for urban land and housing that produced the illegal settlements prompted a series of spontaneous squatter settlements on the shores of Lake Managua. By 1979, there were 36 shantytowns around the lake, housing 9 percent of the city's population (MINVAH, 1982). These settlements posed an even more critical problem due to health hazards issuing from the presence of high-tension electric lines and raw waste dumped into the lake by 17 trunk sewer lines, a problem exacerbated by periodic flooding. The Law of Expropriation of Vacant Urban Land, of December 1981, was designed specifically to create a relocation land resource for residents of the spontaneous settlements.[10] Declaring urban land to be a public resource, the law authorized the taking of unbuilt but developable urban sites having access to infrastructure and basic services but held vacant by owners awaiting a speculative increase in value. The law restricts compensation to the assessed property value, authorizes payments with state bonds, and allows immediate possession of land by MINVAH for projects of "public utility and social interest" (Ley de Expropiación de Tierras Urbanas Baldías, 1981). The juridical basis for the expropriation may be seen as a variation on the well-established principle of eminent domain.

With the legal mechanism in place to secure the land, MINVAH launched a Progressive Urbanization Program to install minimum urban services (graded dirt roads, electricity, latrines, 1 potable water tap for every 20 lots) and to allocate lots to families relocated from the lake shore. Despite the cost of this program, it was pushed forward with some urgency after heavy flooding in 1982 rendered the lakefront settlements even more precarious. Through the program, some 5,000 lots were prepared in Managua in 1982, and a total of 15,478 nationally by the end of 1983 (MINVAH, 1982, 1984).

While its primary emphasis has been infrastructural development, the government has also undertaken some construction of state-built housing, relying primarily on prefabricated units of lightweight concrete and wood wall sections to reduce construction costs, speed production, and cut labor requirements. Known informally as the "massive construction" program, this housing is built in complexes of at least 100 units to exploit serial production techniques. Although production is limited by a variety of factors, and output falls short of plant capacity, the 9,513 units built thus far represent a substantial increase in units per year over social housing built during the Somoza era.[11] Most of the housing has been built in rural areas to support the establishment of agricultural cooperatives and provide resettlement villages for Indians and peasants relocated from the war zones along the Honduran border. Monthly payments for state-built housing in the cities and rural cooperatives are limited to 15 percent of family income, leading to occupant ownership in the form of a "family patrimony," which permits inheritance of the unit by family members but allows the state to control any sale or transfer of title outside the family (Reglamento para la Administración de Viviendas, 1981).

## Perspectives

Despite the evident improvement in living conditions for most Nicaraguans, officials at MINVAH are realistic in assessing their progress to date.[12] The total number of new units produced with state assistance is not keeping pace with the population increase, meaning that most new housing must still be produced through private, unassisted efforts. The level of infrastructural development in the intervened settlements and Progressive Urbanization districts is rudimentary, particularly with regard to sanitary drainage. The prefabricated concrete units of the massive construction program tend to produce a gray, barrackslike environment.

The principal obstacle to housing development remains the ongoing counterrevolutionary offensive, which drains 40 percent of the national budget, disrupts the transportation of materials, and diverts labor resources.

Since the fall of 1984, the intensification of *contra* activity, fueled by ideological and material support from the Reagan administration, has exacerbated the planning problems in Nicaragua. Tens of thousands of people fleeing the frontier war zones have created a new series of squatter settlements, often on precarious sites, in Managua. Urban housing construction has come to a virtual halt as available resources are allocated to protect and stabilize new resettlement villages linked to agricultural production near the war zones to the north. In this context, the conceptual framework of urban housing policy is more significant than the physical results to date. The touchstone of this policy is the treatment of urban land as a social resource rather than a speculative commodity. The objective in terms of housing tenure is individual homeownership that emphasizes the use value of housing over its exchange value. This is accomplished in the state sector through strict controls on resale and in the private sector through rent control and control of credit through nationalization of the banking system.

It is the continued presence of the private sector in rental housing that distinguishes Nicaraguan policy from the Cuban approach and at the same time makes this policy more comparable to the housing system in the United States. Whereas Cuba eliminated most of the private sector in production as part of a clearly stated socialist program, Nicaragua is attempting to achieve social progress in the context of a mixed economy. In the urban housing sector the tools they are using to accomplish this goal all are in widespread use in the United States: rent control, receivership, and expropriation through eminent domain. The difference is in the degree and intent of their application and stems from the conviction in Nicaragua that the private sector exists to serve the public interest, not the other way around.

# Notes

1. A precise figure for the *cuartería* population in Managua was not available as of this writing. Nationally, the *cuarterías* house 8.5 percent of the population (López Román, 1982).

2. Ley de Inquilinato, 1980. For units renting at less than 500 *córdobas* a month, the rent was cut by 50 percent. In Managua, units renting for 500 to 1,000 *córdobas* received a 40 percent rent reduction. These two categories accounted for 93.6 percent of the renter population (MINVAH, 1982). The high percentage of low-rent units indicates that rental housing in Nicaragua was primarily a low-income housing resource. At the time of the law there were 92,052 rental units in the country for a population of just over 3 million (López Román, 1982).

3. The harsher measures taken by Cuba in forcing the sale of rental housing reflect the importance of rental housing as a source of profit extraction by wealthy investors as well as its significance as the principal form of urban housing. As Jill Hamberg notes in the first part of this chapter, rental housing in Cuba accounted for 58.7 percent of the national urban stock and 74.5 percent of the units in Havana. In Nicaragua, rental units during the Somoza dictatorship only accounted for an estimated 28 percent of the national urban housing stock (MINVAH, 1984).

4. Grounds for eviction include rent arrears of at least 60 days, illegal subletting or nonresidential use, damage to the premises, and repossession of the unit for occupancy by the owner or his or her immediate family (Ley de Inquilinato, 1980).

5. The Materials Bank was established by MINVAH in 1982 to complement the Progressive Urbanization Program (described in this article) by providing construction materials with loans amortized over 20 years at 3 percent interest. In addition to the 1,873 "basic modules" of wood wall sections produced in the first year of the program, other materials have been made available thanks in part to donations from other countries, including Sweden, France, and Norway (MINVAH, 1984).

6. State-assisted housing construction in Cuba in the early years included formal self-help construction as well as state-built units. Because Cuba already possessed a substantial urban infrastructure, at least in the larger cities, the self-help programs there went beyond the sites and services approach used in Nicaragua and involved construction of the houses themselves.

7. These settlements covered 772 acres, representing 30 percent of the urbanized area of Managua and 60 percent of its residential land. Nationally, there were a total of 420 illegal settlements at the time of the revolution (MINVAH, 1982).

8. Ley de Repartos Ilegales, 1979. The actual text of the law does not mention eventual title transfer, nor does it use the word "expropriation." Specifically, it gives the state the right to the "intervention, occupation, retention, and administration of the lands and rents" in the illegal settlements.

9. Ley de Titulación de Lotes en Repartos Intervenidos, 1982. Title transfer for lot holders who built houses but rented them out, who had not yet built, or who rented the vacant lot was deferred until such time as they lived on the lot.

10. Ley de Expropiación de Tierras Urbanas Baldías, 1981. While this was the first urban land expropriation measure that was national in scope and the first intended specifically for housing, a series of earlier laws had given the government near-total control over urban land in the center of Managua, much of which had been held vacant by speculators after the destruction caused by the earthquake. These earlier measures included the confiscation of land belonging to Somoza's family and associates, the voluntary donation of urban land in return for forgiveness of present and past taxes, and the expropriation of vacant land in the urban core (Ley sobre Donaciones de Inmuebles

del Casco Urbano Central de la Ciudad de Managua, 1980; Ley de Expropiación de Predios Baldíos en el casco Urbano de la ciudad de Managua, 1981).

11. Factors limiting construction capacity include lack of machinery and heavy equipment; dependence on imported materials, including iron and electrical fixtures; the suspension of AID loans from the United States in 1980 and impaired access to credit generally; and the ongoing war against the counterrevolutionary forces.

Production of state-built housing nonetheless averages over 2,000 units annually, with a habitable area of 44 square meters per unit, as compared with totals under Somoza from 1959 to 1979 averaging 1,600 units annually with an area of only 18 square meters per unit (MINVAH, 1984).

12. Interview with Roberto Chavez, director of Urban Planning, MINVAH, June 22, 1984, Managua. Initial research for this article was conducted during a 10-day visit in June 1984, with a delegation of U.S. architects and planners.

*References*
*Contributors*
*Index*

# General References

This consolidated list of references is divided into two parts. The main body includes all works published in North America and the United Kingdom. The smaller foreign section that follows contains works published elsewhere, principally in foreign languages. These latter documents are for the most part unavailable in U.S. libraries, and including them in the main body of references would have made this quite lengthy list more difficult to use. The numbers in bold type following each entry indicate the chapter(s) where that reference is cited.

Aaron, H. J. 1972. *Shelter and subsidies—Who benefits from federal housing policies?* Washington, D.C.: Brookings Institution. **14, 20**

Abrams, C. 1946. *The future of housing.* New York: Harper & Brothers. **6, 20**

———. 1948. Housing—the ever-recurring crisis. In *Saving american capitalism*, edited by S. F. Harris. New York: Alfred A. Knopf. **6**

———. 1950. The residential construction industry. In *The structure of American industry*, edited by W. Adams. New York: Macmillan. **6**

———. 1955. *Forbidden neighbors: A study of prejudice in housing.* Fort Washington, N. Y.: Kennikat Press. **11**

———. 1957. *A housing program for Pakistan.* New York: UN Technical Assistance Administration. **26**

———. 1965. *The city is the frontier.* New York: Harper & Row. **6**

———. 1971. *The language of cities.* New York: Viking Press. **26**

Abrams, P. 1983. Comment on housing allowances: A critical look. *Journal of Urban Affairs* (Spring). **21**

Achtenberg, E. P. 1985. Subsidized housing at risk: The social costs of private ownership. Paper presented at conference, Housing Policies in the Eighties: Choices and Outcomes, Institute for Policy Studies and Virginia Polytechnic Institute and State University, Alexandria, Va., May 17–18 **28, 29**

Achtenberg, E. P., and M. Stone. 1974. *Tenants first! A research and organizing guide to FHA housing.* Cambridge, Mass.: Urban Planning Aid. **3**

Achtenberg, E. P., and P. Marcuse. 1983. Towards the decommodification of housing: A political analysis and a progressive program. In *America's housing crisis: What is to be done?* edited by C. Hartman, 202–31. Boston: Routledge & Kegan Paul. **I, 20**

Ackerman, J., M. Clawson, and M. Harris, eds. 1962. *Land economics research.* Baltimore: Johns Hopkins University Press. **5**

Acosta, M., and J. E. Hardoy. 1973. *Urban reform in revolutionary cuba.* Occasional Paper no. 1. Yale University: Antilles Research Program. **33**

Adams, E. 1979. 1979 profile of the builders of America. *Professional Builder* (July). **7**

———. 1981. Move to the sun a matter of survival. *Professional Builder* (August). **7**

Adamson, M. 1981. Need a house? Call ACORN. *The Organizer* (Summer). **25**

Agnew, J. S. 1981. Homeownership and the capitalist social order. In *Urbanization and urban planning in capitalist society*, edited by M. Dear, and A. J. Scott, 457–80. New York: Methuen.   **11**

Alford, R., and H. M. Scoble. 1968. Sources of local political involvement. *American Political Science Review* 62:1192–1206.   **22**

Anderson, M. 1964. *The federal bulldozer: A critical analysis of urban renewal.* Cambridge: MIT Press   **14**

Anderson, R. J., and T. D. Crocker. 1971. Air pollution and residential property values. *Urban Studies* 8:3.   **8**

Anderson-Khleif, S. 1979. Research report, MIT–Harvard Joint Center for Urban Studies. Summarized in *Housing for Single Parents.* Research report, MIT–Harvard Joint Center for Urban Studies. (April): 3–4.   **13**

Appelbaum, R. P. 1978. *Size, growth, and U.S. cities.* New York: Praeger.   **8**

Appelbaum, R. P., and J. I. Gilderbloom. 1983. Housing supply and regulation: A study of the rental housing market. *Journal of Applied Behavioral Science* 19:1.   **8**

———. 1984. *Private interferences and public interventions in the rental housing market.* Santa Barbara, Calif.: Foundation for National Progress, Housing Information Center.   **8**

Appelbaum, R. P., and T. Glasser. 1982. *Concentration of ownership in Isla Vista, California.* Santa Barbara, Calif.: UCSB Housing Office.   **8**

Arnold, J. L. 1971. *The New Deal in the suburbs: A history of the Greenbelt town program 1935–54.* Columbus: Ohio State University Press.   **6**

Arthur D. Little, Jr. 1983. *Mortgage refinancing in the regulated housing stock: A survey of 1982 actions.* New York: Rent Stabilization Association. June.   **10**

Ashton, P. J. 1978. The political economy of suburban development. In *Marxism and the metropolis*, edited by W. K. Tabb and L. Sawers. New York: Oxford University Press.   **10**

Association of Metropolitan Authorities. 1984. *Disrepair in the public sector.* London: The Association.   **30**

Baar, K. K. 1977. Rent control in the 1970's: The case of the New Jersey tenants' movement. *Hastings Law Journal* 28:631–83.   **22**

Baer, H. 1983. Thrift dominance and specialization in housing finance: The role of taxation. *Housing Finance Review* 2:4.   **4**

Bahr, H. 1967. The gradual disappearance of skid row. *Social Problems* 15: 41–45.   **2**

———. 1973. *Skid row: An introduction to disaffiliation.* New York: Oxford University Press.   **2**

Baker, R. 1982. A cold hard net. *New York Times* (December 18).   **2**

Baldwin, S. 1968. *Poverty and politics: The rise and decline of the Farm Security Administration.* Chapel Hill: University of North Carolina Press.   **19**

Ball, M. J. 1973. Recent empirical work on the determinants of relative housing prices. *Urban Studies* 10:213–33.   **8**

———. 1983. *Housing policy and economic power: The political economy of owner occupancy.* London: Methuen.   **14, 30**

Barkin, C. 1979. Home, mom, and pie-in-the sky. Master's thesis. University of California, Los Angeles.   **13**

Baron, R. D. 1978. Community organizations: Antidote for neighborhood succession and focus for neighborhood improvement. *St. Louis University Law Journal* 21(3): 634–63.   **26**

———. n.d. *Tenant management: A rationale for a national demonstration of management innovation.* St. Louis: McCormack and Associates.   **26**

Bartholemew, H. 1939. The case for downtown locations. *Planners Journal* 4:32–33.   **6**

———. 1940. Present and ultimate effects of decentralization upon American cities.

*Mortgage Bankers Association of America Yearbook 1940*. Chicago: Mortgage Bankers Association of America.    **6**

Bassuk, E. L. 1984. The homelessness problem. *Scientific American* 251:40–45.    **2**

Bauer, C. 1956. First job: Control new city sprawl. *Architectural Forum* 55:105–12.    **6**

————, ed. 1948. *A housing program for now and later*. Washington, D.C.: National Public Housing Conference.    **6**

Bauer. O. 1925. *The Austrian revolution*. Translated by H. J. Stenning. London: L. Parsons.    **32**

Baxandall, R., L. Gordon, and S. Reverby, eds. 1976. *America's working women: A documentary history, 1600 to the present*. New York: Vintage Books.    **13**

Baxter, E., and K. Hopper. 1980. Pathologies of place and disorders of mind. *Heath/PAC Bulletin* 11:(4):1ff.    **2**

————. 1981. *Private lives, public spaces*. New York: Community Service Society.    **1, 2**

————. 1984. Troubled on the streets: The mentally disabled homeless poor. In *The chronic mental patient: Five years later*, edited by J. Talbott. New York: Grune and Stratton.    **2**

Beauregard, R. 1986. The chaos and complexity of gentrification. In *Gentrification, housing and the restructuring of urban space*, edited by N. Smith and P. Williams. London: Allen & Unwin.    **10**

Bednarzik, R. W. 1983. Lay-offs and permanent job losses: Workers' traits and cyclical patterns. *Monthly Labor Review* (September): 3–11.    **2**

Bell, D. 1976. *The cultural contradictions of capitalism*. New York: Basic Books.    **22**

Bellamy, C. 1979. *Real estate speculation in the South Bronx, a case study: Thomas Cuevas and affiliates*. Report of the New York City Council President.    **11**

Bellush, J., and M. Hausknecht, eds. 1976. *Urban renewal: People, politics, and planning*. Garden City, N.Y.: Doubleday.    **14**

Bemis, A. F. 1936. *The evolving house*. Cambridge: MIT Press.    **6**

Bender, R. 1973. *A crack in the rearview mirror: A view of industrialized building*. New York: Van Nostrand Reinhold    **7**

Bengelsdorf, C., and A. Hageman. 1979. Emerging from underdevelopment: Women and work in Cuba. In *Capitalist patriarchy and the case for socialist feminism*, edited by Z. Eisenstein. New York: Monthly Review Press.    **13**

Benjamin, M., J. Collins, and M. Scott. 1984. *No free lunch: Food and revolution in Cuba today*. San Francisco: Institute for Food and Development Policy.    **33**

Bennett, R. A. 1983a. U.S. provides $175 million to aid 15 savings banks, mostly in city. *New York Times* (January 4).    **4**

————. 1983b. Inside Citicorp: The changing world of banking. *New York Times* (May 29).    **4**

————. 1983c. A daring new world for thrifts in the making. *New York Times* (July 14).    **4**

————. 1983d. Deregulation alters banking. *New York Times* (December 5).    **4**

————. 1983e. Bank of Boston's gamble. *New York Times* (December 21).    **4**

————. 1984a. State panel report due on banks. *New York Times* (February 13).    **4**

————. 1984b. A banking puzzle: Mixing freedom and protection. *New York Times* (February 19).    **4**

————. 1984c. Economic scene: Deregulation's effect at banks. *New York Times* (March 16).    **4**

————. 1984d. Another crisis engulfs the thrifts. *New York Times* (July 22).    **4**

Berg, E. N. 1984. Rise of a national mortgage market. *New York Times* (January 22).    **4**

Berger, B. M. 1960. *Working-class suburb: A study of auto workers in suburbia*. Berkeley: University of California Press.    **6**

Besser, J. D. 1975. The skid row explosion. *The Progressive* 39 (October): 51–53. **2**

Beyer, G. H. 1965. *Housing and society.* New York: Macmillan. **6, 16**

Bienstock, H. 1983. *Adult workers in the New York City labor market.* New York: Center for Labor and Urban Programs, Queens College—CUNY. **11**

Birch, E. L. 1978. Woman-made America: The case of early public housing policy. *Journal of the American Institute of Planners* 44 (April): 130–44. **20**

Black, G. 1983. The 1972 earthquake and after: Somocismo in crisis. In *The Nicaraguan reader*, edited by P. Rosset and J. Vandermeer. New York: Grove Press. **33**

Blake, R. 1985. *The Conservative party from Peel to Thatcher.* London: Macmillan. **30**

Bluestone, B., and B. Harrison. 1982. *The deindustrialization of America.* New York: Basic Books. **10, 27**

———, and L. Baker. 1981. *Corporate flight.* Washington, D.C.: Progressive Alliance. **14**

Blumberg, R., and J. R. Grow. 1978. *The rights of tenants.* New York: Avon Books. **22**

Blumenfeld, H. 1954. The tidal wave of metropolitan expansion. *Journal of the American Institute of Planners* 20:3–14. **6**

Boddy, M. 1980. *The building societies.* London: Macmillan. **30**

Boston Housing Authority. 1983. Unpublished results from the *Tenant Survey.* **20**

Bowles, S., D. M. Gordon, and T. E. Weisskopf. 1983. *Beyond the waste land: A democratic alternative to economic decline.* Garden City, N.Y.: Anchor Press. **I, 10**

Bowley, M. 1945. *Housing and the state.* London: Allen & Unwin. **30**

Bowly, D., Jr. 1978. *The poorhouse: Subsidized housing in Chicago, 1895–1976.* Carbondale: Southern Illinois University Press. **20**

Boyer, B. 1973. *Cities destroyed for cash: The FHA scandal at HUD.* Chicago: Follett. **25**

Boyte, H. C. 1980. *The backyard revolution.* Philadelphia: Temple University Press. **22**

Bradbury, K., and A. Downs, eds. 1981. *Do housing allowances work?* Washington, D.C.: Brookings Institution. **21**

Bradbury, K., A. Downs, and K. A. Small. 1982. *Urban decline and the future of American cities.* Washington, D.C.: Brookings Institution. **10**

Bradford, C. P., and L. S. Rubinowitz. 1975. The urban–suburban investment–disinvestment process: Consequences for older neighborhoods. *Annals, AAPSS* 422 (November). **10**

Brantley, C. 1983. *New York City's services to homeless families: A report to the mayor.* New York: Health and Hospitals Corporation. **2**

Bratt, R. G. 1984. Partnerships assist housing developments. *Public/Private* 2 (Winter): 37–59. **20**

Breckenfeld, G. 1982. The other way builders make a buck. *Fortune* (October 4). **7**

Brodsky, B. 1975. Tenants first: FHA tenants organize in Massachusetts. *Radical America* 9 (March–April): 37–46. **3, 22**

Brooks, A. 1980. Making it easier to get a mortgage. *New York Times* (October 12). **4**

———. 1982. Foreclosing on a dream. *New York Times Magazine* (September 12). **3, 22**

Brown, C. A. 1978. Spatial inequalities and divorced mothers. Paper delivered at the Annual Meeting of the American Sociological Association, San Francisco. **13**

Bruce. A., and H. Sandbach. 1945. *A history of prefabrication.* Raritan, N.J.: John B. Pierce Foundation. **6**

Bruce, M. 1961. *The coming of the welfare state.* London: Batsford. **30**

Building Societies Association. 1985. Bulletin. London: The Association.    **30**

Burnham, W. D. 1980. The appearance and disappearance of the American voter. In *Political Participation*, edited by R. Rose. London: Sage.    **22**

Burtless, G. 1983. Testimony before the Committee on Ways and Means, U.S. House of Representatives (October 18).    **2**

Caplovitz, D. 1967. *The poor pay more.* New York: Free Press.    **11**

Carnoy, M., and D. Shearer. 1980. *Economic democracy.* White Plains, N.Y.: M. E. Sharpe.    **22**

Case, F., et al. 1971. *Housing the underhoused.* Report prepared for Housing, Real Estate and Urban Land Studies Program, Graduate School of Business Administration, University of California, Los Angeles.    **10**

Castells, M. 1973. *Neo-capitalism, collective consumption and urban contradictions: New sources of inequality and new models for change.* Prepared for the international conference on Models of Change in Advanced Industrial Societies, Monterosso al Mare. November.    **14**

———. 1976a. Is there an urban sociology? In *Urban Sociology*, edited by C. G. Pickvance, 33–59. London: Tavistock.    **5**

———. 1976b. The wild city. *Kapitalistate* (Summer): 4–5.    **14**

———. 1977. *The urban question.* Cambridge: MIT Press.    **13**

Center for Auto Safety. 1975. *Mobile homes: The low cost housing hoax.* New York: The Center.    **7**

Center for Community Change. 1971. *The national survey of housing abandonment.* New York: National Urban League.    **10**

Center for Urban Programs. 1974. *Tenant management corporations in St. Louis: The Darst and Carr Square public housing projects.* St. Louis: St. Louis University. July.    **26**

———. 1975. *Tenant management corporations in St. Louis public housing: The status after two years.* St. Louis: St. Louis University. December.    **26**

Center on Budget and Policy Priorities. 1983a. *Soup lines and food baskets.* Washington, D.C.: The Center. May.    **2**

———. 1983b. *Unemployed and unprotected: A report on the status of unemployment insurance.* Washington, D.C.: The Center. October.    **2**

*Centex Corporation Annual Report.* 1982. Dallas: Centex.    **7**

Chapman, G. 1954. Public acceptance of prefabrication. *Appraisal Journal* 22: 56–68.    **6**

Chatterjee, L., D. Harvey, and L. Klugman. 1976. *FHA policies and the Baltimore City housing market.* Washington, D.C.: National League of Cities.    **6**

Checkoway, B. 1977a. The failure of citizen participation in federal housing programs. *Planning and Public Policy* 3:1–4.    **6**

———. 1977b. *The politics of postwar suburban development.* Berkeley: University of California Childhood and Government Project.    **6**

———. 1977c. Suburbanization and community: Growth and planning in postwar Lower Bucks County, Pennsylvania. Ph.D. dissertation, University of Pennsylvania.    **6**

———. 1984. Large builders, federal housing programs and postwar suburbanization. In *Marxism and the metropolis*, edited by W. K. Tabb and L. Sawers. New York: Oxford University Press.    **10**

Christian, J., and T. J. Parliment. 1982. *Home ownership: The American dream adrift.* Chicago: U.S. League of Savings Associations.    **31**

Citizens Commission on Civil Rights. 1983. *A decent home . . . a report on the continuing failure of the federal government to provide equal housing opportunity.* Washington, D.C.: Citizens Commission on Civil Rights.    **21**

Citizens' Commission on Hunger in New England. 1984. *American hunger crisis: Poverty and health in New England.* Boston: Harvard University School of Public Health.    **2**

Citizens' Committee for Children. 1983. *No one's in charge: Homeless families with children in temporary shelter.* New York: The Committee.    2

Clark, L. H., Jr. 1983. Speaking of business: A remembrance of interest rates—and an editor—past. *Wall Street Journal* (July 5).    10

Clark, T. A. 1979. *Black in suburbs: A national perspective.* New Brunswick, N.J.: Rutgers Center for Urban Policy Research.    12

Clark, W., A. Heskin, and L. Manuel. 1980. *Rental housing in the City of Los Angeles.* Los Angeles: UCLA Institute for Social Sciences Research.    8

Clawson, M. 1971. *Suburban land conversion in the United States: An economic and governmental process.* Baltimore: Johns Hopkins University Press.    5, 6

Clay, P. 1979. *Neighborhood renewal.* Lexington, Mass.: D. C. Heath.    5

Cliffe, C. 1982. Seniors and tenants: Decent housing for everyone. *Shelterforce* 7:8–9.    22

Cohen, R., and M. Kohler. 1983. *Neighborhood development organizations after the federal funding cutbacks: Current conditions and future directions.* Report prepared for the Office of Policy Development and Research, U.S. Department of Housing and Urban Development. Washington, D. C.: GPO.    20

Cole, J. 1979. Sweat equity: A study of housing systems by and for the people in the United States and Cuba. *Black Scholar* 11 (November–December): 40–56.    33

Coleman, A. 1985. *Utopia limited.* London: Methuen.    30

Colton, K. W. 1980. Financial reform: A review of the past and prospects for the future. *AREUEA Journal* 8:1.    4

———. 1983. The report of the President's Commission on Housing: The nation's system of housing finance. *AREUEA Journal* 11:2.    4

Community Development Project Information and Intelligence Unit. 1976. *Profits against houses: An alternative guide to housing finance.* London: CDPIIU.    3

Community for Creative Non-Violence. 1983. *Hunger in the land of plenty: A report on human needs and surplus commodities.* Washington, D.C.: CCNV.    2

*Constitution of the Republic of Cuba.* 1976. English translation. New York: Center for Cuban Studies.    33

Conway, D. 1982. Self-help housing, the commodity nature of housing and amelioration of the housing deficit: Continuing the Turner-Burgess debate. *Antipode* 14(2):40–46.    11

Cook, F. J., and G. Gleason. 1959. The shame of New York. *The Nation* (October 31).    11

Cooney, R. S., and A. Colon. 1980. Work and family: The recent struggle of Puerto Rican females. In *The Puerto Rican struggle*, edited by C. Rodriquez, V. Sanchez-Korral, and J. O. Alers. New York: Puerto Rican Migration Research Consortium.    11

Cooper, C. C. 1975. *Easter Hill Village.* New York: Free Press.    20

Crisis Reader Editorial Collective. 1978. *U.S. capitalism in crisis.* New York: Union for Radical Political Economics.    10

Cuban Economic Research Project. 1963. *Un estudio de Cuba.* Miami: University of Miami Press. See also abridged English version: *A study of Cuba.*    33

Cubbin, J. S. 1970. A hedonic approach to some aspects of the conventional housing market. Warwick Economic Research Papers.    8

Cullingworth, J. B. 1961. *The small landlord in Britain.* London: Routledge & Kegan Paul.    30

Cuomo, M. 1983. *1933/1983—Never again: A report to the National Governors' Association Task Force on the Homeless.* Albany, N.Y.: State of New York, Executive Chamber. Reproduced in U.S. Congress. House Subcommittee on Housing and Community Development, 1984, 353–443.    2

Cutler, S. 1974. History, character and recent difficulties of mutual savings banks. In *Public policy toward mutual savings banks in New York State: Proposals for change,* edited by L. Lapidus, S. Cutler, P. P. Kildoyle, and A. L. Castro. New York: Federal Reserve Bank of New York and New York State Banking Department.    **4**

Cutting, M. 1979. *Housing rights handbook*. Harmondsworth, England: Penguin.    **30**

Danneberg, R. 1931. *The new Vienna*. Translated by H. J. Stenning. London: The Labour Party.    **32**

Davidoff, P. 1983. Decent housing for all. In *America's housing crisis: What's to be done?* edited by C. Hartman. Boston: Routledge & Kegan Paul.    **28**

Davidson, F. S. 1979. City policy and housing abandonment: A case study of New York City, 1965–1973. Ph.D. dissertation, Columbia University.    **11**

Davies, J. C. 1966. *Neighborhood groups and urban renewal*. New York: Columbia University Press.    **11**

Davies, R. O. 1966. *Housing reform during the Truman administration*. Columbia: University of Missouri Press.    **6**

Davis, P. J. 1958. *Real estate in America*. Washington, D.C.: Public Affairs Press.    **6**

Dean, J. P. 1945. *Home ownership: Is it sound?* New York: Harper & Row.    **6**

———. 1949. The myths of housing reform. *American Sociological Review* 14.    **6**

DeGiovanni, F., and M. Brooks. 1982. *Impact of a housing voucher program on New York City's population*. New York: Pratt Institute Center for Community and Environmental Development. January.    **21**

Denby, E. 1938. *Europe re-housed*. New York: W. W. Norton.    **32**

Devine, R. J. 1973. *Where the lender looks first: A case study of mortgage disinvestment in Bronx County, 1960–1970*. New York: National Urban League.    **10**

Dialogue Systems, Inc. 1983. *A guide to multifamily homesteading*. Washington, D.C.: GPO. A report prepared at the request of the Office of Community Planning and Development, U.S. Department of Housing and Urban Development. January.    **26**

Diaz, W. 1979. *Tenant management: An historical and analytical overview*. New York: Manpower Demonstration Research Corporation. March.    **26**

Díaz-Briquets, S., and L. Pérez. 1982. Fertility decline in Cuba: A socioeconomic interpretation. *Population and Development Review* 8 (September): 513–37.    **33**

Dietz, A. G. H. 1959. Housing industry research. In *Design and production of housing*, edited by B. Kelly et al. New York: McGraw-Hill.    **6**

Dietz, A. G. H., A. Murray, C. Koch, and B. Kelly. 1959. Construction advances. In *Design and production of housing*, edited by B. Kelly et al. New York: McGraw-Hill.    **6**

Dobriner, W. M. 1963. *Class in suburbia*. Englewood Cliffs, N.J.: Prentice-Hall.    **6**

———, ed. 1958. *The suburban community*. New York: Putnam.    **6**

Dolbeare, C. 1981. Statement before the Committee on Ways and Means, U.S. Congress, House. March 31.    **27**

———. 1983a. The low-income housing crisis. In *America's housing crisis: What is to be done?* edited by C. Hartman. Boston: Routledge & Kegan Paul.    **2, 20**

———. 1983b. *Low-income housing programs and needs: A widening gap*. Washington D.C.: National Low Income Housing Coalition.    **I, 31**

———. 1985. *Federal housing assistance: Who needs it? Who gets it?* Washington, D.C.: National League of Cities.    **1**

Donaldson, S. 1969. *The suburban myth*. New York: Columbia University Press.    **6**

Donnison, D. 1967. *The government of housing*. Baltimore: Penguin Books.    **3**

Donnison, D., and C. Ungerson. 1982. *Housing policy*. London: Penguin Books.    **2, 30, 33**

Donohue, J. J. 1982. Interest rate pressure on the first-time homebuyer: The affordability question. *Mortgage Banking* 42 (May): 10–17.    **22**

Downie L. 1974. *Mortgage on America*. New York: Praeger.    **5**

Downs, A. 1973. *Federal housing subsidies: How are they working?* Lexington, Mass.: D. C. Heath.    **20**

————. 1980. Too much capital for housing? *Brookings Bulletin* 17 (Summer): 1–5.  **1**

————. 1983. *Rental housing in the 1980's.* Washington, D.C.: Brookings Institution.  **I, 2, 10, 15**

Downtown Welfare Advocate Center. 1983. The in-Human Resources Administration's churning campaign. New York: The Center.  **2**

Doyle, F. R. 1978. *The end of the (red) line: A bibliography.* Monticello, Ill.: Council of Planning Librarians.  **10**

Dreier, P. 1979. The politics of rent control. *Working Papers* 6 (April): 55–63.  **22**

————. 1982a. The housing crisis: Dreams and nightmares. *The Nation* (August 21): 141–44.  **22**

————. 1982b. "Rent-a-politician" exposed. *Shelterforce* 7:3–4.  **22**

Dreier, P., and J. Atlas. 1980. The housing crisis and the tenants' revolt. *Social Policy* (January–February): 13–24.  **8**

————. 1981. Condomania. *The Progressive* (March): 19–22.  **22**

Dreier, P., J. I. Gilderbloom, and R. P. Appelbaum. 1980. Rising rents and rent control: Issues in urban reform. In *Urban and regional planning in an age of austerity*, edited by P. Clavel, J. Forester, and W. W. Goldsmith. New York: Pergamon Press.  **3, 8**

DuBrul, P. 1981. Landlords: They never had it so good. *Village Voice* (April 15–21).  **27**

Duncan. S. S., and M. Goodwin. 1982. The local state and restructuring social relations. *International Journal of Urban and Regional Research* 6 (June): 157–85.  **11**

Dworkis, J. 1957. *The impact of Puerto Rican migration on government services in New York City.* New York: New York University Press.  **11**

Eagle, M. 1960. The Puerto Ricans in New York City. In *Studies in housing and minority groups*, edited by N. Glazer and D. McEntire, 144–77. Berkeley: University of California Press.  **11**

Edel, M. 1976. Marx's theory of rent: Urban applications. *Kapitalistate* 4–5:100–24.  **5**

Edelman, M. 1980. *The symbolic uses of politics.* Chicago: University of Illinois Press.  **9**

Editors of *Fortune.* 1958. *The exploding metropolis.* New York: Doubleday.  **6**

Edmonds, S. 1984. House rich but cash poor: An information packet on home equity conversion. Boston, Mass. Department of Elder Affairs. November.  **29**

Edwards, R. 1979. *Contested terrain: The transformation of the workplace in the twentieth century.* New York: Basic Books.  **11**

Ehrenreich, B. and D. English. 1975. The manufacture of housework. *Socialist Revolution* 5.  **13**

Ehrenreich, B., and F.F. Piven. 1984. The feminization of poverty. *Dissent* (Spring): 162–70.  **2**

Eichler, E. P., and M. Kaplan. 1967. *The community builders.* Berkeley: University of California Press.  **6**

Eidlitz, O. 1894 address. *Marc Eidlitz and Son Papers.* New York: n.p.  **7**

Englander, D. 1983. *Landlord and tenant in urban Britain, 1838–1924.* London: Oxford University Press.  **30**

Ewen, S. 1976. *Captains of consciousness: Advertising and the social roots of the consumer culture.* New York: McGraw-Hill.  **13**

Fainstein, N. I., and S. S. Fainstein. 1982. Restructuring the American city: A comparative perspective. In *Urban policy under capitalism*, edited by N. I. Fainstein and S. S. Fainstein. Beverly Hills: Sage.  **10**

Fair Housing Amendments Act of 1979. *Hearings on H.R. 2540 before the Subcommittee on Civil and Constitutional Rights of the House Committee on the Judiciary.* 96th Cong., 1st sess., 1979. Statements of D. S. Days, III, assistant attorney general, Civil Rights Division, Department of Justice.  **18**

Farley, R., T. Richards, and C. Wurdock. 1980. School desegregation and white flight:

An investigation of competing models and their discrepant findings. *Sociology of Education* 53:123–139.   **18**

Federal Home Loan Bank of New York. 1982. *Multifamily balloon mortgage survey analysis report.* New York: Federal Home Loan Bank of N.Y. June 18.   **10**

Federal Reserve System. Board of Governors. 1984. *Flow of funds accounts, assets and liabilities outstanding, 1960–1984.* Washington, D.C.: Federal Reserve System.   **29**

Federal Reserve Bank of New York. 1983. New York State's economic turnaround: Services or manufacturing. *Quarterly Review* 8 (Autumn): 30–34.   **11**

Feins, J. D., and R. G. Bratt. 1983. Barred in Boston: Racial discrimination in housing. *Journal of the American Planning Association* (Summer): 344–55.   **I**

Feins, J. D., R. G. Bratt, and R. Hollister. 1981. *Final report of a study of racial discrimination in the Boston housing market.* Cambridge, Mass.: Abt Associates. November.   **18**

Fellman, G. 1973. *The deceived majority.* New Brunswick, N.J.: Transaction Books.   **22**

Filene, P. 1974. *Him/her/self: Sex roles in modern America.* New York: Harcourt Brace Jovanovich.   **13**

Fisher, R. M. 1959. *Twenty years of public housing.* New York: Harper & Brothers.   **20**

Flahive, M., and S. Gordon. 1979. *Residential displacement in Denver.* Denver: Council Committee on Housing.   **5**

Fleishman, J. L. 1979. *Not without honor: A prophet even in his own country (a case study of the resolution of the St. Louis public housing tenant strike of 1969).* New York: Ford Foundation manuscript. February.   **26**

Foote, N. N., J. Abu-Lughod, M. M. Foley, and L. Winnick. 1960. *Housing choices and housing constraints.* New York: McGraw-Hill.   **6**

Form, W. 1954. The place of social structure in the determination of land use. *Social Forces* 32:317–23.   **5**

Foster, D. 1973. *The origins of the welfare state.* London: Macmillan.   **30**

Foster, H. 1972. Unions, residential construction, and public policy. *Quarterly Review of Economics and Business* (Winter).   **7**

Fox, G. E. 1973. Honor, shame and women's liberation in Cuba: Views of working-class emigre men. In *Female and male in Latin America*, edited by A. Pescatello. Pittsburgh: University of Pittsburgh Press.   **13**

Francescato, G., S. Weidemann, J. R. Anderson, and R. Chenoweth. 1979. *Residents' satisfaction in HUD-assisted housing: Design and management factors.* Report prepared for the Office of Policy Development and Research, U.S. Department of Housing and Urban Development. Washington, D. C.: GPO.   **20**

Francis, J. D., et al. 1982. *National statistical assessment of rural water conditions. Executive Summary.* Department of Rural Sociology, Cornell University. Report prepared for the U.S. Environmental Protection Agency.   **19**

Frech, H. E., III. 1982. The California Coastal Commission: Economic impacts. In *Resolving the housing crisis: Government policy, decontrol, and the public interest*, edited by M. B. Johnson. Cambridge, Mass.: Ballinger.   **8**

Frech, H. E., III, and R. N. Lafferty. 1976. The economic impact of the California Coastal Commission: Land use and land values. In *The California coastal plan: A critique*; edited by M. B. Johnson. San Francisco: Institute for Contemporary Studies.   **8**

Frederick, C. 1929. *Selling Mrs. Consumer.* New York: Business Bourse.   **13**

Fredland, D. R. 1974. *Residential mobility and home purchase.* Lexington, Mass.: Lexington Books.   **22**

Freedman, L. 1969. *Public housing: The politics of poverty.* New York: Holt, Rinehart and Winston.   **14, 20**

Fried, M. 1973. *The world of the urban working class*. Cambridge: Harvard University Press.   **22**

Friedan, B. 1974. *The feminine mystique*. New York: W. W. Norton.   **13**

Frieden, B. J. 1968. Housing and national urban goals: Old policies and new realities. In *The metropolitan enigma*, edited by J. Q. Wilson. Cambridge: Harvard University Press.   **6**

————. 1979. *The environmental protection hustle*. Cambridge: MIT Press.   **8**

Frieden, B. J., and Solomon, A. P. 1977. *The nation's housing: 1975 to 1985*, 103–4. Cambridge, Mass.: Joint Center for Urban Studies.   **3**

Friedman, L. 1966. Public housing and the poor: An overview. *California Law Review* 54 (May).   **21**

Friedman, L. M. 1968. *Government and slum housing*. Chicago. Rand McNally.   **6, 14, 20**

Frobel, F., J. Heinrichs, and O. Kreye. 1980. *The new international division of labor*. Translated by P. Burgess. Cambridge: Cambridge University Press.   **11**

Galbraith, J. K. 1971. *The new industrial state*. Rev. ed. New York: New American Library.   **6**

Gans, H. J. 1962a. Urbanism and suburbanism as ways of life: A re-evaluation of definitions. In *Human behavior and social processes*, edited by A. Rose. Boston: Houghton Mifflin.   **6**

————. 1962b. *The urban villagers*. Glencoe, Ill.: Free Press.   **22, 29**

————. 1967. *The Levittowners*. New York: Vintage Books.   **6**

————. 1982. *The urban villagers*. Rev. ed. New York: Free Press.   **1**

Gappert, G., and H. M. Rose, eds. 1975. *The social economy of cities*. Beverly Hills: Sage   **11**

Garrigan, R. 1978. The case for rising residential rents. *Real Estate Review* (Fall): 36–41.   **8**

Gauldie, E. 1974. *Cruel habitation: A history of working-class housing in Britain, 1780–1918*. New York: Harper & Row.   **14**

Gaventa, J. 1980. *Power and powerlessness: Quiescence and rebellion in an Appalachian valley*. Urbana: University of Illinois Press.   **19**

Gelfand, M. J. 1975. *A nation of cities: The federal government and urban America, 1933–1965*. New York: Oxford University Press.   **6**

Genung, G. R., Jr. 1971. Public housing—success or failure? *George Washington Law Review* 39(4): 734–63.   **20**

George, H., ed. 1962. *Progress and poverty*. New York: Robert Schalkenbach Foundation.   **5**

Getz, V. K., and R. A. Hoppe. Forthcoming. The changing characteristics of the nonmetro poor. *Social Development Issues*.   **19**

Gilbert, B. B. 1971. *The evolution of British social policy 1914–1939*. London: Macmillan.   **30**

Gilderbloom, J. I. 1980. *Moderate rent control: The experience of U.S. cities*. Washington, D.C.: Conference on Alternative State and Local Policies.   **8**

————. 1981a. Moderate rent control: Its impact on the quality and quantity of the housing stock. *Urban Affairs Quarterly* 17(2): 123–42.   **8**

————. 1981b. *Rent control: A sourcebook*. Santa Barbara, Calif.: Foundation for National Progress.   **9**

————. 1982. The impact of moderate rent control in New Jersey: An empirical study of 26 rent controlled cities. *Urban Analysis: An International Journal* 7:2.   **8**

Gilderbloom, J. I., and D. Keating. 1982. *An evaluation of rent control in Orange, New Jersey*. Santa Barbara, Calif.: Foundation for National Progress, Housing Information Center.   **8**

Gilpatrick, E. 1966. *Structural unemployment and aggregate demand*. Baltimore: Johns Hopkins University Press.   **11**

Ginsburg, N. 1979. *Class, capital and social policy.* London: Macmillan.    **11**

Gist, N. P., and S. F. Fava. 1964. *Urban society.* 5th ed. New York: Thomas Y. Crowell.    **11**

Glazer, N., and D. P. Moynihan. 1963. *Beyond the melting pot: The Negroes, Puerto Ricans, Jews, Italians, and Irish of New York City.* Cambridge: MIT Press.    **11**

Glick, P. C. 1957. *American families.* New York: John Wiley and Sons.    **6**

Goetze, R. 1981. The housing bubble. *Working Papers* (January–February): 44–52.    **1**

Goodkin, M. 1974. *When real estate and home building become big business: Mergers, acquisitions, and joint ventures.* Boston: Cahners Books.    **5**

Goodman, J. L. 1978. *Urban residential mobility: Places, people and policy.* Washington, D.C.: Urban Institute.    **22**

Goodman, R. 1979. *The last entrepreneurs.* New York: Simon & Schuster.    **14**

Goodwyn, L. 1978. *The populist movement: A short history of the agrarian revolt in America.* New York: Oxford University Press.    **22**

Gordon, D. M. 1976. Capitalism and the roots of urban crisis. In *The fiscal crisis of American cities*, edited by R. E. Alcaly and D. Mermelstein. New York: Vintage Books.    **10**

———. 1978. Capitalist development and the history of American cities. In *Marxism and the metropolis*, edited by W. Tabb and L. Sawers. New York: Oxford University Press.    **13**

Gray, T. 1979. *Student housing and discrimination.* Santa Barbara: University of California, Santa Barbara.    **8**

Grebler, L. 1950. *Production of new housing.* New York: Social Science Research Council.    **6**

———. 1983. The commission's recommendations on housing finance. *AREUEA Journal* 11(2).    **4**

Green, C. 1982. *Housing single, low-income individuals.* New York: Setting Municipal Priorities Project.    **2**

Greenfield, R. P. 1981. The "Krakers" strike again. *The Nation* (January 3–10).    **25**

Greve, J. 1971 *Voluntary housing in Scandinavia.* Birmingham, England: Center for Urban and Regional Studies.    **31**

Grigsby, W. G., and L. Rosenburg. 1975. *Urban housing policy.* New York: Center for Urban Policy Research, Rutgers University. ARS Publications.    **10**

Groundwork Institute. 1984. *Las Arboledas sketchbook: Design for a new community in Cuba.* Berkeley, Calif.: Groundwork Institute (prepared in conjunction with the Centro Técnico de la Vivienda y el Urbismo, Havana).    **33**

Grubbs, D. 1971. *Cry from the cotton: The STFU and the New Deal.* Chapel Hill: University of North Carolina Press.    **25**

Gruen, C., and N. Gruen. 1977. *Rent control in New Jersey: The beginnings.* Sacramento: California Housing Council.    **8**

Gulick, C. A. 1938. Vienna taxes since 1918. *Political Science Quarterly* (December).    **32**

———. 1948. *Austria: From Habsburg to Hitler.* 2 vols. Berkeley: University of California Press.    **32**

Haar, C. M. 1960. *Federal credit and private housing: The mass financing dilemma.* New York: McGraw-Hill.    **6**

Haber, W., and H. Levinson. 1956. *Labor relations and productivity in the building trades.* Ann Arbor: University of Michigan Press.    **7**

Hacker, A., ed. 1983. *U.S.: A statistical portrait of the American people.* New York: Viking Press.    **2**

Hackney, R. 1984. Community architecture and self-help. In *The scope of social architecture*, edited by C. R. Hatch. New York: Van Nostrand Reinhold.    **27**

Hammond, P. 1982. *Who does rent control control: A history of the passage of rent control in Cambridge.* Boston: City Life.    **24**

Hardy, C. O. 1934. *The housing program of the City of Vienna.* Washington, D.C.: Brookings Institution. **32**

Harloe, M. 1983. The recommodification of housing. In *City, class and capital*, edited by M. Harloe and E. Lebas. London: Edward Arnold. **4**

———, ed. 1977. Introduction. *Captive cities: Studies in the political economy of cities and regions.* London: John Wiley and Sons, New York. **14**

Harrington, M. 1984a. The new gradgrinds. *Dissent* (Spring): 171–81. **2**

———. 1984b. U.S.'s next economic crisis. *New York Times* (January 15). **2**

Hartman, C. 1960. *Family turnover in public housing.* Office of Research, Urban Renewal and Housing Administration, Puerto Rico. **20**

———. 1963. Social values and housing orientations. *Journal of Social Issues.* **29**

———. 1964. The housing of displaced families. *Journal of American Institute of Planners* (November). **I**

———. 1971. Relocation: Illusory promises and no relief. *Virginia Law Review 57.* **I**

———. 1974. *Yerba Buena.* San Francisco: Glide. **5**

———. 1975. *Housing and social policy.* Englewood Cliffs, N.J.: Prentice-Hall. **6, 14**

———. 1979. Landlord money defeats rent control in San Francisco. *Shelterforce* 5 (Fall): 3. **22**

———. 1980. Social planning and the political planner. In *Planning Theory in the 1980's*, edited by R. W. Burchell and G. Sternlieb. New Brunswick, N.J.: Rutgers Center for Urban Policy Research. **5**

———. 1983a. Housing allowances: A critical look. *Journal of Urban Affairs* (Spring): 41–55. **20, 21**

———. 1983b. Rejoinder (to Comment on "Housing allowances: A critical look," by Philip Abrams). *Journal of Urban Affairs* (Spring). **21**

———. 1983c. Review of *The report of the President's Commission on Housing. Journal of the American Planning Association* (Winter): 92–94. **21, 22**

———, ed. 1983d. *America's housing crisis: What is to be done?* Boston: Routledge & Kegan Paul. **3**

Hartman, C. W., and G. Carr. 1969. Housing authorities reconsidered. *Journal of the American Institute of Planners* 35(1): 125–37. **20**

Hartman, C., D. Keating, and R. LeGates. 1982. *Displacement: How to fight it.* Berkeley, Calif.: National Housing Law Project. **I, 2, 25, 27**

Hartman, C. W., and M. Levi. 1973. Public housing managers: An appraisal. *Journal of the American Institute of Planners* 39 (2): 125–37. **20**

Hartman, C., and M. E. Stone. 1980. A socialist housing program for the United States. In *Urban and regional planning in an age of austerity*, edited by P. Clavel, J. Forester, and W. W. Goldsmith, 219–41. Elmsford, N.Y.: Pergamon Press. **20**

Hartz, L. 1956. *The liberal tradition in American thought.* New York: Harcourt, Brace. **30**

Harvey, D. 1973. *Social justice and the city.* Baltimore: Johns Hopkins University Press. **5, 6, 8, 13**

———. 1975. The political economy of urbanization in advanced capitalist societies: The case of the United States. In *The social economy of cities: Urban Affairs Annual Review*, edited by G. Gappert. Beverly Hills: Sage. **4, 10**

Hauser, P. M., and A. J. Jaffe. 1947. The extent of the housing shortage. *Law and Contemporary Problems* 12:3–15. **6**

Hayden, D. 1976. *Seven American utopias: The architecture of communitarian socialism, 1790–1975.* Cambridge: MIT Press. **13**

———. 1977. Challenging the American domestic ideal; Catherine Beecher and the politics of housework. In *Women in American architecture*, edited by S. Torre. New York: Whitney Library of Design. **13**

———. 1978. Melusina Fay Peirce and cooperative housekeeping. *International Journal of Urban and Regional Research* 2:404–20. **13**

————. 1979. Two utopian feminists and their campaigns for kitchenless houses. *Signs: Journal of Women in Culture and Society* 4:274–90.    **13**

————. 1979–1980. Charlotte Perkins Gilman and the kitchenless house. *Radical History Review* 21:225–47.    **13**

————. 1981. *The grand domestic revolution: A history of feminist designs for American homes, neighborhoods, and cities.* Cambridge: MIT Press.    **13**

Hayek, F. A., et al. 1975. *Rent control: A popular paradox.* Vancouver, Canada: Fraser Institute.    **32**

Headey, B. 1978. *Housing policy in the developed economy.* London: Croom Helm.    **31**

Heckler, M. 1984. Statement of Margaret Heckler in "Shelter" (television broadcast). KCTS-Seattle (May).    **2**

Heineman, E. H. 1983. American Express: Symbol of change. *New York Times* (July 13).    **4**

Hellmuth, W. F. 1977. Homeowner preferences. In *Comprehensive income taxation*, edited by J. A. Richman. Washington, D.C.: Brookings Institution.    **15**

Hendershott, P. H., and J. D. Schilling. 1980. The economics of tenure choice, 1955–1979. In *Research in real estate*, edited by C. F. Stirman. Vol. 1. Greenwich, Conn.: JAI Press.    **8**

Hendershott, P. H., and Sheng-Cheng Hu. 1980. Government induced biases in the allocation of the stock of fixed capital in the U.S. In *Capital, efficiency, and growth*, edited by G. M. Von Furstenburg. New York: Ballinger.    **4, 8**

Hendershott, P. H., and K. E. Villani. 1977. *Regulation and reform of the housing finance system.* Washington, D.C.: American Enterprise Institute.    **4**

————. 1980. Residential mortgage markets and the cost of mortgage funds. *AREUEA Journal* 8:1.    **4**

Herzog, J. P. 1963. Structural changes in the housebuilding industry. In Real Estate Research Program, *The dynamics of large-scale housebuilding.* Berkeley: University of California Press.    **6**

Heskin, A. D. 1981a. The history of tenants in the United States: Struggle and ideology. *International Journal of Urban and Regional Research, Housing: Special Issue* 5(2): 178–204.    **22**

————. 1981b. Is the tenant a second class citizen? In *Rent control: A source book*, edited by John I. Gilderbloom. Santa Barbara, Calif.: Foundation for National Progress, Housing Information Center.    **8**

HEW. See U.S. Department of Health, Education and Welfare.

Hinds, M. DeC. 1984. Tax plan clouds future for homeowners and investors. *New York Times* (December 30).    **15**

Hipshman, M. 1967. *Public housing at the crossroads: The Boston Housing Authority.* Boston: Citizens Housing and Planning Association. May.    **20**

Hoch, I. 1972. Income and city size. *Urban Studies* 9(3): 294–328.    **8**

Holin, M. J. 1982. *Co-ops for neighborhoods: A report on the New York City 510 demonstration.* Cambridge: Urban Systems Research and Engineering. October.    **26**

Hombs, M. E., and M. Snyder. 1982. *Homelessness in America: A forced march to nowhere.* Washington, D.C.: Community for Creative Non-Violence.    **2**

Homefront. 1977. *Housing abandonment in New York City.* New York: Homefront.    **11, 16, 26, 27**

Hoover, E. M., and R. Vernon. 1958. *Anatomy of a metropolis.* New York: Doubleday.    **11**

Hopper, K., E. Baxter, S. Cox, and L. Klein. 1982. *One year later: The homeless poor in New York City, 1982.* New York: Community Service Society.    **2**

Housing Assistance Council. 1983. *Preliminary summary of the rural housing data from the 1980 census and supplemental resources*. Washington, D.C.: HAC. October. **19**

*Housing . . . U.S.A.* 1954. New York: Simmons-Boardman. **6**

Housing Workshop of the Conference of Socialist Economists. 1975. *Political economy and the housing question.* London: CSE. April. **3**

Howard, J. T. 1957. Impact of the federal highway program. In *Planning 1957.* Chicago: American Society of Planning Officials. **6**

Howe, L. K. 1977. *Pink collar workers: Inside the world of woman's work.* New York: Avon Books. **13**

Husock, H. 1981. The high cost of starting out." *New York Times Magazine* (June 7). **22**

Industrial Housing Associates. 1919. *Good homes make contented workers.* Edith Elmer Wood Papers. Avery Library, Columbia University. **13**

*The In Rem Housing Program. Fourth Annual Report.* 1982. New York: Department of Housing Preservation and Development. **27**

*The In Rem Housing Program. Fifth Annual Report.* 1983. New York: Department of Housing Preservation and Development. **26**

Interface. 1983. *Keeping industry in New York: An agenda for city action.* New York: Interface. May. **11**

Ipcar, C. 1974. The student ghetto housing market. Lansing Community College, Social Sciences Division. Mimeographed. **8**

Jackson. A. 1976. *A place called home: A history of local housing in Manhattan.* Cambridge: MIT Press. **14**

Jaffe, A. J., ed. 1975. *The Puerto Rican experience.* New York: Arno Press. **11**

Janczyk, J. T. 1980. The potential impacts of high interest rates on the housing industry. *Growth and Change.* 11 (Jan.). **8**

Joe, T., and P. Yu. 1984. Black men, welfare and jobs. *New York Times* (March 11). **2**

Johnson, M. B. 1982. *Resolving the housing crisis.* Cambridge, Mass.: Ballinger Books. **8**

Johnston, R. A., S. I. Schwartz, and T. F. Klinkner. 1977. *General plan implementation: The growth-phasing program of Sacramento County.* Davis: University of California, Davis. Institute of Governmental Affairs, Environmental Quality Series. **8**

Jones, R., D. Kaminsky, and M. Roadhouse. 1979. *Problems affecting low-rent public housing projects.* Report prepared for the Office of Policy Development and Research, U.S. Department of Housing and Urban Development. Washington, D.C.: GPO. **20**

Kain, J. F., and J. M. Quigley. 1970. Measuring the value of housing quality. *Journal of the American Statistical Association* 65(June): 532–606. **8**

Kamer, P., and D. Young. 1981. New York City's competitive position: A review of selected manufacturing service industries. In *New York City's changing economic base,* edited by B. J. Klebaner. New York: Pica Press. **11**

Kamerman, S. B. 1979. Work and family in industrialized societies. *Signs: Journal of Women in Culture and Society.* 4(4): 632–50. **13**

Kantrowitz, N. 1969. *Social statistics for metropolitan New York.* New York: Fordham University Press. **11**

Kaplan, M. A. 1983. Deregulation and new powers in the savings and loan industry: What this portends. *Housing Finance Review* 2:2. **4**

Kaufman, N., and J. L. Harris. 1983. *Profile of the homeless in Massachusetts.* Boston: Governor's Office of Human Resources. Reproduced in U.S. Congress. House. Subcommittee on Housing and Community Development, 1984, 481–504. **2**

Kearns, K. 1980. Urban squatting: Social activism in the housing sector. *Social Policy* (September/October). **25**

Keating, L. n.d. *Reducing the development costs of housing.* Report prepared for the U.S. Department of Housing and Urban Development. Washington, D.C.: GPO.    **8**

Keating, W. D. 1973. *Emerging patterns of corporate entry into housing.* Berkeley: University of California. Center for Real Estate and Urban Economics, Institute of Urban and Regional Development, Special Report 8.    **7**

Keith, N. S. 1973. *Politics and the housing crisis since 1930.* New York: Universe Books.    **6, 20**

Keller, S. 1978. Women in a planned community. Paper for the Lincoln Institute of Land Policy, Cambridge, Mass.    **13**

Kelley, E. N. 1975. How to get your manager to raise rents. Chicago: Institute for Real Estate Management.    **8**

Kelly, B. 1951. *The prefabrication of houses.* New York: John Wiley and Sons.    **6**

Kelly, B., et al. 1959. *Design and production of housing.* New York: McGraw-Hill.    **6**

Kemeny, J. 1978. Urban home-ownership in Sweden. *Urban Studies* 15:313–20.    **31**

Kempton, M. 1982. Sweatshop revival rivals Taiwan on pay scales. *Newsday* (March 19).    **11**

Kerr, P. 1983. A bank's closing can jolt an area. *New York Times* (July 15).    **4**

Kihss, P. 1953. Puerto Rican will to work stressed. *New York Times* (February 25).    **11**

———. 1954. Survey finds new jobs in city exceed influx of Puerto Ricans. *New York Times* (January 16).    **11**

———. 1957. City relief roll held down despite job-hunter influx. *New York Times* (June 2).    **11**

Kilborn, P. T. 1984. Playing the odds on mortgages. *New York Times* (January 24).    **4**

Killingsworth, C. 1950. Organized labor in a free enterprise economy. In *The structure of American industry*, edited by W. Adams. New York: Macmillan.    **6**

King, A. T., and P. Mieszcowski. 1973. Racial discrimination, segregation, and the price of housing. *Journal of Political Economy* 81:590–606    **8**

Kirby, A. 1979. *Education, health and housing: An empirical investigation of resource accessibility.* Hampshire, England: Saxon House Press.    **11**

Kolodny, R. 1973. *Self help in the inner city: A study of lower income cooperative housing conversion in New York.* New York: United Neighborhood Houses.    **26**

———. 1979a. Exploring new strategies for improving public housing management. Report prepared for the Office of Policy Development and Research, U.S. Department of Housing and Urban Development. Washington, D.C.: GPO.    **20**

———. 1979b. Sweat equity urban homesteading in New York. Unpublished manuscript.    **26**

———. 1983. What happens when tenants manage their own public housing. Unpublished manuscript.    **26**

Kristof, F. S. 1970. Housing: Economic facets of New York City's problems. In *Agenda for a city: Issues confronting New York*, edited by L. C. Fitch and A. H. Walsh. Beverly Hills: Sage.    **11**

Krohn, R., and E. Fleming. 1972. *The other economy and the urban housing problem: A study of older residential neighborhoods in Montreal.* Cambridge, Mass.: Joint Center for Urban Studies. Working Paper No. 11.    **8, 10**

Krohn, R., E. Fleming, and M. Manzer. 1977. *The other economy: The internal logic of local rental housing.* Toronto: Peter Martin Associates.    **8**

Krohn, R., and R. Tiller. 1969. Landlord-tenant relations in a declining Montreal neighborhood. *Sociological Review Monographs* 14:5–32.    **22**

Kromer, T. 1935. *Waiting for nothing.* New York: Alfred A. Knopf.    **2**

Ktsanes, T., and L. Reissmann. 1959. Suburbia: New homes for old values. *Social Problems* 7:187–94.    **6**

Lacy, W. H. 1982. Innovation is a key to banks' meeting home financing needs. *ABA Journal* (May 19).    **4**

La Guardia, F. H. 1935. The federal works program and the cities. *City problems of 1935.* Washington, D.C.: U.S. Conference of Mayors.  **6**

Lamarche, F. 1976. Property development and the economic foundations of the urban question. In *Urban sociology*, edited by D. G. Pickvance, 85–118. London: Tavistock.  **5**

Lambert, J., C. Paris, and B. Blackenby. 1978. *Housing policy and the state: Access, allocation and control.* London: Methuen.  **30**

Lansky, S. 1977. *Housing and public policy.* London: Crown Helm.  **30**

Lansley, S., and S. Gross. 1983. *What price housing?* London: SHAC.  **30**

Lapham, V. 1973. Race and housing: A review of the issues. In *Patterns of racial discrimination*, edited by G. M. Von Furstenberg, B. Harrison, and A. R. Horowitz. Lexington, Mass.: D. C. Heath.  **11**

Larrabee, E. 1948. The six thousand houses that Levitt built. *Harper's Magazine* 197:79–88.  **6**

Lasch, C. 1977. *Haven in a heartless world.* New York: Alfred A. Knopf.  **13**

Lasch, R. 1948. What is blocking us: The building industry. *The Nation* (May 15).  **7**

Laurentz, R. 1980. Racial ethnic conflict in the New York City garment industry, 1933–1980. Ph.D. dissertation, SUNY at Binghamton.  **11**

Laven, C. 1984. Self-help in neighborhood development. In *The scope of social architecture*, edited by C. R. Hatch, 104–17. New York: Van Nostrand Reinhold.  **27**

Lawson, R. 1980a. The political face of the real estate industry in New York City. *New York Affairs* 6 (April): 88–109.  **22**

———. 1980b. Tenant mobilization in New York. *Social Policy* 10 (March): 30–40.  **22**

———. 1984. *Owners of last resort: An assessment of the track record of New York City's early low income cooperative conversions.* New York: New York City Department of Housing Preservation and Development. June.  **26**

Lawson, R., and S. E. Barton. 1980. Sex roles in social movements: A case study of the tenant movement in New York City. *Signs* 6 (Winter): 230–47.  **22**

Leavitt, H. 1970. *Superhighway-superhoax.* Garden City, N.Y.: Doubleday.  **6**

Lebowitz, N. H. 1981. "Above party, class or creed:" Rent control in the United States, 1940–1947. *Journal of Urban History* 7:439–70.  **22**

LeGates, R., and C. Hartman. 1981. Displacement. *Clearinghouse Review* 15 (July): 207–49.  **I, 2, 22**

LeGates, R. T., and K. Murphy. 1984. Austerity, shelter and social conflict in the United States. In *Marxism and the metropolis*, edited by W. K. Tabb and L. Sawers, 123–51. Rev. ed. New York: Oxford University Press.  **I, 2**

Leven, C., J. Little, H. Nourse, and R. Read. 1976. Neighborhood change: Lessons in the dynamics of urban decay. In *Housing in America: Problems and perspectives*, edited by R. Montgomery and D. R. Mandelker. 2d ed. New York: Bobbs-Merrill.  **10**

Levin, J. 1952. *Your Congress and American housing—the actions of Congress from 1892 to 1951.* H. Doc. 532. 82nd Cong.  **6**

Levitt, A. S. 1951. A community builder looks at community planning. *Journal of the American Institute of Planners* 17:80–88.  **6**

Levitt, W. J. 1948. More houses and better values. *Journal of the American Institute of Planners* 9:253–56.  **6**

———. 1969. Revolutionizing an industry. In Editors of *Nation's Business. Lessons of leadership: 21 top executives speak out on creating, developing and managing success.* Garden City, N.Y.: Doubleday.  **6**

Liell. J. T. 1952. Levittown: A study in community development and planning. Ph.D. dissertation. Yale University.  **6**

Lilley, W., III. 1971. Washington pressures/homebuilders lobbying skills result in successes, "good guy image." *National Journal* (February 27): 431–45.   **22**

———. 1973. The homebuilders' lobby. In *Housing urban America*, edited by J. Pynoos, R. Schafer, and C. W. Hartman, 30–48. Chicago: Aldine.   **6**

Lindeman, B. 1976. Anatomy of land speculation. *Journal of the American Institute of Planners* 142–52.   **5**

Lindsay, R. 1980. Housing finance in the 1980's. *AREUEA Journal* 8:1.   **4**

Lindsey, R. 1981. Housing costs are turning off flow of Americans to California. *New York Times* (December 31).   **22**

Linson, N. 1978. *Concentration of ownership in Santa Barbara*. Santa Barbara, Calif.: Foundation for National Progress Housing Information Center.   **8**

Lipsky, M. 1970. *Protest in city politics: Rent strikes, housing, and the power of the poor*. Chicago. Rand McNally.   **8, 22**

Lohr, S. 1984. U.S. mortgage securities for Asians. *New York Times* (January 28).   **4**

London. Central Statistical Office. 1985. *Social trends*. No. 15.   **30**

Lopez, A. 1973. *The Puerto Rican papers: Notes on the re-emergence of a nation*. New York: Bobbs-Merrill.   **11**

Lorimer, J. 1978. *The developers*. Toronto: James Lorimer   **5**

Los Angeles County Department of Regional Planning. 1981. *1980 census final population counts by place; 1980 census selected population and housing counts of major and minor statistical area; Los Angeles county population, selected subregions. 1970–1980.*   **12**

Low Income Housing Information Service. 1982. *The Reagan budget and low income housing*. Special Memorandum No. 15. Washington, D.C.: LIHIS. February 15.   **1**

———. 1985. *The 1986 low-income housing budget*. Special Memorandum No. 21, Washington, D.C.: LIHIS. February.   **21**

Lowry, I., J. DeSalvo, and B. Woodfill. 1971. *Rental housing in New York City*. Vol. 2, *The demand for shelter*. New York: Rand.   **9**

Lubove, R. 1962. *The Progressives and the slums: Tenement house reform in New York City, 1890–1917*. Pittsburgh: University of Pittsburgh Press.   **14**

Maffin, R. W. 1983. Letter to Honorable William L. Armstrong, U.S. Senate. January 25.   **20**

Maier, C. 1980. *Recasting bourgeois Europe: Strategies of defense, 1919–1924*. Princeton: Princeton University Press.   **30**

Mainardi, P. 1970. The politics of housework. In *Sisterhood is powerful*, edited by R. Morgan. New York: Vintage Books.   **13**

Maisel. S. J. 1953. *Housebuilding in transition*. Berkeley: University of California Press.   **6**

Malos, E. 1978. Housework and the politics of women's liberation. *Socialist Review* 37 (January–February): 41–47.   **13**

Mandelker, D. R. 1973. *Housing subsidies in the United States and England*. Indianapolis: Bobbs-Merrill.   **3**

Mann, E., and J. J. Salvo. 1984. *Characteristics of new Hispanic immigrants to New York City: A comparison of Puerto Rican and non-Puerto-Rican Hispanics*. New York: Department of City Planning.   **11**

Manpower Demonstration Research Corporation. 1981. *Tenant management. Findings from a three-year experiment in public housing*. Cambridge, Mass.: Ballinger.   **20, 26**

Manzer, M., and R. Krohn. 1973. Private redevelopment and older low rent housing: A conflict of economies. McGill University, Montreal. Mimeographed.   **8**

Marcis, R. G. 1980. Implications of financial innovation and reform for the savings and loan industry. *AREUEA Journal* 8:1.   **4**

Marcuse, P. 1973. Goals and limitations: The rise of tenant organizations. In *Housing urban America*, edited by J. Pynoos, R. Schafer, and C. W. Hartman. Chicago: Aldine. **22**

———. 1978a. The myth of the benevolent state. *Social Policy* 8 (January–February): 21–26. **1**

———. 1978b. The political economy of rent control: Theory and strategy. Papers in Planning No. 7. Columbia University, Graduate School of Architecture and Planning. **3**

———. 1979a. The deceptive consensus on redlining: Definitions do matter. *Journal of the American Planning Association* 45 (October): 549–56. **1, 3, 10**

———. 1979b. *Rental housing in the City of New York, supply and condition, 1975–1978*. New York: Department of Housing Preservation and Development **1, 9, 11**

———. 1980a. The determinants of housing policy. Papers in Planning No. 22. Columbia University, Graduate School of Architecture and Planning. **1, 11, 32**

———. 1980b. *Triage: Programming the death of communities*. Report prepared for the Working Group for Community Development Reform, New York City. **11**

———. 1981a. *Housing abandonment: Does rent control make a difference?* Washington, D.C. Conference on Alternative State and Local Policies. **1, 2, 10**

———. 1981b. The strategic potential of rent control. In *Rent control: A source book*, edited by J. I. Gilderbloom. Santa Barbara, Calif.: Foundation for National Progress, Housing Information Center. **8**

———. 1981c. The targeted crisis: On the ideology of the urban fiscal crisis and its uses. *International Journal of Urban and Regional Research* 5(3). **14**

———. 1982a. Determinants of state housing policies: West Germany and the United States. In *Urban policy under capitalism*, edited by S. Fainstein and N. Fainstein. Beverly Hills: Sage. **32**

———. 1982b. Triage as urban policy. *Social Policy* 12(3). **14**

———. 1983. On the political contradictions of self-help in housing. Papers in Planning. Columbia University, Graduate School of Architecture and Planning. **32**

———. 1985a. Gentrification, abandonment, and displacement: Connections, causes, and policy responses in New York City. *Journal of Urban and Contemporary Law* 28: 195–240. **2**

———. 1985b. The housing policy of social democracy: Determinants and consequences. In *Austrian social democracy 1918–1934*, edited by A. Rabinbach. Boulder, Colo.: Westview Press. **32**

Margolis, R. J. 1973. Metropollyana and rural poverty. *New Leader* (February 5). **19**

Mariano, A. 1983. Home foreclosures jump sharply. *Washington Post* (February 24). **I**

Marshall, H. 1973. Suburban life-styles: A contribution to the debate. In *The urbanization of the suburbs*, edited by L. H. Masotti and J. K. Hadden. Beverly Hills: Sage. **6**

Marshall, S. 1981. *A profile of revitalization projects being implemented by neighborhood development organizations*. Report prepared for the Office of Policy Development and Research. U.S. Department of Housing and Urban Development. Washington, D.C.: Urban Institute. **20**

Marx, K. 1977. *Capital*. Vol. 1. New York: Vintage Books. **11, 32**

Mason, J. B. n.d. A brief history of housing, 1940–1949: Decade of war and progress. National Association of Home Builders Library. Manuscript. **6**

Masotti, L. H., and J. K. Hadden, eds. 1973 *The urbanization of the suburbs*. Beverly Hills: Sage. **6**

Mayer, M. 1978. *The builders*. New York: Norton. **7**

Mayo, S. K., S. Mansfield, D. Warner, and R. Zwetchkenbaum. 1980. *Housing allowances and other rental housing assistance programs—a comparison based on the housing allowance demand experiment.* Part 2, *Costs and efficiency.* Report prepared for the Office of Policy Development and Research, U.S. Department of Housing and Urban Development. Cambridge, Mass.: Abt Associates.   **20**

Mayor's Committee on Puerto Rican Affairs. 1953. *Interim report, September 1949 to September 1953.* New York City Mayor's Office. November.   **11**

*Mayor's management report.* 1983. Preliminary. January. City of New York.   **20**

McAdams, D. 1979. Powerful actors in public land use decision-making processes. Ph.D. dissertation, University of Texas.   **5**

McAdams, D., and J. R. Feagin. 1980. A power-conflict approach to urban land use. Austin, Texas. Unpublished monograph.   **5**

McClean, A. J. 1963. The common law life estate and the civil law usufruct: A comparative study. *International and Comparative Law Quarterly* 12:649–67.   **33**

McDonnell, T. 1957. *The Wagner Housing Act: A case study of the legislative process.* Chicago: Loyola University Press.   **6, 14**

McEntire, D. 1960 *Residence and race.* Berkeley: University of California Press.   **11**

McGrath, C. 1979. The crisis of domestic order. *Socialist Review* 9 (January–February): 12–23.   **13**

McKelvey, B. 1966. *The emergence of metropolitan America, 1915–1968.* New Brunswick, N.J.: Rutgers University Press.   **6**

Meehan, E. J. 1975. *Public housing policy: Myth versus reality.* New Brunswick, N.J.: Center for Urban Policy Research.   **20**

———. 1979. *The quality of federal policy making: Programmed failure in public housing.* Columbia: University of Missouri Press.   **20**

———. 1983. Is there a future for public housing? *Journal of Housing* 40(3): 73–76.   **20**

MeGee, M. 1973. Statistical prediction of mortgage risk. *Land Economics* 45(4).   **10**

Melling, J. 1983. *Rent strikes.* London: Polygon.   **30**

Mental Health Law Project. 1982. *Arbitrary reduction of disability rolls.* Washington, D.C.   **2**

Merritt, S. 1979. *State housing in Britain.* London: Routledge & Kegan Paul.   **30**

———. 1980. *Owner occupation in Britain.* London: Routledge & Kegan Paul.   **30**

Merryman, J. H. 1974. Ownership and estate: Variations on a theme by Lawson. *Tulane Law Review* 48:916–45.   **33**

Meyer, P. 1979. Land rush. *Harper's* 258 (January): 45–60.   **5**

Meyerson, A. T. 1979. The determinants of institutional mortgage investment in Bronx County. Ph.D. dissertation, New York University.   **10**

Meyerson, M., and E. C. Banfield. 1955. *Politics, planning and the public interest: The case of public housing in Chicago.* Glencoe, Ill.: Free Press.   **20**

Meyerson, M., B. Terrett, and W. L. C. Wheaton. 1962. *Housing, people and cities.* New York: McGraw-Hill.   **6**

Mikesell, J., and S. Davidson. 1982. Financing rural America: A public policy and research perspective. In *Rural financial markets: Research issues for the 1980's.* Chicago: Federal Reserve Bank of Chicago. December 9 and 10.   **19**

Miller, H. P. 1965. *Income of the American people.* New York: John Wiley and Sons.   **6**

Mitchell. H. L. 1979. *Mean things happening in this land.* Montclair, N.J.: Allenheld, Osmun.   **25**

Mollenkopf, J., and J. Pynoos. 1973. Boardwalk and Park Place: Property ownership, political structure, and housing policy at the local level. In *Housing urban America,* edited by J. Pynoos, R. Schafer, and C. Hartman, 228–38. Chicago: Aldine.   **8**

Molotch, H. 1976. The city as a growth machine. *American Journal of Sociology* 82:2.   **5, 8**

Moon, M., and I. V. Sawhill. 1984. Family incomes: Gainers and losers. In *The Reagan record*, edited by J. L. Palmer and I. V. Sawhill, 317–46. Cambridge, Mass.: Ballinger.  2

Morton, H. W. 1979. Housing problems and policies of Eastern Europe and the Soviet Union. *Studies in Comparative Communism* 12 (Winter): 300–321.  33

Moskowitz, M., M. Katz, and R. Levering, eds. 1982. *Everybody's business.* San Francisco: Harper & Row.  7

Movimento di Lotta Femminile. 1972. Programmatic manifesto for the struggle of housewives in the neighborhood. *Socialist Revolution* 9 (May–June): 85–90.  13

Muller, P. O. 1976. *The outer city: Geographical consequences of the urbanization of suburbs.* Washington, D.C.: Association of American Geographers.  6

Mumford. L. 1961. *The city in history.* New York: Harcourt, Brace and World.  5

———. 1968. *The urban prospect.* New York: Harcourt Brace Jovanovich.  6

Murie, A. 1983. *Housing inequality and deprivation.* London: Heinemann Books.  11

Muth, R. F. 1973a. *Public housing: An economic evaluation.* Washington, D.C.: American Enterprise Institute for Public Policy Research.  11, 20

———. 1973b. "Residential segregation and discrimination." In *Patterns of residential discrimination*, Vol. 1, *Housing*, edited by G. Von Furstenberg et al. Lexington, Mass.: D. C. Heath.  11

Narparstek, A. 1977. *Neighborhood reinvestment: An annotated bibliography.* 3d ed. Washington, D.C.: U.S. Department of Housing and Urban Development.  10

Nash, G. 1964. *The habitats of homeless men in Manhattan.* New York: Columbia University, Bureau of Applied Social Research.  2

National Association of Home Builders. 1960. The homebuilder—what does he build? *Journal of Homebuilding* 14 (March).  6

———. 1982a. *Land use and construction regulations: A builder's view.* Washington, D.C.: NAHB.  8

———. 1982b. Statistics for new housing construction provided in personal communication from the Research Division, Washington, D.C.  31

National Association of Housing Officials. 1950. *Legislative history of certain aspects of the Housing Act of 1949*, no. N278. Washington, D.C.  6

National Association of Mutual Savings Banks. 1982. *1982 national fact book of mutual savings banking.* New York: The National Association.  4

National Association of Realtors. n.d. *Government regulation and home prices.* Washington, D.C.: NAR, Economics and Research Division.  8

———. 1982. Existing Home Sales, 1981. Washington, D.C.: NAR Economics and Research Division.  31

National Center for Housing Management. n.d. *Public Housing.* Vol. 2. Report of the Task Force on Improving the Operation of Federally Insured or Financed Housing Programs. Washington, D.C.: GPO.  20

National Commission on Urban Problems. 1968. *Building the American city.* Washington, D.C.: GPO.  6, 18

National Committee Against Discrimination in Housing. 1967. *Impact of housing patterns on job opportunities.* Washington, D.C.: The Committee.  14, 18

———. 1971. *How the federal government builds ghettoes.* Washington, D.C.: The Committee.  14

———. 1974. *Fair housing and exclusionary land use.* Washington, D.C.: The Committee.  18

National Farmers Union. 1982. *Depression in rural America.* Denver: NFU. May.  19

National Housing Conference. 1984. *Housing costs in the United States.* Washington, D.C.  2

National Housing Law Project. 1981. *HUD housing programs: Tenants' rights.* Berkeley, Calif.: National Housing Law Project.  21, 29

National Multi-Housing Council. 1981a. *The rent law and legislative activities affecting condominium and cooperative housing.* Washington, D.C.: The Council.   **22**
————. 1981b. The spread of rent control. Washington, D.C.: The Council.   **22**
National Puerto Rican Forum. 1980. *Fact sheets on the Puerto Rican community.* Program Development Unit. New York: The Forum. January 16.   **11**
National Urban Coalition. 1978. *Displacement: City neighborhoods in transition.* Washington, D.C.: The Coalition.   **5**
Nenno, M. K. 1984. Housing allowances are not enough. *Society* 21 (March/April): 54–57.   **2**
Nesslein, T. S. 1982. The Swedish housing model: An assessment. Urban Studies 19:235–46.   **31**
Neutze, M. 1968. *The suburban apartment boom.* Baltimore: Johns Hopkins University Press.   **22**
Nevitt, A. A. 1966. *Housing, taxation, and subsidies.* London: Nelson.   **30**
Newcomb, R., and H. C. Kyle. 1947. The housing crisis in a free economy. *Law and Contemporary Problems* 12:186–205.   **6**
Newfield, J., and P. DuBrul. 1977. *The abuse of power.* New York: Viking Press.   **22**
New York City. Department of City Planning. 1974. *Public and publicly aided housing 1927–1973: New dwelling units completed in New York City.* September.   **11**
————. 1978. *New dwelling units completed in 1976–1977.* June.   **11**
New York City. 1984. *A comprehensive plan for the temporary and permanent needs of homeless families in New York City.* January.   **2**
New York City. Human Resources Administration, Crisis Intervention Services. 1984. *Monthly report, New York City temporary housing program for families with children.* November.   **2**
New York State. Department of Labor. Division of Research and Statistics. 1982a. *Garment industry in New York State.* February.   **11**
————. 1982b. *Current population survey data: New York labor market area.* February.   **11**
New York State. Department of Social Services. 1984. *Administrative closings of New York City public assistance cases.* Albany. September.   **2**
Noble, K. B. 1983. Thrift limits: Cautious rivals. *New York Times* (April 23).   **4**
Northrup, H., and H. Foster. 1975. *Open shop construction.* Philadelphia: Industrial Research Unit, Wharton School, University of Pennsylvania.   **7**
Nove, A. 1983. *The economics of feasible socialism.* London: George Allen and Unwin.   **33**
O'Connor, J. 1973. *The fiscal crisis of the state.* New York: St. Martin's Press.   **4, 11, 27**
O'Connor, P. 1963. *Britain in the sixties: Vagrancy.* Baltimore: Penguin Books.   **2**
Offe, C. 1975. The theory of the capitalist state and the problem of policy formation. In *Stress and contradiction in modern capitalism: Public policy and the theory of the state,* edited by L. N. Lindberg, 125–44. Lexington, Mass.: Lexington Books.   **1**
Offer, A. 1982. *The ramparts of property: Landlords and urban political economy in Britain.* Oxford: Oxford University Press.   **30**
O'Hare, W. P., R. Chatterjee, and M. Shukur. 1982. *Blacks, demographic change, and public policy: Migration trends and population distribution in metropolitan areas.* Report prepared for the U.S. Department of Housing and Urban Development. Washington, D.C.: GPO.   **12**
Olsen, E. 1973. A competitive theory of the housing market. In *Housing Urban America,* edited by J. Pynoos, R. Schafer, and C. Hartman, 228–38. Chicago: Aldine.   **8**
Olson, L. K. 1982. *The political economy of aging.* New York: Columbia University Press.   **20**
Park, R., E. W. Burgess and R. D. McKenzie. 1925. *The city.* Chicago: University of Chicago Press.   **5**

Pattison, T. 1977. The process of neighborhood upgrading and gentrification. Master's thesis, MIT, Department of City Planning. **5**

Paul, B. 1981. *Rehabilitating residential hotels.* Washington, D.C. National Trust for Historic Preservation. **2**

Pearce, D. 1980. Breaking down barriers. Washington, D.C.: Center for National Policy Review. November. **18**

Perkins and Will, and the Ehrenkrantz Group. 1980. *An evaluation of the physical condition of public housing stock. Final report.* Prepared for the Office of Policy Development and Research. U.S. Department of Housing and Urban Development. Washington, D.C.: GPO. **20**

Peroff, K. A., C. L. Davis, and R. Jones. 1979. *Gautreaux Housing Demonstration: An evaluation of its impact on participating households.* Report prepared for the Office of Policy Development and Research. U.S. Department of Housing and Urban Development. Washington, D.C.: GPO. **20**

Pickvance, C. G., ed. 1976. *Urban sociology.* London: Tavistock. **14**

Piven, F. F., and R. A. Cloward. 1971. *Regulating the poor: The functions of public welfare.* New York: Vintage Books. **2, 10**

———. 1982. *The new class war.* New York: Pantheon Books. **22**

Popenoe, D. 1977. *The suburban environment: Sweden and the United States.* Chicago: University of Chicago Press. **6, 31**

Portes, A., and C. Walton. 1981. *Labor, class and the international system.* New York: Academic Press. **11**

Portnoy, F. C., and J. Pickman. 1984. Innovative approaches to low-income housing. *Public/Private* 2(2): 27–35. **20**

Power, A. 1979. *Tenant coops or tenant management corporations in U.S.A.* London: North Islington Rights Project. January. **26**

President's Commission on Financial Structure and Regulation. 1971. *The report of the President's Commission on Financial Structure and Regulation.* Washington, D.C.: GPO. **4**

President's Commission on Housing. 1981. *Interim report.* Washington, D.C.: GPO. **8, 21**

———. 1982. *The report of the President's Commission on Housing.* Washington, D.C.: GPO. **1, 4, 10, 14, 20, 21**

President's Committee on Urban Housing. *Report.* 1968. Washington, D.C.: GPO. **20**

President's Task Force on Food Assistance. 1984. *Summary of findings.* Washington, D.C.: GPO. January 9. **2**

Price, S. C. 1979. The effect of federal antipoverty programs and policies on the Hasidic and Puerto Rican communities of Williamsburg. Ph.D. dissertation, Brandeis University. **11**

Pynoos, J. M. 1974. Breaking the rules: The failure to select and assign public housing tenants equitably. Ph.D. dissertation, Harvard University. **20**

Pynoos, J., R. Schafer, and C. W. Hartman, eds. 1973. *Housing urban America.* Chicago: Aldine. **6**

Rabinbach, A. 1983. *The crisis of Austrian socialism: From Red Vienna to Civil War, 1927–1934.* Chicago: University of Chicago Press **32**

———, ed. 1985. *Austrian social democracy 1918–1934.* Boulder, Colo.: Westview Press. **32**

Rabushka, A., and W. G. Weissert. 1977. *Caseworkers or police? How tenants see public housing.* Stanford: Hoover Institution Press. **20**

Rae, J. 1971. *The road and the car in American life.* Cambridge: MIT Press. **6**

Rainwater, L. 1970. *Behind ghetto walls.* Chicago: Aldine. **20**

Rapkin, C. 1966. Price discrimination against Negroes in the rental housing market. *Essays in Urban Land Economics* (August).    **11**

Richards, C., and J. Rowe. 1977. Restoring a city. *Working Papers for a New Society* (Winter): 54–61.    **5**

*The Richmond school decision: Complete text of Bradley v. School Board of Richmond.* 1972. Chicago: Integrated Education Associates.    **18**

Ridgeway, J. 1984a. The administration's attack on the homeless: Building a fire under Reagan. *Village Voice* (February 14).    **2**

———. 1984b. The Democrats' uphill fight: Down and dirty. *Village Voice* (September 11).    **2**

Ridker, R., and J. Henning. 1968. The determination of residential propery values with special reference to air pollution. *Review of Economics and Statistics.*    **8**

Roca, S. 1980. Housing in socialist Cuba. In *Housing as human habitat.* Vol. 1, *Planning, financing, and construction*, edited by O. Ural, 60–74. Elmsford, N.Y.: Pergamon.    **33**

Roisman, F. 1983. Legal strategies for protecting low-income housing. In *America's housing crisis: What is to be done?*, edited by C. Hartman. Boston: Routledge & Kegan Paul.    **8**

Roistacher, E. 1972. The distribution of tenant benefits under rent control. Ph.D. dissertation, University of Pennsylvania.    **9**

———. 1978. The removal of rent regulation in New York City. Paper presented at annual meetings of the American Economics Association.    **9**

———. 1985. Selling public housing: Should we try? Who will buy? Lessons from Britain. *Hearings before the Subcommittee on Banking, Finance, and Urban Affairs, U.S. House of Representatives.* March 14.    **33**

Rooney, J. F. 1970. Societal forces and the unattached male: An historical review. In *Disaffiliated man: Essays and bibliography on skid row*, edited by H. Bahr, 13–38. Toronto: University of Toronto Press.    **2**

Rose, J. 1973. *Landlords and tenants.* New Brunswick, N.J.: Transaction Books.    **22**

Rose, S. M. 1979. Deciphering deinstitutionalization. *Milbank Memorial Fund Quarterly* 57:429–60.    **2**

Rose, S. 1983. *Social stratification in the United States.* Baltimore: Social Graphics Co.    **2**

Rosen, H. S. 1978. Housing decisions and the U.S. income tax. *Journal of Public Economics* 2 (February): 1–23.    **8**

Rosen, H. S., and K. T. Rosen. 1980. Federal taxes and homeownership. Evidence from time-series. *Journal of Political Economy* 88 (February): 59–75.    **8**

Rosenberg, T. J. 1974. *Residence, employment, and mobility of Puerto Ricans in New York City.* Department of Geography Research Paper No. 151. Chicago: University of Chicago.    **11**

Rosenberg, T. J., and R. W. Lake. 1976. Toward a revised model of residential segregation and succession: Puerto Ricans in New York. *American Journal of Sociology* 81 (March): 1142–51.    **11**

Rosenblatt, R. 1984. Phone interview. Economics and Education Department, Mortgage Bankers Association of America, Washington, D.C. December 28.    **I**

Rosenman, D. 1946. *A million homes a year.* New York: Harper & Row.    **6**

Ross, M. H. 1973. *The political integration of urban squatters.* Evanston: Northwestern University Press.    **25**

Ross, R., and K. Trachte. 1983. Global cities and global classes: The peripheralization of labor in New York City. *Review* 6(3): 393–431.    **11**

Rossi, P. 1955. *Why families move.* Glencoe, Ill.: Free Press.    **22**

Rothblatt, D., D. J. Garr, and J. Sprague. 1979. *The suburban environment and women.* New York: Praeger.    **1**

Royce, J. 1885. The squatter riot of '50 in Sacramento. *Overland Monthly.* (September).   **25**

Ruben, G. 1984. Economy improves: Bargaining problems persist in 1983. *Monthly Labor Review* 107 (January): 33–43.   **2**

Rubey, H., and W. Milner. 1966. *Construction and professional management.* New York: Macmillan.   **7**

Rule, S. 1983. 17,000 families in public housing double up illegally, city believes. *New York Times* (April 21).   **I**

Rural America. 1979. *1978 survey: Self-help housing projects.* Washington, D.C.: Rural America.   **19**

Saegert, S. 1981. Masculine cities and feminine suburbs: Polarized ideas, contradictory realities. In *Women and the American City*, edited by C. Stimson et al., 93–108. Chicago: University of Chicago Press.   **1**

Sakolski, A. M. 1932. *The great American land bubble.* New York: Harper & Brothers.   **5**

———. 1957. *Land tenure and land taxation in America.* New York: Robert Schalkenbach Foundation.   **5**

Salerno, D., K. Hopper, and E. Baxter. 1984. *Hardship in the heartland: Homelessness in eight U.S. cities.* New York: Community Service Society.   **2**

Salins, P. 1980. *The ecology of housing destruction: Economic effects of public intervention in the housing market.* New York: New York University Press.   **14**

Salter, S. 1983. Southeast lags behind nation in the number of housing starts. *Atlanta Journal & Constitution* (January 23).   **7**

Sanchez-Korral, V. E. 1981. Settlement patterns and community development among Puerto Ricans in New York City, 1917–1948. Ph.D. dissertation, SUNY–Stony Brook. May.   **11**

Sanford, E. 1937. Wage rates and hours of labor in the building trades. *Monthly Labor Review* (August).   **7**

Sarokin, W. 1982. *Distressed properties: A study of Bronx savings banks and their handling of "problem" mortgages.* New York: New York City Department of Housing Preservation and Development, Division of Alternative Management Programs.   **10**

Sasaki, H. 1959. Land development and design. In *Design and production of housing*, edited by B. Kelly et al. New York: McGraw-Hill.   **6**

Saulnier, R. J., H. G. Halcrow, and N. H. Jacoby. 1958. *Federal lending and loan insurance.* Princeton: Princeton University Press.   **6**

Saunders, P. 1981. *Social theory and the urban question.* London: Hutchinson.   **14**

Sawers, L. 1975. Urban form and the mode of production. *Review of Radical Political Economy* 7 (Spring): 52–68.   **5**

Schafer, R. 1974. *The suburbanization of multifamily housing.* Lexington, Mass.: Lexington Books.   **22**

Schaffer, A. 1966. *Vito Marcantonio: Radical in Congress.* Syracuse: Syracuse University Press.   **11**

Schaffer, R. 1978. *Mortgage financing in ten New York City neighborhoods.* New York: New York State Banking Department.   **10**

Schechter, H. B. 1984. Closing the gap between need and provision. *Society* 21 (March/April): 40–47.   **2**

Schifferes, S. 1974. Tenants' struggles and housing policy in the 1930s. Master's thesis, Warwick University, England.   **30**

Schlesinger, T. 1980. Trailers: The business. *Southern Exposure* (Spring).   **7**

Schnore, L. 1968. *The urban scene.* New York: Free Press.   **6**

Schriftgiesser, K. 1951. *The lobbyists: The art and business of influencing lawmakers.* Boston: Little, Brown.   **6**

Schulkin, P. A. 1970. Construction lending at large commercial banks. *New England Economic Review*, July/August.   **29**

Schuman, W. 1977. The return of togetherness. *New York Times* (March 20).   **13**

Schur, R. 1980. Growing lemons in the Bronx. *Working Papers* 8 (July–August): 42–51.   **22**

Schur, R., and V. Sherry. 1977. *The neighborhood housing movement*. New York: Association of Neighborhood Housing Developers. January.   **26**

Schwartz C. R. 1977. Unpublished lecture.   **13**

Schwartz, S. I., D. E. Hansen, R. Green, W. G. Moss, and R. Blezer. 1979. *The effect of growth management on new housing prices: Petaluma, California*. Davis: University of California, Davis. Institute of Governmental Affairs, Environmental Quality Series.   **8**

Scobie, R. S. 1975. *Problem tenants in public housing: Who, where and why are they?* New York: Praeger.   **20**

Scott, M. 1971. *American city planning since 1890*. Berkeley: University of California Press.   **6**

Scull, A. 1977. *Decarceration: Community treatment and the deviant—a radical view.* Englewood Cliffs, N. J.: Prentice-Hall.   **2**

Segre, R. 1984. Microbrigades and participation: Cuba. Architecture in the revolution. In *The scope of social architecture*, edited by C. R. Hatch. New York: Van Nostrand Reinhold.   **33**

Seiders, D. F. 1982. The President's Commission on Housing: Perspectives on mortgage finance. *Housing Finance Review* 1:4.   **4**

———. 1983. Mortgage pass-through securities: Progress and prospects. *AREUEA Journal* 11:2.   **4**

Services to Community Action and Tenants and NUPE. n.d. Up against a brick wall: The dead-end in housing policy. London: SCAT–NUPE.   **3**

Shearer, D. 1982. How progressives won in Santa Monica. *Social Policy* 12:7–14.   **22**

Sherman, M., and W. Sherwood. 1984. CLPHA preliminary analysis of the Office of Inspector General's Report on PHA Income Projections: 1977–1972. Unpublished report of the Council of Large Public Housing Authorities (Boston).   **20**

Sherwood, W., and E. March. 1983. *Operating subsidies for public housing: Problems and options*. Boston: Citizens Housing and Planning Association.   **20**

Short, J. 1982. *Housing in Britain: The postwar experience*. London: Methuen.   **30**

Shribman, D. 1983. Loans to families in mortgage pinch approved in House. *New York Times* (May 12).   **4**

Silverman, B. 1971. *Man and socialism in Cuba: The great debate*. New York: Atheneum.   **33**

Simison, R. 1978. Mass-output methods help Fox and Jacobs gain leadership in housing. *Wall Street Journal* (March 29).   **7**

Simon, C. P., and A. D. White. 1981. *The underground economy*. Boston: Auburn House.   **11**

Simonson, J. C. 1981. *Existing tax expenditures for homeowners*. Washington, D.C.: U. S. Department of Housing and Urban Development.   **15**

Sloane, M. F. 1976. *Federal programs and equal housing opportunity*. Report prepared for the Senate Committee on the Judiciary, 94 Cong. 2d sess.   **18**

Smith, N. 1979. Toward a theory of gentrification. *Journal of the American Planning Association* 45 (October): 4.   **10**

———. 1981. Gentrification and uneven development. Unpublished paper, Johns Hopkins University.   **5**

———. 1986. Gentrification, frontier and the restructuring of urban space. In *Gentrification, housing and the restructuring of urban space*, edited by N. Smith and P. Williams. London: George Allen & Unwin.   **10**

Smith, N., and P. Williams. 1986. *Gentrification, housing and the restructuring of urban space*. London: George Allen & Unwin. **2**

Smolensky, E. 1968. Public housing or income supplements—the economics of housing for the poor. *Journal of the American Institute of Planners* 34(2): 94–101. **20**

Solomon, A., and K. D. Vandell. 1982. Alternative perspectives on neighborhood decline. *Journal of the American Planning Association* 45(1): 81–91. **10**

Solomon, A. P., 1974. *Housing the urban poor*. Cambridge: MIT Press. **20**

———. 1981. Flawed analyses of market trends fuel assaults on housing expenditures. *Journal of Housing* (April): 194–200. **1**

Sowell, T. 1981. *Markets and minorities*. New York: Basic Books. **11**

Spence, H. 1981. Interview. *Working Papers* (November–December): 42–49. **20**

Spencer, J. Forthcoming. Sustained mass mobilization as political leverage: The post-World War I crises and the passage of the Emergency Rent Law of 1920. In *From tenant rebellion to tenant management*, edited by R. Lawson. **9**

Spring, B. P. 1959. Advances in house design. In *Design and production of housing*, edited by B. Kelly et al. New York: John Wiley and Sons. **6**

Starr, P., and G. Esping-Anderson. 1979. Passive intervention. *Working Papers* 7 (July–August). **22**

Starr, R. 1976. City's housing administrator proposes "planned shrinkage" of some slums. *New York Times* (February 3). **27**

———. 1977. The changing life of cities. In *How cities can grow gracefully*. Report prepared for the Subcommittee on the City. U.S. House of Representatives, Committee on Banking, Finance, and Urban Affairs. 95th Cong., 1st sess. **14**

———. 1979. An end to rental housing? *The Public Interest* (Fall): 25–38. **22**

Stegman, M. A. 1972. *Housing investment in the inner city: The dynamics of decline*. Cambridge: MIT Press. **10**

———. 1979a. An analysis of the multifamily housing market in "Loisaida": A HUD sweat equity demonstration neighborhood in New York City. Manuscript. January. **26**

———. 1979b. Neighborhood classification and the role of the planner in seriously distressed communities. *Journal of the American Planning Association* 45(4): 495–505. **26**

———. 1981. The President's Commission calls for vouchers: Some reflections and concerns. Comments prepared for delivery at the NAHRO Housing Policy Forum, Washington, D.C., December 9. **21**

———. 1982a. *The dynamics of rental housing in New York City*. New York: Department of Housing Preservation and Development. **1, 2, 9, 27**

———. 1982b. *The dynamics of rental housing in New York City*. Piscataway, N.J.: Rutgers University Center for Urban Policy Research. **11**

Stella Wright Resident Management Corporation and Newark Redevelopment and Housing Authority. n.d. *The Stella Wright story*. Newark, N.J.: Redevelopment and Housing Authority. **26**

Stern, M. J. 1984. The emergence of the homeless as a public problem. *Social Service Review* 58 (June): 291–301. **2**

Sternlieb, G. 1966. *The tenement landlord*. New Brunswick, N.J.: Rutgers University Press. **5, 10**

———. 1970. *Urban housing dilemma* (preliminary draft). New York: City of New York Housing and Development Administration. **9, 10**

———. 1971. Abandonment and rehabilitation: What is to be done? In *Papers Submitted to the Subcommittee on Housing Panels, on Housing Production, Housing Demand, and Developing a Suitable Living Environment*. Part 1. Committee on Banking and Currency, House of Representatives. 92nd Cong., 1st sess. Washington, D.C.: GPO. **10**

Sternlieb, G., and R. W. Burchell. 1973. *Residential abandonment: The tenement land-lord revisited.* New Brunswick, N.J.: Rutgers University Center for Urban Policy Research.   **10**

Sternlieb, G., and J. W. Hughes, eds. 1975. *Post industrial America: Metropolitan decline and inter-regional job shifts.* New Brunswick, N.J.: Rutgers University Center for Urban Policy Research.   **10**

———. 1980. *America's housing: Prospects and problems.* New Brunswick, N.J.: Rutgers University Center for Urban Policy Research.   **1**

———. 1981. *The future of rental housing.* New Brunswick, N.J.: Rutgers University Center for Urban Policy Research.   **2, 14**

———. 1984. Structuring the future. *Society* 21(3): March/April.   **4**

Stone, M. E. 1973. Federal housing policy: A political-economic analysis. In *Housing urban America*, edited by J. Pynoos, R. Schafer, and C. Hartman. Chicago: Aldine.   **6**

———, 1980a. Housing and the American economy: A Marxist analysis. In *Urban and regional planning in an age of austerity*, edited by P. Clavel, J. Forester, and W. Goldsmith, 81–108. Elmsford, N.Y.: Pergamon.   **3**

———. 1980b. The housing problem in the United States: Origins and prospects. *Socialist Review* 52 (July–August): 65–119.   **1, 3**

———. 1983. Housing and the economic crisis: An analysis and emergency program. In *America's housing crisis: What is to be done?*, edited by C. Hartman, 99–150. Boston: Routledge & Kegan Paul.   **2, 20**

———. 1985. Shelter poverty in Boston: Problem and program. Paper presented at conference, Housing Policies in the Eighties: Choices and Outcomes. Institute for Policy Studies and Virginia Polytechnic Institute and State University, Alexandria, Va., May 17–18.   **3**

Stone, M. E., and E. P. Achtenberg. 1977. *Hostage! Housing and the Massachusetts fiscal crisis.* Boston: Boston Community School.   **29**

Storper, M., and R. Walker. 1983. The theory of location. *International Journal of Urban and Regional Research* 7(1).   **11**

Straszheim, M. R. 1973. Racial discrimination in the urban housing market and its effects on black consumption. In *Patterns of residential discrimination*, Vol. 1, *Housing*, edited by G. Von Furstenberg et al. Lexington, Mass.: D. C. Heath.   **11**

Stren. R. E. 1975. *Urban inequality and housing policy in Tanzania: The problem of squatting.* Berkeley: Institute of International Studies, University of California.   **25**

Struyk, R. J. 1980. *A new system for public housing: Salvaging a national resource.* Washington, D.C.: Urban Institute.   **20**

Struyk, R. J., and M. Bendick, Jr., eds. 1981. *Housing vouchers for the poor: Lessons from a national experiment.* Washington, D.C.: Urban Institute.   **21**

Sullivan, B. 1982. *Analysis and assessment of the alternative management programs for New York City's In Rem properties.* New York: Pratt Institute Center for Community and Environmental Development. July.   **26**

Sumichrast, M., G. Ahluwalia, and R. J. Sheehan. 1979. *Profile of the builder.* Washington, D.C.: National Association of Home Builders.   **7**

Sumka, H. J. 1982. Urban homesteading. Paper prepared for the Homeownership Task Force, The President's Commission on Housing. January 11.   **25**

———. 1984. Factors influencing the success of low-income cooperatives. Manuscript prepared for presentation at the annual meeting of the Association of Collegiate Schools of Planning, New York. October.   **26**

*Survey of AFL-CIO members' housing.* 1975. Washington, D.C.: AFL-CIO.   **13**

Susser, I. 1982. *Norman Street: Poverty and politics in an urban neighborhood.* New York: Oxford University Press.   **8**

Sweezy, P. M., and H. Magdoff. 1984. The federal deficit: The real issues. *Monthly Review* 35:11.   4

Swenerton, M. 1980. *Homes fit for heroes*. London: Macmillan.   30

Tabb, W. K. 1982. *The long default: New York City and the urban fiscal crisis*. New York: Monthly Review Press.   11

Tabb, W. K., and L. Sawers. 1978. *Marxism and the metropolis*. New York: Oxford University Press.   13

Taeuber, C., and I. B. Taeuber. 1958. *The changing population of the United States*. New York: John Wiley and Sons.   6

Taeuber, K. 1975. Racial segregation: The persisting dilemma. *Annals of the American Academy of Political and Social Science* 87.   1

———. 1980. Racial residential segregation. Appendix to *A decent home*. Washington, D.C.: Citizens Commission on Civil Rights.   18

Taggart, R., III. 1970. *Low-income housing: A critique of federal aid*. Baltimore: Johns Hopkins University Press.   20

Taylor, A.J.P. 1959. Vienna. In *Encyclopaedia Britannica*, Vol. 2, 747 ff.   32

Taylor, W. 1978. President Carter's urban policy: A critique. *Urban League Review*, No. 2 (Winter).   18

Therrien, L. 1983. Builders find new source of financing. *Washington Post* (July 30).   7

Thomas, D. L. 1977. *Lords of the land*. New York: G. P. Putnam's Sons.   5

Thompson, W. 1977. Land management strategies for central city depopulation. In *How cities can grow gracefully*. Report prepared for the Subcommittee on the City. U.S. House of Representatives, Committee on Banking, Finance, and Urban Affairs. 95th Cong., 1st sess.   14

Tobier, E. 1970. Economic development strategy for the city. In *Agenda for a city: Issues confronting New York*, edited by L. C. Fitch and A. H. Walsh. Beverly Hills: Sage.   11

Treadway, P. 1982. Outlook for housing and mortgages: They'll come back. *ABA Journal* (May).   4

Treuer, M. 1982. *Indian housing, worst in nation*. Boulder, Colo.: Native American Rights Fund.   I, 19

Tuccillo, J. A., with J. L. Goodman, Jr. 1983. *Housing finance: A changing system in the Reagan era*. Washington, D.C.: Urban Institute Press.   4

U.K. Central Statistical Office. 1985. *Social trends*, No. 15. London: HMSO.   30

U.K. Department of the Environment. 1977. *Housing policy: A consultative document*. Cmnd. 6851.   30

———. 1983. *Housing and construction statistics*. London: HMSO.   30

———. 1985. *Home improvement, a new approach*. Cmnd. 9513.   30

U.K. Department of Health and Social Security. 1985. *Housing benefit review*. Cmnd. 9520.   30

U.K. Parliament. 1980. *Second report of the Environment Committee on council house sales*. No. HC 366–I.   30

U.K. Treasury. 1985. *The government's expenditure plans: 1985/6–1987/8*. Cmnd. 9428.   30

U.K. White Paper. 1971. *Fair deal for housing*. London: HMSO.   16

United Nations. Economic Commission for Europe. Various years. *Annual Bulletin of Housing and Building Statistics for Europe*. Geneva: UN.   28

U.S. Bureau of the Census. 1958. *1956 National housing inventory: Components of change, 1950–1956, United States and regions*. Vol. 1, part 1. Washington, D.C.: GPO.   6

———. 1966. *Housing construction statistics, 1889 to 1964*. Washington, D.C.: GPO.   6

———. 1972a. *1970 Census of housing*. Vol. 1. Washington, D.C.: GPO.   8

————. 1972b. *Census of housing: 1970, metropolitan housing characteristics, U.S. and regions.* Report HC(2)-1.    **1**

————. 1975a. *Annual housing survey: 1974.* Washington, D.C.: GPO.    **19**

————. 1975b. *Historical statistics of the United States: Colonial times to 1970.* Washington, D.C.: GPO.    **3, 8, 14, 32**

————. 1979. *Voting and registration in the election of November 1978.* Washington, D.C.: GPO.    **1, 22**

————. 1981a. *Annual housing survey: 1980.* Part C., *Financial characteristics of the housing inventory, U.S. and regions,* ser. H 150-80.    **2, 19**

————. 1981b. *Current population reports,* ser. P-60, no. 134.    **I**

————. 1981c. *1977 census of construction industries.* Washington, D.C.: GPO.    **7**

————. 1981d. *Statistical abstract of the United States.* Washington, D.C.: GPO.    **I**

————. 1982a. *Census of population and housing, supplementary report: Provisional estimates of social, economic, and housing characteristics for states and selected SMSAs,* ser. PHC 80-S1-1.    **I, 1**

————. 1982b. *Annual housing survey: 1979.* Part B, *Indicators of housing and neighborhood quality by financial characteristics, U.S. and regions,* ser. H 150-179.    **I, 1**

————. 1982c. *Annual housing survey: 1980.* Part A, *General housing characteristics, U.S. and regions,* ser. H 150-180.    **1, 19, 29**

————. 1982d. *Current population reports: Characteristics of the population below the poverty level.* Washington, D.C.: GPO.    **19**

————. 1982e. *Statistical abstract of the United States: 1982–3.* Washington, D.C.: GPO.    **2**

————. 1983a. *Annual housing survey. 1981.* Part C. *Financial characteristics of the housing inventory, U.S. and regions,* ser. H 150–81. Washington, D.C.: GPO.    **29**

————. 1983b. *Statistical abstract of the United States. 1984.* Washington, D.C: GPO.    **29**

————. 1983c. *Annual housing survey. 1981.* Part A. *General housing characteristics, U.S. and regions,* ser. H 150–181. Washington, D.C.: GPO.    **29**

————. 1983d. *Annual housing survey. 1983.* Part C. *Financial characteristics of the housing inventory, U.S. and regions,* ser. H 150–83. Washington, D.C.: GPO.    **I, 29**

————. 1984a. *Construction reports, housing starts: March 1984,* ser. C 20-84-3.    **2**

————. 1984b. *Current housing reports, homeownership trends: 1983,* ser. H-121, no. 1.    **2**

————. 1984c. *Current housing reports, housing vacancies: Fourth quarter 1983,* ser. H-111-84-Q4.    **2**

————. 1984d. *Money income and poverty status of families and persons in the United States: 1983,* ser. P-60, no. 145.    **I, 2**

————. 1984e. Press release CB-84-86. April 30.    **I**

————. 1984f. *Statistical abstract of the United States: 1984.* Washington, D.C.: GPO.    **I, 2, 31**

————. 1984g. *Statistical abstract of the United States. 1985.* Washington, D.C.: GPO.    **29**

————. 1985a. *December 1984 construction at $318.7 billion annual rate,* ser. CB85-24. February 1.    **29**

————. 1985b. *New one-family houses sold and for sale, December 1984,* ser. C25-84-12. February.    **29**

————. 1985c. *Housing starts and building permits in January 1985,* ser. CB85-31. February 19.    **29**

————. 1985d. *Annual housing survey. Part C. Financial characteristics of the housing inventory, U.S. and regions.* Washington, D.C.: GPO.    **29**

————. n.d. 1980 census shows an increase in nation's housing costs. News release.    **1**

U.S. Bureau of Labor Statistics. 1940. *Builders of one-family homes in 72 cities*, ser. R-1151.  **6**

———. 1980a. *Earnings and other characteristics of organized workers*. Washington, D.C.: GPO. May.  **7**

———. 1980b. *Occupational injuries and illnesses in 1978: Summary*. Washington, D.C.: GPO. March.  **7**

———. 1981. *Employment in perspective: Minority workers*. Report no. 664.  **11**

———. 1983. *Employment and earnings supplement*. Washington, D.C.: GPO. June.  **7**

U.S. Commission on Civil Rights. 1959. *Hearings in New York*. Washington,D.C.: GPO. September.  **18**

———. 1970. *Federal installations and equal housing opportunity*. Washington, D.C.: GPO. March.  **18**

———. 1971. *Homeownership for lower income families*. Washington, D.C.: GPO.  **18**

———. 1973a. *Fair housing and the law*. Washington, D.C.: GPO. February.  **18**

———. 1973b. *Understanding fair housing*. Publication 42.  **18**

———. 1974. *Equal opportunity in suburbia*. Washington, D.C.: GPO. July.  **18**

———. 1975. *Twenty years after* Brown: *Equal opportunity in housing*. Washington, D.C.: GPO.  **1, 20**

U.S. Comptroller General. General Accounting Office. 1978a. *Housing abandonment: A national problem needing new approaches*. Washington, D.C.: GPO.  **10**

———. 1978b. *Section 236 rental housing—an evaluation with lessons for the future*. Report to the U.S. Congress. PAD-78-13.  **20**

———. 1979. *Rental housing, a national problem that needs immediate attention*. Report to the U.S. Congress. CED-80-11.  **I, 1, 20, 21**

———. 1980. *Evaluation of alternatives for financing low and moderate income rental housing*. Report to the U.S. Congress. PAD-80-13.  **20**

U.S. Conference of Mayors. 1984a. *Status report: Emergency food, shelter, and energy programs in 20 cities*. Washington, D.C.: Reproduced in U.S. Congress. House. Subcommittee on Housing and Community Development, 1984, 445–59.  **2**

———. 1984b. *Homelessness in America's cities: Ten case studies*. Washington, D.C.  **2**

U.S. Congress. Congressional Budget Office. 1981. *The tax treatment of homeownership: Issues and options*. Washington, D.C.: GPO.  **1, 8, 15, 31**

———. 1983a. *Federal subsidies for public housing: Issues and options*. Washington, D.C.: GPO.  **20**

———. 1983b. *Major legislative changes in human resource programs since January 1981*. Washington, D.C.: GPO. 2

U.S. Congress. Congressional Research Service. 1976. *Comparative costs and estimated households eligible for participation in federally assisted low income housing programs*. Washington, D.C.: GPO.  **20**

U.S. Congress. House. Committee on Banking and Currency. 1954. *Hearings on H.R. 7839*. 83rd Cong.  **6**

———. Committee on Banking, Finance, and Urban Affairs. 1981. Deposit Insurance Flexibility Act, H.R. 4603. Hearings before the Subcommittee on Financial Institutions, Supervision, Regulations and Insurance. September 30 and October 1.  **4**

———. 1982. *Depository Institutions Amendments of 1982. Hearings before the Subcommittee on Financial Institutions, Supervision, Regulation and Insurance on S. 2879, H.R. 4603, and H.R. 6267*. 97th Cong., 2d sess. September 21 and 22.  **4**

———. Select Committee on Lobbying Activities. 1949. *Hearings on the role of lobbying in representative self-government*. 81st Cong.  **6**

———. Subcommittee on Housing and Community Development. 1982a. Hearings. June 24.   **25**

———. 1982b. *Homelessness in America.* December 15.   **I, 25**

———. 1984. *Homelessness in America II.* January 25.   **2**

———. Subcommittee on Oversight and Subcommittee on Public Assistance and Employment Compensation of the Committee on Ways and Means. 1983. *Background material on poverty.* Washington, D.C.: GPO. October.   **2**

———. 1984. *Effects of the Omnibus Budget Reconciliation Act of 1981 (OBRA), welfare changes and the recession on poverty.* Washington, D.C.: GPO. June.   **2**

U.S. Congress. Senate. Committee on Banking and Currency. 1954. *Hearings on S. 2889, S. 2949, and S. 2938.* 83rd Cong.   **6**

———. 1968. *Hearings, March 5–20.* 90th Cong., 2d sess.   **20**

———. Subcommittee on the Constitution of the Committee on the Judiciary. 1979. *Hearings on S. 506.* Statement of P. R. Harris. 96th Cong., 1st sess.   **18**

———. Subcommittee on Constitutional Rights of the Senate Committee on the Judiciary. 1976. *Report on Civil Rights 143.* 94th Cong., 2d sess.   **18**

U.S. Congress. Subcommittee on Housing and Urban Development. 1975. *Evolution of role of the federal government in housing and community development.* Washington, D.C.: GPO.   **6**

———. Subcommittee of the Joint Committee on Housing. 1946. *High cost of housing.* Washington, D.C.: GPO.   **6**

U.S. Department of Agriculture. Economic Research Service. 1980. *Hired farmworker housing.* Report prepared by R. Kempe. Washington, D.C.: GPO. December.   **19**

———. Farmers Home Administration. 1980a. *The impact of heir property on black rural land tenure in the southeastern region of the United States.* Washington, D.C.: GPO.   **19**

———. 1980b. *Indian land claims study.* Report prepared by the Institute for the Development of Indian Law.   **19**

———. 1980c. *National farmworker housing study: Executive summary.* Report prepared by InterAmerica Research Associates.   **19**

———. 1980d. *Study of problems that result from Spanish and Mexican land grant claims.* Report prepared by the Natural Resources Center, University of New Mexico, under contract with FmHA.   **19**

———. 1983. *A brief history of Farmers Home Administration.* Washington, D.C.: GPO. February.   **19**

U.S. Department of Commerce. 1983. *Construction Review.* Washington, D.C.: GPO. November/December.   **2**

U.S. Department of Health, Education, and Welfare. 1969. *The role of public welfare in housing.* Washington, D.C.: GPO. January.   **21**

U.S. Department of Housing and Urban Development (HUD). 1972. *National Conference on Housing Costs.* Washington, D.C.: GPO.   **8**

———. 1973. *Housing in the seventies: A report of the national housing policy review.* Washington, D.C.: GPO. November.   **18, 20**

———. 1975. *The dynamics of neighborhood change.* Washington, D.C.: GPO.   **10**

———. 1976. *Housing in the seventies.* Washington, D.C.: GPO.   **14**

———. 1977a. *Statistical yearbook 1976.* Washington, D.C.: GPO.   **8, 18**

———. 1977b. *The urban homesteading catalogue.* Vol. 3. Washington, D.C.: GPO.   **25**

———. 1978. *Final report of the HUD Multi-family Property Utilization Task Force.*   **29**

———. 1979a. *Discrimination against Chicanos in the Dallas housing market.* Washington, D.C.: GPO.   **18**

————. 1979b. *Displacement report*. Washington, D.C.: GPO.    **5**

————. 1979c. *Measuring racial discrimination in American housing markets: The housing market practices survey*. Washington, D.C.: GPO.    **I, 18**

————. 1979d. *Final report of task force on housing costs*. Washington, D.C.: GPO.    **8**

————. 1980a. *The conversion of rental housing to condominiums and cooperatives*. 3 vols. Washington, D.C.: GPO.    **22**

————. 1980b. *1979 statistical yearbook*. Washington, D.C.: GPO.    **20**

————. 1980c. *The supply of mortgage credit*. Washington, D.C.: GPO.    **3**

————. 1980d. *Designing rehab programs*. Washington, D.C.: GPO.    **25**

————. 1981a. *Rental housing: condition and outlook*. Washington, D.C.: GPO.    **20**

————. 1981b. *Residential displacement—an update. Report to the U.S. Congress*. Washington, D.C.: GPO.    **1**

————. 1981c. Survey of mortgage lending activity: 1980. News release.    **3**

————. 1982a. *National housing production report*. Washington, D.C.: GPO.    **19**

————. 1982b. *Recent evidence on the cost of housing subsidy programs*. Washington, D.C.: GPO. October.    **1**

————. 1983a. *Evaluation of the Urban Homesteading Demonstration Program: Final report*. Vol. 1, Summary assessment. Washington, D.C.: GPO.    **25**

————. 1983b. *Neighborhood development organizations after the federal funding cutbacks: Current conditions and future directions*. Report prepared by R. Cohen and M. Kohler. Washington, D.C.: GPO.    **20**

————. 1983c. *Report to Congress*, no. 10. Washington, D.C.: GPO.    **20**

————. 1984a. *Internal audit of income projections used by public housing agencies under the performance funding system*. Washington, D.C.: GPO. January 20.    **20**

————. 1984b. *A report to the Secretary on the homeless and emergency shelters*. Washington, D.C.: GPO.    **I, 2**

U.S. Department of Labor. 1954. *Structure of the residential building industry*. Bulletin no. 1170.    **6**

————. 1959. *Nonfarm housing starts, 1889 to 1958*. Bulletin no. 1260.    **6**

————. 1980. *Annual construction industry report, April 1980*. LMSA.    **7**

————. 1981. *Employment in perspective: Minority workers*. Report no. 664.    **7, 11**

————. 1982. *The employment situation: November 1982*. Release no. 82-454. December 3.    **I**

————. Bureau of Labor Statistics. 1984. *Employment situation: November 1984*. Bulletin No. 84-502. December 7.    **I**

U.S. Federal Housing Administration. 1936. *Underwriting manual. Underwriting and valuation procedure under Title II of the National Housing Act*. Washington, D.C.: GPO.    **18**

————. 1938. *Underwriting manual*. Rev. ed. Washington, D.C.: GPO.    **18**

————. 1942. *Homes in metropolitan districts*. Washington, D.C.: GPO.    **6**

————. 1959. *Hearings in New York City before the U.S. Commission on Civil Rights 349*.    **18**

*U.S. Home Annual Report*. 1983.    **7**

U.S. Housing and Home Finance Agency. Public Housing Administration. 1951. *Low-rent housing manual*, sec. 1021.    **18**

————. 1965. *Low-rent housing manual*, sec. 7.    **18**

U.S. HUD. See U.S. Department of Housing and Urban Development.

U.S. League of Savings Association. 1978a. *Homeownership: Realizing the American dream*. Chicago: U.S. League of Savings Associations.    **3**

————. 1978b. *Homeownership: Affording the single-family home*. Chicago: U.S. League of Savings Associations.    **3**

————. 1980. *Homeownership*: *Coping with inflation*. Chicago: U.S. League of Savings Associations.   **3**

————. 1982. *Homeownership: The American dream adrift*. Chicago: U.S. League of Savings Associations.   **1, 3**

————. 1984. *Homeownership*: *Celebrating the American dream*. Chicago: U.S. League of Savings Associations.   **3**

U.S. Office of Management and Budget. 1982. *Special Analysis G: Tax expenditures*. Washington, D.C.: GPO.   **1**

Upton, L., and N. Lyons. n.d. *Basic facts*. Cambridge, Mass.: Cambridge Institute.   **29**

Urban Systems Research and Engineering. 1982. The costs of HUD multifamily housing programs. Report prepared for the Office of Policy Development and Research. U.S. Department of Housing and Urban Development. Washington, D.C.: GPO.   **20**

Van Bogan, R. 1982a. The case for more mortgage lending by community banks. *ABA Journal* (May).   **4**

————. 1982b. What is the commercial bank's role in real estate lending? *ABA Journal* (October).   **4**

Vandell, K. D., B. S. Hodas, and R. Bratt. 1974. Financial institutions and neighborhood decline: A review of the literature. Manuscript.   **10**

Vartanian, T. P. 1983a. The Garn–St Germain Depository Institutions Act of 1982: The impact on thrifts. *Housing Finance Review* 2(2).   **4**

————. 1983b. Regulation and deregulation of the savings and loan industry. *Housing Finance Review* 2(2).   **4**

Vaughan, T. R. 1968. Landlord–tenant relations in a low-income area. *Social Problems* 16 (Fall): 208–18.   **8, 22**

Vernon, R. 1959. *Metropolis 1985*. New York: Doubleday.   **11**

Von Furstenberg, G., and J. Green. 1970. The effect of income and race on the quality of home mortgages: A case for Pittsburgh. In *Patterns of racial discrimination*. Vol. 1, Housing, edited by G. N. Von Furstenberg, A. R. Horowitz, and B. Harrison. Lexington, Mass.: Lexington Books.   **10**

Wade, R. C. 1959. *The urban frontier*. Chicago: University of Chicago Press.   **5**

Wahl, A. S. 1977. *The eternal slum: Housing and social policy in Victorian London*. London: Edward Arnold.   **11**

Waite, D. C., III. 1981. Deregulation in the banking industry. *Bankers Magazine* (January–February).   **4**

Wald, M. L. 1983. A house, once again, is just shelter. *New York Times* (February 6).   **4**

Walker, R. 1977. Suburbanization in passage. Unpublished draft paper, University of California, Berkeley, Department of Geography.   **13**

Wallace, J. E., S. Philipson, and W. L. Holshauser. 1981. *Participation and benefits in the urban Section 8 program: New construction and existing housing*. Report prepared for the Office of Policy Development and Research. U.S. Department of Housing and Urban Development. Cambridge, Mass.: Abt Associates.   **20**

Wallace, R. 1981. Fire service productivity and the New York City fire crisis: 1968–1979. *Human Ecology* 9(4).   **11**

Warner, S. B., Jr. 1962. *Streetcar suburbs: The process of growth in Boston, 1870–1900*. Cambridge: Harvard University Press.   **6**

————. 1968. *The private city: Philadelphia in three periods of its growth*. Philadelphia: University of Pennsylvania Press.   **14**

————. 1972. *The urban wilderness: A history of the American city*. New York: Harper & Row.   **6**

Warren, H. G. 1967. *Herbert Hoover and the Great Depression*. New York: W. W. Norton.   **25**

Warren, P. 1982. *The effect of voucher-based subsidies on urban public housing author ities*. Policy analysis exercise prepared for the Kennedy School of Government, Harvard University.  **20**

Wayne, L. 1984. Citi's soaring ambition. *New York Times* (June 24).  **4**

Weidemann, S., J. R. Anderson, D. I. Butterfield and P. M. O'Donnell. 1982. Residents' perceptions of satisfaction and safety: A basis for change in multifamily housing. *Environment and Behavior* 12(6): 695 724.  **20**

Weinbaum, B., and A. Bridges. 1976. The other side of the paycheck. *Monthly Review* 28 (July–August): 88–103.  **22**

Wekerle, G. 1978. A woman's place is in the city. Paper presented to the Lincoln Institute of Land Policy, Cambridge, Mass.  **13**

Werner, F. E., and D. B. Bryson. 1982. Guide to the preservation and maintenance of single room occupancy (SRO) housing. *Clearinghouse Review* (April): 999–1009 and (May) 1–25.  **2**

Wheaton, W. L. C. 1953. The evolution of federal housing programs. Ph.D. dissertation. University of Chicago.  **6**

White, J. R., and E. L. Hebard. 1960. *The Manhattan housing market*. Study prepared by Brown, Harris, Stevens, Inc. for the New York City Urban Renewal Board.  **11**

Whyte, W. H. 1958. Urban sprawl. In *The exploding metropolis*, by Editors of *Fortune*. New York: Doubleday.  **6**

Wiktorin, M. 1982. Housing policy and disadvantaged groups in Sweden. *International Journal of Urban and Regional Research* 6(2): 246–55.  **31**

Wilczynski, J. 1977. *The economics of socialism*. London: George Allen & Unwin.  **33**

Wilkinson, R. K. 1971. The determinants of relative house prices. Paper presented to the Centre for Environmental Studies Urban Economics Conference, Keele, Great Britain. July  **8**

Williams, R. 1980. Billion dollar shell game. *Southern Exposure* (Spring).  **7**

Williams, W. 1983. The explosion in bank deposits. *New York Times* (May 1).  **4**

Wilmott, D., and A. Young. 1957. *Family and kinship in East London*. Harmondsworth, England: Penguin.  **30**

Wilson, J. Q., ed. 1966. *Urban renewal: The record and the controversy*. Cambridge: MIT Press.  **6, 14**

Wirz, H. 1979. Back yard rehab: Urban microcosm rediscovered. *Urban Innovation Abroad* 3 (July): 2–3.  **13**

Witte, A. D. 1975. The determination of inter-urban residential site price differences: A derived demand model with empirical testing. *Journal of Regional Science* 15 (December): 351–64.  **8**

Wofford, H. 1980. *Of Kennedy and kings: Making sense of the sixties*. New York: Farrar, Straus & Giroux.  **18**

Wolman, H. 1971. *The politics of federal housing*. New York: Dodd, Mead.  **22**

Women's Work Project. 1978. Women in today's economic crisis. In *U.S. capitalism in crisis*. New York: Union for Radical Political Economics.  **2**

Wood, E. E. 1919. *The housing of the unskilled wage earner*. New York: Macmillan.  **20**

Wright, G. 1981. *Building the dream: A social history of housing in America*. New York: Pantheon.  **27**

Wurster, C. B. 1957. The dreary deadlock of public housing. *Architectural Forum* 106(5): 140–42, 219, 221.  **6, 20**

Zaretsky, E. 1976. *Capitalism, the family and personal life*. New York: Harper & Row.  **13.**

Zeitz, E. 1979. *Private urban renewal*. Lexington, Mass.: D. C. Heath.  **5**

# Foreign References

*The bold numbers after entries indicate in which chapters the works were cited.*

Acosta, M., and J. E. Hardoy. 1971. *Reforma urbana en Cuba revolucionaria*. Caracas: Síntesis Dosmil. For English translation, see Acosta and Hardoy, 1973, in General References. **33**

Acosta Santana, J. 1982. *Teoría y práctica de los mecanismos de dirección de la economía en Cuba*. Havana: Editorial de Ciencias Sociales. **33**

Agüero, N. 1980. La vivienda: Experiencia de la revolución cubana. *Revista Interamericana de Planificación* 14 (June): 160–73. **33**

Alcalde, O. 1985. Transcript of interview with Oscar Alcalde, president of the People's Savings Bank, conducted by Elaine Fuller, writer for *Cubatimes* magazine, Havana. January. **33**

ANPP. Asamblea Nacional del Poder Popular. 1978. Informe del estudio sobre el mantenimiento de las viviendas. AN/II POS/78-DOC. 3-INF. 1. Mimeographed. **33**

Arjona, M. 1981. *La Habana Vieja: Restauración y revitalización. Anteproyecto*. Havana: Ministerio de Cultura, Dirección de Patrimonio Cultural, Departamento de Monumentos. **33**

Banco Nacional de Cuba. 1975. *Dessarrollo y perspectivas de la economía Cubana*. Havana: Banco Nacional de Cuba. **33**

Bauboeck, R. 1979. *Wohnungspolitik im sozialdemokratischen Wien. 1919–1934*. Salzburg. **32**

Bauer, O. 1919. *Der Weg zum Sozialismus*. Vienna. **32**

Beckman, M. 1976. *Building for everyone: The disabled and the built environment in Sweden*. Information to the United Nations Conference on Human Settlements HABITAT. Stockholm, Sweden: Ministry of Housing and Physical Planning. **31**

Brundenius, C. 1981. *Economic growth, basic needs and income distribution in revolutionary Cuba*. Lund, Sweden: University of Lund, Research Policy Institute. **33**

Capablanca, E. 1982. Habana Vieja: Anteproyecto de restauración. *Arquitectura Cuba*, nos. 353–354: 4–15. **33**

Castro, F. 1976. *Enseñanzas de la revolución cubana: Informe al Primer Congreso del Partido Comunista de Cuba*. Bogota: Ediciones Suramérica. English translation. 1977. *Report of the Central Committee of the Communist Party of Cuba to the First Congress*. Havana: Departamento de Orientación Revolucionaria del Comité Central del Partido Comunista de Cuba. **33**

————. 1977. En la clausura del V Congreso de la Asociación Nacional de Agricultores Pequeños (ANAP). May 17. Reprinted in 1979. *Discursos: Fidel Castro*. Havana: Editoria Política. **33**

————. 1978. Discurso pronunciado por Fidel Castro en la clausura del XIV Congreso del Central de Trabajadores de Cuba (CTC), el 2 de diciembre de 1978. *Trabajadores*. December 4. **33**

————. 1984. Speech at the closing session of the First National Forum on Energy, December 4, 1984. *Granma* . December 16. **33**

————. 1985. Discurso en la clausura del VII Período ordinario de Sesiones de la Asamblea Nacional del Poder Popular, el 28 de diciembre de 1984. *Granma*. January 4. **33**

CEE. Comité Estatal de Estadísticas. 1975. *Anuario estadístico de Cuba: 1975*. Havana: Comité Estatal de Estadísticas. **33**

————. 1980. *Anuario estadístico de Cuba: 1980*. Havana: Comité Estatal de Estadísticas. **33**

————. 1982. *Anuario estadístico de Cuba: 1982*. Havana: Comité Estatal de Estadísticas. **33**

————. 1984. *Censo de Población y Viviendas, 1981*. República de Cuba. Vol. 16. Havana: Comité Estatal de Estadísticas. **33**

CEE–DCE. Comité Estatal de Estadísticas. Dirección de Censos y Encuestas. 1977. *Principales características de las viviendas particulares de acuerdo con la nueva división político–administrativa (estimado al 6 de septiembre de 1970)*. Havana: Comité Estatal de Estadísticas. **33**

CEE–DD. Comité Estatal de Estadísticas. Dirección de Demografía. 1979. *Anuario demográfico de Cuba: 1979*. Havana: Comité Estatal de Estadísticas. **33**

————. 1981. *Encuesta Demográfica Nacional de 1979: Características de los nucleos y la familia*. Havana: Comité Estatal de Estadísticas. **33**

Coyula, M. 1982. Conservación y renovación: Aprendiendo de La Habana. Havana. Mimeographed. **33**

————. 1984. Por una noción más amplia de monumento. *Arquitectura y Urbanismo* 5(2): 8–14. **33**

————. 1985a. Vivienda, renovación urbana y poder popular, algunas consideraciones sobre La Habana. Presented in an international event on housing and urban renewal in Latin America, Technical University of Hamburg, Federal Republic of Germany. February 14. Havana: Dirección Provincial de Arquitectura y Urbanismo, Poder Popular, Ciudad de La Habana. Mimeographed. **33**

————. 1985b. Personal communication, July 6. **33**

CTC. Central de Trabajadores de Cuba. 1978. Informe central al XIV Congreso de la CTC. *Granma*. December 2. **33**

CTVU. Centro Técnico de la Vivienda y el Urbanismo. 1980. *Bases del concurso: Concurso nacional de viviendas para cooperativas agropecuarias ANAP–MICONS*. Havana: Centro Técnico de la Vivienda y el Urbanismo. **33**

————. 1983. Presentation of CTVU architects to visiting group of U.S. architects and planners. Havana. January. **33**

————. 1984. *XI Seminario de la Vivienda y el Urbanismo: La construcción de viviendas por esfuerzo propio*. Memoria. Havana: Editorial del Centro de Información de la Construcción. **33**

Czeike, F. 1958 and 1959. *Wirtschafts und Sozialpolitik der Gemeinde Wein 1919–1934*. 2 vols. Vienna. **32**

————. 1978. Wiener Wohnbau vom Vormarz bis 1823. In *Kommunaler Wohnungsbau in Wien*. 2 vols. Vienna (catalogue and narrative for the exposition: *Kommunaler Wohnungsbau in Wien*). **32**

Daun, A. 1979. Why do Swedish suburbs look the way they do? *Human Environment in Sweden* 9 (February). **31**

DCE. Dirección Central de Estadística (JUCEPLAN). 1970. *Censo de Población y Vivienda*. Havana: Dirección Central de Estadística. **33**

DCE–DD. Dirección Central de Estadística (JUCEPLAN). Departamento de Demografía de la Dirección de Estadística de Población y Censos. 1976. *La situación de la vivienda en Cuba y su evolución perspectiva*. Havana: Editorial Orbe. **33**

Díaz de Villalvilla, A. 1984. La vivienda rural y las nuevas formas de producción agrícola. *Arquitectura y Urbanismo* 5(1): 66–69. **33**

DPF. Dirección de Planificación Física, Poder Popular, Ciudad de La Habana. 1984. *Plan Director Ciudad de La Habana*. Instituto de Geodesia y Cartografia.  **33**

Engels, F. 1970. *The housing question*. Moscow: Progress Publishers.  **27**

Estévez, R. 1959. Arquitectos, reforma urbana y vivienda. *Arquitectura*, nos. 309-10 (April–May): 149–55.  **33**

———. 1975. Los Poderes Populares y el plan de viviendas. Formas de ampliar los recursos para incrementar la construcción de viviendas. *VII seminario de viviendas y urbanismo: Tomo II*. Havana: Editorial CEDITEC.  **33**

———. 1982. *La vivienda y el urbanismo en Cuba*. Havana: Centro Técnico de la Vivienda y el Urbanismo.  **33**

———. 1984a. *Análisis de las realizaciones de viviendas en Cuba y en otros países socialistas*. Ponencia presentada en el XI Seminario de Viviendas y Urbanismo, Havana, March. Havana: Centro Técnico de la Vivienda y el Urbanismo.  **33**

———. 1984b. El desarrollo demográfico en Cuba revolucionaria y su incidencia en la demanda y típologia de viviendas y en la densidad poblacional de los conjuntos urbanos. Havana: Centro Técnico de la Vivienda y el Urbanismo. Mimeographed.  **33**

———. 1985a. Transcript of meeting of group of visiting U.S. architects and planners with Reynaldo Estévez of the Centro Técnico de la Vivienda y el Urbanismo. Havana. January.  **33**

———. 1985b. Personal communication, June 14.  **33**

Fernández Núñez, J. 1981. El precio de la tierra, la estimulación y la efectividad de la producción agrícola estatal. *Economía y Desarrollo*, no. 64 (September–October): 179–87.  **33**

Fernández Núñez, J. M. 1976. *La vivienda en Cuba*. Havana: Editorial Arte y Literatura.  **33**

Gomila, S. 1982. El aumento de la densidad poblacional y la optimización de la altura en los edificios de viviendas. Sinopsis de ponencia y mesa redonda No. 10 de la Primera Conferencia Científico–Técnica de la Construcción, July 13–15, Havana. Mimeographed.  **33**

Gomila, S., et al. 1984. Intervención del Centro Técnico de la Vivienda y el Urbanismo en el Seminario Internacional de Arquitectura y Remodelación de Ciudades, Havana, November 8. Mimeographed.  **33**

González, M. 1982. Sobre una posible volaración del suelo urbana. *Arquitectura y Urbanismo* 3 (January–April): 58–61.  **33**

Hautman, H., and R. Hautman. 1980. *Die Gemeindebauten des roten Wein, 1919–1934*. Vienna.  **32**

Heimburger, P. 1976. *Land policy in Sweden*. Information to the United Nations Conference on Human Settlements HABITAT. Stockholm, Sweden: Ministry of Housing and Physical Planning HSB (Tenants' Savings and Building Society).  **31**

Hernández, G. 1962. Las viviendas en Cuba. *Bohemia* (October 12): 94–98.  **33**

HPP. Ministry of Housing and Physical Planning. 1976. *Swedish experiences of self-building, co-operation, consumer research, participation*. Information to the United Nations Conference on Human Settlements HABITAT. Stockholm, Sweden: Ministry of Housing and Physical Planning.  **31**

———. 1980. *Housing, building, and planning in Sweden*. Information to 41st Session of the ECE Committee on Housing, Building, and Planning. Stockholm, Sweden: Ministry of Housing and Physical Planning, in cooperation with the National Housing Board, the National Board of Physical Planning and Building, and the National Institute for Building Research.  **31**

HSB. HSB's Riksforbund. 1975. *HSB Sweden*. Stockholm: HSB.  **31**

International Housing and Town Planning Congress. 1926. *Report, Part 2*. Vienna.  **32**

IUA. International Union of Architects, Cuban Chapter. 1963. *Architecture in countries in the process of development*. Cuban delegation's presentation to the Seventh Congress of the International Union of Architects, Havana. **33**

IUT. International Union of Tenants. 1982. The Scandinavian states support ownership. *International Information* 4 (Fall): 1–2. **31**

Jussil, 1975. Steering mechanisms. In *New Towns and Old*, edited by H. E. Heineman. Stockholm, Sweden: Swedish Institute. **31**

Kainrath, W. 1978. Die gesellschaftspolitische Bedeutung des kommunalen Wohnbaus in Wien der Zwischenkriegszeit. In *Kommunaler Wohnungsbau in Wien*. 2 vol. Vienna. (Catalogue and narrative for the exposition: *Kommunaler Wohnungsbau in Wien*.) **32**

Kasarda, J. 1982. New urban policies for new urban realities. In *Applied urban research*, ed. G.-M. Hellstern et al. Vol. 1. Bonn, West Germany: Bundesforschunganstalt für Landeskunde und Raumordung. **14**

Kjellberg, C., and T. Burns. 1981. Hur Hyrestratter blir bostadstratter i Goteborg. Preliminary report, Stockholm University. **31**

Kozlov, G. A. 1977. *Political economy: Socialism*. Moscow: Progress Publishers. **33**

Lazo, R. 1984. Una institución en pleno desarrollo. *Bohemia* (July 13): 28–31. **33**

Lefebre, H. 1974. *La production de l'espace*. Paris: Editions Anthropos. **13**

Leijonhufvud, S. 1982. Election year '82: New exits from the middle road. *Political Life in Sweden* 15 (December). **31**

Ley de Expropiación de Predios Baldíos en el Casco Urbano del Centro de la Ciudad de Managua. 1981. *La Gaceta*. Managua. December 16. **33**

Ley de Expropiación de Tierras Urbanas Baldías. 1981. *La Gaceta*. Managua. December 14. **33**

Ley de Inquilinato. 1980. *La Gaceta*. Managua. January 2. **33**

Ley de Repartos Ilegales. 1979. *La Gaceta*. Managua. September 26. **33**

Ley de Titulación de Lotes en Repartos Intervenidos. 1982. *La Gaceta*. Managua. January 21. **33**

Ley General de la Vivienda. 1984. *Gaceta Oficial de la República de Cuba*, no. 22 (December 31): 101–22. **33**

Ley sobre Donaciones de Inmuebles del Casco Urbano Central de la Ciudad de Managua. 1980. *La Gaceta*. Managua. January 9. **33**

Lezcano Pérez, J. 1984. Intervención del Jorge Lezcano Pérez, vicepresidente de la Asamblea Nacional del Poder Popular, *XI Seminario de la Vivienda y el Urbanismo: La construcción de viviendas por esfuerzo propio. Memoria*. Havana: Editorial del Centro de Información de la Construcción. **33**

López, J. A. 1984. Consumo y nivel de vida. *Cuba Internacional* (December): 28–33. **33**

López Blanco, A. 1982. El futuro de la vivienda en Cuba. *Arquitectura Cuba*, nos. 353–354: 80–82. **33**

López Román, D. 1983. Control de las rentas urbanas: Caso de Nicaragua. In *Relación Campo-Cuidad: La tierra, recurso estratégico para el desarrollo y la transformación social*. Proceedings of 14th Interamerican Planning Congress of the Sociedad Interamericana de Planificación (SIAP). Mexico City: SIAP. **33**

Lundevall, O. 1976. *Swedish experiences of co-operative housing*. Information to the United National Conference on Human Settlements HABITAT. Stockholm, Sweden: Ministry of Housing and Physical Planning. **31**

Lundqvist, L. J. 1981. Housing tenures in Sweden. National Swedish Institute for Building Research, Gavle, Sweden. **31**

Maciques, J. 1984. Discurso de apertura a cargo del Arq. Jorge Maciques, viceministro del Area Técnica, MICONS. *XI Seminario de la Vivienda y el Urbanismo: La construcción de viviendas por esfuerzo propio. Memoria*. Havana: Editorial del Centro de Información de la Construcción. **33**

Maldonado-Denis, M. 1976. *Puerto Rico y Estados Unidos: Emigración y colonialismo*. Mexico City: Siglo Veintiuno Editores. **11**

Mang, K. 1978. Architektur einer sozialen Evolution. In *Kommunaler Wohnungsbau in Wien*. **32**

Marín, V. 1983. Interview with Victor Marín, head of the Havana Buildings Department (*Control Urbano*), Havana. January. **33**

Marsán, G. 1983. Vivir en la cooperativa. *Bohemia* (November 21): 28–31. **33**

Martín, J. L. 1979. Nuevas vías en la política de construcción de viviendas para area rural en Cuba. Havana: Centro de Estudio y Control del Desarrollo de la Vivienda (CECONDEVI); Trabajo presentado en el Seminario sobre la Vivienda en América Latina, Caracas, Venezuela. September. Mimeographed. **33**

Martínez, M. 1984. Si tu alientas la vida. *Bohemia*. (November 23): 32–33. **33**

MICONS. Ministerio de la Construcción. 1964. *Concurso de vivienda por medios propios*. Havana: Ministerio de La Construcción. **33**

MINJUS. Ministerio de Justicia. 1974. *La vivienda urbana: Su evolución en el derecho histórico cubano y en la legislación revolucionaria*. Havana: Ministerio de Justicia. **33**

MINREX. Ministerio de Relaciones Exteriores. 1965. *Perfil de Cuba*. Havana: Ministerio de Relaciones Exteriores, Dirección de Información. **33**

MINVAH. Ministerio de Vivienda y Asentamientos Humanos. 1982. La Tierra en el desarrollo urbano: Caso de Nicaragua. In *Relación Campo-Ciudad: La tierra, recurso estratégico para el desarrollo y la transformación social*. Proceedings of 14th Interamerican Planning Congress of the Sociedad Interamericana de Planificacíon (SIAP). Mexico City: SIAP. **33**

———. 1984. *Avances del MINVAH 1979–1983*. Managua. **33**

*Moncada's program achievements*. 1966. Havana. n.p. **33**

Muhlestein, E. 1975. Kollektines Wohnen gestern und heute. *Architesse* 14:3–23. **13**

Navarro Alaluf, L. 1983. Notas acerca de las relaciones monetario-mercantiles y el socialismo. *Economía y Desarrollo*, no. 72 (January–February): 201–23. **33**

Novy, K. 1978. Sozialisierung von Unten—Überlegungen zur vergessenen Gemeinwirtschaftsbewegung im "Roten Wein" 1918 bis 1934. Institut für Politishe Wissenschaft der RWTH, Aachen. **32**

———. 1981. Selbsthilfe als Reformbewegung: Der Kampf der Wiener Siedler nach dem 1. Weltkrieg. *ARCH*, no. 55 (February). **32**

———. n.d. Wohnungswirtschaftliche Selbstverwaltung und Selbstfinanzierung—eine ideengeschichtliche Montage. Manuscript. **32**

OECD. Organization for Economic Cooperation and Development. Financial Markets Committee's Working Party on Housing Finance. 1974. *Housing finance: Present problems*. Paris: OECD. **3**

Oleinik, I. 1977. *Manual de economía política del socialismo*. 3 vol. Havana: Editorial Pueblo y Educación. **33**

Pelinka, A. 1977. Kommunalpolitik als Gegenmacht. Das "rote Wien" als Beispiel gesellschaftsverändernder Reformpolitik. In *Kommunalpolitik und Sozialdemokratie*, edited by X. Nassmacher. Bonn Bad Godesberg. **32**

Pérez, H. 1981. Informe ante la Asamblea Nacional acerca del cumplimiento del Plan de la Economía Nacional en 1981 y sobre el Proyecto de Plan para 1982, presentado por Humberto Pérez. *Granma*. December 30. **33**

———. 1982. Informe sobre los resultados principales de la ejecución del Plan de 1982 y los lineamientos y elementos fundamentales de la Propuesta de Plan de la Economía Nacional para 1983, presentado por Humberto Pérez. *Granma*. December 19. **33**

———. 1983. Informe de Humberto Pérez. *Granma*. December 23. **33**

————. 1984. Intervención de Humberto Pérez sobre el Proyecto de Ley de Plan Unico de Desarrollo Económico y Social para 1985. *Granma.* December 29.   **33**

Pérez, L. 1980. The family in Cuba. In *The family in Latin America*, edited by M. S. Das and C. J. Jesser. New Delhi. Vikas Publishing House.   **33**

Philippovich, E. von. 1894. *Wiener Wohnungsverhältnisse.* Vol. 7. Archiv für Soziale Gesetzgebung und Statistik.   **32**

Pirhofer, G. and R. Sieder. 1982. Zur Konstitution der Arbeiterfamilie in Roten Wien: Familienpolitik, Kulturreform, Alltag and Ästhetik. In *Historische Familienforschung*, by M. Mitterauer and R. Sieder. Frankfurt: Suhrkamp.   **32**

Pirhofer, G., and G. Uhlig. 1977. Selbsthilfe und Wohnungsbau. *ARCH* 33 (May): 4ff.   **32**

Pozo, A. 1984. La capital de níquel: Dicen hoy . . . *Bohemia* (December 7): 28–34.   **33**

Proyecto de Ley General de Vivienda. 1984. *Bohemia* (November 9): 20–33.   **33**

Ramírez Cruz, J. 1984. El sector cooperativo en la agricultura cubana. *Cuba Socialista*, no. 11 (June–July): 1–24.   **33**

Regalamento para administracion de viviendas. 1981. *La Gaceta.* Managua. June 16.   **33**

Rioseco López-Trigo, P. 1983. Sin bola de cristal. *Bohemia* (December 16): 3–11.   **33**

Ronmark, K. 1981. *Housing management.* Swedish monograph to the Economic Commission for Europe, Committee on Housing, Building and Planning, United Nations.   **31**

Segre, R. 1980. *La vivienda en Cuba en el Siglo XX: República y revolución.* Mexico: Editorial Concepto.   **33**

————. 1985. *Arquitectura y urbanismo de la revolución cubana.* Havana: Editorial Pueblo y Educación.   **33**

*Seis leyes de la Revolución.* 1973. Havana: Editorial de Ciencias Sociales, Instituto Cubano del Libro.   **33**

Seminario Nacional de Vivienda. 1965. *Arquitectura Cuba*, no. 333: 38–56.   **33**

SI. Swedish Institute. 1980. *Fact sheet on Sweden.* Stockholm: SI. January.   **31**

SR. Svenska Riksbyggen. 1980. *Facts on Swedish housing.* Stockholm: SR.   **31**

Svensson, R. 1976. *Swedish land policy in practical application.* Stockholm, Sweden: Swedish Council for Building Research.   **31**

Tesoro, S. 1982. El misterio de las casas naranjas. *Bohemia* (May 21): 38–40.   **33**

Tribunal Superior Electoral. Oficina Nacional de los Censos Demográfico y Electoral. 1953. *Censo de Población, Vivienda y Electoral. Informe general.* Havana: P. Fernández y Cía.   **33**

Turner, B. 1981. Fair rents in Sweden—Market adapted prices or. . . ? Paper presented at Swedish Institute for Building Research, National Housing Conference. June.   **31**

Uhlig, G. 1981. *Kollektivmodell "Einküchenhaus."* Giessen.   **32**

Ungers, O. M. 1969. *Die wiener superblocks.* Herausgegeben an der Technishes Hochschule Berlin vom Lehrstuhl für Entwerfen VI. March.   **32**

*Urban Reform Law.* 1966. Havana. English translation of law and introduction.   **33**

Vega Vega, J. L. 1962. *La reforma urbana de Cuba y otras leyes en relación con la vivienda.* Havana: n.p.   **33**

Veiga, R. 1984. Informe presentado por Roberto Veiga al XV Congreso de la CTC. *Granma.* February 21.   **33**

Vestbro, D. U. 1979. Collective housing units in Sweden. *Current Sweden.* A publication of the Swedish Institute. Stockholm.   **31**

Vienna, City of. 1978. *Kommunaler Wohnungsbau in Wien.* 2 vols. Vienna. (Catalogue and narrative for the exposition: *Kommunaler Wohnungsbau in Wien.*)   **32**

Vienna, Stadtbauamt. 1960. *Der soziale Wohnungsbau der Stadt Wien.* In *Der Aufbau.* 2 Auflage. December. **32**

Witt-Stromer, H. 1977. *Owner-building of smallhouse-areas and the owners participating in administration and use of those areas.* Report. Smahusavdelningen. Stockholm. **31**

Wulz, F. C. 1976. *Stadt in Veränderung; Eine architekturpolitische Studie von wein in den Jahren 1848 bis 1934.* Stockholm. **32**

# Contributors

EMILY PARADISE ACHTENBERG is a housing consultant working with community-based nonprofit and government organizations in the Boston area. She has recently specialized in issues related to the preservation of federally assisted housing, local regulation of rents and condominium conversions, and the creation of housing trust funds linked to downtown development. She is a member of the Planners Network Steering Committee.

RICHARD P. APPELBAUM is an associate professor of sociology at the University of California, Santa Barbara. The author of two books on urban growth and public policy plus numerous articles on the dynamics of housing markets, Dr. Appelbaum is a member of a national task force on housing policy, affiliated with the Institute for Policy Studies, that is developing an alternative, nonmarket approach to low-income housing needs.

JOHN ATLAS, a public-interest lawyer, is a founder and editor of *Shelterforce*, a national housing publication, and the producer of a video documentary on the housing crisis. He is president of the National Housing Institute and vice-president of the Hackensack-based New Jersey Tenants Organization, which is the largest and most successful statewide tenant group in the country.

DAVID BARTELT is an associate professor of urban studies at Temple University, on leave during the 1985-86 academic year as exchange professor at King's College, University of London. His research focuses primarily on urban housing and community economic development programs in the United States. In the housing field, Bartelt has conducted statistical analyses of abandonment, redlining, and the impacts of the federal Community Reinvestment Act. He has recently completed a survey of various urban economic development strategies used in American cities and of their degree of success.

SETH BORGOS was research director of the Association of Community Organizations for Reform Now (ACORN) from 1977 to 1983. He is the author, with Madeleine Adamson, of *This Mighty Dream* (1984), a pictorial study of mass protest movements in the United States.

RACHEL G. BRATT is an assistant professor in the Department of Urban and Environmental Policy at Tufts University, specializing in housing and community development. She is a member of the Consumer Advisory Council of the Federal Reserve Board and the Multifamily Advisory Committee of the Massachusetts Housing Finance Agency. She received a Ph.D. in Urban Studies and Planning from the Massachusetts Institute of Technology.

BARRY CHECKOWAY is an associate professor of social work at the University of Michigan. He received his Ph.D. from the University of Pennsylvania and taught there, at the University of California, Berkeley, and at the University of Illinois, Urbana-Champaign. His research interests include urban social policy and planning, community development, and citizen participation.

ART COLLINGS is senior housing specialist at the Housing Assistance Council in

675

Washington, D.C., and is on detail from the Farmers Home Administration. He was previously a special assistant for housing policy to the administrator of FmHA.

JOHN COWLEY is a lecturer in political sociology at the City University, London, having previously taught at the New School for Social Research in New York City. He is co-author of *Community or Class Struggle?*, a member of the editorial collective of *Camden Tenant*, and secretary of Camden Square Area Tenants Association. He has been an active participant in housing and community struggles for many years.

CUSHING DOLBEARE is a consultant on housing and public policy, and founder and former executive director of the National Low Income Housing Coalition and the Low Income Housing Information Service. She has been executive secretary of the National Rural Housing Coalition, managing director of the Housing Association of Delaware Valley, and associate director of the Citizens Planning and Housing Association of Baltimore.

PETER DREIER is director of housing for the Boston Redevelopment Authority. He has taught sociology and urban studies at Tufts University and has published many articles in popular and professional journals on political and social issues. With John Atlas, he is currently writing *The Renters' Revolt*.

MARK ERLICH is a union carpenter in Boston. He also has taught and written extensively about historical and current labor issues. He is director of the Massachusetts Carpenters History Project and an editor of the *Labor Page*.

JOE R. FEAGIN teaches sociology at the University of Texas at Austin. The author of fourteen books on urban and race issues, he is currently working on two books on Houston.

JOHN I. GILDERBLOOM is an assistant professor of sociology at the University of Houston. He has worked as a housing consultant to numerous local and state governments, and his research on housing has appeared in *American Association of Housing Eductators, Urban Life, Urban Affairs Quarterly, Journal of Applied Behavioral Science*, and *Urban Analysis: An International Journal*. He is the editor of *Rent Control: A Source Book* and with Richard P. Appelbaum is currently finishing a book, *Dreams and Nightmares: America's Rental Housing Crisis*.

JILL HAMBERG is a doctoral student in urban planning at Columbia University where she is completing a dissertation on housing and urban planning in Cuba. She has lived and worked in Latin America and has taught in colleges in the New York City area. She has consulted in a variety of fields, most recently on issues relating to homelessness.

CHESTER HARTMAN is a Fellow at the Institute for Policy Studies in Washington, D.C. He has taught planning at Harvard, Yale, Cornell, the University of North Carolina, and the University of California, Berkeley. He is founder and chair of The Planners Network, a national organization of progressive urban and rural planners, and has been active in community-based housing and planning issues in the Boston and San Francisco areas. His previous books include *Housing and Social Policy* (1975), *Housing Urban America* (1973; rev. ed. 1980), *Displacement: How to Fight It* (1982), *America's Housing Crisis: What Is to Be Done?* (1983), and *The Transformation of San Francisco* (1984).

DOLORES HAYDEN taught in the architecture departments at Berkeley and MIT before joining the UCLA faculty in urban planning in 1979. She is active as a consultant and practitioner in the fields of housing and historic preservation, as a partner in Dubnoff and Hayden, Santa Monica, and as president of the Power of

Place, Los Angeles. The author of three books on American architecture and urban planning, *Seven American Utopias* (1976), *The Grand Domestic Revolution* (1981), and *Redesigning the American Dream: The Future of Housing, Work, and Family Life* (1984), she is the recipient of a National Endowment for the Arts commendation for exemplary design research. Her work has been supported by a Guggenheim Fellowship and a Rockefeller Humanities Fellowship.

KIM HOPPER has worked for six years as a researcher and advocate with the Community Service Society of New York. He has co-authored articles and monographs dealing with the contemporary picture of homelessness in New York City and nationwide. He is a co-founder and serves on the board of directors of both the New York Coalition for the Homeless and the National Coalition for the Homeless.

JIM KEMENY is a guest researcher at the Swedish Institute for Building Research at Gävle.

ROBERT KOLODNY is the head of Urban Strategies, a nonprofit consulting and technical assistance firm in New York City working on housing and community development problems in the United States and abroad. Previously, he was an associate professor at Columbia University's School of Architecture and Planning. Dr. Kolodny has written widely on public housing, inner-city property rehabilitation, neighborhood preservation, self-help housing, and national urban policy. He has worked with tenant groups and community organizations throughout the country in devising indigenous, bottom-up approaches to neighborhood development.

LINDA KRAVITZ writes frequently about rural development and poverty issues in publications for the Housing Assistance Council, Rural America, and the Agribusiness Accountability Project, among others. She is senior researcher at the Housing Assistance Council in Washington, D.C.

RONALD LAWSON was born in Australia and received a Ph.D. from the University of Queensland (1970). He has been a member of the faculty of the City University of New York since 1971 and is now professor of urban studies at Queens College. His most recent book is *The Tenant Movement in New York, 1904–1984* (1986). He is currently working on a sociological account of Seventh-Day Adventism.

KATHY MCAFEE has been a writer and activist for twenty years. She has done organizing, training, and public speaking on housing, community development, and grass-roots empowerment. Her recent writing has focused on class, power, and economic development in urban America and the Third World.

PETER MARCUSE, J.D. (Yale Law School), Ph.D. (University of California, Berkeley), has been majority leader of the Board of Alderman in Waterbury, Connecticut, and president of the City Planning Commission of Los Angeles. He is now the chair of the Housing Committee of Community Board 9, Manhattan, and professor of urban planning at Columbia University. He has written numerous articles on housing, planning, and international urban development. He is at work on a history of public housing in New York City.

ANN MEYERSON, Ph.D. (New York University), taught housing and urban studies as an assistant professor in the Metropolitan Studies Program at New York University for ten years and was program director between 1981 and 1984. She has also worked as an advocate planner in New York City on behalf of neighborhood groups fighting central business district expansion and gentrification.

GARY ORFIELD is a professor of political science and public policy at the University of Chicago, specializing in national policy and minority rights. He has participated in twelve major school and housing desegregation lawsuits and serves on the board of OPEN, the Leadership Council on Metropolitan Open Communities, the *American Journal of Education, Policy Studies Journal*, and numerous other organizations. His publications include *Must We Bus?, Congressional Power, Toward a Strategy for Urban Integration*, and *Latinos in Metropolitan Chicago* (co-author).

TOM ROBBINS is a Revson fellow at Columbia University. He was formerly the editor of *City Limits*, a magazine covering low-income housing concerns in New York City.

JOSÉ RAMÓN SÁNCHEZ is completing a dissertation in the Politics Department of New York University. He is a lecturer in the Department of Politics, Economics and Society, State University of New York–College at Old Westbury. His research interests include the politics and history of social classes and the city, as well as political and social theory.

STEVE SCHIFFERES received his B.A. from Harvard (1972) and M.A. from Warwick University, England (1975). He worked at Shelter, the National Campaign for the Homeless, from 1975 to 1980, where he specialized in public-sector housing issues and was involved in the implementation of the Homeless Persons Act. Since 1982, he has been making TV documentaries for London Weekend Television, a major commercial TV company in Britain, including its award-winning series on poverty in Britain today, "Breadline Britain." Currently he is working on its sequel, which deals with the wealthy in Britain.

TOM SCHLESINGER is a carpenter and freelance writer in Tennessee.

TONY SCHUMAN, a New York architect, teaches in the School of Architecture at the New Jersey Institute of Technology in Newark. He writes on a wide range of housing design and policy issues and serves on the Steering Committee of the Planners Network.

ROBERT SCHUR, a former New York City deputy housing commissioner, died in 1982. Schur was one of the few bureaucrats who went through New York's government–corporate revolving door backward, winding up in the community, trying to help tenants and groups piece together affordable solutions to their housing problems. The last article he published, in *City Limits* (January 1982), called on community groups to "go back to basics," urging them that no amount of funding or technical assistance would substitute for an organized and committed community.

GLENDA SLOANE is director for housing and community development at the Center for National Policy Review at the Catholic University Law School in Washington, D.C. She chairs the Housing Task Force of the Leadership Council on Civil Rights and is a member of the Consumer Advisory Council of the Federal Reserve Board. Before joining the Center, she was an attorney with the U.S. Commission on Civil Rights and was legal counsel for the President's Committee on Equal Opportunity in Housing.

MICHAEL E. STONE teaches in the undergraduate Community Planning Program and the graduate Human Services Program at the College of Public and Community Service, University of Massachusetts, Boston. In addition to his work on housing affordability, housing finance, and housing policy, he is involved in arson prevention and antidisplacement work and in the development of local strategies for increasing social control and social ownership of housing.

# Index

Abandonment, 6, 17, 22, 96 n.17, 216, 259–60, 424, 442, 472 n.6, 497, 504; and mortgage lenders, 184–201; in New York City, 217; in Philadelphia, 428; and rent control, 180–83, 407, 562; and self-help housing, 459. *See also* Disinvestment; *In rem* housing

ACORN (Association of Community Organizations for Reform Now), 389, 415, 428–46

Adjustable-rate mortgages, xv, 9, 82, 85, 88, 90, 197. *See also* Alternative mortgage instruments

Affirmative Fair Housing Marketing Plans, 310, 315–16, 374

Affordability. *See* Housing costs, as proportion of income

Aid to Families with Dependent Children (AFDC), 19–20, 27, 31, 217, 234, 327. *See also* Welfare assistance

Alexandria, Va., 366

Alternative mortgage instruments, 56, 71, 74

American Bankers Association, 76, 77, 94 n.8, 130

American Indians. *See* Native Americans

American Institute of Planners, 255

Architects, 235, 237

Arizona, 150

Arson, xvii, 6, 216, 217, 408, 410, 413, 424, 497, 499. *See also* Fires

Australia, 275

Baldwin Hills, Calif., 241

Balloon mortgages, 197, 298

Baltimore, 388, 431–32

Berkeley, Calif., 243

Black market practices, 564, 588, 598, 609, 615

Blacks, 189, 190, 203, 204, 206, 214, 222. *See also* Desegregation; Discrimination; Integration; Racism; Segregation

Blockbusting, 6, 112, 118, 298, 302, 316

Boston, xiii, 29, 67 n.9, 169, 320, 344, 347, 349, 350, 367, 388, 389, 405–27, 452, 453, 505, 509

Brooke Amendments, 339

Building and Construction Trades Department, AFL-CIO, 160–61

Building codes, 330

Building materials, 125, 146, 150, 385, 478, 489, 539, 575, 604

California, 39 n.7, 61, 150, 168, 178 n.10, 254, 505

California Housing Action and Information Network (CHAIN), 387, 391

Cambridge, Mass., 167, 411, 421–22

Camden, N.J., 222

Capital accumulation, 188–89, 196, 200 n.5, 466

Capital gains, 266

Capital grants, 529, 570, 572

Carter administration, 318–19

Centex, 147–48

Chicago, 107, 307, 349, 350, 389, 452, 453

Child care, 233, 234, 236, 237, 239, 240, 242, 245 n.1, 368, 388, 400, 403, 471

Cincinnati, 105, 452

Citicorp, 78, 79, 80, 85, 86, 92, 95 n.11, 97 n.21

City Life (Boston), 406, 408, 413, 415–16, 419, 420–21, 425

Cleveland, 113, 423, 452, 453

Closing costs, 491, 493

Collective bargaining, 411, 419, 543

Columbus, Ohio, 438, 441

Commodity nature of housing, 205–10, 358, 393, 407, 614, 629. *See also* Decommodification of housing

Community Development Block Grants, 10, 287, 312, 364, 432, 438, 482, 505

Community facilities and services, 237, 333, 573. *See also* Public services; Social services

Community-owned housing, 63, 358, 412, 413, 414, 486. *See also* Nonprofit housing

*679*